First Among Friends

Supposed portrait of George Fox, 1677. Detail from engraving, after painting of "Quaker Meeting" by Egbert van Heemskerk. See William I. Hull, Benjamin Furly and Quakerism in Rotterdam, Swarthmore College Monographs on Quaker History, no. 5 (Swarthmore, Pa.: Swarthmore College, 1941), 255–58. (Reprinted by permission of the Library Committee of London Yearly Meeting of the Religious Society of Friends.)

First Among Friends

GEORGE FOX AND THE CREATION OF QUAKERISM

H. Larry Ingle

New York   *Oxford*
OXFORD UNIVERSITY PRESS

Oxford University Press

Oxford   New York   Toronto
Dehli   Bombay   Calcutta   Madras   Karachi
Kuala Lumpur   Singapore   Hong Kong   Tokyo
Nairobi   Dar es Salaam   Cape Town
Melbourne   Auckland   Madrid

and associated companies in
Berlin   Ibadan

Published by Oxford University Press, Inc.
198 Madison Avenue, New York, New York 10016

First issued as an Oxford University Press Paperback, 1996

Oxford is a registered trademark of Oxford University Press

Library of Congress Cataloging—in—Publication Data
Ingle, H. Larry (Homer Larry), 1936-
First among friends: George Fox and creation of quakerism/H. Larry Ingle.
p. cm.   Includes bibliographical references and index.
ISBN 0-19-507803-9
ISBN 0-19-510117-0 (pbk.)
1. Fox, George, 1624–1691.   2. Quakers—England—Biography.
I. Title.
BX7795.F7I54 1994
289.6'092—dc20
[B]   93-7660

135798642

Printed in the United States of America
on acid-free paper

for

JAAN AND JON

"Prize your Time for your soul's sake."

PREFACE

George Fox has long needed a biography firmly rooted in the period in which he lived, grew to manhood, and preached the message that pulled together the diverse group of people who made up the Religious Society of Friends, or Quakers. Numerous studies of this important person have appeared, of course, many produced by members of the sect he did so much to found. But almost without exception these studies have been excessively filiopietistic, have tried to squeeze the last drop of meaning (and life) from his "theology" and have amounted to a virtual paraphrase of his *Journal*, available to interested readers for three centuries. Some have written as though the guns of the English Civil Wars and the divisive debates that characterized England's revolutionary era rumbled far offstage, rather than at the center of the period's common life. The authors of such volumes could hardly be critical of Fox or willing to subject their hero to the kind of biographical treatment one might expect in a study of—to name at random one of Fox's contemporaries—Oliver Cromwell. As perhaps the most careful scholar to approach the period bluntly asserted, "There is no real biography of George Fox"; nothing has appeared since Henry J. Cadbury wrote those words in 1972 to alter that assessment.[1]

Interestingly enough, this attitude toward Fox has even infected the wider world of scholarship. When I applied for a grant from the National Endowment for the Humanities to allow me to pursue my research, I was turned down despite numerous favorable reviews. The most amazing response came from a critic who solemnly dogmatized that, given the corpus of Fox's work, the large body of theological commentary on it, and scholarly work on Quakerism in the English Civil War and Interregnum periods, "it would be straining patience to argue that a biography of Fox will tell us anything substantial that we don't already know about the subject." Let the reader judge whether either strain or patience is required to find anything new and substantial here.

This biographical study attempts to rescue Fox from poorly grounded, usually uncritical, and theologically oriented works. It is firmly rooted in manuscript and published sources of the period and brings to the forefront the background that has hitherto been too much ignored. It is based on the hardly novel assumption that a person in the past is, to a large degree, a product of his or her time. It depicts a human being like the rest of us, and able thereby to speak to his contemporaries, but different enough to offer a compelling vision to a portion of his divided society and win their allegiance. If it celebrates anything about

George Fox, it honors his capacity to respond to his times in a way that allowed him and his followers to help mold them. Unlike other works on the man, it is freighted with few explicit lessons, so that the reader is left free to appropriate the countless implicit ones.

During the course of a formidable research task, particularly for one whose field of research and teaching includes other epochs and other lands than England, I have accumulated numerous obligations. My needs, ranging from a magnifying glass to use at the British Library to information on esoteric medical problems, were so great that my thanks can hardly surmount them. I must express my gratitude to Jan Ridley, Peter Cottingham, Elizabeth Salisbury, Walter and Maisie Birmingham, Angela Barlow, Rosemary and Derek Moore, Dennis F. Hall, Joseph Pickvance, Malcolm Thomas, James Pym, Ole Riis, Kim Collis, Maude White, Donald Moates, David L. Smiley, Cathy Aldridge, Thomas Hamm, J. William Frost, Arthur J. Mekeel, Jaan Ingle, Paul Ramsay, Doug Gwyn, Hugh Barbour, Kathleen Denbigh, Donald Rhodes, Edwin J. Bronner, Stephen A. Kent, Yvonne Gee, Lesley (Lel) Bound, Richard Vann, Carole Treadway, Elizabeth P. Brown, Irven Resnick, Paul Schlotthauer, Philip Holthaus, Mary and John Reader, and John Anderson. Geoffrey Makins expertly drew the map. Carolyn Mitchell performed a signal, and I hope not unrewarding, task in reading and critiquing a late version of the manuscript. The following institutions and their staffs were most helpful: British Library at the British Museum, London; Library of the Society of Friends, London; Dr. Williams's Library, London; Institute of Historical Research, University of London; Library of Woodbrooke College; Public Record Offices in London (Chancery Lane), Leicester, Preston, and Kendal; the public libraries in Lichfield, Northampton, Kendal, Atherstone, Whitehaven, and Derby, Great Britain; the public library in Chattanooga, Tennessee; University of Tennessee-Chattanooga Lupton Library; Haverford College Library (Quaker Collection); Swarthmore College Library (Friends Historical Library); Pendle Hill Library; Bequest Committee (Philadelphia Yearly Meeting); Library of Jefferson Medical College of Thomas Jefferson University; Historical Society of Pennsylvania; Faculty Research Committee (University of Tennessee at Chattanooga); and Quaker International Centre, London. My tenure in 1990–1991 as the first Henry J. Cadbury Scholar at Pendle Hill in Wallingford, Pennsylvania, was invaluable because it put me near three excellent libraries and afforded me the most valuable commodity a historian needs: time to write.

Three people made such major contributions to my work that they must be mentioned separately. Neal Coulter, an indefatigable and intrepid librarian at the University of Tennessee at Chattanooga, was always on call to help locate stray tidbits of information I required. James A. Ward, a close friend and valued colleague, constantly encouraged and supported me, taking time away from the history of the Packard Motor Car Company and nineteenth century railroads to listen and advise. My wife, Becky, not only endured me but lived with Fox, too, including a five-month stint in London when she demonstrated that one does not have to be a historian to cultivate the most important characteristic of historical research, namely, the willingness to dig into and learn from the sources. Her continued insistence that my theorizing be based on concrete evidence would serve any scholar well, particularly those who work in rarefied areas where something as elusive as religious faith impinges on human beings.

I have dealt with two perennial problems facing historians of this period—citing dates and quoting seventeenth-century English—by placing the beginning of each year at January 1, quite a change from the England of the time where it began on Lady Day, March 25, and by modernizing grammar, syntax, and spelling to make this tale, I hope, more appealing to late-twentieth-century eyes and ears. Thus, when it comes to the calendar, I am "old style" with slight modifications, but with language I am newfangled. There are problems with any decision in these areas, but I think that, on balance, I have made the right ones.

The problem of converting seventeenth-century English pounds into twentieth-century American dollars is more complicated, and I do not have the final answer. (The interested reader might want to consult the most recent academic source on this problem, John J. McCusker, *How Much Is That in Real Money?: A Historical Price Index for Use as a Deflator of Money Values in the Economy of the United States* [Worchester, Mass.: American Antiquarian Society, 1992].) I have looked at prices in the seventeenth century and tried to find a formula that would relate them to those of the present. For example, Sarah Fell kept a detailed account book of her expenses and income that has been published.[2] Some samples from this book are extremely enlightening: 6 chickens were sold for 12 pence while white bread was a very dear 4 pence; a man's riding saddle cost 94 pence; 1 pound of soap was 4 pence; and Fell paid 4 pence for 2 days of corn weeding. A 1688 estimate gives an annual family income of 38 pounds for artisans or people skilled in handcrafts, such as a weaver, 154 pounds for a lawyer, and 280 pounds for a gentleman.[3] Having considered these figures, I tried to find an average that would be accurate in reflecting these diverse expenses and costs and decided on a rough conversion rate of approximately 1 English pound to 100 American dollars. While this ratio can not be applied in every case, it allows for a relatively accurate figure.

Keys to frequently used abbreviations appear in the bibliography. Because of the vagaries of seventeenth-century printing, I have had to cite material from pages 189–202 of the first edition of Fox's *Journal* by using the printer's signatures. To ground this biography firmly in the soil of Fox's country and to give my readers a taste of the popular views of the time, I have chosen English proverbs common to the seventeenth century as chapter titles. (My source for these proverbs was *The Oxford Dictionary of English Proverbs*, 3d ed., edited by F. P. Wilson [Oxford: Clarendon Press, 1970]).

Chattanooga, Tenn.　　　　　　　　　　　　　　　　　　　　　H. L. I.
June 1993

CONTENTS

First Among Friends

(Map by Geoffrey Makins)

INTRODUCTION

❦

The Sea Refuses No River

George Fox, founder of the Religious Society of Friends, or Quakers, was a significant figure in the history of the Radical Reformation. But he was also more. He sensed a need for, then captured in his movement, the sense of individual responsibility and initiative without which the newly emerging world of capitalism would have had tougher going. His concerns were primarily religious, but he also stressed the secular needs of those left behind by the changing social order. Hence achieving justice, social and economic, was always one of his major intentions, especially in the heady days of the English Revolution. Articulating the spirit of his age, Fox at his most creative pushed the accepted definitions of Christianity to stress new individualistic dimensions and inculcate them in his sect. The fact that by the end of his life the Society of Friends was well on its way to the prosperous respectability it has since enjoyed was no accident.

One major difference between this examination of Fox's life and the rise of Quakerism and most previous studies is that I take seriously these broad themes affecting the Society of Friends, as well as the variety of sources feeding the Society itself. The story I will tell is dramatic, for its subject lived a life that spanned the revolutionary years of mid-seventeenth-century England. Born in 1624 when King James ruled by divine right, George Fox died in 1691, two years after the Glorious Revolution affirmed Parliament's ultimate power to enthrone and dethrone monarchs. No matter that the outward trappings of the monarchy remained the same, the England of 1691, center of a worldwide empire, was a far cry from the little England of 1624. Fox had to respond to the many events that made those changes possible. And if many argue that religious reformers had little direct concern for such world-shaking events as civil wars, glorious revolutions, and the creation of empires, then I can still respond, "Of course, but Fox helped shape public attitudes that either acquiesced in and accepted these developments or opposed and resisted them."

Attitudes, after all, determine how people respond to their world, and Protestantism, one aspect of which Fox championed, was integrally involved with the creation of the new world. Its spirit, the spirit of individualism it promoted, was modern, no matter what the intention of those who fed the new impulse. Fox himself looked backward as well as forward and did not much like what he saw unfolding around him, but in freeing the individual and lending his blessing to many of the changes thus wrought, he had to reap what he had sown no matter that he had intended sowing some other kind of seed. Or to change my metaphor, once the rivulet of Quakerism merged with the larger stream of history, the waters overflowing accustomed channels could not be stopped until the source upstream had run its course. Neither Protestantism in its various forms nor the nation's life would ever be the same again; every important movement has had this impact. The early Fox, who cultivated divisiveness, lived at the juncture when medieval society in England was shattering and becoming modern.[1]

Protestantism naturally splinters. From its beginning, this tendency was both evident and feared. Once the German priest and reformer Martin Luther nailed his Ninety-five Theses to the church door at Wittenberg in 1517 and challenged all comers to debate them, the splintering began. Luther's principle of individual interpretation of the Scriptures presented the established church with the probability that others would follow his path and seek to locate themselves as authorities in matters of faith and practice.

It did not take long for Luther himself to learn from experience what his principles portended. Enflamed by the evangelical and social implications of his teachings, German peasants, beginning in 1524, rose up in armed revolt—labeled by later commentator Karl Marx as the "most radical event in German history."[2] They rebelled to protest paying tithes to absentee clerics and demanded the right to select and pay their own pastors. More broadly, they wanted biblically based standards of justice instituted, standards they believed Luther's calls for religious reform sanctioned.

The fiery explosion of peasant discontent so shocked Luther that the erstwhile reformer hastily published a volatile pamphlet, *Against the Robbing and Murdering Hordes of Peasants* (1525), in which he endorsed smashing the peasants' revolt with an iron mace. Thus the religious radical Luther allied himself with the princely and patrician defenders of the social status quo. His version of reformation, now shorn of much of its revolutionary appeal as a people's movement, retreated into sterile arguments over arcane religious doctrines about the number and types of sacraments, the nature of the Lord's Supper, the mode of baptism, and so on.

The defeat of the peasants in 1525, after about eighteen months of struggle, did not kill the longing for justice that the revolt made manifest. Out of the defeat, the ferment feeding the Radical Reformation bubbled up to produce countless sects and dissenting groups. A more diverse collection can hardly be imagined, and within three decades varieties of religious radicalism had spread to practically every part of Central Europe and beyond, to the Netherlands and England, to Lithuania and to the shores of the Black Sea. A kind of third force beyond traditional Catholicism and mainstream Protestantism, the radical Protestant sects were prevented from triumphing by their own doctrinal and political bickering, bloody official suppression, and their own anarchic tendencies. The Radical Reformation aborted, the longings of its mostly humble adherents still awaiting birth.

By 1580, except in isolated areas, only three main groups—Mennonites, Swiss Brethren, and Hutterites—maintained any kind of organization. The rest of those who had earlier united with the cause of the Radical Reformation had either been forcibly erased from the pages of history or had meanwhile converted to some safer, more socially acceptable version of the new faith.[3] But just as the defeat of the peasants' revolt had not stilled ordinary people's longing for justice, so the virtual demise of the Radical Reformation (a demise represented both by the institutionalization of the three surviving sects and the disappearance of others) did not remove the social, economic, and religious realities that had caused radicalism to flourish in the first place. All that was required for a new bubbling up of radicalism was another set of conditions that would offer people a chance to express and perhaps even to satisfy the kind of yearnings unlikely to be met within the existing order of things.

Such conditions prevailed in England in the middle of the seventeenth century. As with all revolutionary upheavals, the outbreak of the English Civil War in 1642 was unheralded and caught all participants rather by surprise. The struggle seemed at first primarily to be between Parliament and Crown over constitutional issues and taxation but then broadened to encompass elites in local areas who professed loyalty to one side or the other, for one discrete reason or another. Dissolution of the familiar boundaries that had alway marked the country's social and political order caused radical sentiments to erupt during the conflict. For nearly two decades after 1642, therefore, the fundamental question involved who would make the rules, "call the shots," be the establishment.

Even the meanest subject in the kingdom could not escape the implication of this question when the monarch, Charles I, was beheaded on January 30, 1649. The man who told his accusers, "[R]emember, I am your King, your lawful King," had been forced to surrender his life, and to answer, despite his determination not to do so, to what he deemed "a new unlawful authority."[4] The nonmonarchical central power created following Charles's death was not stabilized for more than ten years. Until the dead king's son ascended the throne in 1660, change, basic change, remained always an open possibility for the nation. During the Interregnum this potential for change offered fresh opportunities for men, and women, to drink deeply at the intoxicating springs of individualism and to tap exciting—and threatening—new prospects.

Historians, including this one, have found it easy to celebrate many of the utopian dreamers of the 1650s. Their individualism seems so modern, the new economic forces so promising, the stirrings of equality, democracy, and republicanism so galvanizing, the religious sects so predictive of later ideals of pluralism and tolerance, the efforts of people to control the new order for their collective benefit so exhilarating, that only a person with a stiff carapace of illiberal insensibilities could deny their appeal. These values should be celebrated and defended, of course, for they retain great importance.

But what is too often forgotten is that what a day may bring, a day make take away, and what is given with one hand can be taken away with the other. The progressive and hopeful changes that came with the English Revolution had another side, one that appealed to human selfishness and greed, that undercut the grand ideals the search for change was supposed to enhance and protect. In celebrating bourgeois individualism, the very foundation stone of the emerging capitalist order, later students have not wanted to look long at this darker side.

Charles I knew it by experience, but then he had a personal interest in the matter. A minor literary figure of that age, not much celebrated these days except in sporting circles, also witnessed and commented on how the individualism of Protestantism and the English Revolution undercut traditional values. Izaak Walton, author of *The Compleat Angler*, published in 1653, used his evocative essay on fishing to call into question the new world because it raised up people who did not deserve to be thus elevated. Not more than a dozen pages into his book, he pointed his pen at those he called "men of sour complexion, money-getting men" who spent their time trying to acquire or keep money, and chased about "always busy or discontented." Such people disdained outside authority and could not accept the natural peacefulness of the outdoors or pursue the piscatorial prey. Encounter such a person on the path to a quiet pool, he continued, and "you hardly meet a man that complains not of some want; though he, indeed, wants nothing but his will, . . . and thus, when we might be happy and quiet, we create trouble for ourselves."[5] The conservative Walton wanted to preserve the old world, where one could amble easily along toward a favorite fishing spot, "free from the unsupportable burden of an accusing, tormenting conscience—a misery that none can bear."[6]

Unlike the revolutionaries, Walton did not believe in equality, except insofar as all people shared common and mutual miseries. His ideal state was one in which people would be meek and thankful whether, he pointedly phrased it, "honestly rich or contentedly poor."[7] However much Walton might invoke it, no such utopia had ever existed. So relatively few readers even noticed or paid much attention to his ideal. Hence his book stands as one person's rather idiosyncratic and anguished cry against the new forces undermining the traditional order. Most readers of the nearly countless subsequent editions saw only a quaint, entertaining, and charming little handbook on fishing and seemingly overlooked his trenchant criticism of bourgeois individualism. To neglect Walton, and for that matter Charles I, has almost blinded students of the English Revolution to the darker side of the quest for the ideal reign of equality and justice. Walton, a psychic victim of the revolution, could not celebrate something that was destroying the world he had known.

Not so victimized, George Fox came down finally on the side of the new, the side of revolution and of individualism. To his credit he retained more than a little ambivalence about his choice. Like Walton, he recognized that the new order was destroying the sense of belonging to a community that gave life much of its deeper satisfaction. But he hoped that his movement could recapture this disappearing community, that the spirit of Christ he preached so consistently would call people to a new but different order, one in which the divine spirit sparked ordinary people to revitalize primitive Christianity, replacing the old and channeling the new. This goal, needless to say, turned out to be an illusion. In truth, he and his movement were too much products of their age, riding the stream of history to the uncertain sea called the future.

1

Every Oak Has Been an Acorn

Scenes like the one unfolding in St. Michael and All Angels', a small church in midlands Leicestershire, took place with accepted regularity in all parts of the kingdom. The parish, in the village called Drayton-in-the-Clay, had only a few more than a hundred souls.[1] Church law provided that none be admitted to the sacrament of Holy Communion without reciting the catechism, the articles of faith, the Ten Commandments, and the Lord's Prayer. A child could normally fulfill this requirement and be ready for confirmation at age twelve or thirteen.[2] The hierarchy of the Anglican church positively commanded the catechizing of children, but a rector of Presbyterian leanings like Robert Mason would have considered instilling correct doctrines among his charges an important personal obligation as well. This Sunday, in the late 1630s, one half hour before evensong, Mason had gathered the half-dozen youngsters in the front of the church to go over questions 117 and 118, the ones dealing with a Christian's duty to his or her neighbors. Mason, nearing seventy, could hardly forget his duty to ask probing questions and make sure his young and fidgety pupils grasped the intended meaning of each section; it was a more elementary method than that used at Balliol College at the University of Oxford where the old minister had earned his bachelor's and master of arts degrees, more than fifty years earlier.[3]

The material in questions 117 and 118 embodied an especially troubling point, especially for children in a parish as strongly nonconformist as this one. Mason had become aware of this nonconformity shortly after arriving in Drayton-in-the-Clay in 1606 when some parishioners refused to kneel for communion, a sure sign they had picked up notions of spiritual equality that undercut good order.[4] If Mason wanted to prepare himself to answer any adolescent questions, then he would have consulted William Gouge's *Of Domesticall Duties*,[5] the standard authority on the obligations a person owed to parents, master, clergy, and king. Gouge sharply divided a Christian's responsibilities into outward and inward parts, the better, he made explicit, to rebut dangerous Anabaptist arguments against the authority of masters and the subjection of subjects: "Rule and subjection are matters of outward policy, they tend to the outward preservation of Church, Commonwealth, and family, in this world: but faith, piety, and such graces are inward matters of the soul, tending to a better life." Equality existed, admittedly, in the spiritual realm, yet there remained "a disparity in the other, namely, in civil, and the temporal matters." Christ may have purchased liberty from "the curse and rigour of the moral law," but his sacrificial death, Gouge hurried to add, certainly had not reduced "those degrees which God hath established betwixt man and man, for the good of mankind."[6]

One of Mason's catechists would have been George Fox, son of a weaver with such a strict religious bearing that his fellow villagers sometimes referred to him as "Righteous Christer."[7] As Mason asked his little audience to repeat after him the answer to question 117 ("What is thy duty towards thy neighbor?"), young Fox had no inkling of the implications of the words he recited that day. "My duty towards my neighbor, is to love him as my self, to . . . love, honor, and succor my father and mother, to honor and obey the king and his ministers: to submit my self to all my governors, teachers, spiritual pastors and masters, to order myself lowly and reverently to all my betters." And then together the group intoned: "[T]o do my duty to that estate of life unto which it hath pleased God to call me."

Question 118 asked dutiful catechists to define more specifically what number 117 commanded. The proper answer emphasized willing subservience: "To carry our selves lowly and reverently towards our Masters, being ruled by them, and towards the Ancient, and all our betters." Lest any, particularly the younger children, not fully understand the meaning of the words they were being taught, the catechism spelled out their meaning. "Fathers" included "rich men using their estates aright," and "honor" meant "to give that reverent respect which is due to every superior, whether in authority and powers, in place and calling, or in worth and dignity." The listing went on and on. Masters of apprentices, "whether they be wicked or godly," "wise or foolish," "chastising thee wrongfully or reasonably," must be obeyed without exception. And fathers in the faith— that is to say, ministers—must be honored "with the payment of tithes and duties, which by God's ordinance belong unto them for their maintenance."[8]

These questions and set answers underscored the reality that would dominate the life of George Fox, a reality that led him into conflict with his family, with the religious and political establishments of his day, and finally even with members of the religious society he did so much to shape. Unwilling to submit to authority, unless it be the ineffable and elusive authority of God, Fox was a rebel born. He never integrated into his life the lessons Parson Mason, acting as agent of the established church, tried to teach by way of the catechism. Although he eventually tried to explain the inward workings of his spirit, he was not particularly introspective and left almost no indications that he appreciated the irony of his later attempts to impose authoritative definitions upon a religious community committed, by his own stated principles, to individual experience.

In this sense, Fox was a true heir of the Protestant Reformation and, indeed, of a rich tendency within English church history going back, from the date of his birth in 1624, almost 250 years.[9] The German reformer Martin Luther had enunciated what was to remain the underlying principle of Protestantism of whatever variety, namely, that the individual conscience was finally the ultimate standard in matters of faith and that institutional restraints had to give way before it. However far Protestantism had spread in the more than one hundred years since

Luther's first demand for change in 1517, it had inevitably lost some of its vitality in the process and become secondhand. The catechism's fixed doctrine illustrated how the institutionalization of the reformed faith hindered the growth of true spirituality and stifled or even killed the spontaneity and immediate intensity that Luther had taught Protestants to expect.

Ever alert to the disruptive potential in such an approach, the leaders of the Roman Catholic church resisted it with all the power, secular and religious, they could command. Just as surely, Luther's principle gave dispossessed people of his time and later a handy tool to use against the established order and hence led inevitably to further discontent and disorder. The result was the Radical Reformation, a force that spread over much of Europe and could not be contained, even by the severest repression. Ironically, the person ultimately responsible for this Radical Reformation, Martin Luther, turned against his creation when he realized how much it threatened the received social order. But by then it was too late, for the genie was out of the bottle and could never be put back.[10]

At first glance—and even after a second and longer one—Drayton-in-the-Clay seemed an unlikely place for a genie to reemerge. Situated near the center of the kingdom, the tiny village probably never had more than twenty-five houses. To the west ran an old Roman road from Leicester to Mancetter in the next county, and just a mile to the southwest ran another, the famous Watling Street, which stretched more than 160 miles from the sea at Dover, through London, until it disappeared in the wilds of Shropshire. The eastern midland country thereabout was attractive enough, with a slightly rolling landscape and a long ridge sweeping across the horizon on the distant side of Watling Street. A seasoned traveler in the late seventeenth century extolled the beauty of the area: "You see a great way upon their hills, the bottoms full of enclosures, woods and different sorts of manuring and herbage, amongst which are placed many little towns which gives great pleasure of the travellers to view."[11] The rich clayey soil produced large crops of wheat and beans, allowing others to dismiss the area as "Bean belly Leicestershire."[12] It took three horses—hence the term "three-horse land"—to subdue the unyielding sod. In this region the land was enclosed (or fenced in with hawthorn rows) early so that it could be turned into pastures for sheep and horses.[13]

The heavy soil produced good crops, but it also had disadvantages, particularly regarding roads—described by one traveler as the worst in England. Below Atherstone in Warwickshire, two or three miles from Drayton, even Watling Street was bypassed by the coaches and carriages of the rich: only rough carts were able to make their way along its rutted surface to London.[14] Celia Fiennes, an aristocratic lady who toured the country sidesaddle, allowed that a man on foot would have taken less time than the nearly eleven hours it took her on horseback to trudge through twenty-five miles of mire masquerading as a road.[15] In the summer the clay baked in the fields; in the winter it could become a sprawling bog holding people and beasts tightly in its grip.[16] Such conditions naturally reinforced the isolation of the town's inhabitants.

Yet Drayton-in-the-Clay, now called Fenny Drayton, was too small for its people to remain completely isolated. If Watling Street made them look this way and that, to wonder or to ask what was at the other end, it also provided a way to get beyond the village boundaries and gave direct access to goods produced beyond the parish: villagers could travel to a nearby market town to stock up, as well as to peddle their excess produce. Four miles to the southeast was Hinckley, which every Monday converted itself into one of the region's major horse markets; an even bigger attraction was the fairs held each year on August 12 and the Monday following Twelfth Day in January. With its 150 families, Hinckley was at least six times the size of Fox's home village, and it could even boast a two-master school after the 1620s.[17]

Even closer to Drayton-in-the-Clay, a bit over three miles distant and just over the county line, across Anker River in Warwickshire, lay the smaller village of Nuneaton, which beckoned people of the surrounding countryside to its Saturday market. It too had a grammar school. Coal, a sought-after if expensive fuel, was mined just south of town. People flocked from miles around for the fortnightly and slightly subversive Presbyterian lecture held in the local church.[18] The village of Atherstone, three miles west astride Watling Street, prided itself on a school, run by its Presbyterian vicar, and a flourishing twice-weekly market as well as an annual September cheese fair and plenty of inns to house visitors. When Fox was a boy Atherstone must have looked much the same as it had during the Middle Ages, for the land had not been enclosed by fences and the town was securely cushioned by sprawling fields.[19] Just to the east was the old Roman town of Mancetter with a tenth-century church visible from Drayton across the broad Anker valley. Coventry, crossroads of the Midlands and the kingdom's fourth largest city, boasted a population of some seven thousand and easily attracted people from adjoining counties with goods to buy or sell. Its mercantile reach extended through North Sea ports outward to the Rhine River and to the Dutch, the Flemish, and the Germans on the Continent.[20] Villages hereabouts were honeycombed with religious nonconformists, leading one fifteenth-century chronicler to complain that every second person one met was a heretic.[21]

The lay of the land and the occasional journey to one of the nearby market towns were givens that a person in the second quarter of the seventeenth century took for granted—life was like that and, as far as anyone could tell, had always been so. Still, other physical things in the area suggested other times and other values. If they too were givens—and they were—they had been given by someone else. For example, near Atherstone just two miles up the "Street Way" (the local name for Watling Street) lay a ruined Roman fort, guarding Mancetter, covering about two acres of ground and close enough for a curious boy to find in half an hour as he explored across the low hills. A sharp-eyed explorer could still occasionally spy and pocket a treasured Roman coin. And if a boy's rambles lured him farther down Street Way opposite Hinckley, he might, if he knew how to write, add his scratched initials to those already covering the High Cross—its four columns holding up a gilded globe topped by a cross—that the Romans had raised as a road sign.[22] Such things, however often seen and taken for granted, could easily lead a curious person to think about what was and what might have been in other times and with other people.

Other givens over which average people had little control, but which nonetheless had profound impacts on their lives, included the cycles of weather, harvests, and prices, all related in a complex manner. The one year in four when April did not bring snow to Leicestershire,[23] for example, might mean early crop yields for the lucky few who gambled that getting their beans in the ground early would give them the advantage of a longer growing season, while it penalized the shepherd who waited to shear his sheep by the calendar. One important given was that it was impossible to count on the same given each year. The English economy of the seventeenth century forced people to live on a thin edge between sufficiency and shortages, an unsure situation made worse by ten harvest failures in the last years of the reign of Charles I and the first years of the rule of Oliver Cromwell. Hence food prices from 1646 to 1650 soared 50 percent.[24] Such price increases and related shortages hit first in predominately pastoral areas like Leicestershire, where locally grown food supplies were not as plentiful as in more self sufficient grain-producing regions.[25] The discontent these disruptions occasioned caused food riots and revolts to ripple across the Midlands regularly after suppression of a big revolt in 1607. At that time peasants from nine to twelve miles away—a day's journey—trudged to a selected site to lend their angry voices to local outcries against the fencing off of land and the depopulation it produced.[26]

Regardless of how an individual made a living in Drayton-in-the-Clay, the land itself was the source of everyone's life and property. For farmers who grew wheat or beans, or both, it had to be laboriously broken, planted, and tended before it could be harvested. The land did not produce bounty until it was forced to cooperate with the farmer. If it rooted its subjects in their places, it also caused them to raise their sights beyond the nearest horizon, to recognize that they were a part of the natural world and had to rely on the goodness and plenitude of nature to supply the sunlight and rain necessary for successful crops. Moreover, an eternal quality issued out of the land because it tied a person to ancestors long gone and hinted of sustenance for those yet to come. For those who raised livestock, be they cows, horses, or sheep, the same qualities existed, except they looked for grass. Without grass there would be no milk, no wool, no meat, no work animals, no hay for livestock feed, no ticking for mattresses, not even much manure to lay on the land. Graziers of the seventeen century could readily understand the modern adage that "good grass needs good muck," or its reverse, that good muck needs good grass.[27]

For those villagers whose occupation had moved a step away from farming or keeping animals, people such as weavers, for example, the land was still important. Raw wool came from sheep, of course, but weaving was still not necessarily a full-time occupation, particularly in Leicestershire, an area outside the cloth-making region in this period. Hence it complemented what the farm could provide, so that most cloth makers owned land and kept cattle and sheep. Their skilled work took place after the weather turned cold and the harvests were safely in. Just as the farm tasks required the whole family's efforts, so too did the carding, slubbing, spinning, and warping that went into making a piece of wool cloth. And all that occurred after the usual chores of cleaning, cheese making, and churning.[28]

Another set of circumstances, certainly less mundane, that at least some people in Leicestershire took for granted, centered around certain religious beliefs and practices that the church defined as unacceptable or condemned as heresy. In the middle of the fourteenth century, a popular heresy called Lollardy flourished in the Midlands. Compounded of about equal parts of millenarian ideas, opposition to Roman domination of the church, anticlericalism, and calls for a return to the simplicity of the primitive gospel, Lollardy received its main impetus from a lay desire to control the church. It expressed itself in attacks on priestly prerogatives and such practices as going on pilgrimages and venerating images. That all people had ready access to God without the need for clerical intervention or the use of arcane Latin formulas appealed to an increasingly educated laity who avidly read Lollard translations of the Bible in the common language. With a bit of Bible reading, any literate person could presume to be an equal authority on religious matters with the most learned expositor of Holy Writ.

That was just the problem the astute seventeenth-century observer and philosopher Thomas Hobbes emphasized when he noted that the mere fact of reading the Scriptures led into open disobedience of bishops and pastors: "For after the Bible was translated into English, every man, nay, every boy and wench, that could read English thought they spoke with God Almighty, and understood what he said, . . . and every man became a judge of religion."[29] A less erudite writer warned of the same danger in a London broadside when he pointed out that God had declared himself in Greek and Hebrew—languages reserved for scholars—not in common English.[30] Some dissenting ministers complained that the practice of Bible reading "opened the door to sects and schisms" and led sectarians to decide that anything they thought was the word of God.[31]

Hence the Lollards—the word's root came from a Dutch term meaning "mumbler" or "mutterer," pointing up how they trudged to church services but grumbled about the rites—represented not so much an organized movement as an underground, subversive tendency within English religious life. They survived, even in the face of executions, burnings, and less extreme measures designed to eliminate them. Informal networks of believers, or cells, tied together by secret passwords and word of mouth, radiated outward from Midland centers such as Coventry, over the fields from Drayton-in-the-Clay. Yet another connection between Lollardy and this part of southern Leicestershire was that John Wyclif, the Oxford-educated priest who articulated many of the ideas that sparked the heretical upsurge, spent the last three years of his life exiled to minister in Lutterworth, only a trifle farther away than Coventry.[32] Lollard influence lingered on in the region through an emphasis on a preaching, Bible-teaching ministry within the established church.[33] Protected by powerful noblemen, dissent flourished and made the county the home of heresy and the bane of orthodox churchmen.[34] Nottinghamshire, just north of Leicestershire where Fox would find his first converts, also had a long Lollard history.[35]

Against such a backdrop, it was hardly surprising that a variety of Protestantism approximating Presbyterianism played well in Leicestershire. While some of its leading actors, such as John Willock, rector at Loughborough, had learned their lines from Scottish churchmen, by 1604 the county's laity had taken major roles alongside the clergy, so the Presbyterian script won increasing popularity;

reform built its own audience thanks to the tolerant policy of the diocese's bishops after 1558. The clergy took advantage of this tolerance by inviting laypeople to their "prophesyings" or lectures held to educate ministers.[36] Even after the staunch proponent of Anglicanism John Whitgift became archbishop of Canterbury in 1583 and tried to orchestrate a stricter conformity to the rites of the established church, Presbyterians simply dug down and reformed at the local level. Most Leicestershire ministers tended to be moderates and shunned open involvement in Presbyterian classes or presbyterys, the regional governing bodies, but at least one clergyman refused to conform and persisted in attending his classis or presbytery.[37]

What makes this clergyman so integral to our story was that he served as priest at Drayton-in-the-Clay. The faint trail Anthony Nutter left behind makes him an even more fascinating and intriguing figure. Perhaps a native of Yorkshire but ordained a priest by the bishop of Coventry in 1578, Nutter did not graduate from a university although he may have briefly attended Oxford or Cambridge. His adoption of doctrines and practices that created problems for him demonstrates that one did not have to be a university man to be committed to reform. Four years after his ordination in October 1582, Nutter was invested at St. Michael's in Fenny Drayton, whose sympathetic patron, George Purefey, was lord of the manor and as lay impropriator owned the parish's tithes. (Members of the Purefey, or Purefoy, family were nearly as ubiquitous in the area as good green grass and were staunch Presbyterians.)[38] Presently Nutter found himself in hot water for nonconformity in the face of the new Archbishop Whitgift's efforts to tighten discipline in the church. Nutter refused to read the stated prayers from the *Book of Common Prayer*, refused to require parishioners to kneel for communion, refused to wear a surplice, and refused to use the sign of the cross in baptism or over the ring during the marriage ceremony.[39] These determined reformist stands did not make him a Lollard, but they flowed from the same source as Lollardy, which is to say, a resolute refusal to administer superstitious practices not sanctioned by the Bible. Nutter's obstinacy continued, landing him and seventeen other ministers in prison in 1590 and before the Court of the Star Chamber in Westminster on charges of trying to establish the Presbyterian Discipline as the standard for the church.[40]

Nutter began to attend a classis in neighboring Warwickshire sometime about 1586. Such gatherings were deemed schismatic bodies by church and government officials because they presumed to act in place of bishops as regional authorities over parish ministers. One such underground conventicle in 1589 concluded, if it did not resolve, that neither private baptism nor making the sign of the cross during baptism was permissible. It further held that the faithful should not take communion from the hands of an unlettered minister, though they might listen to a sermon from such a person, apparently on the ground that a layman could read public services as well as a minister. The meeting also provided that no affiliated minister should appear in bishop's court except to protest its unlawfulness. Nutter, one of the fourteen or fifteen ministers with membership in this classis, agreed to be guided by its discipline.[41]

According to his testimony during his trial before the court of the Star Chamber, the classis met voluntarily to further the ministry and consider points of discipline, including to what extent those attending should use the *Book of Common Prayer*. To put the best face possible on this illicit activity, Nutter denied that participants intended to or wanted to break the peace or to challenge the queen's authority by instituting any proscribed form of prayer. They had merely "handled scripture" and explored ways to combat the ultraseparatism called "Brownism," which even these Presbyterian cryptoheretics regarded as a heresy. Moderators had been chosen, he conceded, as well as votes taken, but he could not recall whether the classis had decided that only clergymen associated with it were capable of rightfully administering the sacraments. Whatever they had done, they had certainly not called into question the queen's "whole style" as supreme governor of the Church of England as spelled out in law. Perhaps because of depositions on his behalf given by four of nine prosecution witnesses—depositions denying any subversive intent or practice, including actions pursuant to any "Book of Discipline" or ordination of any priests, elders, or deacons—Nutter and the others got their cases dismissed.[42]

Undoubtedly Nutter's example and influence in his small parish, an influence that extended into Warwickshire by way of the classis, it should be recalled, made him seem even more dangerous to church authorities. In 1593, not long after having his case dismissed in the court of the Star Chamber, he defended one of his parishioners when she refused to be "churched"—that is, submit to being prayed over after the safe delivery of a child—and the following year he admitted to "plucking down the board in the chancel"—presumably a screen designed to shield the sanctuary from the view of the laity. Complaints also filtered up to the bishop that he "does not observe the Book of Common Prayer in all points" and that he mumbled through prayers. Richard Collins, a parishioner whom Nutter charged with swearing, contumely, and absence from the church and the catechism, informed officials that his priest had refused him the sacrament and dared to appear without a surplice. Nutter confessed to the latter minor offense but got away with disciplining Collins without diocesan action, demonstrating how a determined reformer could, within limits, practically usurp his bishop's authority at the parish level. He once handed the contemptuous Collins a copy of the Bible and told him where to turn to find scriptural support for correcting disobedient church members.[43]

Nutter's commitment to his reform principles over the more than twenty years he served Drayton-in-the-Clay wove nonconformity through the warp and woof of parish life. His exemplary teaching and preaching—not to say strict discipline— at the local level made up for his lack of a university degree among peers noted for their advanced education.[44] Just as surely it fed the stiff-neckedness for which such Presbyterian parishes were noted. Over in Ashton, two counties to the northwest, for example, a young devout shopkeeper rebuked his new priest and let him have "my mind to the full: that standing at gospel, with other ceremonies now in use, was a mere Romish foppery, and I should never do it."[45] In Rowton, in Shropshire, the devout complained that their prayers were interrupted by rabble who spent their Sundays dancing under the trees and around the maypole.[46] Of such was the dissenting Presbyterian kingdom made.

With the death of Whitgift and the elevation of the strict Richard Bancroft to the archiepiscopal see of Canterbury, efforts to enforce conformity in dissident parishes redoubled. However ineffective these attempts were in the long run (for Presbyterianism and other species of nonconformity certainly survived), individuals like Nutter suffered in the process. More than ten years after the dismissal of his case by the court of the Star Chamber, he and several other dissenters were called before the bishop's court for violating church order in the way they celebrated divine services and administered the sacraments. To drag out the proceedings, Nutter asked for more time to consider his shortcomings, a delay that failed to change his mind. In fact, while deliberating, he joined another group of Leicestershire clergymen in petitioning the king for further "reformation" in the church.[47] When finally admonished three or four times to right himself, the determined priest instructed his lord bishop by firmly retorting that "whatsoever is the invention of man is not to be allowed in the service of God." While bishops might agree with such views in the abstract, they certainly could not in specific cases such as this one, so on January 30, 1605, Nutter was deprived of his parish.[48]

Thence he moved to West Ardsley (also called Woodkirk) near Wakefield in Yorkshire, one of the hotbeds of nonconformity in the country, where he survived, but hardly flourished, until he died sometime in 1634.[49] (It is a fascinating coincidence that James Nayler, one of the most prominent early Quaker leaders and for a period a rival to Fox, was born and grew up in West Ardsley while Nutter lived there. The circumstance of Nutter's living in two parishes from which these important early leaders of Quakerism emerged highlights his importance in the later genesis of the new sect.) Two items make his later career of interest to us, for they reveal that the policies he pursued in Drayton-in-the-Clay were not aberrations but a part of the man's basic approach. In 1619 he was again presented for nonconformity to the bishop after word got around that he did not require parishioners to kneel to receive communion—indeed, one of the nine members of the neighboring East Ardsley church who came to take communion from Nutter testified that he had absented himself from his home church because he "would never receive the Communion at a reading minister's hand."[50] In 1623 Nutter was brought before his bishop once more for sitting to take communion and again in 1633 for failing to read prayers on designated occasions and not wearing his surplice.[51]

Nutter's theological views, contained in summary notes of three sermons he delivered at Yorkshire "exercises," a kind of monthly theological training school for younger ministers of Calvinist proclivities, point to the basis of his nonconformity. God saved human beings, he affirmed, by divine action alone; those not saved might try to live righteously as a way of extracting salvation from God just as workers or soldiers demanded wages for their toil. ("Whoso seeks just[ification] by good works," Nutter exclaimed in a later sermon, "he makes God a debtor to him. . . . [but] God is debtor to none."[52]) Weakened by sin, however, such feeble and human attempts at righteousness would come to nought, while being freed by grace would bring comfort and assurance.[53] Yet following a sinner's salvation, then God had every right to expect, even require, works "as fruits that [show?] faith [and] inward calm."[54] Nutter put his finger on a dangerous potential in the Calvinism he expounded, for his text (Romans 3: 7–8) told him how the notion of God's election could easily lead people to say that it was permissible to sin so that grace could come of it—or to assume that once one had been saved that one was thereafter free to do anything (a doctrine known as antinomianism). "Not every one," he explained pointedly to his audience of preachers, "who could speak a little Latin" could preach, for it was "no small matter to be a preacher."[55]

These tantalizing notes, sketchy as they are, do offer some insight into what made Nutter the kind of man he was. He demonstrated in his own life and career that the assurance of God's salvation could lead a person to exhibit, as he phrased it, an "inward calm." His reformed Calvinist faith required him to manifest the salvation that God's grace had, however inexplicably, granted him; one sure way of doing so was to stand up for the truth as he knew it. Thus Nutter could defy his bishop regardless of the number of times he was presented for failing to conform to some church ritual for which he could find no justification in the word of God. Satan—he did not name who served the dark spirit, although his allusion to church leaders seems obvious—resembled "an armed man [who] would [try to] bring down the [product?] of the word and preachers."[56] From his own life, Nutter had seen that the powers of the world, represented even by the bishops and archbishops of the church, often sought to inhibit the proclamation of God's word and the kind of discipline it required. His career demonstrated what one of God's chosen servants might expect in a sinful and fallen world.

But Nutter left a nobler legacy than just the hardships he endured: in helping to mold the lives of those who lived in the unlikely hamlets of Drayton-in-the-Clay and West Ardsley, he contributed his share to the mix that made religious reformers like George Fox and James Nayler possible. If they rejected his formal Calvinism—as they would—the sedulity, seriousness, sobriety, and strictness that Nutter and his kind exemplified remained to help form the future, of Fox, Nayler, and the nation. His legacy was a living tradition of principled dissent. Little did he know, of course, that when he spoke at the Yorkshire exercises of how the omnipotent God used the execution of Jesus for the salvation of the world— "God both can and does turn the sins of the wicked, by working out of this more glory"[57]—he had composed his own best epitaph. The consistency of his life certainly showed that a Christian's final allegiance was to the God who acted to turn human foibles into distinct advantages.

The Leicestershire in which George Fox was born and grew to young manhood was a world compounded of both the old and the new: a familiar landscape and styles of rural activity that went back time out of mind—which timelessness could only impart a sense of security to those who knew them—and a slowly evolving and changing religious world. These latter developments, related to points of conflict between local parishes and central church officials as well as to the intrusion of theological positions different from traditional ones, form the basis of most of the story that will unfold here. The world and culture that Fox absorbed as he grew up enabled him to speak the language of ordinary

Englishmen and Englishwomen, particularly dissenters or those so inclined, and to fashion a message to appeal to them. Because he understood his country and had no need to ask questions about it, he could legitimately call into question the inability of its religious institutions to satisfy the needs of those among whom he traveled. Still, his message had to be different enough to distinguish it from that of others, else no one, then or now, would be especially interested in him or it. To be a successful religious reformer one must be in, but not wholly of, one's culture.

Because this study of George Fox naturally concentrates on his efforts to promote and institute religious reformation, the impact of his conflict with old authority and the new religious understandings growing out of it will be at stage center; inevitably his own personal struggles against authority will become intertwined with larger questions of religious change. It is clear from the success of the Quaker movement that Fox was not alone and could speak to the needs of many other individuals. Raised to be obedient to authority, as witnessed by the catechetical training the church expected him to have, he nevertheless responded to a strong call to an allegiance above the mundane. In some ultimately unknown way, both the call and his personal decision to devote his life to its implications grew out of his background and the way he came to understand it. Let the interested observer be forewarned, therefore, not to forget the larger backdrop against which the main story is played out, not only because it is always there to add detail and color but also because through its early influence the human being depicted here carried the past into the future.

2

⊗⅋⅏

Lads Will Be Men

As a child George Fox was something of a prig; as he himself put it, he exhibited "a gravity and staidness of mind and spirit not usual in children." He was serious beyond his years and never strayed from the straight and narrow way. Shunning the company of other children, he never succumbed to the snares that tempted him "almost to despair," never after his eleventh year forgot the "pureness and righteousness" he had adopted by that early age. Both his countenance and speech betrayed a marked "sadness of spirit." Overseen by zealous Presbyterian parents, young Fox learned how "to walk to be kept pure."[1]

His early training took. By the time he was a youth and apprenticed to a shoemaker, he was so downright officious in importuning his fellows that they could hardly endure his company. To escape them and their worldliness, he betook himself to some hidden garret or hid himself in a dark corner.[2] In the last memoir he dictated, he described himself as "afraid" of all, young as well as old, the profane as well as those who professed religion.[3] He adopted as his own the rigid and austere standards of the religious reformers who were trying to change the habits of England. Probably without knowing it, certainly without fully knowing why, he had accepted the authority of people he did not know and had not seen. George was not something of a prig, he *was* a prig, and a little prig at that.

Few of Fox's contemporaries displayed this high level of purity. John Angier, twenty years older and a Presbyterian in Essex and Lancashire, remembered how he was provoked by "bad company, lascivious talk, or excess in the use of the Creature,"[4] and Gervase Disney, who grew up in Lincolnshire, catalogued his boyhood activities of robbing orchards; stealing from his father, brothers, and sisters; talking idly; profaning the Sabbath; disobeying his parents; and breaking the seventh commandment, at least in entertaining unchaste thoughts.[5] Another Presbyterian, Oliver Heywood, raised in Bolton, Lancashire, confessed publicly that he could not "remember the time or age, state or place wherein I was free from sin or perpetuating thereof." So beset was he with lust that he had to walk the fields, praying to be restrained.[6] Even in a unique place free from the world's common temptations, a place like Alcester in Warwickshire, Thomas Beard found himself committing the "black sin" of lying.[7] The famous Baptist preacher John Bunyan could only progress upward from the place where he began his pilgrimage, for cursing, swearing, lying, and blaspheming became, he recalled, almost second nature when he was but nine or ten years old; a ringleader in all manner of vice, he consciously "let loose the reins of my lust."[8] Judging from his *Journal*, either such experiences were unknown to Fox or else he suppressed all memory of them.

What then fashioned the man from the boy? In part it was the nature of the area, the background ambience that people accepted without question. The community, even its local aristocracy, turned in on itself, and its members seemed mostly interested in bettering their lot. The county boasted no large houses, suggesting that extremes of rich and poor were not as obvious as in other parts of England; it was basically a land of commoners. Outsiders scoffed at Leicestershire's serious strivers as "impolite" and looked down on its common people as rattling full of the beans they grew so plentifully.[9] Undoubtedly most people in the Midlands were rude and rough—illiterate, provincial, and narrow. People with the name Fox abounded in the region; one in the fourteenth century was a mayor of Northampton and a Lollard supporter, another three hundred years later even displayed a coat of arms.[10]

Fox's father's craft also played a role in shaping the son. Christopher Fox was a weaver, a skill placing him near the top of the village hierarchy.[11] His occupation inevitably involved other family members; George long after used images suggesting his familiarity with working with wool.[12] Assuming that the operation was a small one—a safe assumption given the size of the village and the consequent size of the local market for his goods—the elder Fox would not have had more than two looms. Unlike the average small weaver, Christopher had enough space in his ample house to locate the loom in a separate room.[13] With their livelihood made within the house, the family had to live close together, finding it impossible to escape one another, especially on the long winter nights from November to March.

When working Christopher sat at his loom with his feet off the floor to pump the treadles. Each time he pushed on the treadles to raise the heddles he had to throw the yarn-loaded shuttle across the width of the cloth, about a yard's distance, grab it on the other side before it hit the floor, and pull the beater firmly against this latest yarn to add to the material already on the loom. Slow and tedious, as well as requiring an unnatural working posture, the process took nearly two hours to turn out a yard at the rate of ten to fifteen throws a minute. When doing broadcloth one and a half yards wide, someone else had to catch and throw the shuttle back across the cloth. After the piece came off the loom, it was scoured in a mixture of domestic and barnyard "liquors" or urine to leech out the remaining oil and sizings; inspected for knots and burrs; taken to a fulling mill where it was soaked and beaten to thicken it and make it shrink. Finally someone stretched it taut and let it dry.[14]

From tagging along with their father to buy wool, either raw or already spun, to catching and throwing the shuttle, to collecting the "liquors" for leeching, the children of the Fox household took part in their father's work. George, oldest of the four children, was born in July 1624. Dorothy came along not quite two years after her brother; John was baptized on December 20, 1629;[15] the birthday of sister Katherine is unknown.[16] As the eldest, George would have been the one his father expected to bear the heaviest burden. Because of such expectations, as well as the normal relationship existing between a son and father, George exhibited ambivalent feelings toward Christopher. In half his specific references to his father—using the terms "natural" or "in the flesh" with "father," both to identify him and to stress that he owed him less than he did to his more recently encountered heavenly parent—he explicitly identified his father as associated with his enemies.[17] He did not trouble himself to record when his father died, an event that likely occurred in the late 1650s.[18] Remembering that the neighbors referred to his father as a "Righteous Christer," a derogatory term underscoring rigidity in matters of religion, and reporting that he had learned righteousness by age eleven, George may have been hinting indirectly at his own natural and continuing ambivalence toward the most important authority in his early years, one from whom he could seldom get away, who dominated his life and who assigned his son necessary, demanding, even unpleasant tasks. One of his future opponents, Richard Baxter, reacted differently when his father was teased as a "Puritan." It cured him of his frivolity of going to maypole dances and led him to appreciate his father's strong convictions.[19]

George's relationship with his mother, Mary, was less uncertain. He remembered her in relation to her family, the Lagos, as though she had better connections than her more plebeian husband, a not uncommon situation, then or now: men are more likely than women to marry up.[20] William Penn, later Fox's traveling companion and co-worker in the Quaker movement, described her as a woman "accomplished above most of her degree" in Drayton-in-the-Clay,[21] but he knew little at first hand about her or her home village.[22] His informant was undoubtedly Fox himself, thus lending added weight to Penn's statement that from his mother George "met with little difficulty," for she was "tender and indulgent over him."[23] In contrast to her husband, George's mother exercised less outward authority and made fewer explicit demands on her son. Fox always prided himself on the lessons he learned by experience. Perhaps because his mother was more indulgent, he responded quickly when she made a request; for example, when she was an old woman and near death he went off promptly to visit her after she asked him to come.[24] With his father, even after he reached adulthood, he had to remind himself that a refusal to obey would lead strangers to comment on his disobedience.[25] Fox saw and learned from childhood experience that a father's will was external and limiting, a mother's permissive and indulgent. This observation, and the way he acted on its lesson in the future, colored his later religious and theological perceptions.[26] Just as important, it helped determine how he would himself respond when he had to act as an outer authority toward people who refused to internalize—or even rebelled against—the values and views he believed to be correct.

To add to his ambivalence regarding his father, when George was fifteen years old, the elder Fox became churchwarden of the parish,[27] the most important lay post in a church and a significant one also in the community. This leadership position, a natural one for a layman with time to think and even read, lent additional emphasis to Christopher Fox's authority and standing.[28] The young Fox might have felt pride in the honor thus done his father, but he might just as well have resented the added power his parent now had, for a churchwarden was a kind of community censor, charged not only with providing the things necessary for public worship but also with presenting to the authorities swearers, scolds, people who lived together without benefit of marriage, unlicensed midwives, and other sinners and minor criminals. Most men refused the honor if they could avoid it.[29] Fox later conceded that his father possessed "a seed of God,"[30] but it apparently never grew. So George must have been pained later when none of his relatives joined him to break away from what he called the "public church," the Church of England, despite their strong Presbyterianism.[31]

His father and mother never indicated the least support for their son's religious convictions and the extremes to which they drove him. Twice, for example, they were ashamed enough when he was committed to prison in Derby to make the journey there to bail him out and to try to reason with him about his error in attacking the priests. Being respectable folk, however strongly committed to nonconformist Presbyterianism, they simply could not understand how a sensible person like their son would invite jail because of his religion.[32] Certainly, at age twenty-six, George should see that. On another occasion, when Fox was preaching in nearby Atherstone, he stirred the locals up so much that they thought him mad and pleaded with his parents to keep him penned up, something they at first seemed inclined to do.[33]

Yet from his family Fox inherited more than the kind of conflicts, both internal and external, common in other households. The family was well off financially, well above the degree associated with people of their class in the village and nation; indeed, they were rich enough to be able to leave money to each of their children.[34] They pledged £100 in bond money to the Derby authorities on their son's behalf, an amount pointing to far-above-average resources.[35] When he took his leave of home at the age of nineteen, George was apparently given enough money to pay for his food, lodging, and travel expenses. Later, fending off an attack from one of their son's critics, his parents reluctantly conceded that he left home with a "great" sum,[36] and Fox admitted frankly that he had "wherewith both to keep myself from being chargeable to others and to administer something to the necessity of others."[37] Clearly he had deep pockets.

And they got deeper. Fox benefited somewhat later from a large legacy that freed him from the need to pursue gainful employment, except for brief periods, for the rest of his life. Unfortunately, no details of this bequest survive. All we know is that he inherited a large sum, equivalent probably to more than $130,000 in modern currency. He called it his "birthright," which if taken literally suggests that it was his inheritance as the family's eldest son.[38] He had no more than started his public ministry when a clerical detractor in a position to know details of the family's position, the minister at Drayton-in-the-Clay, charged he was "full of gold and silver," and his parents allowed as much.[39] By the 1680s some of his critics alleged that he lived off secured funds, something he denied firmly although he just as carefully did not deny having the money. His inherited wealth placed him among that tiny and fortunate minority of English people whose lives were free from the need to earn a livelihood by the work of their hands and the sweat of their brow.[40]

Not as clear as the matter of his inheritance—and that is almost as murky as can be—was where and how Fox received his education. The only specific date he mentioned regarding his early years was age eleven; this he marked as a decisive turning point, when he left his childhood behind. Before age eleven he was taught as a child, suggesting that any formal education he received occurred before 1635.[41] That he learned to read was obvious—his writings and speeches were replete with biblical references; that he was taught to write was less obvious, for his distinctive handwriting—large, broad, and scrawling—was ofttimes not quite readable, and he made up his own spelling rules according to the moment's inspiration. Perhaps like others in the seventeenth century, he was taught to read but not to write, so he had to learn as best he could;[42] certainly, he never excelled at penmanship. Later, one of his followers would redo a scribbled letter before it was sent.[43] Since weavers often placed a book above their loom and read while working, and since the elder Fox could sign his name,[44] George may have learned to scratch out his letters at home.

Fox's spoken and written sentences had a tendency to run on, repeating the same point again and again. He was certainly not familiar with the classical learning that characterized the education of his day. Even supporters sometimes felt the need to explain his ignorance of schoolmen's science, his often "uncouth and unfashionable" expressions that grated on "nice ears."[45] A critic warned listeners to mind the geese when Fox preached, for he "has more subtlety than learning."[46] His use of metaphors and images suggests an interest in matters esoteric. One follower, a self-styled chemist who traveled with him in 1655, remembered how impressed he was when his companion spoke of the "glory of the first body and of the Egyptian learning and of the language of the birds."[47] Fox likewise shared common popular superstitions. Once he tried to convince a visitor who had come to see him in prison that the world was flat because no one had ever reported seeing it bend. When his incredulous guest wanted to know what happened to the sun when it set in the evening, Fox responded that he was not sure but that it probably crossed back under the earth some way during the night to rise at the same place the next morning.[48]

George's childhood gravity did not allow him time for the kind of frivolity that marked other boys' lives. If, like other Leicestershire lads, he ever hunted sourgrass to chew, made a ball out of a pig's bladder, or went bird's-nesting to find beautifully tinted eggs,[49] he left no mention of these pursuits. Instead, he carefully watched his fellows. Most of them, truth to tell, lived remarkably similar dissolute lives—his term for them was "wanton." Being strangers to the private covenant of righteousness to which he had pledged himself, most people he observed ate and drank too much, were quickly devoured by their lusts, lived in filthiness, and, what was worse, loved it. Since his parish was staunchly nonconformist and committed to reformed religion, the dissolute lives he saw there must have troubled him even more. Let a man get hold of a penny and like as not he would end up in the alehouse making merry; were he to get two, he would probably wager on his prowess at bowling.[50] Naturally, Fox steered clear of such wantonness. The rough and tumble of village life was not for him—George ate and drank for his health only and set aside his own special days to fast and to read the Scriptures.[51]

Such youthful shunning of the world's ways made his parents consider sending him off to prepare for the ministry. Sometime, after age eleven, however, a family conclave decided he should be apprenticed to George Gee, a shoemaker who lived in Mancetter, less than half an hour's stroll across the valley west of Drayton. Gee not only trained George in the shoemaker's craft but also let him tend sheep, as well as sell wool and cattle.[52] An apprenticeship, designed to reduce vagrancy and vagabondage, usually lasted seven years. The apprentice meanwhile resided under his master's roof, ate at his table, and received his instruction, not only about the craft to be learned but also on morals, and sometimes even a degree of formal education. The law enjoined him to be faithful to his master, and the community expected him to render good service in return for his training. As much as anything else, this system sought to inculcate and perpetuate the community's standards and values.[53]

Fox remembered his years as an apprentice as being seminal in his own life and important in that of his master. He learned how to manage sums of money and to get along in the give-and-take world of barter and trade. He found the solitude of tending sheep especially appealing. As for his master, "While I was with him, he was blessed," he wrote, "but after I left him, he broke and came to nothing." Hence he prided himself on his ability to drive a bargain that would enlarge his master's pocketbook without having to mislead customers or deal with them wrongly. Before long word got around that the tag George Fox put on the goods entrusted to him was his final price.[54] Fox's comment about his master's misfortune also provides an early example of an unfortunate habit that remained with him throughout his life, namely, his inclination to view his association with a person as redounding to that one's behalf or betterment, hurt or hindrance, depending on the quality of their relations. On occasion this trait led him to gloat about the misfortune of an enemy or opponent and to act as though God would surely punish anyone who dared resist his efforts.[55]

Young George learned how to make shoes well enough to put his hand to that task on the odd occasion when he needed to replenish his funds, and his later associates grudgingly conceded that shoemaking was his trade.[56] A lowly occupation shoemaking may have been—after he became known his critics liked to sneer that he was "a poor journeyman shoemaker," a "blockhead" who "could not live by that trade"[57]—but it was also the kind of craft that offered him a chance to sit by himself, to think, and to reflect on his experiences and observations in the light of his Bible reading. His trade actually encouraged an introspection that led him to trust his own sense of what he should do and be rather than relying on the advice and will of others. He often admonished his acquaintances for their shortcomings, but when they took umbrage at his sermonizing he would withdraw into a corner or hide himself away from those not favored with his insight into their own failings.[58] Fox's individualistic and melancholic temperament was inevitably fed by his apprenticeship.

Shepherding his master's flocks had the same effect. A sheepherder, wrote a contemporary guide, "ought to be of a good nature, wise, skillful, countable, and right in all his doings," but unfortunately few developed these characteristics. A loner like Fox, already differing sharply from his counterparts, was not given to the ill manners, stubbornness, and idleness that marked his fellow apprentices.[59] Just the opposite: Fox now had the time and solitude to sate his desire to understand the world around him. Looking after his flocks in the fields, he had a chance to think and try to place himself in the universe. He observed and discovered important lessons, and later he drew on his experiences while tending sheep. He once recounted how a flock of crows pecked at the body of a dead sheep until they opened its belly and tore at its intestines.[60] In a polemical pamphlet, aimed at those in other churches, he charged that all their prophets had acted "like foxes that have worried the lambs and [instead] have not stood in the gap" to fend off the danger.[61] He learned that each day, whatever it might bring, was equally good, and he lashed out at those who refused to grasp the opportunity thus given to praise God. Just because a day was "rainy or slobby" or frosty or snowy or hot and sultry did not make it an ill day; people who said so "are in the evil, who call the good evil; and thus they are never content."[62]

Herding sheep taught such lessons. For example, yeaning ewes required close attention, regardless of the weather. Like all shepherd apprentices, Fox learned to watch carefully during the blustery February and March nights when sheep gave birth. A ewe might need him to assist her during the birth process. Or perhaps the lamb would be born especially weak, and the alert shepherd would have to be ready to blow life into its heaving nostrils. If the about-to-be born yeanling presented rump first, then Fox would have to reach inside the ewe until he grasped the lamb's feet to pull it out.[63]

Fox went with the sheep to market, negotiating with collectors of road and market tolls along the way.[64] Market days offered people a welcome break from their routine, for folk from nearby villages brought goods to sell and came to take bargains home. Traveling booksellers hawked ballads and pamphlets, and such itinerates always spread news of the latest mysterious natural wonder or rumors about what some distant dissenter had said or done. The voices of buyers and sellers haggling over prices rivaled the shouts of jugglers, tricksters, gamblers, and beer, cider, and perry sellers—all vying for the visitors' scarce pennies. The straitlaced Fox did not regard these occasions as times for frivolity and light living. Probably because of his serious mien and his standoffish ways, other youths and the people he labeled "rude" laughed and jeered at him for his refusal to bet on a wrestling contest, until, fed up with the abuse, he stalked off by himself. Such experiences reinforced his aloofness and magnified the distance he sensed between himself and others around him. To reassure himself about the differences the jeering implied, he took to rationalizing that people generally had "a love to me, for my innocency and honesty," but he recorded no acceptance of his bluenosed prudishness.[65]

In the late summer of 1643 Fox had two related experiences that made him break off his apprenticeship before the end of the usual seven years. The first occurred while he represented his master at nearby Atherstone's famous cheese fair on September 8.[66] While there he ran into a cousin, like himself one who was committed to the dissenting religious faith, and a friend of his cousin. The two invited George to share a jug of beer with them, it being warm and they being thirsty. Fox readily agreed, but after drinking the first pint, the other two decided to see who could drink the most and pledged that the one stopping first would have to cover the tab. Fox was shocked. He had no objections to drinking beer, but these people supposedly adhered to the precepts of sober religion, and now they were engaging in the frivolity of toasting each other and competing to put away the most alcohol. It confirmed his view that self-indulgence permeated every aspect of the society. He was amazed that a cousin who shared his own approach to religion could take part in a drinking contest. Of course he knew such things went on, for he had long tried to separate himself from the loose living around him, but on this occasion he was tested by the world's wantonness. Not for something like this drinking of toasts had he maintained his innocence.

George Fox was not even tempted, so it was no serious challenge. He tossed enough money on the table to pay for the whole jug of beer and then announced that he would leave rather than have anything to do with this little business: "If it be so, I'll leave you." Let those who wanted to act like everybody else do so.

He hurried through the rest of his business and left for home, still visibly troubled by the events of the afternoon, the perversity of the present generation, and how close he had come to being caught up in it. He could not go to sleep that evening—he could not even bring himself to go to bed—so he walked around. He prayed and walked, walked and prayed, and then prayed some more. If there was any hope for the world, he had believed, then it would have to come from the younger generation, people like himself, young people who could see and understand how perverse and wanton things had become and would endeavor to set things right. But what he had witnessed that summer's day was enough to convince him that little could be expected from those who followed traditional paths, whether young or old. Suddenly, though still unsettled, he had a revelation: he saw that he had embarked on a special path through life. He would have to remain separate from the world and its people. "Thou seest," he sensed clearly, "how young people go together into vanity and old people into the earth; and thou must forsake all, both young and old, and keep out of all, and be as a stranger unto all."[67]

Fox's experience, the outward events conditioning the inward measuring, amounted to a turning point in his life and verified what he had known before. He had long been a stranger to all, a person who set himself apart, but his purpose in life had not been clear. The goal remained so dim that he could not glimpse it fully; it was not worked out or opened to him completely. He was still young and his experiences limited, for he had only traveled on his master's business a few times and to places fairly near home. He would just have to await further direction.

Soon, probably the next day after the beer episode, he acted. On September 9, 1643, just two months after his nineteenth birthday, he left home. Breaking off all contact with his parents, he decided to travel and mix with others as little as possible. His route took him roughly down the same Watling Street that passed so near his home. For nine months Fox traveled in the English Midlands and as far south as London, seeking some direction but seldom able to rise above the frustrating feeling of despair that, try as he might through fasting and Bible reading, he simply could not leave behind. Whether or not his original goal was to reach London, the economic center and capital of the country, he ended up there.[68]

Fox's choice of a time for travel did not appear very auspicious, for winter was coming on and England was in the throes of a civil war. One of his contemporaries recalled how during the war he walked better than 110 miles from Hereford to London, lest by riding his horse he risk having it confiscated when crossing military lines.[69] Moreover, the conflict centered in the very Midland counties where Fox went, but strangely his *Journal* never refers to his trip's violent backdrop.[70] He seemed more preoccupied with his personal problems than with issues of wider significance, yet he could hardly have escaped hearing about them and probably participating in the discussions.

The war pitted supporters of the Stuart king Charles and his prerogatives, the aristocratic Cavaliers, against Parliament and its adherents. Starting the year before, in 1642, the fighting originated in a dispute over exactly how much power and authority each branch of the government was to exercise, whether the king had the power to rule as well as reign, tax as well as spend. It did not take long for the issue to broaden into more general questions concerning the role of the monarch within the English government and how powerful the central government should be. Some of the more alert men in the parliamentary ranks presently raised more basic issues such as the kind of church that ought to be established—indeed, whether *any* church should be, the role of the House of Lords, the extent of the right of suffrage, and, before it was all over, the kind of property arrangements the kingdom should enjoy. Intertwined with such broad matters were disputes about innumerable minor matters such as the correct mode of baptism, whether a church should have a written creed or not, the role of the king's advisers, whether a bill approved by the House of Commons had to receive the assent of the House of Lords, and which officeholders should be elected, which appointed.

Debates over such issues served to underscore the extent to which the war had loosed and unsettled everything that had been nailed down and settled before. Every church service, in fact, provided a new opportunity to address broader issues. On Easter Sunday, 1644, at Uppingham, in Leicestershire's eastern neighbor Rutland County, the assistant preacher was set to administer the sacrament of the eucharist when he turned to his congregation, smote himself on the chest, and exclaimed, "As I am a faithful sinner, neighbors, this is my morning's draught," and he turned the chalice up and drank the wine down. And in Nuneaton, just across the ridge from Drayton-in-the-Clay, Vicar Cradock demanded of the Lord: "[D]o not thou stand a neuter; but take one side, that we may see which it is that is thy cause." Such antics led one prominent royalist to mutter out loud, "By which teachers we may guess at the flocks."[71] From Leicestershire thousands of Parliament's supporters, claiming to be situated in the midst of dangers and fears, petitioned the king in June 1642 to settle a "learned and godly" ministry upon them and disarm the papists.[72] Hence as Fox prepared to leave home in an effort to find himself, the nation seemed engaged in a far-reaching argument about where it would finally find itself. The young traveler was surely in a position to witness elemental and local discussions of questions with broad national import.

He might hear and participate in such discussions, that is, if he could avoid involvement in one army or another. Just the right age to become a soldier, Fox and young men like him were targets of the earl of Stamford's order of 1642 that untrained men should report to Leicester for enlistment in his parliamentary army.[73] Fox stayed away, even while others from throughout the staunchly parliamentary area flocked to the colors to serve garrison duty at Coventry.[74] But he could hardly avoid spillovers from the conflict. Ten weeks later, in August, a royalist army of three thousand foot soldiers and six troops of horses under Prince Rupert plundered southwestward from Leicester on its destructive way to Coventry in Warwickshire.[75] The royalist army approached within thirteen miles of Drayton. The Cavaliers depredated the countryside around and were recalled as "debased wicked wretches . . . raked out of hell."[76] If he was not close enough to hear musket shots, then Fox certainly could not miss the smoke from burning houses as the armies passed over land he knew like the back of his hand. The next year Fox decided it was time to leave.

With that decision at the age of nineteen, Fox cut many of the last ties that bound him to his family and ventured out on his own. His travels for his master had given him a glimpse of a world far broader than the one in and around Mancetter, Drayton-in-the-Clay, and the Midlands as a whole; now London beckoned, the center of the country, where the war had freed ordinary people to discuss the religious and political innovations that soon appeared everywhere else. Whether he knew exactly where he would stop is impossible to say, but just getting away would certainly offer an opportunity to explore his growing understanding of his future course and to gain a valuable new perspective of himself. The lad would be a man.

3

⊰⊱

The Longest Way About
Is the Nearest Way Home

In the time-honored way of all pilgrims, Fox realized he had to get away from a locality he already knew too well. His emotional state, certainly, and his nagging desire to understand his place in the world, just as certainly, could hardly be left behind. Yet in a way he probably did not want to think about, his troubling confusion and wonderment would stay with him as he traveled.

From our vantage point, George's itinerary makes little sense beyond the fact that his general path was down Watling Street toward London. He wandered about a great deal in the course of his journey. Maybe he took detours to visit relatives. The chance to replenish his purse by making shoes may have led him to decide to stop in one place rather than going on to another.[1] He may also have followed the cycle of market days from one town to another. On two occasions he chose to stop where parliamentary armies were garrisoned. Many of these soldiers were youths his own age. All had hair cut so unfashionably short that they were tagged "Roundheads," but the young traveler did not cut his own long hair. Fox may have found, as others certainly did, that Parliament's garrison towns offered a haven from the slander that sober religious dissenters faced from royalist neighbors. One contemporary reported how persons noted for piety suffered verbal abuse and even had their personal belongings plundered.[2] Fox did make much of the fact that people he called "rude" laughed at him and that something about him attracted unwanted public notice; the fear he recalled may have come from just this type of harassment.[3]

That he visited towns controlled by Parliament, carefully avoiding royalist strongholds, also hinted at his sympathies in the conflict. He clearly did not share philosopher Thomas Hobbes's assessment that few of the "common people cared much for either of the causes."[4] Later, when the occasion demanded it, Fox could convey the impression that he shared the aims of the parliamentarians.[5] It is not inconceivable that he tried to remain one step ahead of the impressment gangs. Fox may have operated just on the other side of legality, for vagrancy laws prohibited travel without authorization from the parish priest. While this regulation often went unenforced, particularly during harvest time when extra laborers were needed, during a civil conflict zealous authorities could easily use it to exercise control over undesirable strangers,[6] itself a very practical reason to avoid staunchly royalist areas. His travels certainly helped him to come to know himself.

Others could tell something about Fox merely by his outward looks and bearing. His greyish leather outfit, consisting of breeches, doublet, and hat, did not help his appearance, for it associated him with workers and other common folk.[7] It was tough enough and practical too, standing up well in all his travels, but even with the best of care it snagged and pulled against an unobserved thorn or briar, a rough log, a protruding nail. When the weather got warm, it held in body heat and exuded a strong body odor. His eccentric manner and appearance underscored his disdain of human fashion and served to attract the favorable response of others inclined to dissent also.[8] Every day when he got dressed he made his statement about who he was. The broad face, prominent cheek bones, and strong jaw that ran in the Fox family implied a class origin conforming more with his suit of leather than his long hair, a style the aristocratic cavaliers fancied.[9] A bit above average height—taller than five feet, seven inches—and stocky, he had a strong build, powerful enough to separate two desperately fighting men if he desired.[10]

He first stopped in Lutterworth, a village in Leicestershire, only about thirteen miles southeast of Drayton and close enough for him to reach on his first day's walk. He remained there some time, perhaps staying with relatives, certainly soaking up the atmosphere of a town that had sheltered the arch-Lollard John Wyclif more than 250 years earlier. He did not need to visit Lutterworth to find out about Wyclif—in fact, if he had the experience of one visitor a few years later he would not have found a single soul who had heard of him[11]—for English translations of the contentious Latin works that had issued from the heretic's pen were widely available. Fox's mature doctrines mirrored the reformer's call for a return to the simplicity of the original church of Christ and for removal of the special prerogatives usurped by the priests of the church of Antichrist. When Fox thundered that the true church "has been lost, for she has been in the wilderness and the false church has ruled upon the beast's and dragon's power," the echoes from the Lutterworth Lollard's sentiments sounded loud and clear.[12] Later he would endorse the Lollards as God's witnesses in a time of apostasy.[13]

Fox next moved on to Northampton, eighteen miles closer to London and the most powerful parliamentary garrison in the south Midlands. A hotbed of dissenter opposition to the royal cause, Northampton supplied large sums of money to the rebels. Under continuing threats from the royal forces, the citizens of Northampton converted the bridges over the Nene River into drawbridges and repaired the town's protective walls. The threats intensified the sense of discipline its grim-faced inhabitants mustered to defend their town. Northamptonians also labored overtime to shoe the army, making it even more appealing for a skilled shoemaker who was seeking work and money. Townsfolk could forgive the soldiers billeted in their homes when everyone so obviously benefited from the money the shoe industry brought in. As one observer put it, "this town stands on other men's legs." Its market, situated on spacious Market Hill and opened every Wednesday, Friday, and Saturday, was not only a center for trade—shoes, of course, and horses—but also for discussing the latest matters of interest.[14] Perhaps wintering here as 1643 became 1644, Fox lingered long enough to attract the attention of fellow religious sectarians.

The willows on the banks of the Nene were near budding by the time the young itinerant moved six miles southward to the newly liberated Newport Pagnell, now a garrison town, in Buckinghamshire; Newport Pagnell had only the past Christmas Eve fallen to parliamentary besiegers. Always a way station for those on a journey somewhere else, the town immediately became a kind of magnet attracting its healthy share of radical agitators and religious enthusiasts. George Fox, local tradition has it, checked in at the Waggon and Horses public house. Given the excitement in the area, he got an ear- and eyefull every time he went out.[15]

The town's governor, Sir Samuel Luke, a Presbyterian by conviction but fiery in action, commanded the permanent garrison of twelve hundred foot soldiers, and sometimes watched it swell to six times that number. Ordered to pillage the property of the area's royalists and papists, Luke's troops invaded surrounding churches, ripping out statues, tearing altars away from the wall, smashing stained-glass windows, and liberating the silver plate—all for the good of the cause and parishioner education. In the evenings they listened to sermons, many delivered by military men, offering a religious justification for their daily rampages. It was no wonder that law-abiding citizens were soon grousing to Luke about his men's behavior (or misbehavior), particularly after soldiers forced the local minister to flee the town.[16] Officers and common soldiers, another observer reported, constantly exclaimed against ministers as papists and averred that their "steeple-houses" ought to be pulled down.[17] Soon Luke informed London that the people of the region had grown "so malignant" about his troops that he had no power to force them to surrender provisions for maintaining the garrison.[18] The stern Luke saw immorality rampant wherever his men went: "[F]or here women can be delivered of children without knowing men, if they belie not themselves, and men and women . . . lie together and insist it not be adultery."[19] No wonder that when Fox's later antagonist John Bunyan chronicled his own soldiering at Newport Pagnell, he confessed that he felt "the reins to my lust" loosening and succumbed to "all manner of vice and ungodliness."[20]

Luke was just as concerned about "Anabaptistical" elements that threatened to carry his already radicalized army to extremes.[21] Try as he might to make sure that the young conscripts in his army got the right kind of religious training—two sermons each Sunday and another on Thursday, as well as required prayers and Bible reading each morning, were the norm[22]—Luke simply could not keep his charges from hearing the numerous preachers who descended upon the garrison like a flock of dark-coated ravens. One of these preachers was Captain Paul Hobson. Starting life as a Buckinghamshire tailor who preached on the side, he would work as a barber-surgeon in London and eventually emerge as a noted leader among the capital city's Particular Baptists.[23]

What made nonconformist Hobson and his allies such a threat was their total rejection of the notion of an established national church. For them, the true church consisted only of the set-apart body of adult, baptized believers: no more, no less. Any church that presumed to include all the people who lived in a particular parish, just because they lived there, had no claim to being an authentic church of Christ. Hence, strikingly unlike the mainstream churches almost since the beginning of Christianity, Particular Baptists practiced adult baptism only and separated themselves from the apostates around them. In thus opting out of the respectable religious community, they inevitably brought down on themselves the charge of being "Anabaptists" or "rebaptizers," in theological terms people so radical that they rejected the efficacy of previous baptism.[24] Anabaptism also had secular connotations, for it had long since become a label respectable polemicists used to tie their opponents to those German radicals of the previous century who sought to introduce the Kingdom of God in Münster. Such libeling illustrated the depth of fear uneasy moderates exhibited toward those who wanted to move beyond the accepted boundaries of the established religion of the day and promote a faith based on salvation originating in individual experience.

Hobson's sermons, which advocated replacing human reason and the letter of the Bible with a kind of individualized spirituality, got him into almost immediate trouble with Luke and the more moderate parliamentary forces he represented. Baxter, a chaplain, damned Hobson as one of the fountains of antinomianism in the army.[25] It could hardly have been otherwise when the former tailor denied the authority of those who used civil laws to contain the "word of Christ." Let men try to constrain spiritual worship, he preached, and "they take upon themselves the authority and prerogative of Christ," for "civil laws cannot reach Christ's government." "Own truth in the spirit," he advised, "and thou shall understand truth in the letter, but we can never own truth in the spirit, till the truth in the spirit owns us." He took aim directly at the national church: "[T]he Holy Ghost nowhere considers church members under a natural [that is, human] relation, but under a spiritual [one]." A church consisted of those souls, he affirmed, "who through the coming in of Christ are made able to believe in Christ, that they are . . . freely, and voluntarily to give themselves up to Christ, to walk in the acknowledgment of Christ, in or according to his word." No one, he affirmed, could understand the truths Christ imparts unless that one "enjoys Christ within"; "none knows but he that does enjoy it, and none can declare it but he that knows it."[26]

Such a theology, based on the individual infused with the spirit of Christ, one willing to subordinate both reason and the authority of the written word to that experience, foretold a sharp break with established religion—the kind of religion concerned with questions of church order, the real presence of Christ in the eucharist, and even the correct mode of baptism. Hobson wanted, as he phrased it, a community for "people who kiss and embrace one another in spirit, and . . . live in loving and enjoying one another."[27] The nineteen-year-old seeker George Fox, judging from the theology he later formulated, found such ideas particularly exhilarating and inspiring. For more than thirty years, Fox followed the career of the Baptist.[28] True, he left Newport Pagnell before Hobson showed up, but views like the captain's hovered over and infected the army, or so claimed one very unnerved observer.[29] The equally fearful Luke had Hobson locked up.[30]

In June 1644 Fox stopped at Barnet, having traveled thirty-seven miles, the longest leg of his trip, and now only about ten miles from his final destination. Pleasantly sited four hundred feet above the Thames valley on the high road north of London, the town boasted numerous inns commodious enough to house the large number of people who traveled through or who visited for a weekend or a day's outing to flee the ague of the capital. London's "sulphurous air" could cause the most ambitious soul to droop, as Thomas Ellwood, young secretary of the poet John Milton, learned when he went there a generation later and had to escape to the countryside after less than two months.[31] It was not unusual for 150 coaches, not to mention private carriages and wagons, to pass through every day. The Red Lion Inn had welcomed such visitors since the sixteenth century.[32]

In bustling Barnet Fox faced one of the darkest periods of his life. Now nearly twenty, he was beset by "a temptation to despair." It is impossible to determine the exact nature of his temptation, for he was never very specific about it. His depression was probably partly the result of mere homesickness and a sense of guilt for going off on his own and leaving his family, for he did realize that he "had forsaken my relations" and "done amiss against them." Feeling like the biblical Prodigal Son, he became dejected as he saw himself, fleeing from worldly responsibilities, and moaned in his guilt, "Was I ever so before?" Now, he searched his past life in detail to determine if and how he had wronged others. At times he could not face another soul, and so he remained shut away for long periods in his room. In a town swarming with summer visitors and people passing through, Fox probably contrasted the frivolity and lightness around him with the heady excitement and possibility of serious religious reform he had encountered at Newport Pagnell. The difference was a sure prescription for despair in one so finely wrought.

Despair and depression, indeed, were rife in this period and affected numerous sensitive people, especially the religiously inclined. When John Bunyan composed *Pilgrim's Progress*, the very first obstacle he created for his pilgrim to encounter was the Slough of Despond, and before long Christian found himself tossed by the Giant Despair into Doubting Castle's dark dungeon.[33] Fox's despair was probably in part an emotional response to the contempt he sensed directed at him by his social betters in Barnet.[34] The radical Gerrard Winstanley decided that clergymen tormented people into distemper when they taught abstruse church doctrines ordinary folk could not understand. Despondent yet hoping to attain heaven after death, a person, said Winstanley, then "lets go his hold in the earth and submits himself to be a slave to his brother."[35] Such conditions could have an intensely devastating quality and might drive a person to contemplate suicide; in the case of Fox, they made Barnet practically synonymous with despair even when he dictated his memoirs years later.

Likely his state also represented the onset of a kind of delayed adolescence, when the shepherd boy from isolated Drayton-in-the-Clay encountered the possibility of new, different, and perversely appealing ways of life. Barnet was a community unlike any other that Fox had encountered. Hardly a day's journey from London by foot, it had no army garrison, nor was it primarily a market town or noted for any product it produced. The temptations of a town whose citizenry provided whatever its visitors desired must have been numerous for a young man fresh out of the hinterlands, particularly one who prided himself on his strict adherence to righteous living and who worked mightily to deny himself any sensual looseness. Barnet probably had its share of prostitutes who flaunted their charms for those looking for a quick caper.[36]

The lure of sexual adventure, in a distant place, in time of war when moral standards tend to decline anyway, and with a willing partner, may well have been the sinful snare that so depressed Fox. In an unusually candid letter written less than a decade later, he confessed that "I have drunk the cup of fornication."[37] Even if that recollection referred to an incident at some other place and he successfully resisted the temptation to engage in sex at Barnet, he perhaps sought gratification through masturbation, an act regarded as almost as sinful.[38] In the "night season," he certainly knew of alluring whispers[39] of the succubus—to his contemporaries an expression of Satan's wily ways, but to us the perfectly normal sexual dreams of adolescent males. But however normal such fantasies might be, they only aggravated the depression of a boy seeking perfection. Whatever the exact nature of his temptation, when the mature man later reviewed these years for his *Journal*, he was still so haunted by memories of his sins that he could not bring himself even to record the details.

In a deeper sense Fox perhaps despaired because he had not been able to find the way to drop the burden from his back, the burden that warned of youthful inadequacy in the face of so much to be done and that daily reminded him, in the unconscious recesses of his being, of who he was and how massive were the problems he and his society faced. He might remember, two and a half decades later as he dictated his memoirs, that he had kept pure from the age of eleven, but like John Bunyan's pilgrim he also carried a load of sin—except that in Fox's case others could not see the private sack, and he could not shake it off. At Barnet he realized that the most debilitating sin was greater than sex or unseemly deeds: being unable to muster the will to deal with them himself. Surely Despair was a Giant, particularly for a young outlander.

No matter what he did, whether remaining long closeted in his room or moping in the countryside, he could not throw off this despair that plagued him and seemed to prevent him from turning one way or the other. He was immobilized, and that in a town where people were cavorting on a summer's holiday. On the rare occasion when he successfully resisted despair, or as he phrased it, "when Satan could not effect his design upon me that way," then he was baited by specific temptations—though their nature he forever refused to disclose.[40]

For the first time, or at least the first time he thought important enough to record, he visited a priest to "look for comfort." But search as he would, he could find no clergyman who could help him. No priest could offer him what he would not give himself, and he seemed condemned to wander as long as his guilt drove him on. The depression he experienced first in Barnet lurked in the background for many years and had to be resisted lest it pull him down into an irresistible whirlpool. When three years later in 1647 he envisioned "an ocean of darkness and death," he betrayed both his own mental state—the obsessive fear that he was being overwhelmed by an oceanic power beyond his personal control—and the conditions of those around him who were sinking in evil just as surely as they would flounder in a mighty sea.[41]

In this confused state Fox went on to London. Not surprisingly, he found nothing in that metropolis that could relieve him. The cheap plays and sixpenny whores he would have eschewed on moral grounds, although he might have found diversion in seeing a bearbaiting down at the river or the occasional Indian brought back from the colonies across the Atlantic and put on display. Boasting a third of a million people, more than 6 percent of the country's total population, London was the largest city in Europe. With its trade and commerce, its bustling port and eighteen-arch bridge over the Thames, its large number of churches—reputedly 122 in an eight-mile radius—and the seat of government at Westminster, London was a most appealing place for all sorts and kinds. So crowded was the city with carts and carriages that one Londoner exclaimed that the rumble made it appear that "the world ran on wheels."[42] Fox was so impressed with the Thames, with speedy boats going up and down carrying local passengers, that he later used it as a standard to measure other streams' busy commerce.[43]

With the Civil War sputtering along to the north and west, the city took on added importance as the seat of parliamentary government, the obvious place for anyone with a crackpot notion to seek a hearing. Radicalism, political and religious, was everywhere. The press, no longer hampered by royal censorship, spewed forth pamphlet after pamphlet, broadside after broadside, to supply arguments for the literate and bills for the walls. The combined promise and opportunity of the great metropolis made nobles and gentlefolk alike agree with the mere servant who wished, "I hope to see London once ere I die."[44] Only sober Protestants saw things differently. A decade later two from the northern hinterlands, come now as Fox's disciples, quivered in near horror when they surveyed the teeming city for the first time. They wrote down and sent back the words he must have thought: "[O]h, abominable, abominable, [for] deceit, pride, and filthiness abound."[45]

Fox gravitated immediately to the company of religious dissenters in the capital, and a large and varied crew they were. Thomas Edwards, a vigorous Presbyterian enemy of anything that smacked of a radical separatist heresy, compiled a virtual travelers' guide to the religious underground of the era; he uncovered a striking total of 176 heretical errors that were promulgated in the city in the four years preceding publication of his book. The most basic, of course, involved the Bible and its authority, for it did not require a great deal of insight on the part of either dissidents or critics to see that the role of the Scriptures was fundamental to establishing the truth (or falsehood) of Christianity in its protestant variant. As Edwards ran through the catalogue of what he considered to be erroneous beliefs—that the Scriptures were not the word of God, that "the everlasting gospel" allowed all to be pardoned and forgiven, that women might preach as well as men and without preparation or study, that tithes were unlawful—he returned again and again to the dissenters' failure to heed the words of his Bible. Although he could not have known it, in making his list, he also publicized many of the views for which Fox and his followers were to gain notoriety a decade later.[46]

Fox attended services at various churches in the city but spent most of his time with those sectarians called Baptists because an uncle, William Pickering, was a second echelon leader among them.[47] Despite his secondary role among these Baptist dissidents, Pickering had been swept up in a mass roundup of separatists in May 1632, charged with failing to attend his parish church and frequenting instead an illegal conventicle in the home of Henry Dodd. About forty-two dissenters faced a determined archbishop of Canterbury, William Laud, who pontificated about the "dangerous men" scattered throughout the city, but Pickering, when asked to swear before the court, simply but firmly stood his ground: "I trust I have done nothing against the law and [as] for this oath, I do not know what belongs to it, and [I] refuse to take it." For their stand, some of those convicted were confined to prison for up to two years.[48] Such an unwavering witness, could not but serve as a model for Fox.

In 1644 the English Baptist movement was in a crucial stage of flux. Fox had happened by at just the right time to follow a major shift. When Fox described the Baptists he met as "tender," he tried to convey something of their fragile youth and immaturity, their openness to new revelations, their striving in the manner of delicate plants to grow in the harsh new environment the times had presented. The Civil War had opened possibilities for reform few had dreamed of when the first sword was unsheathed. At the top level the Westminster Assembly, which Parliament convened in 1643, was debating and preparing recommendations for the kind of religious settlement the nation should institute; the assembly moved ever closer to an established Presbyterian church. Discussions about the war's purposes and the actions of the army in the field against alleged papists and royalists only reflected similar ongoing discussions at the local level, discussions that in London flourished all the more as royal censorship lessened.

While the Westminster Assembly explored theological niceties such as God's sovereignty and whether an authentic church should have bishops, the Baptists in the nation's capital were in the midst of their own debate, which at once sharpened and blurred the distinctions among various segments of the separatist movement.[49] The subject involved believers' baptism. Fox may have participated in these discussions, although there is no way to know for certain; at least he remembered later that some of the "tender" Baptists tried to get him to remain in London,[50] presumably because they had come to respect him after his time among them and thought he had something to offer their sect. Although the issue the Baptists debated was simplified into the question of whether only adult believers should be baptized, it carried with it far-reaching ramifications for any group trying to remain faithful to the Protestant understanding of faith and English religious traditions. To insist on the baptism of adults only amounted to cutting the last tie with the traditional church and to proclaiming, by implication, a sharp break with those who viewed baptism as a rite to initiate a child into the religious community. Hence espousing believers' baptism also underscored the connection of its proponents with the radical rebaptizers of Münster, with all that implied. By the summer of 1644, as Fox arrived on the scene, these implications were being fiercely debated in a case growing out of the refusal of one separatist, Hanserd Knollys, to have his child baptized. The upshot, after a summer's long disputation, was a succession of champions for believers' baptism and their more-or-less formal consolidation as "Particular Baptists."

Meanwhile, the other major wing of the Baptists, the "General Baptists" with whom Fox's uncle Pickering was associated, was literally exploding with evangelistic fervor.[51] General Baptists, who had always practiced believers' baptism even while forgetting—or denying—their distant Dutch Anabaptist ancestry, absolutely rejected the Calvinist notion that Christ's death benefited only those whom God had elected to save. They received a disproportionate amount of attention from heresy hunter Thomas Edwards. He found especially reprehensible any belief that seemed to promise a leveling among people, such as the mortality of the soul and a ministry open to anyone. Edwards reported how a certain "old wolf" named Clement Wrighter held forth in Westminster Hall that there was no authentic ministry "unless any can show as immediate a call [to] the ministry as the Apostles had."[52] With such an invitation it was no surprise that weavers, smiths, peddlers, and shoemakers, not to mention women, soon flocked to General Baptist meetings and presently preached to congregations that the fearful Edwards numbered to a thousand.[53] Hence the General Baptists seemed an altogether disreputable bunch, existing on the far fringe of the period's numerous sects, refusing to take oaths or to permit marriage with nonmembers, and showing no respect for Sunday.

Fox held himself aloof from formal affiliation with either the Particular or the General Baptists, but he was close enough to both groups to decide that neither young nor old among them lived to the full their religious beliefs. His observations certainly gave him insights into the separatist mentality and allowed him to target Baptist groups later on when he sought converts to his own movement. He may have feared too close an involvement would lead to an identification with the Baptists, and resisted their efforts to include him in their number. He exhibited the same ambivalence toward them that a later follower, the astute Isaac Penington, displayed when he considered the sober people labeled "Puritans": they had, thought Penington, "a precious appearance of God," exhibiting "great sincerity and love and tenderness," yet remained unacquainted with the true spirit of the Lord.[54] In any event, upon receiving word from Leicestershire that his parents were anxious about him, Fox left London for Drayton-in-the-Clay, though his future life's path remained hidden still.[55]

His parents had some ideas about that future life: they wanted him to settle down and find a wife, a course he rejected by pleading he was still a "lad" and had not found what he later called "wisdom." Other acquaintances thought he ought to join the home guard, but he rebuffed that suggestion also, again pleading youth. After this brief visit with his parents, he struck out for Coventry, less than a day's journey southward and a city noted for a strong tradition of religious dissent going back to the Lollards; an active congregation of General Baptists flourished there, but Presbyterians predominated. The secular authorities endeavored to make the city a godly place fit for proper religion, so the tradition was that the mayor should spend part of his Sundays making sure, as one of them put it, that no one idly walked in the park, tippled, or purchased supplies. Coventry had a reputation as a "second Geneva" and could boast a 7:30 A.M. religious lecture every day. Shielded by its parliamentary garrison, the city attracted dissident religious leaders from nearby territory threatened by royal armies, one such none other than the minister from Drayton-in-the-Clay.[56]

It would have been natural for parishioner and parson to have roomed together, but Fox did not name the dissenter with whom he stayed. As in London, he searched out others of "tender" spirit, but he presently found himself less welcome in Coventry than in the capital, for the city's stern religious leaders had little time for Baptists, and even less for people like Fox. Too, his cocksure attitude, fed by the intoxicating atmosphere of London, may simply have rubbed provincials the wrong way. Or perhaps some of the dissenting provincials manning Coventry's garrison from nearby towns like Hinckley, Nuneaton, and Tamworth already knew of Fox and were not very accepting of this would-be prophet from their own region. He likely ran afoul of the coterie of Presbyterians out to suppress dissenters and create in Coventry "true reformed" church values. Before long, he returned home, this time staying for about a year.[57]

Fox arrived about the same time that Nathaniel Stephens, curate of the local church, returned from his own temporary exile. A staunch Presbyterian, a middling scholar, and a well-to-do Oxford master of arts, Stephens had opened himself to Cavalier retaliation—plunder, prison, or execution—by publicly allying himself with Scottish efforts to impose Presbyterianism on England; he subscribed to the Solemn League and Covenant, the price the Scots had exacted from Parliament for joining the antiroyalist side in the Civil War.[58] Later the bookish Stephens, spending sixteen hours a day in his study, honed his scholarly ability into a fine cutting edge to become something of an authority on the book of Revelation. A convoluted book of biblical prophecy dense with possibilities for varying interpretations, Revelation could be penetrated, he wrote, by those "who have come with a sincere mind to find out the truth" since "God will not cease to raise up such."[59] When he wrote these words a decade later, after his run-ins with Fox, Stephens had realized that some would come claiming to have special insight, those "carried so high as to live above ordinances, . . . maintain things apparently contrary to scripture, . . . and rest wholly upon the proof of extraordinary revelation." To control them, Stephens believed the state should suppress blasphemy and force "the profane, the ignorant, and rude body of the people" to come to public places of worship.[60]

With such pronounced views and despite a personality noted for cheerfulness and pleasantness, Stephens was bound to come into conflict with Baptists in his parish, a factor that may help to explain his growing interest in the Apocalypse.[61] Although not formally a Baptist, Fox had clearly been influenced by the sect, and was of course familiar with its positions. He later testified to his own disputes with his pastor. Fox acted toward Stephens and his flock, perhaps even toward his own parents, as though the hair on the sturdy leather suit he had taken a fancy to was turned inward. They were ignorant of authentic Christianity, he snapped in the same breath in which he depicted himself as the "restorer and conductor appointed for the recovery of fallen religion." His officious manner did nothing to improve relations between the two men; attacks by Stephens only reassured Fox that he was in the right.[62]

The substance of a recorded discussion between the two at the time indicated how closely Fox had moved to accepting the foremost General Baptist tenet, the rejection of belief in predestination for the belief that Christ had died for all. Stephens asked the young Fox why, at the point of death, Jesus had cried out, "My God, my God, why hast thou forsaken me?" Fox responded that it was because he bore the sins of every human being, "died for all men, and tasted death for every man, . . . an offering for the sins of the whole world." Since this view was common among those who rejected the Calvinistic idea that God had chosen only a few for salvation, Stephens probably had considered it before, so it is difficult to accept Fox's recollection that his priest told him he had never heard such a thing. But the discussions motivated Stephens to single out Fox's exegeses and adapt them for his Sunday sermons, no doubt to rebut the Baptist position; Fox, though, took umbrage at this backhanded compliment and thereafter regarded Stephens as a threat.[63]

Still unsettled, and still unsettling to those he met, Fox began his travels again, driven by his intention to discover the basis of his despair and to conquer the temptations he simply could not shake off.[64] From priest to pastor, as from pillar to post, he wandered on and on. First he traveled to Mancetter where he had been an apprentice; there a cleric told him to smoke tobacco and sing psalms, neither of which he was willing to try—he did not like tobacco, and he could not sing. Then he discovered that his counselor had broken confidence and told his story; soon even the milkmaids, possibly girls he had known two years earlier, were gossiping about his problems. "Miserable comforters," he muttered as he traveled to seek out a well-known minister in Tamworth, a town guarding the border with Staffordshire and quartering a 250-man parliamentary army force only five miles from the royal garrison at Lichfield.[65] The priest there had only hollow advice, so Fox did not tarry.

One factor that no doubt made him hurry on was military movements in the neighborhood. Leicester's fall to the royalists at the end of May in 1645 sent shivers through parliamentary supporters. Each side began the maneuvering that culminated in the the Battle of Naseby on June 11 and 12. Up to this point Staffordshire had been quiet except for marauding parties from the two aremies. One poor farmer complained that the king's soldiers called him a Roundhead, while the real Roundheads charged him with paying taxes to the royalists—so he lost eleven horses to one side, a team to the other.[66] The collapse of church administration early in the war had already brought dissent out into the open,[67] and with creation of the New Model Army early in the same year radical sects were spreading throughout the soldiery and beyond.

This New Model Army, a people's army, was certainly "new." As time went by, its red-uniformed volunteers, many from the lower orders, rallied to the infectious idea that they were engaged in a war of righteousness and were instruments of the Lord—"with our swords in our hands," they menacingly announced—to carry judgment to every part of the British Isles.[68] One soldier, later a Quaker convert, was convinced that God's spirit was at work in the army.[69] Liberating deer from royalist estates and chopping up popish communion rails for firewood seemed an obvious part of divine judgment to these men.[70] Needless to say, to the minds of more moderate elements, such a force could get quickly out of hand. Hostile royalists liked to sneer about "rawheads" in the "New Noddle Army."[71] Richard Baxter, an army chaplain in the summer of 1645, who abhorred upheaval, was horrified at what he saw in the New Model Army. All the talk about freedom of conscience only led ordinary soldiers, who might have otherwise remained free of contaminating opinions, to begin criticizing all ministers and the churches themselves. Some adamantly refused, as Baxter phrased it, to tie themselves "to any duty until the Spirit leads us."[72]

Camp follower Fox left no record that he encountered such opinions directly, but the fact that he heard the same charges aimed at him pointed to a correspondence between his ideas and those loose in the New Model Army. On occasion he gladly identified himself (and was identified) with members of the New Model Army. Once a number of rank-and-file soliders, favorably impressed with his message, rescued him from a mob armed with stones and staves and shouting, "Down with these round-headed rogues."[73] No wonder an overwrought Baxter rued the army's lasting influence among Anabaptists and Quakers: "If they pulled down the parliament, imprisoned the godly, faithful members, and killed the king, . . . if they sought to take down tithes and parish ministers, to the utter confusion of religion in the land, in all these the Anabaptists [and other sectarians, including Quakers] followed them."[74]

It was a heady time, salad days of an approaching spring for some, herald of an approaching winter for others. Parliament seemed on the verge of winning the war, but royalist garrisons in the area could still make their presence felt and disrupt normal activities.[75] While he listened and learned, Fox still searched for some answer to his personal problems. His despair and the troubling temptations that brought it on drove him to seek out a minister in Coventry who could offer only unapt comments to his questions. "What was the ground of despair," Fox wanted to know, and "How was trouble wrought in man?" His counselor replied with, "Who was Christ's mother and father?", a most unhelpful response. Then, as they walked together in a narrow alleyway and Fox accidentally stepped on the edge of a garden bed, the priest flared up as though someone had set his house ablaze. It was no wonder Fox considered the ministers he turned to "miserable comforters." None of the pastors understood his problems, much less could speak to his condition.[76]

The next authority he visited, John Machin of Atherstone, misdiagnosed Fox's problem as primarily physical and prescribed a course of bleedings. At this point Fox was so severely depressed that he was almost unable to function beyond merely getting through the day. He was "dried up with sorrows, grief and troubles" so that he "wished I had never been born to see vanity and wickedness." The lad who had learned purity by age eleven was now the man ten years older who wished himself blind so he could not see evil, or deaf so he could not hear vain, wicked, and blasphemous words. When other people celebrated the Christ-mas season with feasting and games, Fox's alienation boiled over. He wanted to compensate by giving money to widows and those who had little, but he could not force himself even to perform such simple acts of charity, at least not in the black state his despair had brought him to. He stayed away from marriage feasts lest he be enveloped in the miasma of despair that frivolity had inevitably meant to him since his youth.[77]

Contemporaries who analyzed early Quakers diagnosed this problem as mel-ancholia, an extreme depression caused, they believed, by an abundance of black bile. Enthusiasts who believed themselves filled with the deity and immediately in touch with God were especially inclined to melancholy. This dark malady could be seen in people of high passions, people exhibiting obviously high degrees of fear, or love, or veneration. Indeed, one writer of the period insisted that when the two former characteristics mixed together new heights of veneration would result in paralyzing a person who felt called "to go about some weighty or sol-emn performance in public." Those affected by melancholy might become hyperactive or totally quiescent, so beset either "to cause a tumultuous and dis-orderly commotion in them or so suffocate the heart that motion will be in a manner quite extinct and the party fall down [as though] dead." This state amounted, this authority attested, to "a perfect epilepsy."[78] That this was no over-simplification, promoted for purely propaganda purposes, was indicated when Richard Baxter wrote in his autobiography about how Quakers "have famished and drowned themselves in melancholy."[79]

For Fox it was as though he lived in a dark pit whose walls, made up of writhing things he regarded as evil and deadly—things as usual as Christmas festivities and joyful weddings—hemmed him in and prevented him from moving, even from functioning normally. The folk who enjoyed such frivolous pastimes might bleed when their veins were opened, but not George Fox. His spirit, shriveled and melancholic because of what he saw everywhere around him, would not allow him even to imagine that his dried-up body could give up its precious life's blood.[80] And it did not. Fox had gone beyond despair: he was suffering from angst, sinking into the depths, with nowhere to turn.

4

*Seek Your Salve Where
You Get Your Sore*

As the year 1645 drew to a close and 1646 began, the Civil War in Leicestershire had wound down. Belvoir Castle, long a royalist stronghold and garrison, capitulated, and the king's men at Ashby-de-la-Zouch hauled their colors down.[1] Maneuvering for the best position from which to bargain with his enemies, King Charles presently found himself the prisoner of strict Scottish Calvinists who had one firm demand of all those, be they parliamentarians or royalists, with whom they dealt, namely, that their Presbyterian church be established throughout the kingdom.[2] With Parliament's upper hand thus assured, final victory seemed in reach, as did settlement of the decades-long conflict between court and commons.

As these national developments unfolded, George Fox was nearing twenty-two years of age and seemed closer to resolving his own problems. The most obvious change involved his impending break with the church of Drayton-in-the-Clay, which included his own parents. Fox ceased attending the parish church, having decided that its Presbyterian minister lacked qualifications to hold his position. His decision marked not only a separation from the established church— that was bad enough—but it also signaled Fox's refusal to conform to the moderate Presbyterianism in which he had been reared. Or to put it yet another way, by leaving the church of his community, the uneasy young man substituted his own independent judgment for the collective wisdom and tradition of his small village. He thus lived out in his own life Protestantism's checkered history.

Fox habitually roamed the nearby open fields and orchards during church services, reading his Bible, praying, and wrestling with the forces that tugged and occasionally even tore at his spirit. He recorded numerous "openings," insightful occasions when he suddenly glimpsed how some verse he had read in the Scriptures coincided with his own experiences and wonderings. He had tapped into the tradition that made the inner voice of the spirit supreme over external standards such as church rituals and ministry, as well as the Bible. Minister Stephens, observing such "people of good hope," as he charitably designated them, aptly if sarcastically described the steps of Fox's pilgrimage: "[D]eparted first from the ministry, and then have come to flight from the written Word, and then last of all, to hang upon revelations and extraordinary enthusiasms of the Spirit."[3] Fox's discernment certainly exceeded mere rational or outward forms; he found the deeper his experiences the lighter the weight of his depression.

More and more the malleable Fox gave to his encounters the same authority Protestants bestowed on the Scriptures or Catholics located in the church hierarchy. Without realizing it or, as far as we know, even knowing of the connection, Fox cultivated the same intensely individualistic faith that characterized earlier dissenters from orthodoxy; indeed, even the early Martin Luther, certainly not known for his lack of rigidity in matters of faith, had once compiled a selection of essays about mystical German teachings.[4] His intimate mystical experiences with God led Fox to a theological position that made Christianity a matter of the individual heart rather than of obedience to a hierarchy, an immediate faith based on encounters open to all rather than on some ecclesiastically approved Scripture or rite. Though he was unable to find security in the officially sanctioned way, Fox's spiritual experiences gave him an assurance he had never known before and enabled him to defend his newly discovered and radical faith.[5] Marx's assessment of Luther could just as easily apply to Fox: he "destroyed faith in authority by restoring the authority of faith. . . . He liberated man from exterior religiosity by making man's inner conscience religious. He emancipated the body from chains by enchaining the heart."[6] Gradually, a transformation in Fox's personal life became evident to others around him. The secular peace that seemed so promising for the nation was almost matched now by a growing inner conviction within the young Fox.

In ecclesiastical terms, Fox's principal problem involved the question of authority: where it came from, how it was acquired, and who possessed it. Raised a Presbyterian, yet often having run afoul of Stephens and other ministers, Fox tried to unravel what it was that invested a person with spiritual distinction. The moderate English nonconformists, particularly the Presbyterians, stressed the ideas that a minister required a university education to prepare him to exercise his calling, and that he needed the approval of his peers and formal ordination before he could expound the word of God. The Baptists among whom Fox had lived took the more radical position that anyone, educated or not, man or apt woman, might teach the Scriptures and edify the faithful. Already in his disputations with Stephens Fox had demonstrated his own conviction that without much formal education he was as capable of interpreting the Bible as his university-educated pastor.

Hence one Sunday morning, while his parents and the other parishioners of St. Michael's listened to Stephens explain the word of God in church, Fox had one of his "openings." Instantly his thinking was clarified on this matter of authority. To be bred at Oxford or Cambridge, Fox realized, was simply "not enough to make a man fit to be a minister of Christ." When he tied that revelation to one he remembered from a day or two before, that none were true believers except those who "were all born of God and passed from death to life," he saw that if a professed minister did not exemplify this new birth then he could not be a true minister. Thus neither education nor approval and ordination by a classis invested a minister with authority: only the divine action of God's grace could accomplish that end. His revelation cut the ground from under the established ministry and substituted for it the infinitely broader principle that God could and did—had not Fox himself heard the divine word?—speak to anyone willing to listen.

How liberating that insight was, and how potentially revolutionary! Power over the pulpit, a major instrument of social control where the model of deference to one's betters was regularly enacted through the submission of the parishioners to their "superior," the minister, was thus taken from secular and religious leaders and bestowed, via the ineffable promptings of God's spirit, on any George-come-lately. This principle, Fox told himself now, and later others, "struck at priest Stephens' ministry" and finished it.[7] While not providing the answer to all his personal problems, this revelation gave Fox the base from which to launch his critique of the church—and thereby implicitly undermine the social order it supported.

Fox never wavered from this central idea; from the very first it provided the foundation for his assault on established Christianity. In one sense, it seemed a relatively minor matter—after all, an obvious remedy for an institution with inadequate or hypocritical priests was to reform the structure so that they could be removed and replaced by good ones—but in Fox's mind the issue was far more basic: a single failing called the whole system into question. The churches he took to frequenting, even the more purified churches of the Baptists and other dissenters, he insisted, did not produce true believers; indeed, in leading people to focus on the outward institution, Scriptures, and rites, it usurped the kind of personal revelations he had experienced. As he was, so he wanted others to become: "[A] stranger to all, relying wholly upon the Lord Jesus Christ."

When he revealed his conclusion to his parents, they strenuously remonstrated with their son for cutting himself off from their close-knit community. Fox was troubled by their complaints but hardly deterred from going his own way. When they tried to get him to discuss his problems with Stephens, he explained bluntly that he defined a true believer differently than they did and retreated to solitary isolation in the fields.[8] Fox was gripped more and more by compelling religious experiences that set him apart from others. Certainly, his growing religious independence was leading to deeper and deeper estrangement from his immediate family and the neighbors with whom he had grown up. He was not above flinging at his family a telling biblical quotation: "The anointing which you have received of him abideth in you, and you need not that any man teach you."[9] The rivalry between Fox and Stephens increased after the older man took to visiting Fox's relatives in the region to warn them that George Fox had gone off with those claiming new light on old truths. He was one of those "newfangles." Unable to find anyone else in tiny Drayton-in-the-Clay who appreciated his views—one of the reasons Fox continued his lonely wanderings and searchings about the Midlands—he stood aloof from all: family, church congregation, and acquaintances.[10]

Fox's "openings" began to add to the theological position that later lent notoriety to Quakers. Just as his first opening struck at the pretensions and special claims of ministers, so he had another that reduced churches to the status of mere buildings: God's people, he decided, had no need of a special structure, for together they "were his temple, and he dwelt in them." Hence like Baptists and other radical sectarians, he concluded that the presence of God's spirit was supreme over the churches and temples that human beings built and called holy.

By 1646 Fox had thus announced the position that would become central to the movement he organized and championed. Since true ministers were those born of God's grace, since the temple of God consisted of people so ordered, and since a person's understanding of God came from an inward anointing through intensely personal openings—just as those Fox himself experienced on his wanderings—now, he told others, "the Lord would teach his people himself." He justified this striking heterodox position with the Bible, especially Revelation, which Stephens and other priests insisted was closed to him, but Christ, he responded, "could open the seals" to anyone by a personal leading.

What made Fox's position so significant was the implications of his proclamation, which spoke so directly to people seeking inward assurance in such an unsettled age. The Civil War, after all, had sharply divided the nation's ruling classes, calling into question just where legal authority lay and offering an opportunity for new, and lower-class, leadership to emerge. His message also represented the culmination of almost 130 years of Protestant reformation. When Luther nailed his Ninety-five Theses to the church door at Wittenberg in 1517, he had inadvertently set moving a process that made the individual the ultimate authority in matters religious. Temperamentally committed to the status quo, in social, political, and economic matters, Luther tried to resist the logical conclusions to which others pushed his religious doctrines, but he could not live long enough—much less exercise the necessary authority and influence—to control all that others would do with the ideas he loosed.[11]

When continental Calvinism, which to traditionalists smacked of a kind of international subversion, began to infiltrate England's established church in the middle of the sixteenth century, it brought an ethic that laid on each individual the responsibility of working out a proper response to God's act of salvation. As Calvinists saw it, God required a person saved by grace to be accountable for her or his actions rather than bargaining with the church that submission to ritualistic ordinances would guarantee salvation. In laying the responsibility for righteous living on each individual, Calvinism was a revolutionary doctrine, leveling differences between rich and poor, educated and illiterate, men and women, old and young. Indeed, it suggested that those scorned by the world could be closer to the truth than those acclaimed for their learning, wealth, or outward piety.

Of course, Calvinists, anxious to win acceptance within the established order, made few open references that might be construed as revolutionary, but they had to lay out their general principles. Listen, for example, to Fox's fellow Leicestershireman Arthur Dent, author of *The Plain Man's Pathway to Heaven*, one of the best-known inspirational books of the age, a combination of self-help manual to gaining eternal life and a biting critique of current life. "It is one thing," wrote Dent in 1601, answering an atheist challenge to his Calvinist theology, "to know the history and letters of the Scriptures, and another thing to believe and feel the power thereof in the heart, . . . which none of the wise of the world can have." All outward righteousness availed nothing, he went on, for those who think only of "this world, lands, and leaves [of gold and silver], grounds, and livings, kine [cows] and sheep, and how to wax rich." People like this could, and did, exceed the elect in worldly gifts—and here Dent ticked off his list of laudable virtues; including "learning, discretion, justice, temperance, prudence, patience, liberality, affability, kindness, courtesy, good nature, and such like"—but they were all outward things "and availed not to eternal life." Fancy dress, he specified, was not only bad in itself but also encouraged emulation on the part of the lower orders, "for now we cannot by their apparel discern the maid from the mistress." Being a slave to fashion, however, was not as bad as practicing usury, bribery, rent racking, binding the poor to unreasonable contracts, or charging exorbitant fees, in the manner of so many lawyers, church officers, and engrossers. No wonder Dent believed the gospel had never been so flouted as in his day: "[H]owsoever some make a show of religion, yet they have denied the power thereof." In truth, people might outwardly receive and embrace the gospel, but "by their works they deny [God], and are abominable, disobedient, and to every good work reprobate. This age is full of such carnal protestants."[12]

Like Dent, and Luther and Calvin in their times, George Fox recognized that the established church was the nursery of such carnal professors, but he went beyond them in his conviction that similar offshoots likewise grew in the dissenting churches. Yet he also found that separated believers like Baptists were the most likely people in the Midlands to respond to his message. By 1646, after he had decided that neither an Oxford nor a Cambridge education could make a minister, Fox began gathering disciples.[13] It was as though this crucial opening, echoing Dent's warning to the worldly wise, had convinced him that he was as capable as any to lead others. He found potential disciples everywhere as he wandered northward toward Yorkshire, first into Derbyshire, then veering eastward into Nottinghamshire, particularly hard hit by the fortunes of war,[14] seeking out groups more and more unsettled by the flux of religious and political developments. Parliament had just authorized remodeling the established church organization into a Presbyterian system, a move that prompted resistance because it presaged stricter disciplinary measures against religious dissidents. John Milton, the revolution's prose laureate, expressed a widely held view when he concluded that a "new presbyter is but old priest writ large."[15]

Nowhere was "priest writ large" more important than in the ranks of that debating society called the New Model Army, particularly among a faction known as the Levellers. By 1646, just when Fox was beginning his missionary activities, these Levellers emerged as an independent force. Its members tended to come from the lower middle class; they were what H. N. Brailsford called "the hobnails, clouted shoes, the private soldiers, the leather and woolen aprons, and the laborious and industrious people of England." The Levellers wanted a broad religious tolerance, as well as an array of other political and social reforms, such as the end of feudalism, the supremacy of the House of Commons, and the use of elections to fill practically every office in the kingdom. If the New Model Army was the victorious battle-ax of the Civil War—and it certainly was—then the

Levellers were its honed and sharp cutting political edge. George Fox's movement over the next decade continually brought him into contact with former members of this faction, including its most public leader, John Lilburne. Indeed, to many critics, it seemed that in Quakerism the Levellers had gathered to pray.[16] As late as 1673 even an aristocratic Quaker such as William Penn could sincerely denominate his sect by the label "God's Free-men," a term the Levellers also used.[17]

Discontent about other, more practical matters within the New Model Army, often sparked by Levellers, was rife. Soldiers in garrisons around the country petitioned for payment of long-overdue wages—and making these payments battered even further the chronically strapped Parliament. Hungry soldiers meant weakened discipline; attacks on civilians and theft of their property by soldiers escalated. Bread-and-butter issues easily overshadowed debates about the nation's future government among the rank and file, but such discussions grabbed the attention of literate citizens especially when the army's Levellers, festooned with their signature green ribbons, began their public agitation for their pet reforms, including expansion of the electoral franchise. Before long the New Model Army and Parliament faced off against one another, as each side maneuvered to see which would control the government.[18] The great mass of England's people hovered somewhere between the two factions, clutching tightly to old traditions yet often becoming unwitting actors in the great drama around them. For example, a riot broke out in Canterbury when the New Model Army tried to suppress what it called the "popish festival of Christmas," and helped to ignite the second phase of the Civil War in 1647.[19]

Although most of the discussion centered in and around London, numerous groups of sectarians existed in the Midlands. These dissidents, whether consciously aware of it or not, had a vital stake in the army debates, particularly as they related to continuing religious liberty; if Parliament had its way, dissenters would be legally bound to attend the established church and be subject to its discipline. With the Presbyterian church on the way to being established, Fox paid less and less attention to its ministers and concentrated instead on dissenters who looked at a parson's message rather than whether he had gone to Oxford or Cambridge. Among these poorer folk he found much more openness. As he traveled the Midlands he found audiences of common people, and he headed straight for them, regardless of how strange their notions. He soon learned, however, that their separate preachers could offer him no more solace for his own personal worries than Presbyterians had managed to do earlier.

He passed among people who averred that women had no souls, and he reminded them of how Jesus' mother had said her soul magnified the Lord. Meeting some who followed dreams, he convinced them that they should learn to distinguish between God's word in dreams and Satan's. His usual practice was to rent a room and, except for periodic forays outside seeking people to convince, to keep to himself lest he become involved in an unexpected heated debate. Occasionally he followed his trade of shoemaker when his money ran low.[20] Moving through the Midlands always as a stranger, he saw himself as raised above those he met because his wisdom came from the Lord and he needed no outward assistance. He cultivated, like a kind of second sense, the ability to locate those people who were discontented enough to leave behind those who professed but did not live their faith. Himself raised among people regarded as lowly, he knew that "lowly" people could understand the drift of things and that they could be positive agents in making the world a different kind of place.

Hence he targeted the common people: not common in the sense of "mean," lowly, or degraded—indeed, Fox won only a few of that lowest sort, boasting once to the army's high command that no beggars lurked among his followers[21]— but common in the sense that England boasted so many like them; common in that they fought the battles that won the Civil War; common in that they shared an aspiration that people ought to be judged on their merits and abilities; common in that they shared a conviction that the existing order could not fulfill their hopes and dreams and in fact seemed to punish them for their efforts. They were ubiquitous enough to be invisible. The most numerous group of these commoners consisted of people who got their livings from the land, the same people who watched churchmen or lay impropriators come around to collect those galling tithes at harvest or sheepshearing time: nine for you, one for me. Farmer Edward Muggleston of Swannington in Leicestershire, about ten miles from Fox's home village, was relatively unknown, for example, but he understood well enough what was fair and what was not. One of the earliest of the Quakers to refuse to pay his tithes, he received this dubious distinction in 1652 when he had property confiscated valued at four times the tithes he owed. His goods were seized when he was called to London to testify in a case involving the plundering of a local clergyman during the Civil Wars, a fact suggesting that the church had other reasons to dislike this particular Muggleston.[22]

Another conspicuous set included those engaged in trade, selling things produced with their own hands, such as shoes, woolens, or dressed meat. Many, like yeomen, relied directly on the products of the land for their livelihood. Fox knew their interest, advising that those who followed him would come "to have greater trading, double than ever you had, and more than the world."[23] A smattering of the lower gentry—a justice of the peace here, a schoolmaster or former minister there—rounded out the middling sort of commoner to whom Fox appealed. They were the people who had traditionally not counted for very much, but, thanks to the promise of Civil War rhetoric, they were now ready to line up to be numbered.

Serious and no-nonsense folk they were, people who put a premium on hard work and expected their diligence to pay off. Critics claimed they crept into the trades in London, Bristol, and the market towns and quickly established themselves at the expense of those already there.[24] They never heard Colonel Oliver Cromwell's words, but they did not have to hear him to know the spirit of his advice, for it was in the air: "If you choose godly honest men as captains of horse, honest men will follow them. . . . A few honest men are better than numbers."[25] His army's victory over the royalists seemed endorsement enough of Cromwell's practical sentiments. Potential Quakers, as befitting people trying to better themselves, enjoyed a higher degree of literacy than their neighbors, while many veterans and soldiers, infected by New Model Army discontent, saw in Fox's message a possible solution to their unease. (And he, of course, cultivated soldiers, as late as 1657 still playing to their grievance at not getting paid.[26] The soldiers returned the favor by doing valuable guard duty when Quakers invaded local churches and market places.[27]) Sensing an outlet for their energies, women flocked to the movement. Finally, many who had already moved from the establishment's church to link up with outcast groups like the Baptists could easily take the next step into Quakerism.[28]

Among one group of Baptists in Nottinghamshire, in the tiny village of Skegby just four miles west of Mansfield, Fox's message lodged in the soul of a forty-seven-year-old woman, Elizabeth Hooton, who remained one of his most committed disciples. Like Fox, Hooton had also decided that the Baptists were not upright enough for her; indeed, she had made public statements about their deceit, making her a known dissident even before Fox's arrival. At first her husband opposed her new direction, but soon he too joined Fox's movement. Thereafter regular meetings were convened in the Hooton household, and it became a major base of operation in the area.[29]

Even as he convinced some of those he met, the ups and downs Fox had known since leaving home continued to bedevil him. When plagued by his reoccurring malady—"I cannot declare the misery I was in," he recalled, "it was so great and heavy upon me"—he would seek seclusion in some desolate place where he could read the Bible and fast and not have to see another person. At other times people would flock to hear him, attracted by the rumor that he was a youth with the ability to discern people's conditions; then his own spirit would be inspired by attentive and silent people who practically hung on his every word. But perhaps the next day his tempter would appear again; crashing to earth, he would sense that he had committed some unpardonable sin he could not describe, and he would plunge again into the pit of despair. Up and down, up and down, up and down marked the course of his emotional life. Sometimes he wandered throughout the night. Afterward, looking back on his travail, he decided that God was working in him to purge his soul of sin and make him a new person. Buoyed by this hope, his spirit would once again soar and he knew himself a new person, equal to the prophets, apostles, and writers of the Scriptures.[30]

Such knowledge lent his comments a youthful presumptuousness that he never quite shook off. Thus his depraved contemporaries, he said, "have gotten their words, the Holy Scriptures, in a form but not in their life nor spirit that gave them forth." "Deceit" was the word that came easiest to his lips when he described people like these.[31] With such concentration on human and empty forms no wonder there was so much confusion among those who claimed to follow Christ but could not fulfil his law and command. Fox returned to this theme again and again, for he insisted that opening oneself to the teaching of God's spirit would allow a person to go behind the literal words to find the spirit and power from which they sprang.[32] To "thresh down the deceivers," wrote one of Fox's closest associates, was our first task, "and lay them open, that all people might see their shame, and come to turn from them, and receive the knowledge of truth that they might be saved."[33]

The fact that Fox gathered disciples among those he met suggests that he had something to say that others tossed back and forth on the turbulent sea of an England torn by civil war and revolution wanted to hear. His method drew on a long tradition of English anticlericalism and called people to rely on themselves and their own experiences of the divine.[34] But at twenty-three he still lacked the deep inner conviction that he had left home to find. His parents did not understood their restless son, Stephens's fumbling efforts only demonstrated priestly inadequacies, and none of the nameless preachers and "most-experienced people"—as he labeled other would-be counselors—had helped. True, he functioned on an outward level, winning converts, shunning evil, finding ways to survive physically. But such humdrum matters, even the boosts that convincing another person offered, satisfied not. Was his life to be nothing more than a constant search for a wholeness that crumbled every time he reached out or for an inner calm that could not outlast the next shattering misery? George Fox's life was bearable, but it was not complete. He knew, however, what it could be even if he did not know yet fully how to secure it.

And then it happened. It is not clear whether Fox expected something or not, but he experienced the kind of traumatic event that confirmed what he had been saying to others and the direction his life was already taking. A voice spoke to him, saying, "There is one, even Christ Jesus, who can speak to your condition."[35]

Fox took this bolt as a divine confirmation for what he was and everything he had done. But it was more than that—it also represented the grant of a divine commission for his life's work. This occasion also differed from previous openings, for this time he knew he had heard a voice. In the past he had read the Bible and then through a blaze of insight had come to understand the implications of what he had read. Now the compelling words spoken by this divine voice burned into his consciousness in a way he could never forget. Formerly he had known in part and at a distance, coldly objective; now he "knew experimentally," from his own deep and personal experience. His heart—the words still shout from the page of his *Journal*—"did leap for joy." This was so different, so gripping and compelling, so convincing and assuring, so rich with possibilities, that he pondered its implications long afterward, teased out its meaning, and applied it to the needs of his world, until he had arranged and rearranged it in a way enabling him to live a life of immense power.

As it gave him power, the voice he knew he heard also provided him with a divine confirmation of his life's course that gave him the sure conviction that he was doing what was right. From Samson to Isaiah to Jesus—and now to Fox—prophets convinced themselves that they had heard the divine voice. Contemporary critics and doubters, like Richard Baxter and Thomas Edwards, might sneer that ordinary men and women's claimed voices were imaginary figments, but Fox knew otherwise. Temperamental conservatives might even lament the way the age fed a kind of religious anarchism that flung the door of revelation open to any and every person so inclined, but for those who had had his experience such carping bore no relation to reality. Fox knew: he had heard Christ's voice.

Fox's encounter likewise fit the classic mold of the experience of salvation as described by contemporary Protestants. John Bunyan, for example, warned that one's attempts to live righteously could never save a person; nor would what he called "an assenting of the understanding," "a traditional or historical influence of the words in their heads," suffice. Instead, "it must be by the wonderful, invisible, invincible power, of the Almighty God, working in your souls by his Spirit . . . [to] lay hold on . . . your very souls, and consciences, so effectually, that you may be able by the same faith to challenge the power, madness, malice, rage, and destroying nature" of sin and evil.[36] Fox now knew the power of which Bunyan wrote.

The record does not indicate how long before he resumed his travels Fox stayed to savor his experience, although it was probably not long. Using the episode as a standard to test and to judge later developments, he foreshortened his life in his memoirs to demonstrate how the implications of the words he heard influenced his future decisions. So the meaning did not emerge all at once but was to be found gradually over a lifetime of confrontation and activity. His experience likewise formed the basis of his later theology and the way he looked at his responsibilities.

The first thing he realized naturally involved his own personal needs at the time. He had confirmation that he had been right to believe that his earthly counselors had not helped him because they were enveloped in sin and unbelief. In the expected Calvinist manner, Fox's voice had conveyed the grace of God, coming to enlighten, granting faith and power. As Calvinists believed, this grace had come without the help of anyone, any book, any Scripture, any history or tradition. "Though I read the Scriptures that spoke of Christ and of God," he confessed, "yet I knew him not, but by revelation." Fox saw himself, how he once was and how he was without the encounter with Christ he had just had. Everywhere without this experience of Christ, he saw corruption; people, including Fox himself and despite his best efforts, were lost. "And when I myself was in the deep, under all shut up, I could not believe that I would ever overcome; my troubles, my sorrows and my temptations were so great that I thought many times I should have despaired." But now he recognized that Christ had been tempted by the same devil and had overcome that evil power—Fox could too. Now he knew.

But destined never to be free from temptations, Fox had only an ultimate assurance that he could overcome them. He saw a struggle going on inside himself between the creature who longed for a king's diet and palace and the desire to know the secure comfort that came from thirsting after the Lord and his righteousness. One way represented the ethereal—changeable religion, changeable teachers, changeable notions and doctrines, changeable ways—that offered no security and put people's lives in bondage to every will-o'-the-wisp that happened along. Practically everyone, "professors, priests and people," loved and longed for the very earthly things that Fox tried to rid himself of when he turned to "the unchangeable truth in the inward parts, the light of Jesus Christ," the reality he had just encountered. For this reason he could never forgive those who deceived average people, and by empty and outward forms, rituals, and ceremonies prevented them from experiencing the liberation he now knew.

Fox's experience partook of a mystical joining with the divine, a reality he had sensed was available but which he had never yet been able finally to appropriate. Then he heard the same voice again, addressed this time to the temptation that had plagued him: "Thou serpent! Thou dost seek to destroy the life but can not: for the sword, which keeps the tree of life, shall destroy thee." And now he had a sense of how that sword was Christ, the word of God, and how his own "inward mind [was now] being joined to his good seed that bruised the head of this serpent." His fetters had fallen off in much the same way as those of his contemporary, the radical Gerrard Winstanley, whose Diggers pushed egalitarianism into an agrarian communism. Winstanley experienced his own release when he heard the spirit saying to shattered people like himself, "the seed of all things, which is myself, will bruise that serpent's head, and I will restore thee again. I am thy redeemer."[37] Evidently Fox had felt some insecurity in his previous confrontations with his opponents, but now he was ready: "[T]his inward life did spring up in me to answer all the opposing professors and priests and did bring in scriptures in my memory to refute them with."

This was a security he had never known before. In a world that had become unhinged and that battered him until one day he was beaten down and depressed, the next rising up and exhilarated, he could now know the sure foundation that the love of God provided. He saw death, but it had no sting; he was tempted again—even sinning the unpardonable sin against the Holy Ghost, he judged—but he soared on. "I was filled," he noted of his vivid experience, "with admiration at the infiniteness . . . [and] greatness of [God's] love." God's light bathed him, let him see his troubles, trials, and temptations more clearly than ever before. "As the light appeared, all appeared that is out of the light—darkness, death, temptations, the unrighteous, the ungodly—. . . then, after this, there did a pure fire appear in me." "There is no people convinced of sin, but they are convinced within themselves and with the *light within* them," Fox thundered at a later critic.[38] Bunyan similarly recommended looking intently at one's soul just as one used a mirror to find spots of dirt, because those who "do not know themselves" or "the nature of sin" remained people who emptily profess the words—were mere professors indeed.[39]

In such a mood Fox found it easy to catalogue the confusion, deceit, and falseness of those around him who hated the light, resisted the Holy Ghost, and converted grace into wantonness. Dwelling in the flesh prevented people from understanding what it meant to search for and find God's law written on their hearts: "[T]o speak of these things being within seemed strange to the rough and crooked." But how exhilarating and powerful it proved to be once a person sensed that inward law in the heart. So Fox's special animus was directed at deceitful religious leaders who prated on about the law and the gospel of Christ but who knew nothing of what they spoke except at second hand. Echoing the cry of every antiestablishment dissenter, he averred, "[N]one can be a minister of Christ Jesus but in the eternal spirit, which was before the scriptures were given forth: for if they have not his spirit, they are none of his."[40] Or as Winstanley put it, "[T]hey know not the spirit; they live without upon the earth, upon objects. . . ."[41]

Practically every theme Fox later emphasized appeared in these reflections on his vision. He began, as any relevant theology must, with his own state. Unfortunately for those who would like specifics, he never listed details about his own temptations and sins, but he knew the problem. Like the apostle Paul, he witnessed another law in his "members, warring against the law of my mind . . . for the good that I would I do not: but the evil which I would not that I do."[42] Try as he might, he could not overcome the sense of sin that had weighed him down from his early youth. It had aggravated his bouts of depression and propelled him to seek some solution in the world beyond his village.

But then, when he could find no one to speak to his ragged condition, the grace of God burst on his consciousness and illuminated his plight. This act of grace had come despite his pleas to priests and preachers, despite his prayers, despite his solitary searching, despite even his reading of the Bible, and suddenly he realized that all these things were outward. His trouble was inward and could not be reached by all the external posturing possible—indeed, in so far as these forms misled Fox the seeker to rely on outward means, they positively hindered locating "the unchangeable truth in the inward parts."[43] Addressing those of his critics who put their faith in the Bible, he would later ask, "[W]as there not a word before the Scriptures were written, by which all things were made, and before those words were declared forth?" The answer was clear: "They that had the Scriptures, but not the Spirit that gave them forth, come not to the life."[44]

Fox's own encounter with the spirit was naturally and uniquely his, but it did not differ significantly from what other dissenters believed had to happen for one to know the grace of God—otherwise Fox would have been like a person living in a vacuum and unable to communicate his message to others. The thoughtful voice had wisely spoken to him in a fashion and in words that he had been reared from childhood to understand. For more than 250 years, from the time of the Lollards, English religious rebels had de-emphasized conformity to church-imposed rituals and dogmas and stressed the idea that salvation came when a person lived a righteous life; they transferred the responsibility for salvation from the institution onto the individual. Thus Baxter, for example, hoped to cure "that dangerous disease among the people, of imagining that Christianity is but a manner of opinion and dead belief, and to convince them how much of it consists in holiness."[45]

Fox's experience continued the profound shift that protestantism had introduced into Christianity, a shift marked by a turning away from the community and a turning toward the individual's private needs as the central focus of theological concern.[46] Of course religion had always been in some way an individual thing, but Fox's interpretation of his revelation, both now and later, was going a long way toward making each person's private encounter with God the final test of authentic faith. In a deeper sense than he probably intended, he was making religion intensely personal and private. His very modern position demanded that people stand on their own two feet and, before God, fashion their religious convictions out of their personal experiences. He touched people who thought they did not have a voice and believed that they were not supposed to have one, and he offered them that voice. All that was well and good, surely, but it laid the religious groundwork for a worldview that freed the individual from all sense of responsibility outside his or her own definitions. Fox did not and naturally could not see the connections between the liberating experiences he preached and the unfolding of a world whose excesses he always deplored. But many of those who responded to him understood well enough and understandably so: they aspired to a way of life not hemmed in by traditional structures and saw rich possibilities for themselves within a society caught in the agonizing convulsions of change. Religious individualism gave them a basis for demanding economic and political individualism as well.

Yet it reveals something of Fox's genius that he spoke also to contemporaries who understood religion in the older sense of being bound together. Fox never repudiated this older tradition, at least not in the explicit way he rejected the church's insistence that it alone defined faith, and it lived on just below the surface in the sect he molded, occasionally emerging to war with the individualism he sired. Gerrard Winstanley's synthetic unification of the old tradition with an individual's inward experience was a trifle more creative: "This seed is he that leads mankind into truth, making every one to seek the preservation and peace of others as of themselves. This teaches man inwardly to know the nature and necessity of every body, and to administer to every body accordingly."[47] Yet Winstanley's followers proved unable to ride the cresting wave of those rushing to embrace the modern world's characteristic individualism. So they lasted hardly longer than the blink of an eye, while Fox's Friends survived into the present age. Survival does not prove rightness, but it is a major definition of success.

More than anything Fox had ever experienced, his realization of the primacy of the spirit liberated him from the continual searching that had been his lot for at least the four years he had traveled. While the inner security he now possessed—a security that enabled him to disregard the opinions of those better off and more educated than himself—did not prevent gnawing temptations from returning, it freed him to speak the truth he had experienced in all its simplicity and power. Hence Fox cultivated his ability to make abstractions like God and evil, salvation and sin, liberty and bondage, as real to others as they were now to him.

5

When the Fox Preaches, then Beware Your Geese

On Wednesday, October 30, 1650, Fox was staying in the Derby home of a doctor whose wife he had convinced.[1] He heard the local church bell tolling, calling people to a lecture sponsored by the Presbyterians; numerous outsiders, including an army colonel, had also come for the meeting. After interrupting the service with a compatriot, John Fretwell, a native of Stainsby in Derbyshire, Fox was taken into custody and subjected to eight hours of close questioning. Among other things he asserted, in the course of interrogation, that he was free of sin because Christ had taken it away, a comment bound—if not calculated—to infuriate his staunch Presbyterian inquisitors who held that no person could be free from sin. The two strangers—Fox was listed in the records as a cordwainer and resident of nearby Mansfield—were promptly committed to jail for a term of six months for blaspheming. Actually, the authorities probably cared less about his blasphemy than the appeal his religious message, with its undertones encouraging social insubordination, would have for the lower sorts.[2] Thus he was queried about a female disciple who, it was reported, went looking for a man willing to kiss her.[3] Fox remained in custody, unable to preach publicly, for almost a year.

While in jail, Fox took umbrage that one of his questioners, a justice named Gervase Bennett, applied the label "Quaker" to him and his followers. A derisive term, it was based on the fact that Fox's followers quaked and trembled during their worship, which gatherings they insisted on calling simply "meetings." Fox preferred the name "Children of the Light," a phrase that he claimed Christ had bestowed on them and that they used for many years. He was creative in adopting other acceptable terms, such as "People of God," "Royal Seed of God," or "Friends of the Truth," the latter winning favor and becoming the basis of the modern name, "Religious Society of Friends." He excoriated Bennett for his reproachful description, although he reeled off the names of numerous biblical figures who were said to have also trembled before the Lord. God, he promised, would surely punish Bennett for his mockery."[4]

Fox expected opposition from the authorities. But he also expected others to heed his message, for it spoke to obvious needs. Authentic religion had evanesced like gun smoke during the divisive Civil War years, leaving an emptiness in many hearts. One old man told him that he had been a believer for forty years but had "not tasted the love of God" until his heart was opened.[5] Religion had traditionally functioned as a powerful sanction for the existing order, but encouraged by the possibilities of change during the Civil War and the decline of the established church's coercive powers, English sectarians turned religion into a base for implementing radical change in society. Sparked by Leveller agitation, discussions of the nation's future were common within the ranks of the New Model Army. The soldiers' firm commitment to religious tolerance for dissenters, as well as their demonstrated opposition to clerical pretensions, easily spilled over into the larger society and inevitably fed religious rivalries.[6] Horrified, one heresy hunter reported that common soldiers often listened to sermons that equated the Protestant ministry with papists and advocated pulling down all "steeple-houses."[7] Presbyterians dominated the Westminster Assembly and produced a series of government-approved documents that defined an ascending order of church courts as the final stage of reformation, while their more leftist Calvinist cousins the Independents or Congregationalists moved toward New Light and local church autonomy.[8] The various Baptist sects, positioned even more to the left, eschewed tithes, church buildings, and the established ministry, separated themselves from the world to such an extent that they were popularly considered sneaky "housecreepers," and won from the hypercritical Fox the accolade "tender."[9]

These groups of believers might sound familiar, but many other groups have long since disappeared. Some, like the Fifth Monarchists, radical millenarians who confidently looked for and worked for the immediate establishment of the earthly rule of Christ, were not so much an organized movement as a tendency, particularly among Baptists. They flourished especially after King Charles I was beheaded in January 1649, for this event dramatically exposed the transitory nature of secular rulers. King Charles is dead, they thought, long reign King Jesus! These militants were the vanguard, heralds of the new kingdom.[10]

An even more extreme direction was taken by the Ranters, a shadowy and anarchistic collection of malcontents scattered extensively in the Midlands and the Peak district of Nottinghamshire, the very areas where Fox found his first converts. They carried to its logical end the Calvinist notion that God's election assured a person of salvation no matter what he or she might subsequently do. Hence the Ranters quickly achieved popular notoriety by flouting contemporary moral standards and claiming a mystical union with God. Reported to have uttered radical statements such as "There's no heaven but women, nor no hell save marriage," it was no wonder that the very word "Ranter" became a convenient lash by which opponents of any unconventional movement tried to whip its adherents back into line.[11] Mary Todd, deemed a Ranter, pranced into a room where the Quakers were gathered, pulled up her petticoat, and marched around the room shouting base expressions.[12] The Quakers, who knew something about disorderliness, called any disruptive person a Ranter, and sometimes reacted to one with force. At a meeting in Wellingborough, Richard Farnworth, an early Fox convert, found a Ranter—"the most wickedest one" he had ever seen—coming to disrupt it. Farnworth leaped on him, threw him against the wall, and stuffed a napkin in his mouth; later, however, the Ranter followed Farnworth to the next town and entered his meeting there waving a sword.[13]

The line between religious groups and purely secular groups was a fine one and shifted easily. One tiny group of Levellers, who called themselves "True Levellers" but were popularly dubbed "Diggers," gained notoriety because they raised the issue of property relations in a fascinating and creative act. On Sunday, April 1, 1649, on St. George's Hill up the Thames from London, about twenty or thirty poor laborers dug up and planted some wasteland of the local parish to symbolically demonstrate the people's right to the nation's common wealth. The "light of truth" touched a mystically inclined former Baptist named Gerrard Winstanley and revealed how the earth should be "a common treasury of livelihood to whole mankind, without respect of persons." Although the original Digger experiment was suppressed within a year, imitations sprouted in other parts of the kingdom, including Leicestershire and Nottinghamshire, areas where Fox centered his activities.[14] Even in tiny Drayton-in-the-Clay, Minister Stephens complained that one of Winstanley's pamphlets had attracted too many readers.[15] Later the Digger himself affirmed his conviction that Fox's followers had been, as he told a missionary in London, "sent to perfect that work which fell in their hands."[16]

A more widespread, but amorphous conglomeration was called Seekers, a group of drifting individuals more than anything else. With no organization, no creed, not even a leader willing to admit associating with them, Seekers could be anyone whom uneasy pamphleteers wanted to name. Later, people who found Quakerism congenial remembered themselves as Seekers, but by that time, years in the future, the term seemed generic rather than specific, defining an attitude more than any certain affiliation. Seekers, as one versifier phrased it in a London broadside, "always doubt / Of clearest truths, in Holy Writ laid out."[17] They refused, another critic complained, to "join issue . . . by writing and otherwise."[18] To be identified as a Seeker indicated alienation from both established and dissenting churches, doubt about revealed religion, and inability to find solace from those who presumed to ladle it out. Seekers, much like Fifth Monarchists, hoped to see a dawning spiritual age ruled directly by God. Thus, for one heresiographer, the Seeker seemed a rootless individual who held that no gospel, faith, or ministry existed "unless any can show as immediate a call to the ministry as the apostles had."[19] Few could, and the scattered Seekers seemed destined to continue looking—until a Seeker named George Fox came along to speak to their condition.[20]

For five years, from 1647 to 1652, Fox developed an approach that melded his religious appeal to the social conditions and aspirations of his audience, be they Levellers, Ranters, or Seekers. Inevitably it grew out of a trial-and-error approach, one he perfected in the English Midlands as he wandered hither and yon trying to convert the region's spiritual strays to his religious wisdom. As he traveled around a region he knew well, he responded to popular questings and demonstrated that he had found an answer to the void left by the age's upheavals. He seems to have had some sense of where he could find sympathetic listeners, or at least he cultivated the ability to spot them easily, for as soon as he began his mission he met some "friendly people" in Derbyshire and then others a bit further on in the forested Peak district.[21] Anxious to avoid scrutiny from those in authority, the people he met in their areas illustrated the truth that "people bred amongst woods are naturally more stubborn and uncivil" than those in cleared areas.[22] But to him such people were friendly because he carefully tailored his message to appeal to them, and Fox saw his efforts take hold.

A long-smoldering conflict in isolated Derbyshire offered one example. Enclosing arable land to turn it into pastures had pushed many people off land on which they had always lived; they responded by rioting and tearing down hedges and stone walls. By the summer of 1649 the county's four thousand lead miners were on the verge of revolt. Ore was harder to work in nearly exhausted pits, and formerly independent miners found themselves reduced to piecework. Their new, depressed status did not reduce the pressure from those, lay and clergy, who claimed the right to tithes from miners who dug the ore. The 10 percent tax inevitably weighed heavier as the amount of ore dug decreased. Their sagging condition and the always onerous tithes provoked protests from the miners, no doubt adding to what a later observer called their "strange, turbulent, and quarrelsome" temper.[23] Petitioning Parliament, they claimed to be "seduced by the covetous clergy, [who] believ[ed] their prayers available for the finding of lead." In October upwards of six thousand armed rebels, some forced to subsist on gleanings from the fields, took a "posture of war to purchase their freedom" and were promptly dispersed by Roundhead cavalry.[24]

Fox's message was a "spiritual" one, but to people like these he became a spark, lighting the way to a new age that would be theirs if they abandoned old leaders and followed new prophets. Fox knew how to tailor his message to address the desires of his audience, to use concrete complaints to win adherents for his cause. When he marched into courts to, as he put it, "cry for justice," he surely identified himself with the likes of the miners suing over tithes.[25] When he blasted Thomas Bretland, a dissenting clergyman of Chesterfield, a leadmining center, for "choking" himself on the parish's tithes, he placed himself firmly on the side of the tax resisters, as everyone knew. No wonder the authorities confined him to jail or that his message flourished in the county.[26] In targeting opponents of tithing as his prime audience, Fox learned to identify himself and his emerging movement with the grievances commoners harbored against those who milked them of their property.[27]

Thus when Fox went on to attack lawyers who upheld taking other's property through tithes and ministers who lived off the same tithes while claiming to be curing souls, he chose his targets well. (It should be kept in mind that more than 40 percent of church livings were subject to lay control by impropriators and tithe farmers who collected them on commission for someone else.[28]) These two groups were widely regarded as enemies of the people, so those who heard Fox knew immediately whom he meant:[29] he was questioning the legitimacy of what he sarcastically referred to as these "great professions." And he was convinced that the reasons his clerical enemies disliked him so much was, as he wrote one correspondent, that they were "afraid to have their means rent from them."[30] He had hit upon a creative tactic allowing him to connect the grievances of discontented tillers of the soil, those most affected by tithes, with an appeal to religious dissenters. Let the law be reformed, for example, and people would no longer need human law but live by the law of God that taught each person to see that anyone who wrongs a neighbor harms him- or herself; people would then be "Children of the Light."[31] An old message it certainly was, couched in biblical language that itself bespoke justice, but in the context of the times it addressed concrete and popular material needs and hit responsive chords. The promise of this utopia, of God ruling in and through people's wills, informed Fox's basic critique of the existing order of things and appealed to people who had every reason to distrust the institutions under which they still suffered. He did more than promise change, of course, for he acted consistently in accord with what he preached and exhibited by his every action his disparagement of the old and his commitment to a new order of fairness.

In the background the Civil War rumbled to life again, even if it moved slowly in the Midlands where Fox was busily preaching. In November 1647 the king escaped his captors and, turning the tables on his parliamentary opponents, hastily negotiated a quick alliance with his former Scottish enemies. Scattered royalists took this alliance as a sign to begin their own localized risings, and the Scottish army, hoping against farfetched hope to extend their brand of Presbyterianism southward with the favor of an Anglican king, moved into England. They slogged through the northern Midland area where Fox was winning increasing numbers of converts. Slowed by unsummerlike cold, rain, and wind, the army's progress brought the reality of conflict home to the area and underscored the urgency of Fox's pleas that people must choose between standing either for light and love or darkness and death.[32] Even for those far from the roaring guns, the reality of war was already everywhere, in the one-legged veterans, the weedy crops unworked because the man of the house had been lost in some now-forgettable battle, and the wandering, crazy-eyed refugees.

As Fox crisscrossed the small area from Mansfield to Derbyshire and back again, a region ravaged by the plague as well as by war, his sermons crackled with military and apocalyptic images. He saw, he reported, a great break in the earth out of which clouds of smoke emerged along the fault and then the earth itself, like a giant arising from his slumber, shook; he likened this vision to the shaking of people's hearts as they were convicted of their sins just prior to the sprouting of the divine seed in their souls. In Nottinghamshire he told a gathering of dissenters that the apostle Paul had known an outward law warring against the law of God in his inward mind. In Mansfield, apparently his headquarters, he startled a large meeting of professors—no doubt Baptists—by warning that they spoke only of the outward blood of Christ. "Do you not see the blood of Christ?," he cried. "See it in your hearts," he admonished, so it can "sprinkle your hearts and consciences from dead works." Surely such truth was a "flaming sword."[33]

Words like these attracted dissenters of various kinds, some of whom traveled from far away to hear him. In late 1647 Fox received a deathbed endorsement, a kind of symbolic laying on of hands, from a Mansfield seer identified only as "Brown." A Fifth Monarchist preacher,[34] Brown forecast that Fox would be an instrument of the Lord and that other dissenters would fade away to nothing. This prediction, from one well known as a spiritual leader in the region, apparently had an immediate and visible affect on him, because thereafter Fox's countenance so altered that others now saw him as a different person. For a fortnight people from the surrounding area flocked to see this new marvel of the Midlands and to hear his message. Obviously, Fox got a kind of psychological lift from Brown's endorsement and the stir it produced: "I had been brought through the very ocean of darkness and death"—this image of an ocean was one he often used to describe his continuing temptations—"by the eternal glorious power of Christ." The harvest was clearly ready and his temptations were subsiding. Fox set to reaping;[35] before long the region enjoyed the reputation of being infested with his followers.[36]

In Manchester, Dukinfield, Leicestershire, and Eton near Derby, as well as in Mansfield, Fox saw his preaching take hold in new and exciting ways. His followers began to collect into separate groups, designated as Children of the Light, the formal name Quakers gave themselves.[37] When he interrupted church meetings to accuse, preach, and pray, the very building seemed to shake, while some members of the congregations he visited compared his appearance to someone from apostolic times. Some newly won disciples began to follow his example and go into the churches to attack the ministers and the old ways.[38] When those convinced by Fox's message collected together in their own separate meetings, they came to sense, as a later friendly witness testified, an "agony of the soul" so painful that it had an external effect. Frequently the convert's body would be shaken with "groans, sighs, and tears" as though subjected to the "pangs of a woman in labor." These outward signs bespoke an inward struggle between the forces of darkness and those of light, often culminating in a victorious "sweet sound of thanksgiving and praise."[39]

A harsher critic thought Fox's disciples made noises that reminded him of a bull's roar. Francis Higginson recounted stories of night meetings in out-of-the-way places attracting up to two hundred "in a swarm." Instead of singing or reading Scripture or administering sacraments, the faithful would sit, sometimes for nearly three hours, in silence, until someone presumed to speak under the inspiration of the spirit. Head downcast, with a severe look, and hands striking the breast, the speaker began without warning in a low voice, continuing for as long as the inspiration continued. Listeners hung on every "oraculous" word because, Higginson snickered, "they believe them to be the very words and dictates of Christ." While the speaking continued, some, especially women and children, would fall into quaking fits and swoon as with epilepsy. Lips aquiver, bellies swelled with wind, their bowels loosened as if purged, the worshippers might lie on the ground in such a state for two hours or longer. "'Let them alone, trouble them not,'" Higginson quoted leaders like Fox advising, "'the Spirit is now struggling with the flesh.'"[40]

This Westmorland cleric's description was extreme, but it exaggerated only a little. "Convincement," the term the Children used for conversion, meant to be overcome, and their meetings were gatherings of those who had been overtaken and gripped by God's Spirit. With no obvious leader, the group met in silence to await the promptings of the ever-present Christ. Almost anything was possible:

shaking, quaking, rolling, even stripping. Sometimes nothing of moment was said or done, but an attender might still be touched by the power that seemed collected in the group. One Friend described such a meeting at Grayrigg in Westmorland where a troubled young girl left, sat on the ground, and then cried out in agony, "O Lord, make me clean." Such incidents revealed the Lord's power to the person convinced but also spoke to others, leading them to sense their own needs.[41] At other times, as at Malton in early 1653, nearly two hundred came together and were so moved that, to quote a visitor who was there, "almost all the room was shaken."[42] An evangelist explained how people leaving a steeple-house were astonished to see the Children "trembling and crying" in their meeting.[43] Sometimes three or four who were strong in the truth would appoint a "threshing meeting" to winnow those ready to be convinced from among the heathen.[44] Here, sparked by the presence of opponents, the scene was often more turbulent. At one such meeting a Ranter challenged Fox, who bluntly responded, "Repent you swine and beast."[45]

The first Quakers seldom tried to explain or describe these meetings to outsiders, believing their power had to be experienced. That they grew so rapidly, and as rapidly became notorious to critics, suggested the appeal they had to people unable to find stability in a disorderly world. Inevitably, however, potential Children brought uninformed habits with them when they attended these meetings, so some of Fox's earliest letters counseled restraint. In fact, his first published epistle advised Friends to "love gravity, and soberness, and wisdom," and two years later, in 1652, he warned them to make sure in their meetings that "the wisdom of God guide you" so as "to preserve the truth from suffering by the world."[46] Criticism from outsiders forced them to defend quaking, clearly their most distinguishing characteristic. They found references in the Bible to justify their unconventional behavior but usually preferred euphemisms such as "the power of the Lord" to mask the unruliness of quaking.[47]

At settled meetings where those already convinced came, the experience of seventeen-year-old Stephen Crisp of Colchester was probably typical. Crisp, aware of his own unworthiness, went expecting to get some sense of God's presence, but time and silence dragged on and he took to watching those around him. He certainly could not be like them, he decided, for they were so serious and sober. Concluding that he was wasting time, he started to leave when an inward voice thundered, "That which is weary must die." He returned to his seat, now baptized with the conviction that he must bear Christ's cross, the very thing he had been fleeing all his life. Joy, confidence, salvation came with the intensified willingness of a sobered Stephen Crisp to be crucified to the world and its ways.[48]

Such reactions pointed up how the Children's unconventionality alienated more respectable people. Ignoring these attacks—indeed, using them to advantage—Fox's practices grew increasingly radical. He saw nothing untoward in bringing to meeting a mentally unstable and potentially disruptive person if by chance she could be helped.[49] Building on popular discontent with the religious establishment and the leeway now permitted dissenters, he laid stress on two aspects of the same message, one positive, one negative. On the positive side he proclaimed to people "where their teacher was, within them, the spirit and the light of Jesus. . . . [T]hat Christ was come to teach his people himself."[50] To turn to this light of Christ within them and be faithful to it would transform them into a new people, people able to live in the same state of perfection that Adam and Eve lived in before the Fall. It would give even the meanest person a chance to go deeper into faith than John the Baptist and "come through by the spirit and power of God to Christ. . . . and [be] led by the Holy Ghost into the truth and substance of the Scriptures." Convinced that a person might have "a pure opening of the light, without the help of any man," a conversion experience like the one he had had, Fox preached that no amount of time spent reading the Scriptures could give a person the right knowledge of Christ or the word of God; one must come instead to the spirit that gave them forth in the first place.[51]

Blatantly anti-institutional, his intensely personal appeal called into question the trappings and rituals of organized religion, both in themselves and as part of the social and political order. The very fact of convincing ordinary people that Christ—not a minister, not a bishop, not a member of Parliament—had come to teach them had a radicalizing effect. One of his closest disciples, Alexander Parker, tellingly described the process. People who are convinced, he explained, "come to see the deceit of the priests and the emptiness of their former formal profession and the deadness of it . . . but care must be taken . . . to build them up in that which is holy until they need no man to teach them."[52] Often Fox would fix a person in his audience with a stare almost startling in its intensity, and occasionally he would grasp someone tightly by the hand while he spoke: even scoffers found it difficult to resist such close attention.[53] A story made the rounds that by merely laying his hand on people they would be convinced.[54] Where before there might have been an easy acceptance of things as they were, with Fox's visit an unsettledness came to mark the community.

This side of Fox's message would have made him controversial, of course, among dissenting preachers, theologians, and those who quaked at every itinerant prophet, such as the publicist who attacked "apostolics" because "they now expect a new revealed way / Unknown in Scripture, they have dar'd to say."[55] By itself his charisma would probably not have put him in any danger with the secular authorities or, for that matter, aroused much public opposition. But the social aspect of his sermons, his way of particularizing the evils he alleged, as well as his forceful way of attracting attention, was like waving a red flag to antagonize traditional-thinking authorities and the apathetic masses. Officers of the state would then be drawn into a religious matter threatening the public peace. Fox's style and approach proved to be provoking to the establishment. Indeed, if an audience failed to rise to his provocations, then he interpreted its indifference to his message as an example of "dullness and drowsy heaviness," the very thing he was attacking: "And I told people," he remarked, "they must come to witness death to the sleepy, heavy nature . . . that their minds and hearts might be on things above." Whether met with outright opposition or passivity, he viewed resistence or indifference as an endorsement of the course of action to which he had been called.[56]

Fox, though, much preferred opposition—"a wonderful confusion it brought among all professors and priests." He exulted about hostility aroused by his refusal to doff his hat, because bystanders thereby got to witness the vanity and deceit of the world's people.[57] In Derby, a little county town of twenty-five hundred, he assaulted one congregation by stating that "all their preaching, sprinkling, sacraments would never sanctify a man,"[58] and in Leicestershire he announced his purpose was "to bring people off their old ways, . . . from their churches, . . . from all the world's religions, . . . from all the world's fellowships, and prayings and singings, . . . from heathenish fables, and from men's inventions and windy doctrines, . . . all their images and crosses, and sprinkling of infants, with all their holy days . . . and all their vain traditions." He told owners of public houses that they should not let people have more to drink than they needed; merchants that they should not cheat; teachers that they should teach only serious topics; and all and sundry that they should not take part in wakes, feasts, maygames, sports, plays, and shows, or gaze at stars, watch magicians, and listen to music— otherwise, people would "be nursed and trained up to lightness, vanity and wantonness."[59] His attack was aimed at the very pastimes that had helped make traditional society bearable to many generations of his English fellows. In joining puritanical nonconformists wanting to ban such frivolities, he could hardly have been surprised when some offended people labeled him mad or refused to sell him milk and food.[60]

But angry opponents raged even more about his radical gestures toward social equality, small though he himself admitted them to be. Contrary to the social convention that the plural "you" should be used by an inferior to one's betters, Fox insisted on using the traditional "thee" and "thou" to any single person regardless of status. Nor would he bow and remove his hat or bend his knee to pay obeisance to self-defined social superiors. In probably his most serious affront to customary standards of behavior, he refused to take off his hat to anyone, high or low, king's officer or king's subject, and thereby affirmed that people of all ranks were the same in his eyes. Nothing, he recalled, would so try "all men's patience and sobriety" than this single action, which amounted to open contempt for what society expected. Such activities vividly demonstrated Fox's commitment, in his day-to-day relationships, to the kind of radical equality that a person could extract from the rich egalitarian heritage of Christianity.[61]

When hauled before a court or when he found professors gathered in a church—though he refused to call it a church, using the dissenters' derogatory label "steeple-house" instead—he spoke of oppression and deceit. Once in Mansfield on the edge of Sherwood Forest he heard that local justices of the peace were meeting to inquire into the hiring of servants, one of their administrative responsibilities.[62] When he arrived at the place they were supposed to be meeting, he discovered they had moved on to a town about eight miles away, so he literally ran the distance to exhort the justices to decree that servants should be paid fair wages. He bluntly told others not to take oaths, which he considered forbidden by the biblical injunction not to swear. Such an illegal practice subjected the refuser not only to possible imprisonment but also to a range of other penalties, including denial of the right to sit on juries, to sue for debts, or even to recover stolen goods.[63]

In his home county, at Leicester, he found a disputatious meeting of assorted

Presbyterians, Independents, Baptists, and Anglicans in which a woman dared to rise and ask a question. The minister in the pulpit cut her off with the reminder that he did not permit women to speak in his church. "Do you call this mixed multitude a church?," snorted Fox in defense of the woman's right to ask questions, for he believed a true church to be made up of people separated out of the world. The priest climbed down from the pulpit to dispute with him, causing the whole assembly to collapse in an uproar. Soon little circles of disputants collected all over the building and even took over an adjacent house to argue such fine points as the nature of the church and the validity of infant baptism.[64] Challenging ministers and implying that women's opinions merited consideration was more than enough to label Fox a threat to established religion.

Every symbol of the established church cut Fox to the quick, reminding him of deceit and misplaced authority. When he heard a church bell toll or saw a steeple from afar, he felt something like a "black, earthly spirit" striking at his very life.[65] A ringing bell reminded him of the market bell and how it summoned people to barter and trade—in his view, the ministers were thus setting out their wares, putting a price on the freely bestowed Scriptures, selling the word of God for lucre. For example, he arrived in Nottingham overlooking the Trent River on a Sunday morning in 1649. Headed for the meeting of his group, he spied the steeple of St. Mary's Church, "a great idol," and determined that God was instructing him to go and declaim against it and those gathered there. But first he betook himself to the Quaker meeting, never uttering a word of his plan. He left early and aimed straight for that menacing "steeple-house." (His strategy permitted only one person to bear the odium of disturbing a church service.)[66] Not surprisingly, he found the people barren and the priest a great lump of clay as he stood in his high pulpit. When the priest told his congregation that the Scriptures were the touchstone by which all doctrines and controversies were to be tested, Fox literally could not contain himself, for this amounted to a direct affront to what he considered to be the real authority. "Oh no," he interrupted, "it is not the Scriptures." The Jews had the Scriptures and still persecuted Christ and the apostles; the real authority was the Holy Spirit, the source of the Scriptures, who would lead into all truth. Though subsequent events indicated his words won some assent, the authorities promptly hustled him off to jail.[67]

As with all his later incarcerations, Fox took full advantage of the opportunities this first one presented. Called before the mayor, the aldermen, and the sheriff that Sunday night, he explained his motives and thought he had softened the mayor's attitude, but he nevertheless was sent back to jail. Sometime later the high sheriff of Nottingham, John Reckless, invited Fox to live in his house, an opportunity hardly to be denied. Despite remaining in custody, Fox held large meetings in the Reckless home and succeeded in winning over his host and the entire household. On the very next Saturday the sheriff, now more Quaker than Fox, took himself to the busy marketplace, and marched around calling upon the people to repent, no doubt proclaiming as Children of the Light did in other places, "Repent, repent, woe, woe, the judge of the world has come, Christ is in you all, believe not the priests of Baal, they are liars, they delude you."[68] This spectacle of undermined authority was enough to convince the mayor to hasten

Fox back to the isolation in the jail, which was the unfortunate recipient of the heavy odor wafting from the nearby town privy.[69]

While in jail, Fox encountered a possessed women whose condition allowed him to perform the first of his many recorded miracles.[70] He clearly saw that the way he and his disciples dealt with sick persons—this particular woman had suffered from mental illness for as long as thirty-two years—would offer a way to demonstrate to others the power available to those who followed him. Curing this woman, who had been unsuccessfully ministered to by various clergymen, would represent a divine confirmation of Fox's abilities in striking contrast to his opponents' failure. In her distressed state the woman came announcing that the Lord had told her to "arise, for I have a sanctified people, haste and go to them for thy redemption draweth nigh." The symptoms she evinced—roaring with a loud voice and tumbling along the ground on her stomach—upset other Children of the Light and alienated visitors they tried to attract to their meeting in Mansfield, where Fox brought the afflicted woman after his release. Finally, almost in an act of desperation, Fox and the other Children gathered at Elizabeth Hooten's home in nearby Skegby and on two different occasions met around the roaring body. On the second, after about an hour, they felt a power arise that seemed to cast out whatever demons inhabited the poor woman's spirit: "[S]he rose up and her countenance changed and became white." Watching over her while she recuperated for two weeks, they displayed her to the curious of the neighborhood. Around the immediate countryside this cure caused detractors to think twice before using such labels as "witches," "false prophets," and "deceivers" to describe Fox's adherents.[71] Another cure about the same time likewise testified to Fox's power.[72]

These miracles did not arrest the opposition Fox engendered in his travels, including opposition sometimes from those of the lower orders, his natural allies. In Mansfield-Woodhouse, for example, when he assailed the priest in the church, the "rude" people mobbed him, pummeling him with fists and Bibles and fastening him in the stocks. Interrogating him at a nearby knight's house, some local "great persons" considered him so ill-used that they ignored the mob's threats and set their prisoner free, an action that provoked the rabble into stoning him out of town. Even if he did not win the allegiance of such great persons, their concern did save him, as in this instance, from lower-class opposition. Such a startling failure with some of his usual constituents likely occasioned Fox's "inwardly bruised" depressed state again.[73]

His movement was still inchoate enough that Fox and some confederates, tempted no doubt to be associated with another growing sect, decided to explore theological common ground with a group of General Baptists in Leicestershire. Headed by a prominent itinerant evangelist, Samuel Oates, a young weaver from Norwich, the Baptist group had close ties with a notorious congregation in Whitechapel, London, with which Fox may have come in contact when he was in the capital five years earlier. With the riots and attacks on clergy it occasioned, Oates's evangelistic foray into the Midlands nearly matched Fox's in the level of controversy it produced—in fact, it was more controversial to London heresy hunters because Fox the unknown outlander could hardly compare with the better known Oates.[74] Fox made the first overture to the Baptists, and the two groups met in Barrow, just north of Leicester. According to Fox, the discussion never got beyond mutual questioning—what is faith? who baptized John the Baptist? is one who betrays Christ within equally guilty as the Judas who betrayed him without?—and the confabulation rather promptly broke up but with no lasting recriminations on either side.[75]

Obviously more important for what it revealed of Fox's intentions than for what it accomplished, which was little, the conference marked an attempt to coordinate his growing movement with others of similar views. What most appealed to him about the General Baptists was that they were radical nonconformists who had separated themselves from and wanted no part of the established church, unlike the Presbyterians and many Independents. But even similar institutional approaches could not overcome the two groups' fundamental theological differences. A statement issued by various Baptists in 1650 condemned all those who wanted to replace the ordinances (the Baptist version of the sacraments) by "a God within, and a Christ within, and a word within,"[76] precisely Fox's goal. He insisted that the true faith should be inward rather than outward, that, as he put it to the Baptists during the conclave, the biblical crooked ways must be made straight in one's heart. He left Barrow with his mind settled against any possible merger with the likes of the General Baptists. He had simply expended too much effort for that to be an option now, although his evangelistic efforts among them did not slaken.

Fox also went to Coventry to see a body of Ranters jailed because of their unpopular religious practices and beliefs. Their prevalence in the region as well as their notoriety made them an obvious target for conversion to Fox's views. Roaring, blaspheming, and uttering all sorts of vaporous sentiments, they struck him as positively obnoxious. Like the authorities who had locked them up, he wanted to convince them of the errors of their ways. Fox aimed at splitting the moderate ones away from some of the others who claimed they were God. If they did not know of Fox already, they certainly understood something of his approach, for they quoted him a biblical example of how God had told Peter not to call something unclean if it had been sanctified. Fox preferred to concentrate on their claim to be God and refuted them, he remembered, by pointing out that, unlike them, God knew the next day's weather. While not winning any of them to his view, he implied he had a salutary impact by noting that their leader, skilled and adaptable Joseph Salmon, a New Model Army soldier on his way to becoming a Baptist, presently wrote a recantation and was released from jail. The actual correspondence between the two men's ideas is striking: the prisoner allegorized the Bible, believing that its stories spoke the truth within each person, and even opposed using the sword.[77]

Fox plotted his Midlands missions carefully, arranging to arrive in a town on the special days set aside by Presbyterians meeting in their classes for lectures or on market or fair days. He echoed the millenarian strains of Fifth Monarchists when he told his auditors at a classis in Atherstone, close by Drayton-in-the-Clay that "God was come to teach his people himself" and that they would no longer need "man-made teachers." And at Twycross he demonstrated what the rule of the righteous would mean when he strongly warned collectors of excise taxes against oppressing home craftsmen—"people were much affected" with his warning.

Traveling to Derbyshire, site of the previous year's lead miners' uprising, he discovered that such sentiments boded ill, particularly when the nervous authorities compounded his political views with the religious extremism of the Ranters: More ominous from the establishment's point of view were the few supporters traveling with him. For all the world they must have looked like a roving band of outside agitators. In the context of widespread opposition to paying tithes to support ministers who seemed to grow only richer, his advice to people in Chesterfield that they should "come off all men's teaching unto God's teaching" and obey God rather than humans emphasized the radical implications of his religious message. He and his squad could hardly have been surprised therefore when the provoked mayor confined them briefly before hustling them out of town in the middle of the night.[78]

Fox was not so lucky when he was imprisoned in Derby, for he remained in jail almost a year (his mate Fretwell pleaded that he needed to visit his mother and was released earlier). Jails were not designed, then or now, to be islands of luxury, but seventeenth-century ones were only a bit this side of outright barbarity. Debtors, by definition poor, were about the only permanent residents because most others either awaited trial, release, transportation to the colonies, or execution. That the jailer operated his establishment like a hotel, that is, charging fees for better accommodations and food, gave debtors, who had no money, ample reason to prey on their fellow inmates. Moreover jailers, usually subject to no rules, could be totally arbitrary with prisoners who created problems or who held unpopular views; they could also grant favored inmates more freedom, even the right to a furlough. Judging from prisoner complaints and the fact that many inmates died before trial, jailers often denied them access to food or drink. Close quarters—some prisons were in the basements of castles—and the plague inevitably freed more of the jailed than writs of habeas corpus. To make matters worse, conflicts often surfaced between the sheriffs who were obliged to look after the prisoners and the justices of the peace who were responsible for housing them; at best, this was a sure recipe for inaction, at worst, it left the prisoner in a jurisdictional muddle. The sheriff often operated his jail as a profit-making business, charging, for example, for the charity of removing leg irons. Hence even well-off prisoners could leave their cells broke. It was no wonder that seventeenth-century Britons prayed to be kept out of "four houses, a usurer's, a tavern, a spital, and a prison."[79] Derby's jail was sited over a branch of the River Derwent, at one end of the corn market, exposing its prisoners to damp and filth.[80]

Not surprisingly, Fox bombarded his capturers with missive after missive, filled with complaint after complaint; he even addressed some annoying church bellringers with the warning that their time was too limited to be devoting it to pleasures. But he did not concentrate on such relatively minor matters: to Justice Bennett, who had sent him to jail in the first place, he cried, "Woe be to you greedy men, and rich men; weep and howl for your misery that shall come."

Having watched the haggling in the adjacent marketplace, he upbraided the mayor: "Mercy . . . and justice are cried for in your streets! Oppression . . . is in your streets; but the poor are not regarded." "The Lord is coming with power," he prophesied as though the last days were nigh, "and he will throw down every one that is exalted."[81] Such sentiments were hardly the kind to win him early release.

Fox's turn in jail was not onerous, for he was permitted a constant stream of visitors, with an occasional one attracted from as far away as Yorkshire,[82] and soon got the right to go for walks beyond the walls. The turning point came when the jailor, struck with a sudden sickness he conveniently attributed to divine judgment, begged his prisoner's permission to spend the night with him so they could talk. Fox did not have to be asked twice, for he had already tried to convince his captor to permit him more liberty. Once receiving permission to go outside, he headed straight across the road to the corn market where he preached that the time of repentance had arrived.[83] But whenever he attracted too much attention, he found himself cast into the jail's low and lousy dungeon. Most of the professors who visited him were apparently Calvinists because they debated whether one could be free from sin, with Fox arguing for purity, his antagonists averring that no one could be free from sin while alive. Even his parents came to plead that he follow the less committed Fretwell to freedom: they thought "it was a strange thing to be imprisoned then for religion"—the time seemed near, after all, with the Anglican king dead and Parliament in control, that the Presbyterian church would be the island's established church. They even got the justices of the peace to convene a new hearing for their son, but, stiff-necked, he refused even to consider leaving lest "it blemish my innocency."

By this time Fox had served his six-month sentence, but he was not released, perhaps because it was feared that he would side with the discontented of the area, already disquieted by the lead miners' dispute. Discussion of trying him before Parliament or transporting him to Ireland pointed up these official apprehensions. By July, his ninth month in custody, rumors of war spread through the region and added to local unease. Fox's house of correction was thrown open to men training for the army. Impressed with his commitment to his principles, the soldiers petitioned that he be commissioned a captain and given command over them. The army commissioners, responsible for recruiting and thinking to turn his influence to a useful end, proffered him the position. But he turned them down with the classic comment that he "lived in the virtue of that life and power that took away the occasion of all wars." Still they pressed, pleading that the offer was made out of love and kindness, until Fox, considering it no compliment, flared back, "If that were their love and kindness, I trampled it under my feet." Finally Justice Bennett ordered that money be offered to entice him to enlist, but the prisoner continued to refuse. Thus when the battle of Worcester took place on September 3, 1651, ending the dream of the pretender Charles Stuart that he could take the throne by force, George Fox was safe in the lousy and bedless dungeon his impertinence had brought him to. His abashed parents came to make one last futile attempt to have him released.

Other visitors around the same time served as a vivid reminder that the growing

Quaker movement possessed no immunity from internal problems. Fox faced a challenge to his leadership, one he remembered anticipating three decades later.[84] Headed southward to join the parliamentary army facing off against the would-be Charles II, Rhys Jones and a group of Nottingham Children stopped by to confer with the prisoner. Unfortunately, all we know about Jones comes from his opponents, so it is difficult to get a well-rounded picture of him and his position. Jones exhibited a self-assurance and brassy boldness worthy of Fox himself, so a clash between the two was probably inevitable. Formerly a soldiering Baptist and an early and enthusiastic convert to Fox's beliefs, Jones had taken Fox in his arms and told him that "the Lord had a mighty work through and by him."[85] But Jones took Fox's ideas more literally than Fox intended—he concluded, and preached, that Fox's emphasis on the inward Christ made belief in the historic Jesus virtually unnecessary. Whether he had stopped by Derby to discuss the issue or whether the matter came up after he arrived, Jones directly confronted his incarcerated leader. He protested that the faith as proclaimed by Fox centered on the man who died at Jerusalem. "There was never any such thing," Jones claimed, denying that "Christ suffered there outwardly." Despite the fact that this was his favorite charge against his own opponents, the prisoner pointed out that Jesus *had* suffered at the hands of the chief priests and Pontius Pilate. Jones flung the label "chief priest" at Fox and left insisting that no true prophet, apostle, or holy man ever suffered outwardly.

To Fox and his supporters, Jones and his followers—of their numbers we know nothing—were "Proud Quakers." The precise reason for this prejorative label remains unclear, unless it was because they would not humble themselves to recognize Fox's primary leadership; certainly the Proud Quakers refused to eschew "common fashions and customs" and claimed liberty to "conform to the world to get a livelihood," positions anathema to Fox and his side. Their opposition to Fox's desire that well-off Children aid poor Children implied that they were wealthier than the general run of their cobelievers. Fox considered them little better than Ranters, since they called, as he phrased it, "evil good and good evil." Jones, in fact, claimed no more than Fox, insisting that he too was divinely inspired "to open the spiritual sense of the Scriptures." The Derby dispute did not immediately lead to a final break: for ten years Fox and his supporters tried to entice Jones and his followers back into their sect, but in the meantime the schismatics flourished in and around Nottingham.[86] Twenty-five years later people were still tarring Fox with Jones's reputation.[87]

As his time in jail dragged on, Fox realized that his absence from the movement had left a gap, so he commenced writing letters of counsel and encouragement to Children of the Light. As the years passed these epistles grew in number. The tone of those addressed to the Children, mixing pastoral and devotional advice with admonitions against involvement with the world, cast their author in a somewhat less dogmatic light than his polemical essays and even his memoirs. Lengths varied from brief sentences to pages of exhortations on whatever issue Fox wanted to address at the time. They rambled, did not always clarify the topics considered, and sometimes were internally contradictory. A careful reading is often less efficient than a quick perusal to grasp the author's intent.

Fox dictated most of them, writing a few himself, and then they were copied and recopied and passed from hand to hand and meeting to meeting. Many, either lost or destroyed, are known only from the brief excerpts used to identify the approximately five thousand letters listed in a catalogue of Fox's writings compiled in 1697 by a Friend, Mark Swanner, and published in 1939.[88] Those the author or his associates judged worthy of study or reflection appeared in print at the time and were of course more widely circulated. After the author's death 420, all chosen and some edited to reflect a later generation's moves toward respectability, were published in a folio volume in 1698.[89]

One of Fox's earliest epistles—he dated it "Fourth-day of the First month, 1650" (March 4, 1650)—reflected his irritation with his imprisonment but also his conviction that all was well. "Lord of peace, Lord of joy! thy countenance [support] makes my heart glad," he began. "In the world there are lords many, but to us there is but one God the Father . . . and one Lord Jesus Christ." As pastor to an absent flock he could not forget the oppressor: "In the world are many lords, and many gods, and the earth makes lords, coveting after riches, and oppressing the creatures." He concluded his brief message with a warning to his readers not to be like those who lord it over others: "Oh! that everyone would strive to put down, in themselves, mastery and honor, that the Lord of heaven and earth might be exalted!"[90]

About the same time Fox, though aged twenty-six, was writing like a person much wiser, much older. He directed his followers to listen to the teacher within themselves: "So mind the faith of Christ and the anointing, which is in you." The world's judgment was foolishness, particularly because "love and mercy do bear the judgment of the world in patience." "That which cannot bear the world's judgment," he had learned, "is not the love of God." "O therefore," he counseled, "let not the mind go forth from God; for if it do, it will be stained, and venomed and corrupted." "O therefore you who know the light, walk in the light! For there are children of darkness that will talk of the light and the truth and not walk in it. . . . O therefore mind the pure spirit of the everlasting God, which . . . judges the evil."

The defeat of the royalist army and unsettled political conditions provoked from him a barely disguised millennial message in another epistle. "The Lord is king over all the earth! Therefore all people praise and glorify your king in the true obedience, in the uprightness, and in the beauty of holiness." This king, unlike those who roared and fought with outward arms, spoke in silence: "His voice is sweet and pleasant; his sheep hear his voice, and they will not harken to another. . . . Glory to the Lord God for evermore." In another message to those enduring persecution, the same sentiments echoed: "Triumph above the world! Be joyful in the Lord; reigning above the world. . . . And come out of the world and keep out of it for evermore!"[91] Like the Fifth Monarchists, Fox believed human beings would live in a world ruled by Christ, but unlike them he spiritualized this rule in a way that stressed the way an individual lived and gave little attention to the nature of outward forms. His experience in Derby's dungeon demonstrated what many another prisoner has discovered, namely, that a person's body can be jailed yet his spirit remain free.

When Fox left his cell just before the winter of 1651, having been incarcerated for over a year, he decided to turn toward home, inclined perhaps by his desire to give some explanation to his parents for rebuffing their efforts to free him from prison. On his way back he veered ten miles or so westward into Stafford-shire and approached Lichfield. Here occurred an incident that has always troubled his admirers and followers, particularly those in the twentieth century.[92] A low-lying town whose road ran atop a kind of levee, Lichfield had been the scene of a prolonged seige to dislodge its royalist garrison only five years earlier. The thirty-five hundred shells lobbed at the minster had destroyed one of its three massive steeples.[93] There it stood, a jagged relic of the devastation war had wrought in the land. But the very fact that this exquisite structure still stood testified to Fox of the unfaithness of the present generation. London had ordered it demolished in October, but the initial task of stripping the lead from the roof was proceeding all too slowly, especially in the face of the village's noted "unparalleled loyalty" to the royal cause.[94] If the church in Nottingham with its single spire had reminded Fox of an idol, then the three he recalled seeing on this steepled-house[95] were a virtual trinity of evil. The idea of such evil stabbed at him. He got the clear sense that God required him to go there but to say nothing to his companions. When they came to the house where they were staying, he left them behind and took off, across hedge and ditch as the crow flew, for the city. Coming upon some shepherds, he took off his shoes, despite the wintery weather, and left them with the astonished sheepherders.

Walking the last mile through the squishy soil in his bare feet, he went through the streets, crowded for market day. The traders as usual were busy trying to get the top penny for their goods. The proverb that "love is not found in the market"[96] was painfully obvious that day. With the partially ruined church arching over him, Fox began to shout, again and again, "Woe to the bloody city of Lichfield!" However startled, no one laid a hand on him, not quite sure how such a person might react to attempted restraint. His turn or two around the town finished, he returned to the shepherds, handed them a tip, washed his feet, and put his shoes on again, pleased to have done the Lord's bidding but no doubt anxious to get out of the cold mud.

This seemingly unbalanced action hurt his reputation then and later: his parents iterated they did not approve his course, and a modern admirer has judged him to be "a psychopath of the deepest dye."[97] When he dictated his journal years later, he took pains to justify himself by referring to the bloody Civil War seige of the city and tales of a massacre of Christians on that site during the reign of Roman emperor Diocletian;[98] such a rationalization suggests that he was trying to win some belated respectability for his cause and ignored the fact that Fox's followers, caught up by their conversion and their consuming need to convince others, often acted in disorderly ways. Pronouncing God's judgment on the deceitful world and its evil seemed more important than acting respectably. When John Bunyan wrote *Pilgrim's Progress* two decades later, the aim he took at Vanity Fair, where "wives, husbands, children, masters, servants, lives, blood, bodies, souls" were sold, illustrated how markets discontented sensitive dissenters.[99] And the church, whose ruined steeple set Fox off in the first place, symbolized for him the evil remaining in the existing order of things. Embarrassing it might have been, but there was nothing unusual about acting unconventionally under the sway of intense religious emotions.

After leaving Lichfield, Fox continued his journey to Drayton-in-the-Clay and received there his parents' rebuke. Perhaps he considered remaining at home, but he was soon on the road again. He could have gone to London: with the war over and the country in the hands of a victorious army and a Parliament that promised reform, the capital might have seemed a good choice for the young dissenter. But he decided he was not ready for that challenge—he never forgot the time he had spent there in 1644, the disputations and acrimony, the very size of the place. No, he might be six years older, but he was not quite ready for London. He needed support, more people behind him, a stronger organization, some kind of base. He could not hope to sweep into London all alone.

This time, although he stopped in Mansfield and Derbyshire, he decided that he had spent enough time in the Midlands.[100] Perhaps he feared his notoriety would lead to increased opposition from the authorities—a year shut up in Derby jail had at least taught him to avoid imprisonment if possible. Perhaps his hard work was producing diminishing numbers of converts. Perhaps he was just ready to move on. In the event, if the Midlands seemed less appealing, the north looked like a place ripe for the truth to spring up. Echoing his cry of woe in Lichfield, he moved into Yorkshire preaching repentance as he went. The longest and most important chapter of his effort was beginning.

6

The North for Greatness

In the winter of 1651 when George Fox mounted his horse and turned northward away from Derbyshire, he gave no indication that he sensed anything different about the land, and he certainly did not know what was in store for him
and his movement in the north borderlands. Hence we must take him at his
word: he simply passed into the hill country of Yorkshire, preaching repentance
and searching for more converts to his young movement.[1]

If he had tapped a reservoir of emptiness and found enough response to merit
traveling in the Midlands for nearly four years, then he must have hoped for at
least as much response in the northern counties. Barren and backward, isolated
and fought over by powerful Scottish lairds and English earls, the north country
could boast one large city, York, with a spectacular minster steeple visible for
thirty miles; after that, according to one seasoned traveler, the boasting would
have to stop, for the town, with short, narrow streets, resembled the rest of the
region: mean and indifferent. The area where Fox entered Yorkshire rolled, flat-
tening out to the east where windmills dotted the landscape and the North Sea
lapped against the shoreline.[2] With many streams but few bridges, travel in the
north was mostly by water or horseback; even trade goods moved to market on
the backs of pack horses. Parishes were large, bishops were absentees, clergymen
were ignorant and ill paid, and schools were fewer than anywhere else in the
country. Even though other sections of the country shared these deficiencies,[3]
the area was still regarded as a backwater, ignored and looked down on by more
sophisticated southerners, a place where discontent every so often bubbled up
in the shape of religious revolt.

Since the area was a backwater, its people preferred the known, however troubling, to the unknown, however promising: so they were willing to fight to keep
the status quo. This popular preference, of people "rude of condition and not
well taught the law of God,"[4] had emerged most dramatically during the previous century in an uprising known as the Pilgrimage of Grace. Prompted by economic discontent—bad harvests, cattle plagues, enclosures, and too much money
transferred South into the hands of absentee landlords favored by the Crown—
the Pilgrims protested dissolution of the monasteries and called for ending the
doctrinal innovations that followed in the wake of King Henry VIII's decision to

make himself supreme head of the Church of England. The rebellion spread over the northern counties in the fall and winter of 1536 and 1537, with the number of Pilgrims reaching nearly forty thousand as the result of rumors that the mass would be abolished. The rebels managed to seize York itself, but their end came quickly after their leader agreed to a truce with the king, who then engineered a classic double cross and saved his realm.[5]

The collapse of the rebellion did not mean that the anger it expressed or the conditions from which it arose died out. A hundred years later, when Fox appeared on the scene, abject poverty could still arouse the lower orders to resist paying tithes to ministers or rack-rents to absentee landlords, a situation that made the mass of northerners unreliable allies for the area's gentry who supported the royal cause during the Civil War. In normal times their distance from the centers of religious and civil authority, as well as their poverty, gave people in the region some leeway to live their mean lives with little intervention by out-side forces. After all, as long as they kept reasonably quiet and did not fall too far behind on their taxes and tithes, it little mattered in Canterbury or London what such woebegone people did or did not do. Abstractions, words like "Puritanism" and "predestination," "equality" and "equity," had no concrete meanings for people accustomed to dealing with things they could see and touch. They could understand when a person was treated unfairly, when prices or rents were higher than a person could afford, when supposedly "superior" people demanded obeisance from their "inferiors" who were just as worthy in character. They displayed a close-to-the-earth commonsense approach.

Such an attitude may help explain the persistence of such native heresies as Lollardy and the appeal of foreign religions like Anabaptism in the region. The pope in Rome was too remote to make much difference in their lives. Most believed that trekking to some sacred well or other pilgrimage spot was a waste of time; besides, poor, hard-working northerners had no funds and little time for such excursions. Those infected with Lollardy must have shaken their heads in horrified disbelief when Catholic neighbors did penance by kneeling in icy waters up to their necks.[6] The Roman church's doctrine of transubstantiation likewise conflicted with the commonsense observation that a wafer supposedly embodying Christ himself still tasted like the flour from which it was made. If a person wanted to make the effort to read the Bible in English, then why, one might well ask, did the church insist that the holy book should be open only to those with a knowledge of Latin? And a person did not have to be anticlerical to see through the pretensions of priests, some with no marked advantages over their fellows; their claimed special privileges, ranging from the power to change ordinary wine into Christ's very blood to forgiving sins, certainly did not justify their demands for tithes from the community at large.[7]

It was hardly surprising therefore that the region's people often responded favorably to the preaching of untrained and itinerant evangelists. Three years before Fox's arrival, forty-one of the area's respectable and worried Presbyterian leaders reacted with horror to the flood of "Church-defoliating and soul damning errors, heresies, and blasphemies" inundating the area, publicly pledging to halt with "whatsoever &c may be dear to us" the rising tide of "Anabaptism,

Enthusiasm, Familism, [and] Libertinism," the same doctrines commonly associated with Fox and his Children.[8] Hence the ground had already been prepared for anyone able to connect a call for personal repentance—Christ has come to freely save, teach, and rule his people—to the area's social and economic ills.

Crossing into Yorkshire, Fox stumbled onto already existing groups of Seekers who would harden into the muscle of the nascent movement. Such people he referred to as "tender," a term meaning that people were willing to explore "any ordinance or worship until they had a certain evidence from the spirit of God that his spirit, life, power, and presence was not in it."[9] Fox brought that evidence. To people, as one convert recalled, "of the strictest sect and of the greatest zeal in the performance of outward righteousness," this prophet brought word "that God had given to us, every one of us in particular, a light from himself shining in our hearts and consciences."[10] In less than six months in the north country he succeeded in winning over many future leaders of the Children of the Light, whereas during four years in the Midlands he had recruited only one, Elizabeth Hooten, destined to remain in the front ranks of Quakerism. The Midlands remained the original home of the new sect, but the north was the cauldron out of which it boiled over into the rest of the nation.

Fox's message, a call for people to turn to the inward teacher combined with an attack on social privileges, did not differ from the one he had already delivered in the Midlands. What differed was his audience, already prepared by their history and the area's dissenting ministers, people like those in the Cleveland area who "had tasted of the power of God" and had already collected many dissenters into large meetings. Noting that they carried ale and tobacco to their services, making them "light and loose" like Ranters, Fox admonished them to wait in silence for the Lord to sit with them and gather them together.[11] Durand Hotham of Lockington, the scion of a politically prominent family, informed Fox that he had known the principle of God working in his heart now for a decade. In Balby, just over the border from Nottinghamshire, Richard Farnworth, soon to be one of the most prolific polemical pamphleteers of the movement, discovered, in the words of his first publication, "the light of God in the inward parts."[12] Fox zigged westward to Wakefield and found there former weaver and soldier William Dewsbury, who soon became a leading Quaker preacher.[13]

Just beyond Wakefield Fox encountered the most important of his followers, and his eventual rival, the slightly erratic but brilliant James Nayler. Nayler, eight years Fox's senior, had grown up in the parish of Anthony Nutter, the Presbyterian dissenter who had left Drayton-in-the-Clay earlier in the century. A soldier for eight or nine years who had risen to the rank of quartermaster, he won some fame as a preacher in the New Model Army but had since settled down to farming when Fox appeared on the scene. Later he recorded that about this same time while plowing his field he heard a voice, which he took to be God's, telling him to leave his father's land. Like many another who responded to Fox, he rejoiced at finally hearing "the voice of that God which I had professed as a child but had never known." Hence the Leicestershireman's arrival coincided with Nayler's own conviction that he was being called to the itinerant ministry. Before long his reputation as a gifted speaker and polemicist equaled that of any of the other Quaker preachers, including Fox.[14]

Zagging back toward the east and the coast, Fox established temporary headquarters at the home of locally prominent justice (and former New Model Army captain) Hotham near Beverely, a chronically depressed area.[15] Apparently Fox already had contacts in the area, for first he headed straight for yet another sympathetic army officer, Richard Pursgrove of Cranswick. Pursgrove escorted him to Hotham's house and then proceeded to accompany the stranger to the local Sunday church service. Fox, who presumably wore his usual leathers, expressed pleasant surprise that his host attended the service without wearing the ruffled collar expected of a proper Protestant: "[T]he Lord's power and truth had so affected him that he minded it not."[16]

After the minister, who called himself "Doctor," as Fox disdainfully noted, concluded his sermon, the visitor interjected a message as unconventional as his Sunday attire. Once again he demonstrated his insight into his audience's grievances. He attacked the reverend doctor straight on for taking £300 annually in tithes and then having the gall to preach a sermon based on Isaiah's statement that those who had no money could have wine and milk without price. "Come down, thou deceiver," Fox demanded of the amazed preacher in front of his own flock, "Mayest not thou blush for shame!" The deception revealed and the minister gone, this strange man took as much time as he wanted to direct the assembly to their salvation, "the Spirit of God in their inward parts," their "free teacher," who required no tithes.[17]

In northeast Yorkshire, in the windblown and snowy coastal town of Staithes, Fox delivered the same message but this time launched an even sharper attack against clergy living on tithes. Staithes was a fishing village from which sailors went all the way down the coast to Yarmouth in Norfolk to sell their catch. The local minister's authority stretched out to sea, more than a hundred miles, to net his tenth. Fox either had contacts in Staithes who informed him of their situation, or else he nosed around long enough to find out the facts. However he discovered the truth, he lashed out at the local minister so vigorously for his oppression of his flock that the clergyman fled. Some of the chief leaders of the parish refused to listen to him. But his words evidently hit home because that night a number of the same parish worthies visited him and, hearing Fox out this time, confessed the truth.

A day or two later, having "laid open" a Ranter leader, Fox pummeled Staithes's still-absent clergyman in front of a large gathering. He condemned "false prophets," those who ruled by their wealth, who sought gain from the very haunches of people, who preached for money and taught for filthy lucre. He himself preached "Christ in the hearts of his people, when all these mountains were laid low." This language of the apocalypse, of a coming day of judgment, had a radical edge to it that silenced his critics. His tactic of tapping popular opposition to tithing and then expertly tying it to his religious message won numerous adherents. Meetings soon spread up and down the coast.[18] In Stokesley he dared the local clergyman to come out in the snow-covered street and try his ministry before the populace, but the minister refused. And at Malton when the word got around that he was at the church, a crowd of hundreds swelled the size of the original dozen who had came to hear the minister.[19] Let the heathen rage, the tender responded.

His approach was not always received with approval. Just after Christmas in 1651 Fox ventured into York, the largest city he had visited since London seven years earlier. Naturally he went to the minster and there spoke to the congregation after its Presbyterian leader finished his sermon. Charging that this congregation lived by words alone, he got himself tossed down the steps for his efforts. In the marshy Holderness region of eastern Yorkshire he visited a number of small towns, proclaiming that the day of the Lord had come and that the people should turn away from false teachers to the Christ within. In Patrington his message provoked the active opposition of the local priest who stirred his parishioners to refuse Fox a place to stay and food to eat; nor could he find hospitality outside the town limits. The next morning, after sitting and dozing outside all night amid spiny furze bushes, he rose at first light and headed for the next town but discovered his opponents had moved faster than he. Before the sun was up they dispatched a hefty man with a warrant to warn the next town that Fox was on the way. Returned to Patrington in the company of a guard worthy of a common criminal, but preaching as he went, he was brought before the nearest justice of the peace, a man so given to drink that he was often drunk even early in the morning. The justice, alert enough to see that the suspected vagrant used the familiar "thee" and "thou" to him and had not removed his hat, thought the stranger retarded. Pointing to his hat, Fox asked, "Does this trouble thee"? He took it off, but then clapped it back on his head again, grabbed the justice's arm, and admonished him to repent his evil words and deeds. The justice suspected that Fox might be a spy or a papist, so he ordered him to strip and searched him to see if he carried suspicious letters or documents. Finding none, and noting that his undergarments were not those of a vagrant, the justice ordered Fox released. Vindicated, Fox hiked back to Patrington, where he stayed long enough to intrude into the Sunday service of the minister who had started the whole business and to draw off an embarrassing portion of his church members into a meeting of the Children.[20]

Fox discovered that the contacts he had made among some of the powerful in the region could be used to prevent harassment. Twenty miles up the coast when he appeared at one church, a man punched him in the chest and told him to get out. "Poor man, do you call the steeple-house the church,"? Fox retorted. "The church is the people whom God has purchased with his blood and not the house." From Beverely, Justice Hotham sent a warrant to bind Fox's assailant over to the quarterly court and offered his friend official protection, which, however, he eschewed. Despite refusing assistance, Fox was apparently emboldened by his friendship with Hotham: he targeted homes of eminent people in Holderness to warn them of the need to repent, even though he had to appear at their "great houses" on foot like a nobody. He also pointedly refused to apply to local constables for permission to take rooms in inns, claiming that the custom existed to uncover "suspicious persons but I was an innocent man." On such nights he hunted himself a haystack to sleep in.[21]

Fox insisted on selecting his own time and using his own methods for spreading his message. Critics called Fox "a nimble Mercurialist,"[22] a kind of backhanded compliment that pointed up his pragmatic strategy. At Warmsworth, when the minister thoughtlessly asked him why he had come as he was being hustled out of the church, he halted his expulsion by quickly responding, "[A] question being asked, an answer may be given: I came to witness the Truth, God dwells not in temples made by hands."[23] Once he sat on a haystack for some hours as a milling crowd of anxious auditors awaited some word—a companion spread the whispered reminder that people had also waited for Jesus to speak—until he sensed that the time had come to preach. With conscious casualness, he readily intruded into church services along his path. Sometimes, however, if he was offered a chance to speak from the pulpit, he held back, using the invitation itself as an opportunity to attack established ways. At Pickering, for example, he had a long theological discussion with one of the regicides and a member of the Council of State, the sympathetic Luke Robinson, but he resolutely refused to consider speaking in Robinson's "steeple-house." "I came to bring them off from such things to Christ," he announced, "not to hold up their idol temples, nor their priests, nor their tithes, nor their augmentations, nor their priests' wages, nor their Jewish and heathenish ceremonies and traditions." People had no need of holy buildings and grounds, he said, but only of "the spirit and grace of God in themselves, and to the light of Jesus in their own hearts, that they might come to know Christ, their free teacher. . . ."[24] Like others who raised the radical banner in the mid-seventeenth century, Fox totally rejected the comment that worthies heard at Westminster Abbey: "We must know no law within us, but that which is derived from the law without."[25]

Fox realized that the recent warfare, the king's execution, the Presbyterian church's inability to establish itself, and the religious freedom that arrived in the wake of such momentous developments presented opportunities hitherto undreamed of. Hence he easily grouped hireling priests who exacted their tenth from the people's labor with biblical false prophets and fulminated against preaching for lucre, a practice in sharp contrast to the free teaching offered by the inward Christ. These pointed comparisons marked him as one wanting every Englishman and Englishwoman to join him in turning away from the old ways. A shady line existed between the old religious ways and the old secular ways, so that it was not easy to separate one from the other; Fox, seeing religion as a way of life, never bothered with any such distinction. In a pamphlet he published in 1655, he offhandedly mixed the two spheres, as though one relied on the other. one even required the other. Christ is coming to weigh all things in the balance, he wrote,

and before him the hills shall move and the mountains shall melt, and the rocks shall cleave, . . . and the carnal heart rent; great earth quakes shall be, the terrible day of the Lord draws near, the Beast shall be taken, and the false prophets into the fire must go. . . . Now is the Lord coming to sit as judge, and reign as king, who is the law-giver, . . . now is the sword drawn, which glitters and is so bushed the sword of the Almighty to hew down Baal's priests, corrupt judges, corrupt justices, corrupt lawyers, fruitless trees which cumber the ground.[26]

What was he learning in the north? Using the same militant language, he told the nation bluntly in another pamphlet:

> Woe to the inhabitants of the earth. . . . Torment, torment; woe, woe; plagues, plagues are to be poured forth, and judgement and the wrath of God without mixture poured upon you, . . . and God will be avenged upon the beast and the false prophet. . . . This generation we know, and the generation of the faithful we know: here is a separation between the precious and the vile, between the holy and the profane; so all people weigh and consider in what generation you are: the generation of the righteous shall shine, the generation of the wicked are for the fire prepared to be turned into hell.[27]

"The Lord has spoken," he trumpeted, "who will dash in pieces, and will overturn, until that righteousness be set up, until the earthly part be shaken."[28] Like the writer of Revelation, he was envisioning a new earth that could come into existence only through the action of angry divine agents.

Fox's early theological message consisted of about equal (and tangled) parts of apocalyptic warnings about the Day of Judgment when God's wrath would be poured out on evil masters, tithe gougers, and apostate hierarchs; a sure identification of such reprobates with those who used their social and economic power to lord it over ordinary people; a firm conviction that Christ's spirit was present to teach, lead, and guide those who chose to follow; and, finally, a hope that through the agency of the convinced an age of peace and righteousness was about to dawn on a land that had been too long troubled by injustice, conflict, and war. If the first two parts of his message seemed more directly relevant to objective conditions at the time, then the last two suggested how ordinary people could assist in ordering the new world. More personally, and parochially, Fox was not above identifying his own efforts with the coming new age. In 1658 he had reached the point of reminding those who picked up one of his epistles that it came "from the authority of the Church in England, the pillar and ground of truth, [of] whom Christ is the head. . . . From the true Church, the elect seeds, who are in scorn called Quakers."[29] To speak in this way when no such authority existed only demonstrated Fox's presumption that he and his growing band of disciples possessed the right to speak for the truly, but still ungathered, elect of England.

By the spring of 1652, Fox had walked the length of Yorkshire, concentrating on the eastern part; although he started out on horseback in the West Riding, he early left his mount behind to travel by foot and now naturally complained of being weary.[30] He detoured south into Lincolnshire as he moved westward and found some Friends living across the Trent. Around this time he ran into a charge that was to bedevil him and his fellows continually, namely, that he called himself Christ. In Gainsborough his accusers were so aroused that he leaped on a table to explain that Christ dwelt in all except reprobates and that it was "Christ, the eternal power of God, that spoke in me at that time unto them." But Fox muddled his attempt at explaining what he meant by dubbing his accuser "Judas," thereby starting the rumor that he thought himself to be Christ.[31]

Crossing over the Trent, he came once more to the area around Balby and Doncaster, which he had left more than three months earlier. In the meantime, residents of the region had apparently grown tired of Quaker activities, for now Fox met the most forceful popular opposition he had yet encountered. After dodging clods of dirt and stones in Balby, he went on to Doncaster where his appearance caused a near riot. Here again he was taken before the magistrates, questioned, and then warned that if he did not leave town he would be turned over to the angry mob; apparently he refused to leave, for he was presently thrust out among a stone-throwing crowd. At Tickhill, where he commenced speaking in the church chancel to the minister and parish officers, the clerk smashed him in the face with a Bible and the people hustled him out into the street, tossed him back and forth over a hedge like a shuttlecock, and stoned and beat him until he was bloody. Working his way back to the house where the Children were meeting, he and his compatriots faced down the jeering mob. On another occasion they slept out in the woods drenched by a hard rain to avoid an enraged and armed man bent on doing Fox violence.[32]

Circumstantial evidence suggests that about March 1652, as the cold weather let up, Fox met with his main followers in a formal conclave near Stanley, just north of Wakefield. If so, then it was the band's first general meeting for those from nearby localities. Not only were a number of "great" or "considerable" men at the meeting, but also present were such recent converts, present evangelists, and future luminaries as James Nayler, William Dewsbury, Richard Farnworth, and Thomas Aldam of Warmsworth, the latter in custody and on his way to York jail—that Aldam's escort allowed him to attend Fox's meeting hints at the importance of the gathering. Moreover, by Fox's account, the group explored the same sort of topics usually covered in a Presbyterian classis: "[T]he scriptures wonderfully opened, and the parables and sayings of Christ were expounded, and the state of the church in the apostles' days was plainly set forth, and the apostasy since from that state discovered."[33] Judging from the subsequent activities of those attending, they each decided how and where to proceed.

This coterie of Quakers had been active during the winter, and had made a number of converts among the people of the region. Indeed, the Quakers were attracting considerable attention: it was being said that they had made more clamor in the county than the Scottish army marching through the previous summer.[34] Their activities also explained some of the violent outbursts against the Children. The fact that the opposition centered in the churches, was mobilized by the clergy, and was expressed in religious terms underscored the fears that the coming of Fox and his small but growing band engendered among establishment figures. At the rich church in Wakefield, which had excommunicated Nayler, the Independent minister tried to explain Fox's success by spreading stories that he used secret potions to drug people as he raced from village to village, like some devil's disciple, on a big black horse.[35]

Hallucinogens would be crude tools indeed compared to the actual, sophisticated methods used by the Children. A hostile witness explained how they operated. Entering a town, they spotted a likely prospect and went to his house, saying very solemnly, "I have received a word from the Lord that you should come out of darkness, and be enlightened, that you may be saved and all your house." Quakers recognized that the "vulgar," as this critic deemed them, especially wanted to believe that God cared for them and were thus attracted to the odd or mystical. So the Quakers used uncommon expressions, those with just a hint of mystery about them, unusual terms such as "spiritual worship" and "the light within." The notion that the Holy Ghost taught them, he went on, "makes the common people think them[selves] the best and most valuable persons in the world . . . because it abolishes that distinction which is, and always ought to be, between the priesthood and the laity, setting them both upon equal terms." The minister "is a hireling," they said, "who does nothing but for filthy lucre, preaching only for tithes, pigs, geese, and capons," whereas Quakers freely received and freely gave. Walking in rags, "they railed at riches." So it was no wonder that those considered vulgar became Children.[36]

Their anonymous assailant understood something profound about the Quaker effort to distinguish themselves from others, whether poor, uneducated working folk or well-off Presbyterians. Fox's language was both an evangelistic tool and a unifying force. In trying to fashion a separated body set against the established church, Fox and his cohorts were devising, in a trial-and-error fashion, their own terms for traditional Christian ideas and practices. Village churches they called "steeple houses," while their own church was the "gathering of God's people"; their opponents engaged in "outward" worship that left them part of the fallen world, while theirs was "spiritual, inward" and led them "to walk in the light"; to Fox, clergymen were "hirelings," whereas his followers had no set-apart ministers, at least at this early day; "professors" were those who professed without the Children's "life"; institutional Christians followed the "outward Christ who died at Jerusalem," while Quakers harkened only to the "Christ within." Their language undermined traditional authority and rejected outward conformity as a way to judge authentic religion, while giving Quakers a point of immediate contact with others of their group. The specific terms Fox and the others used were not very original, but their use demonstrated the leaders' awareness that the Children could not tap widespread discontent without a terminology able to legitimize unspoken experiences.[37]

To opponents of the Children, however, Fox's actions more resembled those of a half-crazed fanatic rather than those of God's prophet. A schoolmaster took him for someone who had run away from home. When Fox severely rebuked a group of youths who facetiously lifted their glasses to him in a tavern, one of them menaced him with a club and had to be restrained by his fellows. When he told his host at an alehouse that he was "the son of God," the startled man could think of nothing else to do except send him off to see a group of similar professors, to whom he also preached his message.[38]

His passion to win converts gripped him so much that Fox overlooked his marked success and was wracked by doubts. The divine leadings he knew he experienced had a ring of judgment about them. As he described it himself, "[I]f I did but set up one in the same spirit that the prophets and apostles were in . . . he or she should shake all the country in their profession ten miles about them." Had he not found one, was he not one? Yet the country did not shake. Whether this condition reflected nagging second thoughts about the depth of faith of those with whom he traveled is unclear, but he admitted realizing that merely being able to read the Bible did not enable one to go behind the words to the spirit that inspired it. His old despair returned to haunt him again, or at least he resumed fasting, one remedy he used for his off-and-on-again malady.[39]

For several of those cool, late spring days, as he and his companions moved around hilly western Yorkshire, adjoining Westmorland and Lancashire, Fox continued to fast in an effort to rid his spirit of its burden. Near the border with Lancashire, he and Richard Farnworth came to Pendle Hill, at 1830 feet widely regarded as one of the three highest hills in that part of the country and in sight of the other two.[40] Locals referred to it as a haven for witches. Instead of going around, Fox decided to explore. He apparently left his traveling partner and climbed on alone up one of the hill's steep and stony sides. More likely than not, Fox hiked up the hill enveloped in the thick mist that often covers the hills of this area. But at the top the slightly biting air cleared. It was indeed an unusual day. For a midlander with perceptions sharpened by fasting, the scene from the flat-topped hill towering over the Ribble Valley was energizing. Thirty miles to the west, across the hilly grasslands that rolled on before him, he glimpsed the Irish Sea and its coastline; to the north he saw other and taller peaks. Behind and below him he knew his companion waited, a representative of earlier successes yet in his misty loneliness a striking contrast to the multitudes lost even further down. Fox stood atop if not quite astride the world. "I was moved," he wrote when remembering how he shouted loudly enough so all the people would know that time was short and justice would flow down from the heights, "to sound the day of the Lord."[41] Then looking westward toward the coast, he saw, vividly, the places where numbers of people waited to be gathered. Any doubts Fox had had about his mission vanished like the mists that cleared on Pendle Hill's summit and enabled him to see. Stumbling back down, he found a spring and slaked his thirst, ending his fast. Pendle Hill was a confirmation, the beginning ended.

Fox did not move immediately westward to the places where he had glimpsed people waiting. Instead he turned back north to the rough and hilly regions beyond the Pennine Mountains. The landscape itself seemed positively forbidding, bare and empty. The area had been fought over many times by invading outsiders and was a place where every person had to be ready to fight for kine and kind. This insecure situation bred a fidelity to family and clan more pervasive than any loyalty to some far-off authority. Hence a long tradition of localism survived in the isolated dales of western Yorkshire and fed notions that a natural liberty made people free of outside control, whether from church or state.[42] People traveled the natural, obvious way, up and down the dales, along the tumbling streams, but seldom over the hills to the other side. When Fox and Farnworth moved into the region, the uncertainties at the national level caused some "statesmen," the local term used to describe small landholders, to declare a tithe strike against the tenth normally funneled away to Trinity College down at Cambridge University.[43]

Fox and Farnworth seemed to be searching for such groups of people in the area's nearly hidden dales. When they found dissenters holding a lecture, they stopped to proclaim that Christ the free teacher had no need of hirelings, a reminder that the church was supported by tithes exacted from folk with little enough of their own. In the late 1640s and early 1650s the area seethed with revolts as royalist impropriators squeezed tithes from the people to pay the fines imposed by Parliament.[44] Preaching against tithes thus had a radical edge to it, pointing up their connection with the well-to-do owner of property.[45] On market days the preachers coupled calls for repentence with pertinent cries against merchants who gouged their customers in a time of scarcity and rising prices. Not only his words but also Fox's severe countenance spread public alarm about these intruders. Seldom lingering long enough to be apprehended, he traveled about quickly, sometimes taking a lodging for a night, other times sleeping out on the common land on a hastily gathered bed of fern. On the far edge of Yorkshire, along the Dee River valley, in an area isolated by mountains, he tapped into a veritable underground of dissenters, members of which directed him from one conventicle to another.[46]

Fox was not just stumbling over the rock-strewn hillsides and into fertile valleys like some straying lamb. He was searching out Seekers, looking for likely converts. He found a mother lode. He stopped first at Stonehouses in Dent, a narrow dale eleven mile long, home of six leaders of the tithe strike. The meeting held on that May 31, 1652, consisted of more rich people than "statesmen," so Fox won only a handful to his cause.[47] The next Sunday, he arrived at Borrat on a hill above Sedbergh, in the tow of Richard Robinson, who escorted him the last few miles to meet Gervase Benson, an army colonel, justice of the peace, and man on the make. Disillusioned enough with the direction of national life to allow a group of dissenters to gather at his house that day, Colonel Benson was influential in the area. Once mayor of Kendal, he had served as Roundhead commissioner to seize and sell the estates of defeated royalists.[48] Fox promptly took charge of the meeting and turned it into one he described as "mighty." He converted Benson on the spot. Until his death in 1679 the Colonel put his legal expertise and pen at the service of the Children, particularly as to the testimony against tithes and oaths.[49]

Fox stayed on with Benson. Wednesday he went down to Sedbergh and stormed through its fair as wealthy masters haggled about the fees they would pay for next year's servants. He proclaimed once again "the day of the Lord," a theme equivalent to the "Woe, Woe, to the bloody city" he had employed to judge Lichfield. Now in the atmosphere of the tithe revolt, it took on more radical connotations as he reminded gougers of the weak that their days were numbered because "Christ Jesus is come to reign."[50] He was convinced that the Lord was acting in this age of revolution. Once he told the magistrates of Scotland that in "this mighty day of the Lord . . . [God] hath brought forth much to his glory and given you victory over much and set you above much." Those whom God had thrown down—King Charles and the House of Lords come to mind— "those," he announced, "may take notice."[51] His audience for this message was large. The Presbyterians had taken advantage of the great crowds expected for the fair and set aside the day as one of their lecture days, for ministers and professors also crowded Sedbergh. Fox stood in the churchyard for several hours and preached that the people should pay no attention to hireling, outward teachers. Instead, he admonished them to come out of the old church and into the church of God where "Christ was come to teach his people himself."

Interrupted by an army captain who took offense at his public preaching, Fox found an unexpected defender in the person of Francis Howgill, who commenced a dispute with the officer. A native of Grayrigg about six miles across the Lune River valley from Sedbergh, forty-four-year-old Howgill was a Baptist farmer-preacher, formerly an Independent, and before that educated for the Anglican priesthood. Fox, said this newfound supporter, "speaks with authority and not as the scribes." Another resident of Grayrigg, also an army captain, was likewise convinced, along with a number of others who milled in and out of the churchyard. But a local clergyman considered Fox more than a little crazy for his remarks and told him so to his face.[52]

Word was out that on the following Sunday, June 13, 1652, a large dissenters' meeting would convene at Firbank Fell on a hill commanding the Lune on the Westmorland side. Fox and some of his supporters from around Sedbergh made haste to attend. They found more than a thousand people gathered to hear Francis Howgill, his defender of a few days before, and John Audland, only twenty-two years old, but already enjoying a wide reputation for his preaching skill and invasion of the churches in the region. After the morning messages, when many in attendance had gone to eat lunch, Fox positioned himself on a kind of makeshift pulpit of bare rock next to the chapel—he refused to cross the church threshold—and spoke for three hours until midafternoon. His words differed little from what he had been saying in other places: all could find the spirit of God within themselves and, responding to it, could become Children of the Light, whom Christ would then lead into all truth. This time, however, apparently aware of the significance of this large audience, he buttressed his views with copious quotations from the Scriptures, including the prophets, the apostle Paul's letters, and the gospel itself. He especially attacked the established church, its tithing, hired priesthood, and apostasy since the days of the apostles. "Christ was come," he announced to those who doubted the sanction for his mission, "who ended both the temple and its worship and the priests and their tithes, and now all should harken unto him." Even common people such as those now gathered could recapture "the spirit and power that the apostles were in."[53]

A powerful and liberating message, Fox's words tied the concrete grievances that many insular northerners harbored against the faraway state and established church to a religious appeal placing on each individual the responsibility for breaking with the old world and living in the new. As a more sophisticated convert phrased it, Fox's preaching was about "repentance, and about a light within, and of turning to that, and proclaiming the great and terrible day of the Lord to be at hand."[54] Taking traditional words and symbols that were the common currency of all denominations and melding them into messages that had sharp practical overtones was a wise strategic move. It gave Fox's central message an immediacy and relevance it would not have otherwise possessed. Hence it was no wonder that his band of followers was increasingly regarded as subversive by the authorities.[55]

Audland, six years Fox's junior, took an immediate liking to him and invited him home. On Wednesday, to introduce him to yet another part of the region's underground of dissenters, Audland escorted his guest southward to the Preston Patrick home of John Camm,[56] a well-to-do Seeker since about the time Fox was born, who had traveled the ten miles to Firbank Fell the previous Sunday.[57] That very night Fox attended a previously arranged meeting and preached his usual sermon. Presently he moved back northward to Kendal, one of the flourishing towns of the area, built solidly of gray stone that figuratively crumbled before his assault.[58] Next on his itinerary was Underbarrow, less than an hour's walk west of Kendal over the stony ridge, a journey he made in the good company of the youthful Edward Burrough, whose hometown the small village was. The two men—Burrough was eighteen, Fox a decade older—discussed the older man's preachments and set the stage for Burrough's later conversion. "He spoke the language which I knew not," Burrough remembered, "and it pleased the Lord to speak to me by him."[59]

Fox was not aimlessly wandering around the countryside. At every stop he found a contact who carried him farther westward, toward the area where from Pendle Hill he had seen a great people waiting. Now in Lancashire, an area with a reputation for fear of witch infestation,[60] he found that some of the people he encountered were not very accommodating to strangers. At Stavely, just south of Lake Windermere, the people were "rude"—whether his term described their manners, their social status, or both is not clear—and subject enough to their zealous minister, Gabriel Camelford, that they tossed their visitor headfirst over the graveyard wall. Picking himself up, Fox retreated to a nearby alehouse where some of the congregation gathered between morning and afternoon services. Here he preached that "God was come to teach his people himself and to bring them off from all false teachers."[61]

Fox's words in the Stavely alehouse, like others he had uttered in numerous other places, were at the center of his message. He remained a bit unclear, to be sure, about whether it was Christ or God who had come to teach the people. But such theological niceties did not matter much to him. All he knew, and what he continued to proclaim in the only religious vocabulary he had, was that each individual could experience the inward workings of divinity, which would judge, convict, and empower for goodness—including resisting the tithe man. These convictions Fox had first known personally and then preached far and wide, first in the Midlands, now in the north.

As a result of his latest efforts, his movement had been infused with new blood. In the past six months, since coming into the north and particularly in the past three weeks in western Yorkshire, Westmorland, and Lancashire, Fox had connected with a preexisting network of dissenters and had won the allegiance of an array of fresh talent. Even those whose abilities did not match those of prominent itinerants—for example, James Nayler, Richard Farnworth, William Dewsberry, Francis Howgill, John Audland, John Camm, and Edward Burrough—

still played a key role in their home region, giving Quakerism a secure base and helping to pump new life into it nationally. Fox's success in capturing such people testified to his ability to address their needs and to focus their energies on the cause. If the allegiance of some bordered on worshipful sycophancy (John Audland wrote Fox in 1654, for example, comparing him to Jesus: "Nations shall bow before thee, thousands shall call thee blessed. . . . We boast not but in thee, Lord God"),[62] their talents still helped prepare the way for the movement to go from success to success.

In the Midlands before Fox came north, let it be recalled, the Children of the Light had been led virtually by one person; now with new converts carrying the message farther afield, the movement had outgrown one man and had reached a point where it required some organization. Until now most of Fox's followers lived close to the land, with some, like Francis Howgill, dividing their time between working the soil and preaching the dissenting gospel.[63] As Fox commented about two of them, they tended to be "simple-hearted" or unsophisticated,[64] perhaps not up to the needs he sensed were emerging. The pattern of Fox's travels and the way he contacted and then drew on the talents of those referred to him suggested that he was sizing up the strengths of his followers. The first and most important need of the Children had been to find enthusiastic men and women to carry the word to distant parts: by mid-June 1652, many of these were already at work.

But when Fox stood back and looked at his growing movement, he was forced to recognize that about all it had was a name, a notorious nickname, a localized reputation, and a growing number of scattered but committed supporters willing to proclaim its message or support those who did. His success in gathering the harvest so far only highlighted the need for organization. He needed a way to collect and distribute funds, a headquarters, and an overseer of the entire operation. He needed, and the movement had to have, a person with more administrative experience than most of those he had drawn to the Children.

James Nayler would have made an obvious choice. In Fox's estimation he stood near the front ranks of recent converts,[65] and his successful two-year service as a quartermaster in the New Model Army certainly spoke well of his organizational ability. His recent bout with a tuberculosis-like illness would also have made a sedentary role appropriate. But Nayler's other talents, particularly his brilliant oratory, which Fox had observed, made him invaluable as an evangelist. Moreover, he had financial difficulties that would prevent him from becoming the movement's administrator.[66] No, Nayler would not do.

Perhaps, then, Richard Farnworth? He was one of Fox's earliest converts in the north, and the two had traveled together and knew each other well. Fox was introduced to the region's dissenters by his new friend, who was knowledgable about the area's many competing sects. His preaching, if it followed the substance of his early writings, sounded like Fox's: attacks on the deceit of the tithed ministry, assertions that "the Lord is setting up the ministry of his Son in the hearts of his people," and predictions that "ere long" Christ "shall rule all nations with a rod of iron."[67] A man of conviction who insisted on following the course he believed God had laid out for him,[68] Farnworth owned a ready pen that until his death in 1666 enabled him to turn out pamphlet after pamphlet for the cause. But, like Nayler, Farnworth had talents that were needed in the field and in the rough and tumble of debate. Someone else would have to be found for the administrative post.

Some of the professors he encountered, or was directed to, Fox promptly rejected for any role. At Lindale, for example, site of a very poor chapel just south of Stavely, he met a local constable, Adam Sandys, a strong supporter of Parliament and presumably a likely prospect, but he turned out to be too much like so many other dissenters in refusing to break with the world. Fox was finding that many of the common people of the region shunned religion and embraced the world's ways.[69] Sandys, anyway, was too "chaffy," too light, to join the movement, so Fox moved on, this time turning westward across Furness's low fells.[70]

The next stop Fox recorded was at Ulverston in Lancashire. A trading center with a thriving market, the town lay on the Furness Peninsula in a level area sloping off eastward toward Morecombe Bay. That it was about twice as far from Lindale as the distance he usually traveled before stopping suggested he felt an urge to get there. Perhaps what pulled him forward was the parish's reputation for dissent. If the minister, William Lampit, accurately reflected the position of the church, then it bordered on being a staunchly Baptist congregation, filled with staunch Roundheads. Lampit had entered Oxford in 1621, had been a preacher for more than twenty years, had served in the New Model Army, and had been plundered and thrice imprisoned by royalists. A friend of the notorious Baptist lieutenant colonel Paul Hobson, he had won election to the pulpit of Aikton in neighboring Cumberland, but his tenure there was brief. He had been ejected when the Cromwellian ecclesiastical authorities, trying to impose a centralized system, refused to concede a congregation's right to name its own minister.[71] Judged by its minister, Ulverston was a likely target for Fox's ministrations. He and an unnamed escort headed for the spacious Swarthmoor Hall, whose owners, the pious and sober Fells, had a reputation for accommodating visiting preachers. The Fells lived a mile south of town, where their Elizabethan mansion sat on the edge of a moor on a rather barren and wind-blown site. From the mansion's upper story one could look out over the bay and to the west one could view the Coniston Hills. Its dark paneling and spaciousness contributed to the house's gracious ambience.[72]

The two travelers did not find the master of the house, Thomas Fell, magistrate, judge, vice-chancellor, and zealous parliamentarian, at home when they arrived at Swarthmoor about midweek, for he was in London.[73] Nor was Swarthmoor's lady, Margaret Fell, there to greet them. But in a convenient coincidence, Lampit, now vicar of Ulverstone's St. Mary's, had come to call about the same time that Fox knocked at the door and was admitted by the Fell children and servants. The two men did not hit it off well. Lampit allowed that the visitor was a Ranter who professed Christ in words but would not obey the law. Fox considered the minister "so full of filth" and so much like a Ranter himself that he refused the other's half-friendly overtures. The truth was that, just like Fox, Lampit was strongly attached to his own views and proved too tough to crack.

They clashed too because their ideas were so close. The minister, as he phrased it, "witnessed Christ in him" and conceded Fox "held many great things," the point of their dispute occurring when the Children simply judged him out of the power that Fox exemplified.[74] Fox recalled "a great deal of reasoning" with the minister, but judging from his words, more vitriol than reason passed between the two.[75]

That evening Mistress Fell returned home. Having heard of the Children of the Light when Fox had earlier traveled within twenty miles of her home,[76] she was somewhat taken aback by her unannounced guest's afternoon set-to with the parish minister. If she expected an apology, she got none from Fox, whose flouting of accepted standards of courtesy had already shocked one member of the household.[77] Instead he hurried to present his cause to his hostess, who was either being charitable or was sympathetic enough to allow him to stay the night. The next day Lampit returned to Swarthmoor, and the running argument between him and Fox resumed, with Fell an enrapt onlooker, increasingly wont to take her visitor's side against her regular minister.

A day or so later (July 1, 1652) was market day, which dissenters had set aside as a lecture day. Margaret Fell, a bit unsure of her guest, asked him to attend church with her, but Fox demurred, indicating that he wanted to stay outside until he decided what to do. Set against a hill, St. Mary's church had no steeple to provoke Fox, only a stubby crenellated tower, so he stood back listening to the singing, which finally did provoke him. The hymns were totally unsuited to what he could plainly see was the people's actual state. Lampit seemed absolutely foul. Sensing a divine command to go inside, Fox entered the church, jumped up on a seat, and lashed out at minister and congregation. He claimed to know they were using other's words and other's ways and did not understand the true life and spirit. "God," this stranger announced as though authorized to speak for the deity, "was come to teach his people by his spirit . . . [that] they might come out of their outward ordinances and traditions of men to the light of Christ Jesus."

Ulverston was somewhere near the edge of the world, and intrusions like this did not often occur. Soon the entire congregation was in an uproar. The local justice of the peace shouted for someone to hustle the invader out. But Margaret Fell stared the justice down and surprisingly defended her guest's right to speak, as did the minister himself, who seemed to believe a chance still existed to win Fox over.[78]

The newcomer wore his hair long, perhaps to show that no special holiness attached to the short and fashionable Roundhead style,[79] perhaps to remind people of prophets of old. His critics knew nothing at first hand of ancient prophets; to them long hair marked a Cavalier, and they saw nothing of a refined aristocrat in this person. One guessed he tried to look like Samson the biblical Nazarite, and another reported that his long bush of hair hung in strands by his ears like a fox's tail and that Fox pulled at them as he spoke.[80]

Like all Fox's messages, this one stressed the necessity for a Christian to experience the truth inwardly. Being born a Jew and being circumcised did not make one a Jew, he claimed: being a Jew was a spiritual matter, a matter of the heart. Margaret Fell was so impressed with this message—"I had never heard such before,"—that she, gentlewoman that she was, stood up in her private pew, set off from the rest of the church, to stare down the churchwarden who wanted to remove the interloper. Fox went on. The Scriptures were words of the prophets, of Christ, of the apostles, words they had received from the Lord when they spoke. But mere letters killed, he quoted the apostle, only "the light of Christ in our conscience . . . was our teacher." "Christ says this, and the apostles say this," Fox drove his point home, "but what can you say? Are you a child of Light and . . . what you speak, is it inwardly from God?" He hammered away at the idea that those out of the light were wrong, an indictment that fed an angry mood in the congregation.

Another and entirely different sentiment gripped Margaret Fell. She felt her heart rend as this strange guest made real her own deceitful state and that of the others with her: "We are all thieves; we have taken the scriptures in words. . . . We were but theirs who had stolen the scriptures." Convinced, she knew that Christ Jesus had come to visit that day. Looking around at those sitting in the church, people she had worshipped with for years, she began to cry, then sat down in her pew, unable to hear the rest of Fox's message except for something he was saying about false prophets and deceitful leaders. His preaching was so vividly mesmerizing that it seemed that Fox had literally grabbed the congregation. Most did not want to be touched, and so grew angrier and louder. Some of the visiting ministers were convinced they had witnessed witchcraft or sorcery. After what seemed an age, a churchwarden pulled the intruder outside where he had the last word to those who followed him among the gravestones. Fox accepted this opposition as something a prophet should expect.[81]

Fox returned to Swarthmoor later that night and promptly occasioned a crisis in the household. He preached his message to members of the family and the servants and convinced nearly all of them. Margaret, unsure of what her absent husband's reaction would be to these happenings, was, as she put it, "stricken with such a sadness that I knew not what to do." She too was converted by her guest's incisive unfolding of what she now realized was the truth, but she was still not sure she could hold on to it if her husband turned out to be antagonistic. She knew she would need the Lord's help.[82]

Fell also needed more information. Over the next two days, there must have been deep searching at Swarthmoor, as she and Fox reviewed his movement and its direction. As later events made quite evident, each found much about the other to admire and respect. A practical woman ten years older than Fox, Fell would have wanted to know more about this group she was becoming involved with and what its prospects were. Undoubtedly Fox had answered the same queries before and sensed that her desire for information would lead, as with others, to deeper involvement. So he probably sketched in the Children's origins and development, describing some of those who were a part of the movement, perhaps going so far as to assess their individual capabilities. Likewise, they explored some of the implications of the rapid growth of the movement in the six months since the Leicestershireman had come north. As yet decisions remained tentative. Fox did not want to decide anything without discussing matters with his co-workers, and Fell was not in a condition to commit herself finally until she could discuss matters with her husband. As Fox prepared to depart on a short preaching mission beginning July 3 to towns in the immediate neighborhood, Fell promised to post a letter to Richard Farnworth, inviting him to Swarthmoor.[83]

The stage was thus arranged for important decisions in the brief life of the movement: indeed, insofar as a viable movement requires organization, the Children of the Light was just beginning to take shape. Before coming north, Fox had had only modest success. Now the Children boasted a cadre of committed supporters, and those out on the road were working hard to increase its numbers. Some of its leadership's ties to the world remained intact, true enough (in one minor but telling example, for instance, Nayler slipped into customary heathen ways and referred to the Quaker's "fifth day" as "Thursday"),[84] but creating some kind of organization would help sever them. Moreover, Fox's success in winning Margaret Fell for the cause could only redound to its benefit. Her name and connections, practical organizational abilities and energies, as well as her husband's influence, were all assets Fell brought to the effort. When Fox returned to Swarthmoor within the week from his mission down Furness Peninsula, his latest success must have seemed a kind of divine endorsement for all his northern activities and the growing number of Children he had sired.[85] When his companion Farnworth arrived—would he bring Nayler, perhaps, with him?—the time could be seized. The future beckoned.

So Fox positively exulted that "there is arising a new and living way out of the north" and proclaimed a holy crusade with undertones of the popular millenialism of Revelation: "[T]he Lamb [Christ] had and has the kings of the earth to war with and to fight with, . . . for the Lamb shall have the victory."[86]

7

Put Not Fire to Flax

While waiting for Farnworth to arrive so they could discuss the movement's future, Fox wasted no time beginning preaching missions in surrounding villages. His successes were many, he reports, but "rude" ones continued to resist his efforts. Rumors spread that he bewitched people to win them over. The crusade in the north was clearly on, and it had just as clearly struck fire, immediate fire: Ulverston's vicar, William Lampit, took it upon himself to scout ahead of Fox to warn people about the strange doctrines he preached. Fox headed back to Dent where the tithe revolt smoldered and where he found people still responsive to his message. Preaching at Grisdale, he received word from Margaret Fell that Nayler and Farnworth had arrived at Swarthmoor, so he temporarily banked the coals and returned to Lancashire.[1]

The subsequent discussions were crucial to the survival of the movement. Thomas Fell had returned home and needed attention. Though inclined toward the Independents, he headed the lay list of the "classical presbytery" established in Lancashire in 1646.[2] Fell combined an interest in reformed religion with a close attention to his own worldly interests. He did not miss many chances. A prominent parliamentarian for more than ten years, to the beginning of the Civil War, Fell was fifty-four years old and had sat in Commons for Lancashire since 1645. One of his closest judicial associates presided over the trial of Charles I. Before that he had won appointment to the county committee of sequestration, a post that gave him ready access to information about the holdings of royalist neighbors. His legal training at Gray's Inn in London and his antiroyalist views made him an obvious choice for various judicial posts under the new regime, including vice-chancellor of the duchy of Lancaster and judge of the court of assizes after 1649. In May 1651 he added commissioner to keep the chancery court seal to his portfolio and won the right to exact fees from those with business before the court. His elevation in 1653 to the post of chancellor, with its capital value of £800 (about $80,000), brought him on annual salary of nearly £200—and fees nearly double that. He was certainly one of the region's most powerful men. The chancellor, as head officer and governor of the duchy, usually served also on the privy council. In this tense period Fell found it expedient not to sit when petitions seeking to settle disputed land titles flooded in. A contemporary noted regarding Fell that he enjoyed an "honorable place . . . admitting of much ease and quiet."[3]

Considered a war profiteer by the king's adherents, Fell used the information he was privy to on the sequestration committee to acquire confiscated enemy property valued at nearly £5,000. One who claimed to have suffered at Fell's hands alleged that the judge had inspired his tenants to wage costly court battles against him, presumably to weaken him so that Fell could then scoop up his land cheaply.[4] Even Fell's illiterate sister Alice, orphaned at age eleven and nearly thirty years younger than he, faulted her brother's greed. She charged that he had violated their father's will by failing to provide schooling for her, then forcing her into "servile and hard labor" while retaining her share of the inheritance. The power inherent in his judicial position, she complained, so overawed her that she would have to wait until after his death and her own marriage before trying to secure what was rightfully hers.[5] By the time of his death in 1658 Fell had amassed property enough to make him probably the largest landowner on the Furness Peninsula, with an estate stretching in a continuous band some seven miles from the bay on the east to Duddon Sands in the west.[6]

A man with Fell's influence and power was unaccustomed to being crossed. Even before arriving home on Friday, about the third week of July, he had heard of Fox through Judge Luke Robinson of Yorkshire, a member of Parliament and a person with influence in Cromwell's government. John Sawrey, a local justice of the peace who had witnessed Fox's invasion of St. Mary's Church, had also told Judge Fell that his family had succumbed to Fox's wiles. This intelligence may have lessened his shock but did not mitigate his surprise at the changes he found in his family and household.[7] Fell's mood was not improved when he found two strange men, Farnworth and Nayler, living as guests in his house. Their reassurances and mild manner eased the tenseness of the situation a bit, though not enough to prevent them from offering to leave; Margaret Fell rejected this gesture because she expected Fox to arrive that evening.

Weary from his journey, Thomas Fell went in to eat, with his wife seated beside him, and his children at their music lessons nearby. Fell's uncertainties mounted when Margaret felt herself suddenly possessed, as she put it, by the "power of the Lord" and gripped by a kind of seizure that startled her husband into silence and made the children put aside their instruments. Having completed what must have been an unusual meal, the master betook himself to the parlor, while the wife bustled about waiting for her expected guest. Upon his arrival later in the evening, Margaret interrupted her husband to inquire "if George Fox might come in?" Thomas signaled Fox to enter, and Fox did so, with no ceremony, no greeting, no doffing of his hat, none of the usual courtesies. Farnworth, Nayler, and members of the family crowded behind so they too could hear what Fox and Fell would say.

Fox was in fine form, perhaps because he realized that mere tacit favor from Thomas Fell might prove as valuable as the open support of a dozen lesser men. Margaret certainly recognized that the chief magistrate's influence could bode well or ill for Fox's young movement,[8] and she probably so reminded her guest. His discussion surveyed the history of apostasy since the time of Jesus, a topic likely to appeal to the dissenting Thomas, and he quoted Scripture as proof of his position. Fell, however, changed the subject to more mundane matters, seeking to discover if his visitor, as Judge Robinson had reported after meeting Fox, was in truth a firm supporter of the parliamentary cause. Sensing what Fell wanted, Fox connected himself to Robinson the regicide and others like him: such people when convinced by the spirit of God, he averred, "did see over and beyond the priests of the nation, so that they, and many others, were now come to be wiser than their teachers." "Wiser than their teachers": that statement clearly eroded the ground from under society's institutions and gave individuals control over their destiny. In the context of Fell's career it was certainly a radical position—one that implicitly endorsed his actions in breaking with the established church, serving the rebel Roundhead cause, and confiscating Cavalier estates—but it astutely did not challenge the actual base, economic or political, of the judge's power. Fox not only easily dispensed with the usual genteel courtesies, thus underscoring his disdain for superfluities, but he also knew how to speak expedient words when they were called for. Satisfied, the judge let the case rest. As his wife recalled, Fell "was very quiet that night and said no more."[9]

Fox and the Fell family never won Thomas completely over to the Quaker side, and the judge continued to harbor doubts about the people with whom the rest of his household had taken up. Fox did not help matters much. In the earliest written communication between the two, he scrawled a note bluntly telling Fell that the light did not lay hold of him because "the dark power comprehended you."[10] It was no wonder that before the year was out, Thomas Fell reminded Fox of his uninvited intrusion into his family's life, leading Fox to lash out at him as "a child of disobedience whom the prince of the air lodges in and rules, and your heart is deceitful and not right before God."[11] Margaret Fell also tried unsuccessfully to convince Thomas to join the sect she had embraced.[12] Failing in this, she had to engage in a bit of subterfuge to evade his opposition to something she believed the cause required.[13] Fell's daughter lectured him as though he were a heathen after he encouraged her to marry a particular favorite of his.[14] Such disregard of paternal authority no doubt taught Fell the implications of Fox's promise that people who followed him would become wiser than their teachers.

Still, the sympathy he exhibited toward Fox and his fellow Quakers testified to the broad tolerance and patient understanding of one who might easily have been embittered at his family's involvement with the new sect. Fell served the movement in important ways, lending his family's name to the cause and occasionally interceding with other judges on behalf of leading Children or issuing warrants against those responsible for attacking Fox.[15] Margaret and Fox expected him to lobby members of Parliament on their group's behalf.[16] He even permitted a weekly meeting to be held at Swarthmoor. In fact, only two days after Thomas Fell met Fox, while Fell himself, his groom, and his clerk went to the parish church, Ulverston's first Quaker meeting convened in the Fell parlor with Fox's converts from nearby environs attending.[17] Fell's interest in the development of the movement and his continuing contacts with it certainly did not injure his career with policymakers in London, for he was appointed chancellor after his family's associations with Fox became known. His support caused some Friends to remark on his "loving and tender" patronage,[18] but others pointedly warned him that God "has not called many rich, nor many nobles" or admonished him to be faithful.[19] An uneasy strain always existed between Fell and the Friends.

All Fox chose to write about the next few weeks was that he stayed in the Fell household while, as he recalled, "the meeting there was well settled."[20] Subsequent circumstances, particularly the very important role that Margaret Fell quickly assumed in the life of the young Society of Friends, point to important decisions made at Swarthmoor during this early period. Farnworth and Nayler had come for such a discussion, and the fact that Fox stayed for some time underscored the importance of the gathering.

Margaret Fell's rapid rise in the movement accurately mirrored the qualities of a remarkable person. Her important role testified not only to the willingness of Fox and his male cohorts to include a woman in the top echelon of the group, an unusual development for that day, but also to Fell's notable abilities. Thirty-eight years old when Fox first came to Swarthmoor, she was a well-to-do heiress and landowner in her own right, who had married Thomas in 1632 when she was seventeen. She was the mother of seven children, six daughters and a son, and would give birth to another daughter the year following Fox's arrival. Merely running such a household, particularly with her husband often away at Parliament or on court duties, confirmed her managerial abilities, but Margaret had other qualities that spoke well of her. As a literate woman—a rare phenomenon in the period—and one who oversaw the family's estates and businesses—the Fells not only owned extensive land but also forges to refine iron ore—she had the acumen to play a leading role in the day-to-day workings of the Children. Her fervent commitment to the new faith amply demonstrated her firm determination to balance the needs of her immediate family against those of the new and larger one; if she played the deferential wife before Fox crossed Swarthmoor's threshold, then she certainly did not maintain that role as she accepted more and more responsibilities with the Children.[21]

The circumstances point to a steady growth in these responsibilities, a growth that naturally increased her stature. The Fell home began serving as a letter drop almost immediately as news destined for Fox arrived at Swarthmoor,[22] and by October, only three months after her convincement, leading Children already regarded her as a person whom they should inform about the direction the movement was taking.[23] Soon she was dispatching books for itinerants to distribute.[24] Fox assigned her the task of taking handwritten information from the field and preparing it for wider distribution; either she organized a coterie of copyists or did the laborious work herself.[25] Missionaries sent back news to her about their activities and the converts they were making.[26] She even served as a kind of rehabilitation warden for a woman who needed hard work to subdue the flesh.[27]

Fell's possession of such intelligence served to increase her influence, for in any organization the person with a knowledge of detail occupies a central and powerful position. Her growing store of information about the Children of the Light

and its leadership gave her an importance few could rival. The apparently un-
planned addition of the role of treasurer to her responsibilities in February 1653,
when she hurried money to a jailed comrade who needed funds for food, further enhanced her position. Her intimate acquaintance with the needs and growing dimensions of the movement lent her a self-assurance that contributed to
her authority. She could speak from her own knowledge when she reassured one
doubting correspondent that "the truth will stand when all other things shall be
as stubble."[28] Within a decade royalist informants were whispering that she was
the "chief maintainer" of the sect in the region.[29]

Her influence was enhanced by Fox's own presence in the area. Continuing
his short journeys around Swarthmoor, tethering himself to the spacious house
as his headquarters, he always circled back to keep his finger on the movement's
pulse. He also rested or recuperated there from the physical violence his forays
sparked. On one lecture and market day in Ulverston, for example, Fox was thrust
out of the church by a local justice of the peace and beaten to the ground by a
mob of "rude" people; a blow from a heavy staff across his arm left it black and
blue but did not deter him from returning to the crowded marketplace to preach.
A near-riot ensued because the locals considered themselves threatened by this
outsider's vigorous attacks on the most visible institution of their society, "false
Christianity and the fruits of their priest's ministry." He attacked such evils as
lying, whoring, drunkenness, swearing, and thievery, activities all too common
on relaxed market days.[30] The mob even turned its fury on Thomas Fell's son,
George, who had come to see what was going on. When Fox finally made his
way back to Swarthmoor, he found it turned into a veritable hospital as servants
scurried around to bind the wounds of the injured.[31]

Clearly, this violent episode and similar ones in other nearby towns proved
that his successful preaching had raised local ire, especially among determined
Protestants associated with the new government. Two justices of the peace, one,
John Sawrey from Ulverston, and the other from Lancaster, signed warrants for
Fox's arrest based on charges of blasphemy.[32] Fox was unsettled by the notoriety his efforts had produced and doubted his ability to answer the charges; he
put himself on a strict fast until he gained what he called "dominion."[33] On their
way to Lancaster, the county town, on October 18, Fox and Judge Fell, one of
three jurists scheduled to hear the case, agreed that Fox should be permitted to
speak against the accusations. Forty ministers were present to support the three
ministers who had filed charges against Fox, Nayler, and two other Children,
but favorable questioning from Fell and another judge protected the Quakers.

Couched in doctrinal language, especially the relationship of Christ to the
believer, the dispute obscured the fact that each side had its own unspoken
agenda. The ministerial alliance vowed to silence these threats to their religious
and secular power in the north, as shown by their complaint that Fox and the
others had broached opinions "destructive of the relation of subjects to their
magistrates, . . . congregations to their ministers."[34] When Quakers tacked flyers
on Lancaster church doors warning, "This is the idol's temple where the worship of the beast is upheld, down with it, down with it," they added more fuel to
the ministers' charges.[35] The Children wanted to defend their right to continue

distributing such tracts and preaching in the region while ingratiating themselves with the new powers in Whitehall. In his testimony, Fox, led by the two favorable judges, put his comments that he and Christ were equal in the best light, averring that equality implied two distinct persons. The case was dismissed on a technicality after the complainants could not produce the two witnesses the law required to attest to Fox's alleged blasphemy.[36]

This victory encouraged the Children to move quickly and use the case to shore up their reputation, particularly with those in power in London; they astutely recognized that their movement now had to enter the political arena. Fox and Nayler rushed to inform the public that those threatening them with pistol and sword "never drew a sword for the interest of the commonwealth of England, perhaps against it." And they surely hoped the Council of State would not be distracted, as they ingeniously phrased it, from "the mighty series of glorious providences made out to this infant commonwealth" to proscribe such "humble persecuted Christians."[37] It certainly did not hurt their plea that the chancellor of the duchy of Lancaster, the regicidal John Bradshaw, Fell's superior and close friend, presided over the Council of State.[38] Here was a vivid demonstration of how to adeptly fashion the dispute into "we" versus "them."

Fell's promise that Fox might speak in his own defense gave him the opportunity to attack those who had brought the charges and to air his views to the large crowd the hearing had attracted. Calling his accusers "ministers of the world" who had received their learning at Oxford and Cambridge rather than according to God's will, he went to the heart of the difference between his Children and those who relied on the Bible alone: "The letter of the scripture is carnal, and the letter is death, and kills, but the spirit gives life." That the Friends faced persecution now only demonstrated that wherever Christ became manifest the wicked world plotted against him.[39] Fox, not given to expressing surprise, seemed amazed at the response his speech occasioned, since the hearing room was crowded with the county's influential men, some of them, including the soon-to-be mayor of Lancaster, readily convinced of his truth. Two of the three judges also endorsed Fox's general views, to the extent of remarking that if the spirit and the letter were the same, then the ministers probably carried the spirit around in their pocket. Any lingering depression he felt was quickly dissipated by the successful conclusion of the whole affair.[40]

Fox now anticipated settling some scores. Returning to Swarthmoor after a few days in Lancaster, he dipped his pen in vitriol the better to address a few of his old foes, Justice of the Peace John Sawrey and Vicar William Lampit. He labeled Sawrey the originator of all the persecution that had befallen the "righteous seed," the "truth of God" in the region, and informed him that all the country around smelled his "ill savor." For Lampit, "a deceiver, surfeited and drunk with the earthly spirit" and "a beast wallowing and tumbling in the earth and in the lust," Fox forecast "eternal condemnation" if he did not harken "to that of God in his conscience." In an open letter he predicted the same fate for Ulverstonians if they continued gadding abroad and relying on outward teachers like Lampit: "For the Lord God alone will teach his people, and he is coming to teach them." Thus Fox cleared his conscience.[41]

Until late July 1653 Fox remained in the vicinity of Swarthmoor, making periodic forays into the surrounding countryside to dispute with clerical antagonists, heal the lame, and gather the faithful. He also sent out epistles[42] and received intelligence about northern Baptists who might be potential converts.[43] Word of his successes among the stricter sort of Protestants spread to Cumberland, carried no doubt by epistles he dispatched to the north.[44] He heard that threats were being made against his life, a potential that only moved him to plan to move a company of his followers there.[45] Fox and his party stopped first at Bootle, just over the Lancashire county line, where news of his coming led the regular minister to bring in a London colleague to help him deal with this small invasion. As was his practice, Fox went to the local church on Sunday morning, where he found the visiting minister's words so offensive that he interrupted the service to correct him.[46] The congregation exploded and beat Fox out of the church, one member slamming him across the wrist with what looked like a fence post. The town constable came to the missionaries' rescue and tried to put Fox's attacker in the stocks, but the mob, to Fox's dismay, freed the culprit.

That afternoon Fox and his band returned to the town center. This time Fox, protected by his followers, perched on the market cross where everyone would notice him on their way to church. After the services began Fox and his entourage trooped in. Some of the Children tried to shout the preacher down, but this time Fox waited until the Londoner had finished his tirade against false prophets and anti-Christs and then informed the congregation that such men preached for fleece and preyed upon them.[47] When an uproar again ensued, the constable demanded order in the name of the Commonwealth and succeeded in quieting the congregation, even though the parish minister was so angry he practically foamed at the mouth.[48]

The fact that Bootle's constable, obviously a supporter of Cromwell's government, was favorably disposed to the Children underscored growing ties Fox wished to cultivate with the powers that were. The Roundhead judge Anthony Pearson of Durham had just been convinced and brought his wife to Bootle to meet and travel with Fox. Fox addressed another epistle to army officers, shrewdly citing the apostle Paul's famous command, "[L]et every soul be subject to the higher powers."[49] Once the Quaker missionaries reached Cockermouth—having slowed along the way to convert numerous soldiers—these overtures to the military began to bear fruit, for the ubiquitous "rude" ones who seemed to frequent Fox's meetings were silenced with pointed reminders of the law. The barren, cold, and rock-strewn hills made traveling in this region almost as hard as growing crops, even as they divided communities from each other.[50] But Fox won popular acclaim in these isolated areas by declaring that such and such a woman was a witch. Once he discerned a group of witches working in a field as he passed.[51]

Fox had now reached the northern border with Scotland, an area where violence was so normal that the authorities routinely furnished a dagger to each judge.[52] Protected from the north by the Eden River and Hadrian's ancient Roman Wall, the walled city of Carlisle had been a Cavalier stronghold but now swarmed with soldiers garrisoned there to defend the area from maurading thieves who ravaged both sides of the frontier and made normal life precarious. Wherever he found soldiers of the New Model Army, Fox always found numerous religious sectarians and potential converts. Baptists were numerous in Carlisle and had even infiltrated the army's officer ranks. Quakers had also made inroads among the town population. The city's lower orders chafed under the saintly rule represented by their soldierly protectors, and given a pretext—perhaps rumors that alehouses were to be closed or the popular cockfights were to be banned—they would stage a riot protesting the presence of Roundheads. As a consequence, the political leadership, reflecting newly ascendant Protestant elements, exhibited an insecurity characteristic of latecomers.[53]

The state of the churches was even more unsure. Most of the clergy of the region had already been ejected from their livings for royalist and Anglican sympathies, and so few seemed qualified by strict nonconformist standards that many of the churches of the region remained shuttered and empty. St. Mary's, Carlisle's red sandstone cathedral, was open to all sects, although Presbyterians predominated. An uneasy coalition of dissenters of all varieties tried to maintain some kind of order in the partially damaged church, but found itself pulled apart by mutual jealousy and sharply differing perceptions of the needs of any given occasion. Let a charismatic outsider like Fox appear, and "consternation" would be too mild a word to describe the locals' reaction.[54] Hence when Fox and his following, some of them armed soldiers, marched over the moat and through the Irish Gate from the west in September 1653, they must have resembled another invasion force out to conquer the city.[55]

Baptists and New Model Army soldiers represented important parts of Fox's usual constituents, so he had a ready audience in Carlisle. A Baptist preacher, serving as an army lieutenant, brought most of his congregation to St. Mary's to hear the stranger. Fox was then honorably escorted to the nearby castle, headquarters of the troop stationed in the town, and military drummers summoned the men to listen to his advice that they rely on their inward teacher and forsake violence. Where he could not find such a ready-made audience, he created one himself. On Saturday, the town's bustling market day, he climbed on the cross marking the site of the haggling and proclaimed, "[T]he mighty day of the Lord was upon all deceit and ungodliness and wickedness, and lay away all their deceitful merchandising."

The next day, Sunday, Fox went to St. Mary's and revealed just how frayed were the stitches holding together the city's social fabric. The church was administered by the same coalition that governed the town and that tried to exercise power at the national level. And, as at the national level, these Presbyterians and Independents were uneasy with the growing religious radicalism represented by the Baptists and Fox's Children. Fox's sermon on this day must have been one of his most powerful efforts. He later related how, after announcing that he had come to bring the word of salvation from the Lord directly to them, the assembly of local ruling officials and soldiers shook and trembled, some from fear, some from religious conviction. It seemed the weakened church itself quaked. The magistrates tried to stop him, while their wives went for his long hair, but he was protected by soldiers and other friendly members of the congregation.

Presently a mob consisting of those he labeled the town's "rude" people massed outside. Armed with staves and stones, obviously tired of living under strict military rule, and identifying Fox with the soldiers, they milled around rhythmically chanting "Down with the roundheaded rogues." The crowd threw stones and aimed their cudgels at their oppressors. Only quick intervention by the military commander, who dispatched a file of musket-wielding soldiers into the church to lead Fox and his party through the mob, prevented blood from staining the street in front of the church that Sunday. The now-convinced Baptist lieutenant took Fox to his home that afternoon where a small gathering of his flock and those already associated with the Children had a quiet meeting that resulted in the conversion of others. Ultimately the entire Baptist church in Carlisle went over to the Children.

The next morning the streets of the city were still not calm. The town's leaders had a fresh grasp of the situation and seemed aware that by dealing firmly with the outside agitator they could both keep the mob behind them and also strike a firm blow at the radical New Model Army. The threat Fox represented could not be denied: his attack on marketing practices, his warning that soon such deceit would no longer be tolerated, and his success with the soldiers frightened those who believed in the established order of things.

But the authorities chose to move against Fox on safer religious grounds. In possession of a warrant filed by the cathedral's chamberlain for the arrest of George Fox, "commonly called a Quaker,"[56] the town leaders drew from him the admission that he considered himself God's son, that he had seen God's face, and that God was the original Word, the Scriptures mere human writings. The establishment Calvinist gentry had reason enough to be horrified at such heterodox sentiments. If the unrest of the past few days had not been enough to damn him, then Fox was now condemned out of his own mouth, for blasphemy, heresy, and seducing the good people of Carlisle.[57]

Closely guarded in the jailer's own home, Fox was not immediately charged, nor was he tried before the court of assizes when it convened for its semiannual session. Fox hinted that the judges of the assizes realized that the evidence was too weak to hold him, so they connived with the local authorities to ignore the case and keep him in legal limbo.[58] Until a justice of the peace friendly to the Quakers tried to see the charges and get a hearing before the court, Fox remained at the jailer's house. Clergymen and ladies of the town came to dispute with and stare at Fox, rumored to be facing execution for his crimes.

After the judges of the assizes left town, however, conditions got worse for Fox, probably as punishment for public complaints about his ambiguous status. He was remanded to the city dungeon essentially at his jailer's pleasure. Prisoners like Fox, who had outside support, could get books to read.[59] To hear Fox tell it, the place was little more than a pig sty. It had no privy; the prisoners, both men and women confined together indiscriminately, had to relieve themselves on the floor in whatever private corner they could find. Needless to say, the jail's odor was terrible. Lice infected everyone. The two jailers, both massive specimens, looked and smelled like the men who transported and exhibited bears around the country. The assistant jailer delighted in slapping Fox with a cudgel and forcing him to sing, once so loudly that he drowned out a fiddler. Fox refused to buy the food his keepers sold, a blow at the profits they expected as their right, so they retaliated by beating him back when he tried to approach the high grate to get food brought by supporters. Just before Fox's release, a friendly justice got the assistant jailer incarcerated with the ordinary prisoners for his cruelty.[60]

Fox naturally used his imprisonment to condemn those who upheld such a system. (Two of his legal defenders, Judge Anthony Pearson and Gervase Benson, the latter a former justice of the peace, even required his jailer to post a security bond for good behavior.) Fox's statement, "confounding of the deceit," he characteristically phrased it, went out to be tacked on all the market crosses of the region.[61] Margaret Fell also wrote an epistle for general circulation attacking those in government who professed to favor reformation and liberty of conscience while imprisoning people, like Fox, of "tender conscience." To emphasize the same point, she mentioned that a local supporter of Cromwell, High Sheriff Sir Wilfrid Lawson, whom Fox labeled a "blood sucker," "murderer," and "viper," was spreading rumors that the prisoner would be executed. The campaign to publicize Fox's imprisonment moved Parliament to take note of the situation and inquire of the jailer what was going on.[62]

Fox knew. In a letter to two former mayors of Carlisle, now justices of the peace under the Parliament, the prisoner demanded to know, in his best ironic way, if the foundations were so shaky that his mere appearance meant "the end of Carlisle's religion"? He asked, "[I]s this the end of your ministry, and is this the end of your church?" Their problem—and the obvious reason he had been jailed—he went on, was that the church's true colors had been revealed and people saw it taking away their oxen, fatted beeves, sheep, corn, wool, and household goods for tithes, and giving them to ministers who had done no work for them. He warned the two officials that by mocking and imprisoning God's messengers they would "feel the heavy hand of God and his judgments at last." Those redeemed by Christ out of paying tenths or ninths then "shall reign upon the earth"; "the Lamb and his saints," he concluded, "shall have the victory" and sweep away "all these inventors and inventions that have . . . been set up since the days of the apostles and since the true church went into the wilderness."[63]

Fox's experiences in the border city, particularly his imprisonment, introduced a significant change in his attitude and approach toward the government. Before Carlisle he had hoped that appeals to the ruling powers would convince them to act justly and fairly; after Carlisle he recognized that most of the authorities would not stand with the Children of the Light but were instead committed to the status quo, thereby impeding rule by the godly, at least as he defined them. The year before, for example, he had addressed a letter of admonition to Parliament and the officers of the army whose tone and words suggested that he believed they would, as he phrased it, "give your minds up to God whereby you may stand all in God's counsel."[64] Now he recognized that if the millennium came, then it would not come as the result of official action but through the work of suffering servants who would convince the people to grasp the opportunity before them.

After his Carlisle imprisonment, then, he lost hope that things would gradually get better. So long as the government consisted of men, he now warned, who were "beside [their] senses or wits, irrational," just so long would "people moved of the Lord according to scripture and true doctrine" be falsely imprisoned for making disturbances. And just so long, likewise, would those who tumultuously crowded the streets by the hundreds, "swearing, lying, cursing, and [playing] at vain sports, and talks and jests," be permitted to assemble merely "for pleasure." Leaders like those who had imprisoned him could see no difference between "the precious and the vile, the holy and profane, the godly and the profane, those who fear the Lord and those who fear him not." If his Children of the Light "were of the world," he explained, "the world would not hate us, but we are not of the world, therefore the world hates us because Christ has chosen us out of the world and ... because we testify against the world and the works that are evil."[65]

Fox's forthright testimony was made more feasible by the relative isolation separating the northern provinces from the rest of the nation, but its tone was also strikingly different from the stance of other reformers of the day. Isaac Penington, for example, son of the lord mayor of London who sat at the king's trial, advised submission. "Be content to be slaves," he enjoined those immediately wanting "the full enjoyment of the freedom they have desired and pressed so hard for." His practicality—"the stiffness of the neck and unbrokenness of the spirit chiefly make all our yokes so harsh"—was uninformed by the kind of compelling commitment to which Fox had been called. Surveying his post-monarchical world and fearing a reaction, the pusillanimous Penington saw no possibility that human beings could bring in a new world and did not want them to try. The hoped-for new age would, he hinted, come only through divine activity.[66]

Fox's approach drew no such passive line between divine and human activity: Christ was teaching his Children what to do. For the sake of the new age of righteousness he saw himself as an agent of the divine. But when he attacked the frivolities of traditional village life—gaming, cockfighting, dancing, and imbibing—Fox and his followers drove a huge wedge between themselves and the "rude" people who sought by such means to introduce excitement into the hard work and tedium of daily existence. Fox's stern attitude differed little from the more mainstream Presbyterian and Independent ministers who complained in 1656 about the plays, bullbaiting, football, and gambling that had made the region "a byword in respect of ignorance and profaneness." Indeed, the "Associated Ministers," as they called themselves, may well have been reacting to Fox's successes when they promised to exclude from the sacrament any who engaged in such sinful pastimes.[67]

The change in Fox's attitude toward government reflected new developments in London as well as his personal experiences. On April 20, 1653, Oliver Cromwell, succumbing to his own millenarian fits and deciding to cast his lot with the army and reform, dissolved the Rump Parliament, the desiccated end of the old Long Parliament of 1640. It had proven too conservative for those with grand dreams about the future. At first Cromwell postured in the manner of a newly convinced Fifth Monarchist. When the nominated or Barebones Parliament of 138 godly men convened on July 4, he prodded them with the message, "[Y]ou are called by God to rule with him and for him" and told them that the day had dawned "to usher in the things that God has promised." The new assembly enacted a number of noncontroversial measures, but in reopening the question of abolishing tithes, always an explosive issue, and removing incumbent gentry from their posts as local justices of the peace, the radicals struck at prerogatives enjoyed by influential moderates. Sensing that his support was eroding, Cromwell characteristically temporized and finally decided that God did not favor such precipitous actions. The millenarian plan for the ready appearance of God's Kingdom rapidly faded. Early on the morning of December 12 moderate members met and outvoted their radical parliamentary colleagues, then went home, leaving the increasingly cautious Cromwell behind in London as Lord Protector for life.[68]

These developments in the nation's capital suggested the direction and mood of the country, but they did not immediately concern Fox, who wanted to anchor his movement firmly in the north before returning southwards. His successes were impressive in the valleys and dales of this poor and isolated region and were multiplied by his followers who went on preaching missions of their own. One of the earliest attacks on the new sect, published nearly a year before the Children appeared in the south, complained that hundreds in a trancelike state neglected their usual duties to attend Quaker meetings, the east scurrying to the north and west, the west racing east.[69] For many who watched a tenth of what little they owned siphoned off by a large church or a rich laity, it must have been exhilarating to hear a preacher clad in rough leather and speaking much like themselves declaim, as Fox did in Hexham, that God "would give power to become the sons of God, as he had done to me."[70] And what did people of a lesser sort think when he told them, as he did in an epistle of this time, that the highest religion "must bend and bow" before the light that condemned the world?[71] Critics whispered that the Children shunned large towns in favor of small, isolated places.[72] The character of the audiences targeted—New Model Army soldiers,[73] Baptists,[74] and other dissenting congregations, particularly those in poorer parishes where tithes seemed especially onerous—sent success soaring to their heads. Fox referred, only a bit extravagantly, to the thousands convinced,[75] and Richard Farnworth, who tapped into dogged antitithe sentiment in Yorkshire, remarked that, "the world is all on fire."[76]

Fox also won a reputation for performing miracles, a role naturally expected of God's prophets but of course sneered at by opponents.[77] Although his followers were subsequently embarrassed enough by his reported prowess in performing miracles that they suppressed numerous references to them in his recollections, Fox himself believed that they confirmed the extraordinary power inherent in the movement and he expected them to be printed.[78] To a critic, he cited them as "miracles in the spirit, which are signs and wonders to the world."[79] A most interesting one occurred at Hawkshead on a particularly bitter day. Fox and two teenaged companions, Margaret Fell, Jr., daughter of Thomas and Margaret, and William Caton, a close friend of the Fells, stopped at the home of an acquaintance whose house was much more inviting than those another traveler referred to as the "sad little huts" she saw.[80] The family had a maid and an eleven-year-old son, scabby, dirty, and bent nearly double in a cradle. Already they had taken him to Wells and Bath looking for a cure, but the doctors could not help, so his parents had reconciled themselves to his death. After the boy had been cleaned, Fox laid his hands on the invalid, spoke to him, and then instructed the servant to dress him. Three years later Fox learned that the boy had been healed and had grown straight and tall.[81]

One thing yet remained to be done: tightening up the organizational structure. The need for organization, particularly to control dissidents, within a new religious movement seems to grow naturally as the number of people involved in the movement increases. As early as 1652 Nayler complained about Westmorlanders who were "into words and vain janglings" and had lost themselves that way.[82] In Baycliff, just south of Ulverston, two recent converts got up, as Fox worded it, "into pride and exaltation of spirit" and ran "out from truth."[83] Hence a new tone crept into Fox's epistles during this early period: he began to admonish his followers to maintain unity and keep close to the divine light that would bind them together. Fox had had to deal with this tendency more than three years before in the case of Rhys Jones and the Proud Quakers of Nottingham. But they did not remain subdued and occasionally sent leaflets to nearby towns condemning those still in the mainstream.[84] The evidence of disaffection among new Friends can be read in what Fox condemned in his epistles.

"Keep together in the power up to God" was already his common counsel,[85] but he added advice to "wait upon the unlimited power and spirit of the Lord, which baptizes into one body"[86] and warnings not to succumb to natural impulses or "give not way to the lazy, dreaming mind."[87] He addressed "all Friends who are in the unity"—implying that some were not—and reminded them that they had "one eye, . . . one fire, which consumes all which the light discovers to be evil, and one spirit, which baptizes all into the one body, where there is no confusion, but pureness and oneness."[88] He hinted that some Friends despised the prophecy of women ministers, and he warned them against this error.[89] He denied, and claimed that the Spirit condemned, those who were deceitful and slothful—they were, he judged, "hangers-on, . . . who speak what they are not."[90] Judging others, he wrote yet again, should never be done behind another's back but openly and in the light: "[L]et there be no backbiting among you, . . . meet together, waiting upon the Lord that your minds may be guided by the spirit of God up to God."[91] Such admonitions might sound commonplace, particularly from a religious leader. But these, and others like them, were really more than the usual platitudes. A discerning person and sensitive to the subtle shifts that always mark human behavior, Fox noticed shortcomings among his followers and tried to warn his adherents about their failings.

Yet Fox ironically had himself fed the tendency he condemned. His message from the beginning had stressed that a true Christian must finally rely on his or her own unique experiences. However much Fox hoped the divine spirit would unify honest seekers, he now faced the possibility that an individual's experiences might lead down unique individual pathways. The simple truth was that his message had freed his followers from traditional restraints. This paradox was summed up in the lines of a 1653 epistle addressed "to Friends, that their minds go not out from the spirit of God." "Here," he told his readers, as you join God's life, "you are kept [remain] in the image of God. Not but that you may use the creatures lawfully, but being kept in the image of God, you are kept as kings over all the creatures, and over the creation; here you will see all things and by whom they stand. To the pure all things are pure."[92] That idea was the loose cannon in the Quaker movement, and no Ranter could have said it better. The need to tie this loose cannon down led to the institutionalization of Fox's movement and enabled it to survive. Fox himself had encouraged the diversity that permeated the Society of Friends, and now he had to impose some kind of unity on his movement.

Nowhere did he indicate that he consciously understood how his own preachments had fed the Ranterism that continued to emerge within his movement. The kind of emphasis that began to appear in his writing, however, suggested how troubled he was by his growing sense of the movement's lack of unity, of the spirit of independence, even insubordination, that was beginning to dog a group that freed its members from the usual social constraints. Fox recognized that mere epistles could not by themselves solve the problem. Problems unseen a year before when the movement was small and limited geographically, when he, Margaret Fell, Nayler, and Farnworth had created a kind of headquarters, had now to be dealt with. With Children of the Light scattered across six northern counties and down into the Midlands,[93] with authorized evangelists—not to mention numerous unauthorized enthusiasts—[94] carrying the message hither and yon, and with the growing need for funds,[95] a tighter organization was clearly needed.

Until this time meetings had been collections of people who gathered to wait upon God's guidance in an almost ad hoc fashion. Fox or other evangelists appeared at a local church or spoke in a marketplace, collected an interested group willing to meet in someone's home or barn, preached, and left. Whenever leadership arose, it did so in a rather haphazard fashion. Those areas fortunate enough to find a natural indigenous leader were able to sustain meetings on a regular, weekly basis. Those living in areas that lacked such a natural leader were served by occasional general meetings, convened to gather the isolated faithful. These area-wide meetings gave scattered, isolated Children the sense of being part of a large and viable movement, but they added little to the local, particular meeting.[96]

The first meeting entitled to administer the affairs of separated bodies of the Children was established in Durham in 1653. Called by male members to meet on the first Saturday of each month and to include Friends from the "several" meetings nearby, the group's scope was not spelled out, other than a commitment to consider the "necessities or wants" of each local gathering.[97] These wants likely included concern for the poor among the movement, since in 1654 Fox had condemned Rhys Jones for referring slightingly to this activity in "moon light" meetings.[98] The Durham meeting probably followed William Dewsbury's guidelines laid out for any "particular meeting of Friends, servants, or children of the most high God." Although the term "minister" did not appear, the letter instructed the body of Children—the term "church" was used—to choose one or two persons to have oversight of the needs of the "flock of God . . . not by constraint but by willingness, not for filthy lucre but of a ready mind." A lay ministry was developing, differing significantly from the clergy in both established and dissenting churches.[99] Those selected for "oversight" would oversee the needs of the people and arrange twice-weekly meetings, one on Sunday, one on another day. One purpose of such meetings was "to judge and cut down the deceit" so no member would "walk disorderly." In case the person so treated did not repent, that person would be expelled pending another chance at repentance. In the meantime all association, even eating with the backslider, was forbidden between the expelled member and his former fellows lest "any filthy person dwell in the house of God." The community would see that members' material needs were met and sit as judges if differences arose. Dewsbury prayed that God give his chosen ones the boldness to rule their meetings and "cut down all deceit."[100]

That Dewsbury found deceit prevalent enough to require expelling members of the movement demonstrated that the world's attitudes had intruded into the affairs of the Children of the Light. The same was obvious from the new and worried tone appearing in Fox's epistles. He began to use the word "minister" as a term of endorsement and surrounded it with the aura of authority, almost always divine authority. Thus in early 1654, when he was beset by false prophets like Rhys Jones, he wrote his second epistle specifically addressed to ministers. Much of it was general and admonitory, but there was substance too. "Walk in the light," he advised, "which has converted your souls and brought them to submit to the higher power." Ministers should keep in the light, he stressed, for it "judges down that which is contrary to the light and life. . . . He that believes not, the light condemns him." While his imagery might have seemed obscure to outsiders, those who faced the backbiting, the discontent with female prophets, the deceit that had slipped into local meetings had a way to see: the light, he said, understood time and the world, gave victory over the world, and bestowed on ministers the power of the Lord, "which subdues all [to] the contrary, and puts off the garments that will stain and pollute."[101]

One problem that threatened a dark stain indeed involved the place of women in the movement. Fox never backed down from his insistence that God called women to be preachers and evangelists just as he had traditionally called men. From the very first, when Elizabeth Hooten began to preach and prophesy, women had played an active role among the Children of the Light, and Margaret Fell's position called attention to this reality. Critics of the Quakers thus had an opening that was too good to miss, particularly when the specter of female equality of function raised troubling questions about overturning other traditional relationships between the sexes. The easiest target was, of course, the possibility of immorality among a group allowing women to preach: one critic complained that even conversing with women seduced and drew them away from their husbands, thus "leading captives silly women." This analyst publicized rumors from Wigton of a married Quaker lying naked with another man's wife to illustrate how being united in the spirit expressed itself physically.[102] The results of such reports was easy to predict; an anonymous observer revealed matter-of-factly that Quakers "hold a community of women and other men's wives and practice living upon one another too much."[103]

The role of women raised a related problem that was destined to bedevil Fox's disciples for years: how to control marriages by tightening the meetings' authority over them. The question was bound to arise early, for as soon as a person associated with the Children wanted to be married, procedures become necessary. Fox himself was not married and never evinced much personal interest in sex; he seemed too busy at his calling. The legal situation was fluid. In a gesture to radicalism, the Barebones Parliament legalized marriage before a justice of the peace, an action confirming for all shades of respectable opinion just how far the new regime might go in overturning old landmarks. Fox's Children, of course, had no use for any of the rites of the established church, be they baptism, communion, or marriage. And no one who knew them would expect them to sanction a union before the state's justice of the peace, who might in another situation instigate their arrest. In refusing to recognize the traditional religious ceremony, they ranked themselves with Ranters who sneered that right actions depended upon a person's intentions, and in rejecting civil marriages, they were willing to live illicitly in the open. Hence a wall poster stuck up in London grouped Quakers with mechanics, Ranters, and Anabaptists who would, it read, "obstruct and abolish all decency, order, and form whatsoever in the government of church and state."[104]

Early in 1654 Fox wrote an epistle on marriage whose message was that when God had joined a couple "this marriage is honorable, and this bed is not defiled."[105] But he had also to establish procedures to implement this broad principle. A bit later—the exact date is unclear but it was after Parliament legalized civil marriages in 1653—Fox sent another advisory letter to his followers. It provided that when a couple decided on their intention to marry, but "before anything be concluded," they should confer privately with Friends able to discern if the union could stand in the light. Then with the couple present the marriage could be declared to the meeting, which would inquire to make sure that no other engagement existed. If any impediments were found or if someone opposed the marriage, the case would be referred to a general or regional meeting. Assuming that all blocks were cleared away, the intention could be announced in the market on market day, a way to judge apostates not married in the truth. When all were satisfied, an assembly of Friends would be held at which those in attendance would be free to speak and the couple would "speak as they are moved how that they are in marriage joined together." A certificate would then be signed by those present. The couple were free to declare it to the magistrates or not as they desired.

This method was clearly designed to counter criticism of the way the Children had dealt with the explosive issue of sex and marriage. Fox asserted that he wanted "unrighteousness and filthiness shut out." He also consciously endeavored to justify this procedure by tracing it back to the time before the patriarch Moses found his people had hardened their hearts and were living like beasts. We have now, he exulted, been "redeemed out of the earth [and] come to know it as it was in the beginning": they were now a "peculiar people, the holy and royal seed, the peculiar generation."[106]

In truth, Fox was a bit too optimistic. The problem of human desires had not been solved by merely announcing that Quakers were living in the age of innocence before Adam and Eve sinned. Nor did a more restrictive and inhibiting procedure than the usual vague and less specific rules governing marriages at the time stop public criticisms of the Children.[107] To cite just one example, in 1661 a lawyer in Nottingham charged that Friends "went together like wild beasts."[108] But the marriage problem did force Fox to face the immediate consequences of his preachments on individual inspiration, preachments that removed the kind of constraints people had customarily observed. He then had to fashion new structures and procedures to replace the old ones. The ordering of marriages remained a problem and would return to haunt—and split—the Children of the Light. Local meeting structures stood as legacies of how Fox dealt with dissidents, while his regularized marriage procedures endeavored to remove any basis for public criticism of Quaker couples. Without full awareness of all its implications, he was creating a guiding tradition within Quakerism that would, over time, set narrowing limits on individual liberty.[109]

By March 1654, nearly twenty months had passed since Fox had first arrived at Swarthmoor. The movement had caught fire, the flax was set aflame, but then the burning embers had been banked. This banking loomed as most important, at least internally. He and the small number of people at the center had reconciled a revolutionary principle, that of the right of even the meanest sort to act on his or her own inspiration, with an institutional structure that would serve the Society of Friends far into the future, further indeed than any could foresee at that time. With the experience and success in the north behind them, it was time to take the good news to the rest of the nation, to fan out and proclaim the day of the Lord in the east, the south, and the west. Fox later wrote that God did "move upon the spirits of many [nearly seventy] whom he had raised up and sent forth to labor in his vineyard."[110] More likely, it became clear to him, then to them, that the time had come to see if the flax would burn as fiercely in the east, the south, and the west as it had in the north.

8

As Like an Apple as an Oyster

"An original, being no man's copy," was the way his friend William Penn wanted to remember George Fox after he died. Penn thought Fox's lack of formal education and his inelegant speech were assets allowing him to ignore the jealousy of those who valued mere human wisdom.[1]

Fox's lack of formal training meant that he did not formulate his religious views in the usual academic way, nor was he bound by artificial categories requiring his views to fit a particular theological mold. Despite the fact that he possessed a good library for the time,[2] his writings show few signs that he read the books he owned.[3] His theology grew out of his own experiences, was tempered by his common sense, and was tested against his own selective reading of the Bible. He was not a theologian, nor was he interested in being one—originators of new sects seldom are. First and foremost he was a man of faith. He wanted to communicate his spiritual experiences to his generation, many of whose members shared his own frustrations and goals. Thus he relied on what he considered his inspired intuition and his sense of the way things were, not on theological systems created by mere mortals.

After enunciating a central point, he would ramble, unevenly and unsystematically, over and around it until he almost beat it to death. He was always more repetitive than clear. Like many undisciplined thinkers, he would take a minor point and puff it up until it seemed to become major. Even a casual reading of his *Journal* suggests that he gave equal attention to every idea he believed true, no matter how minor or peripheral to his immediate situation. His output of epistles and pamphlets—more than two hundred were published, and presumably hundreds more were lost[4]—were dashed off to meet whatever concern rose to the top of his mind at a given moment. They read like products of a person more oral than literary, compositions developed while the author was speaking, transcribed, and then hurried off to the printer.[5] He liked to relieve himself by pontificating on all manner of subjects. His views were erratic and subject to shifts over time, as well as to major modifications as he confronted new situations.[6]

From an academic perspective, then and now, these traits were major shortcomings, but they should not detract from our recognition of Fox's essential genius and his skill in being able to speak to his generation's needs. His new faith grew out of the village soil of revolutionary England, and he possessed a special talent that enabled him to articulate his vision for people battered by Civil War and dramatic social changes, people looking for a new faith. For nearly forty years he remained a stormy petrel of England's religious life, drawing healthy numbers of disciples on the one hand, forcing opponents to confront his movement on the other. The controversy he and his Children provoked from preachers, pamphleteers, and politicians underscored the apprehension and fear with which he was regarded in established quarters.

Fox first formulated his position in reaction to the state of the church and professed Christians he witnessed around him. He certainly would not have become a reformer had he not been repulsed by what he saw to be the sorry condition and shortcomings of the religious institutions of his day. When he measured the churches, whether established or separated, against their own professed ideals, he discovered hypocrisy and emptiness. His early effectiveness as an evangelist rested squarely on his ability to slice through the pretenses of pastors, priests, and prelates. Taking direct aim at their flaws, he demonstrated how they added to common burdens, ranging from quite specific grievances like tithes to more intangible ones like putting on airs and insisting on their exclusive right to interpret the Scriptures. A radical egalitarian tone distinguished his message and appealed to people bothered by their government's inability to implement the promises of the cause for which so many had sacrificed in the Civil War. Thus on occasion he pointedly reminded those who had struggled for religious reformation and confidently set up the present government that they were watching a swindle: "[S]uch as once you warred against are now put in authority, which does oppress, imprison, and persecute."[7]

The most obvious example of theological oppression evident in the new order was the "Articles of Religion," approved by Parliament in 1648. Put simply, this document left little or no room for the spirit to blow where it would. Rather than give ground to dissenters like Fox who believed God could lead any individual to apprehend truth, it affirmed the supremacy of the Scriptures. "The whole counsel of God concerning all things necessary for his own glory, man's salvation, faith and life," it insisted in good Calvinist fashion, "is either expressly set down in Scripture, or by good and necessary consequence may be deduced from Scripture." True, its Presbyterian and Independent authors tossed to radical sectarians the sop that the ultimate judge of scriptural interpretation "can be no other but the Holy Spirit," but they immediately tacked on, "speaking in the Scripture," taking back with one hand what they had just given with the other.[8] Such an approach amounted to a monopolization of religious faith by those certified to handle sacred things. The attempt to impose religious uniformity by means of the "Articles of Religion" seriously compromised dissenters' hopes. Even Oliver Cromwell's chaplain complained that those who supported such scriptural oppression "labored to hedge in the wind and to bind up the sweet influence of the spirit."[9]

Documents like the "Articles of Religion" formed the broad canvas on which the English religious settlement was painted and of course colored the specific situation out in the countryside, but Fox found them relatively uninteresting in the 1650s. Unaware of theological niceties and more concerned anyway with obvious matters like tithes and hypocrisy, he concentrated on the practical incongruities that marked his religious world. Most of all he focused on the deceit he saw in the churches. The word "deceit" was seldom far from his lips or his pen. It became a near synonym for every shortcoming he could lay at the feet of church leaders and their followers. With its undertone of hypocrisy and even lying, its hint of commercial trickery and skullduggery, it was the word he needed to use to flay his opponents. Even before his revelation that Christ alone could speak to his condition, he decried "knowledge in the flesh, deceit, and self." The world's knowledge "will conform to anything and will say 'Yes, yes,' to that it does not know." It would lie. It would embrace required forms—outward actions, spoken words, rote repetition of the catechism—without fulfilling "the law and command of Christ in his power and spirit."[10] Priests, he went on, "stood in the deceit and acted by the dark power" and kept the people under it. But he saved his sternest strictures for those deceivers he said had actually heard the voice of God, like Adam's son Cain, "yet turned from the spirit and the word and went into the gainsaying." Such persons had been nourished inwardly by the spirit but deceitfully had taken to covetness, greed, and living on unrighteous wages.[11]

Fox identified deceit with the tendency to embrace and adopt the world's standards. This identification explained why he insisted so strenuously that his followers eschew worldly practices and become a separated people, different from others around them. In an early epistle written in 1652 he advised his followers to "mind the light of God in you and submit to the Lord to be guided by him; lay aside all light words and feigned speeches, hypocrisy and deceit, and love not the world nor the things of the world, for the lord of the world is an enemy to God."[12] His attack on the deceitful practices of the world could be quite specific, even as he undermined the authority the better sort tried to exercise over their lesser fellows. Consider, he advised, men who put gold and silver on their backs, powder their hair, and stick feathers in their caps, and women who paste gold and silver spots on their faces and sport double cuffs: look at how they say, "[H]ere is a gentleman, bow before him, put off your hats . . . this is a brave fellow, a gentleman, . . . are these your fine Christians? . . . Yea, but say the serious people, 'They are out of Christ's life.'" "These are bred up gentlemen," the seldom ironic Fox figuratively pointed, "these are no Quakers, these are called Christians."[13] Serious once more, he pointed out that they do not practice "pure Christianity, but deceive their own hearts with unbridled tongues in a vain religion."[14]

Fox did not limit his use of the concept of deceit, however, to the mere personal. Anyone who was personally deceitful would likely, in this prophet's eyes, deceive and cheat other people. To introduce Londoners in 1654 to the Quakers, Fox expounded their purpose: "[T]o cry against the deceitful merchandise, . . . against oppression and unjust dealing, . . . to cry against you who rule the country . . . and keep not all in order, justice, and equity, where injustice reigns, where justice is not stirring." He warned, "You can not hide . . .

dissembler."[15] Fox naturally targeted markets and fairs for his assaults on deceitful pricing, buying, and selling, warning all, as he phrased it during his early days in the Midlands, "to deal justly and to speak the truth."[16]

Fox's attacks on deceit, combining the personal and the social, implied that his followers, Friends of the Truth, Children of the Light, would form a people who would be personally sober, serious, and stainless, and would live as people called to a new mission within an old society. Rejecting deceit and deceitful ways, they would live by a different ethic, one requiring veracity in conduct and speech. Of course they would go to marketplaces—the usual places to truck and trade— but they would buy and sell by quoting everyone the same price rather than haggling to get the most the market would bear. In handling only fine, licit goods, they would differentiate themselves from sharp dealers who sold products that were spoiled or pirated or immoral. Fox believed honesty and morality would pay off in the long run; he told his followers in 1656 that buyers would come to trade with them "the more, because they know you will not cozen them nor cheat them, then you [will come] to have greater trading, double than ever you had and more than the world." But let those people beware who "cumbered" themselves with riches rather than serving God; they, their minds "clogged" with business, would likely lose what they had.[17] This warning against deceitful unfaith-fulness recommended living the truth as the way to success for commoners who were upwardly mobile and hopeful.

Fox's outspoken opposition to deceitful practices developed from his convic-tion that he was the one specially tapped to announce the "day of the Lord," the time when the world's kingdoms would be swept away and replaced with the Kingdom of God. "The mighty day of the Lord is come," he bluntly informed government officials in 1658, "Christ Jesus is come to reign."[18] The hallmark of the new kingdom would be government by the honest and forthright, the very type people floundering and with no place to go. Gathered out of the world, they would "be able to judge and discern and confound all the deceit of the world and grow up to be as kings, and nothing to reign but what is life eternal, ... treading and trampling all the deceit under your feet."[19] This insis-tence on veracity, on speaking and living the truth in contrast to lying and act-ing deceitfully, became his main message. Its ascendancy over traditional Chris-tian doctrines and creeds helps explain why one of the earliest names for Fox's followers was "Friends in the Truth." The kind of truth he spoke, however, was not limited to mere personal veracity but included also the right to claim authority over the deceitful.

Attacks on deceitfulness were, of course, primarily negative, but as the name of his followers implied, there existed also a positive side to Fox's message. The reason he took such consistent aim at deceit, particularly as related to a person's religious profession, resulted from his own experiences of authentic religion. His dogged lifelong conviction that he had encountered the spirit of God outside accepted channels, without—indeed, despite—the aid of ministers, the Bible, and church institutions galvanized his life and gave him a fearless assurance that he was correct. Hence his use of a synonym like "Light" or "Truth" for God represented a conscious effort to illustrate that authentic religion threw the light of truth on human foibles. It beamed into the murk where humans secreted their thoughts and private actions away from view.

His central theological insight emerged directly from his experience, the mystical conviction of the unalloyed presence of God. He never modified it, whatever his place or state.[20] It was not only that he believed that there was "one, even Christ Jesus, who could speak to thy condition," it was also that he felt the continuing presence of Christ as teacher and guide: "Christ has come to teach his people himself."[21] Fox never bothered to speculate very deeply on the nature of God, the relationship of the man Jesus to the eternal and divine Christ, whether there was a Trinity or not, or whether the Bible was an infallible guide—those were traditional questions of little concern to such a commonsensical man. Indeed, he considered such thoughts "notions," light, airy, ultimately useless, human speculations, and sneered at them accordingly.[22] In the best Protestant and dissenting tradition, Fox required, yea, demanded, a personal response that hearers turn from the old and face the new. Fox's faith in these divine openings, or leadings, convinced him that others could experience the same teacher if they would only open themselves to it.

Fox's conviction about the presence of God was one of the two principles forming the basis of his ideas in the early years of his travels, particularly before 1660. The other, tied closely to, and in a sense growing directly out of, the first, Fox shared with numerous other sectarian dreamers of the 1650s. His unspoken assumption, that his gathered Children of the Light would sweep England—maybe even the world—and reinvigorate the flagging "Good Old Cause" that had won the Civil War and fed hopes of a new order of righteousness, gave to Fox's early thought a millenarian cast and appeal.[23] Although he seldom spoke politically in an explicit way, he illustrated his ideas from examples drawn from the concrete problems people faced, and he offered options patterned after the hopes of numerous contemporaries, including the Fifth Monarchists, who also expected the millennium. Hence he was the articulator for those who only dreamed, the voice of those who were voiceless, the speaker for those who did not speak openly.

Fox usually expressed his certainty that Christ was present to teach and lead those who chose to follow him by advising people to look for the inward light. Every person, he affirmed, possessed this light, a gift of God, which even if obscured still had the power to convict and convince.[24] He put his message most simply in a catechism he composed for children. Belief in Christ and professing the Scriptures were hardly sufficient: "[T]hey do not believe in Christ who do not believe in the light, . . . for the true light . . . is the true Christ." This light, he continued, at once revealed and judged everyone's words, actions, thoughts, and imaginations and gave the person power and strength to overcome evil: "[I]f the light is harkened to, the thoughts and imaginations shall not lodge within you; . . . [it] will let you see yourself and the cross, which is to deny self, and to follow Christ."[25] The light, moreover, "teaches righteousness and holiness, it will keep you from lying [as well as theft, quarreling, gambling, fighting] and not let you lie . . . and lay away all guilt, sin, and uncleanness; . . . it will lead you . . . to cease from men, to be taught alone of God."[26] In one of his few preserved sermons, dating from 1653, he explained that harkening to the light of the spirit would "show you sin and evil, and your evil deeds and actings, and the deceit and false heartedness."[27] Testing even the Bible against this light, he found it true, he told a critic, "because it testifies against sin."[28]

Doctrines and church dogmas were irrelevant in the face of the need for everyone to confront the Christ, at once embodied in and revealed by the light within each person. Candidly confessing that he knew the truth of his conviction before ever seeing it in the Bible, he explained that he apprehended the light and spirit responsible for the Scriptures in the first place: human beings, if his experience was the guide, could go beyond and behind holy writ to the same spirit that originally produced it.[29] Needless to say, giving every Jack, much less Jill, that kind of invitation to individualism caused horrific specters to rise up and haunt more orthodox reformers. To critics like John Bunyan, who charged that stressing an inward Christ led Fox to deny the historic Jesus, Fox gave not an inch. He thundered that "None knows righteousness but within. . . . If Christ who's crucified be not within, and Christ who's risen be not within, I say that you all are reprobates. . . . None knows the Son of God but by revelation and with the light."[30]

While Fox rejected charges that he depreciated the historic Jesus, as well as the Scriptures that related his story,[31] his theological position did add up to a kind of gnosticism, in which Jesus' outward humanity paled into insignificance before the divine and indwelling Christ. In 1657, in a discussion with Sir Henry Vane, former governor of the Massachusetts Bay Colony in New England and a leading Independent, he remarked straightforwardly, as though it was as clear as could be, "the word became flesh but not corrupt flesh."[32] Another critic noted how his passions flared when Fox told him, in a phrase he was wont to use to describe himself, that Christ according to the flesh was the son of Abraham but according to the spirit was the Son of God.[33] Likewise, his method of reaching his theological conclusions emphasized the intuitive and mystical over the historic and creedal, characteristics of a gnostic approach.

The most radical of all Fox's conclusions was his belief that those who came to know the light in the way he described might become children of God. The first statement of this view in the *Journal* virtually paraphrased John 1:12—"For to as many as should receive him in his light, I saw that he would give power to become sons of God: which I had obtained by receiving Christ,"[34]—the kind of gnostic comment bound to lead to controversy and misunderstanding.[35] In his discussion with Vane he stressed the idea that Christ took upon himself the "seed of Abraham," the very same phrase he used when he identified himself with the Son of God.[36] Uttering such comments caused him and his followers to be charged with blasphemy time and time again. But the message of the Gospel of John and their own experience was simply too compelling. John stressed the eternal Christ rather than focusing on the earthly life of the historic Jesus. This New Testament book, often referred to as the "Quaker gospel,"[37] remained a prime source for gnostic teaching.[38] Ecstatic about John's announcement of the Light, Fox easily confused, comingled, and conflated John the Baptist's proclamation of the coming Messiah with the gospel writer's description of the coming of the Word and how that Word infused those who believed.[39] Had Fox foreseen how a few Quakers would come to believe they could literally embody Christ, he might have been more circumspect in his own expression of this idea.

But even if he had known technical words like "gnosticism" or had had the advantage of foresight, criticism such as this made little difference to Fox, who built his theology on his own experience. He did not stop to ask whether any of his ideas had been considered heretical ages ago, for his experience with God transcended in importance anything human beings could say or do about his views. This explains why he could offhandedly refer to himself as the "Son of God." When he found that his meeting with God, the experience of gripping revelation and direct guidance by one demanding his ultimate allegiance, coincided with a biblical passage or two, then so be it—this confirmed that his encounter with God's spirit had indeed made him the Son of God, and so all genuine disciples could be.[40]

Over the ages, Fox believed, "both the order and practice of the true church has been lost" in the wilderness and the "false church ruled upon the beast and dragon's power." Now, he affirmed, the previously vanquished saints, martyrs, prophets, and witnesses, killed by false churchmen, "shall rise again, and the reapers shall go forth and the everlasting gospel [be] preached again to all."[41] Hence Fox, in his untutored fashion that looked forward to modern interpretations,[42] hit upon a way to revive a Christianity lost after centuries of apostasy. Prophet of a mystical way to apprehend truth, he chipped through a Protestant orthodoxy of frozen biblical revelation and proclaimed what Christ had come to reveal: To believe in Christ simply because of the Scriptures is to have "been taught it and received it of man, that is, not taught it by the revelation of Jesus Christ."[43] To believe in the scriptural Christ alone "is to believe as the Pharisees did believe . . . ; but to believe in the light, [then] the life that gave forth the scriptures is seen and Christ is believed in, and here he has the witness in himself and comes to be a child of light and born of God, which birth overcomes the world."[44] Mere words, he averred, never had life unless "first written in the heart of man by God and Christ, and from the spirit they were spoken forth and was known by the spirit of God in others." As he said, "[W]e know the scriptures by the spirit that gave them forth."[45]

As the prophet of a new church dispensation, Fox counterpoised Christ the light, "the end of the prophets, the heir of all things," to moldy bread and vinegary wine stashed away in cupboards: "[H]e is the head of our church, our life, our way, our truth, our sanctification, our justification, our wisdom, our righteousness; this is in us and among us, . . . the royal seed of God, who witness light in us and life in us, and Christ in us." He completely rejected the validity of the sacrament of the eucharist or holy communion, which was not only carnal but played to the deceitfulness that marked so much of the ecclesiastical establishment. Hence he did not hesitate to declare that his movement represented, as he phrased it, "the true church, the elect seed"; indeed, he grandly styled it "the Church in England."[46]

His demonstration of his position on the sacrament was crudely commonsensical, but it dramatically made his point among the folk he wanted to reach. Once he challenged a Jesuit to divide a loaf of bread and a jug of wine, consecrating one half of each, and thereafter allow the people to see if the portions that were the body and blood of Christ resisted molding. The priest's refusal to participate in this experiment was vindication enough for Fox.[47] In the same spirit he ridiculed priests and ministers who claimed that the laity should not, as he phrased it, "meddle with the Scriptures" or interpret them because they did not know Latin or Greek. What then could Jacob the shepherd or Elisha the plowman have to say of divine things, he asked tauntingly? "Stand up, laymen," he demanded of his audience.[48]

Fox thus exhorted each individual to make an immediate decision. As prophet of the dawning new age, his message had an insistence about it that gave ordinary day-to-day choices a far broader significance. Hence each person he encountered, whether personally or through his writings, faced Fox's call to decide about relatively minor matters that would determine the fate of the realm. As individuals elected to break "the bond of inequity," he exulted, its grip would inexorably lessen throughout society.[49] His approach is exemplified in *The Lamb's Officer*, published in 1659 at the very time when the regime of the Cromwells, father and son, was tottering and on its way into history. Addressing leaders of the religious establishment, this pamphlet demanded that priests and vicars plead "Guilty or not Guilty" to a seemingly endless series of loaded questions, which, not so incidentally, served to warn lay readers to be mindful of the insidious practices left behind from Rome's control of the church:

> Have you not been standing [by], when the martyrs, and prophets, and saints' blood has been drunk? . . . from this whore, the Church of Rome, have you not gotten tithes, Easter reckonings, midsummer dues, and glebe lands . . . ? did not the whore set up your schools and colleges, this false church, whereby you are made ministers and gave them names of Trinity College, Jesus College, Emanuel College . . . since the true church went into the wilderness? . . . has not all this swearing since Christ been set up by the false church, the Church of Rome? . . . have you not cast many into prison . . . until death? . . . and where did Christ or the apostles or the true church preach by the hour glass . . . ? are you not such as go in long robes, fashions and lusts of the world, with your ribbons and points, and double cuffs, and wearing gold rings . . . than like unto sober men that preach the gospel?[50]

Hence Fox's approach melded with a personal rigidity that enabled him, once he adopted a position, to force its implications to apply in a variety of situations and for a variety of purposes. For example, the first of his many recorded "openings"—his term for private revelations received from God—revealed that training at Oxford or Cambridge was not sufficient to make a person a minister. From then on, he had no use for the hirelings who took pay for doing what Jesus had commanded should be rendered freely. It made no difference whether such a professor ministered to a tiny dissenting congregation meeting in an airy barn up some isolated dale or preached in a massive gothic cathedral of the established church. Unless such a person obviously spoke with the authority of the living and still-present Christ, then that person was a pretender, full of deceit, and lacking authority.

Fox's rigidity did not apply, however, when it came to responding to threats to the religious order he had created. In this area he proved himself as sure-footed and agile as the wiliest Anglican bishop. When he was confronted with internal rebellion, led by fellow provincial, comrade, and close associate James Nayler, he moved too slowly to deal with the man himself, but he created a structure aimed at preventing anything like that rebellion from happening again. That the organizational structure he perfected worked also to rein in the free style of his followers gave an added fillip to his efforts. It also served to soften the criticism of opponents of the extremes at the edge of the movement—that too was to the good.

There were altogether too many hints of anarchism, or Ranterism, about the approach of allowing people to be guided by something as ineffable as the leadings of some spirit—a spirit of what?—whose wishes no one could document or prove. No wonder Fox's critics fumed and fulminated about the way his teachings loosened the traditional bonds that had held men and women together in a stable social order. Such critics—among them, the sober-minded and conscientious Essex clergyman Ralph Josselyn—sensed that the Quakers' lack of institutional loyalty and commitment served to undermine the social peace. In July 1655, after they first came to his area, Josselyn expressed the essence of the problem as he saw it: "[A]n infallible spirit once granted them, what lies may they not utter and what delusions may not poor men be given up unto?"[51]

Josselyn kept his misgivings within the closed covers of his diary. Others were not so circumspect, trumpeting the news of the Quaker threat far and wide, wherever there were concerned souls with the pittance needed to buy a pamphlet about current problems. Richard Baxter, certainly not usually considered to be an alarmist, wanted no part of the idea that one should wait for the spirit to reveal the truth, for it had already appeared. He recognized that newfangled ideas about freeing people from long-established restraints threatened stability. "I abhor any gospel or religion," he said pointedly in rejecting the idea of apostasy in the medieval church, "that was not made 1600 years ago at least."[52] A group of Baptists, themselves only a short half-step away from the same charge of Ranterism leveled against Fox and his Friends, saw the Quakers as "attempting to lay waste scriptures, churches, Christ, faith, hope, &c, and establish a paganism in England." That warning appeared on the title page of their pamphlet. Inside they rejected the notion that God had come to redeem his people by turning them away from outward teachers so he could teach them himself, even as they sneeringly pronounced anathemas on those who taught others simply to "believe," "love," and "do his will." "Hold fast to the authority of the scripture," they concluded.[53] Even Cromwell's son Henry, who might have been expected to take a longer view, saw the same pattern. "I think," he reported from Ireland in 1656, "their principles and practices are not very consistent with civil government. . . . Some think them to have no design, but I am not of that opinion."[54]

Fox could not answer all such attacks, but when he did he affirmed that Friends who sensed the "power of God in themselves and the spirit," did "know what order is."[55] In 1674, long after the movement had stabilized and turned from its original enthusiastic ways, he would still occasionally take note of people who said that Quakers favored no order. "No government among you," he exploded, "is there not? Yes, the government of Christ, and of the increase of his government there is no end."[56] Fox held that the order of the gospel, under the leadings of the spirit that gave it forth and the continuing counselor who was Christ, could mold a new community, one that could flourish without the usual leadership expected in a church. But that optimistic faith, as events unfolded, was not always to be.

Henry Cromwell wrote his opinion of the Quakers before the watershed Nayler affair occurred during the latter part of 1656. Had he waited nine months, he might have been less sanguine, for Nayler's apostasy thrust a tool into the hands of the Quakers' enemies and helped discredit them among safe and sane folk. More important for my purposes here, it brought Fox himself to the edge of the abyss where he could look straight into the stark potential of his preachments. Without formally repudiating anything he had previously taught, he began giving it a different gloss, shading it so that the startling tinge of ranterish anarchism would merge into the background and safely, he hoped, be hidden from view. The Nayler problem brought him face to face with the threatening possibilities of his own doctrine.

The best example of his post-Nayler thinking appeared in his Epistle 141, which he wrote sometime in 1657, on a topic that had nothing directly to do with theological matters at all. It involved an order for his followers to send accounts of their sufferings to London so the authorities might be informed of the kinds and degree of persecution the Children were enduring. In the process Fox etched out a theory of governing that he applied in this first instance to the regime of Oliver Cromwell. His letter revealed the theoretical underpinnings of his political ideas, but it was even more important for indicating how he wanted to go about solving the problem of authority within the religious community he was intent on preserving. George Fox was thereby carving out his niche as First Friend.

Instructing his Friends to collect their sufferings in each county, Fox told them to lay their accounts before the judges who, he said, "are sent forth from the head and heads of the nation, which nation or nations is to be governed as a family, in justice and truth, and judgment, and righteousness." Nations should be governed in the manner of a family—that was the central issue—and governed with justice and righteousness. Usually Fox was vague about matters like this, but this time he became more specific and detailed. The head of the nation, he went on, gave orders to the judges, "for they are all as his servants" to do his will. The judges then proceeded into the several counties, and the people therein, he said, "are as their families." In a descending order, the judges then gave orders to those below them—justices, sheriffs, bailiffs, constables—until the lowest ranking was reached and all had their orders and did them, for justice and righteousness' sake. All levels, down to the lowest, he explained, "are to look to their places as to their families." This hierarchical arrangement worked well only so long as all acted justly and equally with their families; the very fact that sufferings had to be collected and shown to the judges cried out dramatically that things did not always work as they were supposed to. And that failure underlined why the judges needed the accounts of Quaker sufferings, to call them back to their original mission and purpose. Once adequately warned, the judges would be obliged to act as parents, justly and righteously. And if they then did not, Fox warned, "God, who is just, is ready to plead their cause and to judge and cast out the unjust judges."[57]

This analysis, however well thought through, did not solve the dilemma of the relation between the individual and authority, and it put immensely more power in the hands of human rulers than Fox or his followers had previously been willing to grant. One can look at it two ways, from the standpoint of a ruler limited by the necessity to keep those below content enough to want to remain members of the family, or from the standpoint of a member of the family who was no longer entirely free to go wherever the spirit might lead. In many ways anachronistic in political terms, Fox's assertion certainly did not free the individual in any complete sense, but neither was it totally restrictive. The broad standards of justice and righteousness were not automatically applicable and had to be used in specific situations, but they remained always available for individuals to use to judge their rulers. This expansion of authority was obviously reflective of the spirit of a people who had beheaded their king less than a decade earlier.

What was applicable to the larger community might also be useful for the internal workings of the Society of Friends, especially after it was beset with dissension. The implication that authority descended from the head, to those below delegated to act as parents to the family, could be invaluable for imposing order among the Children. The unorganized and potentially chaotic meetings that had arisen since the first gatherings in the late 1640s could, with some such theory as this in operation, be coordinated to allow the good of the whole, not individual or regional differences, to receive primary consideration. Fox expressed a theory easily adapted and utilized to assure structure enough to enable his Children to survive as a group but not so much as to be stifling. Almost none of the other dissident sects of the period proved able to do this. If an institution's survival is the standard that best defines success, then Fox was eminently successful with this balancing. Lurches—indeed, splits and splintering—would occur in the future of course, but the theoretical base was in place to deal with such problems. It was Fox's major achievement.

9

Out of the North
All Ill Comes Forth

To judge from published reaction to the push of George Fox's Children of the Truth southward, something resembling a new Pict invasion seemed in the offing, and this time no Hadrian's Wall rose to block the incursion. Fox's movement provoked fears in London and encouraged defenders of the established ecclesiastical and political orders to push the populace to reject it. Francis Higginson, a Westmorland minister who watched the Children operate in his county, explained how "Satan's seeds-men" had "crept" into the north the previous summer and seduced multitudes to embrace devilish doctrines.[1] William Prynne, having lost his ears because of two libel convictions, wrote a pamphlet that fulminated against Quakers as "the spawn of Romish Frogs, Jesuits, and Franciscan Friars" who had grown up in the very section of the country where Catholics had always posed a threat.[2] A posthumous edition of Ephraim Pagett's famous *Heresiography* included an attack on the Friends: readers were told that Quakers were an upstart branch of the Anabaptists, "thickest set in the north parts," the dregs of conceited and ignorant common people and prey to those opposing "all laws, magistrates, ancient worship, prayers and sacraments" and subverting the present "holy age, the age of perfection, zeal, and liberty."[3] An anonymous author dubbed them "anti-Scripturalists" and "Libertines" who had begun in the north and now seemed poised to extend their community and their lust for other men's wives southward.[4] A news sheet jibed that a goose wrote in her will, "I give my soul to the sister Quakers, on condition they damm it not, as they had done their own."[5] A broadside shouted that thirty blasphemies flourished in the city and that "Ranters, Quakers, Seekers" broached their heresies daily.[6]

The appearance of pamphlets written by Fox and Nayler, the movement's chief figures,[7] clearly designed to introduce their sect to citizens of the capital city, indicated planning was going forward. Both the tone and language of these pamphlets illustrated some of the reasons the Quaker invasion was looked upon with such apprehension by the establishment. These spokesmen for the Children literally promised to change the way things had been done in the city straddling the Thames. Nayler explained that murmurings against the Children had reached the ears of the Lord, who wanted critics to know that one had been raised up who would "plant in the wilderness and make it a land of springs for the poor and needy to drink at, where . . . the little one shall feed safely."[8] Fox's pamphlet, free of the strained metaphors that usually marred his writing, appeared in London bookstalls in December 1653. Addressing scoffers and scorners who lied and defrauded to amass gold and silver in what he labeled "this great city Sodom and Gomorrah," he promised that their days were numbered.[9] In his angry Amos-like outcry he urged that those he called the "great ones," rising like high mountains and hills, "must be threshed and beaten down."[10]

The first missionary Children to arrive in London, Isabel Buttery and a female companion, came early in 1654, handing out copies of one of Fox's epistles, perhaps the very one just referred to. They quickly contacted an army captain, Amor Stoddard, whom Fox had met seven years earlier during his travels in the Midlands, and began to make converts.[11] They were soon followed by Francis Howgill and Edward Burrough. London was "abominable," Howgill wrote back, "nothing but great words, but filthy deceit."[12] Baptists worried that thousands of Children would roll out of the north and shatter their churches.[13] A broadside of the day listed Quakers, along with Ranters, among the thirty different varieties of blasphemers who daily spread their lies.[14] It is safe to say that the foundations of the new Cromwell regime, into its second six months, did not immediately quiver, although a hall large enough to hold the crowds flocking to Quaker meetings was hard to find.[15] Parliamentarians came to see the show and were astonished by the way these strange Quakers shook, making their chairs and stools tremble.[16] It was their most obvious characteristic.

Of more concern to those in authority were Quaker inroads in the army ranks and evidence from the Midlands that the Children's preaching was feeding unrest. When Cromwell became Lord Protector after disbanding the Barebones Parliament, many soldiers refused to take the oath of allegiance to him and had to be discharged, and others were shifted to Scotland.[17] Riding a borrowed horse, Fox entered Leicestershire, stopping for a large meeting at Swannington on January 3, 1655.[18] A number of Friends, perhaps as many as two hundred, from various parts of the country—Bristol, York, Cambridge, and London—were present. Giles Calvert, a London printer with close ties to the movement, attended the Swannington meeting and returned to London with much new Quaker literature to print. Apparently a number of Baptists and Ranters also attended, and some were converted on the spot.

The authorities' main fear, however, was the subversive ripple the gathering sent through the general population. The visitors proved an insolent lot, disturbing area ministers on Sunday and bluntly telling people that, as two government informants reported, if they "will have their priests, they must shortly maintain them with clubs." By the Quakers' "words of ill favor," the agents went on, "profane persons are confirmed in their atheism, cavaliers encouraged and heightened in their expectations, godly people discontented." When word came that a rebel arms cache had been uncovered at nearby Burton-upon-Trent, the Children scattered, some reportedly sneaking away under cover of a cold and rainy night. Stories that the Quakers secreted pistols under their coats and other rumors were circulating; obviously the movement excited suspicion and fear of subversion.[19]

Fox decided to visit his parents at Drayton-in-the-Clay. As Fox moved through the area, word of his coming spread, giving his clerical opposition time to collect their forces. On Saturday, January 12, after holding a series of successful meetings in the vicinity of his home, Fox arrived in Drayton itself and discovered that his old nemesis Nathaniel Stephens had recruited the staunch Presbyterian incumbent from the adjacent parish of Witherly. They wanted to dispute with Fox. As it turned out, two disputes were held a week apart, with the second led by no less than eight clergymen; both turned into what must have looked and sounded like a bearbaiting or a rowdy stage play. Fox reiterated two main points: he attacked his ministerial foes because they were unable to affirm that they possessed the same spirit that gave forth the Scriptures, and he argued that taking tithes was a denial of Christ, who had come to end such acts of compulsion. He may have gotten the best of the rhetorical argument and the biblical exegesis, but his opponents certainly outdid him in physical combat. Stephens's wife and son, joined by a crowd of more than a hundred, entered the fray. The mob tried to force Fox into the church, stuffed their hands and gloves in his mouth, and once, while shouts of blasphemer and heretic echoed around the churchyard, pushed him down and then piled on. So many rumors about these events circulated around the Midlands that a Fox disciple published a lengthy account of the two brouhahas to defend the Quakers' leader.[20]

Leicestershire exhibited, as one outside observer quickly saw, "much opposition," but Fox stood up well under the pressure. He was determined to test his home county. He rode back northward to Swannington, site of the general meeting that had sparked fears of Quaker involvement in plots against the government. After another large gathering, which again attracted people from far afield, he returned to Drayton. Stephens showed up that night with a band of troopers who would have arrested Fox had he not been in his parents' home. They did take down the names of all those with him as a not-so-subtle warning.[21] There is nothing to indicate what his offense was, but it likely involved a violation of Cromwell's February proclamation making it illegal to interrupt Christian ministers or assemblies.[22]

It would not have been out of character for Fox to try to tease the authorities or provoke them into taking action against him. This time he got his wish after parading through the county town and then moving on to Whetstone nearby for yet another general conclave. At such meetings the Children customarily invaded and disrupted nearby church services. Seventeen soldiers were waiting for Fox; they took him into custody and escorted him back to Leicester. He informed his captors and a group of bystanders that God's Son had been revealed in him, giving him power to understand their condition, and that he was one with God and Christ.[23] The commander of the troops inquired sarcastically if this vaunted "light of Christ" had not been the same light that led Judas to betray Jesus, an interpretation Fox naturally rejected. The officer did offer to release Fox if he would promise to return to Drayton and not attend any more meetings. Fox spurned that proposal lest he appear to be admitting guilt for acts God called him to do. At 6:00 A.M. an armed escort marched him off the hundred miles to the capital.[24]

Fox's arrest indicated that the authorities were worried about the rising tide of discontent the Children represented. Cromwell's decision to dismiss the Barebones Parliament had alienated the social radicals who hoped against all evidence that there was still a chance for ushering in the millennium. Then hardly a month before Fox was seized, a newly energized Lord Protector, increasingly irate because of parliamentary meddling with his plans, announced that he could shorten Parliament's statutory five-month minimum sitting by counting lunar months instead of calendar months. Such a move could hardly cheer those who thought they glimpsed Charles I's ghost stalking Whitehall.[25] The French ambassador wrote his superiors in Paris to tell them about fears in London concerning the increase of Quakers across the land. Pretending that sectarian divisions would prevent them from getting an upper hand sounded to him like whistling in the dark.[26]

Meanwhile, Fox was brought southward. Allowed by his guard to proclaim the day of the Lord in villages and towns along the way, he arrived in London at the end of February and was housed in the Mermaid Inn at Charing Cross. By way of introduction, the press trumpeted stories of how he had seduced Margaret Fell and attracted other women with ribbons that made them rush to him when they wore them. Though in custody, he was allowed to visit London meetings that had sprung up in the past year and a half. When Fox appeared in Whitehall's courtyard, the crowds noted his unfashionable long hair and spread tales that he wore silver buttons.[27] He received so many visitors that the innkeeper complained. Informed that Fox had arrived safely, Cromwell requested an immediate assurance that he would not take up arms against his government.[28] On March 5, the same day he got word of what the Protector desired, Fox composed the first public version of what would become known among his followers as the "Peace Testimony."

"I do deny," he begin, "the carrying or drawing of any carnal sword against any or against you Oliver Cromwell." Thus, the politically astute Fox sought to reassure the nation's leader that he, and by extension the Children of the Light, represented no armed threat to the status quo. He also indicated that while he was personally opposed to participating in war, he recognized and accepted the authority of the state to use the sword. It was, he wrote, "a terror to the evil doers who act contrary to the light of the lord Jesus Christ." "The magistrate," he said bluntly, "bears not the sword in vain." Unlike plotters such as Fifth Monarchists, Fox rejected "wicked inventions of men and murderous plots," but he did so not because he opposed the ends they sought as much as the means they used. He favored "establishing of righteousness and cleansing the land of evil doers," but these goals would be achieved by dwelling in the light "that is immortal [and] that fades not away." Left unsaid was whether he would endorse establishing a righteous state—minus plotting, of course—that would turn its carnal sword against evil. Hence Fox was not a pacifist in the modern sense that he utterly rejected participating in all wars and violent conflicts. He could not imagine himself bearing the sword, at least under present circumstances—he spurned a "mortal crown" like the one some wanted Cromwell to put on—but he also recognized that someone must wield the sword against evildoers.

His references to himself also underscored what can only have been an intentional ambiguity in his letter. If Cromwell reflected on it as he read it, then he realized that the sword Fox laid down in a worldly cause might be used by one seeking to achieve righteousness, even perhaps someone named Fox. Fox signed the letter, "who is of the world called George Fox, who has a new name which the world knows not," and in the text he referred to himself as "whom the world calls George Fox, who is the son of God." This practice of repudiating an old name was not unusual among early Friends. It reflected a desire, upon a person's convincement, to be totally divorced from older, worldly ways and to assume a new identity.[29] But Fox dared venture that his own new identity was as son of God. Here he was not disclosing this information at small meetings of the Children but announcing it to the Lord Protector himself, the one ultimately responsible for enforcing the country's laws against blasphemy. His letter to Cromwell, moreover, implied that his new status at the least allowed him to hold the present regime to a divine standard, at the most suggested that the immortal crown he claimed took precedence over the mortal one that Cromwell figuratively wore, thus permitting him to establish righteousness by using the sword to cleanse the land of its evil.[30]

In an essay he had written two years earlier, addressed "to Margaret Fell and every other friend who are raised to a discerning," he explained that "according to the Spirit I am the son of God." Though the serpent of evil spoke in the first nature, the seed, "which seed is Christ," and which he possessed, would "reign over all the world and comprehend all the world." He described all who received this word, presumably those raised to the proper level of discernment, as gods: "I say unto you: you are gods."[31] These inflammatory words, particularly in an age of great unrest and upheaval, when everything formerly nailed down seemed to be coming loose, explain why Fox and his followers were dogged with charges of blasphemy. Statements like these bothered his critics because he was encouraging ordinary men and women to think too highly of themselves, thereby denying the class arrangement of English society.

As a matter of plain fact, of course, Fox said little that was not contained in the Bible, but he gave it a twist that was not usual in a day when the authorities often chained the Scriptures to the pulpit in church. Merely applying the Bible's promises and standards to everyday relationships was radical enough, but Fox went further: he proposed that at least some people might be elevated to the level of sons of God and thereafter would have the power to judge others, including their betters. (It spoke volumes that when Fox informed the outside world of the disputes at Drayton six weeks earlier he stressed his argument that any person filled with the spirit might legitimately judge all things, including tithes, established ministers, and the use of the magistrate's sword.)[32] Thus when he talked of becoming a "son of God," he meant that anyone infused with the spirit and dwelling in the light, as the human Jesus obviously had, could be like him. Anyone believing and acting on that assurance would truly be emboldened with an idea that would be the source of great power. Fox's version of empowerment helps to explain why middling sorts of common people, those who sensed that their influence within society was not allowed to be commensurate with their abilities, readily converted to the new movement.

This reality, from the standpoint of those in positions of power and authority, was all the more reason for Cromwell to take the measure of this shrewd outlander. Fox had just recently addressed another letter to the Lord Protector that, in typical fashion, combined threats with a subtle effort to win the ruler's favor. On the one hand, he warned that Cromwell must turn aside from his craftiness and subtlety if he wanted to prosper. On the other, he advised the nation's leader, who had only within the year ended a war with the Dutch, that divine power could bring other nations to quake and shudder whenever they proved to be outside God's counsel. His meaning was clear: "[S]tand single to the Lord; . . . you will feel his blessing in your generation."[33]

So Cromwell decided to see Fox immediately, setting the date for their meeting on March 9, only days after he first heard from the prisoner. Perhaps he was intrigued by his correspondent's mystical religion, one that certainly gave him a strong feeling of inner security. Maybe he could find something in Fox that would allow him to square that old circle of balancing the subjectivism of a person's inner experiences and the need for outward authority, something the Protector could use in his dealings with the hordes of sectarians who bombarded him with one complaint or another. He was certainly not above a Machiavellian touch of playing one sectarian off against another. Cromwell also had an interest in divine signs, and Fox surely claimed to have received his share.

In any event, Fox's captors escorted him early Friday morning to the refurbished Whitehall Palace a short distance up the Thames from Charing Cross. The Cromwells had furnished their new living quarters in royal fashion—the only style Englishmen knew for their rulers—with some of the same ornamentation the late monarch had once enjoyed. Tables were laid for every manner of person, from "His Highness" right on down through chaplains and strangers to "Inferiors and Subservants."[34] His recollection tinged with awe, Fox explained that he was taken in to see the Protector even before the grand personage was dressed; it was a signal honor to be allowed to visit one's betters while they were about their toilet. After wishing peace on Whitehall, the visitor repeated what he had said in his last letter. He admonished his host to order his rule by God's will. Indicating that his major concern was the Children's lack of tolerance for those who disagreed with them, Cromwell reminded Fox that they were always quarreling with the ministers. Fox countered by blaming the priests for refusing to accept the truth, preaching for "filthy lucre," and being "covetous and greedy like the dumb dogs." He also tried to explain the difference between those who harkened to the true teacher within and those he dubbed "teachers of the world."

The conversation continued for a good part of the morning. Cromwell was cagey and deliberately wanted his guest to leave with the impression that he agreed with him, even though he refused to pledge himself specifically to anything. He formally released his prisoner and then, as other guests arrived and milled about, invited him to remain to eat, but Fox refused and returned to the Mermaid; Cromwell had not indicated at which table Fox should sit.[35] Such a fete, needless to say, was not the kind of event Fox normally lent his presence to.

At liberty once more, after about two weeks' confinement, Fox resumed his preaching, but he avoided any violation of Cromwell's proclamation against invading churches and interrupting their ministers. Again, as when he was in London a decade earlier, he found the atmosphere exhilarating, and he sought out potential opponents with the zeal of the true believer. He participated in debates with Baptists and the Ranter elements that naturally hovered around the fringes of radical sectarians. He traveled to Waltham Abbey in Essex, a few miles from London, where he preached successfully despite the attacks of the ubiquitous "rude" people who dogged his tracks; this time they broke the windows where he was holding forth. He also targeted soldiers for special attention, going to Whitehall and preaching to Cromwell's guard, winning some converts, including a few people from the Protector's household.[36]

Fox recalled that the Presbyterians, Independents, and Baptists were "in a great rage" because so many people were attracted to the Children. That memory might be laid to a tendency to exaggerate were it not that other evidence points to worries occasioned by the Quakers' success. Richard Baxter, no mean authority when it came to keeping a finger on the religious pulse, published a pamphlet warning mainstream Protestants, such as Independents and Presbyterians, to ignore the Quakers at their peril. Apparently some moderate Protestants took the attitude that since the Children were emptying Anabaptist and separatist conventicles—both desiring no established state church—they could be overlooked. A myopic attitude, thought Baxter: "I had far rather that men continue Separtists and Anabaptists than turn Quakers or plain apostates." Their pride, what we might call "cocksureness," undercut the received order of things. He warned a hypothetical young man attracted by the Children's seeming lack of pride—after all, they wore no lace and eschewed ruffled cuffs—that their spiritual pride was the most killing: they damned ministers who styled themselves "masters," they set themselves above sixteen hundred years of church history, and they considered themselves perfect. When he aimed directly at the Quakers, Baxter took the same approach. The Quakers' demand that ministers possess the same infallible spirit as the holy men who wrote the Scriptures, he sniffed, sounded like "the croaking of your papist guides in that word 'infallible'; that's the pillar of their kingdom, . . . that their church is infallible."[37]

Baxter's chagrin and anger were justified, for Fox gave no quarter. Those who professed Christ but refused to heed his present-day emissaries who taught that he had come now and was manifest, were like the Jews who stoned Jesus, not for his acts but for his alleged blasphemy. And then, skillfully and astutely, he moved directly to address the ties that bound the nation's clergy to the established order, all the way up to anyone who aspired to wear a crown. We, agents of the now-present Christ and speaking his word, he proclaimed, "will make you bare and discover your secrets and take off your crown and take away your mantle and your veil and strip you of your clothes that your nakedness may appear, and how you sit deceiving the nation." In his best millenarian fashion, Fox announced that "the Lord is setting up his throne and his crown, throwing down the crown of man." And echoing Baxter with a new twist, he warned the wise and prudent ones who held forth in their big churches and could not see what the simple Children knew: "[T]he Lord . . . turns the wicked out of the kingdom."[38] These people from the north were something to be reckoned with.

While Fox promised that God would turn the wicked out, he had not given up completely on those, wicked or no, who controlled the machinery of the government. Neither had he indicated just how God would operate in this instance. That soon became clearer. Since 1646, when Presbyterianism for all statutory purposes had become the national church, the authorities had been casting about for some method to exercise control over ministers in local parishes. In the old days bishops discharged that function, but no Presbyterian could acquiesce in returning to such a detested prelatical practice. Yet enforced establishment of a Presbyterian classis would hardly conciliate dissenters ranging from Anglicans on the right to Quakers on the left. Thus in 1652 Parliament created the Committee for the Propagation of the Gospel with the authority to oversee local parishes and their ministers. Two years later, in March 1654, the Committee of Triers, a typically pragmatic Cromwellian solution, emerged. Composed of both laity and clergy, this body was designed to certify whether a given minister could minister in a particular local church. It was not a body, to say the least, whose authority would have been accepted by Fox and the Children.

Yet Fox recommended in a letter to Cromwell and the Triers that they root out the bad and plant the right kind of ministers. He did not say explicitly that Quakers wanted to fill vacant pulpits, but the standards he proposed would have excluded all but the Friends and the most radical sectarians, leaving the ordained clergy out in the cold. Given such an approach, his critics might be forgiven for thinking that the Quakers were a threat to their established order. Perhaps he only toyed with the hope that this new committee could be a vehicle for his Children to ride on to churchly preferment. Nonetheless, the Fox letter suggests that his brief stay in London, the country's center of power, was already giving him tantalizing ideas about how to achieve the future kingdom.

Thus he advised the Triers to exclude all who had already labored in the vineyard and taught for money, were covetous, loved themselves, had the form, but denied the power, of godliness, drank wine, were called master, spoke Greek or Latin, or took tithes and midsummer dues. Fox even named names: he instanced a Lincolnshire vicar who had had a thatcher jailed for thirty-eight weeks because he had not paid six shillings in tithes. The all-inclusive nature of his listing may have been his way of needling the authorities; more likely, he used it to point out that the only people fully qualified to be ministers by biblical standards were his own followers.[39]

One other matter needed attention before Fox was ready to leave Sodom and pursue his evangelistic activities in the south. The Children decided to dispatch missionaries to Europe and to New England, both places where some Quakers had already gone on their own.[40] A fundraising effort was begun almost immediately. The large amounts of money raised for this purpose—nearly £450, or $45,000 in today's currency by the end of the next year[41]—underscored both the generous commitment of these new Friends and also something of their middling economic status. Some grumbling from the north about how such sums were administered was heard, although Fox, who received no funds from the central treasury, escaped the criticism.[42]

To prepare the way for the missionaries, Fox penned a letter to the rulers of all countries, more specifically to the pope and the kings of Spain and France, both staunch Catholics, the latter with a worrisome Protestant minority. The letter expressed the hope that the Children would not be persecuted and warned that God would judge the crowned heads by how they treated the expeditionary force: "[B]e swift to hear and slow to speak and slower to persecute," for the Lord's "fire is going forth to burn up the wicked, which will leave neither root nor branch."[43] Although he would give relatively little personal attention to missionary activities outside England for the next few years, Fox gradually became convinced that only a missionary effort would bring the countries of Europe to gravitate in England's orbit. Thus near the end of Cromwell's reign he condemned the Protector for trifling about small things when, as he put it, "the king of France should have bowed his neck under you [and] the pope should have withered as in winter."[44]

London was now Fox's base of operations, from which he traveled as far as eighty miles to visit the towns and villages of the surrounding countryside, northeasterward to East Anglia, southeastward to Kent, occasionally as far north as Leicestershire, west to Berkshire. Whenever he returned to London, he often stayed at Robert Dring's home in Moorfields. Dring, a linen draper and one of the most influential of the early London converts, allowed his house to be used as a mail drop, as the site of one of the city meetings, and as a place in which the Friends held conferences and strategy sessions. Indeed, the fact that the leading Quaker evangelists gathered at his house on Mondays suggests that already the famous Second Day Morning Meeting, the body of ministers based in London that gradually came to set the agenda for the movement, was emerging (see chapter 13).[45]

By mid-March Fox was in Bedfordshire, traveling with Alexander Parker, a well-educated Yorkshireman who had become his frequent companion. Practically everywhere they stopped, they searched out two groups, Baptists and soldiers. Probably the most important convert was the Baptist minister Samuel Fisher, a graduate of Oxford boasting an annual income of £280, who was converted on June 6. Fisher exhibited a most creative streak when he insisted that on a reliability scale the Bible ranked far below the spirit's leadings for the believer; that was Fox's position too, but unlike Fox Fisher could support this idea by means of conventional scholarship.[46] His newly converted wife was practically beside herself, exclaiming that they could now discern "between flesh and spirit, distinguish spiritual teaching from fleshly [teaching]." Fox was at a meeting in one town or another in Sussex or Kent nearly every day in June. As he had done in the north, he tried to arrive on market days when large crowds could hear him proclaim the day of the Lord.[47]

On June 30, 1655, Fox reached Reading, a place noted for all manner of heresies. He stayed at the well-appointed home of Thomas and Ann Curtis. He was a former army captain and wool draper, she was the daughter of the high sheriff of Bristol; both were accustomed to rich, bejeweled attire. After being convinced—they encountered the Children in Bristol—they ripped the gold buttons off their garments, and Ann exchanged her jewelry and rich gowns for plainer dress. The Curtises opened their home to two Fell daughters and George Bishop, another parliamentary captain who arrived from Bristol to meet Fox. Ann Curtis told Fox and the visitors that all she possessed was theirs. Fox returned their affection by including the Curtises among his closest associates. Many of the town heretics, Baptists and Ranters, came to the meeting and stayed to argue.[48]

Fox now shifted his attention north and east of London, into Essex, Suffolk, Norfolk, and Cambridgeshire. The same patterns obtained as in his other trips: he sought out Baptists, soldiers, and people simply tired of the established church. Other Quaker missionaries had come to the region nearly two years earlier, so Fox possessed the names of converts and others friendly to his sect. The entire area, flat as a dinner plate and easy to ride across, teemed with neat little villages set off by rows of trees. Churches were so numerous that one could often see the steeples of five or six from a given spot.[49] Nearly as ubiquitous if not so visible were underground cells of the mystically inspired Family of Love, a secret, illegal sect that since the previous century had challenged both official theology and church practices. Vaguely communistic, it held that Christ had restored the members to a pre-Adamic state. One widow, perhaps influenced by the Familists, when instructed to walk in the ordinances of God, replied straightforwardly that she could find no comfort in that and would consider herself a hypocrite if she did, "for God dwells in me, and I in him."[50] A woman such as this was obviously a potential Friend. Willing to build on such sentiments, Fox did not discourage the impression that his movement was a kind of Family of Love. After a lengthy session with Fox, a youth of twenty exalted in being part of what he termed a "family of love," of which he considered the leading Friend the head.[51]

Opposition seemed to be mounting in the eastern sections of the country, some of it based on stories of the Children's sexual conduct. Stories circulated about a Quaker who attempted to bugger a mare near Colchester; a bit of doggerel cracked, "Now alas what hope, / Of converting the Pope, / When a Quaker turns Italian. . . ."[52] Christopher Atkinson, a Quaker missionary from Westmorland, caused a scandal by pursuing a woman not his wife. Local Friends required a confession of Atkinson and then disowned him.[53] Supporters of Cromwell in his own eastern region watched the Quaker onslaught and worried that if he did not take firmer action against the internal threat then his shaky regime might collapse; looking anxiously for some firmer action, they were cheered by the jailing of some Children in Cogshall in July.[54] The help Fox received from army personnel in the area, particularly officers, in contrast to the opposition of town officials, suggested that the Quakers were catalysts for disagreement between local desire to keep the lid on and London's willingness to be tolerant. In Cambridge university students were especially rowdy, a situation Fox laid to his attacks on their trade of preaching, hence giving his religious message an economic twist.[55]

Things were also tightening up back in London, even if local leaders in eastern villages thought otherwise. When he returned to the capital Fox found that vigorous attacks on the separated churches, dissenting congregations whose members convened outside the established religious order,[56] were no longer as easy to make as before. Such succinct advice to his clergy opponents that they should "scum off the filth and come from under the thick clay" had produced the inevitable backlash.[57] In April Cromwell issued a proclamation requiring people suspected of ties with Catholics to swear an oath abjuring any connections with Rome or its doctrines. Since Quakers refused to take oaths of any kind, this regulation was now turned against the Children, widely considered by many to be secret papists. Soon less than a dozen of the leading missionaries in the south remained free.[58] Hence Fox correctly saw more ominous implications than locating hidden Catholics when he charged that the Lord Protector had been taken in by locals who did not like Quaker attacks on gaming, cheating, and deceitful merchandizing. Turn the sword against such evildoers, he advised, and aim not at innocent ones who stood athwart priestly aims to "take money now of poor people."[59]

Attacks from local authorities continued, almost without letup. Traveling back to the Midlands, Fox found many Friends imprisoned. He visited Evesham in Worcestershire where a number of Quakers were jailed, and he himself barely avoided punishment in the town's newly built stocks by galloping out of town only a couple of steps ahead of an aggressive magistrate. His horse served him equally well in Warwick. There one member of a mob lunged for his mount's bridle but fell under the horse's hoofs when the horse tossed his head. Fox sped away through the crowded market just ahead of a volley of stones and sticks. His contacts with soldiers this time were few, with Baptists more, details that may have accounted for the opposition he met.[60]

After such forays to the Midlands, Fox returned again to London, both to visit and to rest. He surveyed evangelistic activities in the capital and was elated at what he called "the prosperity of truth" there;[61] already six or seven meetings convened every first day.[62] But he decided not to remain in the city. Perhaps he had an incurable wanderlust or perhaps he simply did not like large cities. More likely, he decided that he was not needed as much in London as in the west, the only part of the country he had not yet visited. Whether he realized it or not, his close associates certainly recognized that something in his style did not go over as well in London as elsewhere. Even when he did succeed with an audience, he had to work so hard that he wore out his voice and stamina.[63]

One obvious reason for the success of the Friends in London was James Nayler, whose many talents seemed to blossom in the cosmopolitan capital after his arrival early in July 1655. As soon as he appeared in what he termed "this great and wicked city where abomination is set," services exploded and people crowded into meeting places. In fact, after being on the scene but two weeks, he was crowing about the way the power in one meeting he attended gave strength to the people to withstand a hail of stones that smashed through the building's windows.[64] Like Fox, he welcomed any opportunity to speak to members of the government, holding one session at a private home where a number of members of the Protector's court showed up. Also like Fox, he found Baptists and soldiers especially responsive to his message.[65] During one meeting among Baptists in Broad Street, a woman looked on astonished as he got the best of a disputant who pleaded illness so Nayler would leave him alone.[66]

From all outward indications, Fox and Nayler got along perfectly, just like any peers who had worked and traveled together off and on for three years. An early convert to the Children and an accomplished speaker and writer, as well as a creative thinker, Nayler had an outstanding reputation both inside and outside the movement. Some ranked him with Fox. Anthony Pearson, a judge who joined the Friends, clearly saw the two as equals.[67] Francis Howgill wrote from Cork that he owed Fox and Nayler his life as one "subject unto you in the Lord, as unto fathers who take care of the family of God."[68] Edward Burrough considered Nayler worthy of "double honor for his work's sake."[69] William Dewsbury, who had an opportunity to watch both Fox and Nayler when they came to Northampton in August, stood back and marveled at the way Nayler "confounded the deceit" of his mixed Presbyterian-Independent-Baptist audience; it was broken to pieces for all to see, he concluded. Fox's accomplishments, if any, got barely a mention.[70]

Unlike many Quaker evangelists, Nayler did not have to disrupt other services to attract public attention. Less than a month after arriving in London he actually received invitations from leaders of dissenting congregations anxious to dispute with one so able and increasingly well known.[71] From his ready pen flowed answer after answer to frequent pamphlet attacks on the Friends. His best-known antagonist was Richard Baxter, and Nayler gave as good as he received in his pamphlet war with Baxter. The number of his responses placed him in the forefront of all the other defenders of the new faith in the next year.[72] Well could he proclaim joyously to Margaret Fell in November that God's "name is becoming very lovely to some, very terrible to others, mightily does it spread."[73]

The radiant Nayler was more than a mere polemicist, and he partially eclipsed Fox in the sophisticated capital. Some people, Friends as well as outsiders, looked on Fox as a bit "strange"—a word used by a close observer and companion— and wondered at the way other Quakers tended to be quiet in his presence and defer to him during meetings.[74] In personal debate Nayler was quick and intelligent. His writings were incisive and polished, whereas Fox in his writings tended to plod and stumble. If not as charismatic, Nayler still attracted a bevy of followers of an intense type, people who practically worshiped him as the harbinger of a new age. They were willing to follow him anywhere and to do practically anything to demonstrate their commitment. Some of the most vocal of these acolytes were women, and this fact led detractors, then and later, to see an insidious influence at work: either he had some mysterious hold over these women or they themselves were temptresses using their wiles to turn his head.[75] Even Fox, who had his own share of female admirers and was noted for a lack of prejudice against women, stooped to using this tactic. To Nayler he lectured, "pluck in your horns, James, and push not against the lambs."[76]

With Fox traveling, a vacuum opened within the leadership. No written rules governed the organization because it was a kind of community of equals, all committed to the same goals and having the interests of the group at heart. Each person's different abilities served the Society of Friends as a whole. Hence it was the most natural thing in the world for the acclaim Nayler garnered to reenforce the view that his talents redounded to the young sect's benefit. The rather free and uninhibited way the organization had worked up to this point gave a wide scope to each Friend's abilities and contributed to the phenomenal early success of the movement. In short, the hands-off policy worked well so long as all agreed on common goals, but it also could produce a many-headed leadership, with too many people going off in too many different directions all at once. Fox had not had to confront challenges to his overall authority from within the center of the movement, so he really did not know how to respond. Looking back on the situation, Fox sensed, as early as the spring of 1655 before Nayler's arrival in London, that something about his friend was different and vaguely troubling, but he could not put his finger on it. Unable to speak to Nayler about such nebulous misgivings, perhaps thinking they were misplaced, he left for the west country late in December 1655.[77]

The question of the leadership was thus left open. Until this point, no one had been formally endowed with authority, the movement having operated by a kind of tacit agreement that Fox's judgment would normally prevail. Thus, for example, in February 1654, John Camm, one of the early northern converts, had, as he put it, "a drawing" that he and Francis Howgill should proceed southward. He did the usual thing and checked with Fox, who told him to go with speed but explained that Howgill was slated to go into Northumberland. Camm accepted that decision as the way things ought to be.[78] Thomas Aldam, another early convert, did not doubt that Fox had the authority to approve books and dispatch evangelists where he saw fit.[79] Disciples also saw him as the obvious person to answer critical attacks on the Children.[80] He was expected to mediate disputes between his followers and to judge who was right.[81] The surviving record indicates that Fox freely gave orders to the itinerants about where they should go, and they usually obeyed him.[82] Thus by 1655 outside observers of the movement regarded "nimble mercurialist Fox" as the movement's chief speaker and leader.[83]

But even as first Friend Fox did not entirely overshadow Nayler, who remained a pivotal figure. Because of his obvious leadership abilities, others naturally looked to him for guidance. Edward Burrough wanted Nayler to look over a paper he had written, "lest some words be imperfect," and as late as July 1656 he was still asking Nayler to review his epistles.[84] Nayler felt free to command Burrough and Howgill to return to London to help with the large throngs that continued to crowd meetings there.[85] After the disquieted Fox left for the west, Nayler remained the most prominent Friend in the city, recognized as such by both insiders and outsiders. Various separated congregations vied for him to put in an appearance, and a lieutenant colonel's followers demanded that he perform a miracle to prove his divine calling. Burrough, John Bolton, and Gerrard Roberts all testified that Nayler's ministry was quite serviceable and publicly supported him.[86] Despite whatever misgivings he had, and as late as May 1656, Fox chose Nayler to go to Yorkshire to meet with some Friends who could not get along with each other. Nayler pledged to go "with speed" but soon returned, for, he said, "I am not free of this place."[87]

It is still not entirely clear what was at the root of Nayler's problem and the movement's problem with him. From all accounts,[88] Nayler's head was turned by his enthusiastic supporters, many of them women. Becoming increasingly unstable, he could not, and did not want to, control their actions. He then broke under the pressures of official repression and imprisonment. Still, his actions differed only in degree and not in kind from those of fellow believers, including Fox himself. Certainly few obvious differences, none of a theological nature, separated Fox and Nayler. The two had been involved in the movement together almost from the beginning, shared many days and nights of traveling, and co-authored pamphlets and epistles.

The first evidence of differences involved the question of what tactics imprisoned Friends should use to win their freedom. Zealous local officials often used a writ of outlawry to coerce recalcitrant Quakers into cooperating with the legal system. Once under such a writ, defendants could be locked away until they purged themselves of contempt for refusing to swear an oath, remove an offending hat, pay tithes, or whatever the offense, petty or major. The most damaging punishment, especially for well-off Friends, was confiscation of the property of anyone judicially designated an outlaw.[89] One such Quaker outlaw, the strong-minded Robert Widders of Upper Kellet in Lancashire, had an estate large enough to be assessed fines of £143 for not paying tithes.[90] Incarceration in the Lancaster jail in 1654 gave him ample reason to be concerned about the sacrifice of his extensive holdings over a matter of principle. Fox recommended that Widders and two others free themselves of the contempt charge, which was, as he saw it, only a technicality. Money, Fox reasoned, "was but earth as would free them from the outward imprisonment." To languish in prison for such a triviality seemed foolish to Fox, so he advised the prisoners to purge themselves of the contempt and then make an issue of the real charges. Nayler did not approve of such moderation, averring that no Friend should cooperate at all with the government and its persecution of the Children.[91]

This disagreement over tactics, however, was hardly enough to explain the deterioration in relationships between the two leaders. Once Fox began to deal with the affair openly, he detailed some specifics but, as was his wont, extrapolated them into broader and less concrete issues. He emphasized two principal problems with Nayler: the damage he and his followers were doing to the public reputation of the movement and the danger he faced for proudly defying God's will. The gravamen of both was something much more threatening, at least to Fox's position within the sect, and that involved Nayler's refusal, finally, to subordinate himself to Fox's authority as leader. As early as February, only a bit over a month after Fox left London, Margaret Fell was giving out that "many Friends have gotten above the power of God in them."[92] A Baptist critic who for his own political reasons mislabeled Nayler the "Head Quaker in England" saw quite well how the theological slipped over into the personal and political. Since the Scripture was not the word for Friends, he explained, "what Fox says is the word it seems."[93] Fox lent support to this view by excoriating Nayler's "subtle, untoward, unbroken, stubborn will."[94]

Fox always tended to assume that those not with him were against him and thus against the truth. In two letters to Nayler written in mid-1656 he used metaphors like "darkness" and "mountain" to describe his former close associate. "I told you," he wrote, that "wickedness . . . was growing into a mountain," betraying the just and the lambs. He claimed to have privately informed Nayler when "the first cloud of darkness was entered into you," but he refused to level open criticism until "I saw wickedness brought to a mountain." This darkness enshrouded others—"that mountain after time broke into mountains and parties"—and "some in London cried against me" and called him a priest for questioning Nayler. Fox catalogued the problem: "[T]he darkness is entered into your disciples . . . and is powered abroad"; they "burst into parties"; they "got up papers and [set] one against another" so that "the way of truth was evilly spoken of and to be a reproach among the heathen," "making tumults and stirring up tumultuous people and mockers and scoffers to sport themselves against the truth." Such cataloguing went on and on, but Fox left no doubt about his conclusion: "I told you, James, it would be a harder work for you to get their spirits down than ever it was to let them up. . . . Your kingdom must down and all this broken to pieces."[95] If Fox, as he claimed, wrote Nayler of his misgivings prior to leaving London, then not a syllable has survived; high levels of lingering acrimony suggest that the matter remained to fester and was whispered about privately among those who knew of the difficulties.

The real problem was that Nayler, however inadvertently, was winning such a fervent band of disciples in London that he was erecting a base of influence that gave him a strength and a prestige independent of Fox's. When Fox referred to wicked mountains and parties crying against him, he really meant that he resented Nayler's growing strength and independence. Nayler doubtless intended otherwise, for he too had the good of the movement at heart. In a sense Nayler became the victim of his own success, as the story of Rebecca Travers illustrates. A woman just approaching fifty and well versed in religious matters, Travers had already marveled at how well this rude country plowman had been able to confound learned London opponents so effectively. When she was invited to dine with Nayler one evening in the company of a supercilious gentleman, she was amazed again at her host's adeptness in giving wise answers to silly questions. At one point, wishing to go deeper, she interposed to ask about what she called "hidden things." Nayler reached his hand across the table, laid it gently on hers, and reassured her in words so penetrating that she failed to notice just how patronizing they were: "Feed not on knowledge, it is truly forbidden to you, as ever it was to Eve; . . . for who feeds on knowledge dies to the innocent life." Rebecca Travers was hooked for life.[96] With this ability to win followers, male and female, and his obvious success in London, Nayler posed a threat of major proportions to Fox. No movement can follow two masters, as Fox realized.

But the west beckoned now. Sending copies of his epistles ahead, Fox tried to prepare the region to the west for his impending appearance.[97] His traveling companions, Edward Pyott from near Bristol and William Salt of London, were more familiar than Fox with what was for him mostly virgin territory. Starting at Reigate and Guilford in Sussex, the trio first headed for the south coast, Chichester and Portsmouth, and then westward to Poole in Dorset. By the end of the first week in January Fox was pushing into Hampshire, his subversive papers popping up in churches and giving the authorities enough anxiety to consider arresting him and his companions.[98]

Fox was so enthralled with the beautiful coastline along this route that for one of the few times in his life he betook himself to endorse—in private, of course—enjoyment of scenic beauty for its own sake.[99] Typically the travelers headed for the local inn and inquired after Baptists and their teachers, all the while keeping an eye out for other "sober" people, the kind who eschewed outward beauty. When they located some, as in Dorchester, they argued about water baptism. In Weymouth they won some Ranters, who converted to more sober ways. Fox was amazed at one captain of horse, the fattest, merriest, most cheerful man he had ever met. He was almost lost but became more serious after the Quaker trio spent long hours on his case.[100]

Away from London, Fox could not keep up with developments there nor watch Nayler at work. By March 1656, he knew that things were not well in the capital, and he wrote Richard Hubberthorne about his concerns. Nayler was better, Hubberthorne reported promptly, more "loving and much nearer the truth that he was." But events at a meeting on Thursday, March 19, at the Bull and Mouth, an Aldersgate inn where the Children rented a gathering place, revealed that others were not as amenable to discipline as Nayler seemed to be. One of them, an enthusiastic woman named Mildred Crouch, held forth for upward of nine hours, until her hoarse voice and the need to relieve herself physically required her to give up the floor.[101]

Fox had more immediate worries than Nayler's activities in London, as ominous for the future as they might be. Increased numbers of Quakers both in London and in the areas where Fox and his companions were traveling gave added concern to the authorities, fearful for the survival of Cromwell's regime.[102] Moreover, by mid-January, the missionaries had moved into Cornwall, England's westernmost county—isolated, backward, and, in Fox's not unbiased eyes, an altogether "dark country." The roads were so narrow that special wagons, long and narrow, plied the few that could handle them, while most accommodated only horses outfitted with special high frames to carry their loads. For one usually so censorious, Fox surprisingly did not mention the almost universal habit of Cornish men, women, and children in puffing pipefuls of burning tobacco.[103] Although the Quakers found few willing to join them, even a small increase in Quaker numbers in this intensely conservative and royalist area heightened general unease and reminded all of the Commonwealth's inability to enforce stability. To deal with this perception, Cromwell during the past May had appointed his brother-in-law, a major-general, to administer the law in the southwest with an unspecified broad grant of powers.[104] Thus attempts by mayors and constables to arrest the Quakers without the use of warrants, such as at Marazion, were to be expected, but even innkeepers in places like Helston turned a deaf ear to their requests for information about local people of good report who feared God. In at least one Cornish village Baptists absolutely refused to hear Fox out about the inward light of Christ.[105]

Responding to these rebuffs in his usual confrontational fashion, the frustrated Fox issued an epistle that was soon circulating across seven parishes all the way to Land's End. "The mighty day of the Lord is come," he warned, and "every one who does not hear this prophet is to be cut off." Those heeding the prophet's message would be freed from "the world's teachers and ways to learn of Christ." It was no wonder that edgy authorities began referring to their "sinful, wicked paper"; a threatened clergyman raised the Catholic specter and accused Fox and his companions of being disguised Jesuits because Pyott wore spectacles. When these strange criers of doom reached St. Ives, Fox went down to see the Atlantic as it crashed onto England's far west coast. Soon facing an aggressive army captain and justice of the peace, Fox's party refused to swear an oath of allegiance or give bond for good behavior; they also sought to justify themselves as "constant, faithful friends to the Commonwealth and in arms for it," an exaggeration as far as Fox was concerned but revealing more than a little about his political slant and aptness.[106]

Captain Peter Ceely promptly put the entire party under arrest and started for Falmouth and Pendennis Castle on the other coast of Cornwall. The governor of the castle who would have had charge of the prisoners was away, so they were housed temporarily in an inn until Ceely determined what to do with his Quaker prisoners. Meanwhile they preached to any crowd who came near enough. At one point the brother of one of Fox's captors barged into his room and pranced back and forth like some enraged wrestler while Fox taunted him to fear the Lord; his tormentor stretched his leg behind Fox's and, shoving him with both hands, tried unsuccessfully to throw the solidly built man.[107]

Ceely then took his three charges to Launceston, the chief town of Cornwall where the court of assizes was scheduled to meet the last day of March, nine weeks hence. The town sprawled up and down numerous hills. Its steep streets, following natural contours, made it nearly impossible to get a clear sense of where one was.[108] But Fox, Salt, and Pyott had no chance to lose their way, for they were quickly locked up. Cromwell's military commander in the region, Major-General John Desborough, who was also the Lord Protector's brother-in-law, seemed disposed to release them if he could extract a promise that they would return to the north. The stiff-necked Quaker missionaries resolutely refused any compromise with mere worldly authority and presently heard the doors to what must have been one of the worst jails in the country clang shut behind them. The charges read like a catalogue of crimes the state could level against any dissidents, whether political or religious: spreading papers tending to disturb the public peace, having no lawful reason for coming to Cornwall, being unable to produce a pass, refusing to give bond for good behavior, and failing to swear the oath abjuring Catholicism.[109]

Thus only a bit more than a year after coming south, Fox found himself again forcibly deprived of the chance to use his considerable skills to travel and win converts for the movement. Isolated from the fuss that Quakerism in London had become, Fox found his usually clear vision restricted, his natural suspicions set to festering, and his leadership diluted through subordinates and the vagaries of a censored mail system.[110] The dangerous men who had come down from the north were now safely shut up, the Commonwealth made that much safer. But with Fox in jail, the lid was on the Children's cauldron. Outside the most fundamental internal challenge the movement had faced added fuel to the blaze.

10

I Thank God and My Cunning

When Edward Pyott, one of the Quakers held at Launceston jail, took up his pen on May 14, 1656, to write to George Bishop, he had strict instructions about what to write. George Fox wanted Bishop, a prominent Bristol Friend, to delay publishing his pamphlet, *West Answering to the North*, because its harsh words about Cornwall were likely to "enrage and obstruct the [Quakers'] service here." After all, Pyott went on, echoing Fox, "the justices have been as yet pretty civil towards us . . . which is to be owned and encouraged."[1] Only the next day Pyott contacted another correspondent, writing that Fox liked the brief prepared for the court but thought it best "to have it go in my name singly."[2] With Pyott signing the brief, Fox could take the high road and retain his stance as prophet of righteousness.

Stuck in far-off Cornwall and isolated in his prison,[3] Fox was forced to use his wits in ways not required before. As it turned out, these qualities, which he had already demonstrated he possessed, would be much drawn upon in days and weeks to come. He would be tempered by having to respond both to external pressures against his young sect and to dissensions threatened to tear it asunder from inside. His advice to Bishop testified to the adept political skill of which he was capable when he dealt with outside forces. Unfortunately, he did not move with the same alacrity or insight when he faced internal problems: he temporized, and he waited an inordinately long time for things to improve, thus permitting dangerous situations to deteriorate beyond repair. However understandable, his temporizing resulted in injury to long-term relationships with close associates, and did not augur well for his leadership within the movement. Fox learned that wits purchased by experience were much more dear than those acquired in other ways.

The mere physical situation of Launceston jail was bad enough. The two-story jail was just inside the city's expansive castle grounds, where the prisoners were sometimes permitted to walk.[4] The jail portion had no chimney and no toilet facilities.[5] At first things were not so bad. The court of assizes did not convene until March 25, so the prisoners had to wait nine weeks after they were interned on January 18. Paying their jailer forty shillings weekly for food and room, they presumed they might preach to others and warn them against such sins as drinking, but when their keeper found that this tactic reduced his profits (from selling alcoholic beverages), he began to take it out on the Quakers. Just before the court sessions he moved them to an area above the worst part of the prison, called Doomsdale; here the floor was made of slats that allowed the stench from below to engulf them. Armed men once invaded their room with orders to confiscate all books and papers. On the day of the trial, as they were taken to the courtroom through the narrow streets, people hung from windows to catch a glimpse of those strange creatures called Quakers.

When the court convened, Fox and his fellows began an acrimonious wrangle with the judge about whether they might continue wearing their hats in accordance with one of their peculiar testimonies. At first they stood quietly and did not respond when visiting Chief Justice John Glynn of England's highest court asked them to uncover. After he pressed, Fox cited various biblical personages who had kept their hats on in court. The judge, no more an authority on curious practices that ran contrary to acceptable court etiquette than he was on biblical exegesis, got so exasperated with the defendants that he all but begged them to remove their hats if they expected justice. If their hats were so offensive, they replied, perhaps Judge Glynn could order a court official to remove them, and besides, they needled this Cromwellian appointee, "Is not liberty of conscience a natural right?" They innocently inquired if any law required removal of a hat. The furious judge fired back, "I do not carry the law books on my back up and down the country, I am not [here] to instruct you." At least twice they were sent out of court so the judge could compose himself, and each time they returned with their hats still in place.

Judge Glynn finally realized he was dealing with a special brand of stubbornness and proceeded without resolving the hat issue. Major Ceely introduced a wholly new element. Ceely reported that the Quaker leader had approached him and proposed that he join in a treasonous plot to bring Charles II to power, with Fox allegedly promising to supply a substantial force for the effort. Defending himself, Fox instantly saw what the chief justice did not, namely, that this new charge was not included among those for which he had been arrested. Moreover, it would have been insane for Fox to randomly pick out an unknown officer of Cromwell's army and endeavor to enlist him in making war against the government. Fox also turned Ceely's charge against his accuser by reminding the court how long Ceely had kept the alleged plot a secret. The judge and the prisoner engaged in a verbal battle over this new charge, the former insisting that the document explaining Fox's arrest should not be introduced into evidence, the latter insisting that of course it should. By now, any sympathy the judge might have felt for Fox was long gone, destroyed by the defendant's willfulness. Incensed, the judge ordered Fox taken from the chamber, shouting after him, "I will see whether he or I shall be master." Glynn finally ended this fiasco by fining the defendants twenty marks (slightly more than £13) for refusing to doff their hats and remanded them to jail until they paid.[6]

Despite the fine and the verbal pyrotechnics, Fox was generally pleased with what he called the judge's "pretty civil" treatment.[7] This leniency may have been one of the reasons that Fox decided to organize a wide-ranging assault on the judicial and ecclesiastical systems. He remained troubled that Friends had quit

Cornwall, particularly when the time seemed ripe for winning large numbers of converts.[8] Fox dispatched orders to the London missionaries, as Pyott phrased it, "to lay it upon them from him" that they should disperse to all the counties and confront the judges and priests in their bailiwicks.[9] Average Quakers, otherwise unknown, answered the call. A Benjamin Maynard appeared in Launceston and promptly got himself arrested for engaging in a seventeenth-century version of a sit-in: he stood silently in a church to protest its unacceptable practices. In nearby Devon, an order issued by an Exeter official charged the Quakers with scattering seditious papers and books across the county, "deluding many weak people, undermining the fundamentals of religion, [and] denying the scriptures to be the word of God."[10] From Bury St. Edmonds came word that Suffolk was so "greatly molested" by the Children of the Light that usually ruthful ministers were speaking openly of cutting throats.[11] These thorny Quakers suggested that the proverb, "A man without religion is like a horse without a bridle,"[12] ought to be amended to "A man without the *right* religion. . . ."

Fox soon felt the backlash resulting from this heightened level of activity. Not only did the jailer verbally abuse his visitors—and, as Fox remembered it, everyone from justices of the peace to curious passersby came to talk with or gawk at them—but he also called them rogues and whores, threatened to break their legs, and even invited them, as one pamphlet trumpeted to the world, "to kiss and put their noses into that which modesty forbears to mention." The jailer brought suit against a local woman who brought provisions for the prisoners and won because the judge instructed the jury that if she came into his house without the jailer's consent she was trespassing. When Maynard was committed to prison, the jailer tossed him into Doomsdale and on April 9 did the same with Fox, Salt, and Pyott. Indeed, if their jail conditions were bad before the hearing, they now became positively ugsome.

As described by the Quaker convicts, Doomsdale more resembled a sty—"a puddle of piss," with filth rising over their shoe tops. When they built a fire of straw one evening in a desperate effort to clear the rank odor, their jailer climbed above them into their own former cell, the one with the slatted floor, and threw dirt and excrement down on them. As a befouling insult he aimed a stream of urine at their feebly flickering fire. Fox did not take all this lying down; he wrote letters to sessions court judges and to Cromwell complaining about their treatment. Like most of his epistles, these letters of admonition and rebuke probably had little impact on those not already in sympathy with him.[13]

Fox realized that it would take more than pronouncing anathemas on his enemies to win this struggle, so he framed a strategy. He played the role of the enraged prophet and directed Pyott to concentrate on enumerating their rights as freeborn English citizens. To protest confiscation of their books, for example, Pyott solemnly intoned, "[O]ur books are our goods, and our goods are our property, and our liberty is to have and enjoy our property, and of our liberty and property the law is the defense." Such an argument, crafted in the first instance for a judge pledged to defend the rights of Commonwealth citizens, also could be broadcast to catch the eye of aspiring commoners across the country who comprised the movement's natural adherents. But Fox could also operate on a purely practical political level. He issued an instruction that such letters be delivered by a person, as he cunningly phrased it, "of some outward esteem to the judge."[14]

One visitor, Will Caton from Lancashire, got in to see the prisoners and stayed several days. His account of his visit offered a glimpse of Fox missed by those who never knew him personally. Caton wrote Margaret Fell that Fox "triumphs in his freedom and liberty, which no man can take from him," a testimony to his endurance. Using his authority, even in prison, Fox asked that any books ready to go to foreign countries be sent to John Audland who was preparing a shipment for France. And, in a likely reference to stories concerning the enthusiastic women surrounding James Nayler, Fox was charitable, noting that "some of them might cease" but were welcome in Cornwall where "they would be glad of women or any in these parts." Caton told Fox how Fell had encouraged him to go to Scotland, to which his host ventured, in his best pastoral manner, that "my service would be little till I came in it" himself; he considered Holland more appropriate. Perhaps as a warning, he lamented what he called the "backwardness" of Miles Bateman, a Friend who had gone abroad. Caton worried about some unstated rumors circulating about him, but Fox reassured him that his "innocency has cleared [him, and] what is past stands justifiable and without condemnation." Fox sensed his need and recommended the long route back to London, along the beautiful coast, so that Caton might "look at it outwardly." The young Caton's elation over the older man's ready acceptance shone though his letter like a light left on for a child on a stormy night: "[W]hen I am with our beloved, in the enjoyment of him, I enjoy you and the rest of the family of love of which he is the head, yet [he] has become servant to all."[15]

Like many others, Caton liked Fox, but unlike them he left concrete examples of what made him appealing—and human. The authorities, though, were searching for a way to rid themselves of the bane called Quakers. The Quakers knew how to make themselves obnoxious when they wanted to: if a jailer referred to them as "rogues," then they retaliated with names like "beast" and "swine." When General Desborough came and listened courteously to their complaints about ill-treatment, they returned the favor by yelling out a window to disrupt a game of lawn bowls a group of officials were playing on the castle green. A strong-minded woman from London confronted the bowlers and the general head on and shouted so loud while berating them that only a trumpet finally drowned her out. In mid-August Desborough repeated his bottom-line position and agreed to free them with a pass good only for a trip north. One judge offered to release them without a pass but then reminded them, in Catch-22 fashion, that the watch for their cobelievers was so tight that they would not get more than six or seven miles. By the end of the month the authorities were leaving the prison doors wide open in hope the prisoners would leave.[16] Refusing to leave or rejecting any compromise, they pledged to endure anything, even banishment, rather than "purchase outward freedom by making a covenant with death and so bring ourselves into inward bondage."[17]

Aware of their continuing value as penned-up martyrs, Fox wrote that imprisoning those who manifested Christ would "make them grow,"[18] and circulated details via leaflets and broadsides to make sure they did. Officials only slowly realized the practical folly of keeping the Quakers locked up. Hugh Peter, a prominent Independent churchman and native Cornishman who advised Cromwell, finally convinced the authorities that "they could not do George Fox a greater service for the spreading of his principles in Cornwall than to imprison him there." Thus on September 13, 1656, nearly eight months after they were jailed, the Friends were freed by Desborough, who did not even extract their pledge that they would go north. Fox's status as a martyr had ended for now.[19] Four days later, as a kind of benediction to the whole sorry affair, Cromwell endorsed liberty of conscience and told Parliament he had "not been unhappy in hindering any one religion to impose upon another."[20]

Fox's management of the situation was expert. It could not be called planning, for he responded to events as they unfolded. But after thirty-three weeks of imprisonment he won an unconditional release. The flow of pamphlets and epistles from his pen focused attention on conditions in Cornwall and the imprisonment he and the others of his kidney were suffering.[21] The Quaker preaching missions that fanned out into the western part of the nation after he ordered missionaries to quit London not only succeeded in winning many to the cause but also forced the government to take extraordinary means to watch for them. Roadblocks were set up to catch suspicious travelers and prevent Quakers from infiltrating the area. Whether Friend or no, every person stopped got a dramatic and personal demonstration of the government's uneasiness in the face of the perceived threat from Fox's Children. The papers that government agents searched for—Launceston's mayor seemed to delight in going through women's clothing and head wraps—were not incendiary, but they could be read as sharpening social distinctions and driving a wedge between classes. For example, Fox pitched one directly at gentry who spent their time foolishly pursuing what he considered "pleasures and vain recreations" and hence "as dogs and swine turned to the vomit." "Weep and howl," he advised, "for the misery that is coming upon you."[22] Condemnations like these were hardly designed to win those so attacked but did appeal to "sober" people harboring distrust of well-off frivolous types.

Fox did not realize that his success in heightening official alarm over the Quaker movement would set in motion events leading to a climax in the James Nayler affair. An air of inevitability surrounded this messy business. As one of Fox's closest co-workers, Nayler had differed little from Fox in his approach to religion. Fox might easily have written, for example, the words Nayler used in early 1656 about people who fulminated against the world's ways but failed to lead others out of those same ways: "[E]ver learning and teaching, but never able to come to the knowledge of the truth, . . . they and the powers of the earth are one against such as take up the cross."[23] Moreover, from the earliest days of his conversion, Nayler had deferred to Fox and his judgment, writing him to get approval of his proposed itinerary and requesting his assistance when he, for example, encountered "vain janglings" in Westmorland.[24]

What differences there were, for instance, in regard to whether Quakers might rightfully take measures to prevent judicial confiscation of their estates, involved degrees of emphasis rather than matters of real substance. Nayler, less willing to compromise for the sake of the outward movement than Fox, deprecated what he attacked as the "outsides" and the "letter" as opposed to the more fleeting inward tuggings of the spirit.[25] If he never viewed Fox as one "outside" who laid down the "letter" of the law, then others in his small band of disciples certainly did. Fox might have coped with Nayler's personal reservations and doubts, but he certainly could not stand by to see the movement—his movement—pilloried and made a byword. Obviously Fox was more acutely aware than Nayler of the need to harness the movement's immense stock of individualism for the institution's interest.

Sects based on personal experience, especially those eschewing textual authority in the manner of the mystical Children, always find it difficult to forestall determined adherents from insisting that their own special revelation is more valid than others'. This reality had bedeviled Protestantism from its onset, and it now confronted Fox in his dealings with Nayler. It would continue to plague the Society of Friends. Neither its inevitability nor the realization that other groups had endured the same thing lessened the trauma of the Fox–Nayler affair for those caught up in it, and both principals nursed serious injuries after it ended. But its ultimate outcome stabilized the movement, and left Fox and his side holding the reins of authority.

With Fox in Launceston the situation in London with Nayler and his followers came to a head by mid-July. Nayler's abilities and appeal attracted a group of disciples who treated him with a reverence others reserved for God alone— or, on occasion, Fox. Martha Simmonds, sister of the radical publisher Giles Calvert and wife of another publisher of Quaker material, himself a Naylerite, had traveled in the ministry and was the principal figure and strongest leader in the small group.[26] She was certainly a powerful woman, a fact that helps explain the degree of opposition to her. In 1655 she suffered imprisonment twice in one week in Colchester; when the authorities clapped her back in jail yet a third time, a fellow prisoner commented matter-of-factly that they could not keep her, for "they will be tormented."[27] An outsider considered her the Quakers' "chief virago," one as likely to disrupt a Shoreditch church service as strew letters through the streets.[28] Like many Children, she spoke in a language that could not be read literally but was peppered with metaphors and images that had meaning to her but to few others. It was easy to see how her enemies—and she had many in and outside the Children of the Light—could consider her a witch. Once when Fox judged a sermon of hers as flowing from her own will and not the divine spirit, she ran to Nayler for support, but he agreed with Fox's criticism.[29] Still she remained close to Nayler and hung on practically every word he let fall from his lips; she regarded him as the rightful leader of the Friends both in London and beyond. His enemies saw him approving nearly everything she did and believed that she exercised some kind of improper power over him. She certainly placed Nayler on a pedestal not large enough both for him and Fox, even applying to him the phrase God used as a self-description to Moses, "I am."[30] Quakers described her later as "whoring from the Lord and his ways."[31]

Few normal people could avoid having their heads turned by such adulation.

Nayler's compatriots saw a man torn inwardly by his commitment to the movement and all it stood for and the acclaim he personally aroused. Physically weakened and emotionally paralyzed, he could not choose between the personal needs
of those whom he had converted and his continued service to the Children as a
whole.[32] He himself did not say anything publicly against Fox or his other associates. His mistake was that he could not distance himself from Simmonds and
her coterie, much less condemn their excesses, which had embarrassed and split
the faithful in London. For Fox, to see the world divided between those who
were for him and those who were against him was as natural as taking his next
breath. Thus Nayler's indecision pushed him beyond the pale as far as Fox was
concerned. After the crisis with Nayler ended, he issued an epistle ostensibly
refuting charges that Quakers were false prophets and the Antichrist, but his
response certainly sounded like his own description of the followers of Nayler.[33]

The dispute broke into the open after mid-July 1656, after Edward Burrough
and Francis Howgill, who had been on missionary service in Ireland, returned
to London.[34] Invading meetings of the Children in the same way rude Ranters
had often done, Simmonds and other Nayler supporters interrupted the speak-
ers by singing, shouting, and trying to dominate the proceedings. No one recorded
exactly what they said, only that it was "low," "filthy," and "out of the life." No
evidence survived that Fox ever heard them, but he accused them later of "poison
and railing speeches against me." To judge from his subsequent condemnation
of Nayler, this clique circulated papers and broadsides and organized parties to
undermine the movement.[35] Burrough excoriated Simmonds and the others as
"out of the truth, out of the way, out of the power, out of the wisdom, out of
the life of God" and—if that was not enough—labeled them "goats, rough and
hairy."[36] Nayler himself was in the north at this time and therefore was not directly
responsible for what his supporters were doing, but upon his return he faced the
consequences of his followers' actions.

Each side, those associated with Simmonds and the weighty Friends Burrough
and Howgill, insisted that Nayler come down on one side or the other. He literally could not, for James Nayler was a broken man: he became ill, trembled night
and day, lying supine on a table, and refused to back Simmonds. Once, according to her, he apologized for his indecision but would not publicly give her his
support.[37] Unable to speak and repudiate his group's disruptive actions, which
continued while he lay disabled for some days, Nayler seemed to his colleagues
to be under Simmonds's influence. Consequently they encouraged him to go to
Bristol where a big event had already been planned for the St. James fair at the
end of July.

Five thousand people attended this gathering. Both Burrough and Howgill
had come from London and were the leading Quakers there; Nayler continued
in a state of walking stupor. Arriving late at the meeting while Howgill was speaking, Nayler came in proceeded by a disciple, Timothy Wedlock of Devonshire.
Wedlock had taken off his hat, which shocked onlookers as a dramatic demonstration that he considered Nayler divine, for Friends did not uncover their heads
unless speaking in prayer to God. "I was almost struck dead," the jolted Howgill
said. Simmonds, who had followed Nayler to Bristol, rose and sang at one point.

The meeting buzzed with astonishment until Burrough quieted things down. Burrough and Howgill cornered Nayler in an effort to convince him to sit with them, but his followers held him back. He would not talk even after they convinced him to go to the house of a mutual Friend—over the protests of his women Friends who roared like bears. Simmonds they physically restrained; she later claimed they threw—or "plucked"—her down the stairs. After a day or two Nayler, now calm and talkative, now weeping copiously, set off intending to go to Launceston to see Fox. Simmonds headed back to London, much to the relief of the other Friends. A couple of general meetings did little to settle the controversy among the Children in Bristol after Nayler's departure.[38]

Nayler never reached Launceston. The roadblocks in the southwest, set up to prevent just such Quaker intrusions, caught him in early August at Okehampton, Devon, just fifteen miles short of his destination, and he was imprisoned at Exeter. He had already started a fast, taking only white wine occasionally mixed with water. His spirits improved to such an extent that he was "willing to bear reproach," or so a fellow inmate described him. The prisoners had been given the right to walk in the garden, which also made things better. Nayler had improved enough to evaluate his situation, explaining, as a Friend reported, that he "saw this thing long before it came, . . . but he knows not how when it came on him he would have hid it." Significantly, two letters went to Launceston over the last two weeks with the same news of Nayler's improvement.[39]

Upon his release Fox did not, surprisingly, rush the fifteen miles to Exeter to see his mentally troubled co-worker. As late as the St. James fair incident in Bristol, he had pooh-poohed the seriousness of Nayler's actions. Nayler had lost his dominion, true, but Fox, as two of his associates described his views, "made not much of it and bade that no Friend should be discouraged."[40] Had he gone to Nayler immediately, he might have prevented Simmonds gaining the upper hand again, for by now she was in Devon where she was nursing General Desborough's ill wife in an effort to win her idol's freedom.[41] Certainly Fox knew now, if he had not known before, what kind of person Simmonds was. Before his release, she and Hannah Stranger, another fervent Naylerite, appeared at Launceston, and the three of them engaged in a free-for-all. Someone had told Fox that Simmonds was referred to as "Nayler's mother," so he rebuked and judged her for this and other acts of insolence. Sarcastically, she retorted that he acted as though he "was Lord and king." Then she told him that his heart was rotten and that he should stop acting so all-wise and bow down to her. Picking up the same theme, Stranger piped in with the dare that if they were devils as he implied then let him make them tremble. Simmonds taunted him with the prediction that he would lose his Children and boasted that Nayler would replace him. Astounded by this experience, Fox could not fathom how Nayler associated with such vituperative people.[42] Still, his pain and anger were all the more reason for him to have hurried to Exeter to see a man he knew and had previously respected. Moreover, the obvious need to find a way to keep the movement unified demanded that Fox take the lead in promoting a reconciliation.

Instead, as Fox himself put it, he "tarried" in Cornwall a full week, his bitterness festering, his conviction growing that Nayler was jealous and biased against him. He visited recent converts and held a large general meeting to which people flocked from as far away as Plymouth on the south coast. Numerous northern missionaries showed up to do service in it.[43] Meanwhile, Simmonds got to Nayler, who under her baleful influence again lost the ability to function.[44] As Fox finally moved toward Exeter, his conviction grew that Nayler must be made to humble himself, admit his wrongdoing, and then repudiate the unrest his followers had caused among the leading Children. Within the next month Nayler became lucid enough to arrive at a conclusion of his own: he sent Margaret Fell the only recorded criticism of Fox he ever made, namely, that Fox wanted to "bury" Nayler's name in order to lift up his own.[45] Whatever his intention in penning this cryptic comment, it was obvious that it would require the utmost tact if Nayler were to be won back to the fold and a public split avoided. Unfortunately, these qualities were in short supply in Fox's personal makeup, particularly toward one he saw as opposing him.

Fox and Pyott arrived at Exeter jail, less than forty miles from Launceston, on Saturday evening, September 20, and spoke to Nayler but said little of substance. Safe to say, Fox did not like what he saw. The next day he joined Nayler and the twenty or so other Quakers locked up in Exeter jail for their regular meeting for worship. He felt compelled to admonish them, singling out Nayler in particular. No record remains of what exactly was said, but he probably spoke in the same rather general terms he used when he wrote Nayler a few days later about "crying against the truth," and being "out of the power of God," and "separated from the power of the Lord God."[46] Nayler was visibly shaken but restrained himself and said nothing. The group kept their hats on when Fox stood to pray and then escorted their leader out. Fox was not prepared for this reaction, or perhaps it merely confirmed his worst suspicions. A dramatic rebuff it was, the reverse of Wedlock's action in Bristol but just as disrespectful and disorderly, the kind of Ranter-like action calculated to infuriate Fox. It rankled, and for twenty years he brooded on their offense: "[T]hey were the first who gave that bad example among Friends." In the future every time someone refused to uncover when a person prayed in a meeting, Fox was reminded at once of James Nayler, "the first who gave that bad example." But Fox again put off directly discussing their differences, to await the new day.

On Monday, September 22, Nayler got permission to leave his prison cell and go to Fox's inn, where he expressed sorrow and contrition for his actions. Fox responded in the same spirit, even commending his colleague's former faithfulness. The interview ended on a positive note, but the mood changed when Richard Hubberthorne, one of the few Fox supporters who had maintained ties with Nayler, walked back to the castle jail with him. Hubberthorne tried to convince Nayler to pull away from his associates, a possibility he rejected out of hand. While the two of them were sitting quietly, Fox came in and spoke to Nayler three or four times, but when Nayler did not answer Fox left. Hubberthorne again pleaded with Nayler to see what he was rejecting by his course of action and his choice of allies, implying that he should be subject to Fox and the truth as Fox taught it; but nothing was resolved. Fox returned and spoke to the entire group of Naylerites, and then he and Hubberthorne proceeded through the wide streets back to the inn. Nayler, like Fox, could not leave the matter alone and came once more to the inn, this time so broken he could not hold back his tears when he recalled the spirit that "could never be separated from him." Fox responded in a similar manner, which must have encouraged Nayler, for he handed Fox an apple as a sort of symbol of their affection. Fox brushed it aside. His rejection, however, did not break the tender outward mood, as Nayler took his leave and returned to jail. A last brief meeting on Monday took place in the castle yard, with Fox reproving Nayler and he endeavoring to justify himself.

Fox sent for Nayler on Tuesday morning, asking him to come to his lodgings where they could speak privately without the Naylerites listening, but Nayler did not come. Fox smarted at this snub, one of the few specific things he held against his former ally.[47] Hubberthorne and Fox then went to the jail and found Nayler, who had a pass from the jailer to go to the castle yard and was exiting through the gate. The prisoner would not return to ask the jailer to permit him to go to the inn, so Fox began criticizing him in the street for his actions, occasioning the first open break between the two. Nayler's anger and loud protestations attracted a crowd of bystanders, both townspeople and prisoners. He shouted at them not to listen to lying accounts and false accusations. They silently turned away. Hubberthorne, accompanied by Pyott, later went back to the jail to see Nayler again. He seemed at once resigned and angry—resigned because, despite what he called "a love in me that would have carried me through fire and water to him," he could not convince Fox to stop believing tales that were simply not true, angry because Fox would not even try to understand. And he would not, he vowed, go to see Fox lest he provoke another sad scene like the one earlier in the street.[48]

Fox came to Nayler one last time, probably on Tuesday evening. The prisoner was on his bed in a recessed area of his cell when they arrived. With little preface, Fox launched into an attack, stressing the set-to in the street. Despite tears and expressions of love from Nayler, the mood was tense and grew more so, as though things were building toward a climax. Nayler proffered another apple, but Fox would not touch it unless the giver could say he was moved by the Lord to present it. Gripping Fox's hand, Nayler asked permission to kiss him. The powerful Fox tried to pull the seated prisoner up to his level, but Nayler would not rise. Fox, feeling slighted and unwilling, as he phrased it, to "receive his show of kindness," deigned not to step down to the lower level. In the manner of a bishop, he held out his hand for Nayler to kiss, a gesture instantly spurned. Then Fox thrust his foot into the pit with the biting command, "It is my foot."[49]

What the outcome might have been if Nayler had kissed Fox's foot is, of course, impossible to say, although it is hard to believe that Nayler would ever have respected himself again had he done so. The scene was certainly not a pretty one, but Fox never evinced the least apology for his role in the denouement. Apologies were never Fox's forte. Moreover, the symbolism of extending his hand for Nayler to kiss, much less his foot, flew in the face of the equality that supposedly characterized a group that Will Caton, in his innocent sincerity, called a family of love. But Fox never relented. The closest he ever came to apologizing for his actions was when he wrote Nayler how, as he explained it, "I loved that of God in you, but your subtle, untoward, unbroken, stubborn will lies upon the good I own."[50] His authority and his position and his judgment had all been called into question by Nayler's followers, if not the man himself, by his refusal to condemn them. Indeed, writing Nayler afterward, he reaffirmed that "with the truth you are judged and condemned. . . . This is the word of the Lord God to you and your disciples." And Fox closed his letter with words that Nayler would know bolstered his authority, those words that bespoke his assumed identity as God's son: "[F]rom him who is of the world called George Fox."[51] When Nayler told Margaret Fell that Fox wished to "bury" his name, he was not far off the mark.[52]

Still, Fox took no public action against Nayler. His inaction reflected a curious approach to leadership. Of course, people in the movement learned through the network of letter writers about what had gone on and lined up on one side or the other, but, like Fox, they said nothing publicly. For example, Francis Howgill, one of the most prominent Quaker evangelists, heard about the Exeter eruption and bluntly wrote a month later to another Friend, "Truly, my dear, James Nayler is bad."[53] Fox agreed—in fact Howgill probably got his information from Fox—yet he never published a pamphlet or distributed a broadside detailing Nayler's actions and shortcomings. Nor did he attempt to discipline his fellow or discredit him publicly. Others who transgressed for some other variety of "filthiness" were disowned or testified against, but Fox was content to rebuke Nayler in person and then stick his foot at him and ask him to kiss it. It was admittedly easier to identify a sexual peccadillo and justify punishment for it than to explain a dispute concerning the subtleties of leadership, but a disagreement involving something as fundamental as the control of a movement surely demanded more than a tongue lashing, sharp as it was. And no penalty, other than Fox's judgments delivered in the heat of argument, was meted out to Simmonds or to Stranger or to Nayler's other supporters. Possibly Fox thought his verbal thrashing would lead them to reform, but he received no such commitment from them. Turning his horse's head eastward, he left his wayward followers to their own devices in Exeter.

Fox headed back toward London, with a stop for a large general meeting in Bristol, the country's second largest city and a major port situated on the Severn River. Lying low against the river, the city had narrow streets covering large underground vaults that served as sewers, a much boasted rarity of the day. But at ground level the streets were dark because the upper stories of the city's timbered houses jutted far enough out over the street almost to touch the ones across the way. The Severn's single bridge, more than four centuries old when Fox arrived, was an exact copy of the famous London Bridge. Most of the bustling metropolis's traffic still moved by fast little boats called "wherries," just as in London.[54]

One of Fox's traveling companions, Edward Pyott, was well-to-do, so he stayed at the Pyott home in a suburb of Bristol, outside the hum of the central city's busy life.[55] Quakerism had made its appearance in the area nearly three years earlier and was already thriving. Fox's advertised Sunday morning meeting attracted upwards of five thousand people, including a number of Baptists who were particularly numerous in the area and came to tease the longhair about the length of his locks and his inability to do all the things he claimed. After Fox put down his principal critic, the meeting became more serious. Fox lashed out at the hired ministry and affirmed his belief that Christ's presence to teach his people now had ended the need for discussion of theological notions about what he called "types" and "shadows" of Christ's appearance. He promised that Christ's appearance in their hearts would lead them into all truth, a commitment that was revolutionary in its implications and underscored again why he was convinced they needed no outward, hireling teachers.[56]

As he moved on through Wiltshire, he again targeted those who preached for money, calling on his listeners to refuse to pay the tithes that supported them, just as they boycotted their temples and colleges. Such appeals, though couched in religious terms for religious purposes, had radical implications for the commoners who listened to this apostle of change.[57] In the back of his mind, as he related in his most contemporary memoir, he knew that judges were using a recent law against vagrants to whip not only people of meager means but even those of a middling sort.[58] A stay in Launceston's infamous jail could convince anyone that the law as applied by Cromwell's government fell unequally on society's different segments.

Fox intended to arrive in London before Nayler, who had been released from prison less than a month after the leader's visit. He and his followers, totaling seven altogether, canvassed streets in Exeter attempting to attract disciples, but their efforts produced meager results.[59] The Nayler group reached a decision that they would convey a "sign" to the area, so as they moved northward and eastward, through Glastonbury and Wells, during the third full week in October, they reenacted Christ's triumphant entry into Jerusalem, with Nayler playing the part of Jesus. Their journey culminated in Bristol on a rainy Friday, October 24, a bit after 2:00 P.M., when they slushed along a nearly knee-deep muddy cartway, James Nayler slumping on his horse in a half-stupor. Two women walked beside him holding his horse's bridle, and a single man led the way. The escorts shouted "Hosanna" and "Holy, holy, holy, Lord God of Israel" in a kind of humming singsong fashion. Surrounded by curious townsfolk, braving the rain to gape at such strange goings-on, the bedraggled little band reached the city's center and were promptly taken into custody. Members of Bristol's Quaker community did not respond to this "sign" and certainly did not flock to Nayler as any kind of messiah, whatever his own unexpressed hopes might have been.[60]

The Bristol segment of the Nayler affair, except for the prisoners' examination, which began the following day, thus ended promptly. Three weeks later Nayler was in London testifying before a committee of Parliament. Although Nayler was carrying a letter from Fox, the one gibing at how he had referred to Martha Simmonds as his mother,[61] it was clear to everyone who examined the situation that his bespattered battalion had little connection with Fox or the mainstream Quaker movement. Friends rushed immediately to control the damage. George Bishop, on the scene in Bristol, held back a letter from Margaret Fell to Nayler lest it fall into the hands of the authorities and thus expose the movement further.[62] Fox saw Cromwell about this time in Hyde Park and a few days later went with Pyott to Whitehall to speak with him again. The Protector was markedly cooler to his guest than he had been on the first occasion they met and disagreed vigorously with him about whether the light of Christ was natural or spiritual. Fox naturally broached his complaints about the way Cromwell's government was dealing with the Children; although he did not record mentioning Nayler, it is difficult to believe the matter did not arise.[63]

No matter what those intimately involved knew or did not know about the Nayler affair, the country's publicists and wags had a field day at the Quakers' expense, which had been Fox's precise worry all along. One pamphleteer jeered that "Archbishop Nayler [was] that false Christ."[64] Ralph Farmer, a Bristol Presbyterian sitting as vicar of St. Nicholas church, where he had been a major target of Quaker enthusiasts, got out a factual if sneering pamphlet to take the local Friends to task for spawning such as Nayler and his ilk.[65] Another Bristol writer denominated Nayler "the Quakers' Jesus," and used his actions to extrapolate "the principles of the Quakers in general."[66] Richard Baxter almost gleefully pointed to Nayler as an indicator of the divisions in the sect.[67] The newspapers of the day, referred to as "diurnals," filled their columns with so many anti-Quaker diatribes that Friends all the way from Kendal in the north to Plymouth in the south began to worry about a backlash. From Plymouth, one wrote, "that about James Nayler has drawn out the minds of many friends in many parts."[68]

Reflecting popular fears of Quakers, Parliament laid aside most of its other business and devoted three weeks in December 1656 to Nayler's fate. The entire affair, and especially the way Parliament handled it, demonstrated how it marked a kind of "Thermidoran" reaction to the sectarian and ideological challenges facing the country.[69] The charge against Nayler was blasphemy. Many erroneously believed that the prisoner had called himself Jesus Christ. The penalty he faced was anything Parliament wanted to exact, up to and including execution. The debate centered as much on the topic of whether an actual Quaker threat existed and the question of religious toleration as the arraigned man's specific crime; the most important question involving Nayler directly was what kind of punishment his crime deserved. Intervention by the Protector near the end of the debate raised a question of parliamentary jurisdiction and found Fox's old nemesis Chief Justice John Glynn instructing Parliament that by sentencing Nayler it could go too far. Nayler's associates were freed, presumably under the theory that since Nayler was the leader he was responsible for the affair.

Parliament was not to be gainsaid in deterring the insidious threat, both under and above ground, that Quakerism seemed to be. Poor Nayler was sentenced to be set in the pillory for two hours, whipped through the streets, and then pilloried for two more hours; he was also to have his tongue bored through with a hot iron and a "B" for blasphemer branded on his forehead. He was then taken to Bristol and ridden through the streets sitting bareback and facing backward on a horse, placed in the the pillory there, and finally returned to London and kept in jail at Bridewell until Parliament chose to release him. That release came almost three years later, in the autumn of 1659.[70]

Fox's attitude toward Nayler remained unforgiving despite the latter's willingness to abase himself for undoing the peace and unity of mainstream Quakers.

His paper advising other Children to freely judge Nayler was kept on a table outside one of the group's London meeting places.[71] Neither Fox nor other leading Friends bothered to sign a petition asking that Nayler's punishment be remitted.[72] Just before Nayler's trial, Fox did cause a statement to be published defending religious liberty and the right of individuals to speak according to the promptings of the inward Christ. His statement, however, was heartlessly neutral regarding Nayler's case, for he succeeded in writing about the Nayler issue without once naming the very person being tried for following his leadings. Moreover, in a postscript he described blasphemy in a way to make his former associate's guilt implicitly clear. It read as though he endorsed anything Parliament wanted to do about the crime: "[I]f the seed of the serpent speaks and says he is Christ that is the liar and the blasphemy and the ground of all blasphemy."[73] Instead of defending Nayler, no more guilty of blaspheming than Fox had been when charged with the same crime, Fox handed the government a definition that left Parliament to decide whether the threat hysterical defenders of the status quo had whipped up merited a guilty verdict or not. Fox's finest hour it was not, particularly because he could have stood with his embattled colleague with no direct risk to himself.

Despite Fox's public support for Nayler's conviction, the seed of the serpent gradually came to repent of the divisions he had caused. In a move unprecedented among the important early Children—certainly Fox never publicly recognized making errors—Nayler formally renounced, as he confessed, "my evil thoughts . . . to be of that which savors of self and not the things of Christ." But he never specifically repudiated his ride into Bristol, the closest he got being his references to the "burden of the spirit of enmity" he had caused within the meetings of the people of God.[74]

Fox's uncompromising position was remarkably short-sighted, as some of the Friends working for a reconciliation between the two recognized. Alexander Parker believed that alienated Naylerites might likely circulate already prepared papers, hence kindling and spreading a fire against the main party of Friends if conciliation were not achieved with their leader. Literally shedding tears as he pleaded with an unhearing Fox "to be tender in this thing," Parker argued that "there are some spirits working to raise up again what was laid in the grave and has no place of repentance."[75] Fellow Quakers came as close to criticizing Fox as any of his party ever did. Another Friend, this one a Naylerite of the first rank, Robert Rich, also tried to get Fox to see the light. A well-to-do merchant and shipowner from London, Rich saw Fox in Bristol and found him to be unbending toward Nayler and critical of Rich because of his support and continued public defense of the jailed Quaker.[76] Rich's subsequent career illustrated the validity of Parker's fear, namely, that the failure to find a way to bring Nayler back would likely drive his followers into nonstop attempts to wrest control of the movement from Fox. In truth, Rich went to his grave in 1679 a determined opponent of Fox and one who joined instead two other dissident groups.[77]

Fox did not openly concern himself with the fallout of the Nayler affair, even though the Naylerites continued their disruptions in London and even in the New World.[78] Instead he traveled and never looked back. Whereas travel for others was a trial, he found it therapeutic. Moving toward his base in the north, Fox gained strength, as though he could find there a way to counteract the slump, psychological and otherwise, that the reaction of the Children to the Nayler affair produced.[79] It was the region where the Quakers seemed more at home; as one wrote longingly from the capital, the Friends there were "rare and precious, very few I find like them."[80] Meetings were large and the people enthusiastic, and Fox sensed that "the Lord's power was eminently manifested." He traveled as far north as Yorkshire, then turned back to visit the Midlands. He did not record a visit to Swarthmoor or Drayton-in-the-Clay, but he approached as close as thirty-five miles to his home village to attend a rally at Edge Hill, where hundreds, including Ranters, Baptists, and the "rude" ones still plaguing his gatherings, heard him speak. Following a roundabout progress that included his first visit to Wales and confrontations there with some Naylerites, he ended up back in London.[81]

Although Fox did not directly connect his next action with the effort to contain Nayler's influence, it laid out the pattern that he would follow in the future when he discovered dissidents maneuvering within the movement. In a letter addressed to Cromwell and Parliament at the beginning of November, he argued that a person must speak when so led by the promptings of the inward Christ. But what if one spoke when no promptings had occurred? Or, more important, when one falsely claimed to be so led? Fox recognized that "where the power of God does not rule and speak, the power of the devil speaks and . . . is tormented at the power of God." He had to find a way to detect when a person spoke falsely and disturbed the group's unity, like a "mere creature," Fox reminded readers, who declared "he is Christ."[82] The dilemma never came out exactly that way in public, of course, for such problems were usually explored in private when close associates candidly surveyed the state of the Society of Friends. Even more basic, of course, was how to determine if someone spoke falsely. Fox had adduced no standards, no criteria, to determine when or if Nayler and his followers stepped over the invisible line that divided authentic promptings from fraudulent illusions: the "filth" and "deceit" Fox and others discerned they recognized by some process they never described. Now Fox had to fix a system that allowed others to see as clearly as he had in Nayler's case, to judge real leadings and detect false ones.

In doing so he crafted an instrument for unity that was his most enduring achievement, precisely because it saved Quakerism from going to oblivion, the way of myriads of other sects in the period. He concluded, without ever offering the rationale for his conclusion, that the individualism that so appealed to a generation of English commoners had to be reined in and a tradition of unity established.[83] The local meeting for business was the instrument he created to achieve this goal. (These gatherings were distinct from meetings held for purposes of evangelization or spiritual edification, which, of course, dated from the earliest days of the Quaker movement.) Given responsibility for overseeing individual Children and carrying on the affairs of the group at the lowest level, they reflected Fox's decision to emphasize unity among his followers. Most clearly revealed in his epistles of 1656, this emphasis was hardly an accident given the divisive events of the Nayler affair after July. "Dwell in peace and unity," he wrote in one; "keep in the seed of peace . . . in which you will all have life and peace, and unity and dominion," he advised in another; "do not gad abroad from the truth within," he preached in a third; and "take heed of jars and strife . . . that you will all have unity," he warned in a fourth.[84] Whom Fox had in mind when he saw disunity arising from those he termed, perhaps a bit enviously, "fair or excellent of speech" his Children would know instantly.[85]

As a matter of fact, the first monthly meeting, the name used to describe each local group and how often it met to conduct business, grew up in the county of Durham in 1653.[86] Apparently restricted to male members, these northern meetings concerned themselves with looking after the poor in each locality and, according to Fox, with seeing "that all walked according to the truth."[87] William Dewsbury left the first recorded instructions to these young meetings regarding the broad scope of their authority. He enjoined them to see that meetings for worship convened twice weekly and to choose as overseers one or two of those "most grown" in the power of discerning. Their principal responsibility involved discipline, "to see that those who come among them walk orderly according to that which they profess." Left intentionally vague, "walking disorderly" gave great leeway for local interpretation. If those so walking did not reform, then Dewsbury recommended they be cast out and shunned, even to the extent of avoiding eating with them. Meetings should also make sure to care for any in "outward want."[88] Obviously the fact that Dewsbury admonished meetings as early as 1653 to discipline those who walked disorderly and to take care of poor adherents meant that the early Children had already had enough experience with each group to know what the situation required.

Thus in 1656 when Fox extended the system of monthly meetings to the entire country, he was building on foundations previously laid. But now the Nayler affair underscored the need for quick action: Fox had to find a way to hem in Nayler's followers' tendency to run out or else watch the movement fly off in every direction before his eyes. In the midst of the Nayler affair, he hurriedly advised Richard Farnworth, "See that Friends be kept in order" and "search out the matter of disorder."[89] This urgency may explain why he passed over the establishment of meetings so rapidly in his *Journal*. Or it may be that when he sat down to dictate his memoirs he was a bit embarrassed that the individualistic principles he had earlier espoused had to be subverted.

In any event, Fox dictated rapidly, remarking simply that he caused at least one representative from each county to meet at Swarthmoor to set up men's meetings.[90] No record remains of exactly when in 1657 this was done, although it was likely during his trip north.[91] (In January he did announce a Easter conclave of all Friends in the ministry; Easter by then was becoming the usual time for gatherings expected to attract participants from across the nation. At it, he could survey the opinions of the Children's public leaders.)[92] An epistle that he directed to be read in all meetings contained the same broad instructions that Dewsbury had given, though with a difference: over, in, and around it hovered the specter of James Nayler. Fox cautioned readers, for example, that those who preached abroad should not evince "a brittle, peevish, hasty, or fretful mind" but remain in the "life and power and seed of God." Always in the church, he

continued, there had been apostate Christians who claimed the right of elder-
ship and unilaterally set themselves up as heads, and thereby "they lose the one
head, which is Christ Jesus." He warned against needless printing of papers, careless words, and traveling around to minister at settled meetings, which tended
to lift itinerants too high. He wanted to keep "settled" meetings untouched by
controversy: "[T]here is a difference between Friends going into the world and
of coming among them who are come to silent meetings and to feed there."
Thus Fox prescribed a quarantine against the deadly virus of Naylerism.[93]

Information regarding establishment of men's quarterly meetings, the next
level above monthly meetings, was even vaguer than information regarding the
lower meetings. Fox said only that he set them up about the same time as local
Friends received authorization to organize.[94] Representing a broader jurisdiction,
usually that of all local bodies within a county, these meetings convened every
three months and assumed a kind of a moral authority over the groups below.
As early as 1653 Dewsbury instructed Friends that if they could not find an
appropriate way to deal with disorderly walkers, then they should turn for help
to those nearby who were righteous and pure in their discerning.[95] Quarterly
meetings, which strikingly resembled the Presbyterian classis or presbytery, in-
stitutionalized Dewsbury's advice and gave the most active Friends in local and
quarterly meetings increased oversight of individual Children, especially any
tempted to mount James Nayler's horse.[96]

Hence a two-level system was erected, a meeting at a local level, a larger and
more distant one a rung higher, forming a systematic check on a potential dissident's outward expression of inward leadings as determined by those gripping
the instruments of power. The Nayler escapade had brought the Friends movement right up to the very edge of the abyss—an abyss of, horror of horrors,
Ranterism. The leaders saw they needed to find a way to impose discipline. That
the need for their system came so soon in the movement's history illustrated
Fox's (and those who sided with him against Nayler) realization of two stark
things: that there existed an extremely disruptive side to the individualistic faith
they proclaimed and that for the survival of the movement they would have to
find a mechanism to preserve it from that threat.[97] On the question of individualism versus authority, Fox had finally come down on the side of authority. It
was, he had decided, the only thing he could do. By the end of 1656, with the
mutilated Nayler lying in his prison cell, Fox could literally thank God and his
cunning for bringing him and the Children of the Light safely to this point and
afterward, the First Friend trusted, into the future.[98]

11

No Time like the Present

With the disgrace of Nayler behind him, Fox resumed his preaching schedule and missionary activities with a vigor redolent of earlier days; he would try, single-handedly, to breathe new energy into his compatriots. His burst of activity, some of it confrontational, suggested he was figuratively thumbing his nose at the Westminster worthies who thought that they had so easily squashed their so-called Quaker threat by throwing Nayler into jail. With his competitor jailed, Fox did not have to attend to that aspect of his movement's internal problems and could concentrate on increasing its numbers and deepening its influence. Wales, where concentrations of Naylerites remained, was one venue, but he also traveled in southern and western England. Before 1657 ended he ventured northward into the dark land called Scotland, seeking not only to convert the natives but also to make contact with the growing number of Quakers in the Lord Protector's army there.

Fox could not know it in advance, of course, but it turned out that the leeway he received from Nayler's incarceration was paralleled by a steady slide in the political fortunes of Cromwell and his Commonwealth. The religious instability that Parliament saw when they looked at Nayler had its counterpart in a growing disenchantment among powerful people with the heady republicanism set loose in 1649.[1] Even Cromwell toyed with the idea of reestablishing an aristocratic House of Lords, just as others pondered the possibilities of reinstituting the monarchy and making the Great Commoner king. Fox had already advised Cromwell to eschew any proffered crown, a course the Lord Protector ultimately chose.[2] This growing conservative mood led Cromwell to remove Quakers from the army and from their positions as justices of the peace. Following Cromwell's death in September 1658, the regime lurched again as son Richard, who took his father's place in Whitehall, saw his strength ebb and found himself unable to fend off conservative and military maneuvering to restore the Stuarts. Fox's followers, and others like them who hoped for further change and deeper reforms, had ample reason to feel more and more disheartened by the reactionary tilt they observed.[3]

Against this ominous background, Fox's evangelistic efforts took on a significance beyond merely finding new converts: if he were successful in winning large numbers of converts, especially among soldiers, then the forces championing the Good Old Cause might somehow reverse the nation's current drift; if the necessary numbers eluded them, then the Quakers, tiptoeing lightly along this side of the line of legality, could shore up their strength and prepare for another day. In this context too, formation of monthly and quarterly meetings offered a convenient way to reenforce and coordinate local efforts. Hence, to publicize the persecution his Children endured, in 1657 Fox instructed Friends all over the nation to record their sufferings if they were arrested for attending meetings or for refusing tithes and not swearing. Significantly, he directed that "a true and a plain copy of such suffering be sent up to London," there to demonstrate to the authorities the extent of the persecution they had ordered.[4]

Official apprehension about religious and other radical forces increased the Protectorate's slide toward a variant of one-party rule that centered more and more power in Cromwell's hands. For all practical purposes, Parliament now amounted to little more than a rubber stamp for Cromwell's decisions and figured less and less in the calculus that was government decision making. The strength of county grandees steadily eroded, as real power locally came more and more to rest in the hands of the army and its officers, like General Desborough in the southwest. The country moved relentlessly toward greater centralization as decisions made in London were implemented in the farthermost reaches of the hinterland, despite the usual bureaucratic inertia and human willfulness.[5]

Ironically, Fox's push for a formal system of monthly and quarterly meetings, capped by the perfectly natural but still inarticulated decision to make London the movement's de facto headquarters, was a mirror image of the political centralization occurring under Cromwell's aegis. When Fox instructed his followers to send up the record of their sufferings to London in 1657, he intended that the authorities would take notice of them. That year the Society of Friends employed a twenty-seven year old Hampshireman, Ellis Hookes, as clerk and a kind of London public relations man.[6] Hiring Hookes not only put a permanent person on the scene of the nation's decision making, it would also work to undercut localism, a process begun when northern money was shifted southward to cover expenses of missionaries two years earlier. The grousing resistance that greeted that decision in the provincial north only served to underscore why further action was necessary. The upshot was that Swarthmoor and its mistress were being eclipsed by London and a hired clerk.

Just as Hookes could watch for budding Naylers, so Fox's epistles in 1657 demonstrated a concern with combating dissent. In the climate prevailing among Quakers in the post-Nayler period, condemnation of strife and images of struggle inevitably invoked memories of the wrangling through which they had just moved. A tempest, Fox wrote, raged upon the sea, and, changing his metaphors, he predicted that the lambs dwelling in patience would have a victory over the beasts of the wilderness regardless of the length of their horns. It was easy to view the patient lambs as Fox's followers and to see the Naylerites as wild beasts, now with their central horn polled. Living the truth would lead a person to remain in love and unity and obviate strife. Where strife appeared, he advised, "[M]ind the light to judge it down and condemn it." Fox called for self-examination to engage in what he termed "the ministry of condemnation in yourselves," a kind of conservative self-criticism leading a person to draw back from overstepping the limits and entering into any disorganizing strife.[7] Such was the new, post-Nayler order.

Renewed missionary activity got under way in January 1657 when Fox and the Lancashire gentleman Thomas Rawlinson departed London and moved southward into Kent, Surrey, and Sussex, heading westward. In the picturesque seacoast town of Lyme they drew up queries attacking those they labeled "mountebanks" for their practice of cheating people and posted them on the town's market cross. They proceded as far southwest as Exeter—Rawlinson had been imprisoned there with Nayler—where a large general meeting of Children from the area convened.[8] Then they angled back north to Bristol where they remained four nights, two with Edward Pyott, Fox's companion and fellow prisoner the year before. Whether their intention was to gauge Quaker support for Nayler or not, they undoubtedly got up-to-date news concerning his lingering influence. Their ultimate destination was Wales, an area where enclaves of Naylerites remained, but Fox and his party suddenly shifted direction to London, via Reading where they picked up the merchant Thomas Curtis, arriving there on March 25, or Lady Day, the traditional first day of the new year. Fox immediately was closeted in at least two meetings with Cromwell, about what remains unclear, although their conversation probably involved the alleged Quaker threat, perhaps even the continued punishment of Nayler. Fox found the Lord Protector, as Rawlinson noted, "very loving," or understanding toward the movement.[9]

When they finally reached Wales, where poverty was so rife that people went barelegged and barefoot and their pathetic thatched huts seemed ready to fall down, they were shocked at conditions. At some places fodder for their horses was unavailable. Fox issued an epistle describing how poor people cried out from their inability to get food, lodging, and apparel, while "rich men and women wear silver and gold." In reaction to the area's poverty, Fox and his associates felt compelled to declare the day of the Lord over and over again. Of course they targeted market days for this announcement because then a town's wickedness and sin was on sale along with foodstuffs and other goods. Their determined proclamation, "Christ was come to teach his people himself by his power and by his spirit," was considered so threatening in Caernarvon that Fox's traveling companion was jailed.[10] "Let there not be a cry of oppression heard in the land," the increasingly radicalized Fox bluntly wrote Cromwell; "[T]he rod of God is manifest in this nation, which is to rule nations." Although he did not expressly name his own movement as this divine rod, he did indicate that its members respected no persons or magistrates unless they demonstrated that they "obey the law and worship God in the spirit." Let Cromwell try himself by that standard.[11]

Fox's companion, John ap John, a native Welshman, had served Separatists of the region as minister. Fox learned to speak enough Welsh to bid a person to fear God.[12] Using ap John's contacts to advantage and also visiting garrison towns where soldiers sympathetic to the Quakers were billeted, the missionaries leveled attacks at those with enough money to wear fancy ribbons on their clothes and frolic at frivolous games and plays. Such charges represented a conscious two-edged strategy, combining an appeal to strict Protestants who had never liked such foolishness and an open identification with those who experienced oppression at the hands of others who cavorted in ostentatious laces and ruffles. Indeed Fox saw the Children's well-known refusal to defer to their social "betters" by addressing them as "you," or bowing, or removing their hats as ways to demonstrate solidarity with the widows and orphans forced to beg up and down the streets in the areas they visited. The same intention came across in their response to a bold Baptist who tried arguing with them at Leominster: to discredit him, a local Friend pointed out that the minister had not only sued him for eggs on which he had refused tithes but that he also employed several journeymen. It was the same, the Quakers asserted, as marrying the Baptist congregation and keeping the world for a concubine.[13]

Fox inched his way northward toward Swarthmoor, stopping in Cheshire to hold a large meeting and to mend some fences that needed repair. The party also stopped at the cities of Liverpool and Manchester. They arrived in Manchester on court day when the town seethed with rough, traditional country people willing to show their rejection of newfangled religious ideas by showering the visitors with dirt clods, stones, and water. Interestingly, Fox did not declare the day of the Lord in Manchester, instead contenting himself with merely rebuking the mob for its impoliteness. Fox was relieved to reach the relatively friendlier climes of Lancaster where he received the plaudits of one of the leading parliamentarians in the area, Colonel William West, long a defender and a kind of Quaker fellow traveler.[14]

Finally arriving at the home of the Fells in late August, after an absence of more than two years, Fox tried to rest, write some epistles, confer with his disciples in the neighborhood, and visit nearby meetings in preparation for his journey to Scotland.[15] But the commodious accommodations at Swarthmoor could not screen him from problems facing the sect. Northern Friends had grown restive about the burden of their large contributions to the common cause, particularly the needs of those going on foreign missions. In May a meeting held near Sedbergh decreed that meetings all over the nation should henceforth contribute to the general expense.[16] Apparently this appeal, endorsed mainly by leaders from the north, did not elicit wide support in the south, a reality that not only rapidly depleted the treasury but also alienated northerners again.[17] Though willing to pay for foreign missionaries, they adamantly opposed funding the expenses of ministers who remained in England, perhaps because most of these "interior" missionaries were now working in the south. Doubts about the administration of their contributions also set the northern Quakers to grumbling. Some questioned whether the two who collected the money, Thomas Willan and George Taylor of Kendal, always carried out the wishes of the region's Friends.[18]

Thus feelings continued to rankle in the north. Two years later the situation still remained in a state of flux, with meetings of Friends trying to protect local prerogatives. A meeting at Skipton held in October 1659 revealed that influential northerners, such as Anthony Pearson, were not willing to follow Fox's directives of 1656 to establish quarterly meetings. They wanted a modified system to prevent constant wrangling over financial matters and explicitly rejected the idea of quarterly sessions located in areas based on the government's artificially defined counties and places. Instead they claimed their right to "join together as may conduce [contribute] to the union and fellowship of the church and the mutual help of one another." They committed themselves to convening with local meeting representatives, as they phrased it, "in the northern parts," at least monthly; these monthly meetings would send representatives to a general meeting, not convening quarterly but two or perhaps three times a year. They also proposed such a general meeting for the rest of the country. Contributions from meetings, whether held monthly, three times a year, or semiannually, could be used to assist all Friends in need and not be limited to ministers alone; this system would tend to benefit those in the north and areas like Wales where economic need was greatest. To justify this last suggestion, the writers diplomatically if a bit disingenuously averred that ministers "will be as much grieved, as others offended, to have a maintenance or hire raised on purpose for them." Finally, they insisted that accounting procedures be tightened up to make sure that a minimum of two persons keep track of all money. Signed by twenty influential northern Friends, the letter delegated Pearson to write a covering letter to Fox and other leading Friends concerning their recommendations, especially the one for a nationwide general meeting. They named Pearson and Gervase Benson, among other northerners, to attend any such national general meeting.[19]

Although this letter would not be written until two years later, it clearly indicates an ongoing concern in the northern parts with the way the sect's finances were being administered. Long isolated from the rest of the nation and looked upon as a backward by more sophisticated southerners, people in the north may have been provincial, but they knew from long experience how to recognize overbearing orders from the south. In this instance the northern Quakers, prompted by Pearson, one of their highest ranking and most politically astute converts, found themselves expressing open discontent with the system of using funds drawn from large areas to support ministers who worked locally. The same concern led them to insist on stricter accounting procedures. That it originated in County Durham and won the assent of Friends from a wide area of the north would certainly demonstrate to the London power brokers just how deeply discontent ran.[20]

Fox was not accustomed to dealing with financial problems generally or with a Society of Friends pocketbook now tightened by northern disquiet. His unfamiliarity with monetary problems became evident when a fire set by a careless boy destroyed the house of William Beame of Scotby near Carlisle just before the First Friend left for Scotland. Informed of the loss, valued at £50, or more than $5,000, Fox immediately showed his concern by ordering a collection taken in the adjacent counties to help Beame to deal with his mishap. Willan and Taylor, both familiar with the accounts, worried privately that another collection undertaken so soon would dry up scarce funds and prevent raising more for expenses already slated. Their appeal for advice to Margaret Fell may also have been an indirect hint to Fox to take care.[21]

Fox's 1657 epistles appealing for unity might have been intended in part to discourage northern unease about finances, although, as in the case of Nayler, he avoided addressing the matter explicitly. The closest he came to money matters was a letter from Swarthmoor in which he spoke of the slothful servant who hid his talent rather than permitted its use for the Lord's service. Expect trials of God's servants, he warned, in the manner of Job: "[F]or the Lord can try you, as he did Job, whom he made rich, [then] whom he made poor, and whom he made rich again." He advised his readers to be content in any state to which they might be brought. To assuage some of the discontent about ministers, he also reaffirmed the radical principle that anyone, male or female, young or old, might minister, prophesy, or pray: "[W]ould God that all the Lord's people were prophets."[22]

Scotland, which Fox and a party of eight, including Lieutenant-Colonel William Osburne entered on September 10, had long been a tempting place for Quakers. For one thing, the government's failure to pay its troops fed discontent in the army, particularly in Scotland, and made soldiers an easy mark for Quaker agitation.[23] Two travelers the previous year had sent back an account that painted that land in dark hues. From Leith, due north of Edinburgh, Francis Howgill and Thomas Robinson wrote of "a dark nation, lost for lack of knowledge and perishing for want of understanding," of a "stiff necked, treacherous, and false hearted people," and of "cowards . . . so stupid . . . and full of feigned hypocrisy and dissimulation." What made the situation even worse from their point of view was that the English army, already extensively infiltrated by the Children, was being purged of its Quaker converts. This expulsion raised Quaker fears that the army would no longer have the will to suppress ungodliness because, as one phrased it, "the spirits of all the ungodly, both English and Scottish," would now be cut loose. About the only bright spot seemed to be that some officers, such as Colonel Osburne, continued to embrace the truth.[24] Forced to live off the population, the army was an alien force in a strange and hostile land, a situation no optimistic military report could change.[25] Cromwell did point out that Scotland's lower classes had benefited under his administration, and lived better now than in the past when they had been ruled by lairds, but that did not stop Scots who supported the Stuarts from sneering about the "Usurper."[26] The few Quakers in Scotland, always hopeful, naturally and openly favored Cromwell.[27]

Fox and his party entered Scotland just north of Carlisle, an area so dangerous because of bandits that a popular saying had it that no one crossed the borders without first making a will. The country, like Wales, had a reputation for its poverty, which gave added poignancy to Cromwell's hope that his policies had helped the poor. One traveler in the same area saw barelegged women and girls, their feet wrapped in woolen blankets and looking sickly, fetching home carts loaded with peat their menfolk had cut. Despite the cold climate, the tiny houses had no chimneys: great holes on the sides let out the smoke from the burning peat. The common food was mostly oat cakes, beaten thin and baked hard, not very pleasing to the English palate. Outsiders quickly decided that Scottish backwardness and poverty was directly related to the seeming slothfulness of the people. Crossing the river Esk, Fox would have seen the common people wading barefoot through the water at low tide, carrying their clothes and shoes to keep them dry.[28]

His *Journal* suggests that Fox had a quicker eye for hypocrisy and deceit than for his surroundings. He targeted especially the ministers of the Scottish Presbyterian church, and seemed particularly pleased to have Robert Widders with him because he thundered against what Fox considered the ministers' rottenness. Alexander Parker and James Lancaster, both frequent companions, and Osburne also came north after the party divided, the other four breaking off to go westward. By Sunday, September 13, they had moved rapidly through Dumfries and Douglas to Gartshore, a small hamlet just half a dozen miles east and north of Glasgow. The few converts were disruptive in the tightly bound communities of the land to the north. In Gartshore, not only did they convince Lady Margaret Hamilton, but Fox also had an open confrontation with some Presbyterian ministers who came to expound the Calvinist doctrine of election.[29] Fox had a lot to say about what he called the folly of this idea, but, judging from a book the Quakers circulated criticizing the ministers of Scotland, he gave even more attention to the inordinate power they had over their parishioners. It was obviously difficult to break into the closed world of Scottish Presbyterianism. Thus he lashed out at the way Scots who had turned Quaker were excommunicated and at what he styled the "club law," or stoning and beatings, used against them. Stressing how the area's ministers used the law—petitioning magistrates to forbid missionaries to come among them, arresting Scots who welcomed Quakers in their homes, and so on—Fox was clearly underlining for London's benefit how the Presbyterian clergymen violated the law of the land, not to mention the principles of Jesus. His caustic words dripping with vitriol, Fox exclaimed, "Oh! How is the beauty of the church of the Presbyterians marred and deformed."[30]

As Fox thus exposed Scottish intolerance, so the ministers' reactions illustrated how they saw the missionaries from the south as spearheads of a new world—and an English world at that—they wanted no part of. It was a world that required religious tolerance and had behind it at least the theoretical support of Cromwell, his government, and the occupying army. Fox knew what he was doing. Consequently, he reported that a mob inspired by a Presbyterian minister had thrown a pan full of water down a soldier's neck.[31] Once word of the Quakers' coming and the threat they embodied got around, an assembly of ministers promulgated a series of statements for their members' assent. Their most important charge, the one ranked first, represented the gravamen of the dispute, not just in Scotland but wherever Fox took his message, namely, that "cursed is he who says every man has a light within him sufficient to lead him to salvation."[32] Those intoning "Amen" to that anathema, assuming they thought about it as they uttered the word, were pledging allegiance to the existing order of things, religiously and politically. Fox's gospel subverted that allegiance. When he maintained that free access to God came through the light that shone in every person,[33] he surely made clergy and established churches superfluous, and that principle easily widened the area of freedom in other social institutions as well.

This message, especially when delivered with an English accent, did not go over very well in Scotland. Nor did the declaration of the day of the Lord break through the opposition and strike a popular chord. The religious establishment presented too much of a solid phalanx against the invaders. Excommunication from the Scottish church had little religious meaning for new Quakers; what did matter was that the action meant loyal Presbyterians would not trade or even converse with the outcasts. Thus in the countryside traveling toward Edinburgh the Fox party could hardly find accommodations, certainly not for love and often not for money. In Glasgow not a single resident came to Fox's meeting, an almost unheard-of development. Even officers of the English army, no doubt reflecting the opposition to Quakers emanating from headquarters, displayed open animosity. At Linlithgow, sixteen miles west of Edinburgh, Fox was astounded when one officer claimed he would have stood guard at the crucifixion of Jesus if ordered to do so; Fox contrasted that comment with others he had heard, probably from Quaker officers, that they would gladly lose their positions rather than turn against the truth. It was obvious that the support he had expected from the officers was eroding. In Leith, site of the army's strongest citadel in Scotland, the officers seemed a bit more favorably inclined, but opposition remained relentless.[34] Despite sounding the truth in sixty different places, Fox was convinced that his opponents were determined to beat Quakerism out of the nation.[35]

Immediately upon arriving in Edinburgh, Fox found a crowd of thousands gathered on Castlehill, a place of execution that loomed above the city, to watch the burning of a woman convicted of witchcraft. It was an appropriate time to declare the day of the Lord, and he proceeded to do so, with few results. Citizens of the proud Scottish capital chafed under English domination and wanted nothing to do with yet another Englishman. The city's council, all Cromwell's appointees anxious to win local favor, promptly ordered Fox to appear before them on Tuesday, October 13. As was his wont, Fox refused to take off his hat and had it lifted from his head by the doorkeeper. The council wanted to know why he had come to Scotland and how long he intended to stay. Fox's answer was a bit disingenuous: "I came to visit the seed of God which had long lain under bondage under corruption," he said, denying any "outward" business. His business, however, had already destabilized the given order of things, as he as much admitted in a written statement he presented after the council ordered him to leave within a week. He compared his persecutors to earlier councils that had judged such troublemakers as John the Baptist, Jesus, and the martyred Stephen, and he condemned them for standing against the truth and siding with those who had stoned and mocked his followers whenever wicked and envious ministers so prompted. But Fox did not test the council's order of banishment by overstaying the week, for he turned west again.[36]

The day after he left, General George Monck, Cromwell's determined military chief in Scotland, ordered all Quakers in the army to register.[37] Monck had long been troubled about the Children's subversive influence within his force.

As far as he was concerned, his army already harbored too many enthusiasts and extremists of every sort. His view was simple: Quaker officers were not fit to command, and Quakers in the ranks would not obey. A subversive element, they were likely to mutiny, as he saw it, "upon every slight occasion."[38]

Fox's careful public words of advice to troops in Scotland did not support Monck's conclusions, but explicit in those words was the broad principle that soldiers were to use the sword only in a just cause. Souls must be subject to the higher powers, he emphasized, but those fortunate enough to rise to that level had the obligation to overturn, chain, and put down "all the powers of darkness, the spiritual wickedness," to use the sword, in other words, for good ends. God would depose, he prophesied, any who repudiated this obligation and allied with the oppressor who had reigned and whom the Lord had already overthrown. Words like these undoubtedly pointed to the conclusion that God had swept aside the previous government for not permitting the Lord to reign: as Fox phrased it, "the Lord laid it as the dust."[39] In a less public letter, he was even blunter: "Who would have ever thought you would have taken part or joined together with them who would have once destroyed you . . . ?"[40] What God had done once God could do again.

Surely Monck, reading such words, could be forgiven for concluding that encouraging such ideas in the minds of ordinary soldiers could easily lead to mutiny. What would happen, for example, if the army were called upon to round up some dissident group like the Children of the Light? Fox's amazement at an officer who would stand by and permit, say, a Jesus to be executed, revealed his assumption that the principle of supporting a just cause took precedence over mere military orders.

Fortunately, Fox discovered that not all the army's officers entertained such views. After Glasgow, he headed for the north of Scotland, again finding the native population almost uniformly hostile. Ambushed from hedgerows bordering the country's narrow roads, Fox's party found themselves dodging angry Scotsmen. Near Stirling irate Presbyterians brandished pitchforks at them. In Stirling itself an armed troop of soldiers stopped them and carried them off to the guard-house, but a few words with some friendly officers resulted in their quick release. At Perth, more soldiers, egged on by antagonistic Baptists, took them into custody, but while they were being escorted out of town, they ended up in the midst of a horse race. Fox found the large crowd irresistible and proclaimed the day of the Lord. The suddenly abashed soldiers thereupon expressed a willingness to go to the hot military graveyard that was Jamaica rather than arresting such men. But they still loaded the Quakers in boats and shipped them up the Firth of Tay to Dundee.

At Dundee it became apparent that a split existed between the English soldiers and their officers, on the one hand, and the civilian authorities, on the other. At the suggestion of some officers, Fox scheduled a meeting in the town hall, a development that led the local council to announce its own session at the same time to deal with town business. The Quakers therefore took over the area around the market cross on a crowded market day, with Parker, Bible in hand and standing astride the cross, warming up an audience consisting primarily of soldiers.

When Fox climbed up and surveyed the market scene, with its haggling and shouting that continued despite the Quaker efforts, he roared with the loudest voice he could muster to condemn their sinfulness and wickedness and announced that this was the day of the Lord. The few converts made in Dundee that market day were primarily soldiers.

Fox and his group then turned southward toward Leith and Edinburgh, in both places escaping arrest warrants. Except at Dunbar on the eastern coast, their audiences remained mostly soldiers of the English army. The city, where fishing was a principal occupation, was also the site of Cromwell's victory over the supporters of the future Charles II eight years earlier. Here, at 8:00 one morning, Fox held a meeting in a churchyard prior to a previously scheduled Presbyterian lecture there. Some of the local citizenry, rich and poor, showed up, along with the usual soldiers, and Fox decided that he had had a good meeting. He left Scotland only a few days and a few steps ahead of Monck's formal order for his arrest.

As he looked back on his experience north of the Tweed, Fox recognized his failure to win over even a small number of the native population, but he put the five months he had spent there in the best light. "For when first I set my horse's feet upon the Scottish ground," he remembered, "I felt the seed of God to sparkle about me like innumerable sparks of fire." But what he deemed a "thick, cloddy earth of hypocrisy and falseness" with "a briery, brambly nature" covered those sparkling seeds and prevented a harvest. He thus concluded that "the husbandman is to wait in patience."[41] That he never returned to Scotland suggests that he knew he had neither the patience nor the energy to break up the clods or clear away the brambles.

Monck's decision to order Fox's arrest underlined the uncertainties growing within the Protectorate. For one thing, Cromwell was ill, so ill that his address to Parliament when it convened in January, in the past so lengthy, this time was remarkably short (indeed, the speaker remarked himself on its brevity): "I have some infirmities upon me, I have not liberty to speak more unto you."[42] Less than nine months later he would be dead. Poor health meant less energy and little direction, and that in turn opened doors of opportunity for those who had long bided their time. Royalists were encouraged by the would-be Charles II's military preparations on the Continent; ships had been promised by the Dutch and men from the Spanish monarch.[43] Fifth Monarchists, those ever-hopeful millenarians who had watched as their April 1657 coup was nipped in the bud, busily examined the mysterious signs of the books of Revelation and Daniel to see if their time was now coming nearer.[44] The religious tolerance that Cromwell had always championed produced a multiplicity of what he conceded were "interests," or sects, each vying for preferment and supremacy. Such an "appetite for variety," he explained in a graphic image suggesting his own irritation, was "as if we should see one making wounds in a man's side and would desire nothing more than to be groping and grovelling with his fingers in those wounds."[45] The groping and grovelling proved trying for many—such as Presbyterians, markedly more conservative than the Lord Protector—and some determined to put an end to the tolerance that had produced it.[46]

Fox's return to his home country, then, came at a crucial time. On the one hand, there were those repelled about the prospects of probing a person's lacerations, particularly when they viewed that wounded person as an England becoming ever more impaired. On the other hand were those who often profited from a policy of tolerance as long as it was adhered to, even if it meant groping and grovelling. The latter group included Fox's Children. They had a stake in protecting the existing order so that it could in turn protect them and allow them to prosper. This stake, however, inevitably sharpened the differences between the contending parties and pricked them into conflict.

Fox's activities now proceeded on two levels. He continued his missionary activities, taking advantage of the religious liberty that existed, even as he kept a close watch on what was happening in the government. Sometimes the two coincided. As soon as he reentered England, he and Anthony Pearson called on several aldermen in Newcastle. A justice of the peace in Cumberland and Westmorland since 1652, Pearson served also as a commissioner of sequestration, making him privy to insider information on the availability of confiscated Cavalier estates; indeed, he had purchased several. He also served as secretary to Sir Arthur Hesilrige, by this time one of the most powerful men in the country. Fox was always anxious to find new followers, particularly among those in powerful positions, but he had a more personal purpose in visiting Alderman Thomas Ledgard, a former mayor known to Pearson through their mutual interest in confiscated lands.[47] Ledgard had attacked the Quakers for destabilizing the social order by neglecting their families, the veritable bedrock of society.[48] What really piqued Fox was the depiction of his followers as "butterflies" flitting over the dales but daring not to venture into town. He determined to see Ledgard and the five Calvinist ministers who supported him and prove them all wrong. Receiving short shrift from all six men, only two of whom bothered to show up, he taunted, "Who are the butterflies now?" And then he was off to the busy market to declare the day of the Lord and to warn that judgment would soon be coming upon them.[49]

To hone the issue even finer for his Newcastle opponents, Fox responded to one of their published attacks on Quakers' ideas. His answer showed how doctrine became easily entwined with questions of political authority. "The scripture," averred Ledgard, "is the lantern of obedience, and it directs men to Jesus." "Obedience" was the all important word. Those who worried about Quakers as threats to the established order focused on their insistence that authority came through the leadings of the ineffable spirit and not the more definite Scriptures; this idea marked them as dangerous Ranters. Fox countered by pointing out that some of those who possessed the Scriptures, like the Pharisees, still walked in darkness and, by implication, could never be obedient to what they did not know. "You who are got up since the days of the apostles, in the apostasy," he insisted, "want [lack] the rule, which is the spirit, in which God the father of spirits is worshiped." Hence the spirit called forth obedience to the rule, which no amount of written Scripture could supply.[50] Fox reiterated this point, but it remained inexplicable to his opponents, particularly because to them it meant the rejection of all rules, not just those of a regime presuming to govern without recognizing the ultimate authority.

Fox left Newcastle to visit meetings in the area. Traveling with Pearson, he stopped by Durham to express his opposition to a proposed college to be built there to train ministers. His objection, of course, arose from his conviction that no training sufficed to make a person a minister, for he believed that one was called and empowered by God for this role.[51] Needless to say, Fox's position did not appeal to northern Presbyterian and Independent ministers whose churches suffered from a paucity of qualified leaders and who saw the suggested college as a means to fill the gap. But his stance very conveniently coincided with the interests of propertied men of influence like Sir Arthur Hesilrige and less powerful men such as Pearson. Having acquired former church and royalist lands, they certainly did not want the government to repossess some of these lands to finance a college from the ground up, however valuable it might prove to be from a religious point of view.[52] Fox gave no indication that he realized how his views comported with the interests of Hesilrige and Pearson, but the latter could hardly avoid knowing it and likely remarked on it to his companion.

At Pearson's behest, Fox went to see Sir Henry Vane, one of the most influential if erratic Protestants in the country, an Independent sectarian who had once served as governor of the Massachusetts Bay Colony in the New World. The authorities had long suspected Vane, a republican, of subversive activity.[53] His religious expressions were similar to Fox's, or at least they wrote in the same biblical style of flowing, mystical metaphors that muddied their meaning.[54] The two argued religious topics to no clear conclusion. Fox's youth—he was not quite thirty-three—surprised Vane, so he may not have taken him as seriously as the First Friend expected. In any event, they both let the sun go down on their anger. Vane remarked later that he would have had his guest thrown out if others had not been present; Fox recorded that Vane "was vain and high and proud and conceited."[55] If Pearson's motive in taking Fox to see Vane was to forge an alliance between them, he failed. The two Quakers returned to Pearson's Ramshaw Hall. They had much to discuss before leaving again to visit meetings of Friends.

Fox spent most of the late winter and early spring of 1658 traveling in the north and retracing his steps of five years earlier into Yorkshire, going by Swarthmoor, and then heading south. In Nottingham he sought out Rhys Jones and the "Proud Quakers." More than eighty showed up to hear him, but Jones himself chose not to appear. Again starting southward to meet his disciples, Fox passed through Leicestershire and Warwickshire, the region where he had grown up, but he did not record a stop with his family, including his recently widowed mother. As he went up and down, he had other things to think about.[56]

By May 11 Fox reached London; he sent an epistle from there to all meetings of his followers.[57] At the end of the month he went to Bedfordshire and the spacious home of Justice of the Peace John Crook, where a general yearly meeting, the first, was due to meet. Crook, having served as a captain in the New Model Army, a position which he parlayed into propertied proprietor of royalist land, won a reputation for sober religion and got himself nominated to the Barebones Parliament.[58] Thousands of Children thronged the area, overflowing his well-appointed estate and nearby towns and inns. Fox used this gathering of ministers and others from all over the nation as a forum to instruct them as to what to do in the current situation.[59] His views, of course, reflected his experiences in Scotland and his travel and conferences with men like Pearson and Crook, as well as his own reading of the existing political climate. His priorities were clearly evident. No matter how determinedly aggressive and seemingly oblivious to practicalities he was when he confronted ministers and magistrates, priests and protectors, Fox had a normal streak about him, one that led him to place a high value on the well-being of the organization he had carefully nurtured for so long. Having left Scotland just ahead of Monck's order to apprehend him and having witnessed lately his inability to reach men like Ledgard, he decided it was time to project a lower profile, build more slowly, and wait for the day of the Lord. His addresses to the three or four thousand who came—easily more than a tenth of his total number of followers[60]—spelled out his conclusions for the movement.

His talks can be read, of course, as sermons pleading for his followers to remain more spiritually faithful, to turn inward and harken to the leadings of the divine spirit. They were certainly that. But set against the context of their time and Fox's recent experiences, they were also more than that. They built on his understanding of the spirit and called his listeners to be alert to and aware of how the spirit's workings would prepare them for a larger mission. His two addresses were suffused, therefore, with Fox's twofold goal: he wanted his followers to remain faithful to his version of faith, and he wanted them to see themselves as a vanguard, living in such a way that others would be convinced by their example. He wanted them, in short, to stand firm where they had been led but to be ready to assume new roles as they emerged.

Fox spoke at least twice. Aware of some dissidents present, probably Naylerites, the astute politician opened with a call for unity, internal unity, a unity against the outside world. God's promise had been made, he said, "to the seed, not to seeds as many, but to one." Let us stand as one, he was saying. To reassure the women, some of Nayler's firmest supporters, he stressed that "all people, both men and women, should feel this seed in them." He made clear that this seed of Christ planted in each heart "was the seed that bruises the serpent's head," a biblical image referring to the ultimate conquest of evil. Then he used seven illustrations, or "types," drawn from the Bible so his listeners would understand the posture they should adopt in a world that he regarded as shot through with evil and destined to be destroyed. In his first six types he described those who had rejected the truth proffered to them. Those who "sit down in Adam in the fall sit down in misery, in death, in darkness and corruption." And those embracing the Jewish law "sit down in that which must have an end and which made nothing perfect." Such people "were drinking of the whore's cup under the beast's and dragon's power"—images from Revelation long identified with corrupt worldly power—and did not live in that power and spirit that fulfilled the prophets and wrote the Scriptures. People sitting down in Christ Jesus were heirs of the promise of the richness of grace and divine kindness, he concluded, and "will inherit substance" and be able to announce to the world the fellowship that still remained a mystery to its people.

Fox spelled out some of the mysteries of his metaphors in his second address.

He recognized that some were pushing to go out into the world to confront the evil they saw there. But right now he counseled caution: "[T]he time is not now, as it was at first [when the Children were young], the time now is otherwise, to settle and stay." He advised that the faithful should sit "still and cool and quiet." "Now there is a great danger to traveling abroad in the world," he said, "except a man be moved of the Lord." Wait in patience, he advised, remain cool, and feel the power of the Lamb. But Fox was not encouraging an escapism motivated by weakness—not at all: refusing to meddle with the powers of the earth, his followers would stand as silent sentinels judging the world's leaders to "answer that of God in them and bring them to do justice." The Lamb's power and authority—Fox often used the word "Lamb" as a synonym for Christ—he saw as the end of the outward law, which originated in the reality of human evil and transgression. He triumphantly concluded, "Christ . . . is the end of the law, bringing those who live in the law of life to live over all transgression."[61] In a pamphlet distributed about the same time, Fox asked, "Are not all foundations to be overthrown that is not according to that of God in every man?" A government based on any other principle faced only confusion and destruction.[62]

Fox may not have intended the overthrow of the government, but it is easy to understand how jittery magistrates might hear or read his words and think otherwise. In truth, he did want a revolution, for he saw his society to be corrupt, evil, and unresponsive to the requirements of justice, whether human or divine. The question begging for an answer was whether the job could be done peacefully or not. On that crucial score, Fox kept his counsel and waited, ever alert and ready to respond to opportunities as they presented themselves. He was prepared, to put it simply, to be a good leader and follow the advice he gave the gathering at Crook's.

The agents of Secretary of State John Thurloe were a bit laggard this time. Three days elapsed before a troop of cavalrymen came to take Fox into custody. Perhaps they were busy with what must have seemed more pressing matters, particularly for people with a penchant for nervousness: a royalist plot was rumored in May and added to the Lord Protector's already precarious position.[63] From Leeds in Yorkshire, a long way from London and Bedfordshire both, worries surfaced that Quakers were uniting with workers to drive tax collectors from the town and planning their rising to occur simultaneously with the capital's troubles.[64] Fortunately, however, Fox was strolling in the garden as the troopers broke into Crook's house and so escaped arrest.[65]

Returning to London in early June, the First Friend grew increasingly concerned about the government's tightening surveillance of his movement and the growing number of arrests of his followers, both in England and Ireland. He visited Cromwell to protest their maltreatment and to warn the Lord Protector again that to take an earthly crown would result in his ruin and that of posterity. He compared compulsory fast days to raise money for foreign Protestants to persecution. These fasts, he concluded, were little more than masquerades behind which the authorities unleashed waves of abuse against his followers. He told Cromwell in no uncertain terms that the Protestants he was endeavoring to help were no better than papists as far as persecution was concerned, and then he criticized England's leaders for the suffering they were imposing on those with whom they disagreed. Toward the end of August Fox himself was taken into custody for a few hours by two zealous troopers. He immediately went to a sickly Cromwell, trying to recuperate at Hampton Court, to dramatize for him exactly how the regime was working. The Lord Protector, whose beloved daughter Elizabeth Claypool had died on August 6, was doing so poorly himself that he could not hear his visitor out and invited him to return later; he already looked like a dead man, Fox remembered.[66] And within days, on September 3, his lucky day, Oliver Cromwell died.

Richard Cromwell was simply not the man to succeed his father. Though relatively free of political attachments, at thirty-two he was young, inexperienced, and irresolute, a man simply not up to the demands of an age of rapid change. The country needed a person with experience enough to handle a nation torn by contending forces.[67] Richard Cromwell's situation grew progressively worse. Needing funds, he called a new Parliament for January. It needed guidance, which he could not give. The members, factious enough already, watched nearly helplessly as the Commons broke apart debating every little tiresome matter conceivable. Determined republicans like Arthur Hesilrige and Henry Vane and commonwealthmen like John Thurloe, who was committed to the kind of regime that existed before the Protectorate, contended with each other and with Cromwellians, Presbyterians, and army officers, themselves divided.[68] With such divisions, it would have required an accomplished Machiavelli to govern, and Richard Cromwell was hardly that.

Parliament could unite on one thing: the Quaker threat. On April 16, 1659, its members debated at length a petition against the imprisonments the Children suffered. "Fanatics," one member called them, while another announced his desire "to whip them home as vagrants." Others complained about the number of Children who flocked into the House chamber. One general stated that disturbers of the peace deserved to spend time in jail but that he did not want to arrest those who refused to swear oaths. After the debate was over and a resolution passed, two or three Friends were called in, their heads properly uncovered, to hear the results; one of these was former justice of the peace John Crook. The resolution stated that their petition had been read but that the House rejected the "scandals thereby cast upon magistracy and ministry," ordering them to apply themselves to their callings and to live lawfully. Denied the right to respond, one was overheard to mutter as he left, "The name of the righteous shall live; but the name of the wicked shall not."[69]

Beyond Westminster, the splits represented in Parliament were exacerbated by religious sectarianism crisscrossing political divisions. The consequent disturbances heightened the fears of those who, terrified, could conjure up dreadful images of the disintegration of the political order. At the other extreme sectarians like the Friends seemed to grasp every opportunity to add to the divisiveness. Fox refused to let the dead Cromwell go to his grave without blasting the new order. The formal last rites cost the financially strapped government perhaps £60,000 to put on the grandest such pageant that English history had ever witnessed. Fox was horrified at the month-long event. The room in which the late Protector lay in state was draped with black velvet, with a raised wax image clad in purple velvet and an ermine cap; beside the figure lay a gilded sword and in its hands a scepter and orb. The confusion surrounding the funeral itself on November 23—it was past nightfall when the day-long ceremonies at Westminster Abbey finally ended and the invited guests stumbled home—did not offend him, but he was incensed by the blaring trumpets, the ostentatious trappings, and the new red coats of the infantrymen who lined the streets, all of which prompted him to speak for the nation's "sober people." "Oh friends, what are you doing," he groaned, "how are you turned to fooleries, which things in times past you stood over." Expect, he warned leaders and people alike, the day of the Lord, for "the swift hand of the Lord is turned against them all."[70]

On the same page of his memoirs in which he recounted his revulsion at such pagan doings, Fox included an epistle to his young followers that marked his response to the shifting mood of the nation. Like many of his epistles, especially those from this period, it could be read two ways, probably the result of intentional ambiguity. Read after the events, the epistle sounded as though he was advising withdrawal and noninvolvement with worldly matters, particularly when a possibility of violence existed. Thus he referred to "Adam's sons" who resembled "dogs, beasts, and swine" when they destroyed each other by "goring, renting, and biting one another." He fulminated against wars and killings and, more fundamentally, the lusts from which they sprung. Considering those who would take up arms for their Zion, Fifth Monarchists, for example, he reminded his followers that Zion needed no such help. Another kingdom, the real Zion, awaited his followers.

By repairing to that true kingdom, Fox asserted, one might "live in Christ, the Prince of Peace, the way of God, who is the second Adam who never fell." Unlike Christ's kingdom, the reign of the first Adam and his children was destined to be destroyed, just as Cromwell's death illustrated human mortality and his funeral demonstrated the moral and spiritual corruption of a regime lurching toward its end. Implicit in his words was the idea that his followers could help bring down this false Zion by withholding their allegiance from it, refusing to pay tithes to it, refusing to abide by its empty forms, refusing to adhere to its meaningless rituals. Their example, preached to all, would then elicit a like response from England's other sober people.[71]

So Fox was coming more and more to eschew violence for the movement, as he had always for himself, but he had not changed his view that the day of the Lord was coming and would be helped along by the Children and the proclamation of their message. He remained as alienated as ever from the larger society: it was corrupt, evil, dominated by Adam's children. He was not above appealing to those in power—particularly when he could make a mockery of their profession of Christianity—nor of reminding them of the suffering they were causing. Let them face their guilt. But he had no illusions about any permanent changes that could be wrought in a state that refused to recognize the higher allegiance he demanded.

Fox's approach took time, but too little of that scarce commodity remained. He and his Valiant Sixty, the collective name given to the missionaries from the north, gripped by a compelling idea that human institutions like the church actually impeded a person's encounter with God, had chalked up an amazingly strong showing: a cadre of committed leaders had created a nationwide organization and gathered thirty thousand or more into the Society of Friends. No other sectarian group of the period could match this record. Indeed, its prospects arguably rivaled those of the established church, which was rent by contending factions trying to gain the upper hand. These achievements had required seven years, double that time if the dating began in the mid-1640s. Having obviously found the words—the day of the Lord, and all they implied about a new people in a new order—that spoke to many, Fox might reasonably hope that if things fell right then the future could be his. As the sands trickled slowly through the 1659 hourglass, the most crucial year of his movement's young life, time would tell.

12

❀

As Easy as Removing
Tottenham Wood

By April 1659 the time had run out for Richard Cromwell's Protectorate. On Thursday, April 21, when the capital's attention would normally have turned to the warming weather that heralded spring, Cromwell requested his commander-in-chief to appear at Whitehall to explain his and the army's opposition. Charles Fleetwood, married to the Lord Protector's sister, simply ignored the summons. Even Richard Cromwell could find a backbone when dealing with a man his father had likened to a "milksop." He sent his bodyguard to bring the commander in by force. They too refused. It was a startling omen. When Cromwell on his own announced a rendezvous of loyal troops at Whitehall to counter one planned by Fleetwood, the men in the ranks would not obey their officers. Still committed to the Good Old Cause, the army was convinced that Cromwell was on the verge of disbanding them so the Stuarts could return and restore the monarchy. Though the young Lord Protector may have been irresolute, he was not stupid. Under pressure he agreed to dissolve Parliament. It was a military coup, pure and simple.[1]

Fox and his followers anticipated the speedy arrival of a new day; after all, one of the expelled Parliament's last acts had been to spurn one of their petitions. The army saw the dawn first. Quickly purged of Cromwell's supporters, including those the dead Oliver Cromwell himself had appointed, its upper ranks began to be filled with those cashiered earlier, including Levellers and Quakers.[2] The churches were next, but as Fox perceived it their dawn was bound to be troubled. He chortled at the irony of the new departure. The papists, he said, addressing his various sectarian opponents, "cry, 'higher power, help, help'" or the mass will end, Episcopalians "cry, 'higher power, help, help'" or common prayers will cease, Presbyterians "cry, 'help, help, higher power,'" or the directory of worship will fall, Independents and Baptists "cry, 'help, help, higher powers,'" or the faith will not stand. "Are you not ashamed," he gibed, "to show you are naked, out of the power and life that the Apostles were in?" Only his followers needed no government to support their efforts, because, he emphasized, "the spirit that gave forth the scriptures teaches us how to pray, how to speak, sing, fast, and give thanks."[3] His epistle bubbled with optimism and a tone of victory.

But later, now embittered, he would chide Presbyterians, Independents, and Baptists for refusing to side with the Quakers in the last days of the Interregnum.[4]

Within days of the upheaval the Children delivered a letter to Fleetwood for transmittal to the general council of officers, the ruling body within the army. The letter expressed hope "for this blessed cause," if only the army did its duty. It prodded the military to "begin where they left the work of the Lord." The letter's anonymous author claimed to represent "a willing people and their numbers not a few" and promised to "cheerfully afford our further assistance to the hazard of our lives and all our earthly concernments."[5] This missive certainly reflected Quaker hopes for the future, and the commitment of the top echelon of the Quaker leadership in London to the army's side. Ever since the mid-1650s, books authored by Children had been cleared before publication with Fox.[6] Thus even if he did not approve of all the sentiments expressed in the anonymous letter, the First Friend did not veto its circulation.

Quaker hopes mounted higher when the army seemed to respond. It promptly summoned the fag end of the Long Parliament, now reduced to forty-two members and appropriately dubbed the Rump. This Parliament, which had tried and executed Charles I, embodied the dreams of those who wanted the Good Old Cause resurrected. It began sitting for its second session on Sunday, May 8, a move that caught strict and sober Protestants unawares. While their opponents muttered, Friends were encouraged, particularly after Parliament received and referred to committee one of their petitions for relief from official prosecution. Rumors that the army would continue to remove wicked men from the officer corps also augered well. A hint of gloating surfaced as Quakers spread the intelligence that homes of Cavaliers and priests were being raided, and some had been arrested. Perhaps a new day had indeed dawned.[7]

Some of the Quakers certainly thought they saw beams of light. Edward Burrough, one of the most committed of all the Quakers in his support for a strong policy on the part of the government against wickedness and for justice, was unreservedly bellicose. In a broadside intended to be posted on walls and buildings, he demanded of the army, "Where is the Good Old Cause now? . . . Have you not forgone it?" He hammered home his view of what the Good Old Cause stood for: it was "for liberty, both in spirituals and temporals," "the just freedom of all peoples," "the establishment of righteousness, mercy, and truth in the earth and taking off all oppressions." The army must stand for these principles. He warned that whoever opposed the Good Old Cause, "[W]e are against them and will engage our lives against them."[8] Richard Hubberthorne, published a series of pamphlets and a broadside to criticize the army and other sectarians for their failure to live up to their earlier commitments.[9]

Quaker critics pounced on such rhetoric. "Hell broke loose," blazed the title of a London pamphlet whose author thought it outrageous that the army might endorse such Quaker appeals and "encourage their ungodliness and blasphemy."[10] A satirical broadside appeared in mid-March purporting to be from a coalition to promote the Good Old Cause, made up of "ignoble men, barkers, cobblers, colliers, draymen, grocers, hucksters, malters, peddlers, sowgarters, tinkers," and assorted mechanics. It warned that if Quakers, Anabaptists, Fifth Monarchists, and Ranters came to power, then "the saints shall possess the earth" and so obstruct and abolish decency and order. Such republicans as Henry Vane and Arthur Hesilrige had supposedly joined Quakers of the stature of Fox, Nayler, and Isaac Penington, son of a former lord mayor of London, to agree to this "Phantique League and Covenant."[11] A bit later, a slightly less excited author alleged that Quakers and Anabaptists had united to turn Parliament out, "setting themselves in their stead to rule all by their giddy heads."[12] City maids pledged their "unresolved virginity" to resist the "dismal looks" of Quakers and other such "conventickling congregations."[13]

Some Children soon got an opportunity to show their mettle. Rumors concerning a royalist coup were stimulated by news that the Stuart pretender touting himself as Charles II was organizing forces from exile across the Channel. On July 31 a force commanded by Sir George Booth, one of many conspirators, rose in Warrington with the announced aim of summoning a free Parliament, the better to turn over to Charles the vacant throne and an orderly country. Despite a Quaker's warning to the authorities in nearby Chester, Booth's men easily marched through that city's gates and occupied the town. Fiery republicans in Parliament redoubled their efforts to muster a militia sufficient to put down the uprising and prevent it from spreading out of the north. Vane laid aside his scruples and forgot his lack of military experience to accept an appointment to raise and command a regiment of volunteers. But then unsure of himself, Vane refused to issue orders to his troops. Fortunately this unusual method of leadership did not have to be tested, for Booth's coup attempt failed, and Booth himself—though disguised in woman's clothes with appropriate stuffing and a wig—was apprehended.[14]

The Children agonized, however much Burrough postured about their willingness to engage their lives for the Good Old Cause. In Bristol, after Parliament tapped seven Friends to recruit men as commissioners of militia, some Quakers thought it permissible to get others to volunteer. Alexander Parker, one of Fox's frequent companions, was torn over the wisdom of this course, even though he personally approved. "I can neither persuade them to it nor dissuade them from it," he explained.[15] In the north, Anthony Pearson, friend of Vane and Hesilrige, was pulled both ways: he wanted to help the goverment, but he did not want to jeopardize his standing with the Children. He accepted a commission in the militia, but refused to wear a sword.[16] Five members of the meeting at Westminster in London, including Amor Stoddard, one of Fox's earliest converts, were designated militia commisioners.[17] Fox claimed that all his followers turned these offers down, thus revealing that he had a selective memory. He publicized his own view of participating in war in an epistle addressed to Friends everywhere. Significantly his pragmatic "No" did not absolutely renounce all warfare on principle. "Take heed," he admonished, "to keep out of the powers of the earth that run into the wars and fighting. . . . Take heed of joining with this or the other." He rejected use of weapons for the simple reason that secular rulers had turned against the just, disobeyed the just, and now found the just pitting them one against another. He carefully left open the possibility that once the state came around to favor God's just cause things could be different. Rumpers prove yourselves, he was saying, and then we shall see. Meanwhile, Friends must dwell in that kingdom with no end and rely on spiritual weapons.[18]

Just as Vane and other republicans recognized the army as the backbone of their regime, the only guarantee of their continued rule, so Fox and the Children sought to increase their influence in it. Fox was in London during the tremors after Booth's rising and continued open discussions with army officers in and around the capital. He had always stood by the army and supported its efforts to win payment of back wages, and this support had made him many friends in the ranks.[19] Now he reminded the nation that Quakers had been unfairly cashiered from the army, and that their only crime had been faithfulness to God.[20] At one sergeant's home he exalted Christ over all, presumably including the state and its shortcomings.[21] He lectured the army on its flaws even as he sharpened the distinctions between the rank and file and those in the government who manipulated them for their own sordid ends. "Oh, when will you throw out all those who have been fed like hogs and swine among you?," he asked in one pamphlet. Addressing those who had championed the Good Old Cause, he charged them with unfaithfulness to the "power of the Lord which once stirred this nation," an infidelity that had prevented them from unfurling their standard in Holland, France, and Spain, and letting it fly over the papacy itself. "And then," he concluded even more expansively, "you should have sent for the Turk's idol, the Mahomet, and plucked up idolatry, and cried up Christ the only king and Lord."[22] The Good Old English Cause would thus have become the good old righteous cause, "for the good of all people, for the releasement of all people out of thralldom, bondage, and capitivity." The army's failure paved the way for a new "inquisition" that had imprisoned an estimated two thousand for conscience's sake in England and had surfaced across the Atlantic, where Congregational authorities, since 1657, had prohibited Quakers from entering Massachusetts Bay Colony. His attacks on deceit, tyranny, and the persecution of the faithful, both at home and abroad, revealed that he saw the army as an instrument of God's judgment, a way to initiate the divine will on earth. It was Fox soaring to his millenarian heights.[23]

As far as is known, Fox did not encourage his followers to join the army, but many of them cooperated with it in one capacity or the other, and he did not rebuke them for their efforts. As we have seen, some served as militia commissioners and recruited soldiers for the army; and some ministers close to the leadership, like Parker, looked favorably on this role. Rumors were rife that Quakers had infiltrated the army.[24] Fox's ideas about the army's mission, including its failure to fulfill its grand historic task, certainly implied that he favored the Children taking an active part in setting it on its rightful course. Those who read his pamphlets or listened to his sermons could be forgiven for concluding that what the army needed was a new dose of leadership, one committed to its grand role. Thus a Welsh Friend wrote to explain why he thought it permissible to join the army.[25] In this as in so many other things he said, Fox's failure to spell out exactly what he meant gave grist to those who wanted to interpret (or misinterpret) him.

Fox's views, written and spoken, did have the effect of driving a wedge between the army and its commanders, the army and whatever civilian authority happened to be in charge in London, the army's current conservative mission and the one embodied in the Good Old Cause. It was no wonder, then, that the Children's continuing influence in the army prompted concern on the part of many higher military officials. In Scotland General Monck saw this threat clearly and tried again to prevent his troopers from attending Quaker meetings. But Quaker infiltration continued. If common soldiers were intimidated by their commander's orders, then officers proved a different matter entirely, some of them even surrendering their commissions to cast their lot with the movement.[26] Even officers on Monck's immediate staff succumbed to the insidious Quaker influence: "[G]reat overturnings there were among them," one missionary crowed.[27]

Fox's *Journal*, written after the event, fails to convey much of the drama and its significance in this crucial period when the Rump government was thrashing about trying to find a firm enough base to maintain its footing. Whatever Fox's hopes, the Rump's republican leaders, men like Vane and Hesilrige with whom he had some contact, apparently made no overtures to him. Indeed, a note of exasperation slipped into his account when he mentioned Vane, a hint from hindsight, perhaps, that the parliamentary leader might have saved himself and his regime and revived the Good Old Cause had he reached out to Fox and the Quakers. Fox displayed the same "I-told-you-so" attitude in a general letter to the "back sliding, hypocritical, and treacherous" leaders who had blithely ignored the warnings he and his followers had preached up and down in churches, markets, and courts. "When you pretended to set up the Old Cause," he allowed, "it was but yourselves, for which you long stunk to sober people."[28]

The practical problems for men like Vane and Hesilrige seemed, in retrospect, to be nearly insurmountable. After Booth's rebellion collapsed, it appeared that any royalist notion of coming to power by force was just a dream. That reality, however, solved only one problem. The army, source of actual power in the nation, was another matter altogether: failure to satisfy its grievances left it discontented, with the potential to cause future problems. Debates about the structure of the government also guaranteed ill will because they inevitably aroused vested interests. The issue of pay arrears for the army always rankled; in some places soldiers simply seized and held militia commissioners until they promised to pay what they lacked the means to deliver. More broadly, the question of the kind of government that could most adequately address all these concerns and assure social peace also proved divisive. Divisiveness, indeed, was in the air. One Quaker tweaked royalist Oxfordians by going naked through the town; another described his society's factions sharply and succinctly, "priests and cavaliers and bad spirits" on one side, "Vane and the best party" on the other.[29]

Overlaying all this was the problem of clashing personalities. Hesilrige and Vane, for example, might agree tactically, but so strikingly different were their personal natures that they rubbed each other the wrong way and irritated others who watched them in action. Vane, a born politician, correctly saw that the Rump had to conciliate the army, the source of its power, while the dogmatic and self-assured Hesilrige was just as determined to force the army to recognize parliamentary supremacy. Hence Vane had no problem with a regiment consisting of sectarians like Quakers and Baptists—indeed, he preferred such men in his ranks—while Hesilrige and many others feared what such a force might do.[30]

By early October the army's sword proved decisive once again, when its officers, angered by Parliament's decision to remove nine of their senior number, mounted another military coup and replaced the Rump entirely. Convinced that the kingdom of God was near, master manipulator Vane survived the coup; indeed he became one of the trusted civilians chosen to sit on a newly created committee of safety to administrate the government. Organized millenarians, the plotting Fifth Monarchists and Fox's more moderate Quakers, made recommendations for nominees to the committee, but their choices failed to win the military's consent.[31] Thus instead of the kingdom of God they envisioned, the millenarians got a regime that lurched from side to side, from pillar to post, from here to there, as it sought and failed to find a middle way between those who longed for order and stability and those intent on introducing radical change.

After the army's second coup, Fox sank deeper and deeper into what he termed "a great travail in my spirit" and "great sufferings and exercises."[32] The question of who was to rule now was uppermost in his mind. Victory over the royalist Booth had settled nothing; indeed, it had aggravated the split in the nation and cleaved Fox's psyche. Margaret, the oldest Fell daughter, living in London and helping to care for Fox, offered her diagnosis that "the North has been much in him." The Children's active opposition to Booth and what that stance committed him and the movement to pulled at him, particularly as the political fabric continued to unravel. Margaret had never seen him so weak, his emotions so out of control. But he could not escape the problem, much less the necessity to grapple with it. Hoping to shake his depressing burden, he left the tense capital on August 26 for Reading and the home of one of his closest associates and traveling companions, Thomas Curtis.[33]

Signficantly when Fox dictated his *Journal* fifteen years later and reflected on his ten-week malady, he tied it directly to his long convalescence at the Curtis home. Although Fox carefully avoided mentioning it, Curtis, a former army captain, had accepted appointment as a commissioner of the militia.[34] The leader's frame of mind was directly affected by this development. Pondering Curtis's decision, and now having a chance to explore it with him, Fox fell into a depressing rumination on human foibles: formerly many people had been tender, he decided, especially after being humbled and convicted by the truth, but now they "were destroying the simplicity and betraying the truth" and exhibiting "a great deal of hypocrisy and deceit and strife."[35] Although his words connected these failures to the dramatic turnings and overturnings of personnel in the government, he was also seeing his own followers becoming more deeply involved—partially as a result of his own teaching. Fox was so down that even his physical condition suffered; no longer his usual robust self, he lost weight and looked weak. Never one to forget a slight, he absolutely refused to see the recently freed James Nayler during his depression.[36]

This mood, expressed in his memoirs, might be considered overdrawn, merely a result of Fox's pique at the Curtis's failure to side with him in the 1670s had he not left another confirmation of his state of mind at the same time. On October 15, while in Reading, Fox wrote to Quaker missionaries in the New World, including two, Marmaduke Stevenson and William Robinson, under sentence of death in Boston for daring to enter that Zion in the wilderness.[37] Designed to bolster the courage of these valiant evangelists, the letter can also be read as part of a dialogue he carried on with himself, an effort to reinvigorate his own faith in a time of personal trial. Advising them, he counseled himself. Dwell in God's power, wisdom, and life, he urged, "that you may have dominion over the world." He reminded them that the "husbandman waits patiently after the seed is sown" and "there is a winter before the summer comes." "Keep in the power of the Lord God," and "the great professors of spiritual Babylon, the mother of harlots, that are full of craft, will be brought down." And his postscript repeated the same assurance: "The Lord is king over all the earth, and Christ has all power in heaven and earth."[38] Fox needed that affirmation almost as much as the doomed Robinson and Stevenson.

His mental state may also have been exacerbated by a realization of a certain waffling on his own part, particularly regarding the question of violence and war. Or, more aptly, Fox's Reading depression drove him to understand his own role in countenancing his followers' involvement in potentially violent conflicts. By always insisting that his followers should commit themselves to the service of truth, service that certainly might be taken to include the Good Old Cause, Fox could hardly be surprised when they decided that army service was permissible. Fox received a poignant letter in early December from a Cardiff Friend whose brother had been named a lieutenant colonel in the militia and wanted to accept the commission because the family thought "he may be serviceable for truth in it."[39] In August twenty-one-year-old George Fell, received orders to raise a troop of horse for "the safety of parliament and Lancashire."[40] On returning to London, Fox flared up at a Friend, not as close to him as the Curtises, who since June had been a militia commissioner. Richard Davis, whom northerners had given charge of money collected for missionary work the previous year,[41] and his wife invited Fox to their home. When she spoke to him, Fox wanted nothing to do with Davis: "I told her," he recalled, "there was no room in her house for me."[42]

Fox's mood was not helped by increasing antagonism directed against the Quakers. He recounted how a mob near London set upon one meeting and beat eighty Friends, tearing their coats from their backs and tossing them into ditches and ponds. In some places disruptive outsiders, beating kettles, throwing rotten eggs, and igniting a gunpowder-like substance, invaded the Quakers' silent meetings. Sometimes anti-Catholic sentiments merged with fears of Quakers in bizarre ways. In Dorchester, for example, during a meeting that included a number of soldiers, the local constable barged in looking for Jesuits. He lifted Fox's hat to determine if it hid a tonsure, a move that shocked the soldiers and helped convert many of them.

A man dressed in a bearskin showed up at a meeting in Somersetshire and created a disturbance by seating himself near the speaker and then cavorting around and bellowing like a bear. But he received his punishment when he stopped to watch a bullbaiting following his escapade at the Quakers' meeting. The bull gored the man under the chin, then tossed his dangling victim above his head. In Norwich, an uneasy mayor refused Fox permission to hold a meeting lest the gathering introduce too much unrest into the community, but Fox found a friendly army officer who made his home available for the meeting.[43]

Fox traveled late into 1659, returning to London early in December where he, as one close observer reported, "reigns in righteousness over all deceit and unclean spirits."[44] Some things undoubtedly elevated his spirits. The army council's decision on December 21 permitting Parliament to reconvene without a House of Lords or a single executive was especially encouraging. The ineffectual committee that had tried to govern since October had proven itself unable to do more than talk about such issues as abolishing tithes and ending persecution of dissenters.[45] Greeted by a brief burst of popular enthusiasm, the newly resurrected Commons might be able to breathe life into the Good Old Cause again. Sympathetic members of Parliament advised the Children to supply lists of sober men suitable for appointment as justices of the peace and promised to appoint them.[46] Nearly ten weeks had lapsed since the explusion of the Rump. Meanwhile, the mood of the country had grown steadily more conservative; presently talk began to be heard and resolutions passed, even in the halls of Westminster, about continuing tithes and reconstituting a House of Lords.[47]

Such talk enraged the First Friend. He labeled discussion of an upper chamber of peers "a dirty, nasty thing."[48] Such sentiments only confirmed the movement's radical reputation, provoking one wag to write, "I laugh to see so many swaying swords / Swear that for zeal they hate a House of Lords: / When quaking cobblers but with half their eyes, / They hope thereby to rule and revilize."[49] Fox and his Children organized another lobbying campaign against tithes. In July they prepared a protest against tithes signed by seven thousand women, one of the first such efforts to use the supposed "weaker vessels."[50] Aimed primarily at outsiders—"the world's people" was the phrase used to describe them—this petition was to be submitted to Parliament at an opportune time.[51] Later one of his critics within the movement charged that Fox had sent letters to all meetings throughout the nation asking that they nominate suitable people, including Friends, to hold the position of justice of the peace.[52]

Fox wrote a pamphlet addressed to Parliament in which he offered specific suggestions for "regulating things." The "Fifty-nine Particulars" listed in the pamphlet reflected his belief that he could appeal to the members' good sense. But to be on the safe side, he published the pamphlet, in hopes of using it to mobilize popular support for his proposals and thus counter the growing conservative mood that seemed to be overtaking the country. The pamphlet reflected his undiminished radical approach and his commitment to the Good Old Cause and its goals, as he understood them. Of the fifty-nine proposals, a majority were firmly grounded in his and his Children's experiences with the authorities, while the others grew out of a broader theoretical commitment to a more just society. Even daring to submit them for the perusal of a public grown tired of such

detailed offerings revealed how Fox the millenarian could be strikingly oblivious to the real world. Yet he had a definite vision, and a person with a vision
impels others to lift their sights too.

To his credit, Fox tried to balance the freedom he espoused with the intru-
siveness into traditional life many of his proposals would require. He never
indicated that he saw the enormous difficulty of such a balancing, and indeed
he did not even endeavor to reconcile these two distinct aspects of his suggestions in the twenty-three-page booklet. He merely tacked on a lengthy plea for
liberty as a kind of addendum, and let it go at that. His pamphlet thus testified
to the muddled way he often cobbled his ideas together. Fox believed he knew
what the nation needed and so he offered his program. The finished product,
however slapdash, was more important than the sum of its diverse parts.

Fox's list of fifty-nine suggestions, not surprisingly, followed no logical order;
they were apparently written down in the order he thought of them. For example, the first three "particulars" called for the removal of penalties against those
who refused to pay tithes to support ministers of a church with which they
did not agree, but not until particular number twenty-eight did he repeat his
oft-stated call for a total repeal of tithes. A number of his suggestions dealt with
various proposals for reforming the law, always a major concern of the era's
radicals. Fox wanted to permit a person to appear in court without an attorney;
to allow a man to wear his hat in court and protect his right not to swear; to
abolish the use of Latin or French in legal proceedings; and to end the death
penalty for a person convicted of stealing cattle, money, or "outward" things.
The "way to take off oppression" and "to bring the nation into a garden, and a
free nation, a free people," he claimed, was to abolish all fee-gougers in the law
courts—chancellors, lawyers, and sergeants-of-arms—and so permit "plain"
people to "decide their business." He held that letting the proud, lofty, or scornful hold office was "to bring the world into a wilderness," and he wanted all
legal fines turned over to the poor.[53]

The Children themselves had experienced many of these shortcomings in the
legal system. Fox also took aim at other practices that had brought him and his
followers into conflict with the law or public sentiment. He insisted that all should
be free to bid others repent or put aside their cheating and cursing in the marketplace; that no one should have his goods taken away for meeting to worship
God; and that no one should be imprisoned for vagrancy when traveling to speak
God's word. He asked that jails be converted into wholesome places and kept
that way so that "prisoners may not lie in their own dung and piss." Jailers should
not be drunkards or swearers.

Fox wanted to enforce an outward equality as a way to move toward an
authentic equality that grew from spiritual equality. A rich man, he reminded
his readers, wore his hat when he went among other wealthy people but wanted
a poor man to remove his as a mark of deference; this discrimination should
cease, so as to "let everyone do justly to his neighbor without respect." He wanted
the nation to provide for poor people, the blind, the lame, and the crippled,
"that there might not be a beggar in England nor in England's dominions." Fines
exacted by lords of the manor should be given to the poor, "for lords have

enough." He also wanted to abolish other badges of customary inequality. Sporting gold lace and costly attire, for example, would be ended and the money thus saved go to clothe the naked and feed the hungry. Unless one's office or service required it, no one should lord it over another by carrying a sword, a dagger, or a pistol.

This method of achieving equality represented a shift in emphasis from a position Fox had taken four years earlier. In a pamphlet written at that time against all professions—lawyers, doctors, and the like—he condemned attempts at leveling by worldly Levellers who had not, he believed, freed themselves from the lusts of the flesh and the darkness of the earth. He was firmly committed, as he wrote then, to "throwing down the mountains and exalting the valleys, raising up the just and throwing down the unjust," but he reproached those who lived in ease and filthiness and away from the light and who postured about equality. They leveled down with their earthly natures, but he wanted a leveling up to the eternal light.[54] Now, in his "Fifty-nine Particulars," Fox added to his moral admonitions and called for the state to pass laws against the outward manifestations of inequality.

Like other serious Protestants, he opposed plays, maygames, playing with dice and cards, football, fiddlings, bearbaitings, cockfights, and horse races, but he went further. Taverns and alehouses should exclude gambling devices, such as cards, dice, or shuffle boards. Even joke books should be banned. Images and pictures should be removed from signs, churches, gardens, and houses. He pontificated against the crosses—"pope's crosses," he snorted—that continued to adorn official seals, coins, even the nation's flag.

Running through Fox's catalogue of his society's evils was the theme that "justice and righteousness exalts a nation, but sin is a shame both to rulers and people." His two most radical proposals were that the nation had an obligation to provide for "all the poor people, blind and lame, and cripples" and that abbey and glebe lands, the "great houses," churches, and abbeys, even Whitehall itself, should be given to these needy people.[55] Although he did not spell out exactly how either proposal was to be achieved, he did recognize that social and economic dislocations associated with England's recent entry into the world of capitalism required new approaches. Once the government had begun confiscating the church's extensive holdings in the last century and awarding them to private individuals, a world with different values slowly began to emerge.

These two propositions, the highwater mark of his radicalism, aimed at dealing with the problems that inevitably grew out of these evolving values and showed him at his most perceptive. Even more important, they initiated a Quaker tendency to seek fundamental solutions for social problems, a tendency that would continually challenge the basic institutions and assumptions of the society in which they lived. While Fox himself never returned to the essential radicalism of this approach, he never repudiated it, and it survived as a method that continued to inspire future followers as they grappled with similar problems in their own different worlds.[56] His radical proposals handed critics new ammunition to use to attack him and his movement. When he and George Whitehead debated a university man in Cambridge in August, one question hurled at Fox was, "Whereas there is some talk by some Quakers of dividing men's estates, and having all things in common, do you believe that is [a] lawful and fitting thing to do?"[57]

The second part of Fox's pamphlet, the last nine pages, addressed people who persecuted others because of their faith. This section was ostensibly addressed to those in the government, whether in London's seats of power or in the lowliest local office out in the countryside, who tried to prevent the Children from following the dictates of their religious faith and experiences. Fox repeated over and over that those who sought to have dominion over another's faith violated the principles of Christ, lived outside the true faith, and worshipped the devil. What he failed to see, however, was that these very people, when they acted sincerely from their own religious convictions, were doing no more than Fox and his followers did when they invaded a market town on market day to "declare the day of the Lord." He apparently did not realize that his strictures against, as he put it, "he who persecutes another about meat and drinks and days" could easily reprove Fox for wanting to deny others the right to play shuffleboard. Fox wanted religious freedom for his own group, and that freedom, he implied, should include the right to restrict the freedom of others when their actions conflicted with his definitions of what was right. Freedom was a good, but so was living in the light. What he overlooked was that others living in what they considered to be the light of the gospel believed they had the right to pursue activities he regarded as reprehensible. In this way, his views differed only in degree from those of the rulers of the Massachusetts Bay Colony: they proscribed and then executed his followers when they felt called to do things that conflicted with the Congregationalists' definition of what was proper.

Fox held that Christ obviated the necessity of coercion because, as he spelled it out, "he destroys the devil, the power of darkness . . . to bring the creature into the liberty of the sons of God." But this liberty did not allow a latitude where anything was permitted, nor did it apply to those acting outside what he called the "Covenant of Light." Fox was far from a modern pluralist or civil libertarian who believes that people should enjoy the right to do anything they want to do, as long as their activities do not impinge on others. His Children of the Light, with their spiritual weapons, would wrestle against spiritual wickedness, but he certainly did not foresee them burning and imprisoning others for their faith, as their opponents did. The reality was, of course, that few of Fox's followers— with the notable exception of James Nayler who had suffered grievously when convicted for blasphemy—were imprisoned for their religious beliefs, narrowly conceived. They almost always endured prosecution because they carried no travel passes or refused to swear, to doff their hats, or to pay tithes. Fox defined religion, commitment to Christ's light, more broadly than others in his day: it expressed itself in opposition to commonplace customs, refusing to swear, removing hats, paying tithes. Fortunately, he never acquired political power and hence never had to decide how to respond to someone beyond the Covenant of Light who violated one of his pet strictures against something like bearbaiting.

At the end of his section on religious freedom, Fox came around once again to what for him was the central expression of religion and the theme of the first part of his pamphlet: equality. Denouncing those who used "thee" and "thou" among themselves but insisted on the deferential "you" when addressed by nonfamiliars, he stressed that this kind of fashion was "outward" and failed to exhibit the kind of "love, life, and faith that works by love [and] envies not." In God's love and wisdom, he emphasized, true "courteousness and kindness and tenderness and stooping and coming down to the [im]prisoned and oppressed . . . are plain and pure and good."[58] If he had not found a way to achieve this good end, he had still composed a powerful statement of the broad goals of his movement.

Any hopes Fox entertained about Parliament implementing his proposals were surely aborted as the political situation worsened in the winter months of 1659–1660. Soldiers openly assaulted their officers, while others, ordered out of the volatile city to the countryside, vowed not to cease agitating until they received their back pay. The Rump was so contemptible that street urchins shouted "Kiss my Parliament" rather than their usual "Kiss my arse."[59] Snipers took aim at soldiers patrolling the streets, and in back alleys silent knifings of stray troopers fed public insecurities. Rumors of conspiracies popped up all over London to underscore how opinion had shifted to favor restoration of the monarchy. The longing for stability simply seemed too much to resist. Absent a massive popular upheaval, Fox had little reason to expect the kind of changes he desired. The many who wanted life breathed back into the Good Old Cause had no actual power, while the fearful but powerful few tried to choke off any sign of its reemergence.

The Rump Parliament, in session from December 26 to March 16, certainly could have received and considered the "Fifty-nine Particulars." Its attention, however, focused on what seemed to most of the country the eminently more important matter of the makeup of future Parliaments. The cry went up for a reconstituted Parliament, "a free Parliament," one that everyone knew would return the Stuarts to power. George Bishop, the single Quaker with experience at Whitehall, saw clearly that the return of the king would mean that all hope for true freedom had vanished.[60] An even more ominous development was military. From Scotland, across snow-covered terrain and in bitterly cold weather, marched George Monck's army on January 1. "Black George," so tagged because of his swarthy skin, had never tried to direct events, but he had always made shrewd use of them to improve his own situation. He supposedly was moving south to protect the Rump's prerogatives; he was being hailed as the country's savior. The army's impending arrival in the capital, even if nothing else happened, boded ill for sectarians like Fox's Friends, for Monck's record contained little evidence of sympathy for them or their ends.[61] In an odd kind of way, Monck's actions can be read as a testimony to the rise of Quaker influence, for "Black George" feared it.[62]

The army from the north reached London on February 3, 1660, and began acting on such fears. Monck's soldiers broke up the Friends' meetings, yanking them out of their meeting places and abusing them in the streets. The general population had little sympathy for the Children, even when it witnessed armed soldiers pulling Quaker men and women into the streets by their hair.[63] Indeed, the population celebrated imposition of a stricter military regime and the practical end of Rump rule. Citizens plied happy soldiers with meat and drink until most of them were drunk all day. The same elated citizens lit bonfires up and down the streets—the weather cooperated by turning almost springlike after Monck arrived—and proceeded to roast chunks of rumps, which they carried up and down the streets on long skewers; one observer counted thirty-one fires along the Strand alone. Republicans scurried for cover. Sir Arthur Hesilrige, still a member of the discredited Parliament, was so afraid of being set upon by angry mobs that at night he crept through the streets without a light lest someone recognize him.[64]

Fox was in London when Monck's army took charge,[65] but he found it expedient to go on a preaching mission shortly after the general settled in at Whitehall. Before leaving, he did attend to one bit of unfinished business, a reluctant reconciliation with a repentant James Nayler. Freed from prison by Parliament on September 8, Nayler hastened to Reading two days later to see his former colleague, but the depressed Fox refused to see him.[66] Fox was adamant on the subject of Nayler and had long been so: previous efforts by friends of both men to effect some kind of reconciliation ran solidly aground on his stubborn determination to have no contact with the prisoner. Fox's hostility encouraged others to circulate papers against Nayler. Alexander Parker worried that these papers would "kindle as great a fire if not greater than ever." Parker begged Fox with tears in his eyes to speak just one word and halt these slanders. "It lies on George Fox," a vexed Parker finally exclaimed.[67]

Upon his release, Nayler took a more subdued role in London than his previous flamboyant reputation, but he was not a person to shut himself away from gatherings of the Children.[68] It would have been almost impossible for him and the First Friend to avoid each other within London's tightly knit Quaker community once Fox returned to the capital in early December, but no evidence of any contacts between them has survived. Finally brought together in the same room in late January or early February, Fox exacted a high psychological price for his follower's apostasy: Nayler had to kneel before Fox and beg forgiveness. William Dewsbury, who had tried hard to find a way to achieve a resolution between the country's two most famous Quakers, was cheered by Fox's "precious wisdom" and the "healing spirit" that spread over those who witnessed the reconciliation.[69]

Judging from his actions, Fox's hopes for the nation and its future were also heightened by Nayler's willingness to submit. But Nayler did not ask Fox's permission before taking his place again in the front ranks of the sect's ministers in London. He thrust himself also onto the literary battleground with a condemnation of those in the steadily weakening Rump, sentiments that might reasonably have come from Fox's pen. Aiming at the nation's rulers who, he said, had "daily waxed fat," hardened their hearts, and stopped their ears, Nayler taunted them for ignoring the signs and wonders that the humble Children of the Light had brought from the Lord God. "You . . . now know not where to hide yourselves from the mighty day that's coming upon you from the God of the whole earth," he concluded.[70]

Fox's tour to Cornwall and the west suggested that he may have entertained some hope of rousing enough opposition in the army to thwart Monck and end the country's movement back to monarchy. But he counted only a few positive results for his labors, including the civility of army officers who attended one of his meeting in Dorchester. In Bristol, however, where a coalition of Presbyterians, royalists, and merchants had held sway for almost six years,[71] Fox found the lines hardening. To his surprise, the army in Bristol had joined with local officials to suppress sectarians. Soldiers swinging their muskets like clubs had attacked Friends in an orchard where they often gathered. Fox's reaction to this blatant attack on the right of the Children to meet was very unusual, unusual enough to imply that he was bending over backward to avoid a confrontation and hoped to win signficant support among Bristol's garrison.

Instead of going himself, Fox dispatched four local Friends, including George Bishop and Edward Pyott, to the mayor to rent the city hall for them on Sundays. The mayor denied he had the authority to act. Fox then ordered his emissaries to contact the army commander in the city to call off his troops. Inexplicably, the four rejected Fox's request and did not go, one of the few times his followers ever dared refuse him. Just as inexplicably, he did not insist that they obey, probably because he had misgivings about stirring up unnecessary animosities. On Sunday a band of soldiers, some with drawn swords, and other intruders shoved into the orchard and pushed to within six feet of where Fox was speaking. But his sermon was so inspired that what he sensed as the presence of God prevented any disruption. The next day four emboldened Quakers reported the soldiers rude behavior to the colonel in charge. He rebuked his troops and hit some of them with the side of his sword. Fox claimed this punishment occurred because his own men had not followed his original orders.

Fox's hopes were buoyed a day or so later by a gigantic meeting at Pyott's suburban home that attracted so many people, Baptists and Congregationalists especially, that the city's streets looked as though they had been stripped bare. His millenarian message that day had overtones relating to events in the nation. He preached that the old worlds of Jewish law and human inventions, the latter of which appeared in the dark period of Christian apostasy, were being superseded by the "Christ [who] was come to redeem, translate, convert, and regenerate man out of all these things." He used a long story to reinforce his theme: The house of an elderly husband and wife was destroyed by their enemy, whereupon workers came every year for one, two, three, four, five years and contracted to repair it, but none did. The old couple paid and paid again until they were impoverished. Christ, Fox promised, would return the couple to the perfect state they knew before their house was damaged. Their Saviour had come to redeem them and to make them and their worldly dwelling perfect, requiring of them neither price nor tithe nor tax nor, presumably, struggle.[72]

It was not difficult to see in this sermon an answer to current conditions in England, the promise that the divine was ready to break into history and take charge of the mess human beings had made. Lest his followers miss the implications of this message, Fox spelled them out in an epistle he designed to be widely distributed. England's recent history demonstrated that earthly kings always faced the possiblity that disillusioned subjects would, to use Fox's term, "unking" them. Thus he saw his Children, male and female alike, being readied to exercise actual political power. "We are of the royal seed," he exulted, "who cannot serve the will and lusts of men and bow and stoop to them." Christ, the ultimate seed, would destroy the old and renew those responsive to his call, setting them up to have dominion once more over God's handiwork. These redeemed ones would, Fox attested, "come to be made kings upon the earth, . . . a terror to evil doers [and] who bear not the sword in vain."[73]

Some of his main followers and close associates acted as though they knew exactly how they might become kings. For example, Edward Burrough, twenty-five years old and determined that the Quakers would take a leading role in shaping a new order, knew what he must do: he issued broadsides explicitly committing the Children to laying down their lives in the struggle for the reforms they espoused.[74] Richard Hubberthorne, who had soldiered in the New Model Army, grew positively apocalyptic in three pamphlets he wrote in 1659. The thundering of God's power, he announced, "is proclaimed to the whole nation, and the nations round about, to take off their bondage" and "to make his creature a free creature and his people a free people."[75] Militia commissioners Thomas Curtis and Anthony Pearson, both Fox's traveling companions, as well as other Children who agreed to recruit men for the parliamentary cause, were walking testimonies to how far some would go to establish a reign of righteousness. With examples like these, it was easy to understand how numerous lower level Friends saw the army as a way to achieve Quaker goals.[76]

Fox's retreat to the hinterland in February was not merely the action of one who did not want to run afoul of the authorities. To the contrary, for the First Friend the turmoil in London proved his conviction that the world's people were again subjecting themselves to one of their periodic upheavals. Himself convinced that God's time was approaching, his actions suggested he wanted to have his own strength renewed by seeking out and winning those who might yet become kings upon the earth. In this context his flaring up at the Bristol Friends for neglecting to contact the colonel and preventing a confrontation with the troops was perfectly understandable: his close confederates did not see that the door to fruitful contact among a strong body of potential supporters had to be kept propped open.

This time, however, the onrush of human events did not wait for God, or at least for God's Children. General Monck found himself riding a wave that swept him onward to more and more political influence. As Richard Hubberthorne read the situation, the "priests and cavaliers and bad spirits" were all for Monck since no one else spoke for them.[77] By the end of February he had been named commander-in-chief of the land forces of the three kingdoms, England, Scotland, and Ireland, and he was also named to the new executive council of thirty-one, the only member elected unanimously. Presbyterians dominated the counsel, and they were known to be fierce opponents of Fox, his coterie, and other sectarians. The council busied itself with negotiations with the heir to the throne, now in Brussels—until April when he moved to Holland—whom fewer and fewer were styling Charles Stuart and more and more Charles II. While the executive council administered affairs with a Presbyterian bias, Parliament legislated the same way. It formally adopted the Westminster Confession of Faith of 1646 for the Church of England on March 2. An ordinance of March 14 authorized division of the counties into presbyteries, and another ordinance passed two days later confirmed ministers in their benefices and declared them entitled to the tithes Quakers detested so much. More ominous still was the call for a new, free, Parliament to meet on April 25. That meant immediate restoration of the monarchy.[78] Blow after blow thus pummeled the Quakers' hopes and Fox's dreams.

About the only hopeful news to be found in this unnerving March was an order from Monck on the ninth that soldiers cease disturbing the Children's meetings. The order had good results for the Quakers, for friendly troopers began appearing at an occasional meeting, although Fox, traveling northward toward his home base and a series of planned conclaves, gave no indication that any were convinced. That was the rub, of course. However much and however often Fox might explain to anxious followers that "the Lord's power was over all . . . and his day shined,"[79] only the army had the power to thwart Charles Stuart's return.[80] Arriving in Gloucester, for example, Fox found some support for Parliament among the ranks, but the loudest cries sounded for the king. Indeed, the royalists were hot to entrap one whose notoriety easily outpaced his horse. Fortunately they did not receive news of Fox's visit until he had already left the town.

Local officials remained alert as Fox moved northward. Stopping by Drayton-in-the-Clay to see his mother, he left only a step ahead of a justice of the peace looking to make his reputation by outfoxing the increasingly cautious Quaker leader. The spring weather, after a very hard winter, had turned fine, and thousands of Children convened on April 22 at a blossoming orchard in Balby, a village just south of Doncaster in Yorkshire. To those fearing a Quaker plot, this gathering was a red flag. What Fox prematurely designated a yearly meeting had just gotten underway when a troop of horse, having traveled all night, arrived from York, more than thirty miles away. They were joined by a company of militiamen, who underscored the locals' concern. Heralded by blaring trumpets, the captain in charge rode through the massed Quakers, wheeled to a halt in front of the stand where Fox was preaching, and demanded that he come down. The argument between the two was lengthy, but at last the captain promised the Children they could continue their meeting with a dozen troopers on guard, for one hour more. In fact, the meeting went on as planned, once the Quakers fed the tired riders and gave feed to their horses. It was, concluded the victorious Fox, a "glorious, powerful" meeting.[81]

Fox was not the only Englishman from the south heading for dark corners of the nation. John Lambert, the general who had crushed Booth's rising the previous year but whose republican sympathies led to a fall from favor, escaped his imprisonment in April. Sectarian hopes fluttered to life. One Quaker, no doubt speaking for others, had already written that he expected "Lambert will join with Vane and the best party."[82] On the April 12 Lambert set out to find enough right-thinking soldiers willing to stand against Monck and monarchy. But "Black George" moved quicker: government troops were as ubiquitous as newborn lambs and as watchful as ewes in the Midlands and the north that fine spring.

They captured Lambert the same Easter Sunday the Quakers opened their gathering at Balby. Others besides Fox noted the connection between his meeting and the anxiety caused by the suspected uprising. Soldiers waylaid two people who had attended the meeting when they were heading back to London and questioned them about their views on Lambert. As late as June the army was still sweeping up Children and others suspected of supporting Lambert. Fox remained scrupulously uninvolved, refusing to sell his horse to some soldiers he passed on their way to Northamptonshire to join Lambert.[83]

Fox had ample opportunity to air these considerations with his followers in late April and early May, for he surely attended enough meetings. In the course of a few days he presided at the gathering of thousands he called the yearly meeting;[84] joined a special meeting for ministers at Warmsworth, just south of Balby; discussed church affairs at a general meeting at Skipton in western Yorkshire restricted to men representing all parts of the country; and finally met with Children from the northern counties at Arnside, Lancashire. As at Skipton, these meetings could not escape considering the state of the church as it was affected by the evolving political situation. Thomas Curtis and Francis Howgill, both central figures in the movement, then joined Fox in traveling the few miles westward to Ulverston and home to Swarthmoor. The topic of their conversations need not be guessed at. Others who came by could hardly have avoided the same matters.[85]

Things looked ominous indeed, as a letter from Will Caton in London related. Caton was level-headed and not given to exaggerating, a factor making the intelligence he sent even more troubling. When Fox opened the letter, he read that troops from the "old army"—whose men were more likely to support the Good Old Cause—were to be dispatched forty miles out of London or disbanded and sent home. On May 8, the day the king's coming was proclaimed, popular acclaim was so great that the ringing bells and blaring trumpets were drowned out. The ceremonies conducted by public officials and the understandably overjoyed gentry were, Caton wrote, "fantastical." Before the proclamation, Quaker meetings had been peaceable and soldier-guards had withdrawn, but Caton was deeply worried now: "I don't know whether this day they will suffer any of our meetings [to convene]; certainly they will not suffer the one at Westminster." Most striking of all, beyond the details, was the underlying tone of Caton's letter, his realization that the Children were wholly set apart from a population absolutely ecstatic with joy and celebration.[86]

Before the end of May, when the king was due to arrive in London, the news grew worse. Imprisoned in Leicester and Nantwich, whipped in Cambridge and Peterborough, the Children faced an enraged population. At a Westminster meeting on May 29, only the timely appearance of troops saved the worshipers from being beaten senseless by an angry mob. That same day Charles II and his two brothers entered the city. They were entirely too much royalty for one plain Friend, whose report begrudgingly described the new monarch as exhibiting "a pretty sober countenance." Yet no matter how the king looked, the "excess and abomination," the "vanity and pride" exhibited by the mobs thronging the city's thoroughfares were inexpressible.[87]

Bitterness burned in the mouths of a few Children, both at the political situation and the timidity of some of their fellow believers. Thomas Salthouse informed those at Swarthmoor Hall a week later that he and Burrough had had good meetings but emphasized what was clear to all, namely, that "the days are evil and the times are perilous." Traveling was becoming more difficult, and to see the poor despised and the proud accounted as worthy was more than a body could stomach.[88] The times were so dark that he confidently expected the movement's adversaries to plan a hand-in-hand struggle against them.[89] Some Children, it seemed, had given up, or at least had left the field to others. From Somersetshire, one still carrying the torch explained that opponents were boasting that the Quakers had "all fled for fear of what would be done to us when the king did come to reign." Laborers were too few, he complained.[90]

Fox once again had a personal taste of the perilous times and what the coming of the king meant shortly after he arrived at Swarthmoor. It was mid-June, and he, Margaret Fell, and a third Friend were sitting in the paneled parlor of the isolated house, surely a haven from the world and its problems. Engaged in conversation, the group was interrupted by a servant who informed them that constables had come to search the house for weapons. No arms were discovered, of course, but the constables arrested the First Friend, took him to nearby Ulverston, and locked him up for the night, a guard nodding off in the fireplace lest the prisoner creep up and out the chimney. The next day, under an armed escort of thirty loyal soldiers, they sent Fox to Lancaster, where he was jailed for nearly five months.[91]

Hence the Quaker leader had plenty of time to think about the failures of the 1650s. The movement had come to its own crossroads, just as the nation was choosing its way. The scant military support Lambert had elicited and the ease with which he was recaptured showed how little actual popular backing existed for an uprising. God had clearly not smiled on a violent coup. And the popular acclaim that greeted the arrival of the new king made the choice to bring him back appear downright democratic.[92] However reluctant, Fox reconciled himself to the lesson these events taught him. Since the general meeting at John Crook's two years earlier, he had watched and waited, reading the signs of the time. He had traveled over much of the country, speaking to local leaders and soliciting their opinions. His preaching about the advent of a new day had attracted many to the movement, and they had committed themselves, honestly and sincerely, to the cause. But in this new day, he had to find new approaches and tread softly, with care.

Facts were complicated things; they could be embarrassing; and in this new context, they might prove dangerous. The central reality was that the tide of events had swept beyond any possibility that Fox's sect could be the catalyst to bring in the day of the Lord or achieve the fifty-nine reforms he had so fervently demanded. Even during the relatively free Protectorate, Quakers commonly faced charges that their goal was to subvert the government and sow divisions among loyal people. During that period Fox could, and did, fulminate against monarchy, but now he had to accept, practically, not just a king but a Stuart king.[93] Now what might dissenters expect with restoration of the monarchy and all it entailed—

such things as reestablishment of the authority of the see of Canterbury, reinstitution of censorship, and enforcement of laws against blasphemy and mandating church attendance? The good old days were gone, certainly, just as surely as the Good Old Cause.

Fox thus prepared to take a sharp right turn, moving away from the millenarian pronouncements and challenges to the status quo that had together marked his public ministry. "Christ has come to teach his people," he had proclaimed convincingly, and now George Fox had been taught himself, by events. He did not blazon his conclusion about—in fact he never explicitly referred to it at all: it was too tender a matter for him to admit that he had been wrong. But in his first surviving memoir, dictated only three years after this period and more than a decade prior to his better known *Journal,* Fox candidly and a bit wistfully evaluated his earlier position. This 1663 comment revealed what Fox thought might have been if he and the other Children had acted differently. Temperamentally unable to admit failure, he never, either before or after, came so close to criticizing his own judgment.

In the days of the Cromwells and the various Parliaments, he recalled, "if I or my Friends had been moved to go into a steeple house and look in any of the priests' faces, their mouths would have been stopped, they would have gone away . . . and they would have come down out of the pulpit in many places. . . . The power of God would have gone so over them, they being so full of deceit, that it would have choked them."[94] Fox and Friends had, indeed, gone into churches and confronted ministers to their faces, so he could not fault himself on that score. His statement seemed rather a lament about a path not taken, as though he reproached himself with the thoughts, "Why did we not do more? We lost our chance." As he saw it now, three years later, their fault was that during the 1650s they had not been vigorous enough to overturn ministers and work a revolution in the church. What applied to the church—an arm of the state, after all—he could just as easily apply to the regime, which he and his followers so often criticized. They had simply not been political enough. They were well organized, better organized than any other of the nation's sects including even the nearly moribund Anglicans; they had a strong cadre of preachers with adherents through the nation and in countrysides and towns and cities, and even in the colonies; they knew how to publicize their views by means of broadsides and pamphlets; they even had sympathetic friends and contacts in high places, including officers in the army. Yet they had failed. The day of the Lord had not appeared as Fox believed it was supposed to.[95] How he must have ached, there in his cold dark cell in Lancaster castle.

13

For the Same Man to Be a Heretic and a Good Subject Is Impossible

The date was January 6, 1661, a Sunday, and one of those minor events occurred that was to have a major impact far beyond the immediate ramifications of the incident itself. A London cooper, Thomas Venner, goaded his church of about fifty to rise in a charismatic, abortive rebellion. As a Fifth Monarchist, Venner had favored the Good Old Cause; he now planned to usher in the Kingdom of God and replace the seven-month-old regime of Charles II with one led by Christ himself. "King Jesus," the insurgents' slogan demanded, "and the [regicides'] heads upon the gate." They took over St. Paul's Cathedral until a combined troop of volunteers and regular forces drove them to retreat, into a wood near Highgate. Emerging three days later, they fought as though the fate of the world depended upon their victory, but most were killed or captured. Their effort failed, to say the least: fourteen of their own heads, including an unrepentant Venner's, were stuck up on London Bridge as grisly warnings to others who might attempt similar rebellious acts.[1] Rumors swept the city, armed men stalked the streets, shopkeepers locked their doors, and shocked citizens retreated to their homes.[2]

Fox and his Friends were not Fifth Monarchists, even if they shared that group's belief in the approaching millennium. Worried authorities, especially Presbyterian and Independent sympathizers who quickly realized that a chance to suppress their opponents had come, did not make fine distinctions between violent, plotting millenarians and more peaceful ones. So sectarians of various types found themselves lumped together with conspirators and suffered increased surveillance and renewed persecution. Exposing the radical religious underground became a priority for nervous officials.[3]

Quakers, already suffering a bad reputation, raised more suspicions than other sects. Reactions to Venner's attempted putsch, puny as it was and doomed to failure, amounted to a preview of the 1660s, indeed of the next quarter century of the life of the Society of Friends and its leader, George Fox. On Monday morning, January 7, he walked in Whitehall and Pall Mall and found the streets full of soldiers and ordinary citizens, all pushing and shoving, the militamen staring at each person as if to see who was part of a conspiracy. Things had not calmed down much by the following Saturday, for twice during the night soldiers raided the house where Fox was staying to arrest him. By Sunday, January 13, he knew immediate action was needed. He and Richard Hubberthorne retired to a Friend's home to draw up a statement explaining the Quaker position in regard to the tense situation.[4] If not immediately, the movement gradually turned in on itself, partially to survive, partially because its leaders and most members lost their millenarian conviction that they could revive a primitive Christianity and enable the saints to rule. The post-Restoration Society of Friends, no longer a movement, was reduced to fending off attacks and guarding its sectarian peculiarities from outside contamination.[5]

After 1660 Friends—seldom billing themselves as "Children of the Light" anymore—evolved into a sect markedly different from the creative, exuberant, and confrontational company of the turbulent and exciting 1650s. Leaving behind their enthusiastic and ecstatic escapades, they gradually withdrew from confrontations with society at large and became concerned with their internal problems. To a large degree, they separated themselves from the outside world. In truth, the Restoration raised the curtain on a sober second act for Fox's movement, "the second period of Quakerism,"[6] during which the Society of Friends matured and thereby assured its survival after its heady early days. And George Fox, whose spiritual experiences had done so much to form and shape the movement, oversaw and directed the second act. During the 1650s he had had to share the spotlight with a cast of other luminaries, such as James Nayler, but now he held center stage alone, with the light focused solely on him, until he married Margaret Fell in 1669 and thereafter brought her to center stage with him.

In the first weeks after the Restoration, it certainly did not appear that things would play out that way. Fox remained in the relative safety of Swarthmoor less than two weeks before being carried off under guard to Lancaster.[7] The dungeon under the dark brown and grey castle, which stood next to the church on the city's highest hill, was his destination; he was imprisoned there until the end of September.[8] The castle and the church dominated the city, one a sprawling symbol of secular power, the other jutting a gothic hand upward as a reminder of God's overarching power. From his cell Fox could not see the fells he had been forced to leave more than fifteen miles across Morecambe Bay.[9] Jails of the day did not totally isolate inmates from the outside world, but Fox nevertheless felt frustrated when he could not keep up with things going on in the capital. The regular post from London usually arrived on Saturday, and when he did not receive letters he demanded explanations.[10] Even Margaret Fell, who hurried to London in hopes of using her family's influence to secure the First Friend's release, did not escape his censure when her letters failed to reach him quickly enough.[11]

The authorities were worried about the Quakers who had swarmed into the area for the meetings Fox had so recently attended. Interviewed by a former Roundhead mayor and member of Parliament now overseeing the castle, Fox faced charges that he had brought hundreds of outsiders into the region at a particularly troublesome time and that he harbored treasonous intentions toward the new king—a "Common Enemy to his Majesty," he was labeled.[12] His inquisitor even suggested that he would welcome another war in hopes of plunging the nation into blood once again. Fox's denials did no good: he was remanded to jail and was refused his request to see a copy of the charges leveled against him.[13]

An intensive lobbying operation to convince the king to free Fox was launched immediately. Fox wrote a pamphlet in which he reminded his readers that his jailer had received a major's commission from the parliamentarians and had carried arms for them; he, on the contrary, harbored "nothing to the king but love." The political point was clear: he was being held by the very people who had borne arms against the current king and martyred his father. Fox also testified that he had renounced the use of weapons and had "never learned the postures of war."[14] Still, he could be defiant; he was not afraid to warn king and Parliament by advising both to consider the fate of "such as have been in authority before you, whom God has vomited out because they turned against the just."[15]

Margaret Fell made much the same point in milder language in a letter she mailed to the king before leaving Swarthmoor. While pressing for religious liberty, she warned that "the people of God, called Quakers," had limited patience; they would "love, own, and honor the king, and these our present governors, so far as they do rule for God and his truth and do not impose anything upon people's consciences."[16] Fell also informed the nation's magistrates of the injustice of keeping Fox in jail,[17] and she and Ann Curtis, whose royalist father had been executed by parliamentary order nearly two decades earlier, secured an audience to see the king. At one point Curtis offered to take Fox's place in the gloomy Lancaster dungeon.[18] Charles seemed favorably impressed with Curtis's mien, but General Monck, rewarded with a dukedom for his role in restoring the king, advised Charles that Fox should not be given special treatment. The king, who could hardly forget his father's bloody fate, wanted to win the support of peaceful dissidents; indeed, in his pre-Restoration Declaration of Breda he had promised "liberty to tender consciences."[19] This high-sounding commitment did not lead to Fox's unconditional release but it did result in an order to Lancaster that the prisoner be freed on a writ of habeas corpus. But red tape and local jealousies kept Fox jailed until late September.[20]

Lancaster officials wrangled over who should pay the expense for Fox's escort to London. Finally they decided to let him and two Friends go on their own, secured only by a promise to show up on the right day. Detouring first by Swarthmoor Hall, the group headed south.[21] Fox held a number of meetings in the Midlands, not even two miles from Drayton-in-the-Clay, but recorded no visit to his mother. He did note that the meeting in Frandley was so large that it had to be moved outside into the autumnal air, a vivid reminder of his movement's continuing strength. He arrived in London during the third week in October just as the regicides were being executed at Charing Cross before giddy crowds of onlookers.[22]

Friends around the nation certainly had nothing to be giddy about—indeed,

Fox only now felt himself fully freed from the burden of last year's depression. His followers were likewise depressed: promised throughout the previous decade that the day of the Lord was near and that a new kingdom of peace and justice was about to be born, they naturally saw the Restoration as a sign of God's disfavor. Moreover, the restoration of the monarchy suggested that Fox had been wrong. To prevent too many from falling away, he composed an epistle of reassurance while still in Lancaster castle. Friends should not be troubled, he advised, by the change in government, for "what is now come up, it is just with the Lord that it should be so." He predicted that a brighter day would dawn; until then, any murmuring and distrust of God's will would provoke "thunder down from heaven, . . . and his enemies shall be astonished and the workers of iniquity confounded." Yet he muted his hope for a new order even as he refused to give it up totally, and he warned that those who did not don garments of righteousness would be amazed once the divine and mysterious hand began to work its will.[23] When he communicated messages like this one to his followers, he was trying to woo back those who had run for cover, had decided to sit on the sidelines, or, worse, like Anthony Pearson, had defected. The Restoration divided Quakers into two groups: those who found reassurance in Fox's message to trust in God and the inevitable workings of God's will, and those who expected the Society of Friends to take a more militant stance.

It is clear that as 1660 drew to a close Fox was being forced by circumstances to reassess his earlier views, particularly regarding the use of violence. Having determined to move away from outright advocacy of political and social reforms as one way to protect his movement, Fox still needed to develop other survival tactics. He sought a strategy that comported with the movement's past yet responded to the diverse attitudes within the movement, attitudes ranging from Burrough's and Salthouse's to those who had quietly retreated. Late 1660 was a time of deep concentration and struggle for the First Friend. He had to find a way that would simultaneously preserve his sect, convince the authorities of its peaceful intent, and yet allow the friends to remain true to their brief history.

One key step Fox took was to give up his earlier view that it was permissible to use the sword in the cause of justice. His gradual shift on this question, from the acceptance of the use of violence as a means to achieve a just society to a refusal to approve the use of violence under any circumstances, represented the other side of his method of coping with the new world after the Restoration. To deemphasize social reform would mean retreating to a greater emphasis on "spiritual" and relatively safer religious matters. To adopt what moderns call a "pacifist" stance would send a message to hostile and suspicious authorities that they need not worry about the Friends' ultimate aims. Hence embracing new ends in this new situation all but required changing the practical means.

Fox began his retreat from activism before Venner made his valedictory promise that he would be vindicated by the immediate return of Christ, but the Fifth Monarchist uprising and the scare subsequent to it formed the immediate backdrop for retrenchment. In 1660, probably soon after Charles had taken the throne, Fox issued a broadside devoted primarily to explaining why his followers refused to swear oaths. In this handout he buried a sentence that showed him inching toward a rejection of force, except for a "war with the devil and his works." "To plot and confederate or to raise insurrections," he wrote, "we utterly deny, . . . though we cannot swear to this."[24] The same approach, indicating one of his definitions of the devil's works, underlined his continued willingness to view the sword as a legitimate instrument for a righteous cause. Thus he cautioned Charles that permitting vanities like plays and maygames showed that the king bore his sword in vain. If the king had a sword to wield, he implied, then let him wield it for a worthwhile purpose.[25] On another occasion he defined this worthwhile purpose as keeping the peace and protecting people's estates, both fascinating reflections of his followers' aspirations.[26]

This pragmatic approach worked until Venner's rebellion changed the calculus. Before there had seemed to be little practical need for Fox to modify his position. He was freed from jail in September, then the charges against him were dismissed in October. The king not only continued to be conciliatory but was out-and-out sympathetic: he ordered that other Friends be released from jail and decreed that they should not be punished for wearing their hats in court or for failing to attend church. Charles seemed to be so favorably disposed to the Quakers that his chief ministers, most of whom were unbending opponents of the sect, were embarrassed by their monarch's indulgence toward its members.[27] During one interview with Margaret Fell the king's advisers hustled him out of the room when he began to make promises that they believed ran contrary to the statutes officials were using against the Quakers.[28]

Thus royal sympathy hardly translated into tolerance. Neither did it prevent officials from rounding up likely suspects. Venner and a compatriot had barely been drawn and quartered when the government issued a January 22 proclamation for Scotland in which Quakers, Anabaptists, and Fifth Monarchists were all lumped together as dangerous sects because of their "cruel tenets and bloody practices." The new order permitted the authorities to seek out meetings of these malcontents and arrest them.[29] When Quaker homes were searched in Yorkshire, papers were discovered that seemed to indicate a nationwide intelligence network backed up by a series of local meetings; both fueled already frantic suspicions. The frenzy with which many officials went about uncovering threatening elements led Charles on January 17 to attempt to control excesses by forbidding searches or seizures without a warrant. His efforts, however, were too puny in the wake of the near panic: the secretary of state undercut the king by pointing out that all over the country efforts were being made to disarm and arrest the fanatics.[30]

Fortunately, the First Friend could move with much more swiftness than the king and, in this instance at least, expect to carry along most of those under him. On January 21, two days after Venner's execution and fifteen days after his rebellion, Fox and eleven other Friends issued what later became known as the "Peace Testimony." Their haste was justified, not only because of the danger of persecution, but also because they had been told that a document granting freedom to imprisoned Quakers awaited only the king's signature. Fox and Hubberthorne wrote the text,[31] with the latter certainly improving on the First Friend's usual rambling style. Francis Howgill and Gerrard Roberts, a London businessman and prominent minister, also signed the document. The signers did not include such militants as Edward Burrough or Thomas Salthouse, those such as Thomas Curtis who had served as militia commissioners, or, for that matter, Margaret Fell, Ann Curtis, or any other woman. The men who did not add their names may have had misgivings about the message or may have wanted to follow developments before finally making up their minds. Or they may have simply been out of town and beyond reach. As for the omission of women, the matter may have been considered too important for their participation, either from a public relations or an internal standpoint. Fell, a likely signer, was in London at the time, and Curtis was as near as Reading. The declaration, from first line to postscript, was a clear effort to deal with the worsening political situation as Fox's Friends faced it.

The declaration's title underlined its writers' intent, as they put it, to remove "the ground of jealousy and suspicion" regarding "the harmless and innocent people of God, called Quakers." No general meeting or constituted body of the Society of Friends issued the pronouncement: its authors presumed on their own authority to speak for all Quakers when they affirmed their principle that "all bloody principles and practices we . . . do utterly deny, with all outward wars and strife, and fightings with outward weapons, for any end, or under any pretence whatsoever: and this is our testimony to the whole world." Denying also that they would ever be led to do what the spirit had once and for all forbidden, the statement specifically overruled Fox's earlier position that the sword might be wielded in a just cause. The authors marshalled a raft of biblical citations to show that Christ had commanded followers from the beginning not to fight with outward or carnal weapons. With a backward glance at the Fifth Monarchists, they affirmed that since Christ's kingdom lay beyond the present world they could not fight. Nor would they plot, and they denied ever having done so. They also claimed to have consistently eschewed outward weapons, but here the signers spoke accurately only for themselves, certainly not for Burrough, Curtis, and the like. Still, the struggle to achieve justice had not ended, albeit the Friends would employ a different kind of arms: "[O]ur weapons are spiritual and not carnal, yet mighty through God, to the pulling down of the strongholds of sin and Satan."[32]

In a historical sense, the declaration represented a major shift from the position Fox had articulated since 1650. While in Derby jail, he specifically exempted himself from participating in wars when he rejected a request from a group of soldiers that he take a captaincy. He quoted the apostle James that wars and fighting grew from lust, and he told them that he lived in a state that took away the occasion of war.[33] His position thus remained a personal one and was never used to judge his followers. Indeed, as we have seen, he never rebuked a single Quaker who joined the army, recruited militiamen, or raised arms for those engaged in furthering the Good Old Cause. More important, Fox had repeatedly recognized, most recently within the last year, that a magistrate who bore a weapon might permissibly use it in a just cause. He did not deny, and never would deny, the right of a nation's rulers to wield weapons in the defense of a just cause. The problem was in defining such a cause. In this particular instance he justified the use of weapons for suppressing maygames and drunkenness. Fox never made the kind of unequivocal pacifist demand that another Quaker, Agnes Wilkinson, addressed "to all who wear swords" in a 1653 epistle. She advised "all who handle a sword and take up carnal weapons ... to strip yourselves naked of all your carnal weapons and take unto you the sword of the Spirit, for the Lord is coming to judge men."[34]

Fox remembered the declaration as one "to clear us from all plots and contrivances."[35] His recollection underscores the context for the statement, a period during which Quakers aroused such official suspicion that they were set upon and abused while doing nothing more unusual than going to market.[36] But what was written for the nonce quickly became a standard summary of Quaker practice. It was translated and published that same year in Holland and Germany, and it was eventually given a prominent place in Fox's *Journal*.[37] Within a decade Quakers were claiming that it was common knowledge that they shunned violence.[38] Critics thus identified Quakers with refusing to lift the temporal sword.[39] Only a few years later other sectarians would adopt the same approach.[40]

Fox carried around in his head the memory of all those, including himself, who had already suffered in the more tolerant period of the Protectorate. (In this regard, it is easy to wonder if he swallowed hard before he signed the statement Fell had taken to London the year before for the king, the one listing a tongue bored through among the sufferings Quakers had undergone during the previous twelve years.[41] Only James Nayler, after all, had endured such a fate.) He had served time in the pestilential jails at Derby, Carlisle, and Launceston. He had suffered from deprivation, cold, damp, filth, and terrible smells. He had been verbally and physically abused by his jailers. And he had also suffered abuse from magistrates and constables in town after town across the nation. He wanted to make sure that other Friends did not experience the same things in the new decade.

There was also a deeper reason, one that went a long way toward explaining why the declaration of 1661 was embraced by most of Fox's followers then and cherished by Friends as time passed. "So we," Fox and Hubberthorne wrote, "whom the Lord has called into the obedience of his truth, have denied wars and fightings and cannot again any more learn it."[42] Pragmatism was fine, but Fox had been driven by the situation to go deeper; he saw now that he and his followers must give up the sword totally and forever. Rooted in his experience of being called, which formed the backdrop of his response to the situation, the statement never needed revising. In a booklet he wrote seven years later, he amplified his ideas about obedience to the divine will, even as he affirmed his belief that heeding God's will would allow one to achieve the practical result of victory over evil. Christ's command, he said, "is to you, to love one another, for that edifies the body and overcomes the evil; ... that is the law of love that is to be among Christians." Hence one who wronged others or enemies was clearly "out of Christ's mind, power, and command."[43]

Not everyone within the Society of Friends agreed with the declaration, but only one boldly published his objections. Isaac Penington, son of one of the judges at the trial of Charles I, a man of wealth and repute, had become a Friend in 1658. He never aspired to be in the inner circle of decision makers, but he flourished a facile pen and produced works that when printed and reprinted rivaled Fox's own.[44] "A down right good man," one favorably disposed critic called him.[45] In 1661, probably responding to the "Peace Testimony," he published a tract dealing with what he deemed "A Weighty Question" concerning whether rulers were obligated to protect the innocent. He admitted that fighting came by Adam and Eve's fall, but he averred that magistrates were authorized by God to rule and defend those too innocent or too weak to fight: women, the infirm, children, those "forbidden by the love and law of God written in their hearts," even priests. Having parried, he thrust with Fox's prior principle, asserting that, given the sorry state of the fallen world and the inability of many to allow God to defend them, the sword might honorably be "borne uprightly" to "suppress violent and evil-doers."[46]

At least one Quaker wanted Fox to go further and oppose war taxes, accusing him later of inconsistency in countenancing exclusion of members who served in trained bands and then approving payment of taxes.[47] But as far as Fox was concerned, the matter was closed and the principle established, despite how Quakers like Penington might complain. The First Friend had to move on. A week after the "Peace Testimony" was published, he appealed again to Friends to collect lists of their prison experiences so they could be submitted to the king and his council.[48] The matter of sufferings that Quakers were enduring at the hands of official and unofficial persecutors would remain a continuing concern,[49] for Fox recognized that if the Friends could demonstrate enough cases of unfair and illegal treatment to the London authorities, then they might assure a speedier redress of grievances. Acting in a more systematic and thorough manner than any other group at the time, Fox and his Friends thus compiled a record of sufferings that proved increasingly useful as legal precedents.[50] He used the same collection to illustrate Quaker testimonies against tithes and oaths, sometimes finding biblical figures who disregarded social customs, and sought thereby to sway public opinion.[51]

Moreover, Fox saw the sufferings of himself and his followers not as evidence of wrongdoing on their part but as a sign that they were faithfully following God's will. He applauded when Quaker William Sympson followed his advice to run unclothed through Cambridge streets to show startled crowds that they too would be stripped naked. He exulted when Robert Huntington wore a horse's halter so Presbyterians in Carlisle could see that they too would be restrained. And he approved constable Richard Sale's march into a Westchester church carrying a lantern and a candle to illuminate its darkness.[52] You are a dauntless people, he announced triumphantly, "who never feared them, whose backs were not unready but your hair and cheeks prepared, . . . as knowing it was your portion in the world."[53] The same principle, working in reverse, made him gloat over the misfortunes that beset his opponents. When one regicide was drawn and quartered, Fox relished how the same Colonel Francis Hacker had sent him under guard to London in 1654. Now he had his just, if sad, due.[54]

In December 1661 Fox took time to survey the expansion of Quakerism across the world. He found it spreading and making contacts on four continents, wherever people, as he put it, "have a thirst for God." In the West Indies, in Jamaica, Barbados, Nevis, and St. Kitts, he found Friends flourishing under the liberty obtaining there. The picture was not as rosy on the North American mainland, particularly in New England where laws had been enacted prohibiting Quakers from entering the Massachusetts Bay Colony. The forthcoming appearance of veteran evangelist Elizabeth Hooten and her companion Jane Brooks in Virginia would test reports that things were proceeding well there. Many Friends languished in prison in Scotland, but numbers were increasing there. The movement was also growing in Ireland. Will Caton had contacted the prince of the Palatine in Germany and found him loving, and another Friend had visited every German prince, securing a declaration of tolerance from at least one. In Denmark, where an order had been issued denying entrance to any Quakers, a missionary had confronted its ruler with a call for repentance. Two Friends had been banished from Egypt but had resumed their journey to find the legendary African ruler, Prester John. In Turkey, the English ambassador had refused protection to two Quakers, causing them to be deported.[55] Rome, where the heart of Catholic Europe continued to beat, had long been a target for Quaker evangelism but resisted all their efforts. Now Fox heard that another Quaker had died in Rome's prisons.[56]

Even these far-flung activities did not fully satisfy the First Friend, who recognized a need to retreat in England, but saw no such need elsewhere. He informed William Ames, who had already moved on from Holland to Germany, that "a seed of God" needed to be gathered in eastern and northern Europe, in Poland, Russia, Hungary, and Sweden. An obviously irritated Will Caton complained to Fox that Holland also had numerous seeds to be harvested, that he had just learned Dutch well, and that he was the only Friend left to watch over the "tender hearts" they had convinced. For himself, he sensed little of Fox's concern; perhaps he could lay it on someone there in England, Caton counseled.[57] Fox had better luck with Samuel Shattock, a Quaker who had been excluded from Boston under threat of death should he return. King Charles, importuned by Edward Burrough, agreed to order Masssachusetts governor John Endecott to release all imprisoned Quakers and return them safely to England. In a brilliant stroke of irony, Shattock was tapped to deliver the word to an overruled and chagrined Endecott.[58] Fox found time also to confer with the visiting governor of Connecticut about tolerance there.[59]

John Perrot was a missionary whose career once he returned to England created massive problems for Fox. Perrot's most notorious challenge, which involved the question of whether a man should take off his hat when another Friend prayed in a meeting, was of no great moment in itself.[60] But under vigorous massaging by strong egos, it rapidly erupted into the kind of divisive issue that bedevils every movement based on individualistic and mystical apprehensions of reality. For Fox personally, it amounted to a replay of the episodes of Rhys Jones and his Proud Quakers and of Nayler and his followers' messianic pretensions. Perrot even looked like Nayler, for he grew a Jesus-like beard.[61] If Fox thought he had solved the problem of authority with Nayler's humiliation and submission, then he was certainly wrong, for his problems with Perrot raised the same issue: who would rule? But there was a vital difference this time around. The struggles before had been Jones versus Fox and Nayler versus Fox, but now it was Perrot versus Fox and the machinery he had created to exercise control and oversight of the Society of Friends. And the situation outside the organization was also different this time. The threat of renewed persecution drifted in and out like morning fogs over northern fells and put a premium on unity. Fox should certainly have learned enough to find ways to avoid division, which would only make the Friends more vulnerable to outside attacks.

Perrot had a valued record among the early Quakers.[62] Edward Burrough sang his praises in the Irish missionary service: "Eminent in the nation," were the words he used to describe Perrot in early 1656, when he needed someone who could write quickly and serve well in the common Quaker tactic of facing down ministers in Ireland's churches. Perrot turned out to be just the person.[63] Another associate lauded his "beautiful life" and "the virtue and sweetness of the clear life of God manifest" in him.[64] A younger contemporary considered him a person of "great natural parts."[65]

In mid-1657 Perrot and five other missionaries left for Italy and the eastern Mediterranean. Perrot visited Venice and Rome; he spoke in synagogues—trying Latin as a common language to his audiences—and was interrogated by members of Catholic religious orders, particularly after he landed in the hands of the Inquisition. Later transferred to a place designed for mental patients, he remained incarcerated for three years, until 1661, when he returned to London. Unless he exaggerated, his punishment was horrendous: he was chained by the neck so he had to sit, stand straight, or lie down at the same spot, and he was regularly flogged with a pizzle, a bull's penis, dried for effectiveness. It was hardly surprising that eventually he began to act like his mad fellow inmates.[66] When he returned to England, he dubbed himself "Theor John," a name from Greek apparently suggesting he viewed himself as an emissary sent for a special religious duty.[67] Yet in his surviving letters he appears as a humble, conciliatory, and peaceful person, one who shrank from contention and strife. "Surely God casts me not out because of my own nothingness, emptiness, or unworthiness," he affirmed almost Job-like, "but because of his love, he loves me."[68]

Perrot's physical, spiritual, and emotional suffering and isolation in Rome were surely traumatic. His experiences in the Eternal City convinced him that he had a divine revelation that called into question, as he explained in one epistle, "all the customary and traditional ways of worship." Thus he announced an "express commandment from the Lord God in heaven" requiring him "to bear a sure testimony against the custom and tradition of taking off the hat by men when they go to prayer to God." It was bad enough that this revelation conflicted with accepted Quaker practice, which permitted men to wear their hats at all times except when someone prayed. Even worse was that Perrot carried the Quaker conviction that God was in both men and women to its logical extreme. First he applied the apostle Paul's advice to the Corinthians that women keep their heads covered in prayer to men also. And then he warned those who upheld a distinction that "the Lord God will not hold you guiltless."[69] He asked bluntly from Rome, "[W]hat is the difference between the fleshly head of carnal man and a carnal woman, and which of them does God most respect?"[70] This aspect of his challenge underscored how Fox's Friends had embraced a common social practice as well as biblical injunctions that women keep their heads covered, thus eroding their vaunted commitment to equality. Whether this emphasis by itself attracted women to Perrot or not, he, like Nayler, enjoyed a notable success with them.[71]

This imputation hurt and hurt badly. It pushed Fox into a corner from which he lashed out in a way that revealed some of his deepest assumptions about women and their nature. To one leading supporter of Perrot, John Harwood, who defended men leaving their heads covered like women, Fox denigrated women: "And so you would bring all men to sit like a company of women," he taunted, "and so you would bring all into a form under the penalty of curse." Men must "stand in our liberty in the power of God before hats were." Women could not enjoy that same liberty because Paul had ordered their heads covered; men wearing hats amounted to an empty and accursed form, while for women it was required.[72]

The sting of the same Perrotist charge led Fox to produce one of his most illogical and internally contradictory epistles. Without mentioning Perrot by name, he stumbled badly as he tried to explain Paul's advice and the two failures of Quakers as regarded covering one's head: why they subordinated their broad principle of living above all forms to the apostle's time-bound statement and the unequal requirements for men and women. He did not succeed in either goal. Fox condemned those who circulated papers about the hat, "jangled" that "comely" Quaker practices were "heathenish and Romish," and spread their janglings around the nation. But the only way he could explain Paul's distinctions between men and women was to say that the worldly Corinthians had not known the power of God, a description Quakers would never apply to themselves. Thus in accepting Paul, he denied equal treatment. He again admonished his followers to live in the power of God, "the state of Adam and Eve before the fall," when such head coverings were immaterial. But to admit that hats on or hats off made no difference now gave the argument to Perrot, and that he could not do. So his justification of the Quaker practice, living after the Fall as they did, was that it led to "order, comeliness, and decency," which meant that they must reject Perrot's janglings. His conclusion illustrated his unease, for implicitly he came down on Perrot's side—"The church of the Romans fell away by running into outward things. . . . And the apostle reproved them. . . . And therefore, all dear friends, keep in the power of God over all outward things"—which was the very thing Perrot recommended.[73] Thus did Fox demonstrate that the dispute really involved his authority, not a question about covering or not covering heads, be they male or female.

Fox replied publicly to the issue of women. He did not stoop to do so regarding a London group that merged with Perrot's challenge. A small clique had become convinced that power was unduly concentrated in the hands of a few men at the center and that Fox, as leader, countenanced and perhaps even encouraged this evolution. Compared to their opponents, this group had little influence and less power. They ultimately lost their struggle to change the direction of the Society of Friends, which meant that they disappeared into the back pages of history. The leader of this group was John Pennyman, an inveterate Fox hunter originally from Yorkshire. By 1661 he lived in London, making a prosperous living as a woolen draper. It has never been established what the root cause of his disagreement with Fox was, although he made no secret of the fact that he disliked the First Friend and distrusted his supporters. Pennyman's actions hinted at an almost pathological hatred of authority, but he apparently was lucid and convincing enough to win support from others—at least a goodly proportion of Friends in local second-echelon positions shared his malady.[74] For example, he identified as accomplices men of the stature of Nicholas Bond, a government official who started and housed the meetings in the Strand and in Greenwich;[75] John Osgood, a young linen draper who served over the years on numerous yearly and monthly meeting committees;[76] and William Penington, merchant and brother of Isaac.[77] Thus he claimed the support of most of the main men's meeting in London.

By the time Perrot appeared in London, the principal concern of this group was what they alleged to be lies contained in the accounts of the sufferings that Fox had solicited and Ellis Hookes, the paid clerk of the Friends in London, had compiled, written, and published. Knowing that by singling out Hookes they would raise questions about Fox's role also, they took on the clerk. To force him out, they tried convincing the men's meeting in London to declare him incompetent and reduce his salary. In November 1662 they called Hookes before them and, as he explained, "dealt pretty hardly with me." They demanded all the papers submitted for the proposed book of sufferings, but he claimed that they were private communications and offered to let them see only those for London and its vicinity. The insurgents had not learned much about the power of incumbents, for now someone identified only as "an ancient Friend of Fox's" intervened on Hookes's behalf and the salary was paid. Then Fox and Amor Stoddard, both influential ministers, and Gerrard Roberts and Gilbert Latey, probably the two most powerful figures in London's Quaker administration, moved in, and Hookes kept his post. So chagrined were the dissidents that they retreated to a wood three or four miles outside the city, where they loudly (but safely) bemoaned what they considered "the sad degeneracy of the leaders."[78]

Pennyman continued to snipe at the leadership until his death in 1706. His associates seemed to have made their peace with the establishment, but in 1661 they supported Perrot's challenge. Galled by the Quakers' willingness to view Fox as "Lord and Lawgiver," as Pennyman succinctly phrased it,[79] they would accept help from anyone who might happen by. And Perrot happened by. Whether they agreed with him in all particulars or not was beside the point; it was enough that they saw in him a powerful and articulate challenger who could assist them in reducing the influence of the few men who exercised so much power within London's Quaker community. Pennyman's reference to Fox as "Lord and Lawgiver" may also have reflected a brooding discontent with the expedient compromise imposed by the "Peace Testimony" of 1661. In these ways, Perrot acted more as a spark to a pile of tinder already there than as someone introducing a new concept.

It is easy to see, therefore, how Perrot could set Fox's teeth on edge. The unforgettable Nayler business was never far from Fox's mind; the need to preserve unity in the face of outside persecution was his main concern; and the possibility that a new crisis would peel off adherents faster than a sheepshearer could cut wool in the spring frightened him. For Fox, Perrot looked exactly like the internal challenge Quakers feared most—he was a Ranter, an unrestrained, obstreperous, institution-destroying individualist. Fox also knew, certainly better than Perrot did, the nature of the discontent with his leadership. He did not want the tinder to catch fire. Thus when Perrot got to London in late July, Fox was girded and waiting. The dispute was carried on in theological terms, but it really involved that nagging old question of power and who had the right to exercise it. Having already warned the itinerant by letter that a "great judgment will come upon you,"[80] Fox now had a chance to spell out exactly what he meant.

Fox did not wait long. On Perrot's very first night back in the capital, they met at Gerrard Roberts's home, where the traveler had come, he said, "to wait upon the Lord." Fox did not begin with the charge of Ranterism and disobedience but instead started by indicting Perrot on more mundane matters, such as the exorbitant expenses he had run up during his four years away from England. Fox specifically mentioned £20 loans to two women Friends jailed in Malta and the cost of shipping books and letters from Rome. If Perrot was correct in reporting that he said little, then Fox surely talked a lot, for he did not halt the interrogation until 2:00 A.M. The next night Fox's accusations continued until 1:00 A.M., with Perrot responding only that he had heard it all the night before. Fox recruited two other Friends a day or so later to assist in what could only be described as a continuing effort to make the new arrival confess to wrongdoing. On the matter of the expenses, Fox claimed that spending so much would lead people to think that Quakers were "moneyed." Perrot argued that he had spent no more money than ministers who had remained in England, and certainly not enough to equal the cost of publishing Fox's hefty tome, *A Battle-Door*, the principal purpose of which was to argue that "thee" and "thou" were common in many languages.[81] Pressed hard, Perrot burst into tears and agreed to ask his wife to draw on her estate and repay the disputed funds. He asked for a conclave of ministers to hear his side of the dispute, but Fox dismissed that request, as did his old partner in Ireland, Edward Burrough, when it was broached to him.

At some point the matter of wearing hats finally surfaced, the witness defending himself with, "the Lord required it of me." "A breach of unity," Fox snapped at this ranterish heresy. Perrot, having reached the essence of the dispute, countered with, "[I]f I should do otherwise, then I should sin." True unity, he said, consisted not in something outward like a hat, "but in the spirit only." He would not stand, he went on, "in opposition to any man who could say by the word of the living God that he was moved to take off his hat in prayer," but anyone who sought "to make ... an absolute enforcing rule, law, or tie for another man's conscience [as he considered Fox had done], I did conclude that you were not right in that particular." Hence what he wanted most of all to avoid was imposing a rule that prevented, as one supporter emphasized, Quakers from being "left to the order of that spirit which first convinced them."[82]

Fox was not won over. To the contrary, he was convinced now more than ever that Perrot needed major attention if he was to see the error of his ways. When Francis Howgill, who had known Perrot in Ireland, arrived in town, he was dispatched to talk to his former associate at Roberts's house. Howgill's words, however tempered by long acquaintance, had the same purport as Fox's. He also mentioned the hat, the hard words, and verse—Fox had earlier charged Perrot with sending "hard words" in both prose and verse back from Rome—and ventured a new issue, namely, that Perrot had written, as he recounted it, "the secrets of my mind" to George Fox the younger. This young man, boasting the same name as the First Friend, had staked out a more radical position than the one now in vogue. Only two months after Charles II's return, sounding like a determined Fifth Monarchist, he explained to the king that God's decree was "to disthrone him and to take the kingdom myself."[83] He also took aim at those who "soared up above the sphere, / In words, in carriage, or in action" and thus "gave the Seed no satisfaction." Although he mentioned no names, in this context he probably had his namesake in mind.[84]

Perrot's response to having written verses was very odd, although it was possible that, since he knew some of his mail from Rome had been opened and read by others, he was being sarcastic: "If they had offended any Friend in England, when I sent them from Rome, if any had, brother-like, turned the sense of them into prose, to have taken off the offense from any, I believe that I should have taken it dearly well." And the same was true, he iterated, with any alleged "hard words." Having been out of the country, he contended to underscore the obvious, "I was innocent and unknowing in the matter"—all the more reason for his fellows to "give the sense of my writings otherwise."[85]

This series of grillings occurred within the first week Perrot was back in London, but as yet no public action had been taken against him. Perrot continued to travel and suffered arrest in Canterbury.[86] In September Fox, William Dewsbury, and their dissident met with some missionaries from New England and found their hearts knitted together.[87] Almost obsequious in his manner toward Fox, Perrot explained that "I am as innocent as a worm in writing and as full of love as my upright heart can contain," but he firmly refused to back down and admit he was wrong.[88] "Hard as flint" was the way one on Fox's side described him.[89] In his approach Perrot differed sharply from Nayler, who had tended to lose his voice as soon as he was confronted. Perhaps Fox was not yet sure of what course of action he should follow, or perhaps he hoped that time and reflection would woo the dissident back. He certainly knew that Perrot was erecting a power base in London, and that he had some influential supporters, both inside and outside the Society of Friends. For example, he set up evening meetings in the city, which, while not unusual, did indicate that he was not willing to subordinate himself to the oversight of influential local Quakers.[90] Moreover, Isaac Penington, who had publicly opposed Fox on the use of arms, was close to Perrot and entertained him at his well-appointed home at Chalfont.[91] Two years later Penington published a long reflective essay in which he ventured that the Society of Friends, like ancient Israel, had become too well-off and self-satisfied, thus straying from its earlier purity.[92] There were even tantalizing hints that Perrot and the king were on friendly terms; at least Charles once had him released from prison and granted him an audience during which he wished him well.[93]

At first Perrot found the questionings he had undergone so grueling that, he complained to Fox, "you have wearied my soul with contentions."[94] But during a trip into Essex in November his spirits were buoyed enough for him to address a general letter to the Friends in London asking for a meeting on November 19 to deal with the question of the hat.[95] In what he termed was a "very sweet and precious meeting"—perhaps because "the counsel of God's uniting spirit" led him to refer to neither hats nor caps—the assembled Friends decided he was free of any renting and dividing spirit. He left no record of whether he kept his hat on when William Dewsbury and John Crook prayed, and the meeting ended on a positive note.[96]

Perrot wanted to continue this drift toward reconciliation. Thus, before leaving on a planned trip to Bristol at the beginning of the year, he appeared on Monday, December 30, at the Roberts home for the regular Second Day Meeting of Ministers. A number of supporters, John Pennyman and John Osgood, for example, came with him.[97] The growing influence of the Second Day Meeting was not artificial or forced but represented a natural evolution. From an effort originally designed to make sure that local meetings in the London area had ministers each Sunday, it was developing into a committee of men who assumed an oversight of all Quaker activities in the capital.[98] Its tone was set by regular attenders at its meetings, men characterized by access to nationwide contacts and information, a broad outlook, and an understandable view that these qualifications made them obvious leaders. Thus as time went on and more and more activities, such as publishing, centered in London, the Second Day Meeting extended its influence deeper and deeper into the hinterland. Therefore it was only natural that the ministers of this meeting would have a say in the wrenching dispute over wearing hats.

Thus this meeting, dominated by those Perrot's supporters called "the elders," embodied a major test for Perrot, the climax of the entire affair. Practically all the issues in the dispute were aired fully, and the dissident-turned-diplomat played his audience superbly. Perrot began by entreating them to send him off to Bristol with their blessings. Probably speaking metaphorically, he claimed that he put his neck under Fox's feet, "requesting, beseeching, and begging your love." Fox was willing to grant this request if the supplicant would "do so and so." Perrot refused, lest love be purchased and not granted freely. Francis Howgill, having only recently read two of Perrot's papers on the hat issue, commented that if he had read them before then he would have said nothing. Revealing his practical concern, Fox called on those assembled to live in "love and unity together," for they "had many enemies abroad, and it was not a time for us to have a contest among ourselves."

But the issue of authority was always present, even if below the surface. Two conflicting points of view became obvious, one that desired the utmost latitude for individual leadings and interpretation, the other insisting on the individual's submission to outside authority. Perrot read from a letter he had written to a woman in which he stated that obedience to God was fundamental and that if

God should command him, as with Hosea, to take a harlot with syphilis then he would do so, "though it would be the hardest thing under the sun." Fox could not believe that God would command such a thing under the gospel but, despite a plea that he do so, uncharacteristically put off judging the notion. If Fox believed it impossible for God so to command, Perrot deferentially affirmed, "I would find it impossible to obey it." Hubberthorne preferred that the matter "might be better unwritten than written," and Perrot agreed to bear his judgment. Perrot then spoke and prayed, whether with or without hat is unknown. He firmly exalted God and denigrated the unredeemed. But then he broke the aura of good feelings by commenting that even the most learned needed God's teachings daily. This startled the sophisticated Londoners and others anxious to put a respectable mask on a Quaker face marred by an unseemly and radical reputation. One replied, "[T]hat was to make ignorance," and another and then another repeated the charge. Sensing his mistake, Perrot asked to be allowed to go, and Hubberthorne replied, "John, you seem to desire our love, then stay." The dissident left with a promise to meet them two hours after the next day's meeting at the Bull and Mouth tavern.[99]

The crowded meeting beside the tavern the next day was, according to one critical participant, as "glorious a meeting as ever I was at." Isabel Harker, an ardent Perrot supporter, sensed that its "love, which flowed from and burst out and ran over in the chosen vessel, will not easily be lost."[100] But this spirit did not survive the subsequent short walk to William Travers's house. Fox, Howgill, Hubberthorne, and George Whitehead, a younger leader destined to be a dominant force in the Society of Friends for another fifty years, met with Perrot and some of his disciples. There, with the others sitting by silently, Hubberthorne opened with aspersions against Perrot's comments of the previous day. The flabbergasted man in the dock mumbled that he did not remember everything that he had said during their long session and appealed for others to help him. Apparently they did, for all except Hubberthorne cooled off, and the meeting arose shortly when a German doctor and his wife interrupted. But Perrot did not escape that easily. A select group insisted he go into an upper room, where Hubberthorne expressed his bitterness about the hat issue and said a number of hard things, but the others, including Fox, embraced Perrot and wished him well on his journey.[101] But he got no endorsement for his trip and later termed the expressions of love, at least from Fox and Howgill, as "pretended."[102]

Given what happened almost immediately after Perrot left London, he and Harker either misinterpreted the actual situation or else, and more likely, the Quakers at the center decided to deal with him finally only after he left. Perrot had already planned to stop at the home of Isaac and Mary Penington in Buckinghamshire for a ten-day retreat from the trials he had been through in London. He had hardly arrived when one letter after another started to arrive from the capital. The letters rehearsed the hat question once more, warned that he would be punished, and predicted that the magistrates would pick him up. When the recipient of these missives got to Bristol, he found that other letters had been sent to prejudice the Quakers there against him.[103] An epistle from Fox to all Friends was also being circulated. The First Friend proclaimed that he "was moved of the Lord God to write." Backed by such supreme authority, he coupled Perrot with Nayler and them both with the Ranters, all of whom had kept their hats on when Friends prayed. He condemned their "dark, earthly spirit" in one sentence, their "dark, subtle, and sophistical spirit" in the next, their "cankered, rusty spirit" in a sentence farther on. While acknowledging that they acclaimed their love and wanted their liberty, he damned both their claim and their desire as feigned and insincere. Finally, he concluded that their actions allowed people to point to the Quakers and see their divisions, but God "looks upon them and the world as one against the truth and power of God."[104]

The personal aspersions now waxed. When he went west, Perrot caught up with rumors that he preached Islam or had been won over by priests on his way home from Rome through France. Others whispered that he was a "grievous adulterer" or, worse, a Cavalier.[105] He certainly did not help himself with the mainstream Quakers when he published a short pamphlet in 1662 suggesting, from its title page on, that other denominations could unite in "pure amity" with the Quakers.[106] Even his mid-1662 decision to voluntarily accept deportation to Barbados so he could get out of Newgate prison drew Fox's ire. "To publish such a book before he goes" was, Fox fumed, "the way of the false prophets . . . [who] have gone and told the world if there had been any weakness among Friends." The First Friend thundered that Perrot ought to go back to his wife, saddled with £500 of debts, and "not throw his excrements and dung among Friends."[107]

When Perrot shipped out to the colonies, he extended his influence into a new part of the world and found a safer base. His departure certainly did not end the matter. The controversy died down, but then revived off and on throughout the 1660s and into the next decade. From the Netherlands, Benjamin Furly, the businessman who had corroborated with Fox on *Battle-Door*, sent letters back home to propose that Quakers stop arguing about something as insignificant as whether to remove the hat or not.[108] No one heeded his advice. Perrot himself went to Maryland and Virginia, there to create more problems for those in authority within the Quaker movement.[109] An eruption occurred in England in 1673 when William Mucklow, a former Quaker from Surrey, published *The Spirit of the Hat: or, The Government of the Quakers*. All the leading Friends were concerned about this new outbreak, but William Penn was assigned the task of replying to Mucklow's frontal assault on the power of the Second Day Meeting.[110] Despite all this obvious evidence of continuing unrest, those around Fox continued to insist that the Society of Friends was unified. They took especial exception to their opponents' attempts to define parties within the sect. Terms like "Foxonian," "King George Fox," or "G. Fox and His Party" were abusive libels that did not reflect reality as they preferred to see it.[111]

The vehemence and illogic that characterized Fox's attitude toward Perrot explained a great deal about the Society of Friends after 1660. Experiencing a defeat in his longing for the Good Old Cause, Fox made the compromises that he found necessary in order to convince the authorities that they had nothing to fear from his group. In his effort to preserve an organization that had helped give meaning to the lives of many of his countrymen and countrywomen, there was nothing especially reprehensible about changing course and tacking for expediency's sake. What he failed to see, however—more accurately, what no one could see—was that in taking the long, institutional view he was vitiating a major part of the force that gave his movement its spectacular successes during the 1650s. In a more subtle way, the January 1661 "Peace Testimony," a compromise regardless of what it was called, set a precedent that encouraged others to demand that he recognize their right to compromise. George Fox, as the result of his personal makeup and his personal history, was simply not a man who could compromise easily, particularly when the compromise involved something as important to him as his power and influence inside the movement he had shaped and molded. The "Peace Testimony," after all, did not call his authority into question or threaten his role within the movement; but the hat question, minor as it seemed to be, did both.

Isaac Penington, who had watched his politician-father make decisions on matters of moment that ultimately cost him his head, understood this situation. Convinced that the Friends had been chosen by God as divine instruments, he remarked on what he deigned to call the "contemptibleness of the vessels" sent for the task, vessels "for the most part mean as to the outward, . . . of no deep understanding or ready expression, but very fit to be despised everywhere by the wisdom of man." They did not even have the usually expected acquaintance with the deep mysteries of religion. What they had done, he went on, was to preach "repentance and about a Light within, and of turning to that and proclaiming the great and terrible Day of the Lord to be at hand." That nicely summed up the Quaker gospel of the 1650s. And they had prospered, he exclaimed. But now, after those necessary compromises, "their danger is greatest"; they had grown proud, "richly adorned with the ornaments of life and come to have the power itself in [their] hand to make use of." No wonder Penington predicted that "some great and eminent ones" would fall in Israel.[112] And no wonder too that Fox and other Quaker leaders who had been labeled "heretics" by religious and government officials in the 1650s should now try to impose the heretic label on fellow Quakers who refused to submit to their authority.

14

*More Belongs to Marriage
than Four Bare Legs in a Bed*

George Fox's marriage to Margaret Fell took place at the end of the 1660s. The union marked a personal culmination, even if it did not change his life very much. Marriage is an almost perfect metaphor for his final years in this decade. And if the metaphor identified a struggling marriage, then it would be even more apt. There was little evidence of elation or excitement on either his or his wife's part—rather than a new beginning it seemed a continuation of the way things had been. The new marriage was an old marriage. The events to which he had to respond also remained more troubling, a kind of nagging bother, than anything pleasureable. Unrest and dissent, despite the fact that Perrot was out of the picture in the New World, still existed within the Society of Friends, calling forth an ongoing effort to deal with them. Complicating this unease was the legal situation, one bringing down on the young sect the full force of the government. A marriage that does not work can seem like a prison when the couple is hemmed in and unable to squeeze free. Fox spent nearly three years in prison, his wife-to-be a year longer, and she was sent back to jail a second time before the decade's end.

There was one other thing that troubled Fox, more subtle, but just as devastating as his other burdens. In the 1640s and 1650s, he had lived in an exhilarating period when the problems he faced were the same as those faced by others excited by the search for a better relationship with God and their fellows. He had grown to maturity in a time of uninhibited hope, of pure excitement, such as freshens and enlivens a new marriage with love and joy. But now, in the 1660s, his "openings," as he continued to call them, did not seem nearly so relevant to the day-to-day aspect of his problems. However much human beings had to deal with details, God did not come in them. If God led Fox, for example, to know how to deal with a John Perrot, he still was not able to use God's help to silence Perrot or his dissident followers. His authority had been challenged, and now his problems ground him down more. He had made his commitment, and now he had to make it work, under conditions that seemed never to get better. In the 1660s the forty-six-year-old leader suffered the worst period of depression he ever experienced.

Fox's problems were highlighted at a 1662 worship meeting at Broadmead in Bristol, a meeting that turned out to be the most notorious one he ever attended. The debate that subsequently swirled around it had little to do with what he said but rather with the way he acted. Things were tense for Quakers in Bristol that summer Sunday morning; simply by meeting together they were breaking the law of the land. The so-called Quaker Act had become effective that May. It prohibited more than five persons from gathering for any religious exercises contrary to the rites of the Church of England. The members of the Bristol meeting knew they were breaking the law, but they believed that they themselves, not the authorities, should define their religious life. Under such conditions Quakerism was not a faith for the fainthearted. Word that Fox would preach at the meeting had spread through the area, partially because hundreds of people had already visited him at the local home where he was staying. The previous week he had attended the meeting and had spoken after one of his oldest traveling companions, Alexander Parker, was taken into custody for breaking the law.

That Sunday, July 27, was a hot day, hot even for the last week of July. Magistrates had let it be known that they intended to catch the wily Fox they had missed the week before. Fox was thus aware that the trained band, citizen soldiers sometimes used to enforce the law, would be ready for him, so he sent John Stubbs, another companion, and some others to scout out the meeting. Near the meetinghouse they encountered a file of musketeers, whose sergeant politely stopped them and sent them back. They watched his troop march to a nearby Baptist church and arrest its minister for violating the Quaker Act. Stubbs hastened to the home of Edward Pyott, where Fox was staying, and reported the morning's events. Fox considered and then directed one Friend, Edward Bourne, to go on to the meeting but to come at noon and meet him in the field outside the meetinghouse. Then Fox, with two Friends walking ahead of him, left in time to make the rendezvous. As instructed, Bourne met them, and moments later they were joined by Dennis Hollister, one of the best known local Quakers and a Parliament member during the Interregnum. As they walked toward the meetinghouse, Hollister expressed his misgivings. He asked Fox if he really wanted to go into the "very mouth of the destroyer." Fox said he did.

When they arrived, they found that two Friends had been posted at a mostly unused door to watch. They greeted Fox, and the three entered. The gathering was unusually large. Some of the congregation had come from other parts of the country, Bristol being conveniently located near Wales and the west. Few had known for sure that Fox was coming and ripples of excitement ran through those present there. A woman was speaking, but after Fox and his fellows entered she immediately stopped, and Fox began his discourse. Later he remembered that he prayed and then preached that all could see that the God of Israel would surely deliver them. Fox, obviously clear about what he wanted to say, finished and stepped down.

At this point the meeting was interrupted by a young man who had left to check on the troops outside when Fox arrived. Pushing through the crowd to the speaker, he whispered that he had overheard one of the guards vowing that they would get Fox this week. Fox then left, probably departing by the same door through which he had entered, for the trained band was guarding the main entrance. As he left, he told Stubbs, George Bishop, another local and influential member, and some others to "keep in the meeting," probably to prevent mobs of panicky people from rushing out. Stubbs and the others returned and held the meeting for a bit longer until it ended at the regular time, but before the strangely laggard authorities initiated their raid. No one was arrested, much to the relief of those who thought that Fox would be apprehended.[1]

There seemed nothing particularly unusual about this meeting of July 27. Indeed, it ended peacefully and escaped the problems—invasion by armed soldiers, beatings, imprisonments, and so on—that often greeted an open violation of the law by England's intractable minority of Friends. By these standards the Bristol meeting was downright decorous.

Eighteen years later, however, this particular meeting became the subject of debate when one of those present that day, now an opponent of George Fox, used his actions to suggest that he lacked the kind of personal integrity that merited the acclaim or the leadership role he enjoyed. William Rogers, a Bristol businessman who attended his leader's wedding, believed that Fox was a hypocrite who violated his own long insistence that Quakers forthrightly and honestly accept the sufferings that the practice of their faith required of them. Rogers argued that when it came to confronting the authorities head on, Fox deliberately sought to avoid those he knew were going to arrest him: he let others bear the risk while he sneaked down the stairs and out the back door. To act as he did in Bristol suggested to Rogers that Fox could, would, and did act in a similar fashion elsewhere. Thus Fox was no leader, certainly not one worth following; he was a charlatan.[2]

This incident and the controversy it produced indicated that the years after the Restoration were times of increased peril for George Fox and the Quakers. As undisputed leader of the Society of Friends, the First Friend found himself facing a new situation, one fraught with pitfalls: he had to sustain and strengthen the organization in the face of this outside pressure, rally his followers despite the desire of some of them to compromise with the authorities, and shape his institution to bear the weight of this ongoing struggle. He had learned a valuable lesson from his experiences with Nayler and Perrot: he knew now that he had to subordinate the individualism of the early days to the needs of group survival in the present and future.[3] There was a certain irony to his situation, for the man who had himself been tagged a Ranter during the 1650s now turned that politically loaded term against any who crossed him. Moreover, in doing so, he inevitably cast his lot with a class of people who had looked askance at the rude and crude vessels who had brought Quakerism's early message to the nation. Isaac Penington's reading of the movement's forced maturity firmly anchored its experience within the broader tradition of sectarian history.[4]

There was, in addition, a woman whose influence and knowledge Fox came increasingly to rely upon. By the end of the decade of the 1660s, George Fox and Margaret Fell would become husband and wife. Fell's first mate, Thomas, bequeathed her not only his extensive estate but also the influence he had so carefully cultivated during his life. As widow of the deceased chancellor of the duchy of Lancaster, highest legal post in the county, and mistress of Swarthmoor Hall and the extensive lands associated with it, Margaret Fell was a member of the local aristocracy, accustomed to having her say heeded. Over the years, since that fateful day in June 1652 when she had become convinced of the truth Fox preached, Fell's role in the sect had grown steadily. An astute woman who knew her way amid worldly affairs, she stood for many years at the center of an ever-broadening network of correspondents who informed her of developments in the far reaches of the Quaker empire. Her role exemplified the truth that knowledge gives power. Friends, then and later, conferred upon her the title of "nursing mother" of the movement,[5] but she was much more than that: her status and experience gave her a ready supply of self-assurance in her dealings with people. Although there is no indication that she even met Perrot, she addressed a letter of condemnation to that dissident.[6] Not only did she deal with powerful men, even kings, in behalf of her cobelievers, but within the Society of Friends she also doled out assignments like a Quaker bishop.[7]

Regardless of her power, Fell deferred to Fox, both about her own family matters and her role within the Quaker movement; or perhaps it would be more accurate to say that they relied on each other, building on a growing respect for the other's judgment. Less than a year following her husband's death in October 1658, the widow Fell was soliciting Fox's advice about one of her horses.[8] About the same time, just as he went into the deep depression that overtook him near the end of the Protectorate, he expressed his need for a letter from her.[9] She likewise needed him. On her first trip to London in 1660, she noted that a decision about how long she should remain did not rest on her own desires—or pocketbook, for she found it necessary to borrow expense money. Her visits to government officials, as well as her work superintending publications ranging from disputes with Baptists to addresses to the king, made her a valuable person in the capital, and she quite willingly awaited Fox's wishes about when she should return to Lancashire. Do not let up in pressing the king, he forcefully wrote.[10] She ended up staying fifteen months, until September 1661, when Fox finally decided, as she said, that her release was ordered by the Lord.[11]

Neither Fell's lobbying, nor the presence of Fox, nor the publication of addresses and petitions could prevent Parliament from having its way with dangerous sectarians. Quakers had never been popular—they were too puritanical, too stiff, too principled when it came to the traditional frivolities, maypoles, morris dancing, and the like. Now those who made the new rules did not permit themselves to be fettered by niceties like religious tolerance. Given the divisive role religion had played in the two previous decades, unity was an ideal espoused by most, pluralism hardly conceivable. Protestants of all varieties did not like a policy that might open the way for Roman Catholics to worship freely, which was one of the king's goals in opting for leniency. Others, like Richard Baxter, wanted a church broad enough to appeal to moderates like Presbyterians, but narrow enough to suppress more radical sects. Thus during the 1660s a succession of new laws was added to the books to deal with dissenters; at the same time older laws, long ignored, especially those requiring oaths of allegiance, were enforced.[12]

Thus various oaths, of allegiance, of compliance with the Anglican church, of disavowing taking up arms against the king, and so on, were used to persecute the Quakers. The Friends' refusal to remove their hats when they stood, seldom meekly, before a magistrate, was judged to be a provocative act. The Quaker Act prohibited public, non-Anglican religious gatherings, as we have seen, if more than five adults were present. A Quaker household might invite five outsiders in for a meeting, but this alternative did not allow for much evangelization and was not at all satisfactory. Persons charged with violating the law might be convicted without a jury trial if they confessed, or if the justice of the peace received a sworn statement from a witness, or "notorious" evidence of the meeting existed. The punishments imposed for violations of the Quaker Act ranged from fines to confiscation of goods, to imprisonment; if those on trial would not swear to uphold the state, then the death penalty could be applied. The famous Five Mile Act of 1665, although aimed at ordained clergy, was broad enough to allow zealous officials to use it against obviously unconsecrated, unswearing Quakers. According to this law, a person "pretending" to holy orders and already convicted of preaching in an unlawful assembly who would not swear to refrain from taking up arms was prohibited from coming within five miles of a town.[13]

Unlike other dissidents, who usually scurried for cover or feigned conformity to the religious establishment, the Friends continued to hold their meetings openly, as at Broadmead. They would continue to meet, one Friend insisted, in the numbers God called together.[14] Hence any announced or regular gathering was fair game for a strict constable or justice of the peace; if the Quakers tried to restrict their meetings to their own adherents, zealous authorities planted spies who would give testimony about the illegal conventicle. In periods of relative quiet Quakers might be allowed to meet in peace, but if rumors of a plot surfaced or a suspicious outsider appeared to meet with the group, the authorities would spring into action. Ellis Hookes described enforcement of the Quaker Act in one such incident in October 1662. On Sunday, October 26, at 10:00 A.M., armed troops appeared at London's meeting places and swept up 104 Quakers, all men save three women, and carted them off to jail; those not jailed were beaten or abused as they were forced into the streets outside. The apparent cause of the crackdown was a story of a rising. Crowds of people shouted, "They must all be banished," as the victims were marched away at pike point.[15]

Jails filled up quickly with large numbers of Quakers. When the prisoners got to Newgate, they were tossed into a huge, high-ceilinged room with a pillar in the center. They strung hammocks around the room from the central post to the opposite walls to a height of three stories. Sleepers at the two upper levels went to bed first, hoisting themselves along the pillar and gripping the ropes of the lower hammocks as they made their way to their places. Around the floor other beds for the sick and infirm were laid. The noxious vapors in the room were conducive neither to sleeping nor good health. One prisoner died. The young and inexperienced Thomas Ellwood, secretary to John Milton, found it especially loathsome when the jailers parboiled the heads of three dead plotters in preparation for displaying them at various points in the city. The roundup of October 26 netted a shady interloper who decided that however bad conditions were he could live better in jail on the food supplied to the Quaker prisoners by their fellow Friends than he could outside. Until Ellwood reported him, he often carved the meat and chose the best cuts for himself. Confronted by the sheriff and told he would be transferred and housed with other felons, the imposter, who had kept his hat on, swept it off his head and bowed low to plead that he was in fact a Quaker; by that customary but un-Friendly gesture he revealed himself as an imposter.[16]

After stiffening the Quaker Act in 1664 to make it cover all nonconformists, prosecution of members of Fox's sect increased. Within a year five London meetings alone produced over 2,100 arrests of Quakers whose only crime was being at worship, although it was probable that some of these imprisonments included people incarcerated more than once.[17] Outsiders could not believe what they were seeing. A correspondent of Richard Baxter's, pointing out that the Quakers were about the only people willing to suffer, chided him because his published prediction of their early demise had backfired and was being used to discredit him.[18] Baxter himself marveled that the Quakers' habit of coming to a meeting likely to be raided and sitting in absolute silence marked them as "poor deluded souls," but he grudgingly conceded their courage: "[T]hey were so resolute and gloried in their constancy and sufferings that they assembled openly, . . . and were dragged away daily to the common jail and yet desisted not, . . . so that the jail at Newgate was filled with them." The critical Baxter also admitted that many were attracted to the Society of Friends because of the good example of those who bore up under the suffering,[19] a conclusion later supported by scholars.[20] Fox recognized the value of publicizing the persecution of his sect and badgered his disciples, particularly Hookes, to continue compiling lists of those who had been mistreated for submission to king and Parliament.[21]

But the First Friend did more. Recognizing that principled stands could go a long way in swaying even hostile officials and that a united front against these laws could lead to their modification, he penned some of his most powerful and persuasive writings to encourage his followers. Filling up the jails, Fox saw clearly, would lead to ultimate victory. Undoubtedly written to strengthen some of the weaker brethren, his letters breathed with the reassurance that the Quakers were on the side of right, their enemies in league with evil. He thus sought to erect a barrier to set his followers apart from the rest of their society and give them a compelling and overarching justification for taking unpopular and illegal positions. His position differed markedly from that of other radicals, such as John Milton and John Bunyan, who would not risk frontally challenging the authorities.[22] Just the first lines of some of his letters conveys the determination he wanted to instill in his supporters:

"In the power of God that is everlasting and does remain in this your day of trial"

"Look above all sufferings that are outward"

"All you prisoners of the Lord for his truth sake and for keeping the testimony of Jesus Christ against all the inventions, traditions . . . that are in the fall"

"In the power of God and his immortal seed dwell"

"Trust not in man nor in the arm of flesh"

"All you that have known the way of truth and tasted of the power of the same and now turn back into the world's fashions and customs, you stop them who are coming out of the world"

"Keep low in the power and your eye in the seed that destroys the devil and his works."[23]

During the 1660s these admonitions and calls to be faithful filled Fox's epistles. The principle of the remnant willing to challenge the world remained, an idea held over from the previous decade, but he limited its impact. Fox now regarded the world as a place where the struggle was on a personal level, where each person made a discrete decision to take a stand. For each person, of course, the call to discipleship was still a major, existential one—and laced with dangerous consequences—but there was little of a group commitment except to rally around, support, and succor those who were suffering. A call to personal righteousness replaced the proclamation of the day of the Lord. Still and all, in trying to hold Quakers apart from the larger society and insisting that they live by a different standard, Fox's words had a clearly subversive ring. Parliament's determination to muffle such dissidents because they shattered the allegiance expected of loyal subjects was thus understandable.

This new and more subtle form of Quaker radicalism was underscored by Fox's demand for liberty of conscience, a concept that received little of his attention in the 1650s. His followers knew, he emphasized, that persecution was not new, for they had experienced it before. But now he appealed to Anglicans, Presbyterians, Independents, and Baptists to love one another and to lay aside thoughts of banishing, burning, or hanging those with whom they disagreed. Stressing the law's inability to effect more than outward acts, he used his idea that a person's actions reflected one's inward condition to insist on religious liberty: one should have liberty to believe because, he asserted, "the inward man brings the outward man conformable to the righteousness and to a righteous man's state, which the outward law was not made for." Only Christ could rule the heart and change a person's outward actions. And he blended in just a touch of his curious brand of anarchism by stressing that the law was made for sinners and disobedient people, not for those who knew "that Christ is the end of the law for righteousness sake."[24] This argument certainly did nothing to reassure the authorities—at least no rush to repeal restrictive regulations was evident— so Fox issued an essay justifying religious tolerance with examples drawn from the Bible and English history, but that also failed to produce positive results.[25]

Fox's new attitude toward the state and its officials showed up in a number of other ways. The Quakers tended to cooperate with the authorities even if such cooperation resulted in more arrests. For example, a justice of the peace raided a meeting in Buckinghamshire attended by Thomas Ellwood and asked those in attendance to give their names. They readily complied, and the justice then arbitrarily chose six, three women and three men, to be sent to Aylesbury jail.[26] This practice drew the fire of critics of Fox and his leadership, who thought that worshipers should remain silent and make it more difficult for constables to make arrests or enable some attending to escape in the confusion.[27] But Fox told his followers to give the spies who came among them no cause for fear and asked them to recall that God had caused the walls of Jericho to fall down at the blast of a ram's horn.[28] Although he continued to be highly critical of the injustice of the Quaker Act, for example, Fox also used pragmatic arguments when addressing Parliament. In a broadside he pointed out that a small gathering would more likely lead to conspiracy than one with hundreds of people and a cross-section of views.[29]

Fox continued to travel to meetings, but he took precautions to prevent arrest. In so doing, he sometimes violated his own advice to his followers that they bear persecution unflinchingly. But his followers wanted him to remain free to give the guidance they believed only he could offer: "You are more than a thousand of us," they told him.[30] Believing that facing down the authorities was the only way to achieve a victory for his sect and for religious tolerance, Fox displayed a great deal of courage in the early 1660s. Yet he also knew, as his followers certainly recognized too, that the times called for a healthy dose of prudence. It would have been senseless for him to throw aside all caution and rush into what the Quakers called "the dragon's mouth."[31] By avoiding jail himself, Fox opened himself to the charge that he recommended to others a course he was unwilling to adopt himself.

For a while Fox carried a letter from a well-connected sympathizer vouching for him. In Swannington in Leicestershire on September 2, 1662, he was arrested while ostensibly visiting a widow in whose house nine others from as many families had just happened to gather. Taken to the county town, he found that six of seven other cobelievers had already been rounded up, but he did not use his letter. The group of arrested Quakers finally numbered about twenty. The group refused to swear the oath of allegiance to the king: "I never took any oath in my life," expostulated Fox. He also argued before the court that they could not be charged with violating the law since they had not been arrested at a meeting. With some irony, he explained that the last time he had been arrested in Leicester it had been for allegedly plotting to restore King Charles. The jury found the Quakers guilty of refusing to swear. Fox painted a dramatic picture of preaching to the crowds thronging the streets as they were taken from court to jail. But he did not have to show his letter, since those of the group arrested for refusing tithes were freed from jail almost as quickly as they had been convicted. Headed for London, he detoured westward back to Swannington to wave his missive before the eyes of the constable who had originally arrested him before he went to another meeting.[32]

In Tenterden in Kent Fox tried a different strategy and used his considerable talents to tie his would-be persecutors into knots. Having traveled in East Anglia in the winter, he was headed south and then west. After a large meeting that attracted Friends from a wide area as well as many not yet convinced, he and his traveling companions were taken into custody. At court he successfully countered the arguments of the justices who heard his case. Had he come to make a disturbance, they queried? "I did not come to make a disturbance," he answered. Well, they responded, the law prohibited Quaker meetings, and they showed him the act. But he craftily answered, "That [law] was against such as . . . held dangerous principles, and therefore that was not against us, for we held Truth and our principles were not against the government." The judges then argued that he was against the king. Fox countered with the statement, "I, for my part, had been cast into Derby dungeon many years ago . . . because I would not take up arms against him." After a bit more dickering, during which Fox repeated some of the debate over the bill in the House of Lords sympathetic to dissenters, the mayor of Tenterden, sitting with the justices, suggested that Fox be allowed to go on his way.[33]

On another occasion on May 31, 1663, at Poulner on the Hampshire border with Dorset, Fox engaged in a bit of subterfuge to prevent being captured. When a trained band of militia came to check on a large and previously scheduled monthly meeting, Fox successfully avoided detection by hiding in a nearby field of grain. Seventeen other early arrivals from the surrounding countryside were taken, but the meeting went ahead as scheduled. While Fox was holding forth that afternoon, a spy, dressed so gayly he stood out among the plainly dressed Quakers, showed up but presently left to report to the magistrate. Realizing that the man had to walk a mile and a half to Ringwood to report on the gathering, and that the constable would then have to return, Fox ended the meeting early. He then went to a nearby Friend's home before resuming his journey westward again. Later he heard that the constable died from a leprosy-like illness, and the wealthy men comprising the militia lost their estates, both fates the First Friend considered richly deserved.[34]

After Poulner Fox headed westward again. He set a grueling pace, traveling parallel with the coast, covering almost 180 miles in a week, and holding meetings every day. At Topsham in Devon his party linked up for a time with Margaret Fell and two of her daughters, and then he crossed into Cornwall, still in his mind a "dark country."[35] Fortunately, he noted that the meetings they attended as they traversed the far west, moved into Bristol, and then passed into Wales were all quiet and not bothered by the trained bands he had found elsewhere. At Bristol he met up with Fell again, she not having detoured into Cornwall, and together they made their way northward to Yorkshire and the other northern counties before returning to Swarthmoor.

In York, Fox found some Quakers who were tempted to join in a rumored antigovernment military plot, contrary to his announced condemnation of such activity. Government spies had kept tabs on religious dissidents who were angry because their dissenting ministers had been ejected from their church livings. The dissidents wanted to hold the king to the Declaration of Breda, which had promised liberty of conscience, and reinstitution of a more godly magistracy and ministry. At least twenty-six plotters were executed.[36] While resting two weeks at Swarthmoor, Fox issued a firm reminder to his followers that they should not be involved in such goings-on lest they compromise the recent "Peace Testimony." He sent copies of the reminder to various magistrates in the region to, as he phrased it, "take all the uneasiness out of their minds concerning me."[37] In a number of places in the hilly and isolated country of the north he kept one lucky step ahead of armed searchers trying to find him. After hearing that Carlisle's deputy governor was on the watch for him, for instance, he did not go into town to visit some Quakers in jail. Instead, he dispatched a letter to them enclosing a copy of his warning against plotting.[38]

The country seemed under a constant cloud that summer: the rain fell, it was said, nearly every day and added to the nation's unease. Northern streams became raging torrents.[39] Fox's epistle warning against plotting did little to reassure anxious officials who saw floods of Quakers wherever they looked. A Kendal informant estimated that their meetings, located about eight miles apart all over the countryside, weekly collected more of Fox's "cubs" than anywhere else in the country. And Fox's perambulations reenforced royalist fears that Quakers would rise if their leader gave the word.[40] The frustrated Kendal sessions court offered £5 to anyone who would turn Fox in. (The First Friend, reluctant to underestimate his own worth, remarked that Jesus had been sold for much less.) Thus he was not surprised when he returned to Swarthmoor and discovered that a troop of men had been there looking for him, and that they had even forced chests and trunks to make sure that he was not hiding in them. This action stepped over the boundary into the impermissible. That night in bed he decided to have it out with the local justice of the peace, Colonel Richard Kirkby, under whose authority the house had been searched.[41]

Kirkby, surrounded by those whom Fox later slightingly referred to as "gentry (so-called)," warned his visitor to remain at Swarthmoor. He said Fox would not be bothered if he did not hold any large meetings there. Fox refused to agree to any such restriction on his freedom of movement or the right, as he saw it, of local Quakers to convene at Swarthmoor for their meetings. When Kirkby invoked the Quaker Act, Fox responded with the reminder that his followers were peaceable and presented a threat to no one. Outwardly at least Kirkby and some of the others standing around seemed convinced, so Fox left.[42]

Whatever good feelings developed during this discussion did not last long. Justices of the peace in Lancashire were beginning a determined push to rid the region of Quakers.[43] A few days later Fox received a summons to appear before another justice. Having decided that permitting himself to be arrested would relieve some pressure on northern Quakers, he did not attempt to escape even though he claimed to have known of his impending arrest at least a day ahead of time. This time Margaret Fell accompanied him. Under questioning, he denied knowledge of any plotting. The interrogation grew quite heated with words like "rebel," "traitor," and "papist" resounding in the room. Like many such sessions, this one veered quickly into other areas, and the Quaker leader found himself being quizzed about whether he knew the languages discussed in his *Battle-Door*, an indication that someone was keeping tabs on his writings. But when it was over and done with, Fox refused to take the oath of allegiance and was cited to appear before the court of sessions in Lancaster. He and Fell went back to Swarthmoor to await its convening in January 1664.[44]

On Tuesday, January 12, 1664, the quarterly court of sessions met. Situated high on a hill, Lancaster dominated the surrounding countryside. A keen-eyed person could see into both Cumberland and Yorkshire—the one to the west, the other just eastward. Pendle Hill rose in the east and was visible when the clouds blew away. The town was old and decaying. George Fox and Margaret

Fell crossed the bridge over the Lune River as they rode in from outlying Ulverston. The cobblestone street leading up to the castle was steep and slippery enough to cause even the surest-footed horse to stumble and threaten its rider.[45] Of the three justices, only one, Colonel William West, had any sympathy for the Quakers. One judge remarked that they intended to proceed smartly against the regime's enemies. Fell had already made an effort to influence the court and prevent Fox and about ten other Quakers from being convicted.[46]

Little likelihood existed that they would be freed, for Fox and his compatriots did not blench before the judges. Fox rose and faced the bar with his hat firmly in place on his head, staring at the judges as they rustled into their places. When a deputy notified those in the crowded court to keep silent, Fox waited until the room was hushed and then said twice, "Peace be with you." It was not, needless to say, the best way to influence the court on his behalf. He was questioned about plots and his attitude toward them; he denied any knowledge of plotting and noted that he had published papers in which he warned his followers not to join in them. But because he refused to swear to the oath of allegiance, he was committed to the castle's dungeon. Ten other Quakers joined him there that day for the same offense; by the end of the week about twenty more Quakers would be added, some for not paying tithes. It did not matter that Fox affirmed that "allegiance did not lie in oaths but in truth and faithfulness"—the court recognized oaths alone.[47]

Fox was incarcerated until September 1666, spending nearly thirty-one months in jail, first in Lancaster Castle until April 1665, and then in Scarborough.[48] It was his longest incarceration, and his fortieth birthday passed by underground. The cells were about twelve feet square, with something like a shelf for sleeping, and pitch dark when the oak door was closed. The only heat came from a fireplace in the hall outside the thick walled cells. "A cold, raw, unwholesome place" was how he described the jail. His imprisonment was relieved by three additional hearings and the comradeship of the numerous Quakers who were sent down. Some of his fellows were released, some died in custody. Fox tried to use this suffering to the best effect. One prisoner, sentenced for refusing to pay tithes to a lay impropriator, the royalist countess of Derby, died after two and a half years of confinement, and his body was turned over to fellow Friends for burial. The Friends who carried his body the thirty miles south to Ormskirk stuck up notices on every market cross they passed to tell the reason for his death. Jail offered opportunities for theological disputes, for Quakers were not the only dissenters behind the castle's bars. One dissenter considered the Quaker leader especially obstreperous.[49] Fox made sure that accounts of his trials were published in pamphlet form, and he continued to issue epistles during this period.[50] He also found time to dictate the 126 pages that were to become his first memoirs.[51]

Staying in jail failed to soften Fox, if that was the court's intention. Two months and two days after he was first confined he appeared before the court of assizes, the next highest judicial body after the court of sessions. As usual, Fox refused to swear, insisting that as a Christian he could not be loyal to Christ and take an oath. He also wore his hat. And he rebuked the elderly judge on the bench when he peered down and again inquired, "Sirrah, will you take the oath?" Fox shot back, "I am none of your 'Sirrahs'"—a term typically used by a superior when addressing a social inferior—"I am a Christian."[52] Fox noted that for the judge "to sit there and give nicknames to prisoners . . . did not become his gray hairs or his office." A little later the judge almost used "Sirrah" again, but he checked himself. Fox tried reminding the court of the king's Breda Declaration promising religious liberty but got nowhere with that strategy. The last word naturally came from the judge, who remanded Fox to the dungeon until he was ready to swear. In a gesture of conciliation, he was brought up two days later to see if he had changed his mind. Thus he remained in jail.[53]

Margaret Fell had been arrested by this time for refusing to take the oath before the justices of the peace, so she appeared in the court of assizes before the same judge, Thomas Twisden. As the widow of a prominent jurist, however, Fell received preferred treatment; she was allowed to sit on a stool on a cushion with four of her daughters lined up beside her. Fell spoke directly to the jury, ignoring the fact that she had not, and would not, take the oath. She deigned not even to remove her gloves so she could swear on the Bible. The exasperated Twisden, who had bent as far as he could to prevent her from going to the dungeon, finally had to order her removed. Just before being pulled away, she uttered words revealing her perception of herself: "I was bred and born in this county."[54]

Fell was not numbered among the fifty-one other Quakers whom Fox counted as suffering various legal penalties in Lancashire. Ordinary folk all, they had had their goods—a pewter bowl here, a goose there, a mare and a fine somewhere else—confiscated for a variety of faults, such as failure to attend church or refusal to pay tithes. This catalogue contained crimes easy enough for other north country commoners to comprehend.[55] In the basement jail sat those who had been cited to court but refused to swear or who had been convicted of other crimes. It filled up, almost emptied out, and filled up again; there was a constant flow of people in and out. Men and women were confined in the same area. The floor of the dungeon, according to Fox, looked and smelled liked it was a "Jakes house" or privy. The jailer did not supply beds and some of the prisoners had to sleep on the bare floor. No distinction was made between those charged or convicted of felonies and those imprisoned because of their religious views, a fact making life in the cramped area even more trying for the Quakers.[56]

At the end of August the court of assizes met again. Fell and Fox were brought back into court to see if they were now ready to swear. Neither would. Fell tried to find out exactly what information the churchwardens had given that resulted in her indictment, but she got nowhere. Asked what church she attended, she replied, "the Church of Christ," and then she asked the judge if he would "have us to turn from that which we have borne witness to so many years and turn to your church, contrary to our conscience." Convicted by the jury, Fell was adjudged guilty of praemunire, a catchall offense like contempt of court allowing confiscation of her property and imprisonment at the king's pleasure.

Then the judge turned to Fox. The courtroom was crowded with Lancashire's elite, come to town for the assizes to discharge their legal business. Fox naturally did not swear. Referring to the requirement that the court endorse its own proceedings, the judge wanted to know if Fox would have them swear that the two Quakers had taken the oath when they had not. The defendant provoked laughter in the courtroom by countering, "Would you have these men to swear that I refused the oath?" Never one for frivolity, he wheeled around to those laughing and asked if they wanted to turn the court into a playhouse? He managed to get the original indictment against him dismissed by pointing to a number of factual errors, including reference to the fifteenth year of the king's reign, not the correct sixteenth, and the judge had to admit that because of the faulty indictment Fox was technically free to go. But he did not have the opportunity to leave, for the judge immediately demanded that he take the oath of allegiance, which he again refused. By afternoon Fox was again behind bars.[57]

Fox's prison conditions got worse after the summer session of the court of assizes. The jailer placed him in solitary confinement in one of the castle towers. His new cell was open to the wind and rain, and was often filled with the castle's smoke. Fox shivered, choked, and vainly tried to stuff something in the window to keep the elements out. His linen underwear—he did not mention his leather suit—could hardly keep him warm because it was constantly soaked through from rain. He paced in his cell, for exercise and to keep warm. He wrote almost no letters or epistles that year, either because he was kept totally isolated or because he could not keep his paper dry. For such a prolific correspondent this isolation must have been as psychologically draining as it was physically debilitating, for he could hardly walk when he was finally taken out of the tower. He mentioned two visions, one foretelling the plague, which came later that year, and the Great Fire of London. Fox spent the winter of 1665 in this miserable situation, longing for the next assizes session in March. The days surely dragged by, even as he told himself that the Lord's power was over all.[58]

Fox honed his skills as a jailhouse lawyer as he waited, carefully examining his indictment for errors. When court convened and the jury was sworn, the defendant immediately got into a wrangle with Judge Twisden, who was less patient with Fox this time. Fox enticed the judge to concede that the oath was to be administered only to subjects of the realm and then pointed out that the word "subject" had been omitted: since Fox was apparently not recognized as a subject, he averred he could not be asked to swear. Twisden, at his temper's end, ordered, "Take him away, jailer, take him away." In absentia, Fox was then convicted and subjected to praemunire. At the beginning of May 1665, he was moved to the east coast.[59]

Fox was in no condition to do much traveling. Nearly unable to sit on the horse the sheriff provided, he shuddered every time one of his guards lashed the horse to make him prance. When the party finally reached Bentham, inside Yorkshire, only sixteen miles away up and beyond the Lune River valley, even the guards could see that their prisoner was too weak and weary to go on without some bedrest. But before long they had him up again and pushed on at least ten more miles to just outside Settle. While stopped the next night, some Quakers got in to see their leader, and then the party pushed on to York, almost all the way across the northern part of the country. In York Fox got some much-needed rest, and the town's amicable governor also discussed religion with him during his two-day stay.[60]

From York, the party moved on to Fox's destination, Scarborough, thirty-five miles away on the North Sea coast. He had been there twice before, but then he had been free, now he came under the king's control. The group stopped half-way, at Malton, and his escorts allowed some Quakers to see Fox. It was too late to go to the castle when they arrived, so the prisoner was put up in the inn with an armed guard. The lingering daylight of a May evening offered members of the party a chance to catch a glimpse of the spectacular town, if only out a window. Scarborough, situated on a high cliff falling off to the sea, was dominated by its church and castle, perched on the plunging peninsula. The weathered stone walls of the latter had stood for more than five hundred years, but having been stormed twice during the late wars were now partially ruined. Cows and sheep grazed on the steep slopes of the castle grounds. There was a sea wall in the shape of a half-moon just off shore to shelter the harbor and the fishing vessels moored there. Early morning mists from the cold ocean sometimes blotted out the town from the castle. In the fifteen months he was in Scarborough, Fox saw all this, but he was not allowed to go down to the beach to try the spa water that the locals took as a purgative.[61]

Indeed, Fox needed just the opposite of a purgative—he needed food, rest, and warmth, but he got none. His first room was comfortable enough; the second one was open, requiring him to spend his own funds to try to stop the weather from coming in; the third was the worst of all, almost unliveable. It had a permanently open window and no fireplace or chimney, so his bed linens, his clothes, everything he owned stayed wet that winter. The cold mist and wind made him literally numb. When he built a fire to try to keep warm, the smoke was everywhere. As was usual in jails, he had to pay for his food, but officials would not let Quakers bring it in, so he had to employ a townswoman to fetch his bread and some wormwood to steep in his water. Once when he was particularly ill from the cold, he acquired some elecampane beer, a bitter, strong drink used as a tonic and stimulant, but his guards sent him to see the deputy governor and drank it up while he was gone. On another occasion, a fellow inmate, a bit tipsy from his own beer, challenged him to fight. Fox stuck his hands in his pockets and turned his cheek toward his tormentor and told him to go ahead and hit, but the subdued prisoner turned away. When rumors spread of a rising anywhere in the country, a guard threatened to dangle him over the wall and drop him into the sea below. Not permitted visitors or mail, unable to write—his fingers swelled up until one was as large as two—"I was as a man buried alive," he ruefully recalled.

About the only thing, and a small one at that, that made Fox's fifteen months in Scarborough bearable was the influx of people who came to stare, bait, and challenge him. He gloried in the excitement of debate and dispute. Moreover, the appearance of visitors brought him temporary release from his frigid room. Catholics, Presbyterians, Anglicans, public officials—all came to have a round with the Quaker. With Catholics he discussed the alleged infallibility of the pope, learnedly citing a church father to show that an early bishop of Rome had sacrificed to idols; with Presbyterians he refuted the doctrine of limited atonement by simply asking whether Christ had died for all sinners; with Anglicans, who questioned the Quakers' method of marriage, he pointed out that Jacob and Isaac had been joined with their wives before an assembly of God's people rather than by a priest. He also began to get on better with the governor of the castle, who in 1666 promised to put in a good word for Fox when he attended Parliament.[62]

Fox had other assistance elsewhere. Margaret Fell, though still in prison in Lancaster, was writing letters for Fox; Ellis Hookes was using his contacts in London to lobby for his leader's release; and one Friend in Essex had contacted a member of the House of Lords on his behalf. The arguments they made to the king for granting the prisoner his freedom involved his continued insistence that he had never countenanced plotting and that he would pledge not to do so in the future. They also explained that he was ready at all times to discover plots. Their most intriguing claim was that Fox "was an instrument of discovering a plot in Yorkshire."[63] He himself never mentioned uncovering a plot, nor is there any other indication that he reported one. The claim itself indicated how much some Quakers were backtracking.

The order for Fox's release was signed on September 1, 1666. When he left Scarborough castle, some of his guards, referring to his unbroken spirit, remarked that he was "stiff as a tree." They might well have been referring to his physical body as well, for Fox had endured the worst imprisonment he would experience. He was never again as robust as he had been. Months later he was still commenting on how weak he was, how he was so stiff he could hardly bend his legs to mount his horse. But he never lost the sense that God made his oppressors pay for their misjudgments and the hardships he had suffered. From the Great Fire of London, which raged for three days beginning September 2, to the deaths, illnesses, and other misfortunes that plagued guards, inmates and visitors, who had tormented or offended him, he drew a feeling of vindication, covering two full pages in his journal with a listing of what had happened to those who had abused him. To assuage perhaps a tincture of guilt, he explained that "I could but notice how the hand of the Lord turned against those my persecutors."[64]

It took almost three months, until nearly the end of November, for Fox to arrive in London. He moved more slowly now because of his physical condition, but also because he wanted to determine what had transpired among his followers in the three years he had been locked away. Nothing out of the ordinary occurred as he traveled southward, preaching as he went, finding soldiers dogging his path, not as potential converts but watching for any hint of a plot. An apprehensive Kendal critic predicted that his release would only embolden other Quakers, whose antisocial attitudes seemed to him exemplified by their lack of sorrow about the many churches that had been lost in the Great Fire.[65] Archenemy Colonel Kirkby offered £40 for Fox's arrest, which meant that his imprisonment had made him dearer by eight times the £5 previously offered; he did not comment on his increased value. He stopped to visit with his family as he passed Drayton-in-the-Clay on the Warwickshire border: his mother was at least sixty, and he wanted to see her. His meetings were generally large and often attracted people from nearby counties, thus enabling Fox to get a sense of the state of local meetings.[66]

Two overlapping problems emerged that led Fox to increase his organizational efforts. Both were rooted in an excess of local autonomy and a paucity of authority extending from the center, for dissent within the Society of Friends continued to burgeon. In his post-Scarborough travels, Fox found himself again facing people who, to use his phrase, "had run out." Perrot's followers still kept their hats on during prayer, an expression of individualism that Fox approved less now than before. Other dissenters, their particular points of dispute long since lost to us, circulated handwritten epistles to convince others that they, not their orthodox cobelievers, had the truth. He spent entire days with some of these dissidents, trying to convince them to write papers condemning their actions. Putting monthly meetings in place for disciplinary action, a course he had long advised, would nip this problem early and at a local level. It spoke volumes about the loose organization of the Quakers that whole counties, like Huntingdonshire and Leicestershire, had never established these meetings. Some northern areas had had them since Nayler's day, but the weakened apostle's extensive campaign in 1666 and 1667 suggested that Friends there had simply not heeded his advice to organize disciplinary meetings to control dissenters, or else they had fallen into disuse.[67]

This longing for stability was not limited to Fox. Indeed, it was made manifest in May 1666, while he was still imprisoned at Scarborough. Nearly a dozen Quaker leaders convened in London that May to ponder on the fate of what they called the "Church of God." They issued a document entitled "A Testimony from the Brethren," and ordered it to be read in all meetings and kept permanently for reference. Once free, Fox found no fault with the sentiments expressed by such staunch allies as Richard Farnworth, Alexander Parker, and George Whitehead; certainly their views comported with his own actions following Perrot's challenge.

Farnworth, the document's author, and the ten other signatories viewed with alarm numerous open and closeted enemies who, they said, despised a rule "without which we . . . cannot be kept holy and inviolable." They laid down regulations to prevent the subversion of the good order of the Society of Friends. Separatists should exercise no office within the society, should acquiesce in the judgment of overseers about what the truth required, should be prevented from traveling in the ministry and spreading errors, and should submit any writings for approval to "faithful and sound Friends" so "that nothing but what is sound and savory" might go before the public. Asserting their own special ability to see what they deemed "the workings of [God's] spirit and of those who are joined to it," they defined themselves as repositories of authority within the organization. Their authority stretched backward, they instructed Friends in all meetings across the nation, to "the wise men and the prophets whom God sanctified and sent among you."[68]

That these leaders assumed the role of patriarchs and apostles with the exclusive right to interpret faith, history, and practice for the faithful did not go down well with all Quakers. George Bishop, a patriarch himself as far as longevity in the movement was concerned and near the end of a full life, dissented firmly from what he considered their usurpation of power rightfully reserved to the spirit. Charging that they used "outward things" such as papers and strivings to bolster their power, he implied that Friends had advanced beyond the early church, which had centralized authority in the hands of apostles and elders. "We have not now things in the disposition of [one] person," he told them in no uncertain terms, "but according to the power that moves in every one." As Bishop recognized, the ruling made it more difficult to change the patriarchs' definition of Quaker life, unless one was, of course, a member of this male, London-based establishment.[69]

Fox thus had forceful backing for his reassertion of the role of monthly meetings for discipline: he was determined that localities without such meetings would establish them. London was the venue for his experiment. It had a Two Week Meeting for discipline, but as the number of Quakers in the capital increased, this body was unable to handle all the problems that arose. Too, as the insurgency of John Pennyman and his coterie so dramatically illustrated in the early 1660s, a single meeting could be captured by a group of dissidents and turned against the main group. Fox's most immediate concern was to restrict those he and his supporters referred to as having "walked disorderly or carelessly, and not according to truth," a quaint way to describe people who did not obey the rules. There was certainly plenty to do. In Southwark meeting, south of the Thames, for example, a man attacked marriage, lived with a woman to whom he was apparently not wed, and wore his hat when he testified. A woman had "spoken flightily of Friends and Truth" and had "too much familiarity" with a doctor; a man—"Ranter-like," the minutes recorded—tried to entice another to leave his wife so he could take up with her. Both the woman involved with the doctor and the "Ranter-like" man claimed the liberty that came from divine revelation. Fox targeted just these kinds of presumptive activities as he moved to make sure that meetings for discipline were set up. It was, he insisted, "the Gospel-order."[70]

The other problem involved marriage, from the beginning a major point of controversy with people outside the sect. If Fox worked it right, he might be able to deal with both problems at once. Given that Friends eschewed traditional marriage practices, holding that men and women might be wed by simply stating their intentions before a meeting of the faithful, they opened themselves to charges of adultery by conservatives and others in society at large. Quakers' beliefs naturally attracted the attention of theologically-minded commentators, but it was their social oddities, including rumors of peculiar practices in sexual matters, involving sex, that propagandists used to paint lurid pictures and thus damn their subjects in the eyes of right-thinking people. One of the first published attacks on the young movement misrepresented Quaker belief in marriage in the spirit as a form of sharing wives and husbands and repeated a tale that a Quaker in Wigton lay with a woman not his wife.[71] The frequent parallels that opponents tried to make between Quakers and the infamous Family of Love were rooted in attempts to stoke fears that the former would convert all England into the latter.[72]

In 1653, only months after she had thrown her lot in with the Children, Margaret Fell found herself shielding a Friend from a charge of adultery.[73] The same year Fox issued an admonitory epistle advocating a "joining together with the light," but his recommended procedures left too many loopholes for those who wanted to exploit them for their own advantage (See chapter 7).[74] Traveling missionaries, hoping to stop the mouths of critics, importuned the leaders to correct this oversight, at least so magistrates would be aware of the Quaker approach to marriage.[75] But not enough was done in this regard in the 1650s.[76] Sometimes the courts waded in to sort through the morass.[77] At other times so-called "disorderly spirits" boldly intruded into meetings and stood up to declare themselves wed.[78] The matter grew worse when some Quaker missionaries followed the logic of their position and sided with open malcontents. Two went so far as to endorse a Ranter's view that marriage, by the world's custom, often resulted from human lust, even as they affirmed that a true marriage came into existence when witnessed by an assembly of God's people.[79] Not until 1661 did a formal Fox pamphlet on the subject of marriage finally appear.[80] As late as 1679 he still needed to do research on the question's historical roots.[81]

At the same time Fox was also thinking about new roles for women. Characteristically, he began to talk first in general terms, perhaps testing his followers to see what they thought of his ideas, perhaps unsure himself about what role women's meetings would finally play in the evolving scheme. Women's meetings devoted to charitable projects had existed in London for a decade or better, but he did not at first propose to extend this system to the entire nation. True, in 1666 he issued a circular letter exhorting women to organize themselves into meetings, but he spoke only in the broadest terms about "service" and "duty," warned against "talk and tattle" as though women were especially susceptible to these vices, and hoped that women "may be in their services and places." In other words, he limned no more specific responsibilities for women than others who wanted to limit women to the kind of nurturing that suited their motherly nature.[82] Nor did he act immediately to press even this moderate approach.

Fox's hesitancy was underscored on his trip to Ireland in the summer of 1669, for he left no record of any concern for women's meetings there.[83] Instead he worked to tighten up discipline in the already existing men's meetings.[84] His journey, his first overseas, lasted three months. Ireland had been a battleground on which the English and Irish had bled each other for at least five centuries.[85] The English were usually the aggressors, particularly in Fox's time, for true Cromwellians could hardly abide the thought of Irish papists, and believed that forced conversion to the true religion, if not extermination, was the solution to the Irish Catholic problem.[86] Irish land was confiscated and given or sold at low rates to English settlers willing to bear living among the island's understandably resentful and unruly natives. Almost all the Quakers in Ireland had settled there after emigrating from England. Some of them, like William Edmundson, the so-called "Apostle of Irish Quakerism," were such avid Cromwell supporters that they gave their children martial names like Hinderance and Trial.[87]

With four Friends, including James Lancaster, who would later go with him to America, Fox sailed from Liverpool on Saturday, May 8. Having left his horse behind, he had walked a good distance to the dock and arrived hot and worn out, but unlike most of the other passengers his party did not become sick, except when the ship's cook was lost overboard. When they arrived in Dublin on May

10 they were not searched, an unusual enough omission that others remarked on it. Fox laid it to the fact that "the power of the Lord chained all the custom masters." The land had a peculiar odor, faintly resembling corruption, he said, but his cryptic comments do not indicate whether it was because of the blood the Irish had shed resisting the English or the blood the English had spilled trying to subdue the Irish. He quickly began a tour of all the meetings around the island.

The entire expedition had a slightly furtive air about it, as though Fox wanted to avoid detection. He kept a wary eye out for spies or scouts who might want to apprehend him, and, contrary to his practice in England, he avoided contact whenever possible with royal officials. The local authorities, many emigrants themselves and beholden to London, had received information of Fox's coming and were on the lookout for him. They had issued a sort of wanted poster containing his description, including information about his hat, long hair, clothes, and horse. Thus Fox avoided public places, like inns. Soon after his arrival he warned English Friends not to write lest they alert the constabulary to his whereabouts.[88] And he was so secretive about this Irish trip in his *Journal,* not published until 1694, that it is still impossible to trace his steps in Ulster where twelve meetings existed.[89]

In staunchly Roman Catholic areas, presumably where the arm of English law was not so strong, Fox was not as circumspect; in fact he was publicly contemptuous. In his first direct encounter with large numbers of Catholics Fox took the part of an ugly invader. In one unnamed town, for example, he goaded a crowd in the streets by offering to pay two pennies to a priest to have a mass said for his horse. "The candles had a mass, and the lambs had a mass," he asked, "why might not his horse have a mass?" He badgered townsfolk to bring their priests "forth and try their God and their Christ that they had made of bread and wine." But danger lurked in these areas: in some places he heard of "Tories," stealthy highwaymen who threatened any English people they encountered.

Leaving Dublin on August 11, Fox sailed on a storm-battered sea back to Liverpool.[90] Again, unlike most of the other passengers, he did not get sick, despite having gone without sleep for three nights before leaving. He was pleased with himself and his efforts. He had not encountered any of Perrot's hat supporters, and he had helped put in place the beginnings of a national organization for the Society of Friends in Ireland. Things seemed to be going well, particularly since he had finally reached a decision on a major matter while away.

Fox had decided to marry Margaret Fell. Accounts of the long discussions leading up to the event, which took place in Bristol on Wednesday, October 27, 1669, sound like a dynastic union with God as an involved third party. There certainly were no passionate feelings on either side; perhaps both were getting too old for passion. As leader of a group faced with persecution because of its peculiar ways, the forty-five-year old Fox was seldom given to emotions: displaying any now seemed less important than acting as a model for his soon-to-be recommended marriage procedures. Indeed, he approached what should have been a moving occasion, grounded in love and mutual affection, with all the excitement of someone completing a business deal. In both his memoirs and an explanatory letter addressed to Children of the Light everywhere, he spoke of being "commanded" to take Fell to wife, of his marriage testifying to "the church coming out of the wilderness, and the marriage of the Lamb before the foundation of the world." He wanted it to be understood that his was an "honorable marriage and in an undefiled bed," no doubt to lay to rest ugly rumors of sexual misconduct between the two.[91]

Ten years older than Fox, the mother of eight children, Fell opened her home to the First Friend almost from their earliest contact. If one who traveled so much could be said to have a residence, then Swarthmoor Hall was his. Not only were the two regularly in touch when he was absent, but Quakers could write to Fell at Swarthmoor to learn about their leader's movements. A strong woman, Fell knew all the important people of the group and their activities as well or better than Fox himself, for she was the movement's postmistress. Her writings, like Fox's, are marked by a self-righteous tone that would have made her unappealing except to one who shared her outlook. As mistress of a large estate and widow of the chancellor of the duchy of Lancaster, she saw no contradiction between elegant living and the Quakerism she adopted. Tales of her penchant for satins and gold and silver lace reached as far as Scotland. "She is one," said a critic, "who is past the cloud."[92] Although socially she stood far above Fox, the trust he exhibited by bringing her so promptly to the forefront of the sect's leadership in 1652 served the group well. She responded by becoming his ardent defender— on the rare occasion he needed defending—and they drew closer through the tasks to which they jointly put their hands. However much their relationship lacked passion, they knew each other well. The stars may not have sung when they were married, but members of Margaret's family made no secret that they had expected and wished for it over the years. The only exception was her son George, who did not hide his misgivings about his mother's religious convictions as well as his father Thomas had.[93]

About six months before the couple first notified the Bristol meeting in mid-October of their intentions, Fox brought the matter up with Fell, when they met in London before he went to Ireland.[94] She agreed to marry him, but they waited until he concluded that God had commanded them to go ahead. Margaret Fell was a wealthy woman, with income from a handsome annuity left by her father, but Thomas's will provided that in case of her remarriage she would lose Swarthmoor Hall, its grounds and gardens, and fifty adjacent acres to her daughters.[95] That detail had to be taken into consideration. Fox made sure that the daughters understood that he sought no material advantage from the union, and they allowed their mother to continue to occupy the home place, which the new husband would continue to use as he always had.

The Quaker marriage procedure, normally slow, moved along speedily for the First Friend and his intended. On Monday, October 18, the couple appeared before the Bristol men's meeting to state their intention, accompanied by Margaret's six surviving daughters and her four sons-in-law, as well as an array of outsiders, including George Whitehead and the recently convinced William Penn. All naturally embraced the idea and gave it their approbation. Whitehead alluded to reports of misconduct that had circulated in the north about the couple—

Fox deprecated these tales with the term "jumble"[96]—and indicated his pleasure in uniting with their wishes. More directly, he noted that only those whose spirits had been "seasoned by the power of God" were fit to judge such things.

Three days later a joint meeting of men and women heard the same assurances. Fox discussed the state of marriage, expanding on what he had been thinking and had written in his unpublished epistles on the subject; the scribe recorded that all were so moved that he could not take the leader's words down. Son-in-law Thomas Lower obliquely referred to "children who are yet to be born," but whether this was a prediction of children for this new union is unclear. The bride-to-be described herself as "spotless, chaste, and undefiled to the Lord." Stressing that marriages after Adam and Eve had been false and apostate, Penn insisted that this one represented the first parents' purity as it was before the Fall. On Friday, October 22, a local Friend announced publicly the end of the procedure, including an examination by at least one private men's meeting.

The following Thursday, with the preliminaries finally over, the marriage itself occurred in a regular meeting for worship. After all that had gone before, the ceremony itself was anticlimatic. Penn, for example, left to catch a ship for Ireland the day following the public announcement.[97] After the couple spoke their simple promises—Fox, holding Margaret's hand, pledged to take her "in the everlasting power and covenant of God, which is from everlasting to everlasting and in the honorable marriage, to be his bride and wife," while Margaret noted that she took him "in the unalterable word and in the presence of God, his angels, and us his holy assembly"—the marriage was accomplished. Fox's new wife then prayed, and a number of those in attendance added their testimonies. At the conclusion, ninety-four witnesses signed the certificate to certify what had transpired. Even the certificate was composed to make the point that this ceremony accorded with what Fox considered the ancient practice of dispensing with a minister, for it instanced Ruth and Boaz's and Jacob's marriages from the Bible.[98]

Life did not change much for the newlyweds. They stayed together about ten days and then separated, Fox traveling back through the counties toward London, his wife heading north to home. Swarthmoor, for all its physical appeal and quiet isolation, was simply too far from the capital control center of Quaker activity, and Margaret, conscious of her northern roots, felt the need to look after the property and serve as an overseer of what she called the "holy, eternal truth" there. She wrote nothing to suggest that she rued Fox's choice to forsake their "outward habitation" and "deny ourselves of that comfort,"[99] but subsequent events point to her consuming and painful disappointment in this respect. In Fox's mind, the needs of the organization required him to remain in the south, something his wife would have to accept, and outwardly did. Since their marriage aimed to epitomize the pure union of Adam and Eve before they fell, he could take physical closeness or leave it, as he explained to a sober neighbor, an old Puritan, who knew him and his family.[100]

This attitude was not shared by Margaret Fox. At age fifty-five, she could not have another child, but she wanted one very badly indeed, perhaps to show doubters inside and outside the sect that her marriage enjoyed divine favor. Her marriage prayer certainly indicated that she believed God could do anything; it also included an intriguing reference to the offspring of the Lamb's wife: "[T]he freeborn of that womb of eternity is coming out of the wilderness to be comforted and nourished, and to be nursed and clothed with the eternal free spirit of the living God."[101] Undoubtedly this referred to the church, but Fox had all along insisted that it, the relationship between Christ and his bride, the church, prefigured all true marriages. It would have been perfectly normal for Margaret, married to one viewed as God's prophet, to quickly and easily slip into seeing their marriage as naturally playing a role in begetting a new creation, perhaps an actual child. In any event, after she returned to the north following ten days with her new husband, she began to notice signs that she was pregnant for the tenth time. Then in April she was carted off again to Lancaster jail under a renewed imposition of praemunire, partially engineered by her own son who was bitter about her marriage to Fox and wanted to use it to gain control of his father's estate.[102] Conditions in the castle had not improved since she left it two years before, so it was no wonder that she remembered that for most of this time she was, as she put it in her memoir, "sick and weakly."[103] Being in jail was depressing enough, but she also had the family problem of son George hanging over her, as well as the fact that Fox did not come to help her.

For Fox's absence, Margaret had herself partially to blame, for she kept her secret to herself: there is no record that George had any idea of his wife's news. Giving birth to a child, however, was not something easily hidden, especially in the crowded jails of seventeenth-century England. As the nine months of her pregnancy dragged on, word leaked out, and a handful of people came to know of her condition. Eight and a half months after the marriage, in mid-July, a Friend in London wrote William Penn, still in Ireland, of the surprising news of Margaret Fox's condition. The letter, however, was intercepted by the authorities and never reached its intended recipient's hands. But no baby was born because there was no actual pregnancy.[104] Margaret had convinced herself that she was carrying a child, a condition known as pseudocyesis, imaginary or false pregnancy.[105]

Not knowing any of this—at least as far as the record reveals—Fox continued his travels, patching up the ragged edges of local meetings so they had the strength to respond to threats from both official prosecutors and internal dissenters. Introspection and self-reflection was not a part of his makeup, no matter how often he recommended it to others. The closest he ever came was the occasion years before when he heard a voice saying, "[T]here is one, even Christ Jesus, who can speak to your condition." Now, in 1670, having long since come to understand his condition, he plodded on. He might reel from his ordeal as a prisoner, but he managed to survive and carry on. Even marriage, which for other men represented one of life's high points, did not change his outward activities or affect his personal habits any more than changing his leather clothing. But this bearing up exacted a psychic toll, and one that would have to be paid. Part of the bill had already been rendered to Margaret, whose imagined pregnancy testified more eloquently than words to the weight on her mind following the marriage.

15

What Is a Man but His Mind?

In the middle of George Fox's fifth decade, when he was forty-six, he underwent another one of those spells of depression that he struggled with throughout his life. Whether it was the worst one he ever experienced or whether simply more information survived regarding this episode, he reached the bottom in the fall and winter of 1670. Returning from a preaching mission in the counties around London, he arrived in Hornchurch east of the city and literally fell apart. He described himself as "so oppressed" he was unable to speak to a scheduled meeting and momentarily unable to hear or see. By the time he made it back to Stratford, where his condition worsened, he was thought to be near death. When his nurses refused to heed his call for his clothes, considered a sign he knew he was ready to die, he railed at them. He insisted on going to Enfield, northeast of London, where he lodged throughout the winter at a widow's home, sometime site of the local meeting.[1] His attending in-laws wrote to Swarthmoor about his "distemper," a common term indicating a double derangement of mind and body, and the fevers that made his body shake as though invaded by malaria. In early October, stepdaughter-in-law Margaret Rous thought he was getting better, but in November he was too weak to be moved across London to her home in Kingston.[2]

Physically and mentally exhausted, Fox was too weak to stand. At first male Quakers tried to help him, but he abruptly decided that he wanted only "sober women" as attendants. Local Friends acceded promptly to this whim, so two women remained around the clock. Withdrawn and silent, he roused himself enough when the mail was due to inquire if a letter had come from his wife, still jailed at Lancaster.[3] Occasionally losing track of time, he hallucinated about Presbyterians and Baptists, his ancient antagonists, and saw them gnawing at human bones, trying, he sensed, to get at him. He struggled against these evil apparitions until, in a paranoiac reaction, he imagined himself a storm-tossed Jonah with huge maneaters darting around him.[4]

Fox's mental tribulations were not totally divorced from reality, for outside his room the government endeavored once more to suppress dissenting religious groups. Even moderate Presbyterians could not avoid surveillance and arrest. Indeed, on the first Sunday after a new law, the second Conventicle Act, tightening prohibition against religious conclaves of more than five people, became effective in May, an informer reported the gathering at Gracechurch Street meeting. Fox was arrested after he spoke and then taken before the lord mayor. Released after the spy refused to testify, he rode off on the journey that concluded so suddenly with his illness.[5]

Hence, clearly troubled by the persecution going on outside his sickroom, he imagined himself to be like the apostle John who recorded his own fantasies in Revelation, Fox's favorite biblical book. He envisioned the appearance of a new Jerusalem, home of those responsive to his preaching. "Without the city," he saw clearly, "are the dogs"—"ugly slobbering hounds" prowling about like government agents. But within was the light, the truth, and, the ecstatic Fox exalted, "the gate stands open night and day so that all may come in" to a shelter large enough to hide everyone. Beyond he saw false churches, false cities, filled with false Christians who had degenerated from true love, faith, and righteousness. Having always drawn sharp black-and-white distinctions between his followers and those who spurned him, Fox in his delirium wanted to hope that the persecution happening outside would stop, and that Christ would ultimately reign over his persecutors. His union with Margaret Fell became somehow intertwined in his mind with Revelation's rich imagery concerning the Lamb's marriage: "Oh, the heavenly Jerusalem," he rhapsodized, "the bride is come down, the marriage of the lamb that must go over all the false cities that have gotten up since the apostles' days." "Thou, O blessed God, has seen all these things," he all but shouted in exultant conclusion.[6]

In his tortured mind that dark winter, Fox confused this vision of religious liberation with sexual longings from which he himself had not been totally released. Perhaps he wanted to sire the offspring of the Lamb that would free humanity and himself from the chains of sin, darkness, and death. In his visions he saw himself walking in a field with his followers, whom he directed to dig at a certain spot. Finding a room filled with people straining to get out, he freed them. Then he instructed his disciples to dig again, and the same thing happened. But at a third digging, Fox descended into the hole and found a vault with a treasure, and a woman sitting dressed in white. He felt himself being followed and, turning, saw another woman, who held his hand against the prize. The very clock seemed to speed up, and his pulse raced, until he slapped her hand away and warned her not to touch the treasure. Time slowed down, and the temptation vanished.[7]

For one so troubled, Fox did not regard these visions as something to be ashamed of or to hide, as moderns might do. To him, they represented divine visitations that helped him see what he had to do. The glimpse he received of the new Jerusalem, for example, led him and two associates to formulate a set of intricate and tortuously uninteresting calculations to demonstrate that the heavenly city was ten times the earth's size. Compiling his memoirs five years later, he included a long commentary on his vision as though it possessed as much validity as Revelation, as for him it probably did; he just as naturally assumed that those who studied his life would value it also.[8] Likewise, he interpreted his visions of the earthbound people and of the white-clad woman in a way to give them broader religious significance and blocked the latter's obvious sexual implications. Little did he know that time thwarted this effort, for the manuscript on which it was written deteriorated over the years and Fox's interpretation of his dreams was lost, never to be recovered.[9]

The important thing about Fox's visions was that they ended, and he got well. His imprisonment and the ill health that followed it, the government's prosecution of Quakers and its implications for the future, the nagging dissidents inside the movement and the demands they made on his energy, his marriage and Margaret's inflated hopes regarding it, and his well-hidden but obvious need for reassurance about his adequacies, as both leader and husband—these all played a part in bringing on his latest bout of depression. But these millstones did not pull him under, for he began functioning again in time. His travail, the mental agony more serious than the physical agony, made him more human, more like the rest of his fellows, and his victory over his trauma added something to his stature.

Still, Fox's inability to deal openly with his problems, his tendency to transform anxiety into depression and associated physical malaise, offers us a striking insight into the way Fox coped. His unconscious wrestled with his burdens in dreams and visions, because he was unable to confront them openly, or, as far as we know, discuss them with others. A sense of inadequacy and a fear that others would see what he knew about himself lay somewhere near the center of his being. Even in reporting his dreams he sought to assuage these doubts, having his disciples reassure him, "George, you find out all things."

By March 1671 Fox was better, well enough to clear his desk in preparation for a trip across the Atlantic to the colonies. He prepared an epistle on marriage, one indicating that even at this late date he was not ready to give women's meetings a part in the process, for he talked only about the exclusive role of the men's meetings.[10] In June he reaffirmed an enhanced role for women's meetings but gave them no part in marriage procedures.[11] Meanwhile, he also sent twenty-five-year-old William Penn, then sitting in hellish Newgate prison, a firm reminder that some of his time should be spent preparing an answer to an Irish anti-Quaker attack.[12] Before leaving for America, he lobbied for Margaret's release, sending two women to plead with the king on her behalf. Before he left in August, she was freed and came to London to stay with him at the home of Margaret and John Rous in Kingston-upon-Thames. Fox also visited one of the Quaker schools he authorized in 1668—designed to teach, he explained then, "whatsoever things were civil and useful in the creation,"[13]—this one for girls in Shackelwell just outside London.

The trip to "the plantations," as the colonies were then called, was a significant one for Fox. The colonies often attracted the most adventurous Britons, those most intent on proving their worth and mettle against an unknown environment or in comparison to their fellows left at home. Fox had already staked out a claim to being an adventurer. Outwardly he had nothing to prove to anyone: the success of his movement testified to his prowess. He never commented on the transformation the trek into the wilderness worked in him, but it emerged from the account he left. The change occurred because on the western side of the Atlantic Fox was no longer an outsider trying to get in, or, as he often was at home, a hunted man. The provincial plantation authorities, worthies such as assemblymen and governors, did not hound him: instead, they listened to him respectfully and weighed his opinions. His reaction was reciprocal, and he gave them little to wonder about: everywhere he remarked on "people of account," of "note and esteem," who took him seriously.[14] At his first stop, in Barbados, he set up some household meetings, and rather than proclaim the liberating gospel of the day of the Lord, he encouraged masters and mistresses to control their servants, black and white, a "great service," he reflected, for the island. No doubt the governor, a Colonel Coddrington, saw it that way, for he and Fox exchanged both professional and social visits thereafter.

Thus the transatlantic trip continued a turning inward regarding matters of religion and social values. One purpose Fox had in going in the first place was to eradicate pockets of Perrot's followers who survived across the ocean. He had already written Marylanders that they had once been a "pretty people" but had now run after the hat.[15] And on Long Island a recently arrived Londoner, the wily George Dennis, stirred up his fellow Quakers to an anti-Fox frenzy. Six months before the leader was to arrive, Dennis was unburdening himself of a long handwritten attack on Fox at the half-yearly meeting. The First Friend wasted no time in dealing with such insubordination.[16] Though an internal affair, it pointed to his determination to maintain the status quo. Likewise, in Barbados he carefully positioned himself on the side of the ruling order, this time on the volatile issue of slavery. The tone of his recollections points to the likelihood that the acclaim he enjoyed from noted and esteemed people turned his head and reenforced his decision to moderate any criticism of the established order. Fox, once a supporter of the Good Old Cause, was making the compromises necessary for living in the world he and others like him had not prevented from coming into being.

Fox's party was a large one, thirteen in all, including two women. William Penn, a Quaker only three years and just out of Newgate, accompanied Margaret and others to Gravesend to wave the seafarers off, and she went on to the Downs off Deal. Fox spent the night of August 13, 1671, in that Kentish town, the last moments he shared with his wife for two years. He referred to the ship, the *Industry*, as a yacht, a light ship designed especially for important people, and he may have already bought an interest in it; at least later he was a shareholder in the ship.[17] Ocean voyages of the day, especially on small leak-prone ships, were not to be undertaken lightly. This one left in mid-August, early in the hurricane season, and headed for the exact area where they arose. The sea was capable of infinite changes. One day it was as smooth and flat as a meadow, with fish leaping up as finny escorts for the vessel as it lazed along in the doldrums under a hot sun. Another day, or even later the same day, great hills and valleys might form as swells rolled across wide expanses, and the hapless boat would find itself sinking into the troughs between great waves and then being raised to great heights before sinking again. Sudden blustery winds could blow hard enough to crack a mast, as happened to the *Industry* off the Scilly Isles. Yet again, a storm could send tons of water smashing onto a small deck, with streams of water trickling into every dry place on board.

Even without storms, life on ship made seventeenth-century journeys no pleasure trips. Once nearly overtaken by a Moorish pirate, the *Industry* fortunately
escaped when a cloud enveloped pursuer and pursued and a strong wind separated the two.[18] Clothes became dank and smelly, meals were every day the same,
barreled fresh water ran short and tasted bad, quarters were cramped, tempers
were often on edge. Another first-time seafarer, as Fox was, remembered how
landfall promised water to drink, to bathe in, and to wash foul clothes.[19] Passengers aboard the *Industry* fell ill but briefly revived by eating an occasional dol-
phin they hooked. Having to man the pumps day and night kept the pumpers,
sometimes working at seven hundred strokes a half hour, in good health. The
blazing sun, especially for a ship becalmed, recalled the old tale of how the sun
could force a person to shed the lightest clothes much quicker than his brother
wind could tear them off with mighty blasts. The humid ocean air seemed heavy
and sometimes smelled like a sulphurous hell.[20] One could not escape rain in a
storm, and it was just as difficult to hide from the torturing heat.

When not pumping the bilge or holding meetings—Fox and his followers
worshipped regularly throughout the voyage—the Quakers delved into the mystical meaning of such improbables as the four rivers that Genesis mentioned as
flowing from the Garden of Eden. Where the Quakers convened is not clear, but
probably not in their cabins. Fox's legs swelled so much he could not get his
slippers on; his skin split, itched, and burned. Five weeks into the journey he ate
some tainted meat and began vomiting. He boasted about not being seasick, but
his already weakened condition left him worse off than others who were. Some
fasted, a decision made easy by the worsening state of the food. Any bird that
looked as though it came from land raised hopes that Barbados was close. When
the ship finally reached Carlisle Bay at 10:00 P.M. on October 3, Fox, though still
ill, quickly headed for shore and the house of a local Friend. His hasty action
only retarded his recuperation, and for three weeks more he suffered pain, swell-
ing, and a general bloatedness. His companions worried that his old distemper
might reappear.

Barbados, easternmost of the West Indian islands, measured only about 160
square miles but rapidly became the stopping-off place for Quakers going to the
New World. A moderate climate and land perfect for growing highly profitable
sugar cane caused its population to increase to sixty thousand, two-thirds black,
and made it, as the governor crowed to Charles II in 1666, "the fair jewel of
your Majesty's crown." The trend toward larger plantations held by fewer hands
made it home to some of the wealthiest men in British America. Quakers prospered on the island; in 1681, a decade after Fox's arrival, one official described
them as "often very rich." They did so well because, like other planters, they did
not hire whites to work the cane fields, relying instead on cheaper slave labor.
Barbadian Friends averaged twelve slaves per household, more slaves than Quakers anywhere. The isle's second largest denomination, they owned five meetinghouses.[21]

Quaker numbers and influence made officials on Barbados uneasy. Ever since
1660 complaints had been heard that the Friends did not bear a fair share of
defense costs. Officials moaned that every convert weakened the colony. Quaker

wealth, all thought, surely made them well able to finance a regiment to help fend off attacks. Thus, despite their prominence, the unloved Barbadian Friends often paid fines or were jailed for violating milita regulations.[22] The unpopularity and doubts about this rather strange religious group gave the First Friend something to worry about. Indeed, this hostility naturally rubbed off on him. Nearly three years later, ugly anti-Fox rumors about his "debauched and bestial" sexual practices with Barbadian women had traveled from the island to New England.[23]

Another matter was John Perrot, who had died in Jamaica a bit over six years earlier but whose influence lingered on almost everywhere Fox set his foot. Fox's determination to create men's and, more significantly, women's meetings "in the order of the gospel," as he customarily phrased it, was his response to the Perrotists. Exercising discipline, these new meetings would see that Friends avoided such disorderly practices as permitting men to wear hats when they prayed. Fox also wanted them to deal with sexual immorality, an ever-present danger on the island, judging from his warnings. He told the first women's meeting in Barbados on October 28 that men with "the evil custom"—he referred specifically to blacks and Indians but did not exclude whites—"in running after another woman [when] married to one already" should be forced to break off their illicit relationships.[24] Some of Fox's party fanned out to other islands, carrying the same message.[25]

Their meetings attracted not only large numbers of Quakers, nearly one hundred at the women's meeting alone, but many of "the world's people." Some of these Fox labeled "considerable persons," men like justices of the peace, assemblymen, military officers, the governor; one judge, owner of 166 slaves, rode fourteen miles to hear Fox speak and then became a Friend.[26] The Quakers were held in suspicion in Barbados because they condemned local clergy as lying hirelings, interrupted church services,[27] and held meetings with slaves. Fox went into action to improve his sect's reputation. He soon realized that their stand on the slave question counted most with the island's powerful elite.

Fox thus decided to clear Quakers of the charge that their appeals to slaves undermined the foundation of Barbadian society. He also wanted to address the charge that Quakers were dangerous heretics, people whose very theological tenets made them untrustworthy. The result was his famous "Letter to the Governor and Assembly at Barbados," a document later used again and again for half the purpose for which he issued it: to assert Quaker orthodoxy.[28] Thus most of those commenting on his letter ignored his repudiation of the "wicked slander," as he called it, that by merely meeting with blacks Quakers were "endeavoring to make the Negroes rebel." Instead they concentrated on the theological pledges that, in the main, made the Friends sound as firmly orthodox as any Christian who ever recited the Apostles' Creed.[29]

The document's aim was to demonstrate that Quakers offered no threat to the established order, and that they adhered to traditional Christian beliefs, including God's creation of the universe, Jesus' virgin birth, his crucifixion for human sins, and his resurrection. The theological section was hardly remarkable, although it did add an important Quaker twist by stressing that Christ "is now come . . . to rule in our hearts . . . , which makes us free from the law of sin and death." Lest any discern here a hint of antinomian Ranterism, Fox went on to emphasize acceptance of the authority of the Scriptures as, was twice repeated, "the words (not word) of God."

Of more concern to the ruling authorities of Barbados was the portion of the letter that addressed the "lie," as Fox termed it, that Quakers promoted slave unrest. In a colony, where potentially insubordinate blacks comprised two-thirds of the population, whose economic well-being rested squarely on slave labor, and whose social cohesion depended on black's submission to their white masters, this matter was more critical than the subtleties of theological beliefs. Fox took great pains to explain that Quaker meetings for slaves taught them "justice, sobriety, temperance, charity, and piety, and to be subject to their masters and governors," not prescriptions for insurrection.[30] Quakers, he reassured his readers, "utterly abhor and detest in our hearts" any thought of slave rebellions. Indeed, Friends followed biblical injunctions to teach submission in family gatherings that slaves, as "a very great part of the families of this island," were required to attend.

In a later pamphlet addressed to ministers on Barbados Fox criticized them for devoting so little attention to slaves that they became unruly. Sextons prevented blacks from entering their churches, he charged, while Quakers were teaching them to "yield subjection to their masters and those over them."[31] The lesson was plain: Quakers' slaves were more law-abiding than those of other Christians. Fox was basically arguing that to Christianize blacks made them more submissive and subservient. In this respect, Fox's thought reflected a maturing of the slave culture and acceptance of a new view that no contradiction existed between Christianity and slavery. Hence Christians might hold slaves, at least for the time being—and that time always retreating into an indefinite tomorrow—so that Christians might legitimately be enslaved by others of their faith.[32] The authorities had nothing to fear about Fox's work in Barbados. The former exponent of the Good Old Cause was here at his conservative best—or worst.

Fox spelled out his approach to the slave issue in a sermon delivered at Thomas Rous's house where he was recuperating. It was Saturday, two and a half weeks after the weakened leader had arrived in Barbados, and a collection of his followers had come to wait upon him so he did not have to spend his energy traveling to them. Fox admitted having been troubled by slavery and race since his arrival—Barbados was his first encounter with matters racial—and noted that he had wondered how to bring righteousness out of an institution that could easily produce mischief. His method was to spiritualize the issues. Any person transgressing the laws of God, even the children of Israel, could be accounted sinful, or black, he asserted: it was possession of Christ, not race, that marked the differences between white and black, God's children and Ethiopians. He ventured, though he carefully did not endorse outright, the idea that after a term of thirty years owners might free slaves "who served them faithfully" and "whom they bought with their money." Until then, let Friends preach Christ to their Ethiopians; then they would be free in the thing that mattered, their spirits, regardless of their earthly status.[33] "All are God's free men who walk in the truth," he counseled his slave and free followers about spiritual liberty, "so it is Christ the truth who does set free and at liberty."[34] Two years later he asked Barbadian Friends for "a black boy of your instruction that I may see some of your fruits, and as I shall see, I shall make him a free man, or send him to you again," presumably still a slave.[35]

Fox was no social egalitarian, as his views on slavery revealed. He was too much a child of his time, even if part of that time trumpeted the Good Old Cause, to countenance a complete upturning of the social order. He never modified his view that wealth, rightly obtained, and the wealthy, rightly ordered, had a rightful place in society. In one epistle he bluntly instructed families that "he who has more of the earth than another, that makes the master." He understood that the best servant or child or slave was the one who internalized the master's values. Thus he assured masters, "[W]hen you are away they are the same as when you are with them." Masters should rule in love, of course, and should receive counsel from those below them, but they were the final authority. To this built-in contradiction was added a corollary: on the one hand, masters had every obligation to give orders to others, yet on the other hand, Fox set standards for masters: that they rule in love, wisdom, and patience, without tyranny, hastiness, or willfulness. Fox even suggested that slaves might call masters to account, if ever they dared.[36] This idea gave the Barbados powers-that-be ample reason to fear his approach, for they sensed that, no matter how conservatively he couched his Christianity, it contained seeds of their peculiar institution's destruction.[37]

On January 8, 1672, Fox and his entourage sailed for Jamaica, about twelve hundred miles and ten days to the west, just south of Cuba. The largest English possession in the West Indies, the island had been the site of Quaker missionary activity since soon after William Penn's father seized it from the Spanish in 1655. One Fox companion called it "that debauched wicked Sodom." Pirates used it as a base to harass Spanish treasure galleons, but English policymakers also had licit plans for the island. They hoped sugar, as well as other tropical products such as tobacco, would make Jamaica one of the major suppliers of such goods to Europe.[38] Quaker numbers swelled rapidly in Jamaica in the years before 1700. To further this influx, in 1662 the government promised freedom from serving in the militia, a policy instituted, dropped, and then reluctantly reinstituted not long before Fox appeared.[39]

The Quaker leader apparently found little to disturb him during his stay on Jamaica, during which he traveled hundreds of miles around the verdant Isle of Springs. Staying only seven weeks, he left behind a fellow traveler, Solomon Eccles, to oversee the rapid growth of Quakerism. He remained on the lookout for Perrotist elements, for that renegade had responded to England's "Western Design" for the area. Jamaica's governor conferred twice with the Quaker leader as did a military official, and they parted with mutual good feelings. Fox inaugurated disciplinary meetings for men and women to control dissidents and instituted seven new meetings for worship. More satisfying, no doubt, was the public submission of a Perrot lieutenant, Jane Stokes, who had carried her chief's message to North America itself and caused mainstream Friends much trouble.

The next destination for Fox was Maryland. The ketch on which the Fox party took passage to the mainland was beset with troubles, mostly caused by bad weather, before they lost sight of land. A week of sailing against the wind passed before Jamaica's rugged and volcanic Blue Mountains finally sank below the horizon. Passing Cuba's Isle of Pines, a mainstay broke, and the canvas sails fell, littering the deck. On two occasions storms hit so hard that the crew tied the rudder and let the ship plunge on before the wind. It required better than five weeks of rigorous sailing in treacherous weather before the ship finally reached Virginia. The Fox party sailed up Maryland's Patuxent River on April 20.

A frontier area, Maryland was sparsely settled, with a 1670 population of some sixteen thousand, dominated by a small elite. Its planters, some large landowners, but most owning small holdings, lived near the numerous navigable rivers surrounded by their acreages and their workers: free, indentured servants, and slaves. All seemed eager for a break from their hard life. Fox and his missionary band offered such excitement, and thanks to the Catholic proprietors' policy of religious tolerance, Quakers were welcome. Tobacco was the chief crop, but Marylanders had not yet defined their system of black servitude as precisely as governments in the West Indies.[40] Fox's outreach to slaves in the Indies did not continue when he got to the continent, for he evinced more interest in exotic Indians than acculturating Africans. The whites in Maryland were not an insecure minority—in Talbot County, where Quakers were numerous, slaves made up only about 10 percent of the population[41]—and had little reason to fear uprisings. Fox did not need to prove that Quakers could help slaves conform to their plight. Not forced to deal with the slavery question, he did not.[42]

Fox got to size up the Maryland elite even before his party landed. A local delegation, including a lawyer and a former sheriff, came out to visit. When their boat sank in a sudden squall, leaving his visitors stranded, Fox organized a worship service that impressed them. The Marylanders were further impressed when one of the Quakers risked his life to get word ashore about their plight and lack of food. Once the entire group was rescued, Fox went off to a meeting in West River that lasted four days and attracted the Speaker of the Maryland assembly and a member of the governor's council. Here again Fox instructed provincial Friends on the advantages of men's and women's meetings, something John Burnyeat, who called this meeting, had not done.[43] A now-enlarged party next sailed across Chesapeake Bay and up the Eastern Shore's Choptank River where Fox visited another meeting and conferred with a company of Indians. They seemed as interested in his message as he was to meet them.

Burnyeat related disturbing news of Perrotist unrest among Quakers on Long Island, New York. Attending the October half-yearly meeting at Oyster Bay, he had watched almost helplessly while two newly arrived London Friends, George Dennis and his wife, made allegations against Fox. Now Fox and Burnyeat rushed overland in order to reach Long Island in time for the next half-yearly meeting in mid-May.[44] Through Maryland and the swamps and woods of New Jersey they hurried, sleeping in Indian villages as they traveled. They seemed always to lodge with chiefs, never with ordinary Indians, and shared their meager fare. They arrived on time, and on May 17 the six-day event opened. At first Fox found Dennis convincing in his denials of stirring up last fall's meeting. But then Burnyeat, assuming the role of prosecutor, proved that Dennis had in fact disrupted the meeting. The Long Island Quakers, no doubt prodded by Fox, promptly turned their backs on the wayward brother.[45] After a trip back to Flushing, Fox sailed across Long Island Sound to Rhode Island at the end of the month.

Rhode Island was a heretic's haven and heaven. Fox was as depressed about the numbers of Ranters he found there as he was impressed about the absence of priests and the prevailing religious tolerance. First founded by malcontents from neighboring Massachusetts in 1636, the colony adopted the unheard-of policy of granting political and religious liberty to practically all sorts and kinds. For a generation it had been nicknamed "Rogues' Island" or "Island of Errors."[46]

Roger Williams, the colony's founder and a power in its affairs until his death at age eighty in 1683, was himself so rigid that he found it difficult to get along with anyone in religious matters; the Friends' reputation for a free-wheeling theology made it impossible for him ever to hit it off with them. Considering them the worse kind of antinomians, nearly anarchists, he castigated them as "anti-Christian," "blasphemous," "scornful," "censorious," and tossed the catch-all label "Ranter" right back at them for encouraging women to strip naked.[47] But Quakers had been living in Rhode Island for more than two decades by the time Fox arrived.

Upon arriving in Newport, the colony's capital, Fox discovered that Rhode Island's leading officials, from governor through lieutenant governor and judges down through local justices, were all Friends. Some of them had just won office after outraged citizens reacted to efforts of the Williams faction to stifle criticism and collect taxes. The First Friend lodged at the home of Nicholas Easton, the new governor; held a series of protracted meetings, including a general one that pulled Quakers in from all over New England; set up men's and women's meetings; blessed the wedding of Joseph Bryar and Mary Gould with his presence;[48] and gloried in his accolades. Concerned with the number of Ranters he found, he held one meeting for them alone. An irascible Roger Williams, his teeth on edge, licked his political wounds and determined to have it out with the Quaker invaders.[49]

Actually Fox and Williams had much in common, in both their styles and their ideas. Blunt and forthright, disdaining the niceties of polite society, they were principled and argumentative men, and each insisted on the rightness of his own convictions. Both profoundly disliked hireling ministers. Williams was a committed democrat politically, if less willing than Fox to adapt these principles to his religious predilections—he deemed allowing women to speak in church as something he called "will worship."[50] He referred to himself as a "Seeker." They each wanted an active government, though Williams was not as thorough-going as Fox, who had glimpsed the possibilities of a true revolution at home. Both found much to respect in Indian ways and wanted Europeans to deal justly with the Native Americans. Curiously, they got on better with the aboriginals, despite the gulfs of cultural differences and language, than they could with each other or with those of their own people with whom they disagreed on theological matters; each, in other words, only practiced tolerance up to a point of ideological closeness. Fox thus reserved his choicest anathemas for any adherent who dared carry his principles too far, while Williams, unable to vouch for his wife's salvation, refused to take communion with her.[51]

Temperamental similarities between these two bulldogs of religious broadmindedness disappeared once Fox arrived. Williams boasted of having read Fox's massive 1659 response to his critics, *The Great Mystery of the Great Whore*, as well as, he claimed, 120 English attacks on the Quakers: Fox had not impressed him. To refute Fox's errors and discredit the recently elected opposition, Williams proposed a debate, but the Quaker left Rhode Island on July 28 before the invitation arrived.[52] Nearly two weeks later three Quakers substituted for Fox, and the debate went on. Fox was the whipping boy, for Williams concentrated on him and what he termed his erroneous ideas, especially his ideas concerning the nature of Christ and whether the Bible was the word or words of God. The Rhode Islander came across as a diligent—and long-suffering—researcher, quoting the *Great Mystery* at length and complementing Fox as the Quakers' "greatest writer," "greatest preacher," and, somewhat backhandedly, "the most deified whom I have heard of."[53]

Inexplicably Fox now turned south and did not go into other parts of New England. He thus omitted visiting Massachusetts, site of the most dramatic persecution his followers had faced in the New World. Mary Dyer, friend of the arch-antinomian Ann Hutchinson, was one of four Quakers who paid with their lives for their evangelistic activities in Congregationalist Massachusetts.[54] Fox did send a letter and books to Connecticut's governor, John Winthrop, Jr., with the hope that the Nutmeg Colony would not persecute Quakers.[55] That the general meetings in Newport laid the foundation for a yearly meeting for churchly discipline in New England also obviated the need for him to tarry longer. So he ordered the homeward-bound William Edmundson, one of his traveling companions, to go north into the rest of New England while he sailed away.[56] At his departure, Edmundson thought Fox more healthy and cheery than he had seen him in years.

After dodging mosquitoes at Fishers Island and enduring drenching rain in an open boat, Fox and party landed on Shelter Island inside Gardiners Bay on eastern Long Island, there to meet with refugee Quakers from the area and a large contingent of Indians. The latter were so impressed with the message Fox brought that they agreed to a fortnightly meeting at which the local Friend who owned the island would read the Bible to them. Some Indians also told Fox that those of their race who had adopted the religion of the New Englanders were worse off than before. Embracing Quakerism was no doubt a better course, they admitted, but they held back, fearing that the other professors would hang them. A week after leaving Rhode Island, the Quakers set out in their open boat once again, this time aiming for Oyster Bay, but they encountered a storm that hurled them back across the sound to Fishers Island. Meetings at Oyster Bay, and a bit later in mid-August at two towns, Flushing and Jamaica, in the former New Netherland, were well attended by prominent locals. John Stubbs and John Burnyeat, who had traveled with Fox since Maryland, left now to return to New

England. Retracing his earlier path, Fox again turned southward, across the mouth of the Hudson, to New Jersey.

The deep bogs and steep places near Shrewsbury gave that rural area the name of Purgatory, an apt-enough description, thought Fox, particularly after the horses got so winded going up and down hills that their riders had to let them lie down to catch their breath. Purgatory for Fox also meant that dissident elements had infiltrated local meetings, so he used the occasion of the September 2 general meeting to institute men's and women's meetings. They would be of "great service in keeping the gospel order," he exalted, and seeing that "all walk as becomes the gospel." He did not, however, address the purgatory called slavery despite the fact that well-to-do Shrewsbury Quakers used blacks for both domestic and field work.[57] Unlike Barbados, here no public insecurity about the numbers of blacks existed.

Before leaving Shrewsbury Fox demonstrated the miraculous powers expected of a religious prophet in the seventeenth century by healing a man thought to be suffering from a broken neck. Thrown from his horse, John Jay was taken for dead by Fox and his companions. Fox, placing Jay's dangling head between his knees, put one hand under his chin, the other behind his head, and raised it two or three times until the victim began to breathe again. The next day, the itinerants, including the now-cured Jay, rode on the sixteen miles to Middletown, crossed a river astride a tree, and held a meeting. It seemed a dramatic and divine endorsement of Fox's abilities and leadership for all concerned.[58]

They moved southward, sleeping outside and trying to dry themselves beside their smoldering fires when they were unable to stay with friendly Indians. Skirting the future site of Philadelphia, they arrived, tired and weary, at New Castle, in the present state of Delaware, only recently taken by the English from the Dutch. No Quakers resided in the small village or anywhere around, but the governor invited Fox to lodge at his home and threw it open for a meeting on Sunday, September 15. Despite evidence that some of those who attended were convinced, Fox eagerly pushed on to Maryland, the center of American Quakerism in 1672. He left the following day for the Eastern Shore.

Fox remained there for more than a month. Preaching was productive, and meetings were crowded. He was pleased that many of these people had already heard of him. Native Americans listened to him through a translator and told him that they sensed he was an honest man. Once someone counted so many boats thronging tiny Tredhaven Creek that it seemed to resemble the busy Thames. On October 3 a general meeting for all Maryland opened, with nearly a thousand people, many of them people of rank and quality, in avid attendance. The men's and women's meetings he had established the previous year were still functioning, a reassuring sign that machinery was in place to prevent upsurges of Ranterism. When they moved up the Bay toward Annapolis, he discovered that some responsibility for discipline was still his, and he met with some disorderly walkers.

By early November Fox and his group had worked themselves around to the western shore and sailed again into the Patuxent River where he had landed a year and a half earlier. On November 5 they left Maryland, alternatively rowing and sailing, for Virginia and then Carolina. Settled only in the eastern tidal areas near convenient water transportation, each colony resembled Maryland economically and socially. Virginia, of course, was the principal mainland colony from an imperial point of view, but its Quaker population was minuscule compared to the other Chesapeake center. By this time its recorded history as an English outpost stretched back nearly three-quarters of a century, and its society had stratified into sharply distinct classes with a sophistication absent in Maryland. Few Quakers had emigrated to the colony, so Fox simply avoided most of the area bordering the Chesapeake and landed on the James River just north of Carolina. Spending only ten days in Virginia, he held only three meetings, one of which drew some justices of the peace and a militia colonel, and organized a meeting for discipline among the few Friends left behind.

Carolina, at least the northeastern corner where Fox was headed, was for all practical purposes a part of Virginia and literally a backwater. Almost totally isolated because of nearly unnavigable shallow rivers and sounds, it was consequently settled by spillovers, Indian traders and trappers, poor dirt and hog farmers. The first Quakers, immigrants from the north, came on the scene in 1665. The Henry Phillips family settled along the Perquimans River, one of the numerous streams that divided the lowland into fingers jutting out into Albemarle Sound. Quakers were noted for being stiff-necked and stubborn, qualities they shared with the few other hardy souls who eked out a living from the unpromising thin soil of the area.[59]

The region was watery, which may explain why Fox once explained God's judgment to a group of Indians with the story of Noah and the Flood. The party waded through swamps, including the Great Dismal Swamp, and streams too shallow for boats, hardly a pleasant business in late November and early December. As in the other places Fox visited, he took special care to seek out Indians, once using one to prove to a disagreeing doctor that all people have consciences that prod them to know right from wrong. Similarly, public officials came to hear him at public meetings, some having heard stories about him from back home: one queried him about a reported miracle in Cumberland. A captain Nathaniell Batts, whom Fox identified as a former governor of Roanoke but who was actually a fur trader and land speculator, was recruited to deliver a message to the principal Indian tribe of the region, the Tuscarora.[60] In his eighteen-day stint in Carolina Fox organized no meetings, although he met with some Friends who had not kept to the truth, as he described them.[61]

Upon leaving Carolina, Fox traveled back to Maryland. A day or so after Christmas in 1672 he encountered the first and only opposition from civil authorities on his entire trip. A sheriff in Virginia came to take him into custody but, being won over, let him go on up the Chesapeake. Winter was now hard on the land, and Fox and his party found themselves trudging through snow, facing freezing rain, sleeping outside, and waking to find water frozen by the fire. When they finally got back to what had become their home base, James Preston's home on the Patuxent River, Fox was convinced that they would have frozen to death had they not made it when they did.[62] They scheduled a general meeting, and a day or so later another one in an area where there had been no Friends before;

the few who came had to struggle through the deepest snow that people there had ever seen. At night it was so cold that Fox bundled up in all his clothes. To make matters worse, at the end of January 1673 Preston's house burned down, and Fox lost all his clothes, books, and other possessions. For three nights they had to sleep under the bleak sky.

Fox held numerous meetings in the next five months back and forth across Chesapeake Bay. He had decided to wait until after a general meeting for Maryland scheduled for May before finding a ship to transport him back home. Occasionally he took a week off to catch up with his correspondence. He sent letters to Maryland's governor and its assembly explaining about what Quakers said instead of taking oaths. Other letters reminded Ranters that "God's people have no liberty nor freedom," and told established ministers that true ministers served without charge.[63] Despite meetings in wigwams and tobacco houses and conferences with "ruling men" and Indian chiefs, he left no indication that he noticed the 7–10 percent of the population who were black. At the men's and women's meetings on May 17 Fox went over the state of the Society of Friends in Maryland with those in attendance.

Four days later, following what he termed a "glorious" meeting attended by members of the governor's council, Fox boarded the *Society of Bristol,* the ship that would take him back to England. Select Maryland Quakers stayed on board that night, wanting to spend as much time as possible with their leader before the ship weighed anchor the next morning for Bristol and home. The voyage down the Bay was slow because of contrary winds, so it was May 31 before the ship passed the Virginia capes and headed into open water. The eastward sailing was especially stormy: once waves hovered like mountains over the vessel and crashed down with the noise of roaring cannons; the sailors, their leading passenger reported, said they had never seen such a storm. Fox knew that God was nearer than the water and would preserve them and claimed he never worried.[64] The eastward winds did move the ship quickly across the Atlantic; they arrived in four weeks, a bit less than half the time it had taken to go the other way. Only Robert Widders and James Lancaster of the original thirteen who had set out returned with Fox; the saddest absence was that of Elizabeth Hooten, his first convert more than twenty-five years earlier who had died in Jamaica.

The trip had been a valuable one for Fox. Aspiring to see Quakerism develop into a worldwide movement, he had looked eastward to Europe and Asia as well as westward to the New World as places to implement his vision. He did not know that the English-speaking world, the bulk of it across the Atlantic, would become the main overseas home of his fellow believers, indeed in some ways would drain the metropolis of its Quakers; but he had now seen the site of this great reversal.[65] Elated about the number of convincements in America, he had a sense now of his followers there and of their problems, and they knew him. Soon more and more letters asking and giving advice would be going back and forth between them and him, even as he set up a regular network to channel books from England to Quakers in the colonies.[66] Ranterism had not been stamped out—it seemed almost endemic to his movement—and dissidents would continue to arise, but the machinery had been put in place to deal with the problem.

Fox got off a letter to Swarthmoor the very day he arrived in Bristol, June 28, to let Margaret know that he had arrived safely in the city where they had wed four years earlier. She, two daughters, and a son-in-law, Thomas Lower, came down to Bristol to meet him. William Penn, who had married Gulielma Springett, daughter of Mary Penington, while Fox was away, brought his bride along, and other Friends came too, especially from London, to provide a sober Quaker contingent for the bacchanalia called St. James Fair in July. Fox's sermon was a powerful one. He spoke of three teachers, the God who had taught the first parents in Eden, the serpent who had tempted them to evil, and the Christ who bruised the serpent's head and spoke to and led those who had chosen to follow him.[67]

Fox needed all the power he could muster, for conditions in England were not as fine as those in the colonies. For one thing, the House of Commons, angered over the king's Declaration of Indulgence suspending laws against dissenters—his attitude had become clear the previous September when he pardoned 491 Quakers—passed the restrictive Test Act in March 1673. Aimed at Catholics, including the king's brother, the duke of York, it required officeholders to swear allegiance to the Crown and to renounce the doctrine of transubstantiation. The Quaker leadership early saw that this law could be applied to them because of their testimony against oaths and protested vigorously but ineffectually against it.[68] Parliament's determination to enforce religious conformity boded ill for Fox because it created an atmosphere that made non-Anglicans of all stripes suspect.

More ominous for the peace of the Society of Friends was the trouble brewing over women's meetings and Fox's leadership. Although he did not mention encountering any problems in Bristol, Friends in that city had raised questions nearly two years earlier about his epistle on establishing these meetings.[69] Twenty miles outside Bristol, however, he came face to face with unrest about the new departure. A Wiltshireman, Nathaniel Coleman, speaking for a number of others, had questions about women's meetings; he pointed out that the apostle Paul had forbidden women to speak in church, stressed that women's meetings would lessen the authority of male elders, and, more basically, insisted that God commanded men to rule their wives. These were harbingers of the very kind of questions that would wrack the Society of Friends throughout the next decade.

Fox's response reflected his view that Friends lived in an age beyond the letter of the law as Coleman quoted it. Bluntly he told his challengers that Paul had referred to women's role after the fall of Adam and Eve and that now, Christ having restored human beings to the age before the Fall, things were different. Living in the image of God, both men and women could be helpers, he affirmed, one with another, and thus bypass and abolish all differences of roles that encrusted the old age. With a twist of circular reasoning, Fox asserted that any man's desire to rule women indicated that he was living in the time of the Fall—in other words, do as I say, or your refusal demonstrates that you have not entered

Christ's new age of righteousness and are not a real Quaker. Coleman did not seem convinced by this logic, and he stormed out of the meetinghouse, determined to take his case to Quakers at large. But just outside the door he sensed, as he later confessed, that "the fire of the Lord did burn within" and saw "the angel of the Lord with his sword drawn in his hand," so he returned to recant and beg Fox's forgiveness. Thus was opposition cleared for a monthly meeting for women in Wiltshire.[70]

But this opposition had an unforeseen result: it drove Fox toward a more conservative stance on issues involving power arrangements among Quakers. This posture was not evident immediately because he gave little indication that he realized the opposition to women's meetings ran as deeply as it did. The minor to-do in Wiltshire he had put down easily enough. He found when he got to London that dissidents had published pamphlets against the main body, but they were promptly answered.[71] True, he worried enough in the autumn to leave Margaret and her daughter Rachel at the Rous's house in Kingston and briefly go preaching in nearby Essex and Surrey. Arriving back in London, he "set all things straight among Friends," as he strongly remembered, but he evinced more concern about a wave of imprisonments occasioned by Quakers opening their shops on holy days and fast days.

With Margaret and Rachel, Fox rode the fifteen miles to Rickmansworth and Basing House, the commodious and always open home of William Penn. Thus did Fox cultivate close personal ties with this important convert. Penn lived in a staunchly royalist area—one older house on the site had instructions, in French, scratched on each windowpane, "Love loyalty"—a decision reflecting something of the man himself. The house had a walled garden, a large lawn, an impressive stand of beech and linden trees, and more than enough room for its frequent guests.[72] Penn's background marked him for this grand style. As a young blade of twenty-one, he watched his father, an admiral, consorting with royalty, and once served himself as his emissary to Whitehall and a nightshirt-clad Charles II.[73] He dressed suavely, spoke well, and almost always acted the aristocrat, even to the extent of being a bit of a dilettante, particularly when it came to education. Well-traveled and knowledgable, he was a cut above the rest of the coarse first generation of Quakers, particularly George Fox.[74]

Yet Penn chose, against vigorous paternal opposition, to join the scorned Quakers, his decision speaking for his integrity and commitment to the dictates of his conscience. He brought characteristics to the Friends no others among them enjoyed. A few, such as George Bishop and Anthony Pearson had political experience; some, such as Margaret Fell and Mary Penington, came from the gentry; and others, such as John Crook and Gerrard Roberts, were wealthy. But William Penn's background marked him as the sect's first convert who combined all of these characteristics with more than a passing acquaintance with the nation's top rulers. As it turned out, Penn became a vigorous and prolific polemicist, who more than held his own in the Quaker struggle against dissidents inside and detractors outside.[75] His was not yeoman's service but literally noblesse oblige, causing an occasional Friend misgivings about a haughtiness in his manner.[76]

Two things resulted from the influence of Penn, and both showed the moderating influence of someone from his social position. Penn knew kings and courtiers, Parliament members and government ministers. As he rose within the highest reaches of Quakerdom, he made sure that records of sufferings included the testimony of people of account in each county, the better to convince royal officials of Quaker complaints. Because of him, a more sophisticated approach emerged, based on the assumption that the nation's social system was a good one and would respond to an obvious injustice—only a Quaker from Penn's high background, used to hobnobbing with officials he believed to be fundamentally benign, could initiate such a new departure.[77] More important for the internal development of Quakerism was the moderate tone Penn encouraged in a movement formally given to excesses. He abhorred the tendency to anarchism, or Ranterism, always flaring up on the fringes. Fox disliked these tendencies too, but his opposition was much more practical—he simply did not want them undercutting his own power. Penn's aristocratic temperament was offended by the spiritual egalitarianism Quakerism promoted. "God has given greater judgment to his church," Penn pontificated to a hat-wearing libertine, "than the individual members of it."[78]

This same approach was reenforced after the 1667 convincement of another young aristocrat, the Scotsman Robert Barclay of Ury, south of Aberdeen. Four years Penn's junior, Barclay was born in 1648. Both their fathers had supported the royalist cause in the Civil War, but the Scottish soldier, unlike Penn's naval officer father, did not switch sides after the republican triumph, perhaps because his family was related to the Stuart monarchs. Neither son had to earn a living. Both sons studied for a time in Paris, both had a talent with words and left literary monuments attesting to their abilities, both used their talents in the interest of order within the Society of Friends, and, most important, both pitched their tents with the ill-educated and rough-hewn George Fox and so helped assure that Quakerism would not expire as so many other revolutionary sects did. Barclay, more traditionally educated than Penn, proved the more adept theologically and produced an enduring work on Quaker thought, *An Apology for the True Christian Divinity*, although his *Anarchy of the Ranters and other Libertines*, published in 1676, showed him at his polemical best.[79]

The addition of these two noblemen brought to the front men with an array of abilities. In constructing a formidable intellectual defense of Quakerism, this second generation supplied the London leadership with the means to sustain themselves against the most serious challenge the movement had yet confronted. Earlier, Fox had had to deal with challenges, from Rhys Jones, James Nayler, and John Perrot, almost by himself. Things were different now. Thus as he and the family took leave of the Penns to go north late in 1673, things looked better. His followers were increasing in the area, his usual moroseness had lifted, and he intended to stop at Drayton-in-the-Clay to visit his seriously ill mother while Margaret went on to Swarthmoor.[80] He knew, of course, from his London stay and from talking with Penn, of the budding controversy between provincials and those who upheld centralized authority. But he did not know how serious this problem was nor how much he would soon owe the reinforced leadership of the

Society of Friends. Nor did he realize when he arrived for a meeting in lawyer John Halford's barn at Armscote, less than forty miles from his mother's home, that another imprisonment awaited him.[81]

As in the 1650s, the authorities were again worried about sectarians, particularly those attracting large groups. Worcestershire, where Fox stopped, was where Richard Baxter had attempted to prevent any dissenters from infiltrating the county, a strategy thwarting Quaker efforts there in the 1650s. A variety of citizens now approached Henry Parker, justice of the peace from Evesham, to report that upward of four hundred were congregating, some of them ominously from the north, and that the notorious George Fox had come from London to teach them. One minister complained about losing a greater part of his parishioners, people who harkened to the ridicule Fox heaped on their often-absent and tithe-gathering officiant.[82] On December 17, 1673, Parker ordered local constables in nearby areas to apprehend any persons traveling without permits and send them to Worcester.[83] Accompanied by a local minister from Honington, a village close by Armscote, Parker himself showed up at Hawford's house after the Wednesday meeting ended. The clergyman melodramatically used a staff to block the open parlor door and prevent all the suspects from escaping, while yelling for Parker to do his duty. One local offered to submit to arrest as surety for the appearance later of Fox and and his son-in-law Thomas Lower, but Parker hustled the two off to Worcester.[84]

In the deteriorating jail by the Severn River the prisoners waited nearly a month for a hearing. Fox and Lower orchestrated an unprecedented public relations effort to have some higher authority, right up to the king, order their release on a writ of habeas corpus. One Quaker, a Surrey justice of the peace, took a fistful of documents to Charles, finding him sympathetic but too "timorous" to threaten his relations with an increasingly hostile Parliament. Lower's brother, physician to the court, intervened for the two Quaker prisoners, and Penn's aged mother wrote the lord lieutenant of the county in an effort to secure their release.[85] At the January hearing Parker paraded his charges, pointing out that arresting two outsiders was preferable to fining local citizens for attending illegal conventicles. Fox argued that the people from the north, London, and Cornwall were all of the same family. Surprisingly sympathetic sentiments emanated from the court of assizes bench, but the judges clearly worried about the notoriety that Fox and his party had brought to the region. Said the chairman, as he half-pleaded for the First Friend to take the oath of supremacy, "Mr. Fox, you are a famous man."

Such a demand was the very thing that Fox's associates sought to avoid.[86] Not swearing could bring punishment on him for praemunire, the offense under which Margaret had been imprisoned three years earlier and which for all practical purposes made the convicted person an outlaw subject to loss of property and incarceration at the king's pleasure. But no one doubted what Fox would do. Not only did he spurn the oath—though he did pledge allegiance to the king and denied the pope—but he also refused to give surety to return for the next assizes session if released. He had hardly left the courtroom before penning a letter to associates in London relating the latest developments and instructing them to see if they could extract two or three words from the king for his release. If not, he went on, then "you may obtain the other [habeas corpus] as privately and suddenly as may be, before Parker gets up to prevent it." In truth the judges were rather favorably disposed toward their prisoner: they did not find him guilty of praemunire but held him over until the next session of the assizes.[87]

Until his final release after fourteen months in February 1675—Fox was twice freed briefly on writs of habeas corpus and allowed to go to London—the situation was a trying experience for all concerned. In resolving not to swear, Fox was ready to remain isolated in prison. He rejected any idea of a pardon, lest he implicitly acknowledge guilt. His stance meant that the struggle for his freedom had to be carried on at the appellant level in London. Determined supporters soon found themselves working at cross purposes and probably prolonged his ordeal. As his incarceration dragged on and the legal maneuvering became more convoluted, the London directorate called in outside legal aid, something that Fox might have vetoed earlier had he not already resorted to the same strategy.[88] The ordeal worsened when the prisoner fell ill, for a time becoming so weak he could hardly utter a word and needed air in his closed dungeon.[89] Tempers and levels of tolerance grew short.

Margaret, finding she could do little in Worcester, soon left for Swarthmoor. Her absence fed Fox's anger about what he considered her failure to understand his own determination to stay in prison. "When I was taken, you began to fall on me with blaming me," he rebuked her, "and I told you that I was to bear it, and why could you not be . . . content with the will of God? And you said some words and then were pretty quiet."[90] Later, out of prison temporarily on a writ and importuned for interest on some money Margaret had borrowed, he grumbled that she had gotten too deeply in debt.[91] Lower's wife Mary also expressed her irritation when she did not hear from her spouse. Her husband rushed to reassure her that their time was taken up with meeting visitors and writing papers, including one by Fox defending women's meetings that he enclosed to be copied and circulated. He added that although Fox was well, his stomach had given him some trouble, a rumble of future ill health.[92]

The prisoner left the Worcester jail at the end of January on a writ of habeas corpus issued from the King's Bench in London. Free for two months, at the end of which he had promised to return to Worcester, he spent some time with his in-laws the Rouses, in Kingston-on-Thames.[93] The Quakers decided that they should focus on the issue of swearing, and explain the Friends position in hopes of winning both public and offical support. Fox wrote a letter to the king, explaining how he was willing to bear the same penalty for not adhering to his "nay" and "yea" as those who perjured themselves under oath, while across the English-speaking world Friends distributed a pamphlet that explained why they refused to take oaths.[94] Other Quakers buttonholed every available official in hopes of finding someone who would intervene to save Fox from having to return to Worcester.[95]

But return he had to, on March 31, 1674, three days before he was due to appear in court. The judge proved lenient, binding him over to the court of sessions at the end of the month and permitting the obviously infirm Fox to remain free as long as he did not leave town. Thomas Street, chief judge of the court of sessions and a member of Parliament, was hostile, although he allowed Fox to address the jury and explain that his travels in the area had no sinister purpose. So many Friends from Bristol, London, and elsewhere were in attendance that the courtroom took on something of the atmosphere of a Quaker meeting. Street's fellow jurists, clearly moved, freed the prisoner after he spent less than two hours in jail. Granted liberty until the court's next quarterly meeting, Fox left for London, where he attended a meeting of ministers and stayed until July 9.[96] When court resumed Fox was convicted of failing to swear, despite numerous objections both by the defendant and a lawyer who spoke for him during the hearing. Street found him guilty of praemunire, which meant imprisonment until the king was pleased to release him.[97]

Fox's condition continued to deteriorate. Margaret came down from Swarthmoor in August. She and Lower busied themselves trying to get an order for the First Friend's release, but their efforts were fruitless. Fox seemed to be verging on another breakdown—he saw himself "among the graves and dead corpses"—because the efforts of his supporters had proved to be so ineffectual. Support for a parole for Fox wheedled from his old nemesis Justice Parker produced no position result. In October Margaret left for London to personally plead with the king, but Fox's adamant refusal to accept a pardon foredoomed her chances of success.[98] By December she was sounding desperate. Pressing for pity, she told an official that for twenty long weeks she had no way of "knowing that I should find him alive."[99]

A month later, a writ of habeas corpus called for the prisoner to appear before the King's Bench in London, but he was required to arrive before the court's term expired on February 12. The sheriff, off on county business, dragged his feet, and Fox was not physically up to riding the ninety or so miles by horseback. When a slow coach become available on February 4, and after two attorneys pledged a hefty £500 security to indemnify the sheriff, the party hurried to the capital, arriving on the eighth, only four days before the deadline. But the chief justice acted with dispatch when the matter finally reached him; he ruled that numerous errors in the indictment justified releasing Fox. With hardly a minute to spare on the last day of the term, Fox was freed after fourteen months in custody.[100]

Awaiting the adjournment of Parliament and the convening of the yearly meeting in late May, Fox recuperated at the Rous's house in Kingston with his wife. The mail brought pleas from Swarthmoor wanting to know when to expect the couple's return. The family offered to send fresh horses on ahead to meet the travelers. Since Fox had not been home in a decade, they wanted his favorite wine bought and time to bottle the cider and strong beer they were readying for him. The two Foxes naturally wanted to attend the May 1675 yearly meeting before returning north. In the meantime Fox traveled down river to London, preparing pamphlets and epistles to influence public opinion and the deliberations of Parliament.[101]

In the face of the divisions splitting the country's Quakers, the yearly meeting initiated decisive action, but the First Friend did not take a very public role.

He did not sign the epistle condemning the "disorderly proceedings of some professing the truth," nor the memorandum authorizing a meeting for sufferings, soon to become the most powerful body in English Quakerdom.[102] On his own he sent an epistle to quarterly meetings to make sure subordinate meetings were seeing to the needs of poor Friends and so preventing families from "decaying," a safely noncontroversial admonition.[103] Despite Fox's low profile, the yearly meeting's actions would never have won approval without his endorsement and support. He termed the session "a glorious meeting in the everlasting power of God."[104]

Following the yearly meeting, the Foxes and Margaret's daughter Susannah took the coach and progressed north along much the same route George Fox had followed when he first came to London more than thirty years earlier, through Barnet, Newport Pagnell, and Northampton. His mother was dead by now, and he had no reason to stop at Drayton-in-the-Clay. The party detoured to Coventry, arriving at Lancaster in time for the men's and women's quarterly meetings. Accompanied by members of the Fell family, come to meet them from Swarthmoor, they proceeded carefully, even with the tide out, across the perilous sands of Morecambe Bay. When they sighted the manor house, jutting upward into the breezy summer air from its rather barren surroundings, they knew they were nearly home.

It was Friday, June 25, 1675,[105] nearly twenty-three years since the itinerant George Fox had first seen that house, making his way down Furness Peninsula from the north. Then having appointed himself chief spokesman for a little band of disparate seekers, he had searched for a place to anchor a movement that he believed would shake the whole country around. Now the matured movement was a church of far-flung dimensions and diminished fervor, its headquarters the mightiest city of Europe, capital of a growing empire. Its leader, weakened and needing a period of recuperation, was returning to rest at the secluded site of his salad days. But, given his past, he would not be idle. Soon he turned his attention to the internal challenges facing his Society of Friends.

16

❦

A Man May Cut Himself
with His Own Knife

George Fox returned to the north, weary, half-ill, and needing to recuperate. But he was not a person to remain idle, particularly when facing a major challenge. Over the course of his half-century Fox had learned that control of the past allowed a person to grasp the present and shape the future. So he set about making sure that he knew the past—his own as well as the movement's—in order to cope with the malcontents who were working havoc among northern adherents. Thus he began work on an autobiography, recording his life and his recollections of the movement's past. Dictating to his son-in-law Thomas Lower, he carefully went through the correspondence that Margaret had kept over the years—a sure way to jog his memory. He noted on each missive that he had read it, who the author and the recipient were, the approximate date, and often his decision about the letter's disposition, whether it should be recopied or destroyed. Both his *Journal*, which was not published until after his death, and the notations he added to the letters naturally reflected his view of the controversies in which he had taken part. To assure himself that posterity had the correct version, he modified some letters to make them say what he wanted them to say.[1] He also took time to compose detailed instructions for dealing with his large literary legacy.[2]

His *Journal* is a classic of religious literature, with a vigor reminiscent of the man himself. Although to moderns it sounds repetitive and too discursive to hold one's steady attention, it has an air of authenticity about it. It moves from here to there, but it does so without clear logic or certain plan; one section is a kind of jumble of ideas important to Fox at the time of writing; another offers a pastiche of incidents selected to illustrate a religious truth more basic than mere factual accuracy; and still another presents a hodgepodge of immediate insights into the ways of God, and of human beings in relation to the divine. Hardly a theological treatise, the *Journal* is a sprawling account of mystical experiences, encounters with opponents, travels into practically every corner of the country, and aggressive attacks on his opponents. It is a shambles, but one version or another has been in print since 1694.[3]

Edited by Thomas Ellwood and published three years after Fox's death, the *Journal* had the advantage of being close in time to its subject's life. It appeared under the guidance of those in the central leadership, men committed to putting a cautious, respectable face on their sect's turbulent history. Under their supervision, Ellwood toned down or omitted many events they considered most bizarre. Knowing the outcome, he made Fox into a person enabled by superior foresight to triumph over his opponents. The first sixteen pages of Fox's memoir were also lost or destroyed, so we have to rely on Ellwood's account of his leader's early life. (The "Spence Manuscript," which includes the dictated material from which Ellwood worked as well as letters and epistles interspersed throughout, was not published until 1911.) For the years after 1676 Ellwood's story consisted primarily of reprinted documents, supplemented by material kept by one of Fox's traveling companions and others. Ellwood had a trained and careful ear for language—he served John Milton as secretary and reader after the poet became blind—but the desire to depict Fox as a moderate inevitably meant that he had to soften sometimes rough edges and reduce the vigor and firmness of the real man. Just as surely, the sanitized Fox who emerged from the *Journal* fed the institution-building efforts of his successors, a useful process now as then.[4]

The *Journal's* backdrop was the conflict raging among Friends. Plumbing his memory, Fox found weapons to hurl at opponents. On the very first page, in answer to one caviler, Fox boasted that he had known pureness and righteousness from the age of eleven.[5] He calculatedly wrote minor dissidents out of his movement's history or reduced their roles. He grouped some lesser figures with major challengers like Nayler and Perrot and, lest his judgment be questioned, reduced the roles of friends who had been close to him, like Thomas and Ann Curtis and Anthony Pearson, but had since become his enemies.[6] He seemed to delight in cataloguing misfortunes befalling those who crossed him, such as when he related how the butcher who derided Friends died with his swollen tongue dangling out of his mouth.[7] In these and other ways his memoir was as polemical as anything he ever wrote.

It also served to distort the actual record, for Fox naturally placed himself at the center of the movement, even in the 1660s and 1670s when his travels to the colonies, lengthy imprisonments, and debilitating illnesses forced him to step aside and permit others to bear more responsibility for the Quaker sect. Thus Fox assumed a role that made him less the architect of the Society of Friends than its public defender, even its lightning rod, one who protected the movement by becoming the target of all those who would do it harm.[8] He knew what the movement needed: a series of local meetings, strengthened at the county level by quarterly meetings; centralized bodies to oversee and coordinate the meetings all over the country; and a way to draw more on the talents of women. He did not admit it, of course, but he lifted a page from the book of old critic Richard Baxter, who had organized Worcestershire ministers into an association. Fox was well aware, for example, of how ministers thronging a meeting overawed weaker attenders.[9] When he heard about differences in Scotland, he immediately sent off a letter in which he advised ministers to meet to keep unity so "that you might treat of things that tend for peace."[10] But he did not fill in the details. He held back, letting others take the initiative for shaping the organization in line with his expectations, and then he stepped to the front to champion it publicly.

Fox was not averse to permitting others to bear some of the burden of decision making, particularly when their decisions closely reflected his own wishes. The leaders who had come to the fore in London, some old, some new, were more interested in details than Fox. They knew how to implement their leader's vision, and he lent his approval. But more important than lending approval, he spent his prestige to assure that opponents did not thwart what he recognized was needed to hold the institution together. A lesser man than Fox would not have seen the wisdom in taking a back seat at this point, and instead would have insisted on his prerogative. That he understood the necessity of keeping a lowered profile underscored his essential genius.

The First Friend certainly did not abdicate his rule of the Quaker movement. In fact his decision to establish women's meetings sparked the tinder under the so-called Wilkinson–Story split, thereby giving inchoate discontent an issue upon which to focus."[11] Women's occasional separation for worship had a long history,[12] perhaps because some meetinghouses made no provision for them among the ministers, lest visitors wonder, as it was quaintly put, "at this class of gifts." When they spoke they stood on a tub or stool.[13] Some Quaker men made no secret of the fact that they preferred women to remain silent.[14] So, except in London, women had little responsibility for meeting affairs, a situation reflecting the way things had always worked in the church. The paucity of women's names on surviving meeting documents from the early years silently testifies to the locus of actual power. In 1666, when Fox dispatched his epistle exhorting men's meetings to establish counterparts among the women, he offered few details about what he expected the women to do, nor did he act to implement his initiative. Later, he remembered affirming in 1668 that both men and women were heirs of all the gospel authority that adhered to the meetings, but once again he gave no guidance as to what he meant precisely or what he thought should change. Traveling the countryside in the late 1660s he devoted the bulk of his time to erecting men's meetings for administering discipline.[15] As late as 1670 he composed an epistle that explicitly emphasized the male role in collecting sufferings.[16] He clearly expected the men to make the major decisions and administer discipline.

In June 1671, as he made plans to leave for the New World, Fox moved toward a firmer position on women's roles. Margaret was in the capital with him as he worked on his epistle. Five years earlier she had composed the century's foremost exposition of churchwomen's rights, *Women's Speaking Justified*.[17] Modest women, Fox had observed, did not feel free to speak of what he termed "women's matters" among men, and modest men certainly did not desire to pry into purely female concerns.[18] To deal with this reality and expand women's roles, he took as a model the London experiment, now nearly a decade and a half old. He dispatched a circular letter recommending that women establish separate meetings as, he prodded, "they have in other parts." Then they could visit widows and orphans, oversee children put out as apprentices, and contribute from the money they accumulated to meet the needs of the poor. Noting that they should inform the men of any needs they could not meet, he implied that the men would exercise final oversight, especially over large expenditures. Despite this nod in the direction of male authority, he affirmed that "man and woman, being both in the power and seed [of] Christ Jesus . . . are both helpmeets" for each other. That is, each needed the other to perform different but equally important functions "in the household of faith." He even advised the women when to convene—at 10:00 A.M., once or twice monthly—and to worship quietly until someone "whose mouth the Lord opens" spoke up or confessed.[19]

Quaker processes cranked slowly. It was November, with Fox already in the New World, before his letter on women began to produce results. Emboldened by the First Friend's ideas about women, the women of Bristol converted their existing meeting for worship into a monthly meeting concerned with the things Fox had suggested. One of the women involved was Isabel Fell Yeamans, daughter of Margaret Fox. Without asking leave of their two-week meeting governing body, all male of course, the women publicized their newly expanded gathering. The men's meeting was shocked by the women's actions and laid practically everything else aside to devote the bulk of its November 27 agenda to the matter. One leading merchant, William Rogers, was especially angered: he demanded to know why the women had proceeded on their own. A committee of six, including some of the most powerful Quakers in Bristol, was instructed to attend the next women's meeting and come back with an answer.

Claiming they had acted because the men's meeting had sent Fox's letter on to them, the women split over what to do. After some discussion they deferred, as they compliantly put it, "to the wisdom of God in the Friends of the men's meeting." Pleased with this capitulation, the thirty men, with no women attending, reaffirmed the women's "duty to mind only those things that tend to peace." They decreed that no women's monthly meeting be scheduled until they all, men and women together, reached unity on the question. To make sure everyone understood where power resided, they ordered three women leaders, including Yeamans, to deliver their decision.[20]

To William Rogers, such feminine upsurges boded ill for the Society of Friends. Even critics acknowledged that Rogers, from a well-off trading family, had a well-deserved reputation as a firm upholder of discipline, and that he possessed a ready wit and alertness. He and Fox knew each other well.[21] His was the first open challenge to the new order, which had been promptly acceded to in the north.[22] Rogers would eventually become the main anti-Fox writer within the Society of Friends,[23] but that role was still in the future. For now, he had stalled the movement to establish women's business meetings, carrying all the men with him and winning at least the women's public acquiescence, but the matter would rise again: the broader point transcended women's meetings and involved who was to determine the contours of the faith, the individual or the larger body. A later dissenter summed it up well when he advised, "[L]et no men (nor WOMEN especially) rule over you, neither receive their traditions nor doctrines further than manifested by the truth in your own hearts and in the Scriptures."[24]

Fox took no part in the Bristol controversy, for he was in Barbados. But while there he made a startling announcement, that couples seeking to be married must have their proposed union examined twice by both men's and *women's* meetings, appearing first before the women.[25] When he had been married two years before in a ceremony consciously designed to exemplify the preferred procedures, he and Margaret had gone to the men's meeting first and only later to a joint meeting of men and women. Why Fox chose Barbados to unveil this dramatic new expansion of women's roles is unclear. Perhaps, recognizing the plan's potential for feeding unrest, he wanted to start in a far-off corner of the world and let his revolutionary idea filter slowly back home. Perhaps he saw this strategy undercutting the Perrotists, who enjoyed strong support from women. Whatever his reasoning, he was notably quiet about the idea of women's meetings helping to rule on proposed marriages upon returning, perhaps believing that if the opposition was not deliberately stirred up tempers would cool.[26] Only in February 1676, nearly five years in the future and long after disaffection broke out, did Fox finally issue an epistle spelling out the new requirement.[27] Other male authorities were also uncustomarily oblique about this new role for women. True, the epistle of the 1675 yearly meeting defended women's meetings in general terms, rebuking those who called them into question, but it neglected to address what many male Quakers considered the demeaning requirement that men seek approval for marriage from women.[28] Nor, in his long sermon to the yearly meeting, did Fox mention this new authority for women, contenting himself with the curiously circumspect statement of his belief that "many times women's business is not proper to men." Mentioning no one by name, he also endorsed those who helped women serve God.[29]

After Bristol's suppression of its women, it was clear that dominant males would not accede easily to the new departure. Reports trickled in, not to the London center of power but to Margaret Fox, of just how adroit threatened men could be. In the north she positioned herself as champion of women's meetings: In fact, with George in America, she became the country's foremost proponent of the innovation, writing and traveling in its behalf. One whom she encouraged, Jean Simcock in Cheshire, immediately ran head-on into the wily response of an insecure but determined male establishment. The women of her quarterly meeting approved a paper that they forwarded to the men's meeting. But knowing of, and resenting, Fox's outside intervention, the itinerant James Parke, a northerner who served in the higher reaches of London's central bureau, deliberately held the floor for so long that time expired before the women's idea could be considered. Though rebuffed, the undaunted Simcock vowed to bring the proposal up again.[30] The point was, of course, that even men of importance only half-heartedly supported women's meetings and would use their skills to thwart them.

Margaret Fox, acting as catalyst, thus brought the issue of authority to a froth. In late January 1673, while George was still abroad, she raised the issue of what role women's meetings should play in marriages at the Westmorland quarterly meeting in Kendal. Armed with a prepared paper, she took on the men of the area who opposed a broadening of women's role in the Quaker movement, particularly John Story, their acknowledged leader. A Westmorlander who had suffered imprisonment while working as an evangelist in the south, Story was not present, so it was up to his cohort John Wilkinson to bear the burden of the defense.[31] Margaret had a long list of complaints against the local male leadership: they did not allow women to pass on marriages; they compromised the testimony against tithes; they did not publicly announce meetings for fear of informers; they refused to permit condemnations of disorderly walkers to remain in the record books;[32] they censured those who sang, sighed, or groaned under religious ecstasy during meetings; and, the dispute's gravamen, they undermined the central bodies, calling them "courts of judicature" and "sessions" imposed by human will. The flash point of Margaret's attack, all recognized, was the males' objection to the new role for women's meetings in marriage procedures.

The dissidents had answers to these charges, some of which the wife of the First Friend considered as personal affronts. Whether compelling or disingenuous—and there were both kinds—the responses reflected a conflict over authority: whether those in provincial Westmorland were to set the rules or those in London, at headquarters. This fundamental difference emerged clearly when Margaret Fox alleged that Story had circulated and thus endorsed an old Anthony Pearson ranterish-sounding paper, in which it was stated that the way of truth resembled a ship at sea, blown wherever the spirit (wind) should take it. Story embraced this idea but denied knowing it was Pearson's. Like other malcontents, Story had problems with anyone, particularly outsiders, trying to hem in his leadings from the spirit. He and his separatist supporters portrayed Margaret Fox as such a villain that a backlash forced them to explain their vigorous attacks on her.[33]

Let it be said, the Society of Friends' leaders did try to determine how local groups operated, not only regarding broad matters like those that concerned Margaret Fox but even on local questions of how meetings should organize. For example, later, in December of the same year, a delegation of London worthies, including George Fox himself, out on a furlough from prison in Worcester, appeared at Jordans, Buckinghamshire, to help split the monthly meeting so, they claimed, to better accommodate those living at a distance. Thus in this case, Quakers from the London center interferred at the local level to set territorial boundaries for meetings, up to now strictly a local prerogative.[34]

The men at the center were a varied yet complementary group. With a commerical and professional bent, men like George Whitehead, William Penn, James Claypoole, and Ellis Hookes were gradually displacing the more rough-hewn rustics from the north and west as principal decision makers in the Society of Friends.[35] In 1673 George Whitehead was thirty-seven years old. The longest lived of the first generation, he would be a key figure in the Quaker movement for more than forty years. A successful businessman, he could appear smug and opaque, with an air that he knew things unavailable to lesser mortals. A prolific writer and ardent controversialist, he won a reputation as "the wheel within the wheel." His influence approached that of Fox.[36] Shrewd James Claypoole, a merchant with far-flung interests, never let his eye stray too far from the main chance. He was always alert, he admitted, to "improve" £1000 or £2000 to "very great advantage."[37] The aristocratic William Penn brought his talents, his know-how, and his contacts with outsiders to the task before them. Men like Alexander Parker and Thomas Salthouse used their wide travels and acquaintanceship with divers Friends to advantage. Ellis Hookes, so long involved in the Quaker bureaucracy in London, had so much self-assurance that he never hesitated to lecture outlying Friends about their shortcomings.[38]

The evolving institutional arrangements elevated Fox's priorities to the level of law and drew numerous complaints. By the time the issues that underlay the schisms of the 1670s crystallized, a powerful new executive body was in place in London to meet the challenge. This collective, variously known as the "Morning Meeting," the "Second Day's Morning Meeting," or the "Ministers' Meeting," had its roots in the gatherings of ministers who met in private London homes in the mid- and late 1650s to make sure local Quaker groups all over the country enjoyed the services of a recognized minister. Their work led to familiarity with all the Quaker evangelists, itinerant ministers, and settled ministers, and knowledge about their capabilities and weaknesses. Over time the London group gradually acquired more authority, and hence more power. Control over the spoken word, or at least who spoke it, soon expanded into control over the written word. Early on, Fox decreed that if Friends intended to publish anything concerning the Quaker movement, they should forward their manuscripts to London for inspection and approval.[39] Hence at 8:00 A.M. on Sunday and at 10:00 A.M. on Monday, those who claimed status as ministers of the Society of Friends met at the rooms of some London Friend's house.[40] This meeting became the first dispenser of denominational discipline.

Although the Morning Meeting concerned itself primarily with overseeing publication of books—implementing a 1666 directive that "faithful and sound Friends" see that "nothing but what is sound and savory" go out into the world—it easily ventured into other areas. At one of its first recorded meetings, for example, it instructed Friends in the counties to find candidates for Parliament who would support liberty of conscience and remove all "oppressive and popish laws."[41] It also flexed its muscles. On December 27, 1675, sitting at Claypoole's, the meeting directed William Penn to review a paper written by Fox and "fit it for the press." Thirteen months later it appointed a committee to read and correct one of the First Friend's contributions before it was printed.[42] Fox became angry at another Morning Meeting decision. In April 1676 he growled petulantly about the "evil savor" when it forbade Friends to read a firm letter he had written on the dispute involving women's meetings. The central body's assumption of such an authority over local meetings exemplified, he snapped, "a spirit that is too high."[43]

To an outside observer, even to the average Friend, the identity and reach of a Quaker group established about this time merged with that of the Morning Meeting. This more representative body, the Meeting for Sufferings, was also dominated by a relatively few well-off gentlemen in London. In fact, it amounted to a mere expansion of the Morning Meeting, which specified that as many of its members might serve in the new body as they desired.[44] It met first on June 22, 1676. Given that the Meeting for Sufferings also convened weekly, usually on Friday at 10:00 A.M., it by necessity consisted of men resident in the capital who were allowed to act for Quakers beyond the city. For example, William Meade, Margaret Fox's future son-in-law, served as representative from London, Durham and Northumberland, and New England.[45] Sometimes it acted with as few as three or four members present.[46] It also contained a shadowy central committee of twelve, two drawn from each of six London meetings, whose jobs included making investment decisions about gifts and legacies and making sure that Hookes's salary was paid.[47] The membership of these groups overlapped with that of the Morning Meeting—Penn and Whitehead served on both—and the Meeting for Sufferings rapidly became the Society of Friend's executive committee.

It had roots in the sect's past, its very name illustrative of Fox's determination to collect and publish accounts of persecution of Quakers and to challenge the Restoration state to treat the Friends more justly.[48] By the late 1670s its power to speak for the organization as a whole and to guide the yearly meeting gave its members an influence that could not be denied. Some in the west—for example, in Bristol, London's natural rival—and more in the north, who saw their influence diminishing, resented the Meeting for Sufferings and the Morning Meeting because they were eroding the autonomy of local meetings. Critics complained about the emerging hierarchy and demanded the names of those responsible for the new departure. Some opponents demanded recantations from the London "governors" of the Society and denounced them for usurping God's power and spirit.[49] When Ann Travers, an influential Friend, petitioned that some funds collected for relief of suffering be allocated for dispensing by women's meetings, she watched helplessly as the matter was buried until it was not heard from again, a time-worn tactic of those occupying positions of power.[50] Likewise, private members held some of the Society's funds, which they presumably could use as they saw fit until they were needed.[51]

Thus did blessings abound whence authority flowed. The centerpiece of Quaker discipline was the 1666 "Testimony from the Brethren," signed by eleven of the most powerful Quakers centered in London, excepting only Hookes. It announced that those who would not submit to the central leadership would be denied. Its hectoring tone used verbs like "declare" and "testify," with "warn" and "charge" thrown in for good measure.[52] Critics, even outsiders, claimed that it handed Fox and his "Representative Body" the powers of pope and councils.[53] About the same time, Fox sent each meeting a statement consisting of nineteen specific points, but they were rather more pastoral than prescriptive. Of course, he dealt with wearing hats—"the old rotten principle of the Ranters," he called it—and recommended that "tale carriers" who sowed dissension be reproved, an unapt behavior most often associated with women.[54] But his focus centered more on looking after the poor and widows; recording sufferings; keeping books for marriages, births, and deaths; and buying burial grounds.[55] It did not exude the same lordly air of the 1666 "Testimony from the Brethren," and its counsel never elicited any discontent.

Before Fox returned from America, the London power brokers had rushed to scotch rumbles of dissent and defend their leader. They were aware, as Claypoole wrote later in another context, that "high places are slippery, and more snares attend him who governs than him who suffers."[56] In a letter signed at the yearly meeting in 1673, thirty-six Friends took aim at those who despised centralized authority. Their warning was clear: those Friends who did not surrender their private judgments to the will of their "brothers" were in error. "The Lord," the brothers concluded, "has laid it more upon some in whom he has opened counsel . . . (and particularly in our dear brother and God's faithful laborer George Fox)" to render discipline.[57]

At the end of the yearly meeting in May 1675 the London leaders again sought to head off the developing crisis by warning Friends of what they termed the "disorderly proceedings of some professing the truth." Their listing represented a summary of the tangle of disputes tying up local meetings, particularly in the west and north. Marriage and matters of gender were the largest single category of the twelve items covered; they ranged from a reaffirmation of the practice that Quakers not marry first cousins, through a reminder that marriages be cleared twice by women's and men's meetings, to advice that meetings watch couples to make sure that "all foolish and unbridled affections" be speedily brought under God's judgment. More important, the letter averred that women's meetings, just like men's meetings, had been set up with God's counsel and sharply admonished those who sneered at them as "synods" and "popish impositions." The letter reiterated the policy that Friends not flee persecution and that meetings be open to all and publicly announced; likewise the "ancient testimony" against tithes was reinforced. Violators of such testimonies—"disorderly walkers"—should have their names recorded. The meeting endorsed "serious sighings, sensible groaning and reverent singing" if in unity with gospel service. Finally, it appealed to Friends to avoid contention, utter few words, and flee the world's fashions, language, and spirit. This statement's weight came from men of the stature of Alexander Parker, George Whitehead, William Penn, and Thomas Salthouse.[58]

In a fundamental sense this letter dealt with issues that illustrated the maturity of the Society of Friends. But it also revealed that Quakers were not always able to live together as friends. The storms associated with Rhys Jones, James Nayler, and John Perrot had been small compared to the one the Society of Friends now faced. The current challenge was more far-reaching, both in geographical extent and in the number of points disputed by the London authorities and those Quakers all over the country who challenged London's right to make policy for the entire Society of Friends. However much they were right when they appealed to the original message of Quakerism—and much truth, let it be noted, adhered to their critique—the challengers, who looked to the past, were engaged in a losing struggle with the London leadership, who looked to the future, and knew that if it was to survive the Society of Friends had to resist the luxury of unrestrained individualism. A balance was being struck, a balance without which the Society of Friends simply could not endure: a degree of individualism had to be sacrificed for the greater good of what had evolved from a loose confederation of like-minded dissenters into a sect, and now into an institution.

This growing institutionalization became the object of widespread attack. Jeffery Bullock, a disowned Friend from Sudbury, fumed that Fox and the elders in the Meeting for Sufferings were setting up false practices. He lectured that "your visible church government is altogether anti-Christian" because "every member of the church of God is to be both ruled and governed by the measure of God's spirit that is in them." Bullock insisted that he was not opposed to all visible church government, only to that government that failed to grow out of the spirit of life in an individual's own particular experience. Delighting in quoting Fox against himself, Bullock skillfully highlighted the essential problem for one who had so eagerly stressed the sufficiency of the light of Christ within.[59]

Compared to Francis Bugg, also a former Friend, Bullock was niggardly in output. With great joy over many years Bugg published his string of attacks on the leadership. From 1680 to 1724, forty-four long years, this beefy wool merchant from Suffolk needed seventy-eight books to catalogue all his disagreements with Fox and the establishment; his life consisted of little else than spewing anti-Quaker venom.[60] He concocted disagreements out of such matters as his claim that leading Friends postured about treating all alike but, he alleged, required apprentices to approach them bareheaded.[61] Bugg's catchall of complaints finally caught fire over the old bugaboo of marriage, an issue that easily shaded into questions of gender and women's roles. Bugg told his aunt that he turned against Fox because of the requirement that marriages go twice to women's meetings before approval by the men. This, claimed Bugg, amounted to setting up women's government.[62] "Take heed, beware of novelty, / And of female authority," began a poem in one of his pamphlets.[63]

Although Rogers and Bugg were the hornets of the anti-Fox party, a more moderate Friend from Mortlake in Surrey, William Mucklow, first stung the Quaker establishment into action. Six years Fox's junior, Mucklow privately circulated a letter in mid-1672 containing thirty-eight queries dealing with the fundamental issue as the dissidents saw it: liberty of conscience in the face of centralized decision making. Although his letter has not survived, Penn's comprehensive answer did.[64] Mucklow used his letter as the basis of a well-reasoned book the following year when he assailed the plans the "Foxonians" had in mind for the Society of Friends. Charging the party of Fox with taking a leaf from the papists, Mucklow took the long view. "In all ages truth has not been persecuted as truth but as error," and this, he impugned, was now happening. "In the true church unity stands in diversities," he said, "but in the false, unity will not stand without uniformity." Those who forbade wearing a hat during prayer, the specific ruling that most irked Mucklow, had the gall to claim that "the spirit, and not the scripture, is the rule." Yet they insisted that judgments about the right course were to be determined not by an individual's own leadings but by church fiat: "[T]hey lay down this as the infallible rule, that the body will have a true sense, feeling, and understanding of motions, visions, revelations, doctrines, &c, and [it is] therefore safest to make her my touchstone in all things relating to God."[65] If the hat question was indeed the minor matter Penn asserted,[66] then why cut off those who refused to wear it, wondered this thoughtful critic.

Penn rushed to defend Fox. "There is either such place as a Christian society," he expertly divided the question, "or there is not." If such a body existed, then it must have the power to enforce its decisions about seemingly minor, "needless," questions, such as wearing a hat. "Deny this," pronounced Penn, "and farewell to all Christian church order and discipline, yea, and truth itself, for it is an absolute inlet to Ranterism and so to atheism, near whose borders this author dwells." Fox never referred to "liberty of conscience," Penn emphasized, believing that consciences enslaved by the world were not free and that only the inward conscience, released from sin's thralldom, was liberated to know and do right.[67] "'We must not judge consciences,'" Fox noted sarcastically, quoting his critics. The apostles certainly judged consciences, whether they were seared or tender; they judged faith, whether dead or living; and they judged worship, whether of beasts and dragons or of God. Let a person desiring true liberty live in Christ's gospel, he concluded simply.[68] For Penn and Fox, people did not know their real interests, which a superior and more competent authority was obliged to drill into them.

The entire controversy had more than a little irony about it. Fox and the original Children of the Light had won a first hearing from men and women who longed to be freed from the overlordship of men asserting superior wisdom and authority, men with no use for individualism and willing to use rank power to govern. Now members of the Society of Friends were being told by the very people who had originally brought them a message of liberation that they should kowtow before a new establishment. With success and growing membership, the leaders of the Society found themselves faced with the same challenges they had earlier hurled at others in a similar position. They realized now, as they did not and could not before, that some system of authority was absolutely necessary for a religious institution to survive, even if the members of that institution eschewed it. Critics delighted in taunting Fox and his supporters on this point. They "once cried for liberty of conscience," Thomas Crisp jeered, declaring that "none must perform any worship but as taught and led thereunto by the Light in their own hearts." "But having gathered a people now, say they, submit to your elders; and if [you do] not conform to his orders for conscience sake then [you are] willful, stubborn, out of the universal Spirit and Truth, enemies, rebels, accursed from all eternity."[69] History's muse could only smile at the irony.

A cornered Fox, however, was in no mood to smile, and certainly not at himself. He deplored talk of liberty, especially if it conflicted with stability. "God is a God of order," he thundered, "and not of confusion." Let truth judge and exclude malcontents who, like Adam and Eve, succumbed to the blandishments of the devil, "the world's god," "the power of death and darkness and confusion."[70] Dissidents might just as well deny the very gospel itself, he warned Wiltshire Friends, as to deny its rightful order.[71] He came to believe that in a church governed by Christ there should be no strife, and if there was, then Christ was not governing.[72] As the number of second-generation Quakers who surreptitiously paid tithes or struck deals with collectors rose, Fox took to emphasizing "our ancient testimony." Since exact numbers were unknown, he demanded an inquiry "concerning all such among Friends as do pay tithes."[73] The yearly meeting echoed the same position when it bemoaned "that where any decline their testimony [against tithing], . . . they do thereby increase the weight and burden of sufferings on them that are faithful."[74]

On the subject of women's meetings, George Fox did not look back. His stance was not something tacked on to his ideas; instead it grew out of his fundamental nature. Indeed, on one occasion, to underscore his strong views on the subject, he did the unheard-of and referred to himself in print as a woman. Writing to Catholics who boasted that they could go without food longer than his Quakers, he asserted that "I, the writer of this, who am a woman," had once fasted twenty-two days. If a mere woman could do that, then Quakers could certainly go without food longer than Catholics.[75] Just as he was sure that anyone who denied women's meetings denied the gospel itself, he insisted that a woman was, as he patiently explained to an audience in Barbados, "a companion, an equal in the holy image of God, for the man a meet help in righteousness." Let Baptists, Presbyterians, and Independents prate about their new state, Quakers would show it forth, demonstrating that Christ, "the second Adam," had restored his followers to the full equality the first parents enjoyed before the Fall. This equality freed neither men nor women to act licentiously. In restoring human beings to their prefallen state, Christ, he stressed, had brought them back to "one man and one woman, not many."[76] He felt nothing but disgust, he wrote, for "all men who hunt after women, from woman to woman, and also women whose affections run sometimes after one man and soon after another."[77]

Fox obviously did not shrink from discipline, but first he sought to deal with Quaker dissent in a pastoral way—an unusual approach and one demonstrating his ambivalence. He had already criticized his wife for her rather high-handed excursion into Westmorland.[78] Perhaps earlier disputes had taught him something, or, more likely, the shifts of some close associates to the side of the discontented led him to hope that conciliation might staunch the hemorrhage.[79] Hence in early 1675, just before being freed from prison in Worcester, he shivered in the cold castle yard for hours while conferring with John Story and John Wilkinson, accompanied by Thomas and Ann Curtis, formerly two of his closest friends who had sided with the dissidents. The weather may have been chilly and the intention reconciliation, but the air quickly heated up. Ann Curtis, a sometime volunteer to take Fox's place in prison, set the First Friend's teeth on edge by oozing about "Dear John Story," while his jailmate and son-in-law Thomas Lower promised to prove Story a liar. Fox thrust at the Two Johns, the label attached to these two leading dissenters, that if they did not back down he would declare against them as strongly as he had testified against the clergy; they parried that they would "not make an idol of him" no matter how many letters he might send into their base in the north. Although Lower thought Fox a "burdensome stone" for the dissenters, they went away complaining that the son-in-law had been the heavy.[80]

The bloodletting grew worse. By the mid-1670s dissent permeated meetings all over the country, with discontent feeding discontent. In Reading, the meeting split, with Thomas Curtis leading those who broke away from the original meeting when it sided with the Londoners. It did no good to remind him how he had once cautioned a group of Quakers around his table that any who crossed

Fox would end up "blasted and withered."[81] Fox was incredulous at the Curtises and their failure to support the establishment. Their central problem was, as he told them, that "you do not stand for the faith of Christ" and "have let loose your spirits among the young against the ancient."[82] In Wiltshire criticism of women's meetings led some Quakers to attack men's gatherings and even the practice of owning meetinghouses.[83] Soon old papers written by Nayler and Perrot were reprinted to bolster pleas for liberty.[84] In some locales the dissidents expanded men's meetings to include women, an unacceptable tactic in the eyes of the mainstream group.[85] But recognizing the cogency of this move, Fox took pains to try to answer the argument that separate meetings for the sexes denied equal treatment; he asserted that physical separation did not mean that the two groups could not unite in spirit.[86] Bristol meeting, where William Rogers was still a force, was threatened with schism, and by 1678 a separate quarterly meeting had surfaced in Lincolnshire.[87] Even the small Dutch meeting was divided over the issue of registering marriages with the civil authorities.[88]

Each side used stories about the other's derelictions to convince fence sitters. One tale that Fox's party spread related how a man at his wedding stood and announced, "Master Story, I take such a one to be my wife" and afterward toasted Story with "I will drink to thee" and doffed his hat.[89] The secessionists countered that in repeating this false story Fox had called the couple "whores" and "rogues."[90] At one point Story allegedly reported that before Fox came to the north in 1652 he had been a preacher among the Ranters.[91] Others attacked Fox for referring to himself as the son of God.[92] In the closest he ever came to admitting an error, Fox confessed that two decades earlier he might have acceded to a proposal that people buy tithes from their holders to avoid having to pay the tax.[93] A critic pointed out that some Fox supporters had put aside their wives because they had been married by a minister, the implication being that families meant nothing to zealous Foxites.[94] Fox insisted that he wanted women to rule on marriages to check disorderly practices like the one in which a Gloustershire couple found a schismatic willing to certify their marriage with a "pitiful certificate."[95] An undertone of class crept into the dispute when a Fox adherent pointed to the dissaffected Quakers as "rich in wit and wealth."[96] Both sides could play that game. The dissidents charged that the aristocratic Penn, contrary to Quaker practice, wore a wig. Fox defended Penn, explaining that he did not wear a wig out of vanity but because he had lost all his hair after a youthful bout with smallpox.[97]

In a sense Fox watched these developments from the sidelines, for the years had taken their toll on the First Friend. He was vigorous enough in his writings, and he continued to condemn Quaker schismatics and issue refutations addressed to their errors. But his isolation in the north had not helped. Illness plagued him—he was so weak that he could hardly walk outside[98]—and rest seemed almost impossible, what with visitors from England, Scotland, and abroad.[99] His colleagues in London took to wondering if he was seeing clearly. To them, he seemed unable to understand how he was viewed as behind the centralization of power and that agreement on other issues would not end the controversy.[100] In his letters, they found a curious mixture of vituperation against Wilkinson and

Story and kind gestures toward others just as bad. Indeed in a single month, December 1676, he sent the Curtises two missives, one conciliatory, one censorious.[101] When the movers of the Second Day Morning Meeting finally got the dissidents to agree to a northern conference to explore the issues dividing the Society of Friends, Fox might have been expected to ride the twenty-five or so miles to the site at Sedburgh. Penn begged him to go to defend his put-upon wife, if nothing else, but the weakened leader refused.[102] Margaret did attend with a daughter and son-in-law, choosing to speak for herself; Penn, who stayed over at Swarthmoor on his way north, accompanied them.[103] Fox may have been too busy with work on his autobiography to attend the meeting. He now realized that this controversy was just another of many that had dogged the movement from the start. "It was for the trial of Friends of their standing to God," he explained philosophically, and "it would pass the way after them who have gone before."[104]

The 1676 meeting at Draw-well, home of a firm Fox supporter, stretched over four days in the April spring, and attracted wide attention. But Fox had little hope for a positive outcome and dispatched a strong antiseparatist letter even as the Quaker factions crowded into the plaster-walled house overlooking the Lune River valley.[105] A broadly worded understanding, capable of being interpreted in various ways, was issued when the conclave ended, but it did not, as Fox guessed, settle the dispute.[106] The two Johns, Story and Wilkinson, visited Swarthmoor afterward, finding the leader in no mood to listen to talk of separation, even though he deemed himself "tender" toward them. In emphatic language, he lectured them about how they had denied the spirit by which they were first convinced and told them that they bore the blood of others whom they had drawn into separation—"that was and is the word of truth," he upbraided them.[107] The Draw-well "condemnation," as the dominant group too hastily termed it, quickly unraveled and itself fostered further acrimony.

The tragedy was that, despite the reams of paper expended in the dispute and the maledictions the participants too readily used, the issues might have been resolved if Fox and his side had made the effort to listen to the dissidents and be more conciliatory. Because the two-sided argument carried on the old debate over the relative weight to give to individual consciences as opposed to institutional arrangements, and because the Quaker movement was marked by original, even revolutionary, ideas, the Friends might have found a new way to move forward. Rogers, Story, Wilkinson, and their followers did not set out to be schismatics. They believed themselves to be continuing along the path Fox had first proclaimed. As Wilkinson expressed it in a memorial to Story, "[F]orms men placed religion in were not only empty and dry, without virtue and life, but also a snare and of evil effect."[108] Many dissidents had no fundamental objection to women's meetings, which had always been accepted in the movement; they simply did not want women's meetings to be instruments of London power extending into the hinterland. Why, they wanted to know, did an arrangement that worked in urban London, giving women a separate and necessary role there in taking care of the poor, have to be extended to rural areas in the north, where travel was difficult and laborious?[109] And they had a point. Story instructed his followers to exclude no one, male or female, from acting on behalf of the poor and sitting in any meeting to set policy on the matter.[110]

Beneath and behind all the fury the schism generated, Fox may have recognized that he had a tiger by the tail, and that he was in no position to ride comfortably but was unable to turn it loose. His ambivalence toward the schismatics, mounting attacks one day, pulling back the next, suggests his realization that the critics did have a point, however much he would not concede it. The next year, 1677, just following the yearly meeting, the heavyweights of the Society issued one of their toughest condemnations against the rebels. Their chosen words, like "obdurateness," "self-will," "pernicious jealousies," "secret smitings," and "evil designs," echoed some of Fox's favorites, but his name was not among the nearly seventy signatures. His striking absence from the long list implied that he wanted no public part of what smacked of an illegitimate effort, though he was certainly present at the postyearly meetings where the matter was discussed.[111] But as First Friend, he still stood against challengers to his authority and the authority of the central bodies in London. What he desired, as he patiently explained the next year, was that Story remain in the "low estate" he was in when he was originally convinced—"low" meaning, of course, that the farmer-dissident should recognize Fox's authority now as he had at first.[112]

Fox could hardly wash his hands of the whole affair, for he confronted the opposition whenever he traveled, though less frequently than in the past. Fortunately for the authority of the power brokers in London, Story, the principal sectarian in the north, died in late 1681, and Wilkinson sank into inactivity.[113] Rogers began circulating some of his exposés of leading Quakers in manuscript. He would produce pamphlets until well into the next century, but he was not as prolific as Francis Bugg. Fox and others hurried to respond to his charges.[114] (Interestingly, James Claypoole, one of the rich and powerful Quakers near the center of power, did not permit Rogers's schismatic views from interfering with their lucrative business arrangements.)[115] In Reading Thomas Curtis held out until 1693, by which time his old companion Fox had died, with the separate meeting lingering on until 1716.[116] The Morning Meeting announced that on principle it would no longer receive money from rebellious meetings, and thereafter increasing numbers of recantations came in from secessionists wanting to return to the fold.[117]

By late March of 1677 Fox felt well enough to leave Swarthmoor and head north to bolster the faithful and ferret out schismatic opposition.[118] Leonard Fell, a longtime Lancashire Friend, and Margaret and her daughter Rachel accompanied him part way. In the rugged dales of Westmorland and western Yorkshire he visited local meetings and attended quarterly sessions, sometimes having to trudge through early spring snowdrifts. It was no wonder that he had to dismount frequently and rest.[119] Three weeks later, the two women having returned home, he was in York and writing of his spiritual exhilaration (and physical exhaustion) at being back in the saddle again: "I am in my holy element and holy work of the Lord! . . . though I can not ride as in days past." His meetings were, he reported, uniformly large, precious, and united. From York, he struck out for the south, aiming to reach London in time for the yearly meeting in early June, although he tarried nearly four days in the immediate vicinity of Drayton-in-the-Clay. He did not feel well, a condition caused partially by the general state of his health but also by the constant demands on his time. More than once his disciples, as well as the need to confer with opponents, kept him up later than he wished; when finally in bed, his head ached all the way down to his teeth. During the course of the yearly meeting, Robert Barclay, who the previous year summed up the establishment's attitude toward the schismatics in his significantly titled *The Anarchy of the Ranters and other Libertines*, had a face off with William Rogers.

Fox remained aloof from that debate, an abstention that epitomized his continuing unease about the struggle. Where he stood was not in doubt—he was with the forces of order against those demanding liberty—but his attitude toward the participants suggested that he realized how his own teachings had fired the discontent. Curiously, despite his numerous epistles and public attacks on the dissidents, he tried to maintain his distance from the formal resolutions that his colleagues in power in London aimed at their opponents. Permitting others to pronounce some of the anathemas, he wanted to remain an avenue of reconciliation open to those who had gone wrong. This stance demonstrated a maturity connected more with experience than age, a result of organizing the movement's early history and reflecting on its meaning. Now he knew—had he ever doubted it?—that controlling the story of the past helped determine the way people of the future would act.

17

❧❦

The Fox Runs as Long as He Has Feet

In April 1683 one of George Fox's female disciples, visiting London from Cambridge, came to see her leader. Ann Docwra had heard from a hypercritical relative that Fox lived as well as any knight in England, was as big as two or three, and spent his time dozing, in a near stupor from liquor and brandies. She found a big man, true, taller than the average, big boned, his face rounded, a bit on the fat side, but not incapacitated, either by liquor or languor. When she approached, he was dining, his fare this day a piece of salty beef the size of a man's hand, his drink a beer flavored with wormwood, a bitter aniselike herb. Docwra declined an invitation to eat—she did not care for the food—though her host, she understood, ate it regularly. He moved stiffly, and his hands and fingers were so puffy he could not write. Fox, feeling her critical eye, told her that she should not look to him but to the light and grace of God in her own heart by which she would see the truth and its enemies. Docwra left impressed.[1]

The scene Docwra described might have been written in at any time during the last fifteen years of the First Friend's life. Except for two brief trips to the Continent and one more visit to Swarthmoor, he spent the bulk of that time in London. His desire to travel, even his deep need to visit supporters, had to give way to the reality of his physical state. His bloated condition, with puffy face, hands, and body, and the juniper berries he used for medication, suggest that he was suffering from what was then called dropsy, the retention of fluids in the body, what we call congestive heart failure.[2] On his worst days he was totally inactive, and even on good days he had far less energy than in the past. But by remaining in the capital he could participate in the decision making of the sect with a minimum of activity.

The presence of Fox's in-laws, the Rouses, just down the Thames at Kingston, and the Meades, near Romford in Essex, enabled him to escape some of the capital's hurly-burly. With each passing year the dissident Quakers posed less of a threat to the London leadership, which gradually consolidated its position. The elder statesman Fox did not stand completely above the struggle, but he contented himself with periodic pronouncements supporting the leadership. His energy level remained high enough for him to dictate regular admonitory epistles, leaving the impression that he was more involved in the administration of the Friends than he actually was. Sometimes, instead of attending committee meetings, he had to be content with sending recommendations.[3] Compared to previous, almost frenetic, years, Fox's activity certainly lessened.

Fox had no home of his own, preferring to stay with various leaders or in-laws.[4] William Meade, a moneyed Friend and something of a sharp dealer,[5] had homes in London and in the nearby countryside,[6] and always made Fox welcome, particularly after he wedded Sarah Fell in 1681. Fox stored books, papers, and personal items at the Meades', a sleeping hammock at the home of another Friend, his saddle and bridle at yet another's.[7] He also farmed out parts of his fortune to those who knew more about investing than he did, and leased his flock of sheep to someone else. One Quaker with whom he often stayed, Benjamin Antrobus, a linen draper, kept £100, or $10,000, to help with Fox's expenses, and the ubiquitous Ellis Hookes oversaw other parts of his business. Like many English fortune seekers, Fox was enamored of putting his excess cash in shipping and sank more than £120 in two barks. He lent better than £50 to two traders from whom he received the profits.[8] The aging Fox took a lively interest in such financial matters, so much so that he was not above importuning members of the Fell family when he wanted them to pay their debts.[9] His interest in money matters led Fox's opponents to whisper, and then shout from the housetops, that he had secreted a portion away from the tithe collectors, as well as advised others to do so.[10] After the king granted William Penn the colony called Pennsylvania in 1681, Penn gave Fox a lot in Philadelphia, 16 acres of land in the suburbs, and 1,250 acres in the back country, but Fox never took up the gift nor profited from it.[11] As he listed these possessions, he carefully instructed his agents to keep quiet about them, aware of the embarrassment this intelligence might cause both him and the movement if widely known.[12]

After the yearly meeting in June 1677, only weeks following his return to London, Fox's attention turned to bolstering Friends on the Continent, particularly in Holland and Germany. Prospects on the other side of the North Sea had long attracted Fox and his followers, and missionaries had early gone to the United Provinces abutting the Zuider Zee, continuing a tradition of close ties between Protestants there and in England. Targeting Mennonites, an Anabaptist group attracted by the tolerant Dutch, the Quakers found that their usual tactics won few converts.[13] Traders did start Quaker meetings in scattered ports along the North and Baltic seas, in towns such as Emden, Hamberg, Lübeck, and Danzig. The small returns did not prevent internal dissension: in fact, small numbers sometimes exacerbated conflict. On almost the same day in September 1676 that Robert Barclay wrote Penn about the need to send someone to Holland to mediate a dispute about registering marriages, Fox was taking pen in hand to advise Dutch Friends to live in peace among themselves.[14]

Thus during the yearly meeting a delegation of leading Quakers laid plans to sail to the Continent. Fox certainly was First Friend, but the stern-looking Quaker contingent's gray clothing covered sterling pedigrees of birth, intellect, and material attainment. The two aristocrats chosen for the mission, Penn and Barclay, had already contributed much to the intellectual defense of the faith.

Accompanying them was Scottish scholar George Keith and his wife Elizabeth; he was perhaps the most brilliant Quaker of the second generation, and she was the daughter and widow of university professors.[15] George Watts, an extremely wealthy member of the Meeting for Sufferings, a Londoner with whom Fox often stayed, also joined the expedition,[16] as did Isabel Fell Yeamans, Fox's daughter-in-law from Bristol. Two prominent Quaker merchants from Colchester with family and trade ties across the water completed the main party. Fox did not miss this opportunity for commerical contacts, directing Sarah Fell to send some iron ore from the Fell forges for him to show around.[17] On July 26, before first light broke, the Quakers' ship raised anchor, reaching the Dutch shore the following night.[18]

The party moved quickly, staying for Sunday meeting in Rotterdam on July 29, and then hurrying on to Leiden, Haarlem, and Amsterdam. Part of the journey was made in a canal boat pulled by a horse walking ahead on the shore, something different enough for Fox to remark on. Neither Fox nor any of the other English leaders could speak Dutch so they had to rely on interpreters. Although some Mennonites came to the appointed public meetings and seemed interested, no convincements occurred.

On August 2 Holland's first quarterly meeting convened in Amsterdam, with converts present from other parts of the country. The distinguished visitors, it now became clear, had come to inaugurate a system of disciplinary meetings parallel to those in England, in hopes of preventing the problems that had plagued the Friends in England. The new church's charter provided for a yearly meeting that would draw Quakers from Holland and Germany, stretching through the Palatine along the Rhine River valley all the way to Lübeck and Danzig on the Baltic Sea. Beyond referring to this broad expanse of territory, the bulk of the rules for the continental yearly meeting set out how to deal with a member who had "walked disorderly." Interestingly, nothing was said about marriage requests having to go before the women's meeting, although the English Quakers affirmed that the authority of the men's and women's meetings originated with God and the gospel. The following day, in what they called a select meeting, one limiting participation to ministerial leaders, the visitors from England suggested that the locals be tolerant of those desiring to register their marriages with the secular authorities, but they did not resolve this festering dispute.[19] Continental Quakers, they decided, might publish any book already approved in England, but should grant to a chosen few among themselves the power to authorize local Quaker publications.

With a nod at dissidents back home, Fox and his cohorts admonished the Dutch to "avoid unnecessary disputes about words, which profit not, but keep in the love that edifies." While counseling unity amid his hosts on the Continent, Fox sent an epistle home to England in which he scolded "loose earthly spirits" among the English Quakers. Some of these spirits were sniping at Fox's traveling companion and close friend, Robert Barclay. The Scottish aristocrat's early release from jail caused other Quaker prisoners to complain that undue influence in high places had gotten him freed in April ahead of them. Fox wrote to remind those still incarcerated that outward suffering was only one kind of suffering, and noted that Barclay, after all, had a great love for the Lord.[20]

The visiting Quaker luminaries split up after the general meeting, with Penn, the Keiths, and Barclay heading east into Germany, on their way to Mannheim on the Rhine, while Fox and a Dutch interpreter turned northward to towns in Friesland and Germany. (Fox wrote a letter to a royal sympathizer, Elizabeth, the half-Stuart princess palatine of the Rhine and abbess of Herford, for Isabel Yeamans to deliver. He was happy that one of such quality would become, in biblical terms, "a fool for Christ.") The few Friends in this region lived along routes plied by English and Dutch traders. The absence of Friends meant that Fox occasionally had to take meals and find a bed in inns they passed. The area contained lots of strict, sober Calvinists, some Baptists, and some members of the Reformed church, many of whom were anxious to dispute with the visiting Quaker.

The low-lying, fertile land was flat as a plate here and stretched off lush and green in all directions. Passing into Germany on their way to Friedrichstadt, a tiny town on the Treene River in Holstein, the party encountered bands of soldiers who inspected travelers at nearly every crossroads. Fox was not impressed with the people of Lower Saxony. He received no positive response from the area's Catholics, long subject to the rule of the bishop of Münster, a prelate depicted in cartoons as half-warrior, half clergyman.[21] Fox labeled them "dark." At Hamburg, the largest city they visited, he found a foolish woman who had spoken against him during the Perrot controversy. He noted that she had paid for her sarcasm, in which she had compared him to Moses, by enduring the plague the dozen years since. At other times summer showers soaked them to the skin as they sloshed along in open wagons.

Friedrichstadt had been founded by Dutch dissenters and had attracted an English Friend. The hamlet, pleasantly sited between two rivers, benefited from its location on the route across Schleswig-Holstein and boasted a flourishing meeting.[22] Here Fox organized separate groups for men and women to allow Quakers to deal correctly with marriages and to minister to the poor. A Baptist preacher made himself irritating with slanderous attacks. As the traveler turned back south, he was more optimistic about the state of this meeting than any others he visited outside the United Netherlands.

Eager to get back to Amsterdam and link up with the Penn mission, the Fox party put in two straight twenty-hour days and covered better than forty miles a day. Traveling in heavy rain, they found themselves having to drive through deep water. Once when their young guide would not go on, the already tired Fox took the team's reins and, helped by stronger Friends holding the wagon back with strong ropes, plunged forward through the rushing water. How pleased this bedraggled and soaked little group must have been when they finally arrived at Emden and boarded a ship on September 5 to take them to Holland.

Travel now became easier for the English visitors. Their boat to Leeuwarden arrived at 11:00 P.M., but the city's gates were closed, and they had to spend the night sleeping on the boat. Penn was waiting for them at Harlington, where meetings for men and women were organized. The English Quakers engaged in a dispute with a Mennonite physician, Galenus Abrahamsz, about the necessity for a messenger of Christ to perform miracles. The implication was that Abrahamsz would be convinced if one of them staged a miracle. Penn carried most of the burden of the debate, insisting that the Christian gospel had been proved once by miracles and needed no further validation. The discussion went poorly, especially because the translators had difficulty in rendering abstractions into Dutch. Though eager to do his part, Fox had to stop several times because he was suffering from shortness of breath, a symptom of his dropsy.[23] Neither Quaker disputant said so, but it was clear that the time for their own miracle working was over: the late seventeenth century was an age for organization, not an age for enthusiastic wonders.

The Quaker party split up again, with Penn returning to Germany, and Fox and his party continuing on to Amsterdam, whence Isabel Yeamans and the Barclays returned to England on September 17. Fox waited for Penn's return, residing at the home of a wealthy widow and early convert, Gertrude Diricks Nieson, who had interpreted for him and was considering returning with him to England. He sent a letter with the departing Friends cautioning English Quakers against the dissidents gathered around John Story and dispatched another letter advising his followers in Danzig to order his books from Amsterdam. On September 26, at the monthly meeting, he must have sensed that the large congregation listening to him was better educated than those he usually addressed, for he admonished his audience that no one could know God's mind by reading or studying history. Almost every day he conferred with a person interested in the Quaker sect or attended a meeting. Everywhere he went he stressed the idea that the gospel of Christ could not be known by "studying nor by philosophy," but only by revelation.

On October 7 Penn and his party returned to an Amsterdam he described as "much alarmed" and marked by "great curiosity in some," presumably over Fox's work. "God's gospel bell was rung," Penn noted regarding the meetings they scheduled. At least one of the private gatherings with some Dutch worthies was carried on in Latin, with the learned Penn and Keith of necessity taking the lead, allowing Fox to enjoy a much needed break. Abrahamsz also showed up for another round of discussions. Penn had some difficulty in making out just what the Dutch physician's point of view was, though he considered him and his followers "the most virulent and obstinate opposers of truth in this land." To Fox, Abramhamsz seemed confounded. As though to respond to his earlier request for a miracle, a woman Fox described as crawling on hands and knees for fourteen years began walking normally; he told her to beware of pride and advised her to be humble and lowly.

Toward the middle of October Fox and Penn left for Leiden and Rotterdam, passing through The Hague, the country's neat little capital, where they got such a poor reception that Penn could only sputter about its lust and pride and pray to the Lord for strength. With more than a hint of sarcasm, Fox labeled it "the greatest village in the world." The last four or five days the English Quakers spent in Holland Fox dictated pamphlets; one was addressed specifically to the Jews of

Amsterdam, a group he remained convinced could be reached.[24] On October 21, 1677, the Quaker party—Fox, Penn, the two Keiths, and Gertrude Nieson and her children—left with about sixty people on a leaky packet boat for Harwich. It turned out to be a rough voyage. Great waves breaking over the small boat washed some sailors overboard, and those remaining worried about their lives.[25] The journey was made easier by the presence of a convivial colonel and some people Fox considered "eminent persons." The passengers finally disembarked, three days and two nights later, on October 23. Fox may have been too exhausted to write his wife, for Penn sent first word to her about the group's safe arrival.[26]

Fox's life hereafter fell into a routine, a wise decision that allowed him to conserve his energy. London became his base, the various Quaker committees his arenas of operation, the homes of family and Friends respites from too much involvement in controversies with the government, other religions, or dissident Quaker groups. As an elder statesman, somewhat above it all, he was listened to with respect by his colleagues, and he knew that his presence in a meeting in the hinterland was welcomed, but he also recognized his physical limitations. It required two long weeks for him to travel from Harwich to London, not only because he proceeded slowly but also because he wanted to visit meetings in that part of the country. At Colchester, an attractive city spread out over the low ground of eastern England, for example, he found a prosperous and flourishing meeting—nearly one thousand people showed up to hear the legendary Fox— and succeeded in convincing some seduced by the dissidents to return to the fold.[27]

In London on November 9, Fox eagerly took up his routine. Practically every night he stayed at a different Friend's home, and he began attending the weekly Meeting for Sufferings, for the first time regularly. His close associates were the men whose hands guided the Society of Friends' decision making: Penn, Whitehead, Hookes, Gerrard Roberts, Edward Mann, William Gibson, John Bolton. Theirs was a community of interest, developed out of long contact and an understandable desire to keep the Society of Friends intact and orderly. Eleven days after his arrival back in London, Fox went with Penn and Gibson to confer with a pair of Buckinghamshire schismatics in a fruitless effort to woo them back.[28] But he just as willingly shifted to others the responsibility of some sensitive matters.[29] He also evaluated manuscripts for the Second Day Meeting. The meeting deferred to him and other Friends with seniority when a particularly controversial proposal came up—such as whether to reprint an edition of James Nayler's writings; significantly, the meeting decided not to, lest they be seen as feeding discontent.[30] He prodded the meeting to make sure that only approved books went from the printers to Quakers in the countryside and to condemn ranterish and atheistical authors masquerading as Friends.[31]

Fox's activities and reputation were such that he epitomized for dissidents all the problems they had with the Society of Friends. To the schismatics, his followers were "the fruit of a dark spirit" and responsible for decisions leading to centralization of the sect,[32] even though he carefully shied away from taking a public role however much he might defend the London center's decisions. In Buckhamingshire, just west of London, a group of rank-and-file Friends adamantly resisted control from the capital and delighted in demonstrating their contempt for the authority claimed for women's meetings. One couple, for example, appeared before the women's meeting but refused to return and hear its answer, and a Daniel Akehurst told anyone who would listen that Fox had been moved by a fake spirit when he set up women's meetings.[33] When Fox came to Thomas Ellwood's home close by Beaconsfield to meet in January 1678, such naysayers, as his *Journal* recorded, aimed their arrows at him but did not hit because of his acuity.[34] But other critics groused that he would not respond to them nor agree to a conference; they worried that he might die and never answer them.[35] And when Fox spoke, he did not give them the sought-for answer: they wanted abjurations and confessions; instead, they claimed, he tongue-lashed them as "whores and rogues, drunkards and swearers."[36]

Fox's activity in the south, particularly in the Wiltshire towns near Bristol in the winter of 1678, was quite tiring. Almost every day he huddled with people who wanted to see him, one day with dissidents, the next with loyalists. Fox and his supporters could never be sure the schismatics would let them use their meetinghouses. He held a number of trying conclaves with his old associate William Rogers, who was busy writing a book attacking the mainstream and rapidly becoming the dissidents' chief spokesman. But Fox did not attend a session that Penn convened on February 1, 1678, in a major effort to resolve the crisis. (Nothing came out of this gathering, other than a lengthy document, parts of which read like a formal treaty negotiated between two hostile powers.)[37] Each encounter seemed more contentious than the one before, and Rogers could not be convinced to desist. Fox thought of him as "a restless, envious, malicious, imperious spirit."[38] The opposition, which seemed irretrievably lost, insisted on publicizing these gatherings, something those in power did not want and Fox deplored.[39] The same thing happened in Bristol after he met with John Story, who broadcast accounts of the encounter as far north as Yorkshire. Fox thought his antagonist distorted their session but agreed that charity was needed on both sides.[40] Both groups understood that whoever controlled the publicity would win the fence sitters, but since the dissidents were in a small minority, their responses hinted at desperation.

Fortunately not all Fox's encounters wore so heavily on him as those in Wiltshire. Whitehead, Keith, Penn, Penington, and a stream of leading Quakers joined with him for periods of time, to be replaced by others eager to be part of what seemed almost like a royal progress. Many of the Friends he visited wanted him to stay longer, and he sometimes had to pull himself away. Wherever he went, he continued to sense, as he told his wife, that "the Lord's power is over all." Still, as February neared its end, Fox decided to end his travels and began to head slowly eastward toward London.[41]

Fox made a noteworthy stop on the way at palatial Ragley Hall, east of Worcester in Warwickshire, home of the most aristocratic convert to Quakerism, Anne, Viscountess Conway. A dabbler in matters esoteric, she attracted an assortment of people who could spark and hold her interest while they took advantage of her fortune, one of them the learned Cambridge Platonist Henry More, another the Belgian alchemist and mystic Francis Mercurius van Helmont.

Judging from More's and Conway's assessments, these pottering highbrows delighted in observing Quakers turn away from their exuberant past and don respectablility—"emerged above that low beginning," as More pointedly put it.[42] When Fox and Friends embraced this lot, they failed to recognize that they were implicitly giving support to the schismatics' attacks on the movement. To his credit, Fox later saw this problem and repudiated van Helmont.[43]

But not yet. George Keith, apparently the first Quaker to meet Conway, recognized in the early 1660s that Platonism neatly meshed rationalism and mysticism to give them an affinity with his new faith. He tried to visit Ragley Hall annually, almost frequently enough to become a member of the Conway circle, and now he introduced Fox into this scintillating group. Fox and the viscountess hit it off well: he and his companions were invited into the lady's darkened chamber—even though her husband rarely enjoyed this privilege—where she, ill and seeking diversion, enjoyed their lively discourse and insisted they stay on.[44] The world-traveler van Helmont, conversant in German, assisted Keith and Fox to answer a book written in that language and then rode with them to a meeting in nearby Stratford-upon-Avon. Fox's sojourn at Ragley stretched over nine days at the end of March, indicating that the years had burnished enough rough edges off the leather-clad old sheepherder to allow him to mingle easily with his social betters.

Fox wanted to attend the yearly meeting in London and moved east to the home of son-in-law William Meade, arriving on May 7. He attended meetings in some places along the way, and visited Friends and associates in others. He stayed overnight at Barnet on the last day of April, where a rush of memories from three decades before must have flooded back, but he remained typically closed-mouthed about his inner feelings.[45]

In the capital, meanwhile, fears were mounting among members of Parliament about the future of the monarchy and, indeed, of the country. Extreme Protestants feared that James, duke of York, Catholic heir to the throne, would try to impose his faith on England and Scotland when he succeeded his brother as king. Speculation about this possibility heightened suspicions that Catholics and other dissenters seeking religious liberty were united in a cabal to overturn the established order. Almost from the beginning of the Quaker movement, its opponents had linked Quakers to Roman Catholics, charging both with subversion. This supposed connection, though laughable from the Quaker perspective, had recently been embraced by some casual observers because of the known friendship between William Penn and the duke of York. By this time Penn rivaled Fox as the most well-known Quaker, so his association with Catholics proved damning for local officials in such out-of-the-way places as Derbyshire.[46] Penn bluntly denied to a parliamentary committee in March 1678 that he was, as he phrased it, "an emissary of Rome and in pay from the Pope." But refusing to be the "common whipping stock of the kingdom," he decried the injustice of the whip raised against both Quakers and Catholics and appealed for religious liberty for both.[47] Defending religious liberty for despised papists only reenforced public notions of Catholic–Quaker collaboration.

Religious liberty for all had long been a goal of Fox, especially after 1660 when he realized that Quakers would not convert the nation.[48] The persecutions suffered at the hands of zealous local officials likewise concerned Friends who came to London for their yearly meeting in mid-May.[49] Fox and his followers struggled now on two fronts, with the more tolerant king against a suspicious Parliament and with schismatics who demanded total liberty of conscience within the movement. Fox gave no indication that he appreciated the irony in this situation: to the contrary, he added to it. Hence when he arrived in London, he went almost immediately to Westminster to argue that Quakers were not Catholics and were not a threat to the state, and to demand that Parliament halt persecution of Quakers.[50] He wrote the king of Poland, pleading for toleration for Danzig Quakers.[51] (So impressed was the king that he reportedly informed his advisers that though they had spent much time and money on education, they "could not write such a letter.")[52] Meanwhile he proceeded to lecture Quaker schismatics again for rallying against his prescriptions. To oppose rules in the church, he insisted, revealed the same attitudes of those in biblical times who resisted the authority of the spirit of God, an authority that emanated, now as then, from holy men of God.[53] Such opponents exemplified, he emphasized in another missive, "a loose spirit" and "a stubborn will," ones, he implied, that would have "man ruling over the woman as Adam did over Eve in the fall."[54] He was convinced that the liberty they desired was a "false liberty, out of light, power, spirit, grace, truth, and the word of God."[55]

After the yearly meeting Fox began a slow journey north, one requiring eleven weeks to arrive at Swarthmoor. He spent some time in Leicestershire and in the western part of Yorkshire. A pleasant surprise was the low level of movement dissent. In fact he estimated that in three hundred miles of travel he found only three Quaker schismatics, at least after leaving Hartford where so-called evil spirits required extended attention. There the issue, which reverberated for another year, involved disorderly marriage procedures and the refusal of some to recognize the power of women's meetings. Fox's advice was forthright: outlaw the obstinate ones. Except for accounts of his set-to at Hartford that beat him north, the rest of the trip was uneventful, and Fox arrived at Ulverston to greet his anxious wife on September 11.[56]

For the next year and half Fox stayed close by. He arrived just as a civil suit involving the disposition of Thomas Fell's estate was going to chancery court, twenty years after Margaret Fox's first husband, once chancellor of the same court, had died. Put simply, the matter concerned whether Margaret's son George, estranged from her because of her involvement with the Quakers, and his heirs owned parts of the estate after his mother remarried. The suit offers a fascinating insight into the willingness of George and Margaret Fox to use a court system to which he attached adjectives like "evil," "corrupt," and "unjust," for their own advantage. They filed a suit against George Fell's son and wife a month before Fox returned to Swarthmoor. The defendants countered by citing the recent excommunication of other members of their family by the bishop of Chester for spurning his authority. Not surprisingly, Fox figuratively thumbed his nose at this churchly annoyance and evinced no open remorse or fear at being formally cut off from the established church. The Quaker heirs of Thomas Fell and Fox won the final judgment: Margaret Fox and her daughters retained the disputed land.[57]

The few surviving letters of this period indicate that Fox worried about the lingering separatism among some Friends, once even having a vision about it. William Rogers had circulated manuscript copies of his book, *The Christian Quaker*, but it was hard to come by in the north because his scattered supporters had to copy it by hand. Containing documents to support its personal attacks, the book was a frontal assault on the London power brokers and others like Fox who, Rogers charged, feared liberty of conscience. Fox orchestrated answers to it, instructing Robert Barclay, a frequent correspondent these days, to stop those "dirty spirits."[58] Eight other Friends worked on a comprehensive response, *Anti-Christian Treachery*, but it did not appear for another seven years.[59] Barclay wrote a handwritten answer to Rogers's book, and no copy survived, but Fox was impressed enough when it arrived in April 1679 that he dispatched it immediately to Bristol. He kept a finger on the schismatic challenge and was elated when he heard that things were going poorly for the outsiders.[60] A letter he sent to Lady Conway suggested that his head had not been entirely turned by her station, for he wrote how pleased he was that she turned from, as he not so delicately phrased it, "this dunghill world of vanity and vexation of spirit."[61]

Fox's stay at Swarthmoor gave him more time to write. Examination of his epistles from this period shows his method. Becoming interested in a topic like, say, the differences between the Old Covenant of the Jews and the New Covenant of Christ, he would write numerous letters exploring the biblical and doctrinal basis of the distinctions he found. He would then publish a pamphlet based on ideas he had first articulated in his letters.[62] Working on a study of marriages, for example, he instructed a young associate in London to search books on the topic, to find out what the apostles and the Church Fathers had said about procedures, and whether a priest was required in the early church to validate a marriage.[63] He then published his book on marriages, with appropriate citations, even page numbers (his researcher got no mention).[64] An indication that Fox realized his books would have more credibility if based on research appeared in a pamphlet he wrote to a Muslim, because he referred to the Koran to support his position.[65] At one point he began to study Hebrew, the better to explore the Old Testament.[66]

Fox did not spend all his time at Swarthmoor. Sometimes he stayed at Marsh Grange on the other side of the Furness Pennisula. In this ancestral home of his wife, separated from the rude world by massive gateposts topped with stone balls denoting the family's genteel beginnings, lived Margaret's daughter Mary, her husband, Thomas Lower, and their growing family of little girls. The youngest Lower daughter was newly born when Fox arrived.[67] Here he could not only play the doting grandfather, but he could also dictate letters for son-in-law Lower to write out.[68]

In early March 1680 Fox took leave of his adopted family for what would be the last time.[69] Perhaps he sensed that he would not return to the north again, for he struck out eastward to York, where he visited Friends who were in prison and attended the quarterly meeting, before starting south for London. Dissent was simmering in York, apparently independent of the schismatics in the west and south, but involving the same issue: the question of how much authority central bodies should have over local meetings and the Friends in them. The point of controversy was that old bugaboo marriage, specifically, the rule that twelve months should elapse before a surviving spouse might remarry. The minority wanted to permit immediate remarriages and raised the broader principle of who was to make decisions, the individual or the men in London laying down the law.[70] Fox addressed this issue in his "brave opportunity" at the quarterly meeting. The body itself wanted to enforce the requirement to wait a year. Fox admonished members to act according to their assigned places in the church. The dissidents paid little attention and established separate meetings. Five years later he was still fulminating that such who created tumult and disorder were serving the devil, for "Christ's government," he affirmed, "is a peaceable government, and there is no strife in it."[71] When one schismatic quoted Luther, Calvin, and the pope against him, he dismissed that tactic as "silly."[72]

Fox went south very slowly, arriving in London in time to attend the yearly meeting in May. He later noted that "many of the dirty spirit" were present, but the majority repudiated them. Flexing their muscles, they would not appoint a committee to discuss disputed matters.[73] Fox took an active part in the Morning Meeting, reviewing others' books, occasionally speaking to one Friend or another about revising something he had written.[74] When warm weather came, Fox visited meetings around London, using the Rous home at Kingston-on-Thames as a base. At Hartford, a center of discontent two years before, he encountered John Story and pointedly attended the local men's and women's meetings to lend them his endorsement.

When Parliament convened in autumn it was gripped by fear of a rumored "popish plot." That the King's brother, James, heir to the throne, was a Catholic fueled fear of all manner of Catholic conspiracies. Stories of bombs in churches, mysterious night riders, and armed Catholics fed popular hysteria, and a majority in the Commons seemed ready to exclude James from the throne. Talk of another civil war surfaced, with the omens serious enough to produce worrying.[75] Fox played no direct role in this partisan infighting. Instead he and his fellow believers lobbied to counter allegations that they were plotters and to end the penalities such accusations occasioned. While Fox formally denied giving aid or comfort to enemies of His Majesty's government, Penn was presenting a petition to Parliament. Quakers, he patiently explained, were safe and sane; they were not Ranters, whom the government might justifiably choose "to rebuke and chastise."[76]

Inevitably, however, Quakers suffered, and suffered doubly, as initiatives on tolerance swung back and forth between Parliament and the Crown, with each of them changing sides on the question and squeezing dissenters in the middle. For example, arrests of Quakers in London and Middlesex jumped from 15 in 1680 to 441 in 1683.[77] The two Foxes figured in these statistics, for in mid-1681 both husband and wife found themselves confronted with a case transferred from Lancaster involving failing to pay their small tithes. With son-in-law William Meade by his side and after seeking the advice of an attorney, itself suggestive of the sophistication Quakers had developed in dealing with the legal system, Fox privately visited all four judges scheduled to hear his case and won a dismissal.

At the 1681 yearly meeting Fox delivered a sermon that was remarkably free of even oblique references to strife, either inside the movement or in the larger society.[78] The problems presented by internal dissenters had not, of course, entirely disappeared. Immediately following the annual gathering Fox sent an epistle to quarterly meetings reminding them that Christ was bishop, king, and shepherd and admonishing his followers to subject themselves to the one who had bruised the serpent's head. The message was obvious: good Quakers followed their leader. The First Friend took the same message to meetings in the region near London throughout the next year. But with external legal persecution continuing, internal disorder seemed less important for the moment.

Thus by 1683 Fox and other Friends were dashing here and there, like a harried fire squad, in an effort to keep meetings open. This response took on nearly heroic proportions as they struggled to gain the right to meet openly. On March 18, for example, Fox found officers forbidding admission to the Gracechurch meeting, so, as he had done two days before, he stood on a chair in the street and spoke to what he guessed were thousands of people, all amazingly quiet and respectful. Meetings held outside that spring and summer became almost more common than those held indoors. Sometimes the assembled Quakers had to worry about citizens who invaded and disrupted their services. Fox was arrested on Sunday, October 7, for preaching at an illegal conventicle and then taken before a judge, but he was promptly released. Now in his sixtieth year, Fox found the constant drain on his physical strength exhausting and noted with appreciation when the Quakers met outside and the constables generously provided a stool for him. Despite his weakness—or perhaps because he showed so much inner strength in ignoring it—his associates testified that his spiritual concern helped produce deep, divinely gathered meetings.[79]

Fox was not well and did not always conserve his strength. After the 1684 yearly meeting, on the spur of the moment, he decided to go again to Holland and attend the annual gathering there on June 8.[80] He reached Colchester on June 1, when a big meeting was planned, but only with a determined effort could he muster the energy to attend. Weakened by a cold, he rested two days before leaving for Harwich and the trip across the Channel. Alexander Parker and George Watts, who had private business contacts in Holland already,[81] accompanied their long-time Friend and made his trip easier. The Dutch Quakers, though few in number, were divided by disputes, and Fox had to mediate, another drain on his energy. He reassured one of Rotterdam's local officials that Friends would not permit his orphaned Quaker nieces to marry and lose their inheritance. It was the desired answer, so Fox rode home stylishly in his host's chariot.[82] Fox stayed in Holland, traveling to Friesland in the north, for about six weeks, before returning to the Meades' home in Harestreet. For more than a month he rested and recuperated from the strain of the trip.

The rest of the fall and winter Fox remained close to London. He still showed signs of excess fatigue, caused by having to deal with continuing problems within the movement. One nagging problem was a dispute between two Quakers over the ownership of part of New Jersey and the policies to be implemented there. Extending back to 1675 when Penn, apparently directed by the London leadership, had tried to arbitrate,[83] the affair dragged on, complicated by the Quakers' inability to govern the colony because they only held title to the land. Fox in early 1680 appealed to Barclay to press his royal kinsman to grant the inhabitants the right to govern themselves.[84] The dispute eroded the morale of Quakers in the colony and led to meeting after meeting among the top echelons of the London leadership in the autumn of 1684 and afterward. Fox's attention to these meetings, like those in Holland, drained his strength, so much so that in the fall he took Sundays off.

Trials for the gradually declining Fox came from all sides. Rumors reached London that Swarthmoor Hall had been invaded by local officials who hoped to force Margaret Fox into calling a halt to the weekly meetings held there. She was fined £100, partially for praying and preaching in her own house, and twenty-four cattle were confiscated.[85] To petition the king and be with her husband, she came to the capital in November.[86] News continued to arrive about official affronts at Swarthmoor, for her son-in-law Daniel Abraham was slapped by an officer as an armed force carted off wheat from the barn.[87] His wife's presence did not change Fox's physical condition: he continued to be weak and unwell. The sufferings of his disciples also continued. One, Richard Vickris, was sentenced to death in Somerset for not attending the Anglican church, although a friendly justice finally freed him on a writ of habeas corpus. Informers swarmed into meetings in London.[88]

Fox did visit some meetings in and about London, although he spoke less and stayed for briefer periods now. But he still found energy to compose more than his quota of epistles to great and small, dictating ten hours one October Sunday, from 11:00 A.M. to 9:00 P.M. Sometimes, as when he and his wife stayed with the Meades, he did not get out of bed all day. In December and January the couple retreated to the Rouses for a month at Kingston, doing little but resting. He seldom walked or rode horseback these days, instead going by coach or chariot sent by one of his well-to-do Friends. On March 16, 1685, Fox escorted Margaret down to the inn called the Swan with Two Necks so she could take the Monday coach north to home. For the sixty-year-old Fox and his seventy-year-old wife, it must have been a sad parting, neither knowing whether they would see each other again.

As the two embraced and waved their good-bys, changes in the wider world portended a markedly new situation for them and the sect they had done so much to nurture. Charles II, whose erratic policies these last years were responsible for releasing wave after wave of persecution aimed at dissenters, died in February. His much-feared brother, the vain James, quietly if grandly ascended the throne, and an anxious Anglican Parliament assembled in mid-May. The new king was eager to grant Catholics and other dissenters freedom both to worship and to take part in the nation's political life, a practical approach reflecting almost exactly what Quakers had long urged. He did not intend to impose Catholicism on his subjects; he believed his faith would naturally win their hearts. But the king's intentions sparked opposition from the majority and fueled more rumors of plots.[89]

Fox quickly began cultivating his contacts with James, instructing Robert Barclay on what to say to the king.[90] Penn used his friendship with James to advantage and concluded that the Friends were benefiting from it.[91] Such activities pointed to a burgeoning moderation in the sect. The leadership did not want to antagonize members of Parliament or other people in the government, even deciding not to report that officials were defrauding the king's treasury of fines levied against the Friends.[92] Fox admonished his followers, as he put it in an epistle, to keep out of "bustlings and trouble, tumults, outrages, quarrels, and strife." But with his unswerving eye focused on the need to be consistent and to stand up to persecution, he also told them to continue to gather in the name of Jesus, regardless of what the law against conventicles might say. Like the 1661 "Peace Testimony," this warning was designed to lift public suspicions that lingered over the Friends because of their supposed association with rebellious elements. Fox's approach to Parliament was to join with members of the Meeting for Sufferings and the yearly meeting to petition that active persecution be halted.

After the yearly meeting Fox, tired from the heat, throngs of Friends, and heavy business, took an eight-week holiday in the country in nearby Kent and Essex. His weakened body, his *Journal* recorded, was simply not "able to bear the closeness of the city." Before leaving, he had to be bled. While on vacation he was offended by some of the current fashions he saw, fancy clothes decorated with gold and costly jewels, revealing clothes that clearly violated the apostle Paul's injunctions that women dress soberly. In condemning this lack of modesty, he cited outward professors like Richard Baxter who looked askance at such displays and quoted one who inquired of a woman displaying her bare neck and breasts, "[W]ill you sell this flesh?" "No," replied the shocked fashion maven. "Then," the professor ordered, "shut up your shop."

Fox's health was not helped when he was pulled into a shadowy but simmering personal and political dispute among those in the higher reaches of the Society of Friends. In 1674 William Penn and William Meade had been defendants in one of the more noteworthy trials in English history, one establishing the principle of an independent jury,[93] but political differences thereafter drove the two apart. Penn was an intimate friend of the king, while Meade was highly critical of James, his Stuart pretensions, and his fellow believer's closeness to the king. To make this matter even more trying for Fox, Meade was his son-in-law, his host on numerous occasions, and a strong right arm in the central organization, where he was linked with such heavyweights as George Whitehead.[94] When Penn, since 1681 proprietor of his own colony in the New World bearing the family name, was absent, the dispute quieted down, but in October 1684 Penn returned to England. Meade began spreading tales, some apparently relayed by a critic in Pennsylvania, Christopher Taylor, one of Fox's oldest Friends. Penn believed that Fox, like others in the inner circle, had been taken in by such rumors and was "very plain" with his elder, at least as he described his tone. That seemed to end the matter, at least for a time.[95] It did not change the reality that Fox remained closer to Meade than to Penn: he saw the former daily, establishing an intimacy he did not enjoy with the latter, who was more a close professional associate.

Still Fox realized that Penn and men of influence like him had played and would continue to play important roles in winning the movement the acceptance he longed for. Thus excitement ran through the Quaker community like a flash fire on March 15, 1686, when James II issued a pardon to all those imprisoned because of failure to attend the established church; as a result of this pardon, upwards of sixteen hundred Quakers saw the free light of day, some for the first time in years. Although this proclamation did not so much indicate the king's principled opposition to jailing dissenters as his wish to split his opponents, the yearly meeting in May was ecstatic. An excited Fox blessed the Lord for King James,[96] though he privately gave Barclay major credit for getting the king's ear.[97] Undoubtedly he told Penn the same thing. "The hearts of the king and rulers have been opened," he exulted immediately following the gathering. But acutely aware of a Quaker tendency to resist authority—the latest examples being those worrisome York Friends, quarreling over marriage regulations—Fox warned, "and let none be lifted up by their outward liberty."

As a matter of fact, most of the schismatics had quieted down. Meetings in York, Bristol, Reading, and a few other smaller places were still divided, true, but many dissidents had abjured their divisiveness,[98] some returning to mainstream meetings, some joining other churches. Yet Fox's epistles continued to dwell on the need for unity in the years following 1685 to underscore his sense that the movement harbored a congenital tendency toward division. For example, in June 1687 he asked the Meeting for Sufferings to close ranks and deal with unrest in London meetings occasioned by what he called "a spirit of separation."[99] He wrote earlier that those who had heard their shepherd's voice should heed the bishop in their souls, as well as the outward elders whence arose spiritual care. John Wilkinson received one of his letters, with a plea that he seek the true light before it was too late, as did one of the Yorkshire dissidents.[100]

The nation too was moving toward more unity, even if, for the king, in an unforeseen and unwanted fashion. In April 1687 James highhandily promulgated a declaration of indulgence for dissenters without leave of a Parliament he seemed to delight in ignoring. The yearly meeting the following month had reason once again to be ecstatic, almost obsequiously so. Penn may have had to wheedle expressions of thanks from other dissenters; but he certainly did not have to pressure the grateful Quakers. They noted the king's "great compassion," his "princely speech," his "Christian declaration," even as they described themselves as "faithful subjects" who promised to pray that he be preserved and that Parliament concur with him. When Penn presented their address to His Majesty, he added his own, more effusive, fillip. The king had found a principle centered on, as Penn put it, "good nature, humanity, Christianity, and the good of civil society," one likely to bring "security to him beyond all the little arts of government," words that James wanted to hear and hoped would come true.[101] Unfortunately for the king, his declaration did not win over Parliament. Within eighteen months his crown was legally transferred to his elder daughter, Mary, and her Dutch husband, William, while James sailed to exile in France. It was, the English never tired of boasting, a bloodless, "Glorious Revolution."

Fox had wanted James to remain on the throne. But he had doubts about some Friends, probably including Penn, who seemed to be corrupted by their proximity to the seat of power.[102] The First Friend also realized that a period of tolerance was not an unalloyed plus. So he warned, just after the yearly meeting, about a "great danger in a time of liberty of . . . ease and looseness and false liberty." Despite fatigue and hoarseness, aggravated by the annual gathering, Fox slowly toured meetings near London, sometimes trying to settle the differences that dogged them. In Hartford, for example, he dealt with dissidents once again and was so wearied that he went to bed for three days at Henry Stout's house. His prayers and exhortations were briefer now, as Fox struggled to keep his weakened body going. He rested fifteen weeks, for the whole summer, at the Meades' house in Essex, and came away so refreshed that he could once again ride horseback, at least for short distances.

By late 1688 Fox's condition was worse. He wore glasses now, and his congestive heart failure was much more troublesome. On one occasion he literally caught himself reeling in a London street and had to be put to bed. He slept little, one day cheery, the next, as his daughter-in-law observed, "perfectly weak." He would go to a meeting, have to leave early, perhaps after just forty-five minutes, and arrive home weary and light-headed.[103] But his poor health did not prevent him from dictating epistles to his followers, more than a few emphasizing one of his oldest themes, that hireling ministers turned people from the true light of Christ in their hearts. Judas, he pointedly emphasized in another, was the first hireling. Fox also took aim at those who had problems with central office regulations on marriages, warning again against any union of first cousins.[104] Having already delineated his wishes for his literary executors, in October he prepared his last will and testament; the previous year, referring to himself as a "gentleman," he had arranged for some recently purchased property near Swarthmoor to go to the Ulverston Friends for a meetinghouse.[105] Aware that news of this gift might lead to criticism, he cautioned against bruiting word of it about, even to all the trustees. Hints remain that Fox was following his wife's sometimes imperious wishes in this matter, for she wanted to keep the Ulverston Friends, who had met at the Swarthmoor Hall since 1653, under her wing.[106]

Despite his strictures against hirelings, a slightly more tolerant side was emerging in Fox's old age. For example, he initiated a correspondence with John Norris, an Anglican priest and author with ties to Cambridge Platonists like Henry More. It was easy to see why Fox found Norris appealing. Depreciating book learning, Norris emphasized the idea that a person should subordinate human knowledge to the light existing in one's soul. Hence he recommended that a blind woman attend to moral development and not worry too much about abstract ideas. But Fox thought that Norris was implying that mere mortals should not talk about wisdom, a position that would end evangelism and all chance of winning converts to Quakerism.[107]

Perhaps Fox's more tolerant attitudes reflected the spirit of the age. In May 1689 Parliament passed an Act of Toleration, granting dissenters the right to worship freely and freeing Quakers from the necessity of swearing to most oaths. Fox had pulled himself out of his sickbed in March to join other Friends, Whitehead and Meade especially, in lobbying Parliament to support toleration. The professionalism with which these once-despised Quakers approached their task was highlighted by the fact that they took a room near Westminster to house their activities. (Penn remained in the background: since the outster of James II he no longer had much clout in matters governmental.) After the yearly meeting in May Fox was again exhausted and retreated to the Rous home at Kingston to recuperate. King William's personal surgeon examined Fox in September before he returned to London for a few weeks on his way to the Meades in Essex. Here during the winter he felt so poorly he could not go the half mile to the local meeting, even in the family chariot; the locals therefore came to the house to hear his brief testimonies. The Meeting for Sufferings occasionally sent proposed public statements to him at the Meades for his examination and approval.[108] Wife Margaret, seventy-six but not as feeble as her husband, visited him in April, making her ninth and probably most wearing journey to London.

As the couple watched their bags being loaded into the Meade chariot on Monday, April 21, 1690, and then left for London, Fox could not know that he would never return. Although he had lately taken to looking backward, he usually did so to examine and learn from the history of the movement he had done so much to shape: he seldom did so to reflect on his own problems. Immediately ahead of him, this year in June, was the yearly meeting and, despite his slowly but steadily weakening condition, some more visits to local meetings. Kingston, and the Rouses, was an obvious destination, and he went there for two weeks in May. On May 29 he even attended a wedding. Margaret departed for home a month later, but George Fox left no record to suggest that he missed her. He went back to Quaker business immediately. "I have stood in the seed and power of Christ," he explained, "and the wicked [and the schismatics] have shot their arrows at me."[109] That statement could easily stand as his valedictory.

◈ ❦ ◈

A Good Life Makes a Good Death

For the next nine months Fox spent most of his time within a small fan-shaped area in London and just to its north, swinging eastward as far as Waltham Abbey and Chesham in the far western suburbs. The handle of this fan lay on the north side of the Thames just off Gracechurch Street, a property on which the White Hart Inn had stood until the Great Fire of 1666 totally razed it. The Quakers purchased this lot and constructed a large meetinghouse, secluded enough from the main thoroughfares to offer the solitude their silent gatherings required. Some of the most prominent Friends in the capital built houses nearby, where, because of their proximity to mercantile and financial centers, they not only lived but carried on their trade. The area, just on the edge of the City, exuded prosperity.[1] The houses were substantial, three or four stories high, with oblong leaded glass panes; and trees added a rich, leafy ambiance to the neighborhood.[2] Henry Gouldney, a young and wealthy Quaker who also owned a home in suburban Hertford, lived in one such house. Fox stayed at both Gouldney residences numerous times throughout the summer and autumn. He attended meetings most Sundays and an occasional session about larger concerns, including lobbying Parliament members, but most of his time he tried to rest. In October he was saddened by the deaths of Robert Barclay, only forty-three years old, and his traveling companion in America, John Burnyeat.[3]

On January 10, 1691, Fox arrived at the Gouldney residence late in the afternoon. It had been a busy week, with the First Friend attending a quarterly meeting and a Meeting for Sufferings. He was tired, but that night he found the strength to dictate a letter encouraging Friends in Ireland to bear up under the fighting that country was undergoing as a result of James II's military efforts to win back his throne. Friends in England, Fox hastened to reassure his readers and perhaps also himself, "are in love, unity, and peace," as they were also in Europe and the New World.[4]

The next day, First Day, Fox went to Gracechurch Street meeting—he and his followers usually called the street Gracious, lest they use the term "church"—and, as he usually did, he preached a sermon and prayed. He assured his audience that he felt well, better than he had for some time, but after the meeting broke up, Fox complained of pain near his heart. It was a cold day, and the cold air seemed to strike his chest; he began to shiver. Still, he remarked to a group as he hurriedly left, "I am glad I was here; now I am clear, I am fully clear."

When he got back to the Gouldneys, only a few doors away, he lay down, his usual habit. Getting up shortly afterward, he found that he felt no better and had to lie back down. When he arose once more, he commenced to groan after a few minutes, his body gripped with cold, but the stubborn Fox had to be forced into bed. Within two hours, by 5:00 P.M., his strength began to fail noticeably. The early winter darkness hovered like a shroud.

Fox sensed that his time was short, and, by way of giving final instructions, he asked to see some of his associates. To them—Penn, Whitehead, Stephen Crisp, and a few others—Fox requested that books and the truth be spread abroad. "All is well," he tried to assure them, "the Seed of God reigns over all and over death itself." But his mind was also on the movement and the unity he had struggled so hard these last thirty years to achieve; thus he emphasized the message that "the Seed reigns over all disorderly spirits." He strained to speak, repeating that the Lord's power was over all. When conscious, he spoke often to Robert Barrow, a Lancashire Friend, who tended him most of the time.

By Tuesday evening, January 13, now into the third day of his illness, Fox was growing weaker, although he did not complain. Five Friends, the most prominent being Penn, lying low because of treason charges, were there. A little after 7:00 P.M., he grasped Barrow's hand and expressed his hope that his Friend would give his love to those among whom he had traveled. Between 9:30 and 9:45, he shut his eyes, closed his mouth, characteristically firmed up his chin, and breathed his last. He did not fight the inevitable and looked as though he had just fallen asleep. "He died as he lived, a lamb," wrote Penn, a bit too charitably, to Margaret Fox, far away at Swarthmoor.

It would have been contrary to Quaker practice to have presented Fox lying in state, but for the next three days, until Friday at noon, Friends found ready admission to the Gouldney home to see the body, "the pleasantest corpse that ever was looked upon," thought Barrow. After the regular Third Day meeting, leaders of the Society of Friends gathered to prepare for the funeral rites they had to endure. This session was interrupted by the tears and groans of men of the stature of Penn and Whitehead, people whose emotions were usually under tighter control. One elderly participant explained that he had buried his parents, his wife, and many children without shedding a tear, but now, "I am overcome," he cried, "I shall never forget this day's work."

On Friday, the meeting room and the courtyard outside were thronged, with the crowd overflowing into Gracechurch and Lombard streets. More than four thousand people had come to the funeral service, so many they had to strain to hear the dozen men who spoke of their departed Friend. The meeting held for two hours. At its end, the body, shrouded in the wool required by English law to discourage imports of linen, and confined in the simple lightweight wooden coffin recommended for heavy corpses by local Quakers,[5] was carried by thirty-six Friends, six from each of the London monthly meetings. Carefully remaining to one side of the streets so as not to disrupt busy foot and coach traffic, the procession walked three by three northward toward Bunhill (Bonehill) Fields, the ancient burial ground the Quakers had purchased in 1661. Two hours elapsed before the last of the long line of grievers made their journey of barely a mile.

Silently they trudged up Lombard Street, passed Threadneedle and Cornhill streets in the financial district, and then moved into Moorgate, turning left into Whitecross Road to enter on the other side of the cemetery. The winter afternoon's dull sun, setting at 4:19 P.M., was almost gone before they arrived. Bunhill Fields already contained the final resting places of such Quaker notables as Edward Burrough, Francis Howgill, and Richard Hubberthorne, and now a fresh grave awaited its newest addition. The good-sized field could not contain the crush of mourners, though the "world's people" present held back and watched from outside. At the graveside five Friends, again including Penn and Whitehead, testified, and the body was lowered into its final cold resting place. "Dust to dust. . . . "[6]

George Fox's death did not close an era in the history of the sect he did so much to form, for the Society of Friends continued to breathe his spirit and life. His successors were destined to relive the contradictions he left them. Even as he died, a dispute was brewing across the water in William Penn's land between George Keith and the religious leaders of the colony, one demonstrating that Quakerism had trouble with the theological right as well as the antinomian left.[7] As Fox's legacy, the Society of Friends reflected both the individual, radical Christian approach he championed, most obviously in the years before 1660, and the determined, more realistic and authoritarian stance he found necessary when dealing with dissidents. Fox was not the kind of man to attempt to resolve the contradictions these two poles implied, and he let them alone, never seriously trying to make them mesh in any logical fashion. Indeed, he never indicated he understood how his own unfocused experiences of the divine spirit fed these two currents; they continued to shape, and sometimes divide, his movement as far as one could see into the future.

This reality, poignant as it might be, did not lessen Fox's essential genius. From his intensely spiritual experience of the inward leadings that he identified with Christ, he fashioned a message that spoke to his contemporaries. This message challenged the (un)established order of the Cromwellian Interregnum in a way no other movement of the time did. Seldom interested in political give and take, Fox had no systematic plan about what to do with his creation and responded in his characteristic trial-and-error way to the challenges that his movement provoked. Fortunately his creativity enabled him and his movement to endure. Uninterested in governing, he did not seek secular power, having faith that the jolts and tugs of the spirit would lead him out of whatever morass he stumbled into. Again, if he did not totally and completely extricate himself, he was able to muddle through, and his institution survived, strong enough to deal with the next crisis. In these ways, too, he was first among Friends. Life, and history, went on.

Notes

Preface

1. Henry J. Cadbury, ed., *Narrative Papers of George Fox* (Richmond, Ind.: Friends United Press, 1972), 96.

2. Norman Penney, ed., *The Household Account Book of Sarah Fell* (Cambridge: Cambridge University Press, 1920), 167, 277, 371, 407, 427.

3. Reprinted in Peter Laslett, *The World We Have Lost: England before the Industrial Age*, 2d ed. (New York: Charles Scribner's Sons, 1971), 36–37.

Introduction

1. Christopher Hill and Edmund Dell, *The Good Old Cause: The English Revolution of 1640–1660*, 2d ed. (New York: Augustus M. Kelley, 1969), 20.

2. Karl Marx, *Selected Writings*, ed. David McLellan (Oxford: Oxford University Press, 1977), 69.

3. The best and most complete study of the radical side of the Reformation is George H. Williams, *The Radical Reformation* (Philadelphia: Westminister Press, 1962). Chapter 4 covers the peasants' revolt.

4. Charles Petrie, ed., *The Letters, Speeches, and Proclamations of King Charles I* (New York: Funk and Wagnalls, 1968), 244–45.

5. Izaak Walton, *The Compleat Angler*, 2 vols., ed. James R. Lowell (Boston: Little, Brown, and Co., 1889), 2:281.

6. Ibid., 2:278–79.

7. Ibid., 2:285.

Chapter 1

1. Population figures in seventeenth-century England are notoriously difficult to obtain. Two figures form the basis of my educated guess here: in 1603 the parish church had ninety communicants, excluding children not confirmed, of course, and in 1670 there were twenty-three households in Drayton-in-the-Clay, which at an average of five to the household would yield slightly more than one hundred people. For these figures, see W. G. Haskins, ed., *Victorian History of the County of Leicester*, (London: Oxford University Press, 1901–), 3:169, 172 (hereafter cited as *VHC* followed by name of county).

2. John E. Booty, ed., *Book of Common Prayer 1559*, (Charlottesville: University Press of Virginia, 1976), 288–89. On teaching the catechism, see George Harford and Morley Stevenson, ed., *The Prayer Book Dictionary* (London: Waverly Book Co., [1912]), 156, 659.

3. On Mason, see Joseph Foster, ed., *Alumni Oxonienses, 1500–1714,* 4 vols. (Oxford: Parker and Co., 1892), 3, and 4:983; C. E. Welch, "Early Nonconformity in Leicestershire," *Leicestershire Archaeological and Historical Society Transactions,* 37 (1961–62): 32, (hereafter cited as *LAHS Transactions*); and T. Joseph Pickvance, *George Fox and the Purefeys* (London: Friends' Historical Society, 1970), 21–22.

4. One authority even asserts that the whole village was in a virtual revolt against the establishment a few years before Fox's birth; see E. K. L. Quine, "The Quakers in Leicestershire, 1648–1780" (Ph.D. diss., University of Nottingham, 1968), 6.

5. William Gouge, *Of Domesticall Duties* (London: George Miller, 1634).

6. Ibid., 602.

7. [Thomas Ellwood], *A Journal or Historical Account . . . of George Fox* (London: N. p., 1694), 1. Unless otherwise noted, I will refer to and quote from this first edition of Fox's *Journal.*

8. John Mayer, *The English Catechisme Explained* (London: Miles Flesher, 1635), 424–36.

9. On this fascinating topic, see Claire Cross, *Church and People 1450–1660: The Triumph of the Laity in the English Church* (N.p.: Fontana Press, 1987).

10. On this topic, see Williams, *Radical Reformation.*

11. Celia Fiennes, *Illustrated Journeys of Celia Fiennes, 1685,* ed. Christopher Morris (London: MacDonald and Co., 1982), 145.

12. Thomas Fuller, *History of the Worthies of England,* 3 vols., ed. P. Austin Nuttall (London: T. Tegg, 1840), 2:225.

13. My description of the area is drawn from Alan McWhirr, "Archaelogy in Leicestershire and Rutland 1979," *LAHS Transactions,* 54 (1978–79): 71; Jenkyn Edwards, *Fenny Drayton: Its History and Legends* (Nuneaton, England: Chronicle Press, 1924), 3; M. W. Beresford, "Glebe Terriers and Open Field Leicestershire," *Transactions of the Leicestershire Archaeological Society* 24 (1948): 101, 105 (hereafter cited as *TLAS*); Joan Thirsk, *Agricultural Regions and Agrarian History in England, 1500–1700* (London: Macmillan Education, 1987), 13; and Joan Allen, *Our George: The Early Years of George Fox, the Quaker: 1624–1645* (Nuneaton, England: Bethany Enterprises, 1990).

14. *VHC: Warwick,* 4:126.

15. Fiennes, *Journeys,* 145.

16. On conditions in Leicestershire and what it was like to grow up there, albeit from a modern perspective, see H. St. G. Cramp, *A Yeoman Farmer's Son: A Leicestershire Childhood* (Oxford: Oxford University Press, 1986).

17. Joan Simon, "Town Estates and Schools in the Sixteenth and Early Seventeenth Centuries," in Brian Simon, ed., *Education in Leicestershire, 1540–1940: A regional study* ([Leicester, England] Leicester University Press, 1968); 4, 14; H. P. R. Finberg, ed., *The Agrarian History of England and Wales,* 8 vols. (Cambridge: Cambridge University Press, 1967–), 4:492; *Magna Britannia et Hibernia* 6 vols., (London: Elizabeth Nutt, 1720), 2:1350.

18. John Ogilby, *Britannia; or, An Illustration of the Kingdom of England* (London: J. Ogilby, 1675), 164; *VHC: Warwick,* 4:172–73; Ann Hughes, *Politics, Society and Civil War in Warwickshire, 1620–1660* (Cambridge: Cambridge University Press, 1987), 10, 20, 81.

19. *VHC: Warwick,* 4:126–27; Allen, *George,* 21–22.

20. Hughes, *Politics in Warwickshire,* 12–17; Allen, *George,* 11.

21. David L. Mosler, "A Social and Religious History of the English Civil War in the County of Warwick" (Ph.D. diss., Stanford University, 1975), 38, 43; Allen, *George,* 11.

22. John Nichols, *History and Antiquities of the County of Leicestershire,* 4 vols. in 8 (London: J. Nichols, 1795–1815), 4:121, 287, map opp. 424.

23. N. Pye, ed., *Leicester and its region* ([Leicester, England]: Leicester University Press, 1972), 104.

24. W. G. Hoskins, "Harvest Fluctuations and English Economic History, 1620–1759," *Agricultural History Review* 16 (1968): 17–19.

25. Alan Everitt, *Change in the Provinces: The Seventeenth Century* (Leicester, England: Leicester University Press, 1972), 36. Everitt ventured that the rise of religious enthusiasm may have resulted from insecurities produced by such shortages.

26. Andrew Charlesworth, ed., *An Atlas of Rural Protest in Britain, 1548–1900* (Philadelphia: University of Pennsylvania Press, 1982), 34–39.

27. On these themes, see the evocative work by Cramp, *Yeoman Farmer's Son*, esp. 43–44, 52–53.

28. E. Lipson, *History of the Woollen and Worsted Industries* (London: A. and C. Black, 1921), 73, map opp. 220; Finberg, ed., *Agrarian History*, 4:218; G. D. Ramsay, *The Wiltshire Woolen Industry in the Sixteenth and Seventeenth Centuries*, 2d ed. (London: Frank Cass and Co., 1965), 15.

29. Thomas Hobbes, *Behemoth, or the Long Parliament*, ed. Ferdinand Tönnies, 2d ed. (London: Frank Cass and Co., 1969), 21–22.

30. *A Gagge for Lay-Preachers* ([London]: N. p., 1652).

31. Thomas Good to Baxter, 9 February 1655, Baxter Papers, 2:92, Dr. Williams's Library, London.

32. On Lollardy, see Cross, *Church and People*, chaps. 1, 2; John A. F. Thomson, *The Later Lollards* (London: Oxford University Press, 1965), chaps. 4, 12; A. G. Dickens, *Lollards and Protestants in the Diocese of York 1509–1558* (London: Oxford University Press, 1959); K. B. McFarlane, *John Wycliffe and the Beginnings of English Nonconformity* (London: English Universities Press, 1966).

33. A. Betteridge, "A Brief History of Free Churches in Leicestershire and Rutland" (Unpublished paper, n.d., Public Record Office, Leicester), 2 (hereafter cited as PRO followed by name of city).

34. T. Joseph Pickvance, "A Man of Vital Religion," *Friends Quarterly* 9 (1955): 146; Allen, *George*, 11.

35. *VHC: Nottingham*, 2:278.

36. A fine study of these developments in Leicestershire is C. D. Chalmers, "Puritanism in Leicestershire, 1558–1633" (Master's thesis, University of Leeds, 1962), 21, 25–30, 61, 65–66, 70.

37. Ibid., 83, 86; Cross, *Church and People*, 148–49.

38. Mosler, "Social and Religious History," 58, 72–73, 77, 126, 135.

39. The most convenient account of Nutter and Purefey is Pickvance, *Fox and the Purefeys*, 6–19. See also C. W. Foster, ed., *Lincoln Episcopal Records, 1571–1584* (London: Canterbury and York Society, 1913), 44; and C. W. Foster, ed., *The State of the Church in the Reigns of Elizabeth and James I* (Lincoln, England: Lincoln Record Society, 1926), xxii–xxiii, xxxi, 47, 298. Apparently Nutter knew some Latin; see the notes of a sermon he delivered after he left Leicestershire in Elkanah Wales, "Notes of Sermons," Add. MS 4933A, fol. 100, Dept. of Manscripts, British Library (hereafter cited as BL).

40. Foster, ed., *State of the Church*, cxxxi.

41. Ronald G. Usher, ed., *The Presbyterian Movement in the Reign of Queen Elizabeth as Illustrated by the Minute Book of the Dedham Classis, 1582–1589* (London: Royal Historical Society, 1905), xxix, 17–18. Nutter's involvement with the Warwickshire classis has suggested to one authority that he had to search outside his county to find a group of ministers with views advanced enough to satisfy his reform impulses; see Chalmers, "Puritanism in Leicestershire," 90–91.

42. For a transcript of the trial, see John Strype, *Life and Acts of John Whitgift*, 3 vols. (Oxford: Clarendon Press, 1822), 3:275–84. The question as to whether Nutter in effect testified for the prosecution is dealt with effectively in Pickvance, *Fox and the Purefeys*, 12–13.

43. Chalmers, "Puritanism in Leicestershire," 97, 100–103.

44. Ibid., 263.

45. William L. Sachse, ed., *The Diary of Roger Lowe* (New Haven, Conn: Yale University Press, 1938), 121.

46. Richard Baxter, *Reliquiae Baxteriana*, (London: N.p., 1696), 2.

47. Chalmers, "Puritanism in Leicestershire," 122.

48. Foster, ed., *State of the Church*, 363–66, cxxxi.

49. Again, on this period, see Pickvance, *Fox and the Purefeys*, 16–19.

50. Ronald A. Marchant, *The Puritans and the Church Courts in the Diocese of York, 1560–1642* (London: Longmans, 1960), 42.

51. John A. Newton, "Puritanism in the Diocese of York (excluding Nottinghamshire), 1603–1640" (Ph.D. diss., University of London, 1955), 32.

52. Wales, "Notes of Sermons," Add. MS., 4933 B, fol. 179–80, Dept. of Manuscripts, BL.

53. Ibid., fol. 203.

54. Ibid., fol. 179–80.

55. Ibid., Add. MS. 4933 A, fol. 100.

56. Ibid.

57. Ibid., 4933 B, fol. 179–80.

CHAPTER 2

1. John L. Nickalls, ed., *Journal of George Fox*, rev. ed. (Cambridge: Cambridge University Press, 1952), 1, 4 (hereafter cited as Nickalls, ed., *Journal*); Gerard Croese, *The General History of the Quakers* (London: N.p., 1696), 12–13. Apparently Fox's mother encouraged him in his "singular temper"; see Nickalls, *Journal*, xxxix.

2. Croese, *General History*, 15.

3. George Fox, "How the Lord by his power and spirit did raise up Friends," in Cadbury, ed., *Narrative Papers*, 9.

4. *A Narrative of the Holy Life, and Happy Death of . . . John Angier* (London: N.p., 1685), 84.

5. Gervase Disney, *Some Remarkable Passages in the Holy Life and Death of Gervase Disney* (London: J.D., 1692), 34–35.

6. Oliver Heywood, *Autobiography*, 4 vols., ed. J. Horstall Turner (Brighouse, England: A. B. Baynes, 1882), 1:153–55.

7. Thomas Beard, *The Holy Seed*, 3d ed., ed. Joseph Porter (London: N.p., 1715), 10, 17.

8. John Bunyan, *Grace Abounding to the Chief of Sinners* (London: J. F. Dove, 1827), 10–11.

9. A. M. Everitt, *The Local Community and the Great Rebellion* (London: Historical Association, 1969), 20–21; *Oxford Dictionary of English Proverbs*, 3d ed., F. P. Wilson (Oxford: Clarendon Press, 1970), 718–19.

10. Allen, *George*, 33–34.

11. Allen (*George*, 33–36) makes more than the meager evidence warrants out of the details available about Christopher Fox. For example, she infers from his title that he

trained apprentices and put out piecework to others. She also repeats a tale that he was lord of the manor of nearby Chilvers Coton in Warwickshire. No evidence supports such suppositions.

12. See, for example, his reference to a jailer cudgeling people as though "he had been beating a pack of wool," in Norman Penney, ed., *Journal of George Fox*, 2 vols. (New York: Octagon Books 1973), 1:126 (hereafter cited as Penney, ed., *Journal*).

13. Finberg, *Agrarian History*, 4:60–61. On houses in the area, see William G. Hoskins, "The Leicestershire Farmer in the Sixteenth Century," *TLAS* 22 (1944–45): 33–94.

There is a photograph extant, taken about 1900, of a since-destroyed two-story, at least four-chimneyed, house locally considered to be Fox's birthplace (copy in possession of the author; see the slightly stylized but mostly accurate drawing after this photograph in L. V. Holdsworth, *The Romance of the Inner Light* [London: J. M. Dent and Sons, 1932], opp. 2). It seems clear from the photograph that the brick and timbered house had been enlarged to almost double its original size at a later date. Judging from its size and configuration, the Fox home had a central fireplace, probably with two hearths, one to heat the public "hall" or living room and one to heat the parlor, where Christopher's loom may have been located. The Fox house was unusual in that it had two doorways, apparently one into each room; this arrangement would have permitted access to the workplace with minimum disturbance to the other part of the house. There were only three windows on the front, two in the upper story, where the family slept, and one below, probably a "fire window" added to give some light to the fireplace area. Of course, there may have been windows in the rear and on the ends of the house, but these are not visible in the picture. On the central fireplace house plan, see R. W. Brunskill, *Illustrated Handbook of Vernacular Architecture*, 3d ed., (London: Faber and Faber, 1987), 106–07, 198.

A contrary tradition persisted in Fenny Drayton until at least 1924 that Fox's birthplace had long since been torn down, probably near the end of the eighteenth century, so it is impossible to prove that the picture depicts the actual house; see Edwards, *Fenny Drayton*, 31–32.

14. On the process of weaving, see R. Patterson, *Wool Craftsmanship through the Ages* (London: International Wool Secretariat, [1956]), 7–11.

15. Edwards, *Fenny Drayton*, 34.

16. Nickalls, ed., *Journal*, 753. One author found up to five Fox children from somewhere; see A. Neave Brayshaw, *The Personality of George Fox* (London: Allenson and Co., 1933), 7.

17. *Journal*, 134–35; Richard Farnworth, *Spirituall Man Judgeth All Things* (London: N.p., 1655), [2]. See *The Works of George Fox*, 8 vols. (Philadelphia: Marcus T. C. Gould, 1831), 2:19, for a formal epistle addressed to his parents. Others exhibited similar feelings toward their fathers. Ellis Hookes, six years Fox's junior, explained on the day before his own sire became terminally ill, "I never knew him so kind"; see Ellis Hookes to Margaret Fell, 1 Oct. 1672, Swarthmore MS., I, 55, Library of the Society of Friends (hereafter cited as LSF).

18. Fox's statement that he came into his birthright "in the other power's days," a phrase he used to describe the Cromwellian period, is the basis for this conclusion; see William Rogers, *The Christian-Quaker* (London: N.p., 1680), pt. 5, 47. Fox also referred to his father in 1655 as an "old man"; see Farnworth, *Spirituall Man*, [2].

19. Richard Baxter, *Reliquiae Baxterianae* (London: N.p., 1696), 2.

20. Northern Warwickshire contained a large number of Lago families, but it has proved impossible to connect any of them directly with Mary. The economic status of the Lagos ranged from substantial landowners to penniless weavers (Joseph Pickvance, letter to the

author, 22 April 1989). For a survey of the region's Lagos, which yields little hard information, see Allen, *George*, 36–39.

21. Nickalls, ed., *Journal*, xxxix. It remains unclear in what areas Mary Fox was accomplished, whether in lineage, education, moral standing, or spiritual insight.

22. Mary Fox died on January 7, 1674 (see entry in "Bishops Transcripts," Fenny Drayton, 103, PRO, Leicester), while Penn did not become a Friend until late in 1667.

23. Nickalls, ed., *Journal*, xxxix.

24. Ibid., 672–73.

25. Ibid., 189.

26. One scholar has remarked on the "feminist" nature of Fox's theology; see Phyllis Mack, "Feminine Behaviour and Radical Action: Franciscans, Quakers, and the Followers of Gandhi," *Signs* 11 (1986): 457–77.

27. "Bishops Transcripts," Fenny Drayton, 135, PRO, Leicester.

28. Baxter, *Reliquiae Baxterianae*, 89.

29. John Addy, *The Archdeacon and Ecclesiastical Discipline in Yorkshire, 1598–1714: Clergy and the Churchwardens* (York, England: St. Anthony's Press, 1963), 21.

30. Nickalls, ed., *Journal*, 1.

31. William Sewell, *A History of the Rise, Increase and Progress of the Christian People Called Quakers*, 3d ed. (Burlington, N.J.: Isaac Collins, 1774), 7. On the family's Presbyterianism, see Pickvance, *Fox and the Purefeys*, 28. Fox continued to try to convince his family. In 1653 he intended that his sister in Leicestershire receive a copy of a paper he was having published; see Francis Howgill to M.F., 1653, Barclay MS., 76, LSF. Much later Robert Barclay sent copies of his defense of Quakerism to the sisters; see Robert Barclay to Fox, 9 May 1679, in *Reliquiae Barclaianae* (N.p.: 1870), 44.

32. *Journal*, 41, 46. His parents may have been among those who considered Fox mentally unbalanced because, as he put it, he "stood for purity, and righteousness, and perfection"; see *Journal*, 46. In 1655, during a visit to Drayton when he stood up to a group of eight priests including Nathaniel Stephens, George did receive a kind of general endorsement for his firmness in debate from his father: "My father, though he was a hearer and follower of the priest, was so well satisfied, that he struck his cane upon the ground, and said: 'Truly I see, he that will but stand to the truth, it will carry him out' "; see *Journal*, 135. A more contemporaneous account suggests that he embellished the story a bit for his *Journal*; see Farnworth, *Spirituall Man*, [3]. So close was Fox in his early years to Presbyterianism that, even after an opening led him to question it, he boggled at rejecting their requirement that ministers be educated; see *Journal*, 5.

33. Norman Penney, ed., *Short Journal and Itinerary Journals of George Fox* (Cambridge: Cambridge University Press, 1925), 13. Once in his travels he came near home, and his family seemed offended and put off with him; see *Journal*, 54. Likewise when Fox's itinerants stayed within minutes of Drayton-in-the-Clay and crisscrossed the area, they never deigned to stop by his former home; see Thomas Taylor to George Fox, 16 March 1655, Swarthmore MS., III, 30, LSF.

34. John Pearson and John Blaykling, *Antichristian Treachery Discovered, and the Way Block'd up* (N.p.: [1686]), 129. No record remains to indicate exactly when Christopher Fox died, but he was dead by 1670, when tax records listed Mary as a widow; see George F. Farnham and Albert Herbert, "Fenny Drayton and the Purefey Monuments," *TLAS* 14 (1925–1926): 104. Traditionally, and after 1660 legally also, a weaver's widow had the right to carry on her late husband's trade; see Antonia Fraser, *The Weaker Vessel* (New York: Alfred A. Knopf, 1984), 98. For averages in the seventeenth century, see Gregory King's table, reprinted in Laslett, *World We Have Lost*, 36–37.

35. *Journal*, 41.

36. Nickalls, ed., *Journal*, 1. It is significant that Ellwood omitted this confession from the first edition of Fox's *Journal*.

37. *Journal*, 3, 5. On at least one occasion he refused to accept money from an admirer and rebuked him for offering it; see Penney, ed., *Short Journal*, 16.

38. As regards Fox's finances, the principal sources outside hints in the *Journal* are Rogers, *Christian-Quaker*, pt. 5, pp. 47–49, and Pearson, *Antichristian Treachery*, 128–29, 131. Rogers, a former influential Friend, claimed that the amount was £1200–1300, but admitted he did not know the precise figure. His charge represented an inordinately huge sum, would place Fox's family in the upper ranks of English society, and conflicts with other things he said and did. On the other hand, by his own admission he did have an inheritance, he seldom if ever earned a living, and he readily gave money away and had to spend a lot on traveling, with little or no evidence of support from the Children.

The discussion of Fox's funds, which in itself was not a major issue between the parties, came up as a consequence of the Wilkinson–Story controversy (See chap. 16). Fox penned a reply to Rogers, but it has not survived, although both Rogers and Pearson quoted from it, the latter in championing his leader; see Pearson, *Antichristian Treachery*, 129. In his defense of Fox, the more circumspect Thomas Ellwood did not mention the question of money; see Ellwood, *An Antidote against the Infection of William Roger's Book* (London: N.p., 1682). Pearson also admitted that Fox's relatives, presumably his brother and sisters, possessed "something" that belonged to him but which he permitted them to keep; see Pearson, *Antichristian Treachery*, 132. Fox gave partial credibility to this last point when, near the end of his life, he began to make arrangement for the disposition of his property. In a letter to his brother John Fox and a nephew, he made reference to the money one of his sisters was holding, money she "had of her father and mother which was mine," as he phrased it. He also implied that the principal was earning interest; see Penney, ed., *Journal*, 2:352. A nineteenth-century biographer, with no indication of how he arrived at his figure, estimated that Fox inherited £800; see Henry Tuke, *Memories of the Life of George Fox*. (Philadelphia: Benjamin and Thomas Kite, 1815), 309. Finally, the size of the reputed Fox home also pointed to the family's healthy financial condition; see note 13.

39. Nickalls, ed., *Journal*, 1.

40. J. F. C. Harrison, *The English Common People: A Social History from the Norman Conquest to the Present* (London: Croom Helm, 1984), 113; Laslett, *World We Have Lost*, 36–37.

41. *Journal*, 2; Croese, *General History*, 13. A recent scholar asserts that Fox attended school in Billesdon, something that simply can not be substantiated; see Brian Simon, "Leicestershire Schools, 1625–40," *British Journal of Educational Studies* 3 (1954–1955): 50. Another author speculates that Fox received only a limited education because he may have suffered from dyslexia, but that possibility is merely an inference from other things known about Fox; see Cecil W. Sharman, "George Fox and his Family, I," *Quaker History* 74 (1985): 4. Atherstone, three miles distant, boasted the nearest school, certainly close enough for him to attend; see *VHC: Warwick*, 4:127. Its master was Obadiah Grew, a well-known Presbyterian dissenter with a master's degree from Oxford; see Mosler, "A Social and Religious History," 38–39. Allen (*George*, 45–48) speculates, with little evidence other than the coincidence of contemporaneousness and proximity, that George Abbot of nearby Caldecote, a member of Parliament for Tamworth, took a lively interest in the young Fox's education.

42. A contemporary reported that Fox "had some smattering of letters, and could write something of a hand, though but little before he was a Quaker"; see William Mather, *A Vindication of Wiliam Mather and His Wife* (London: B. Aylmer, 1701), 12.

43. Alexander Parker to Isaac Penington, 15 Feb. 1668, Penington MS., IV, 5–6, LSF.

44. Baxter, *Reliquiae Baxterianae*, 89; "Bishops Transcripts," Fenny Drayton, 135, PRO, Leicester. Neither of the other two churchwardens was able to execute his signature.

45. Croese, *General History*, 13; William Penn, "Preface," in *Journal*, H2, I2. Naturally critics stressed the lack of learning they found among Quakers. For only one example, see John Gauden, *A Discourse Concerning Publick Oaths* (London: R. Royston, 1662), 9.

46. J. G., *A Just Defense and Vindication of Gospel Ministers and Gospel Ordinances* (London: W. G., 1660), 9.

47. Norman Penney, ed., *"The First Publishers of Truth"* (London: Headley Brothers, 1907), 278. This comment, the only one of its type I have found, may suggest that Fox had some contact with the secret and magic body of knowledge called Rosicrucianism, which emerged on the continent in the seventeenth century and reached England about the time Fox was growing to manhood. On the Rosicrucians, see Frances A. Yates, *The Rosicrucian Enlightenment* (London: Routledge and Kegan Paul, 1972). More likely, Fox's associate, Edward Bourne, read his own views into Fox's statements and reported them later that way; on Bourne, see Penney, ed., *Journal*, 2:384.

48. Nathaniel Smith, *Quakers Spiritual Court Proclaim'd* (London: Langley Curtis, n.d.), 7.

49. Cramp, *Yeoman Farmer's Son*, 100, 102, 137.

50. For examples, see Sachse, ed., *Diary of Roger Lowe*, 15, 28.

51. *Journal*, 2; "How the Lord," in Cadbury, ed., *Narrative Papers*, 9.

52. Nickalls, ed., *Journal*, 2. The tradition that Gee was Fox's master cannot be absolutely confirmed, but it goes back a long way. For one example, see *A Parallel between the Faith and Doctrine of the Present Quakers, and that of the Chief Hereticks of the Church* (London: John Nut, 1700), 5.

53. Margaret Davies, *The Enforcement of English Apprenticeship: A Study in Applied Mercantilism, 1563–1642* (Cambridge: Cambridge University Press, 1956) 6–7, Appendix I; and Lipson, *History of Worsted Industries*, 28–30.

54. *Journal*, 2.

55. For only one example, involving Justices Sawrey and Thompson, see Nickalls, ed., *Journal*, 140.

56. Thomas Ellwood, *An Antidote against the Infection of William Roger's Book* (London: N.p., 1682), 201–2.

57. Francis Bugg, *Pilgrim's Progress, from Quakerism to Christianity* (London: W. Kettleby, 1696), 33; and [Samuel Young], *The Foxonian Quakers, Dunces, Lyars and Slanderers, Proved Out of George Fox's Journal* (London: N.p., 1697), 20. See also Charles Leslie, *Theological Works of the Reverend Mr. Charles Leslie*, 2 vols. (London: W. Bowyer, 1721), 2:355, and [Theophilus Evans], *History of Modern Enthusiasm, from the Reformation to the Present Time*, 2d ed. (London: N.p., 1757), 76.

58. Croese, *General History*, 15.

59. Leonard Mascall, *The First Book of Cattell* (London: John Harrison, 1605), 203.

60. Penney, ed., *Journal*, 1:195.

61. Fox, *To All the Nations under the Whole Heavens* (London: N.p., 1660), 1.

62. Fox, *Concerning Good-Morrow, and Good-Even: The World's Customs* (London: N. p., 1657), 11.

63. Mascall, *First Book*, 233–34.

64. Peter J. Bowden, *The Wool Trade in Tudor and Stuart England* (London: Macmillan and Co., 1962), 17–18.

65. *Journal,* 2.

66. Henry J. Cadbury, ed., *Annual Catalogue of George Fox's Papers,* (Philadelphia: Friends Bookstore, 1939), 31 (item 162A), 33 (item 2A); for the date of Atherstone's fair, see [Daniel Defoe], *A Tour Thro' the Whole Island of Great Britain,* 3 vols. (London: G. Strahan, 1727) 2:132.

67. *Journal,* 3.

68. Ibid.; Sewell, *History,* 7.

69. Nehemiah Lyde, *A Narrative of the Life of Mr. Richard Lyde of Hereford* (London: N. p., 1654), 7.

70. On the war in the region, see R. E. Sherwood, *Civil Strife in the Midlands, 1642–1651* (London: Phillimore and Co., 1974).

71. [William Dugdale], *A Short View of the Late Troubles in England* (Oxford: The Theatre, 1681), 569, 570–71.

72. *A Petition Praying for Reconciliation between King and Parliament* (N.p., n.d.), Broadside.

73. *A True Relation of the Transaction of the Commands of Both Houses of Parliament in the Execution of the Militia in the County of Leicester* (London: N.p., 1642), 1.

74. Baxter, *Reliquiae Baxterianae,* 45.

75. *A True Relation of Prince Rupert His Forces* (N.p., 1642), 1–2; *A Continuation of Certain Speciall and Remarkable Passages from Both Houses of Parliament* (London: N.p., 1642), 3.

76. Everitt, *Local Community,* 12–13.

Chapter 3

1. One defender reported that on a later occasion Fox paused in his travels to work as a shoemaker in Nottinghamshire; see John Whiting, *Persecution Exposed in Some Memoirs Relating to the Sufferings of John Whiting,* 2d ed. (London: James Phillips, 1791), 442.

2. Baxter, *Reliquiae Baxterianae,* 44.

3. *Journal,* 2–3.

4. Hobbes, *Behemoth,* 2.

5. *Journal,* 80.

6. Joan Parkes, *Travel in England in the Seventeenth Century* (Oxford: Oxford University Press, 1925), 256–67. Fox's priest was in exile when he left home, so he would not have been able to acquire a pass even had he tried.

7. For example, Derbyshire lead miners wore leather; see [Defoe], *Tour,* 3:51. On the color of Fox's clothing, see Penney, ed., *Journal,* 1:187–88.

8. Evans and Evans, eds., *Lives,* 52.

9. Sewell, *History,* 14; John Nickalls, *Some Quaker Portraits: Certain and Uncertain* (London: Friends Historical Society, 1958), 19.

10. *Journal,* 171. I have extrapolated Fox's height from a comment in the *Journal,* 224*, that once when he was talking with Cromwell, the Lord Protector sat on a table so he would be as tall as Fox. Cromwell stood about five feet, seven inches; see Antonia Fraser, *Cromwell: The Lord Protector* (New York: Alfred A. Knopf, 1973), 63.

11. [Defoe], *Tour,* 2:132.

12. *To All Freinds and People in the whole of Christendome* (London: N.p., n.d.), 28. Edward Burrough in 1661 made the parallel with Lollardy even more explicit. He catalogued fourteen doctrines, ranging from the assertion that altar bread was nothing more than a common bread to the uselessness of baptizing infants, that Quakers shared with Wycliff's

followers; see Edward Burrough, *Memorable Works of a Son of Thunder and Consolation* (N.p., 1672), 801–4. I am endebted to Joseph Pickvance for calling my attention to this reference.

13. Cadbury, ed., *Annual Catalogue*, 158 (item 5128G).

14. *VHC: Northampton*, 3:12, 24–25, 29; Everitt, *Local Communities*, 13–14; Celia Fiennes, *Through England on a Side Saddle* (London: Field and Tuer, 1888), 96; Committee of Both Houses to Commander of the Army, 2 Aug. 1648, *Calendar of State Papers, Domestic, 1648–49*, 230.

15. Joseph Staines, *The History of Newport Pagnell and Its Immediate Vicinity* (Newport Pagnell, England: C. Tite, 1842), 84; *VHC: Buckingham*, 4:410. There is a dubious assertion, based on absolutely no visible evidence, that Fox's message—whatever it was in 1644 (not 1643, as the author also misstates)—"astonished" soldiers garrisoned at Newport Pagnell; see Reginald L. Hine, *Relics of an Un-Common Attorney* (London: J. M. Dent and Sons, 1951), 150.

16. Staines, *Newport Pagnell*, 80, 92, 94–95. A more recent scholar has stressed the moderation of the troops, the radicalizing influence of the local population; see Anne Laurence, "Bunyan and the Parliamentary Army," in Anne Laurence, W. R. Owens, and Stuart Sim, eds., *John Bunyan and his England, 1628–88* (London: Hambledon Press, 1990), 17–29. Regardless of the source of such influences, they were present in the town.

17. Thomas Edwards, *Gangraena* (London: T. R. and E. M., 1646), pt. 2, 5.

18. H. Roundell, "The Garrison at Newport Pagnell during the Civil Wars," *Records of Buckinghamshire* 2 (1861–1862): 355.

19. Vera Brittain, *Valiant Pilgrim: The Story of John Bunyan and Puritan England* (New York: Macmillan, 1950), 84.

20. Bunyan, *Grace Abounding*, 11.

21. See his comments in Roundell, "Garrison at Newport Pagnell," 357–58.

22. Brittain, *Valiant Pilgrim*, 83.

23. On Hobson, see Edwards, *Gangraena*, 89–92; W. T. Whitley, "The Rev. Colonel Paul Hobson," *Baptist Quarterly* 9 (1938–1939): 307–10; and Richard L. Greaves, *Saints and Rebels: Seven Nonconformists in Stuart England* (N.p.: Mercer University Press, 1985), 133–56.

24. For a fine treatment of the Particular Baptists, see Murray Tolmie, *The Triumph of the Saints: The Separate Churches of London, 1616–1649* (Cambridge: Cambridge University Press, 1977), chap. 3.

25. Baxter, *Reliquiae Baxterianae*, III.

26. Paul Hobson, *A Garden Enclosed, and Wisdom Justified Only of Her Children* (London: James and Joseph Moxon, 1647), 5, 11–12, 22–23, 45.

27. Ibid., 92.

28. At least a correspondent assumed that Fox knew where Hobson lived; see Thomas Robertson to Fox, n.d., in "A. R. Barclay Mss," *Journal of the Friends' Historical Society* 50 (1963): 167–68.

29. Baxter, *Reliquiae Baxterianae*, III.

30. Hobson, *Garden Enclosed*, [iii].

31. Thomas Ellwood, *History of the Life of Thomas Ellwood* (Philadelphia: Joseph Rakestraw, 1808), 133.

32. *VHC: Hertfordshire*, 2: 329–30; John A. R. Pimlott, *The Englishman's Holiday: A Social History* (New York: International Publications Service, 1976), 33.

33. John Bunyan, *The Pilgrim's Progress*, 2d ed., ed. Roger Sharrock (Oxford: Clarendon Press, 1960), 14, 113–14. On the matter of despair in this period, see Christopher Hill,

The World Turned Upside Down (Harmondsworth, England: Penguin Books, 1976), 171–75, and Christopher Hill, *A Turbulent, Seditious, and Fractious People: John Bunyan and his Church* (Oxford: Clarendon Press, 1988), 68, 184–87.

34. On this valuable point, see James Turner, "Bunyan's Sense of Place," in Vincent Newy, ed., *The Pilgrim's Progress: Critical and Historical Views* (Liverpool, England: Liverpool University Press, 1980), 91–110.

35. George H. Sabine, ed., *Works of Gerrard Winstanley*, (Ithaca, N.Y.: Cornell University Press, 1941), 568–69.

36. Carl Bridenbaugh, *Vexed and Troubled Englishmen 1590–1642* (New York: Oxford University Press, 1968), 366–74.

37. Cadbury, ed., *Annual Catalogue*, 36 (item 6,80A).

38. On this point, see Michael R. Watts, *The Dissenters* (Oxford: Clarendon Press, 1978–), 1:187. Another scholar, admitting his conjectures, proposes that Fox may have relieved his sexual frustrations by masturbation at the same time his interest in religion increased; see Stephen A. Kent, "Psychological and Mystical Interpretations of Early Quakerism: William James and Rufus Jones," *Religion* 17 (1987): 262, 272n86.

39. *Journal*, 6.

40. For all this period, see *Journal*, 3.

41. Nickalls, ed., *Journal*, 19. It is true that Fox's vision in 1647 included the victory of an ocean of light and love over the dark tide, but his experiences had not yet matured enough to lead him to the second half of the vision.

42. Quoted in Selma R. Williams, *Divine Rebel: The Life of Anne Marbury Hutchinson* (New York: Holt, Rinehart and Winston, 1981), 27.

43. "The American Journey of George Fox," *JFHS* 9 (1912): 20.

44. See Bridenbaugh, *Vexed Englishmen*, chap. 5; the quote is from 161.

45. Francis Howgill and John Camm to Fox, 27 March 1654, in "A. R. Barclay Mss," *JSHS* 48 (1957): 134.

46. For his listing of errors, see Edwards, *Gangraena*, 18–37.

47. While Fox did not mention his uncle's given name, referring to him only as "Pickering," the most obvious candidate for this designation was the Pickering named William; see William J. Collins, "The General Baptists and the Friends," *Baptist Historical Transactions* 5 (1916–1917): 69; and "Records of the Jacob-Lathrop-Jessey Church 1616–1641" in *Baptist Historical Transactions* 1 (1910): 214.

48. Champlin Burrage, *The Early English Dissenters in the Light of Recent Research* 2 vols. (Cambridge: Cambridge University Press, 1912), 2:311–12; "Records of Jacob-Lathrop-Jessey Church," 215. On this persecution, see also Tolmie, *Triumph*, 17.

49. I follow Tolmie, *Triumph*, chap. 3, for the complicated history of this discussion among London's Baptists.

50. *Journal*, 3.

51. On the General Baptists, I follow Tolmie, *Triumph*, chap. 4.

52. Edwards, *Gangraena*, 81–82.

53. Ibid., 86–87.

54. *Letters of Isaac Penington* (Philadelphia: Friends' Book Store, n.d.), 28.

55. *Journal*, 3.

56. Edmund Calamy, *The Nonconformist's Memorial*, 2 vols., ed. Samuel Palmer (London: W. Harris, 1775), 2:112; Levi Fox, ed., "Diary of Robert Beake, Mayor of Coventry, 1655–1656," in Robert Bearman, ed., *Miscellany 1* (Oxford: Dugdale Society, 1977), 115, 117–18, 136; Watts, *Dissenters*, 1:14, 50, 71; Hughes, *Politics in Warwickshire*, 80, 311. It is fascinating to speculate, given their later strained relations, about the possibility that Fox

had gone to Coventry partially to inform his minister that the coast was clear and he could return home.

57. *Journal*, 3–4; Hughes, *Politics in Warwickhsire*, 311; Mosler, "A Social and Religious History," 198; Baxter, *Reliquiae Baxterianae*, 45.

58. On Stephens, see *Dictionary of National Biography*, 18:1066 (hereafter cited as *DNB*), Calamy, *Nonconformist's Memorial*, 2:112–14; and Nichols, *Antiquities in Leicestershire*, 4:318. In 1664, after losing his living in Drayton-in-the-Clay and moving to Hinckley, Stephens paid taxes on nine hearths, the second highest number in the area, a clear indication of his wealth; see Clifford Thomas, *History of the First Congregational Church in Hinckley* (N.p., 1962), 19.

59. A. C. Bickley, *George Fox and the Early Quakers* (London: Hodder and Stoughton, 1884), 17; Nathaniel Stephens, *A Plain and Easie Calculation of the Name, Mark, and Number of the Name of the Beast* (London: Ja. Cottrel, 1656), 13.

60. Ibid., 252–53, 260.

61. Calamy, *Nonconformist's Memorial*, 2:112–14. For a fascinating suggestion that one Baptist with whom Stephens came into conflict was Gerrard Winstanley, the famous Digger and later Quaker sympathizer who may have visited Drayton-in-the-Clay, see *DNB*, 18: 1066. Stephens also disagreed with John Tombes, the minister noted as the "literary champion of believer's baptism in England"; see Nathaniel Stephens to Baxter, 25 April [no year], Baxter Papers, IV, 158, DWL. On Tombes, see Tolmie, *Triumph*, 53.

62. Croese, *General History*, 19, 23.

63. *Journal*, 4. Fox's comment to Stephens also suggested his early "adoptionist" view of the nature of Jesus: he had to bear the world's sins "as he was man, but died not, as he was God." For a published version of a January 1655 dispute between Fox and Richard Farnworth on the one hand and Stephens and a group of Presbyterian clergymen on the other, see Farnworth, *Spirituall Man.*

64. Much later in a fragment of manuscript—at what exact time it is impossible to tell—Fox dated, as he phrased, the rise of truth in Leicestershire with this period, that is to say, 1644. See Penney, *Journal*, 2:338. This recollection is probably incorrect, given the fact that Fox's nearly paralyzing sense of despair at the time made it highly unlikely that he could convince anyone else of something he had not finally settled on himself and that obviously had brought no relief to his own troubled spirit.

65. Hughes, *Politics in Warwickshire*, 195.

66. D. R. Guttery, *The Great Civil War in Midland Parishes* (Birmingham, England: Cornish Bros., [1950]), 60.

67. D. H. Pennington and I. A. Roots, eds., *The Committee at Stafford, 1643–1645: The Order Book of the Staffordshire County Committee* (Manchester, England: Manchester University Press, 1957), lxxi; *VHC: Stafford*, 3:116.

68. On the New Model Army, see H. N. Brailsford, *The Levellers and the English Revolution*, ed. Christopher Hill (London: Spokesman Books, 1976), 143–52; quote from 148.

69. Richard Hubberthorne, *The Real Cause of the Nations Bondage and Slavery, here Demonstrated* (London: N.p., 1659), 4.

70. Harrison, *Common People*, 203.

71. Richard Hubberthorne, *The Common-Wealtsh's Remembrancer* (London: N.p., 1659), 25.

72. Richard Baxter, *Practical Works of Richard Baxter*, 23 vols. (London: James Duncan, 1830), 1:49–51.

73. *Journal*, 109. The incident occurred in Carlisle in 1653.

74. Baxter, *Practical Works*, 1:94–95.

75. Hughes, Politics in *Warwickshire*, 248, 257.

76. *Journal,* 4–5.

77. Ibid., 5.

78. Philophus Parresiastes, *Enthusiasmus Triumphatus; or, A Discourse of the Nature, Causes, Kindes, and Cures of Enthusiasme* (London: J. Fletcher, 1656), 25–26.

79. Baxter, *Practical Works,* 1:90.

80. *Journal,* 5. One modern authority has emphasized that emotional disturbances can drive the body's blood away from its periphery and thus prevent a person from bleeding; see Warren C. Middleton, "The Psychopathology of George Fox," *Psychology Review* 38 (1931): 310.

CHAPTER 4

1. Sherwood, *Civil Strife,* 209.

2. Austin Woolrych, *Battles of the English Civil War* (London: Pan Books, 1966), 141–42.

3. Stephens, *Plaine and Easie Calculation,* 267. Numerous efforts to connect Fox with such continental mystical groups as the Family of Love or radical Anabaptists, while academically interesting, have been unable to adduce convincing evidence of tie-ins. As Stephens recognized, there was a kind of natural direction to the development of "extraordinary enthusiasms of the Spirit." It would be more accurate to say that rather than intersecting with continental movements Fox ran parallel to them.

4. John Bossy, *Christianity in the West, 1400–1700* (New York: Oxford University Press, 1987), 107.

5. On this theme, see the important work by Steven E. Ozment, *Mysticism and Dissent: Religious Ideology and Social Protest in the Sixteenth Century* (New Haven: Yale University Press, 1973), esp. the "Introduction."

6. Marx, *Selected Writings,* 69.

7. *Journal,* 5. The fact that Fox remembered his opening coming on Sunday morning while everyone else was at church underscored his conviction that his revelation had as much validity as anything going on in St. Michael's.

8. Ibid. Quaker historians beginning with William C. Braithwaithe have tended to deemphasize the sharp rebukes the young Fox aimed at his parents (see his *Beginnings of Quakerism,* 2d ed. [York, England: William Sessions, 1981], 32), an understandable desire but clearly unwarranted by comments such as this one.

9. 1 John 2:27.

10. *Journal,* 5–6. Interestingly, Fox began to claim an authority concerning "Revelation," the same book of which Stephens published his own extensive study. If Fox did not rebel against his natural father, he certainly did against his spiritual one.

11. On this point, see Williams, *Radical Reformation,* and Ozment, *Mysticism and Dissent,* 17–25. The most convenient study of Luther is Roland H. Bainton, *Here I Stand: A Life of Martin Luther* (New York: New American Library, 1955).

12. Arthur Dent, *The Plaine Mans Path-way to Heaven* (London: N.p., 1610), 18–22, 59, 139–40, 203. On Dent, see Maurice Hussey, "Arthur Dent's 'Plaine Mans Path-way to Heaven,'" *Modern Language Review* 44 (1949): 26–34.

13. *Journal,* 8, 17. Indeed, there is one unsubstantiated tradition that Fox had collected followers even earlier, while he was in Newport Pagnell in 1644; see Brittain, *Valiant Pilgrim,* 78.

14. *VHC: Nottingham,* 2, 291.

15. Cross, *Church and People,* 201–5.

16. On the Levellers, see Brailsford, *Levellers;* quotation from p. 10. Quakerism's crit-

ics, of course, were elated to find Levellers among Friends; see, for example, John Ward, *Diary of the Rev. John Ward, A.M.*, ed. Charles Shevern (London: Henry Colburn, 1839), 141. Later Fox publicly condemned the Levellers for concentrating on things of the earth rather than "that which overturns the earth, and . . . raises up the just and throws down the unjust"; see Fox, *A Declaration against all Professions and Professors* (London: N.p., 1655), 4.

17. *Collection of the Works of William Penn*, 2 vols. (London: J. Sowle, 1726), 2:211.

18. On this crucial period, see Barry Coward, *The Stuart Age* (London: Longman, 1980), 192–99.

19. Patrick Collinson, *The Birthpangs of Protestant England: Religious and Cultural Change in the Sixteenth and Seventeenth Centuries* (New York: St. Martin's Press, 1988), 41.

20. Whiting, *Persecution Exposed*, 442.

21. Fox, *To the Councill of Officers of the Armie and the Heads of the Nation* (N.p., [1659]), 5.

22. Joseph Besse, *A Collection of the Sufferings of the People Called Quakers*, 2 vols. (London: Luke Hinde, 1753), 1, 350. Muggleston was apparently rather well-to-do, for at least three general meetings were later held in Swannington, probably at his farm. The seized goods were valued at more than £8, well over $800 in today's terms.

23. Fox, *Works*, 7:126.

24. *Remarks upon the Quakers: Wherein the Plain–Dealers Are Plainly Dealt with* (London: Walter Kettilby, 1700), 2.

25. Quoted in Christopher Hill, *God's Englishman: Oliver Cromwell and the English Revolution* (Harmondsworth, England: Penguin Books, 1975), 64.

26. Fox, *This is to all Officers and Souldiers of the Armies in England, Scotland, and Ireland* (London: N.p., 1657), 2.

27. Richard Farnworth to M. F., 12 Dec. 1652, Swarthmore MS., III, 45.

28. For a thoughtful analysis of the social background of early Quakers, see Richard T. Vann, *The Social Development of English Quakerism, 1655–1755* (Cambridge, Mass.: Harvard University Press, 1969), 47–87. Vann's findings should be balanced by reference to Barry Reay, *Quakers and the English Revolution* (London: Temple Smith, 1985), 20–26. See also T. A. Davies, "The Quakers in Essex, 1655–1725" (Ph.D. diss., Oxford University, 1986), particularly his point that the Quaker missionaries appealed to already existing dissenters, some of whom had already run afoul of church discipline (13–30), and Alan B. Anderson, "Lancashire Quakers and Persecution, 1652–1690" (Master's thesis, Lancaster University, 1990), 78.

29. Emily Manners, *Elizabeth Hooton: First Quaker Woman Preacher (1600–1672)* (London: Headley Brothers, 1914), 3–5.

30. *Journal,* 6–8, 14.

31. See, for examples, *To All that Would Know the Way to the Kingdom*, in *Gospel-Truth Demonstrated* (London: T. Sowle, 1706), 5, and *Journal,* 19.

32. *Journal,* 7.

33. Fox, *Works*, 3:17.

34. James F. Maclear, "Popular Anticlericalism in the Puritan Revolution," *Journal of the History of Ideas* 17 (1956): 443–70.

35. *Journal,* 8.

36. John Bunyan, *"The Doctrine of Law and Grace unfolded" and "I will pray with the Spirit,"* ed. Richard L. Greaves (Oxford: Clarendon Press, 1976), 66–67, 135.

37. [Gerrard] Winstanley, *Winstanley: The Law of Freedom and Other Essays*, ed. Christopher Hill (Hammondsworth, England: Penguin Books, 1973), 230.

38. Fox, *The Great Mistery of the Great Whore Unfolded* (London: N.p., 1659), 63.

39. Bunyan, *Doctrine of Law and Grace*, 13.

40. *Journal*, 8–12. Fox's description and explication of his vision sound like the words of admonitions in his later sermons.

41. Winstanley, *Law of Freedom*, 228.

42. Romans 7:20, 23.

43. *Journal*, 9.

44. Fox, *The Priests and Professors Catechisme* (London: N.p., 1657), 12–13.

45. Baxter, *Reliquiae Baxterianae*, 92.

46. On this theme, see Bossy, *Christianity in the West*, esp. 167–71.

47. Winstanley, *Law of Freedom*, 222.

Chapter 5

1. Regarding the proverb I use as a chapter title, an opponent of Fox used this adage against him a decade later; see J. G., *A Just Defense and Vindication of Gospel Ministers and Gospel Ordinances* (London: W. G., 1660), 9.

2. On this point, see Herbert W. Schneider, *The Puritan Mind* (Ann Arbor: University of Michigan Press, 1958), 70–73.

3. The fullest account of the arrest and trial appears in [John Camm and Francis Howgill?,] *An Answer to a Book which Samuel Eaton Put up to the Parliament* (London: N.p., 1654), 53–55.

4. Penney, ed., *Journal*, 1: 5–8; Fox, *Possession above Profession* (N.p., 1675), 13. On another occasion, Fox assigned joint credit for the term to Colonel Nathanael Barton, a Presbyterian preacher in Derby, who also signed the complaint against him; see Fox, *Cain against Abel, Representing New-England's Church Hierarchy in Opposition to Her Christian Protestant Dissenters* (N.p., 1675), 27.

5. Penney, ed., *Short Journal*, 4.

6. Brian Manning, "The Levellers and Religion," in J. F. McGregor and Barry Reay, eds., *Radical Religion in the English Revolution* (New York: Oxford University Press, 1986), 65–90.

7. Edwards, *Gangraena*, pt. 2, 5.

8. Theodore C. Pease, *The Leveller Movement: A Study in the History and Political Theory of the English Great Civil War* (Gloucester, Mass.: Peter Smith, 1965), 77–81.

9. Nickalls, ed., *Journal*, 392; James Nayler, *Deceit Brought to Daylight: in answer to Thomas Collier* (London: T.L.,1656), 19–20. On Quakers and Baptists, see Craig W. Horle, "Quakers and Baptists, 1647–1660," *Baptist Quarterly* 26 (1976): 344–62.

10. B. S. Capp, *The Fifth Monarchy Men: A Study in Seventeenth-Century English Millenarianism* (Totowa, N.J.: Rowman and Littlefield, 1972).

11. Quote from Hill, *World Turned Upside Down*, 227.

12. Richard Hubberthorne and James Nayler, *A Short Answer to a Book called the Fanatick History* (London: N.p., 1660), 9.

13. Thomas Goodaire to William Dewsbury, n.d., in Henry J. Cadbury, ed., *Letters to William Dewsbury and Others* (London: Bannisdale Press, 1948), 20–21.

14. Winstanley, *Law of Freedom*, 157, 127; Hill, *World Turned Upside Down*, 113–50. For an unsatisfactory attempt to prove that Fox borrowed many of his ideas from Winstanley, see Winthrop S. Hudson, "Gerrard Winstanley and the Early Quakers," *Church History* 12 (1943): 177–94. Winstanley remained close to the Baptists, or at least a Quaker missionary in London in 1654 connected him with them; see Edward Burrough to M. F., 1654, Caton MS., III, 143–47, LSF.

15. Stephens, *Plaine and Easie Calculation*, 267.

16. Burrough to M. F., 1654, Caton MS., 3:143–47, LSF.

17. *A Catalogue of the Severall Sects* ([London]: R. A., 1647).

18. [John Jackson], *Strength in Weakness; or, the Burning Bush not Consumed* (London: J. Macock, 1655), vii.

19. Edwards, *Gangraena*, pt. 1, p. 82. On the Seekers, see J. F. McGregor, "Seekers and Ranters," in McGregor and Reay, eds., *Radical Religion*, 121–29, and in relation to Quakerism, Hugh Barbour, *The Quakers in Puritan England* (New Haven, Conn.: Yale University Press, 1964), 31–32.

20. One sympathetic contemporary, John Tombes, a leader among those opposing infant baptism, claimed to have "good evidence" that Quakers had formally been Seekers; see John Tombes to Baxter, 4 April 1655, Baxter Papers, 2:90, DWL. On Tombes, see Tolmie, *Triumph*, 53, 62, and Penney, ed., *Journal*, 1:448.

21. *Journal*, 6–7.

22. Quoted in Helen Forde, "Derbyshire Quakers 1650–1761" (Ph.D. diss., University of Leicester, 1977), viii.

23. [Defoe], *Tour*, 3:43.

24. On economic conditions in Derbyshire, see *VHC: Derby*, 2:174–75, 331–32; on miner unrest, see Brailsford, *Levellers*, 565–67.

25. *VHC: Derby*, 2:332; *Journal*, 25.

26. Penney, ed., *Journal*, 1:1, 393.

27. On this point, see Barry Reay, "Quaker Opposition to Tithes, 1652–1660," *Past and Present*, no. 86 (1980): 98–120, and Nicholas J. Morgan, "Lancashire Quakers and the Tithe, 1660–1730," *Bulletin of the John Rylands Library* 70 (1988): 61–75.

28. Christopher Hill, *Economic Problems of the Church: From Archbishop Whitgift to the Long Parliament* (Oxford: Oxford University Press, 1968), 144.

29. Harrison, *Common People*, 198.

30. Fox to Margaret Fell, 1653, Swarthmore MS., VII, 103, LSF.

31. *Journal*, 18–19.

32. Woolrych, *Battles*, 150, 158, 160–61; *Journal*, 22.

33. *Journal*, 14–15, 17; Gervase Bennet and Nathaniel Barton to Darby House of Correction, 30 Oct. 1650, *Journal*, 32; *VHC: Notthingham*, 2:292.

34. Alexander Gordon, "George Fox in the *Dictionary of National Biography*," *Journal of the Friends' Historical Society* 2 (1905): 68.

35. *Journal*, 13–14.

36. Samuel Eaton, *The Quakers Confuted* (London: R. White, 1654), viii.

37. Robert Barclay, *The Inner Life of the Religious Societies of the Commonwealth* (London: Hodder and Stoughton, 1876), 261–62.

38. *Journal*, 14–17.

39. [Robert Barclay], *Barclay's Apology in Modern English*, ed. Dean Freiday (N.p.: Hemlock Press, 1967), 256.

40. Francis Higginson, *A Brief Relation of the Irreligion of the Northern Quakers* (London: T. R., 1653), 11–12, 15–16.

41. George Whitehead, *Christian Progress* (London: J. Sowle, 1725), 3.

42. Richard Farnworth to Margaret Fell, Jan. 1653, Swarthmore MS., IV, 83, LSF.

43. Thomas Holme to Margaret Fell, Mar. 1654, Swarthmore MS., IV, 83, I, 189, LSF.

44. *Works of Fox*, 7:23.

45. Penney, ed., *Short Journal*, 8.

46. *Works of Fox*, 7:16, 22.

47. See for examples, George Fox and James Nayler, *A Word from the Lord, unto all the fithlesse* (N.p.: 1654), 9–10; Nickalls, ed., *Journal*, 18, 19, 44, 331, 361.

48. Hugh Barbour and Arthur Roberts, eds., *Early Quaker Writings, 1650–1700* (Grand Rapids, Mich.: Eerdmans, 1973), 204–5. For one of the best studies of early meetings, see Rosemary Moore, "The Faith of the First Quakers: Their Thought and Practice before 1660" (Ph.D. diss., University of Birmingham, 1993), chaps. 2, 3.

49. Penney, ed., *Short Journal*, 2–3.

50. Ibid., 1, 6.

51. *Journal*, 18, 21–22.

52. Alexander Parker to Margaret Fell, 22 July 1656, Swarthmore MS., I, 165.

53. Higginson, *Brief Relation*, 19.

54. [R. Blome], *The Fanatick History: or An Exact Relation and Account of the Old Anabaptists, and the New Quakers* (London: J. Sims, 1660), 115.

55. *Catalogue of the severall Sects.*

56. *Journal*, 22.

57. Ibid., 24–25.

58. *VHC: Derby*, 1, 184; Penney, ed., *Short Journal*, 4.

59. *Journal*, 23–25.

60. Penney, ed., *Short Journal*, 6.

61. *Journal*, 24. On the radical implications of these gestures, see Richard Bauman, *Let Your Words Be Few: Symbolism of Speaking and Silence among Seventeenth-Century Quakers* (Cambridge: Cambridge University Press, 1983), 46–56.

62. On justices of the peace, see Craig Horle, *The Quakers and the English Legal System, 1660–1688* (Philadelphia: University of Pennsylania Press, 1988), 28–32.

63. Ibid., 49.

64. *Journal*, 16–17; Penney, ed., *Short Journal*, 3.

65. Such symbols, particularly church bells, affected other sectarians the same way and led Parliament to forbid ringing them for pleasure or pastime on Sunday; see Hill, *Turbulent People*, 265.

66. By 1652 Fox had elevated this course to the level of a conscious strategy. In a letter advising his followers, he suggested that three or four or six leave the meeting and proceed to any "unbroken places" and there "thresh the heathenish nature" as a true service to the Lord; see Fox, *Works*, 7:22–23.

67. [Defoe], *Travels*, 3:15.

68. Higginson, *Brief Relation*, 13.

69. *Journal*, 26–27; Penney, ed., *Short Journal*, 1–2.

70. On Fox and miracles, see the reconstructive work of Henry J. Cadbury, ed., *George Fox's Book of Miracles* (Cambridge: Cambridge University Press, 1948). As Cadbury makes clear, both Quakers and their opponents expected those who lived in the apostolic age to perform miracles.

71. Penney, ed., *Short Journal*, 2–3.

72. *Journal*, 27–28. A modern authority on seventeenth-century medicinal practices has denominated Fox the best practitioner and a pioneer of such nondirective healing techniques in his day; see Michael MacDonald, *Mystical Bedlam: Madness, Anxiety, and Healing in Seventeenth Century England* (Cambridge: Cambridge University Press, 1981), 217.

73. *Journal*, 28.

74. Tolmie, *Triumph*, 76, 78; Barclay, *Inner Life*, 256–57.

75. *Journal*, 28–29.

76. Hudson, "Gerrard Winstanley," 180.

77. *Journal*, 29–30; on Salmon, see Hill, *World Turned Upside Down*, 217–19, and Richard L. Greaves and Robert Zaller, eds., *Biographical Dictionary of British Radicals in*

the Seventeenth Century, 3 vols. (Brighton, England: Harvester Press, 1982–1984), 3:134 –35. Salmon—"a great enemy of the truth"—"bewitched" some Children later in Barbados, when he slyly eschewed ranterism and enticed Quakers into his camp. "He has gotten the form of truth in words the most that ever I heard any," wrote Henry Fell to Margaret Fell (3 Nov. 1656, Swarthmore MS., I, 66.) Later Quakers, Fox included, would be charged with blasphemy for allegedly claiming divinity.

78. *Journal,* 30–31; Penney, ed., *Short Journal,* 3–4.

79. J. E. Thomas, *House of Care: Prisons and Prisoners in England 1500–1800* ([Nottingham, England]: University of Nottingham, 1988); *Dictionary of Proverbs,* 310.

80. H. Hutton, *History of Derby* (London: J. Nicholas, 1791), 49.

81. Unless otherwise indicated, my account of Fox's imprisonment is taken from *Journal,* 32–53; Penney, ed., *Short Journal,* 4–5; Penney, ed., *Journal,* 1:2–14.

82. *Journal,* 54.

83. See the map of Derby in John Speed, *The Counties of Britain: A Tudor Atlas,* ed. Nigel Nicholson (New York: Thames and Hudson, 1989), 62.

84. Fox, *All Friends everywhere This is the Word of the Lord Unto You All* [London: John Bringhurst, 1683], 4.

85. Oliver Hooten, undated memorandum, Portfolio MS., X, 42, LSF.

86. On Jones, see James Nayler to Fox, 1654, Swarthmore MS., III, 75; Fox to Rice Jones, 1660, Swarthmore MS., VII, 104; Fox to Jones, [1654], Penington MS., IV, 80, LSF; Whitehead, *Christian Progress,* 120–21; William Smith, *Balm from Gilead* (N.p.: 1675), 192; Penney, ed., *Journal,* 1:10–11; *Journal,* 281*–82*. By 1657 Fox was misstating the position he had reported Jones taking in 1650.

87. Anne Conway to Henry More, 29 Nov. 1675, in Marjorie H. Nicholson, ed., *Conway Letters: The Correspondence of Anne, Viscountess Conway, Henry More, and Their Friends, 1642–1684* (New Haven, Conn.: Yale University Press, 1930), 407–09.

88. See the preface to Cadbury, ed., *Annual Catalogue,* iii–v.

89. *A Collection of Many Select and Christian Epistles, Letters and Testimonies* (London: N.p., 1698).

90. Fox, *Works,* 7:16.

91. *Journal,* 38–41.

92. For the best example, see William James, *Varieties of Religious Experience* (New York: Modern Library, 1936), 8–9, who referred to it as the action of a "psychopath and *détraqué* of the deepest dye." Another authority called Fox's antics at Lichfield the work of "a nervous invalid" who obviously needed the services of a physician and a psychiatrist; see Middleton, "Psychopathology of Fox," 296–316. Quaker historians have, of course, exhibited more than a little embarrassment about this incident: some, like William Sewel (*History*), Elbert Russell (*The History of Quakerism* [Richmond, Ind.: Friends United Press, 1979]), John Punshon (*Portrait in Grey: A Short History of the Quakers* [London: Quaker Home Service, 1984]), and Elton Trueblood (*The People Called Quakers* [New York: Harper and Row, 1966]), omit any reference to it at all, while others attempt to explain it away: Barbour, *Quakers in England,* 117, and Barbour and J. William Frost, *The Quakers* (New York: Greenwood Press, 1988), 344, think it reflected "an unconscious memory" or "a subconscious memory" of the martyrdom of two dissenters in Lichfield, one sixty-seven years, the other a dozen years before Fox's birth (Barbour also wants to move Lichfield from Staffordshire into Leicestershire; see *Quakers in England,* 268). Barbour and Roberts, eds., *Early Quaker Writings,* 619, and Brayshaw, *Personality of Fox,* 8–9, speculate that Fox's mother must have told him about the execution of these people, one of them possibly an ancestor, in Lichfield. Cecil W. Sharman (*George Fox and the Quakers* [London: Quaker Home Service, 1991], 75–76) simply writes it off as so unique to account for.

But let Braithwaite (*Beginnings,* 56) have the last word on the matter in his comment on Fox's own attempted rationalization: "This *ex post facto* explanation, with the help of a piece of unreliable history, is of course worthless."

93. Fiennes, *Through England,* 90; Sherwood, *Civil Strife,* 215–16; Charles E. Stringer, *A Short Account of the Ancient and Modern State of the City and Close of Lichfield* (Lichfield, England: T. G. Lomax, 1819), 71.

94. C. H. Josten, ed., *Elias Ashmole 1617–1692,* 5 vols.(Oxford: Clarendon Press, 1966), 2:588, 653, 780; 3:1046. On Lichfield's political leanings, see Council of State to governors of Northampton, Lichfield, and Coventry, 14 July 1649, *Calendar of State Papers, Domestic, 1649–50,* 231–32, and Ra Parker to unknown, 8 Sept. 1651, *Calendar of State Papers, Domestic, 1651,* 416.

95. The fact that there were only two steeples in Lichfield in 1651 contradicts a significant detail as he remembered it and thus serves as a warning about the reliability of his *Journal* as a whole. Either he had been to Lichfield before the war or visited it after the third steeple was rebuilt following the Restoration; he fails to mention any other visit to the town—indeed he implies (*Journal,* 53) that he did not know the name of the place when he came upon it. Only two scholars have noted this discrepancy: one, Henry J. Cadbury, in his *Friendly Heritage: Letters from the Quaker Past* (Norwalk, Conn.: Silvermine Publishers, 1972), 208, did not comment on it; the other, Brayshaw, *Personality of Fox,* 25, speculated that the stump of the demolished spire may have jutted high enough for Fox to mistake it for the real one or that Fox may merely have connected three spires with Lichfield. Two others included a modern picture of the cathedral, with three steeples of course; see Barbour and Roberts, eds., *Early Quaker Writings,* 51.

96. *Dictionary of Proverbs,* 491.

97. James, *Varieties of Religious Experience,* 9.

98. A latter-day disciple found a 1649 reference that a pool of water near Lichfield mysteriously turned red; see Beatrice Saxon, "Notes and Queries: 'Woe to the Bloody City of Lichfield,'" *Journal of the Friends' Historical Society* 41 (1949): 86–87.

99. Bunyan, *Pilgrim's Progress,* 88–97.

100. *Journal,* 53–54.

CHAPTER 6

1. *Journal,* 54.

2. Fiennes, *Through England,* 58–59. Unless otherwise indicated, my account of the northern counties is from the description in Barbour, *Quakers in England,* 72–84, and in Christopher Hill, "Puritans and 'the Dark Corners of the Land,'" in Christopher Hill, *Change and Continuity in Seventeenth-Century England* (Cambridge: Harvard University Press, 1975), 3–47.

3. The point against the traditional easy generalization is made effectively by A. G. Dickens, in *Lollards and Protestants in the Diocese of York,* 1509–1558 (London: Oxford University Press, 1959), 1–7.

4. A. G. Dickens, *The English Reformation* (New York: Shocken Books, 1974), 126.

5. Ibid., 124–28; Cross, *Church and People,* 65–69.

6. Bossy, *Christianity in the West,* 52.

7. The "Introduction" in Dickens, *Lollards and Protestants,* 1–15, is especially suggestive on these points.

8. "Memoirs of the Reverend Mr. Elkanah Wales," Add. Ms. 4460, BL.

9. Richard Hubberthorn [?], n.d., Portfolio Ms., 2:81, LSF. Despite later critics who tried to identify early Quakers with Roman Catholics (see, for only one example, Edward

Cockson, *The Quakers Pedegree Trac'd; or, Some Brief Observations on their Agreement with the Church of Rome* [London: Edw. Ebets, 1703], 51), Fox concentrated his efforts on Protestant dissenters. For the location of Catholic and dissenting areas in the northern uplands, see John Bossy, *The English Catholic Community, 1570–1850* (London: Darton, Longman, and Todd, 1975), 88.

10. Fox, *Works,* 3:11–12.

11. Penney, ed., *Journal,* 1:20–22.

12. Richard Farnworth, *A Discovery of Truth and Falsehood* (London: N.p., 1653), title page.

13. Penney, ed., *Journal,* 1:399.

14. The most recent work on Nayler is William G. Bittle, *James Nayler, 1618–1660* (York, England: William Sessions, 1986), but see also Emilia Fogelklou, *James Nayler: The Rebel Saint, 1618–1660* (London: Ernest Benn, 1931). There is biographical information in James Nayler and George Fox, *Saul's Errand to Damascus* (London: N.p., 1653), 31–32.

15. *VHC: Yorkshire East Riding,* 6:91, 98, 105.

16. Fox's followers were not the only dissenters who opposed the collars and cuffs of proper Protestants. A woman in London, for example, interrupted a preacher with the demand, "Why do you wear cuffs? Neither our Lord nor his disciples ever taught in cuffs"; see S. R. Gardiner, *History of the Commonwealth and Protectorate, 1649–1656,* 2 vols. (New York: AMS Press, 1965), 2:248.

17. *Journal,* 55–56.

18. Ibid., 58–59.

19. Penney, ed., *Short Journal,* 9–10; *Journal,* 61.

20. *Journal,* 64–67; Penney, ed., *Short Journal,* 7; Penney, ed., *Journal,* 1:30–32.

21. Penney, ed., *Journal,* 1:32–33. He was well aware of the need to have a horse if he wanted to impress those who lived in great houses; see *Journal,* 54.

22. Donald Lupton, *The Quaking Montebanck; or the Jesuite turn'd Quaker* (London: E. B., 1655), 17.

23. Thomas Aldam to Justice——worth, [1652], Portfolio MS., XXXVI, 118, LSF.

24. Penney, ed., *Journal,* 1:401; *Journal,* 62–63.

25. Quoted in Tai Liu, *Discord in Zion: The Puritan Divines and the Puritan Revolution, 1640–1660* (The Hague: Martinus Nijhoff, 1973), 121.

26. Fox, *To all that would know the Way to the Kingdome* (N.p., 1654), 5.

27. Fox, *News coming up out of the North, Sounding towards the South* (London: N.p., 1655), 5–6, 9.

28. Fox, *The Glorie of the Lord Arising, Shaking Terribly the Earth, and Overturning All, Until Righteousness Be set up* (London: N.p., 1655), 1.

29. Fox, *An Answer to a Paper which came from the Papists Lately out of Holland* (London: N.p., 1658), 51, 61.

30. *Journal,* 54, 67.

31. Ibid., 67–68. Fox also referred to himself as the son of God in a 1654 letter to Oliver Cromwell (Penney, ed., *Journal,* 1:161, 425), in a statement of charges made against him when he was in prison in 1660 (Penney, ed., *Journal,* 1:381), and in an undated epistle (Swarthmore MS., II, 55, LSF). There is no reason to doubt Fox's explanation here nor to be surprised at the rumors his preaching fed. He naturally wanted to enhance his authority, he did emphasize over and over again that "Christ has come to teach his people," and he could get carried away by the conviction of his special calling. In the 1660 statement he suggested he was "the son of God" because he was "led by the spirit of God." Moreover, other Friends, the most famous being James Nayler, made statements or engaged in activities intended to suggest the same status. Hence such charges were under-

standable and went with the territory whenever imprecise people, filled with the conviction that they had a great mission, set out to convey the depths of their experiences to others; see H. Larry Ingle, ed., "George Fox as Enthusiast: An Unpublished Epistle," *Journal of the Friends' Historical Society* 55 (1989): 265–70.

32. *Journal*, 68–69, 71; Penney, ed., *Short Journal*, 10, 14–15.

33. *Journal*, 70; Penney, ed., *Journal*, 1:402.

34. Penney, ed., *Journal*, 1:38.

35. *Journal*, 70; [Defoe], *Travels*, 3:85–86.

36. *Remarks upon the Quakers: Wherein the Plain-Dealers Are Plainly Dwelt with* (London: Walter Kettilby, 1700), 4–5, 9–10.

37. On this point, see Bauman, *Let Your Words Be Few*.

38. Penney, ed., *Short Journal*, 17.

39. Penney, ed., *Journal*, 1:39–40.

40. Although a number of hills rise higher in the region, an old adage—"Ingleborough, Pendle, and Penigent / The three highest hills between Scotland and Trent"—underscores its prominence; see *Dictionary of English Proverbs*, 404. Moreover, its redundant name, from the Celtic word for hill, underscored its prominence.

41. Some (for example, Nickalls, ed., *Journal*, 104n) have interpreted his statement figuratively, but given the fact that other hills had the same effect and that his words were in character, it is reasonable to take Fox literally; see *Journal*, 256*. William Penn also recounted that Fox shouted as though he had a great audience. *Journal*, Hf.

42. David H. Fischer, *Albion's Seed: Four British Folkways in America* (New York: Oxford University Press, 1989), 622–29, 777–78.

43. On the tithe revolt, see David Boulton, *Early Friends in Dent: The English Revolution in a Dales Community* (Dent, England: Dales Historical Monographs, 1986), 24–26.

44. Anderson, "Lancashire Quakers," 39.

45. On this point, see Margaret James, "The Political Importance of the Tithes Controversy in the English Revolution, 1640–1660," *History* 26 (1941): 1–18.

46. *Journal*, 72–73; Penney, ed., *Short Journal*, 17; Penney, ed., "*First Publishers*," 311.

47. Boulton, *Early Friends*, 27–29.

48. Ibid., 22–23.

49. Penney, ed., *Short Journal*, 279; Penney, ed., *Journal*, 1:42. For a list of Benson's works, see Joseph Smith, *A Descriptive Catalogue of Friends' Books*, 2 vols. (New York: Kraus Reprint, 1970), 1:249–50.

50. Fox, *To the Protector and Parliament of England* (London: N.p., 1658), 61.

51. Fox, *This is to all Officers and Souldiers of the Armies in England, Scotland, and Ireland* (London: N.p., 1657), 3.

52. *Journal*, 74. For Howgill, see Penney, ed., *Journal*, 1:404.

53. *Journal*, 74–75. On Audland, see [William Evans and Thomas Evans, eds.], *The Lives of Early Friends* (Farmington Falls, Maine: Friends of Jesus Christ, 1986–), 1:294–95.

54. John Barclay, ed., *Selections from the Works of Isaac Penington* (London: Darton and Harvey, 1837), 196.

55. See Cockson, *Quakers Pedigree*, 37–38. On this theme, see Reay, *Quakers and English Revolution, passim*.

56. On Camm, see [Evans and Evans,] *Lives*, 287–94.

57. Penney, ed., "*First Publishers*," 243.

58. On Kendal's appearance, see Fiennes, *Through England*, 158–59. On Kendal's importance to the new movement, see Penney, ed., *Short Journal*, 280.

59. *Journal*, 76; Elisabeth Brockbank, *Edward Burrough: A Wrestler for Truth, 1634–1662* (London: Bannisdale Press, 1949), 24; quotation on 25.

60. *Dictionary of Proverbs*, 441. Fox himself was charged with witchcraft in the area a few months later; see *Journal*, 94.

61. *Journal*, 77; Penney, ed., *Journal*, 1:406; *VHC: Lancashire*, 8:281.

62. "John Audland to George Fox, 1654," *Journal of the Friends' Historical Society* 26 (1929): 41.

63. For a listing of the occupations of Fox's leading associates, see Ernest E. Taylor, *The Valiant Sixty* (London: Bannisdale Press, 1947), 42–43.

64. *Journal*, 76.

65. This conclusion is extrapolated from Richard Farnworth to Fox, 1652, Swarthmore MS., III, 53, LSF, and the fact that Nayler was among the first two to follow Fox to Swarthmoor Hall. On this letter, see H. Larry Ingle, ed., "A Letter from Richard Farnworth, 1652," *Quaker History* 79 (1990): 35–38.

66. On Nayler's qualities in these regards, see Bittle, *Nayler*, 5–6.

67. Richard Farnworth, *England's Warning Peece Gone Forth* (London: N.p., 1653), 4–6, 16.

68. Farnworth to Fox, 1652, Swarthmore MS., 3:53, LSF.

69. W. K. Jordan, *The Social Institutions of Lancashire: A Study of the Changing patterns of aspirations in Lancashire, 1480–1660* (Manchester, England: Chetham Society, 1962), 111.

70. *VHC: Lancashire*, 8:269; Penney, ed., *Journal*, 1:47, 406.

71. W. Lampit to John Musgrave, 15 and 16 Oct. 1650, in John Musgrave, *A True and Exact Relation of the Great and Heavy Pressures* (London: N.p., 1650), 20–23. See also B. Nightingale, *The Ejected of 1662 in Cumberland and Westmorland, Their Predecessors and Successors*, 2 vols. (Manchester, England: University of Manchester Press, 1911), 2:613, 624–25, 629–30, 635.

72. For a description of the topography of the area and of Swarthmoor Hall, see Maria Webb, *The Fells of Swarthmoor Hall* (London: Alfred W. Bennett, 1865), 1–5.

73. Margaret Fell, *A Brief Collection of Remarkable Passages and Occurrences Relating to . . . Margaret Fell* (London: J. Sowle, 1710), 2.

74. Howgill to Margaret Fell, 1652, Barclay MS., 75, LSF. Despite strong words, Lampit emerged as much more conciliatory in this interview than Fox depicted him.

75. *VHC: Lancashire*, 8:342, 346, 354; Penney, ed., *Journal*, 1:47, 406; Penney, ed., *Short Journal*, 19.

76. Margaret Fell to [Priest Camelford], [1653,] Spence MS., 3:135, LSF.

77. Sewel, *History*, 117.

78. Ibid.; *Journal*, ii–iii, 77–78; Penney, ed., *Short Journal*, 19 (I have tied together the quotation from the last two sources).

79. Sewell, *History*, 147.

80. Leslie, *Works*, 2:357; Lupton, *Quaking Montebanck*, 17.

81. *Journal*, ii–iii, 78; Fell to [Camelford], [1653,] Spence MS., 3:135, LSF.

82. In addition to her sadness, Fell experienced what she described as a "great heaviness and judgment" after her convincement but before her husband arrived home; see *Journal*, iii.

83. These conclusions are mainly extrapolated from Farnworth to Fox, 1652, Swarthmore MS., 3:53, LSF. Also see Ingle, "Letter of Farnworth." Farnworth was at his home in Balby, Nayler at his in Wakefield; see Farnworth to Nayler, 6 July 1652, Swarthmore MS., I, 372, LSF.

84. James Nayler to Fox, 1652, Swarthmore MS., 3:60, LSF.

85. *Journal*, iii, 78–79.

86. Fox, *Works*, 7:20. Occasionally, Fox referred to himself obliquely as the "Lamb"; see *Journal*, 245*.

CHAPTER 7

1. *Journal,* 79–80.

2. For the traditional view of Fell, see Webb, *Fells,* 422–28; Isabel Ross, *Margaret Fell: Mother of Quakerism,* 2d ed. (York, England: Ebor Press), 3–5; Bonnelyn Y. Kunze, "The Family, Social, and Religious Life of Margaret Fell" (Ph.D. diss., University of Rochester, 1986), 27–30, 89–90.

3. On officers of Lancashire and Fell's appointments, see Robert Sommerville, *Office-Holders in the Duchy and County Palatine of Lancaster from 1603* (London: Phillimore, 1972), ix, xi, xix, xxi, xxix, xxxi, xxxiii, 2, 95; and Robert Somerville, *History of the Duchy of Lancaster, 1603–1965,* 2 vols. (London: Chancellor and Council of the Duchy of Lancaster, 1970), 2:59–60.

4. Blackwood, *Lancashire Gentry,* 94, 141. Fell's purchase of royalist lands underscored his already substantial wealth, for rich Londoners usually outbid poor locals.

5. Records of the Chancery Court of the County Palatine of Lancashire, PRO, London, PL6/26, no. 170. Margaret Fell filed an answer to her sister-in-law's suit and admitted at least some of the charges. Unfortunately, the ink has washed off half the answer, making it impossible to determine her exact response; see PL7/47, no. 50, PRO-L. No disposition of the suit has been found.

6. Webb, *Fells,* 425.

7. Fell, *Brief Collection,* 2–3.

8. Fell to [Camelford], [1653,] Spence MS., 3:135, LSF.

9. *Journal,* iii–iv, 80.

10. Fox to Judge Fell, [1652,] Swarthmore MS., VII, 74, LSF. Margaret Fell seemed to have shared this exasperation when she considered her husband's refusal to embrace one the rest of the family welcomed, in the words of Braithwaite (*Beginnings,* 104), "almost as a new Messiah." In a letter written shortly after the visitor left Swarthmoor, she excoriated an unnamed person who had rejected Fox. "My own dear heart," she wrote to Fox, "though you have shaken the dust of your feet at him who would not receive you nor is not worthy of you, which shall be a testimony against him forever, yet you know that we have received you with our hearts and shall live with you eternally. . . ."; Margaret Fell to Fox, 1652, Spence MS., 3:25, LSF. These sentiments might have applied to the parish minister, but since the letter was signed by every member of the Fell household, including servants, except husband Thomas and son George, it is probable that the unnamed person was the nominal head of the house.

11. Fox to Thomas Fell, 1652, in Cadbury, ed., *Narrative Papers,* 133–34.

12. James Nayler to Margaret Fell, 1653, Swarthmore MS., I, 85, LSF.

13. Margaret Fell to Gerrard Roberts, 21 Oct. 1657, Spence MS., 3:49, LSF. This particular incident dealt with a book Margaret had written, one she feared her husband would think "light of" and try to suppress.

14. Margaret Fell, Jr., to father, [1656,] Swarthmore MS., I, 42, LSF.

15. See, for example, *Journal,* 88.

16. Margaret Fell to husband, 18 April 1654, Portfolio MS., XX, 52, LSF. Perhaps she doubted him, for she braced him up lest he let Fox's letter "lie at thy door."

17. *Journal,* iv, 80.

18. See, for examples, A. Parker to Margaret Fell, 22 Feb. 1655 and 17 Feb. 1657, Caton MS., 3:258–64, 305–06; and 21 July 1655, Swarthmore MS., I, 162, LSF.

19. Thomas Aldam to Fell, 1653, Swarthmore MS., III, 41, LSF.

20. *Journal,* 81.

21. On this point, see Kunze, "Family, Social and Religious Life," 40–42, 87. The available evidence simply does not offer much insight into the Fells' relationship before 1652.

22. Nayler to Margaret Fell, 1652, Swarthmore MS., 3:192, LSF.

23. Nayler to Margaret Fell, 26 Oct. 1652, Swarthmore MS., 3:2, LSF.

24. Farnworth to Margaret Fell, 12 Dec. 1652, Swarthmore MS., 3:45, LSF.

25. Fox to Margaret Fell, 1653, 7:42; Fox to [M.F.,] 1653, Swarthmore MS., VII, 103, LSF.

26. Taylor to Fox, 18 May 1653, Swarthmore MS., 3:29, LSF.

27. Aldam to Margaret Fell, 30 Oct. 1654, Swarthmore MS., IV, 89, LSF.

28. Margaret Fell to Thomas Fell, 18 Feb. 1653, Portfolio MS., XX, 52, LSF.

29. Daniel Fleming to J. Williamson, 28 Jan. 1664, in Norman Penney, ed., *Extracts from State Papers Relating to Friends, 1654 to 1672* (London: Headley Bros., 1913), 188–89.

30. Fox to Ulverston, 1652, in Penney, ed., *Journal*, 1:99–101.

31. *Journal*, 85–86.

32. On the two, see Penney, *Journal*, 1:61–62, 408, 409. The precise charges appear in Russell S. Mortimer, "Allegations against George Fox by ministers in North Lancashire," *Journal of the Friends' Historical Society* 39 (1947): 15–17.

33. Penney, ed., *Journal*, 1:72.

34. See their petition to the Council of State in Fox, James Nayler, and John Lawson, *Saul's Errand to Damascus*, in Fox, *Works*, 3:587–88. The words of this petition were being used as late as 1696 to attack Quakers; see Francis Bugg, *The Quakers Set in their true Light* (London: C. Brome, 1696), 9.

35. Higginson, *Brief Relation*, 32.

36. Fox's answers are in his *Works*, 3:588–97. According to one source, Fox's statement that he was equal to God, the basis of the charge, was made in a private session with one of Lancaster's most prominent ministers: no witnesses, no conviction; see Higginson, *Brief Relation*, 2.

37. Fox, *Works*, 3:586–87.

38. Somerville, *Office-Holders*, 2.

39. Fox, *Works*, 3:592, 597.

40. *Journal*, 89–90, 92. The mayor apparently was not firmly convinced; see Penney, ed., *Journal*, 1:413.

41. These letters, as well as similar ones, are in *Journal*, 94–101.

42. A number of 1652 and 1653 epistles were written in this period. Epistle 20 is dated at Swarthmoor, 31 Jan. 1653; see Fox, *Works*, 7:27–29. On the date, see Braithwaite, *Beginnings*, 116n3.

43. Thomas Hunter to Fox, 14 Mar. 1653, Swarthmore MS., IV, 209, LSF.

44. Fox, *Works*, 7:43–45, 48–49.

45. *Journal*, 102–5.

46. The question of when Fox disturbed church services has received more attention than it deserves. Legally, and as an accepted practice in most Protestant parishes, laity could speak to the congregation after all the sand had run through the minister's hour glass (See Braithwaite, *Beginnings*, 133; Penney, ed., *Journal*, 1:400). In an effort to deemphasize the unrest the radically unconventional Fox brought to villages and towns, he and his followers often found it expedient to stress that both the legal authorities and the vigilantes who opposed and attacked them were reacting to their message, not to any violation of the law. Thus, for example, of three sources that describe what happened at Bootle, only one, and that closest to the event, mentions that Fox, as he put it, "was moved to speak in his [the minister's] time"; see Penney, ed., *Short Journal*, 27. The other two suppress this vital detail; see *Journal*, 104; Penney, ed., *Journal*, 1:108. Clearly the Fox of the mid-1670s and later editors decided that the unruly and illegal activities of twenty years earlier were an embarrassment that might better be forgotten. This practice has

continued among commentators; see, for examples, Penney, ed., *Short Journal*, 284; Barclay, *Inner Life*, 274–79; and *John Stephenson Rowntree: His Life and Work* (London: Headley Brothers, 1908), 387–88. The fact is that Fox (and other Quakers), in this instance as in others, readily broke the law whenever they thought the situation to require it.

47. Most likely the substance of Fox's attack can be found in Epistle 38, which was written about this time, uses the same phrases, and propounds the kind of rhetorical questions ideally suited for an oral appeal against the ministry: "Now all people, take notice! . . . Who are the hirelings now, whom the scriptures speak of? . . . Who seek for the fleece, and clothe themselves with the wool now, and so make a prey of the people? Where are the hirelings now? The priests preach for hire, and the prophets prophesy for money"; see Fox, *Works*, 7:46. The parallel illustrates that Fox's writings were often published versions of what he said orally.

48. Penney, ed., *Short Journal*, 27–28.

49. Penney, ed., *Journal*, 1:96–98. Fox stressed that a law that violated a pure conscience was against God.

50. Fiennes, *Illustrated Journeys*, 169.

51. *Journal*, 106–8; Penney, ed., *Short Journal*, 30.

52. Fischer, *Albion's Seed*, 771.

53. Colonel Charles Howard, fined £4,000 for warring against Parliament, now snuggled up to his former opponents and became governor of Carlisle; see *VHC: Cumberland*, 2:292.

54. Ibid., 2:94–95.

55. On the city, see Fiennes, *Illustrated Journeys*, 172.

56. See the chamberlain's account reprinted in Nightingale, *Ejected*, 1:179.

57. *Journal*, 108–10; Penney, ed., *Journal*, 1:114–16, 417; Penney, ed., *Short Journal*, 31–33, 285.

58. *Journal*, 110.

59. George Taylor, memorandum, 1654, Swarthmore MS., I, 215, LSF.

60. *Journal*, 110–13, 117. On jails and jailers, see Horle, *Quakers and Legal System*, 33–34, 147–49.

61. *Journal*, 113–17.

62. Penney, ed., *Journal*, 1:116–20, 126.

63. *Journal*, 114–15; Penney, ed., *Journal*, 1:418–19.

64. Penney ed., *Journal*, 1:79–85.

65. Ibid., 1:127–30.

66. Isaac Penington, *A Voyce out of the Thick Darknesse* (London: N.p., 1650), preface, A3ff.

67. *VHC: Cumberland*, 2:95, 482.

68. Coward, *Stuart Age*, 219, 222–25.

69. The *Querers and Quakers Cause at the Second Hearing* (London: I. G., 1653), 45.

70. *Journal*, 119.

71. Fox, *Works*, 7:50.

72. Penney, ed., *Short Journal*, 34.

73. In addition to Fox's *Journal*, see Nayler to Margaret Fell, 1654, Swarthmore MS., III, 6; Richard Farnworth to Margaret Fell, 12 Feb. 1652, Swarthmore MS., III, 45; George Whitehead to Fox, 1653, Swarthmore MS., IV, 90, LSF. Farnworth reported that soldiers surrounded Friends so they might safely read their epistles.

74. In addition to Fox's *Journal*, see Nayler to Fox, 1653, Swarthmore MS., IV, 71, and John Stubbs to Elizabeth Stubbs, n.d., Swarthmore MS., IV, 160, LSF.

75. *Journal,* 118.

76. Farnworth to Brethren, 1653, Swarthmore MS., IV, 229, LSF.

77. See Higginson, *Brief Relation,* 29. Critics, of course, demanded miracles as proof of God's favor (see Samuel Eaton, *The Quakers Confuted* [London: R. White, 1654], 14) but refused to accept them.

78. Penney, ed., *Journal,* 1:348. On this topic, the most thorough study is Cadbury, *Fox's Book of Miracles,* esp. 38–44, 95.

79. Fox, *Works,* 3:37.

80. Fiennes, *Illustrated Journeys,* 168.

81. Penney, ed., *Journal,* 1:140–41; Cadbury, *Fox's Book of Miracles,* 125.

82. Nayler to Fox, 1652, Swarthmore MS., 3:60, LSF.

83. *Journal,* 103.

84. Ibid., 127–28.

85. Fox, *Works,* 7:51.

86. Ibid., 53.

87. Ibid., 56.

88. Ibid., 58.

89. Ibid., 43.

90. Ibid., 67.

91. Ibid., 61–62. In the text "meet" is "met," an obvious mistake.

92. Fox, *Works,* 7:38.

93. Fox's epistles often included references to, as he put it in one, "Friends everywhere abroad scattered"; see, for example, *Journal,* 125.

94. Who, for one instance, was the Thomas Hunter in Northumberland in 1653? See Hunter to Fox, 14 March 1653, Swarthmore MS., IV, 209, LSF.

95. "Setting up menes meeting in Bishoprick," [April] 1653, Swarthmore MS., II, 17; Margaret Fell to friends, 1654, Thirnbeck MS., 1, LSF.

96. At one point, perhaps as early as 1653 (see Cadbury, ed., *Annual Catalogue,* 40 [item 19, 10A]), Fox did recommend that general meetings adjudicate differences between members in particular meetings; see Fox to Friends of the Truth, n.d., Thompson MS., 55–56, LSF. My view is that the early date is suspect.

97. "Setting up menes meeting in Bishoprick," [April] 1653, Swarthmore MS., II, 17, LSF. The sixteen male signatories also said "great sums of money" were needed and proposed a collection the next Sunday.

98. Fox to Rice Jones, [1654,] Penington MS., IV, 80, LSF; Penney, ed., *Journal,* 1:147.

99. One of the few statements on the early Quaker ministry is Henry Clark, *A Description of the Prophets, Apostles and Ministers of Christ* (London: N.p., 1655).

100. See William Dewsberry to Friends, 1653, Swarthmore MS., 3:19, LSF. The letter also has Fox's initials, "G.F.," which were probably added later. Fox did indicate that he endorsed the letter's recommendations by scrawling on the back that the letter should be "engrossed" or copied for distribution. On the letter, see Braithwaithe, *Beginnings,* 140n4. Braithwaite dated it March 1653/54, but it is unclear from the document itself how he arrived at that time. A likely "4" in the date has been marked through and a "3" inserted.

101. *Journal,* 124–28.

102. *Querers and Quakers,* 25, 49. See also *Certain Quaeries and Antiquaeries, Concerning the Quakers* (London: N.p., 1653), 8.

103. *The Quakers Terrible Vision; or, the Devil's Progress to the City of London* (London: N.p., 1655), 4.

104. *A Phanatique League and Covenant, Solemnly enter'd into by the Assertors of the Good Old Cause* (N.p., 1659), Broadside.

105. Fox, *Works*, 7:79–80.

106. Fox, "Concerning Marriages," n.d., Thompson MS., 56–57, LSF.

107. On this point, see Fraser, *Weaker Vessel*, 371–72.

108. Nickalls, ed., *Journal*, 422. The judge ruled against this position.

109. On this point, see Paul P. Gilmartin, "George Fox's Contribution to the Role of Community in Discernment of Spirits" (Ph.D. diss., Catholic University of America, 1967), 184, 186, 190, 194–95.

110. *Journal*, 124.

CHAPTER 8

1. William Penn, "Preface," *Journal*, H2–3.

2. On Fox's library, see the series of articles beginning with John L. Nickalls, "George Fox's Library," *Journal of the Friends' Historical Society* 27 (1931): 2–21.

3. Thus the Quaker scholars' parlor game of trying to determine whether Fox was influenced by the Family of Love, the Anabaptists, or medieval mystics, to point out only three examples, is a bit beside the point except as an academic exercise. The contrary view, that Fox was well read, is asserted by Joseph Pickvance, *A Reader's Companion to George Fox's Journal* (London: Quaker Home Service, 1989), 11.

4. The major listing is, of course, Cadbury, ed., *Annual Catalogue*.

5. Ever since the seventeenth century his followers have endeavored to systematize his theological musings and thereby risked distorting his views. The first to attempt the project was former Scottish Presbyterian and Jesuit-trained Robert Barclay, who produced his *Apology for the True Christian Divinity* in 1676 (the current edition is *Barclay's Apology in Modern English*), and the most recent systematizer is Douglas Gwyn, *Apocalypse of the Word: The Life and Message of George Fox.* (Richmond, Ind.: Friends United Press, 1986), written from a perspective allowing no sense of historical development, despite its subtitle. See H. Larry Ingle, "On the Folly of Seeking the Quaker Holy Grail," *Quaker Religious Thought* 25 (1991): 17–29. The best modern introduction to Fox's theology is Aimo Seppänen, *The Inner Light in the Journals of George Fox: A Semantic Study* (Tampere, Finland: Department of English Philology, University of Tampere, 1975). See also Geoffrey F. Nuttall, *The Holy Spirit in Puritan Faith and Practice* (Oxford: Basil Blackwell, 1947), chap. 10.

6. Most of those who have tried to extrapolate a coherent theological position from Fox's writings—and hence found it necessary to superimpose artificial categories—have overlooked this important point; hence they have written as though a phrase he used, say, in 1653, was just as applicable and true, or even truer, as one that was employed thirty years later. But, the only way one can understand someone who lived as long as Fox and wrote as much as Fox did is to look at him and his writings historically.

7. Fox, *A Warning from the Lord to all such as hang down the head for a Day* (London: N.p., 1654), 1–2.

8. *Articles of Christian Religion, Approved and Passed by both Houses of Parliament* (London: N.p., 1648), 5–6.

9. Quoted in *DNB*, 17:1111–12.

10. *Journal*, 7.

11. Ibid., 19.

12. Fox to Friends, 1652, Portfolio MS., IX, 10, LSF.

13. Fox, *The Priests Fruits Made Manifest* (London: N.p., 1657), 3–4. Similarly, Parliament considered forbidding painting faces and wearing patches on one's face; see Fraser, *Cromwell*, 400.

14. Fox, *Something in Answer to all such as falsly say, The Quakers Are No Christians* (London: Andrew Sowle, 1682), 20.

15. Fox, *News coming up out of the North, Sounding towards the South* (London: N.p., 1654), 6.

16. *Journal*, 25.

17. Fox, *Works*, 7:126.

18. Fox, *To the Protector and Parliament of England* (London: N.p., 1658), 61.

19. William Dewsbury, George Fox, James Nayler, and John Whitehead, *Several Letters Written to the Saints of the Most High* (London: N.p., 1654), 14–15. (I have transposed the two main clauses of this quotation.)

20. Quakers, particularly those of the twentieth century, have spilled more ink over the question of Fox's mysticism than was ever required. Indeed, in many ways it can be said that this question delineates the major (and sometime unacknowledged) division among modern Friends. Those who sneer with the canard that mysticism begins in mist, has "I" in the middle, and ends in schism represent one end of the spectrum, while those who insist that Fox preached a "universalism" abstracted out of his time and place stand at the other. For those seeking a guide to wade into this rather arcane debate, see Melvin B. Endy, Jr., "The Interpretation of Quakerism: Rufus Jones and his Critics," *Quaker History* 70 (1981): 3–21.

21. Although the popularization of this phrase has lately been identified almost exclusively with Lewis Benson—see his *Catholic Quakerism: A Vision for All Men* (Philadelphia: Philadelphia Yearly Meeting, 1968)—it was always there to be plucked from Fox's *Journal* and was earlier stressed as the essence of his message in Ernest E. Taylor, *The Valiant Sixty* (London: Bannisdale Press, 1947), 13.

22. *Journal*, 13. On this point, see Seppänen, *Inner Light*, 38, and Ingle, "On the Folly."

23. On this topic, see H. Larry Ingle, "George Fox, Millenarian," *Albion* 24 (1992): 259–76.

24. *Journal*, 22.

25. Fox, *A Catechisme for Children* (London: N.p., 1657), 3, 5–6.

26. Fox, *To all that would know the Way to the Kingdome*, 1, 3–4.

27. Dewsbury, *Several Letters*, 16.

28. Fox to Priest Stookes, n.d., Swarthmoor MS., VII, 50, LSF.

29. *Journal*, 22–23.

30. Fox, *Great Mistery*, 206–7.

31. See Fox, "Answer to them that say Quakers deny the scriptures," 1654, Swarthmore MS., VII, 76, LSF.

32. Penney, ed., *Journal*, 2:313.

33. Fox to [Clement Writer], 1656, Swarthmore MS., VII, 16, LSF.

34. *Journal*, 22.

35. On this theme, see Ingle, "Fox as Enthusiast."

36. Penney, ed., *Journal*, 1:313. On Fox's view of himself in this regard, see Ingle, "Fox as Enthusiast." I have found only one occasion in which Fox responded to a criticism of his use of this phrase. In 1663, answering a former Quaker's pamphlet, he turned the disagreement into an ad hominem attack, lecturing John Harwood with the words, "Your actions and fruits have manifested whose son you are and yourself to be ignorant of the Scriptures and the spirit that gave them forth"; see Fox, *The Spirit of Envy, Lying, and Persecution Made Manifest* (London: N.p., 1663), 2. It was not a satisfactory answer.

37. See Howard H. Brinton, *The Religious Philosophy of Quakerism: The Beliefs of Fox, Barclay, and Penn as Based on the Gospel of John* (Wallingford, Pa.: Pendle Hill Publications, 1973).

38. Elaine Pagels, *The Gnostic Gospels* (New York: Random House, 1979), 119.

39. Fox, "The Lord is risen," 1677, Richardson MS. (transcript), 393–95, Quaker Collection, Haverford College (hereafter cited as QC).

40. Fox wrote an epistle explaining—certainly not *defending*—his position on this issue. See Fox, "Lord is risen," 393–95.

41. [Fox], *To All Freinds and People in the Whole of Christendome* (London: N.p., n.d.), 27–28.

42. For a statement of Jesus' approach that offers a fascinating comparison with Fox's, see Thomas Sheehan, *The First Coming: How the Kingdom of God Became Christianity* (New York: Random House, 1986), esp. 58–62.

43. Fox, *Concerning Revelation, Prophecy, Measure, and Rule, and the Inspiration and Sufficiency of the Spirit* (N.p., 1676), 18.

44. Fox, "To believe of a Christ," Portfolio MS., XXXIII, 117, LSF.

45. Fox, *This is a Controversy Betwixt the Quakers and the Papists* (N.p., 1664), 2–3.

46. Fox, *An Answer to a Paper which came from the Papists Lately Out of Holland* (London: N.p., 1658), 12, 51, 61. For only one example of Fox's frequent references to the carnality of sacramental bread and wine, see Fox, et al., *A Declaration Against all Popery and Popish points* (N.p., [1655]), 27.

47. *Journal,* 288.

48. Fox, "It is a common saying," 1663, GFF's Epistles, MST, Folio Demy, 56–59, LSF.

49. Fox, *Warning from the Lord,* 1.

50. Fox, *The Lambs Officer Is gone forth with the Lambs Message* (London: N.p., 1659), *passim.*

51. Ralph Josselin, *Diary of the Rev. Ralph Josselin,* ed., E. Hockliffe, Camden Society Publications, 3d. series, vol. 15 (London: Camden Society, 1908), 112.

52. Richard Baxter, *One Sheet Against the Quakers* (London: Robert White, 1657), 3.

53. Christopher Feake and John Pomroy, *A Faithful Discovery of a treacherous Design* (London: H. Hills, 1653), title page, 46, 52.

54. Thomas Birch, ed., *Collection of the State Papers of John Thurloe,* 7 vols. (London: N.p., 1742), 4:509.

55. Fox, *The Spirit of Envy, Lying, and Persecution Made Manifest* (London: N.p., 1663), 6.

56. Fox, "As for our Silent Meetings," 1674, Richardson MS., 239, QC.

57. Fox, *Works,* 7:135–36.

CHAPTER 9

1. Higginson, *Brief Relation,* 1. Higginson was well known among Friends, one of whom referred to him as the "dragon's mouth"; see Thomas Lawson to Margaret Fell, 17 July [1655], Swarthmore MS., I, 244, LSF.

2. William Prynne, *A New Discovery of Some Roman Emissaries* (London: N.p., 1656), 4. On this topic, see Stephen A. Kent, "The 'Papist' Charges against the Interregnum Quakers," *Journal of Religious History* 12 (1982): 180–90.

3. Ephraim Pagitt, *Heresiography,* 5th ed. (London: N.p., 1654), 136.

4. *Quakers Terrible Vision,* 3–4.

5. *Mercurius Fumigofus,* 20–27 Dec. 1654, 246.

6. *A List of some of the Grand Blasphemers and Blasphemies* (London: Robert Ibbitson, 1654), Broadside.

7. Higginson, *Brief Relation*, 1, 3.

8. Printed in [John Jackson], *Strength in Weakness; or the Burning Bush not Consumed* (London: J. Macock, 1655), 11. See also James Nayler, *The Power and Glory of the Lord Shining Out of the North; or the Day of the Lord Dawning* (London: N.p., 1653).

9. Fox, *News coming up out of the North*, 11–13. George Thomason picked up his copy on December 21; see *Catalogue of the Pamphlets . . . Collected by George Thomason*, 2 vols. (London: British Museum, 1908), 2:50–51.

10. Fox, *The Vials of the Wrath of God* (London: N.p., 1654), 7. The full statement was reprinted in *Works*, 4:27–31.

11. William Evans and Thomas Evans, eds., *Friends Library*, 14 vols. (Philadelphia: Joseph Rakestraw, 1837), 11:300. Within months, Buttery proved an embarrassment to the movement, having been arrested and committed to Bridewell for selling books in the streets on a Sunday. She was also apparently involved with the earl of Pembroke; see Howgill and Anthony Pearson to Margaret Fell, 10 July 1654, Caton MS., III, 181–85, LSF.

12. Howgill and Camm to Fox, 27 March 1654, in "A.R. Barclay Mss.," *Journal of the Friends' Historical Society* 48 (1957): 134. For this period, see Braithwaite, *Beginnings*, 159–62.

13. Edward Burrough to Margaret Fell, 1654, Caton MS., III, 143–47, LSF.

14. *A List of some of the Grand Blasphemers and Blasphemies Which was given into the Committee for Religion* (London: Robert Ibbitson, 1654), Broadside.

15. Burrough and Howgill to Margaret Fell, 2 Oct. 1654, Caton MS., III, 161–63, LSF.

16. Roger Williams, "George Fox Digg'd Out of His Burrowes," in *The Complete Writings of Roger Williams*, 7 vols., ed. J. Lewis Diman (New York: Russell and Russell, 1963), 5:45.

17. *Journal*, 123.

18. Robert Widder to Margaret Fell, 1654, Swarthmore MS., IV, 100; John Whitehead to wife, 3 Jan. [1655], Thompson MS., Writings, 195–96, LSF.

19. *Journal*, 131; William Sheffield and Thomas Cockram to Protector, 9 and 21 Jan. 1655, in Birch, ed., *Thurlow Papers*, 3:94, 116.

20. My account is taken from Farnworth, *Spirituall Man*, supplemented by Penney, ed., *Journal*, 1:152–59. The Witherly Presbyterian was John Chester, a Cambridge graduate who was ejected in 1662 after two laboring men testified he opposed infant baptism and the king; see Matthews, *Calamy Revised*, 113–14. Significantly, Farnworth—and Fox himself, for he wrote a goodly portion of the *Spirituall Man*—did not mention Fox's subsequent arrest.

21. Fox's memory as recounted in his various journals is somewhat confused here (see *Journal*, 135–36; Penney, ed., *Journal*, 1:158–59; Penney, ed., *Short Journal*, 38), so I have mainly followed the more contemporaneous letter of Alexander Parker to Margaret Fell, 1 Feb. 1655, Swarthmore MS., IV, 234, LSF, written prior to Fox's arrest.

22. On the proclamation and Cromwell's mood, see Fraser, *Cromwell*, 572–73. The proclamation caused nearly immediate concern among the Quakers; see George Taylor to Margaret Fell, 26 Feb. 1655, Swarthmore MS., I, 214, LSF.

23. Fox, Sufferings at Lester, [1655], Swarthmore MS., VII, 171, LSF. Fox accepted the support of one onlooker, Ranter Jacob Bauthumley.

24. *Journal*, 136.

25. Fraser, *Cromwell*, 511, 515.

26. Bordeaux to Cardinal Mazarin, 4 Feb. 1655, in Birch, ed., *Thurloe Papers*, 3:123.

27. *Perfect Proceedings of State Affaires*, 22 Feb.–1 March 1655, 4491–93.

28. Parker to Margaret Fell, 10 March 1655, Caton MS., III, 265–66, LSF; *Journal*, 137.

29. See, for one example, Aldam to Thomas Fairfax, 1654, Portfolio MS., I, 8, LSF.

30. Penney, ed., *Journal*, 1:161–62.

31. There are two manuscript copies of this epistle: Swarthmore MS., II, 55, and Caton MS., II, 48–49, LSF. See also Ingle, "Fox as Enthusiast." The fact that the essay was addressed to those "raised to a discerning" suggests that, whether intentionally or not, Fox was thinking of a two-tiered level of insight, one for the few acute enough to understand such deep mysteries, the other for the average adherent still unable to appreciate them. That the essay was never published, and also that the earliest edition of the *Journal* dropped all reference to his statement in the letter to Cromwell, points to the disquiet that Fox and Friends later felt about their early enthusiasms.

The same embarrassment—and in these cases, it would not be inappropriate to call it a historical cover-up—is evident in the effort Fox made to excise and emend letters addressed to him in the 1650s when he was going through his correspondence in the 1670s; this correspondence later became the Swarthmore Manuscripts. For a discussion of this approach, see H. Larry Ingle, "George Fox, Historian," *Quaker History* 82 (1993): 28–35.

32. Farnworth, *Spirituall Man*, 6–22 (Fox signed one part of this book, and since the portion I cite is in the first person, he was its likely author).

33. Penney, ed., *Journal*, 1:163–65. Other Quakers had the same message for Cromwell: John Camm, for example, wrote him in 1653 that the Lord would trample all the powers of the earth who refused to stoop to him; see John Camm to Oliver Cromwell, 1653, Swarthmore MS., IV, 115, LSF.

34. Whitehall's furnishings are described in Fraser, *Cromwell*, 458–59.

35. Parker to Margaret Fell, 10 March 1655, Caton MS., II, 265–66; *Journal*, 137–38; Penney, ed., *Journal*, 1:166–68; Penney, ed., *Short Journal*, 38–39.

36. *Journal*, 139–40; Penney, ed., *Journal*, 1:165–70.

37. Richard Baxter, *Quakers Catechism; or, the Quakers Questioned* (London: A. M., 1655), iv–v, xiv–xvii, 8–9.

38. *Journal*, 141–43. One can almost date some of Fox's epistles, both published and unpublished, by the way he took a liking to a particular set of words, using them over and over again, then discarding them and finding others. For example, in 1653, he wrote an epistle that advised "stand naked and bare and uncovered," very much like this one; see Fox, Epistle, 1653, Swarthmore MS., VII, 40, LSF.

39. Cross, *Church and People*, 202, 212–13; *Journal*, 147–49.

40. On this topic, see Braithwaite, *Beginnings*, chap. 16.

41. "Accounts of moneys received for the service of truth," 1656, Swarthmore MS., I, 397, LSF.

42. Fox to Friends in the North, 1656, Swarthmore MS., VII, 137, LSF. Twenty years later, when he went through the archives of the movement, an irritated Fox still fumed about the criticism, scribbling on the back of one letter a notation that coupled the complaints with Nayler, Perrot, John Pennyman, and other schismatics; see Thomas Willan and Taylor to Margaret Fell, 14 July 1655, Swarthmore MS., I, 239, LSF.

43. *Journal*, 146–47. The first mention of missionary activity outside the British Isles was in 1655; see Penney, ed., *Journal*, 2:325–26.

44. Quoted in Braithwaite, *Beginnings*, 440.

45. On this point, see Parker to Margaret Fell, 3 April 1655, Swathmore MS., I, 161, and Burrough and Howgill to Margaret Fell, 27 March 1655, Caton MS., III, 164–69, LSF.

The fact that a good bit of money was obviously being raised by 1655 for a significantly increasing number of evangelistic missions, both foreign and domestic, suggests a corresponding increase in centralizing decision making. For examples, see Penney, ed., *Journal*, 2:325–27. Likewise it helps explain local questioning about the uses to which the money was being put. On Dring, see Barbour and Roberts, *Quaker Writings*, 590.

46. On Fisher, see Hill, *World Turned Upside Down*, 259–68.

47. Parker to Margaret Fell, 18 June and 6 July 1655, Caton MS., 278–86, 287–92; *Journal*, 150; Penney, ed., *Journal*, 1:182–83. For Parker, see Dilworth Abbott, "Alexander Parker," *Journal of the Friends' Historical Society* 8 (1911): 30–32.

48. Parker to Margaret Fell, 6 July 1655, Caton MS., III, 287–92; *Journal*, 152; Penney, ed., *Journal*, 1:185, 430–31, 441; Sewell, *History*, 286. The Curtises are not mentioned in this section of the *Journal*, presumably because both later "ran out" and opposed Fox.

49. Fiennes, *Illustrated Journeys*, 77.

50. On the Family of Love, see Alastair Hamilton, *The Family of Love* (Cambridge: James Clarke and Co., 1981), esp. 120. On the area, particularly Cambridgeshire, see Margaret Spufford, *Contrasting Communities: English Villagers in the Sixteenth and Seventeenth Centuries* (Cambridge: Cambridge University Press, 1974), esp. 282–83, 351–52.

51. William Caton to Margaret Fell, 23 July 1656, Swarthmore MS., I, 313, LSF. On Caton, see Penney, ed., *Journal*, 1:421. Fox never identified himself with the Familists, followers of Jacob Boehme, even though at least one Quaker expressly defended him as the northern prophet about whom the German mystic had written more than a quarter century before; see Francis Ellington, *Christian Information Concerning these Last times* (London: N.p., 1664), 10–12. (Ellington's book had almost the same title as one by Boehme.)

52. *A Relation of a Quaker, That to the Shame of His Profession, Attempted to Bugger a Mare near Colchester* (N.p., n.d.), Broadside.

53. Richard Clayton to Margaret Fell, 12 July 1655, Swarthmore MS., I, 30, LSF; *Journal*, 153.

54. *Diary of Josselin*, 15:111–12. One Quaker apprehended was James Parnell; see *Journal*, 152–53.

55. On local disagreements, see *Journal*, 152–55.

56. See his epistle addressed to gathered churches in *Journal*, 161–63.

57. Cadbury, ed., *Annual Catalogue*, 50 (item 23,202A).

58. Howgill to Margaret Fell, March 1655, Caton MS., III, 176–78, LSF. Craig Horle, comp., "William Caton MSS., Volume 3: Listing and Index," 1975, LSF, concludes that this letter is misdated by a month.

59. *Journal*, 163–65. Some Quakers worried that the law would threaten their property, real and personal; see Taylor to Margaret Fell, 12 May 1655, Swarthmore MS., I, 236, LSF.

60. *Journal*, 166–71.

61. Ibid., 171.

62. Taylor to Margaret Fell, 2 April 1655, Swarthmore MS., I, 219, LSF.

63. Burrough and Howgill to Margaret Fell, 27 March 1655, and Parker to Margaret Fell, 10 May 1655, Caton MSS., III, 164–69, 267–72, LSF.

64. James Nayler to Margaret Fell, 1655, Swarthmore MS., III, 81, LSF. Contrary to what Bittle says (*Nayler*, 77, 217), Nayler could not have reached London before July because Fox did not arrive at Reading until the last day of June.

65. Nayler to Margaret Fell, 3 Nov. 1655, Swarthmore MS., III, 80, LSF. Still, one close observer thought that Baptist converts to Quakerism were few, at least as compared to Seekers; see John Tombes to Baxter, 4 April 1655, *Baxter Papers*, 2:90, DWL.

66. Whiting, *Persecution Exposed*, 176.

67. Pearson to Margaret Fell, 9 May 1653, Swarthmore MS., I, 87, LSF.

68. Howgill to Fox and Nayler, 18 Jan. 1656, Portfolio MS., III, 83, LSF.

69. Edward Burrough to John Bolton and Richard Davis, 20 Nov. [1655?], Markey MS., 79–82, LSF. See also Burrough to Margaret Fell, 1655, Swarthmore MS., III, 17, LSF.

70. Dewsbury to Margaret Fell, 3 Sept. 1655, Swarthmore MS., IV, 139, LSF.

71. Parker to Margaret Fell, 28 July 1655, Caton MS., III, 293–94, LSF.

72. Bittle, *Nayler*, 79–81.

73. Nayler to Margaret Fell, 3 Nov. 1655, Swarthmore MS., III, 80, LSF.

74. Parker to Margaret Fell, 10 May 1655, Caton MS., III, 267–72, LSF. Fox also tended to act a bit more cautiously in London than elsewhere, seldom interrupting church services, for example, and not causing the clamor that usually accompanied his preaching; see Croese, *General History*, 1:68.

75. On this theme, see Christine Trevett, "The Women around James Nayler, Quaker: A Matter of Emphasis," *Religion* 20 (1990): 249–73.

76. See, for examples, Caton to Margaret Fell, 23 July 1656, and Fox memorandum, n.d., Swarthmore MS., I, 313, 2:42, LSF.

77. *Journal*, 167, 171; William Goff to Thurlow, 10 Jan. 1656, in Birch, ed., *Thurlow Papers*, 4:408.

78. Camm to Margaret Fell, [c. Feb. 1654], Caton MS., III, 479–80, LSF.

79. Aldam to Fox, n.d., Swarthmore MS., III, 19, LSF. Braithwaite (*Beginnings*, 134) dated this letter in 1653.

80. Thomas Taylor to Margaret Fell, 1 July 1653, Swarthmore MS., I, 16, LSF.

81. Henry Fell to Caton, 27 May 1656, Swarthmore MS., IV, 265, and Burrough to Fox, n.d., Barclay MS., 161, LSF.

82. For examples, see Thomas Stubbs to William Dewsbury, 27 Dec. [c. 1654], 15 Sept. 1655, in Cadbury, ed., *Letters to Dewsbury*, 18–19, 38–39.

83. Lupton, *Quaking Montebanck*, 17.

84. Burrough to Robert Dring and Gerrard Roberts, 21 Jan. 1656, Markey MS., 103–4, and Burrough to Nayler, 12 July 1656, Portfolio MS., I, 43, LSF.

85. Willan and Taylor to Margaret Fell, 5 April 1656, Swarthmore MS., I, 268, LSF.

86. Nayler to Fox, [1656], Swarthmore MS., III, 76, LSF. This letter is an interesting one, misdated 1654 by Fox but clearly written after the recipient left London. Nothing indicated that Nayler sensed that Fox had doubts about him, and he wrote with the utmost confidence and comradeship, even requesting that Fox write a man who no longer seemed interested in the Friends.

87. Nayler to Margaret Fell, 1 June [1656], Swarthmore MS., III, 82, LSF. I am following Braithwaite (*Beginnings*, 244) in dating this letter, despite Fox's date of 1655. Fox's action in directing Nayler to Yorkshire calls into question Braithwaite's willingness to read the listing in Penney, ed., *Journal*, 2:334, so as to date his defection in June 1656. It is also unclear exactly what the issue in this dispute was. It probably involved the reluctance of northern Friends to have their contributions for missionary activities distributed from London; see Fox to Friends in the North, 1656, Swarthmore MS., VII, 137, LSF.

88. Of course, almost all the accounts about the Nayler affair were written by the ultimate victors, those who sided with Fox against Nayler, or outside critics eager to prove the worst about the hated sect. There is also clear evidence that the sources were manipulated by Fox when he was going through the archives of the movement in the 1670s. On this topic, see Ingle, "Fox, Historian." The Fox party's management of the sources led one historian to venture the hypothesis that Nayler, not Fox, was the real founder of the Society of Friends and that evidence to the contrary had been suppressed; see

Winthrop S. Hudson, "A Suppressed Chapter in Quaker History," *Journal of Religion* 24 (1944): 108–18. Obviously arguable, that position is too extreme.

89. On writs of outlawry, see Horle, *Quakers*, 42, 54, 61n71.

90. On Widders, see Penney, ed., *Journal*, 1:295–96; Sewell, *History*, 86–87.

91. Robert Widders to Margaret Fell, 1654, Swarthmore MS., IV, 29, LSF.

92. Ann Dewsbury to Margaret Fell, 1 March 1656, Swarthmore MS., IV:142, LSF.

93. Thomas Collier, *A Looking-Glasse for the Quakers* (London: N.p., 1657), 17–18.

94. Fox to Nayler, 1656, Cook MS., 53, LSF.

95. Fox to Nayler, 1656, Swarthmore MS., I, 382, and Fox to Nayler, Sept. 1656, Portfolio MS., XXIV, 36, LSF.

96. Whiting, *Persecution*, 175–77.

97. John Disbrowe to Thurlow, 12 Feb. 1656, in Birch, ed., *Thurlow Papers*, 4:531.

98. William Goff to Thurlow, 10 Jan. 1656, in Birch, ed., *Thurlow Papers*, 4:408.

99. Caton to Margaret Fell, 23 July 1656, Swarthmore MS., I, 313, LSF.

100. *Journal*, 171–73; Penney, "First Publishers," 80.

101. Hubberthorne to Fox, 20 March 1656, Swarthmore MS., IV, 12, LSF. This letter has been misdated a year by nearly all who have looked at it. On the identity of Mildred Crouch, see Robert Rich, *Hidden Things Brought to Light on the Discord of the Grand Quakers among Themselves* (N.p., 1678), 13.

102. Thurloe to Henry Cromwell, 12 Feb. 1655, in Birch, ed., *Thurloe Papers*, 4:530–31.

103. Fiennes, *Illustrated Journeys*, 41, 204.

104. Thomas Carlyle, ed., *Oliver Cromwell's Letters and Speeches*, 4 vols. (New York: Charles Scribner's Sons, 1899), 3:201.

105. *Journal*, 175; Penney, ed., "First Publishers," 20; *The West Answering to the North in the Fierce and Cruell Persecutions of the manifestation of the Son of God* (London: N.p., 1657), 1. In the latter source, Fox claimed to be traveling from Cornwall to Bristol, which, although generally true, still misstated his immediate intention, for when he was arrested he was headed away from his supposed destination.

106. *Journal*, 175–76; *West Answering*, 3.

107. *Journal*, 177.

108. Fiennes, *Illustrated Journeys*, 212–13.

109. Penney, ed., *Journal*, 1:210; Fox, *West Answering*, 4–6.

110. Fox believed the authorities were watching the post so as to entrap them; see Camm to Margaret Fell [ca. June 1656], Caton MS., III, 478–79, LSF.

CHAPTER 10

1. Edward Pyott to George Bishop, 14 May 1656, Original Record of Sufferings MS., 610, LSF (hereafter cited as ORS). For Bishop's authorship of this pamphlet, see Cadbury, ed., *Narrative Papers*, 19n. The fullest study of Bishop shows how Fox orchestrated his follower's experienced political acumen to produce a pamphlet that was a virtual anthology of the violation of Quaker rights; see Maryann F. Castelucci, "An Experience of Defeat: George Bishop, from Soldier to Quaker during the English Civil War and Interregnum" (Ph.D. diss., City University of New York, 1990), 163–65.

2. Pyott to ?, 15 May 1656, ORS MS., 505, LSF.

3. By June Fox was asking for letters; see John Audland to Margaret Fell, 20 June 1656, Caton MS., III, 448–49, LSF.

4. For a drawing of the castle grounds, see L. V. Hodgkin, *A Quaker Saint in Cornwall: Loveday Hambly and her Guests* (London: Longmans, Green and Co., 1927), opp. 13.

5. Josiah Coale to Fox, 12 Jan. 1664, Barclay MS., 64, LSF.

6. My account of the trial is taken from *Journal*, 180–85; Penney, ed., *Journal*, 1:211–16; Fox, *West Answering*, 15–29. Fox claimed that a Captain Bradden told him that Ceely was angry because once when he walked on the castle green Fox rebuked the major for what he told him to his face was his "hypocrisy and rotten heartedness"; see *Journal*, 185. Such language, however true, was not the way to win friends and influence people, as this incident shows.

7. Pyott to Bishop, 14 May 1656, ORS MS., 610, LSF. Fox still judged that Glynn was lacking in humility and told him so; see Cadbury, ed., *Annual Catalogue*, 60 (item 192B).

8. Caton to Margaret Fell, 23 July 1656, Swarthmore MS., I, 313, LSF.

9. Pyott to Bishop, 18 April 1656, ORS MS. 305, LSF. Within a month, many were making the long trek to the southwest. "Kings," one declared, "shall lay down their crowns before him and present their gifts unto him"; see Howgill to Margaret Fell [late May 1656], Caton MS., III, 173–75, LSF.

10. Fox, *West Answering*, 34, 76–77.

11. Henry Haynes to Thurloe, 5 July 1656, in Birch, ed., *Thurloe Papers*, 5:188.

12. *Dictionary of Proverbs*, 507.

13. Fox, *West Answering*, 35–37. An example of his letters is in *Journal*, 201*–3*.

14. Pyott to ?, 15 May 1656, ORS MS., 505, LSF; Pyott to John Gwynn, 14 July 1656, in *Journal*, 189–200, quotation at 190. The differences between Fox's approach and Pyott's can best be seen in the letters they addressed to John Desborough in *Journal*, 215*–17*. Pyott also made a strong statement favoring liberty of conscience in another letter to Desborough, calling it a "natural" and "fundamental" right granted to those who "profess faith in God by Jesus Christ"; see Penney, ed., *Journal*, 1:238–39. Ellwood did not associate Fox with this letter in the *Journal*'s first edition, probably because he realized that Pyott was its author. In the copy of the letter that appears in Penney's edition of the *Journal*, Fox wanted it to appear that he was the joint author and added his initials at the same time he wrote on the back of the letter, "in the presen at lansendenton in corwall 1656 read over"; see Pyott to Desborough, 1656, Spence MS., I, 146, LSF. Although he no doubt influenced Pyott's thinking, the evidence is too slim to grant him coauthorship.

15. Caton to Margaret Fell, 23 July 1656, Swarthmore MS., I, 313, LSF.

16. Parker to Margaret Fell, 19 Aug. and 13 Sept. 1656, Swarthmore MS., I, 166, 167, LSF. These letters are reprinted in Hodgkin, *Quaker Saint*, 196–203.

17. Thomas Salthouse and Miles Halhead to Margaret Fell, 9 Sept. 1656, Caton MS., III, 89–91, LSF.

18. Fox, Robert Rich, and William Thompson, *Copies of Some few of the Papers given into the House of Parliament in the time of James Naylers tryal there* (N.p., [1657]), 6.

19. *Journal*, 187, 217*. On Peter, see Raymond P. Stearns, *The Strenuous Puritan: Hugh Peter* (Urbana: University of Illinois Press, 1954). Ten days before their release they were arranging to get mounts for traveling but were unsure where they would go; see Pyott to Bishop, 2 Sept. 1656, ORS MS., 301, LSF.

20. Thomas Carlyle, ed., *Oliver Cromwell's Letters and Speeches*, 4 vols. (New York: Charles Scribner's Sons, 1899), 3:294.

21. See the numerous entries in Cadbury, ed., *Annual Catalogue*, 55–62, for some indication of how much he wrote during the first nine months of 1656.

22. *Journal*, 201*, 217*–18*. Extensive Quaker inroads in the west caused one alarmed observer to label this time "the evening of the world"; see *The Quakers Quaking* (London: N.p., 1657), 1.

23. James Nayler, *Love to the Lost* (1656), in George Whitehead, ed., *A Collection of Sundry Books, Epistles and Papers Written by James Nayler* (London: J. Sowle, 1716), 323–24.

24. James Nayler to Fox, 1652, 1654, Swarthmore MS., III, 60, 73, LSF. See also Nayler to Fox, 1653, Swarthmore MS., III, 71, LSF.

25. Whitehead, ed., *Sundry Books*, 269–72, 322. George Whitehead, who knew Nayler well, attested that he preferred "the ministration of the Spirit above that of the letter"; Whitehead, ed., *Sundry Books*, vii.

26. On Simmonds, see Kenneth L. Carroll, "Martha Simmonds, a Quaker Enigma," *Journal of the Friends' Historical Society* 53 (1972): 31–52.

27. James Parnell to William Dewsbury, 16 Dec. [1655], in Cadbury, ed., *Letters of Dewsbury*, 40–42.

28. Lupton, *Quaking Montebanck*, 19.

29. Hubberthorne to Margaret Fell, 26 July [1656], Caton MS., III, 364–65, LSF.

30. Francis Howgill to Margaret Fell, 21 Oct. 1656, in Henry J. Cadbury, ed., *Swarthmore Documents in America* (London: Friends Historical Society, 1940), 28–30.

31. Ralph Farmer, *Sathan Inthron'd in his Chair of Pestilence* (London: N.p., 1657), 11.

32. The earliest and most balanced analysis of Nayler, written sixty years later by one who knew him, is Whitehead's "Epistle" in Whitehead, ed., *Sundry Books*, iii–xxiv; see also Fogelklou, *Nayler*. There may have been a strain of extremism in the Nayler family. At least on a September Sunday in 1659, it was reported that his brother William interrupted London's Savoy church with a bellowing noise that sounded to some like the devil; see Danson, *Quakers Wisdom*, 3–4. To a different critic, Nayler denied that he had a brother who had ever come within fifty miles of London; see Hubberthorne and Nayler, *Short Answer*, 8–9.

33. See *Journal*, 226*–31*.

34. Howgill to Margaret Fell, [late May 1656], Caton MS., III, 173–75, LSF. Ironically, they came to the capital because Nayler called for their help in April; see Willan and Taylor to Margaret Fell, 5 April 1656, Swarthmore MS., I, 268, LSF. On July 12 Burrough was still submitting his epistles to Nayler for clearance; see Burrough to Nayler, 12 July 1656, Portfolio MS., I, 43, LSF.

35. Fox to Nayler, 1656, Swarthmore MS., I, 382, and Fox to Nayler, Sept. 1656, Portfolio MS., XXIV, 36, LSF.

36. Burrough to Simmonds, n.d., Markey MS., 120–21, LSF.

37. Farmer, *Satan Inthron'd*, 10–11; Hubberthorne to Margaret Fell, 26 July [1656], Caton MS., III, 364–65, LSF.

38. Howgill and Burrough to Margaret Fell, 13 Aug. 1656, Caton MS., III, 132–36, LSF; Howgill and John Audland to Burrough, 2 Aug. 1656, in "A.R. Barclay MSS.," *Journal of the Friends' Historical Society* 43 (1956): 90; Farmer, *Sathan Inthron'd*, 11.

39. Thomas Rawlinson to Margaret Fell, 23 Aug. 1656, Swarthmore MS., III, 12, LSF. I am inferring from Rawlinson's letter that he informed Fox in his letters that Nayler was improving, although no such letter has survived. Anne Downer, a kind of "girl Friday" for Fox (*Journal*, 187), was in Exeter when Rawlinson wrote and planned to return to Launceston.

40. Howgill and Audland to Burrough, 2 Aug. 1656, A. R. Barclay MS., 323–24, LSF. According to them, Fox wanted to see Nayler at Launceston immediately. As a consequence of their reading of Fox's mood, Howgill and Audland advised Friends in London to be quiet and let the matter simply "cease and die."

41. Farmer, *Sathan Inthron'd*, 11.

42. Fox to Nayler, n.d., Portfolio MS., XXXI, 132; Hubberthorne to Margaret Fell, 16 Sept. 1656, Swarthmore MS., III, 153, LSF; Howgill to Margaret Fell, 21 Oct. 1656, in Cadbury, ed., *Swarthmore Documents*, 28–30. Fox's letter was found on Nayler after his arrest in Bristol and was read at his hearing. Hubberthorne's letter averred that Simmonds had been brought to confess, but Fox's letter did not indicate that he believed she had repented.

43. *Journal*, 219*–21*; Thomas Turner to Margaret Fell, 1656, Swarthmore MS., IV, 123, LSF; Fox to Nayler, Sept. 1656, Portfolio MS., XXIV, 36, LSF.

44. On this point see, Hubberthorne to Margaret Fell, 16 Sept. 1656, Swarthmore MS., III, 153, LSF.

45. Fell to Nayler, 15 Oct. 1656, Spence MS., III, 38–39, LSF. This letter can be found in Ross, *Fell*, 396–98. Unfortunately Nayler's letter to Fell, which had come to her hand, has been lost or was destroyed, so there is no way to know in detail what he might have said or to put it in context.

46. Fox to Nayler, Sept. 1656, Portfolio MS., XXIV, 36, LSF. William Salt, who, it will be remembered, later "ran out," was also traveling with Fox; in typical fashion, his name was omitted from much of the record as a kind of punishment for his errors.

47. Fox to Nayler, Sept. 1656, Portfolio MS., XXIV, 36, LSF.

48. Nayler later affirmed that, as he said, "all along he had testified against that spirit that led into strife, division, and made rent among the people of God"; see M. T. and Roger Hebden to Dewsbury, 13 June [1657], in Cadbury, ed., *Letters*, 23–25.

49. My account of the Exeter meetings between Fox and Nayler is taken from *Journal*, 220*; Nickalls, ed., *Journal*, 268–69; and Hubberthorne to Margaret Fell, 4 Oct. 1656, *Journal of the Friends' Historical Society* 26 (1929): 13–15. Bittle's account of these incidents (*Nayler*, 96–99) has at least three factual errors: Fox was released from Launceston on September 13 not September 9; the differences were not discussed in any major way on Saturday evening; and it was Tuesday, not Wednesday, morning when Fox asked Nayler to come to see him.

50. Fox to Nayler, 1656, Cook MS., 53, LSF.

51. Fox to Nayler, Sept. 1656, Portfolio MS., XXIV, 36, LSF.

52. Twenty years later when he was going through the movement's archives, Fox took the time to edit material about Nayler or letters that referred to him in laudatory terms. See, for examples, Willan and Taylor to Margaret Fell, [1656,] Swarthmore MS., I, 294, and Fox, "To all the elect seed called quakers," 1656, Portfolio MS., X, 30, LSF. This last document is quite revealing, for its first line reads, "1676, This was given forth in j:n: his dayes," and has numerous emendations in Fox's hand that would have made no difference to anyone except those in the future examining a historical document. Of course it can not be proved, but the likelihood is that Fox or others destroyed letters that put Nayler in a better light.

53. Howgill to Margaret Fell, 21 Oct. 1656, in Cadbury, ed., *Swarthmore Documents*, 28–30.

54. Fiennes, *Illustrated Journeys*, 192–93.

55. Penney, ed., *Journal*, 1:424.

56. *Journal*, 221*–22*; Penney, ed., *Journal*, 1:443.

57. *Journal*, 222*–23*.

58. Penney, ed., *Short Journal*, 48.

59. Howgill to Margaret Fell, 21 Oct. 1656, in Cadbury, ed., *Swarthmore Documents*, 28–30.

60. My account is taken from George Bishop to Margaret Fell, 27 Oct. 1656, Swarthmore MS., I, 188, LSF, and Farmer, *Sathan Inthron'd*, 2–3. Bittle (*Nayler*, 102) plau-

sibly concludes from his study of the affair that Nayler and his group had decided on the "sign" before they left Exeter and proceeded to carry it out. There is no contemporaneous evidence directly supporting this conclusion, although Nayler did tell a parliamentary committee later that God had used him for a sign (*Nayler*, 116.) Given Nayler's obviously diminished mental state, it is not clear to what extent he was fully involved in the decision, if, in fact, one was reached.

61. Fox to Nayler, n.d., Portfolio MS., XXXI, 132, LSF. Nayler denied having made this statement; see Farmer, *Sathan Inthron'd*, 14–15.

62. Bishop to Margaret Fell, 27 Oct. 1656, Swarthmore MS., I, 188, LSF; see also J. Audland to Margaret Fell, 1 Nov. 1656, Caton MS., III, 452–54, LSF.

63. *Journal*, 223*–24*.

64. E. D., *Innocents No Saints: or, a Paire of Spectacles for a Dark-Sighted Quaker* (London: N.p., 1658), 3.

65. Farmer, *Sathan Inthron'd*. On Farmer, see Braithwaite, *Beginnings*, 171; Bittle, *Nayler*, 67–68; and Joseph Smith, *Bibliotheca Anti-Quakeriana* (New York: Kraus Reprint, 1968), 175–76.

66. William Grigg, *The Quaker's Jesus* (London: M. Simmons, 1658), title page.

67. Baxter, *One Sheet*, 11.

68. Willan and Taylor to Margaret Fell [1656], and Arthur Cotton to Fox, 18 Nov. 1656, Swarthmore MS., 1, 294, 4:163, LSF.

69. On this point, see Ronald Hutton, *The Restoration: A Political and Religious History of England and Wales, 1658–1667* (Oxford: Clarendon Press, 1985), 122.

70. Bittle, *Nayler*, chapters 5 and 6, gives a full account of Nayler's trial and the issues surrounding it. He died about a year after his release, on October 21, 1660, nearly four years to the day after riding into Bristol.

71. Rich, *Hidden Things*, 38. Rich claimed to have the paper beside him as he wrote.

72. For the petition, see Penney, ed., *Extracts from State Papers*, 21–23.

73. Penney, ed., *Journal*, 1:263–66. It is interesting that of the three major studies of Nayler, not one noticed that Fox was condemning their subject here. And, of course, none of those who have written about Fox have noted it. Even Robert Rich, who sought every shot to use against Fox and remarked favorably on the paper, overlooked the postscript's import; see Rich, *Hidden Things*, 39.

74. Nayler to "dearly beloved people of God," n.d., Portfolio MS., XXXI, 132, LSF.

75. Parker to Margaret Fell, 15 June 1658, Caton MS., III, 313–17, LSF.

76. Rich, *Hidden Things*, 38–40. Rich not only defended Nayler while he was being tried before Parliament, he went so far as to lick the martyr's brow after a "B" was scorched into it; see Bittle, *Nayler*, 142.

77. On Rich, see Penney, ed., *Journal*, 2:467–68.

78. Caton to Margaret Fell, 17 March 1657; Henry Fell to Margaret Fell, 14 April 1657; Richard Roper to Margaret Fell, 20 Oct. 1657, Swarthmore MS., I, 316, 1:69, III, 131, LSF.

79. Barbour, *Quakers in England*, 65–66.

80. Roper to Margaret Fell, 20 Oct. 1657, Swarthmore MS., III, 131, LSF.

81. *Journal*, 224*–25*; Penney, ed., *Journal*, 1:262–63. Apparently a number of Nayler supporters lived in Wales, for Fox remembered some more a bit later in Cardiff; see *Journal*, 245*.

82. Penney, ed., *Journal*, 1:265. Nayler, it should be emphasized, never claimed he was Christ, even though his followers had certainly demonstrated their belief that he was. Fox enjoyed the same reputation with some of his own followers, a reputation that proved rather embarrassing after Nayler's trial; on this point, see Ingle, "Fox, Historian."

83. On this point, see Gilmartin, "George Fox's Contribution," 184–88, and Arnold Lloyd, *Quaker Social History, 1669–1738.* (Westport, Conn.: Greenwood Press, 1979), 21. Another scholar has argued that Fox's "intensely authoritarian attitudes" led him to create systems of meetings designed to suppress individualistic inspirations; see Nicholas Morgan, "The Quakers and the Establishment, 1660–1730, with specific reference to the North-West of England" (Ph.D. diss., University of Lancaster, 1985), xxii.

84. Fox, *Works,* 7:120–29.

85. Ibid., 7:128.

86. "The seting up the menes meeting in Bishoprick 1653," Swarthmore MS., II, 17, LSF.

87. Fox, "Concerning our Monthly and Quarterly and Yearly Meetings," 1689, in John Barclay, ed., *Letters, &c., of Early Friends* (London: Harvey and Darton, 1837), 311–17.

88. Dewsbury to Friends, 1653, Swarthmore MS., III, 19, LSF.

89. Fox to Farnworth, 6 Aug. 1656, Portfolio MS., XXXVI, 140B, LSF.

90. Penney, ed., *Journal,* 1:266. Interestingly, this information was not revealed until 1911 when the Penney edition was published.

91. Braithwaite (*Beginnings,* 322–23, 332) dates this meeting in the summer of 1657, but his reasons for assigning this time to it, despite the information in his note, remain unclear. Lloyd (*Social History,* 3), though otherwise quite good on this topic, fails to mention the Swarthmoor gathering and thus avoids the problem.

92. Hubberthorne to Margaret Fell, 20 Jan. 1657, Caton MS., III, 398–99, LSF.

93. Fox, *Works,* 7:126–29. About the same time and just after the Nayler affair, in November, at Balby in Yorkshire, another meeting of elders convened and issued the most detailed rules yet; see Braithwaite, *Beginnings,* 310–13. Although Fox was in the area, he does not mention that he attended this conclave. It is hard to imagine that he missed it.

94. Penney, ed., *Journal,* 1:267. Braithwaite (*Beginnings,* 322–23) again dates the quarterly meetings from 1657.

95. Dewsbury to Friends, 1653, Swarthmore MS., III, 19, LSF.

96. One scholar referred to Fox's system as having "spiritualized the Presbyterian system," a bit of an overstatement; see George A. Johnson, "From Seeker to Finder: A Study in Seventeenth-Century English Spiritualism before the Quakers" (Ph.D. diss., University of Chicago, 1948), 313.

97. On this point, see the valuable work of Pamela M. C. Oliver, "The Quakers and Quietism: From George Fox to Thomas Story" (Master's thesis, University of Melbourne, 1972), 21–22. Another scholar has found that after Nayler's fall, the doctrine of individual perfectionism, which encouraged his extremism, gradually disappeared from Fox's epistles; see Ruth M. Lavare, "The Early Letters of George Fox, 1650–1660" (Ph.D. diss., University of California, 1954), lxxxiii.

98. Fox himself cited with approval the description of himself as cunning (as well as a pun on his name) when he quoted people in Wales exclaiming, "Oh . . . he is a cunning fox"; see Penney, ed., *Journal,* 1:276.

CHAPTER 11

1. For some flavor of the parliamentary distaste with Quakers and Quakerism, see Thomas Burton, *Diary of Thomas Burton,* 4 vols., ed., John T. Rutt (London: Henry Colburn, 1828), 1:168–73.

2. Penney, ed., *Journal,* 1:267.

3. Ibid., 1:263. See also Richard Hubberthorne, *The Good Old Cause Briefly Demonstrated* (London: N.p., 1659).

4. Fox, *Works*, 7:134–35.

5. On this point, see Wilbur C. Abbott, ed., *The Writings and Speeches of Oliver Cromwell*, 4 vols. (Cambridge, Mass.: Harvard University Press, 1947), 4:372–73.

6. Norman Penney, "Ellis Hookes," *Journal of the Friends' Historical Society* 1 (1903–1904): 12–22.

7. Fox, *Works*, 7:136–38.

8. *Journal*, 245*.

9. Thomas Rawlinson to Margaret Fell, 26 March 1657, Swarthmore MS., III, 11, LSF. William C. Braithwaite, who also noted this letter, guessed the two discussed whether Cromwell should assume the crown, certainly a possibility, but it seems unlikely that Fox interrupted his journey to return to London to advise on a matter of state, particularly one on which the Lord Protector already knew Quakers' views. Given Fox's concern with the sufferings his followers were enduring, it seems more likely that they discussed the government's attitude toward religious dissenters in general and the Quakers in particular. For Braithwaite's analysis, see *Beginnings*, 438–39.

10. Fiennes, *Journeys*, 158–59; Penney, ed., *Journal*, 1:280, 281, 282–83, 284–85, 449; Penney, ed., *Short Journal*, 50; Cadbury, ed., *Annual Catalogue*, 64 (item 36C).

11. Fox to Protector, Speaker in Parliament and Magistrates, 1657, Markey MS., 320, LSF.

12. Penney, ed., *Journal*, 2:106.

13. Ibid., 1:285–86; *Journal*, 253*.

14. Robert Widders to Fox, 1654, Swarthmore MS., IV, 41, LSF.

15. *Journal*, 259*–61*; Cadbury, ed., *Annual Catalogue*, 58 (item 124B); Penney, ed., *Journal*, 1:412.

16. Penney, ed., *Journal*, 2:337. For an excellent survey of this problem, see Braithwaite, *Beginnings*, 321–23.

17. Epistle, From men's meeting at Skipton [c. 1657], Willan and Taylor to Margaret Fell, 12 Sept. 1657, Swarthmore MS., II, 18, I, 301, LSF. (I am following Braithwaite, *Beginnings*, 323, in dating the former letter in 1657 despite Fox's date of 1656.)

18. Willan and Taylor to Margaret Fell, 9 May and 12 Sept. 1657; and Caton to Margaret Fell, 30 June 1658, Swarthmore MS., I, 297, 301, 317, LSF. For another indication that northern Friends were muttering about deceit, see Farnworth to Howgill and Burrough, 4 Oct. 1656, in "A.R. Barclay MSS.," *JFHS* 32 (1935): 62.

19. Epistle, General Meeting of Friends of the North at Skipton, 5 Oct. 1659, Portfolio, XVI, 2. See Braithwaite, *Beginnings*, 328–32, for a differing interpretation; an account, from the same general point of view, of the fits and starts in the establishment of meetings can also be found in *Epistles from the Yearly Meeting of Friends*, 2 vols. (London: Edward Marsh, 1858), 1:iii–xxviii.

20. This interpretation differs from that of Penney, ed., *Journal*, 1:470, and Barbour and Roberts, eds., *Early Quaker Writings*, 605. On Pearson, see Amy E. Wallis, "Anthony Pearson (1626–1666)," *Journal of the Friends' Historical Society* 51 (1966): 77–95. When Pearson decided to leave the Society of Friends and return to the Anglican church, it may have reflected some of his frustration over this issue.

21. Willan and Taylor to Margaret Fell, 12 Sept. 1657, Swarthmore MS., I, 301, LSF.

22. *Journal*, 265*–67*.

23. George Monck to Thurloe, 21 March 1657, in Birch, ed., *Thurloe Papers*, 6:136.

24. Willan and Taylor to Margaret Fell, 12 Sept. 1657, Swarthmore MS., I, 301, and Howgill and Thomas Robinson to Taylor, 14 July 1656, Portfolio MS., II, 77, LSF. On Osburne, see Penney, ed., *Journal*, 1:451.

25. Monck to Thurloe, 10 Feb. 1657, in Birch, ed., *Thurloe Papers*, 6:52–53.

26. See Cromwell's order of 27 July 1657 to allow confiscation of straw for army horses in Scotland and his speech to Parliament on 25 Jan. 1658, in Abbott, ed., *Writings of Cromwell,* 4:386–87, 718–19.

27. Timothy Langley to Thurloe, 19 Sept. 1658, in Birch, ed., *Thurloe Papers,* 7:403–04.

28. Fiennes, *Illustrated Journeys,* 172–73.

29. Nickalls, *Journal,* 315–18; Penney, ed., *Journal,* 1:408, 452.

30. See *The Doctrines and Principles of the Priests of Scotland,* reprinted in Fox, *Great Misery,* 513–52; quotation from 548.

31. Ibid., 515. He implied the soldier was a Quaker but did not say so explicitly.

32. *Journal,* 270*.

33. In this context, see *Journal,* 271*.

34. *Journal,* 271*–72*, 276*; Penney, ed., *Short Journal,* 51; George B. Burnet, *The Story of Quakerism in Scotland, 1650–1850* (London: James Clarke and Co., 1952), 40.

35. Margaret Fell to Gerrard Roberts, 21 Oct. 1657, Spence MS., III, 49, LSF.

36. *Journal,* 273*–75*; Burnet, *Quakerism in Scotland,* 37.

37. Statement of eight Quakers, 20 Oct. 1657, Swarthmore MS., IV, 237, LSF.

38. Monck to Oliver Cromwell, 21 March 1657, in Birch, ed., *Thurloe Papers,* VI, 136.

39. Fox, *This is to all Officers and Souldiers,* esp. 1–6; quotations from 5, 6.

40. Fox to Monk, the rest of the officers, Souldiers, Priests, and Magistrates, n.d., Swarthmore MS., II, 25, LSF.

41. For the Scottish trip, see *Journal,* 276*–81*, Penney, ed., *Journal,* 1:296–309, 452–54, Penney, ed., *Short Journal,* 51–53, 290.

42. Abbott, ed., *Writings of Cromwell,* 4:708. On this period generally, see Godfrey Davies, *The Restoration of Charles II, 1658–1660* (San Marino, Calif.: Huntington Library, 1955).

43. Abbott, ed., *Writings of Cromwell,* 4:708–09.

44. On this group, see B. S. Capp, *The Fifth Monarchy Men: A Study in Seventeenth-Century English Millenarianism* (Totowa, N.J.: Rowman and Littlefield, 1972).

45. Abbott, ed., *Writings of Cromwell,* 4:717.

46. On this point, see Reay, *Quakers and English Revolution,* chap. 5.

47. "Anthony Pearson" in Greaves and Zaller, eds., *Dictionary of Radicals,* 3:15–17; Roger Howell, Jr., *Newcastle upon Tyne and the Puritan Revolution* (Oxford: Clarendon Press, 1967), 175.

48. Roger Howell, Jr., "The Newcastle Clergy and the Quakers," *Archaeologia Aeliana,* ser. 5, 7 (1979): 200.

49. *Journal,* 281*; Penney, ed., *Journal,* 1:454.

50. Fox, *Great Mistery,* 410–11.

51. *Journal,* 281*—next verso (no pagination).

52. Howell, *Newcastle and the Revolution,* 331–32; Howell, "Newcastle Clergy," 202.

53. Henry Cromwell to Thurloe, 6 Feb. 1655, in Birch, ed., *Thurloe Papers,* 4:508–9. On Vane, see J. H. Adamson and H. F. Follard, *Sir Harry Vane: His Life and Times, 1613–1662* (Boston: Gambit, 1973).

54. For an assessment of Vane's style of religious writing, see Adamson and Follard, *Vane,* 325–26.

55. Penney, ed., *Journal,* 1:312–14.

56. *Journal,* 282* and verso opposite (no pagination).

57. Fox, *Works,* 7:157–58. The epistle contained many of the sentiments he expressed at the upcoming yearly meeting. His *Journal* (286*) dates his arrival in London after the yearly meeting.

58. On Crook, see H. G. Tibbutt, "John Crook, 1617–1699: A Bedfordshire Quaker," *Publications of the Bedfordshire Record Society* 25 (1947): 110–28.

59. Penney, ed., *Short Journal*, 54. As to whether this was the first yearly meeting, Braithwaite concluded that this conclave was a yearly meeting for ministers, and therefore one for religious purposes, as distinct from a yearly meeting for elders, which concentrated on business matters; see Braithwaite, *Beginnings*, 331–34. Although I am not altogether convinced of the validity of this distinction, for present purposes any differences, if such there were, do not detract from the interpretation I give here. For Fox's own description, albeit written thirty years later, see his "Concerning Our Monthly and Quarterly and Yearly Meetings," in Barclay, ed., *Letters of Early Friends*, 310–17.

60. The number of Friends in the British Isles is notoriously difficult to ascertain, so the best estimates are no more than mainly educated guesses. The two most recent scholars, Hugh Barbour and J. William Frost, *The Quakers* (New York: Greenwood Press, 1988), 33, would not even hazard a guess. Earlier, Barbour (*Quakers in Puritan England*, 182) suggested at least twenty thousand by 1657, presumably including those in the colonies as well as the metropolis. The latest to estimate is Reay (*Quakers and English Revolution*, 27), who ventured 35–40,000 by the early 1660s. One contemporary hostile critic with no reason to underplay his estimate—indeed, just the opposite—said there were 30,000 in the year he wrote; see J. G., *A Just Defense and Vindication of Gospel Ministers and Gospel Ordinances* (London: W. G., 1660), iv. Hence it seems reasonable to conclude that Fox's audience at Crook's easily represented one-tenth of the Children who lived in England, Scotland, Wales, and Ireland.

61. *Journal*, 282*–86*.

62. Fox, *The Law of God, the Rule for Law-makers* (London: N.p., 1658), 32.

63. Abbott, ed., *Writings of Cromwell*, 4:822–23.

64. Thomas Harrison to Protector, 7 July 1658, in Birch, ed., *Thurloe Papers*, 7:242.

65. *Journal*, 286*.

66. *Journal*, Aaa.190–Aaa2.195; Abbott, ed., *Writings of Cromwell*, 4:849, 861, 864. Fox had earlier addressed a kind of pastoral letter to Claypool; see *Journal*, Aaa.189–90.

67. See the portrait of Richard Cromwell in Davies, *Restoration*, 14–17.

68. Ibid, chap. 4.

69. Rutt, ed., *Diary of Burton*, 3:66, 4:440–46.

70. *Journal*, Bbb2.200. On the funeral, see Abbott, ed., *Writings of Cromwell*, 4:873–75; Davies, *Restoration*, 41–42.

71. *Journal*, Bbb2, 200–202.

CHAPTER 12

1. On this period, see Davies, *Restoration*, 82–84, 188. For the best overview of this period in its relation to Friends, see Reay, *Quakers*, chap. 5.

2. Davies, *Restoration*, 86–87.

3. Penney, ed., *Journal*, 1:329–33.

4. For an example, see *Journal*, 204–6.

5. *A true Copie of a Paper delivered to Lt. Gen. Fleetwood to be Communicated to the General Council of Officers* (London: N.p., 1659), title page, 4, 7.

6. Aldam to Fox, n.d. [bound with letters in the mid-1650s; author died in 1660], Swarthmore MS., III, 54, LSF. See also Willan and Taylor to Margaret Fell, 6 Dec. 1656, Swarthmore MS., I, 293, LSF. For an example of a Friend seeking Fox's approval of a manuscript addressed to the nation's rulers, see John Whitehead to Fox, 20 Nov. 1659, Swarthmore, MS., IV, 178, LSF. Smith (*Descriptive Catalogue*, 1:910–11) lists no such pamphlet for Whitehead, so Fox may have disallowed it.

7. Thomas Rawlinson to Margaret Fell, 11 May 1659, Swarthmore MS., III, 10, LSF.

8. Edward Burrough, *To the Whole English Army* (London: N.p., 1659), no pagination.

9. On Hubberthorne's stance, see Ingle, "Richard Hubberthorne and History: The Crisis of 1659," *Journal of the Friends' Historical Society* 56 (1992): 189–200.

10. Thomas Underhill, *Hell broke loose: or an History of the Quakers, Both Old and New* (London: N.p., 1660), iii.

11. *A Phantique League and Covenant, Solemnly enter'd into by the Assertors of the Good Old Cause* (N.p., [1659]), no pagination.

12. J. G., *Just Defense*, iii.

13. *A Declaration of the Maids of the City of London, etc* (N.p., [1659]).

14. Davies, *Restoration*, 135–37; Adamson and Follard, *Vane*, 391–92.

15. Parker to Fox, 7 Aug. 1659, Swarthmore MS., III, 143, LSF.

16. Penney, ed., *Extracts*, 138. In this later testimony before a London court Pearson claimed to have no interest in the conflict between king and Parliament, between "a kingdom and a free state." These options revealed his sympathies, regardless of his denial. One visitor to Pearson at this time, though describing him as a "wicked lad" and prone to deceit, still endorsed his usefulness to the Children's cause in Durham noting, "he bears good stroke." Howgill to Burrough, 1659, in "A. R. Barclay Mss.," *Journal of the Friends' Historical Society* 35 (1938): 99. As late as May 1659, his coreligionists endorsed him for another term of justice of the peace; see George Taylor to Roberts, [May 1659], in Penney, ed., *Extracts*, 111–12.

17. Rich, *Hidden Things*, 29.

18. *Journal*, 202–03. Fox took this same general approach in a formal epistle of 1659; see Fox, *Works*, 7:168–69. See also Fox to Friends at Bristol [1659], Swarthmore MS., VII, 157, LSF. My interpretation of Fox's views differs from that of the most recent historian who has looked at the matter (Peter Brock, *The Quaker Peace Testimony, 1660 to 1914* [York, England: Sessions Book Trust, 1990]), because his definition of pacifism is simply too narrow and modern: "refusal to bear arms stemming from a belief in the virtue of nonviolence and in the origin of war lying in human lust" (14). Thus he is willing to excuse Fox's approval of the magistrate's use of the sword in a good cause.

19. Fox, *This is to all officers*, 2.

20. Fox, *To the Councill of Officers*, 5.

21. *Journal*, Bbb. 197.

22. Comments like this suggest that Fox operated with non-Christians on two levels. Engaging in a formal dialogue, he could be quite charitable, but when he spoke to people who accepted his Christian presuppositions, he was less tolerant. For an undue emphasis on the former approach, see N. I Matar, "Some Notes on George Fox and Islam," *Journal of the Friends' Historical Society* 55 (1989): 271–76.

23. Fox, *To the Councill of Officers*, 1–3.

24. On this point, see the cataloguing in Reay, *Quakers*, 88–91.

25. Frances Gawler to Fox, 26 Nov. 1659, Swarthmore MS., IV, 219, LSF.

26. Caton to Fox, 20 Dec. 1659, Swarthmore MS., IV, 268, LSF.

27. Caton to Willan, 14 Nov. 1659, Swarthmore MS., IV, 279, LSF.

28. *Journal*, Bbb. 197, 204–06.

29. Edward Jeffreys to Baxter, 30 July 1659, Baxter Papers, III, 138, DWL; Hubberthorne to Margaret Fell, 21 Nov. 1659, Caton MS., III, 400–403, LSF.

30. Davies, *Restoration*, 157.

31. Ibid.

32. Fox's account of this malady is in *Journal*, Bbb. 198–99, 213.

33. Margaret Fell, Jr., to Mother, 27 Aug. 1659, Spence MS., III, 2G, LSF. Although

this source does not mention the Curtises specifically, there were no other Quakers resident in Reading with whom Fox was so intimate.

34. Sewell, *History*, 88; Reay, *Quakers*, 88. It should be noted that Fox punished Curtis after their later falling out by downplaying his part in Quaker history in the *Journal* version of events.

35. Relations between Fox and Curtis remained close, and in February 1660 they traveled together to the southwest; see Parker to Margaret Fell, 29 Feb. 1660, Swarthmore MS., I, 169, LSF. It is hard to believe that they failed to explore the question of involvement with the militia during that long journey.

36. Nayler to Margaret Fell [1659], Portfolio MS., XLI, 22, LSF.

37. On this development, see Rufus Jones, *The Quakers in the American Colonies* (London: Macmillan and Co., 1911), chap. 4. Stevenson and Robinson were hanged on October 27, 1659, and never saw Fox's letter.

38. Fox, *Works*, 7:178–79.

39. Gawler to Fox, 26 Nov. 1659, Swarthmore MS., IV, 219, LSF. Fox's note on the back of the letter, "which gf for bad and said it was contraye to ouer princables for our wepenes ar spirituall and not carnall," reflected a later attitude. The letter reveals that he was being confronted with requests from sincere followers who sensed a contradiction between the "service of truth" and involvement in the military: the former he insisted on, the latter he had not discouraged. He addressed this issue also in Fox to Friends in Bristol [1659], Swarthmore MS., VII, 157, LSF.

40. Minutes of Council, 19 Aug. 1659, in Penney, ed., *Extracts*, 116.

41. Barclay, ed., *Letters*, 286n–87n.

42. Penney, ed., *Journal*, 1:343; Reay, *Quakers*, 88. I am rejecting Fox's date of 1658 for this incident because he was not, as far as we otherwise know, "weak and in great sufferings" then, nor was there a cloud over Davis at that time; on the contrary, he had just been one of those selected as treasurer.

43. *Journal*, 203–4, 206–7.

44. Margaret Fell, Jr. to Margaret Fell, 3 Dec. 1659, Spence MS., III, 65, LSF.

45. Hubberthorne to Margaret Fell, 21 Nov. 1659, in Barclay, ed., *Letters*, 73–74.

46. Fox, *Spirit of Envy*, 4.

47. *Journal*, Bbb.199; Davies, *Restoration*, 187, 256–63. Few believed the Rump's promise to protect the ministry by continuing tithes; see *The Diary of Samuel Pepys*, 11 vols., ed. Robert Latham and William Matthews (Berkeley and Los Angeles: University of California Press, 1970), 1:27.

48. Fox, *To the Councill of Officers*, 7.

49. *England's Murthering Monsters* (N.p., 1659), Broadside.

50. *These several Papers was sent to Parliament* (London: N.p., 1659).

51. Memo, General Meeting, Skipton, 5 Oct. 1659, Portfolio MS., XVI, 2, LSF.

52. John Harwood, *To All People That profess the Eternal Truth of the Living God* (N.p., 1663), 4. Fox's denial of direct involvement with this scheme rings true; see Fox, *Spirit of Envy*, 4. For lists of such nominees, see Penney, ed., *Extracts*, 6–13, 105–15.

53. For another critique of the legal system, see Fox, *Law of God*.

54. Fox, *A Declaration against all Professions and Professors* (London: N.p., 1655), 4.

55. Fox, *To the Parliament of the Comon-Wealth of England* (London: N.p., 1659), 3–14.

56. For two examples, see *John Bellers: His Life, Times and Writings*, ed. George Clarke (London: Routledge and Kegan Paul, [1987]), and Susanne Gowan, George Lakey, William Moyer, and Richard Taylor, *Moving toward a New Society* (Philadelphia: New Society Press, 1976).

57. Richard Blome, *Questions Propounded to George Whitehead and George Fox* (N.p., [1659]), 6.

58. Fox, *To the Parliament*, 14–23.

59. Latham and Matthews, eds., *Pepys Diary*, 1:38, 40, 45.

60. Castelucci, "Bishop," 65.

61. On this period, see Davies, *Restoration*, chap. 14, and Adamson and Follard, *Vane*, 408.

62. Reay, *Quakers*, 97–98; Hutton, *Restoration*, 71.

63. Henry Fell to Margaret Fell, 7 Feb. 1660, Caton MS., III, 242–44, LSF; E. B. to W. M., n.d., in Barclay, ed., *Letters*, 75–79.

64. Latham and Matthews, eds., *Pepys Diary*, 1:38–39, 52, 55, 60.

65. Fox was still there as late as February 7; see Henry Fell to Margaret Fell, 7 Feb. 1660, Caton MS., III, 242–44, LSF.

66. Margaret Fell, Jr., to Mother, 12 Sept. 1659, Spence MS., III, 59; Nayler to Margaret Fell [1659], Portfolio MS., XLI:22, LSF.

67. Parker to Margaret Fell, 15 June 1658, Caton MS., III, 313–17, LSF. Efforts at reconciliation can be followed in Braithwaite (*Beginnings*, 271–74), although he neglects to illustrate the depths of Fox's continuing opposition.

68. Margaret Fell, Jr., to Margaret Fell, 12 Sept. and 29 Oct. 1659, Spence MS., III, 59, 63, LSF; Hubberthorne to Fox, 24 Sept. 1660, in Barclay, *ed., Letters*, 82–84.

69. Dewsbury to Margaret Fell, n.d., Swarthmore MS., IV, 134, LSF (Braithwaite, [*Beginnings*, 274n1] dates this letter in early February); Rich, *Hidden Things*, 37. Though this latter source is hostile and was published nearly twenty years later, Rich, one of Nayler's most public supporters, was in a position to know, and Fox's demand that the freed prisoner kneel does not sound out of character. A decade and a half before Rich another Fox critic and prominent early Friend, John Harwood (*To All People*, 6), made the same charge. When confronted with this last allegation, Fox equivocated, denying that he ordered Nayler to kneel before him, but averring that if a wrongdoer wanted thus to confess before the Lord, "I shall never deny it nor call it idolatry"; see Fox, *Spirit of Envy*, 9.

70. Whitehead, ed., *Collection of Books*, 592–93. Margaret Fell reported matter-of-factly on Nayler's reemergence as a spokesman; see Margaret Fell to Fox, 31 July 1660, Portfolio MS., XXIII, 37, LSF.

71. Castelucci, "Bishop," 125–26.

72. *Journal*, 206, 210–12.

73. Fox, *Works*, 7:164–66. Fox's conviction that his followers would be kings on the earth was not new. In October 1653 he reminded them that they would "judge and discern and confound all the deceit of the world, and grow up to be as kings"; see Fox, William Dewsbury, James Nayler, and John Whitehead, *Several Letters Written to the Saints of the Most High* (London: N.p., 1654), 15.

74. Barry Reay, "The Quakers and 1659: Two Newly Discovered Broadsides by Edward Burrough," *Journal of the Friends' Historical Society* 54 (1977): 101–11.

75. Richard Hubberthorne, *Real Cause*, 2. The other two pamphlets were *The Good Old Cause Briefly Demonstrated* (London: N.p., 1659) and *Common-Wealtsh's Remembrancer*.

76. On this point, see Reay, *Quakers*, 88–91.

77. Hubberthorne to Margaret Fell, 21 Jan. 1659, Caton MS., III, 400–403, LSF.

78. Davies, *Restoration*, 293–97, 304, 313.

79. *Journal*, 212–13.

80. Davies, *Restoration*, 318–19. The top reaches of the army's hierarchy moved quickly

to shore up loyalty by requiring officers to sign an engagement to support parliamentary decisions; Davies, *Restoration*, 314–15.

81. *Journal*, 213–14. On the weather, see Hockliffe, ed., *Diary of Josselin*, 134.

82. Hubberthorne to Margaret Fell, 21 Jan. 1660, Caton MS., III, 400–403, LSF.

83. *Journal*, 214–15; Davies, *Restoration*, 334–36; Parker to Fox, 7 June 1660, Swarthmore MS., III, 143, and Edward ? to Fox, 1 May 1660, Portfolio MS., I, 54, LSF.

84. Braithwaite, *Beginnings*, 333–34, sorts out the confusion about yearly meetings.

85. Penney, ed., *Journal*, 1:355–56, 358.

86. Caton to Willan, 7–8 May 1660, Swarthmore MS., IV, 261, LSF.

87. Hubberthorne to Fox, 29 May 1660, Swarthmore MS., IV, 18, LSF.

88. Salthouse to Margaret Fell, 5 June 1660, Swarthmore MS., III, 168, LSF.

89. Salthouse to Fox, 19 Nov. 1660, Swarthmore MS., III, 174, LSF.

90. Salthouse to Margaret Fell, 29 June 1660, Swarthmore MS., III, 167, LSF.

91. Penney, ed., *Journal*, 1:358–59.

92. On this point, see Hutton, *Restoration*, 113.

93. One Friend, later disowned for his chronic naysaying, made this point; see John Pennyman, *A Short Account of the Life of Mr. John Pennyman* (London: N.p., 1696), 85–86.

94. Penney, ed., *Short Journal*, 56.

95. My conclusions have been provoked by Hutton, *Restoration*, 119–23. For a Quaker's brief review of the nation's history during the 1650s, see Richard Hubberthorne's in Hubberthorne and Nayler, *Short History*, 16–23. See also Ingle, "Hubberthorne and History."

CHAPTER 13

1. Latham and Matthews, eds., Pepys, *Diary*, 2:11; Capp, *Fifth Monarchists*, 199, 206; Hutton, *Restoration*, 150–51.

2. Latham and Matthews, eds., Pepys, *Diary*, 2:9.

3. This radical underground has been explored by Richard L. Greaves in two books, *Deliver Us*, and *Enemies under his Feet: Radicals and Nonconformists in Britain, 1664–1673* (Stanford, Calif.: Stanford University Press, 1990).

4. *Journal*, 229–31.

5. This interpretation differs only in emphasis from that of Richard L. Greaves, "Shattered Expectations? George Fox, the Quakers and the Restoration State, 1660–1685" (paper delivered at George Fox Commemorative Conference, Lancaster University, 26 March 1991), for he stresses that the defense Fox and the Quakers mounted against their persecutors proved that they were not totally demoralized.

6. This is, of course, the title of the second volume of the standard history of the Quaker movement: William Braithwaite, *The Second Period of Quakerism* (London: Macmillan and Co., 1919).

7. The dating of his stay at Swarthmoor is extrapolated from *Journal*, 216, and Fell, *Collection*, 4.

8. Fox's recollection that he was a prisoner for twenty weeks apparently referred to the date near the end of October when he was set at "full liberty" after a London judge acted on a writ of habeas corpus (*Journal*, 228–29). Also see Hubberthorne to Margaret Fell, 24 Sept. 1660, in Penney, ed., *Journal*, 1:364–65.

9. Finnes, *Illustrated Journeys*, 164.

10. Hubberthorne to Fox, 31 July 1660, in Barclay, ed., *Letters*, 84–85. Many adherents, including Hubberthorne, visited their imprisoned leader; see Hubberthorne to Mar-

garet Fell, 25 Aug. 1660, in "Richard Hubberthorne to Margaret Fell, 1660," *Journal of the Friends' Historical Society* 29 (1932): 72.

11. Margaret Fell to Fox, 31 July 1660, Portfolio MS., XXIII, 37, LSF.

12. Fox, *The Summ of such Particulars as Are Charged against George Fox in the Mittimus by which He Stands Committed* (N.p., [1660]), 1.

13. *Journal,* 217–18; Penney, ed., *Journal,* 1:463.

14. Fox, *Summ,* 2–3.

15. *Journal,* 219–21; other letters are at 223, 224–25. He also advised the king not to permit frivolities like maygames and drunkenness to play havoc with "them that do well"—otherwise, he warned, "you do bear the sword in vain" to allow such abominations; see *Journal,* 225.

16. Fell, *Collection,* 202–10. This letter, composed on June 5 before she left for London, is interesting. Fox probably advised her on its contents, for he signed it, the only one of the fourteen signatories not in the capital before Fell personally delivered it on June 22. Buried in the statement, in the penultimate paragraph, was a passing reference to "our testimony against all strife and wars and contentions" (209); how far it applied to those who refused to rule for God remained ambiguously unstated.

17. Margaret Fell to the magistrates, n.d., in *Journal,* 221.

18. Margaret Fell to Fox, 17 July 1660, in Penney, ed., *Journal,* 1:372–73. By the next week Fell had had three meetings with the king; see Margaret Fell to Pearson, 24 July 1660, Spence MS., III, 54, LSF.

19. Arthur Bryant, ed., *Letters, Speeches and Declarations of King Charles II* (London: Cassell, 1968), 85.

20. Margaret Fell to Fox, 31 July 1660, Portfolio MS., XXIII, 37, LSF; *Journal,* 221–23, 226. Fell also left for royal perusal three copies of one of Fox's oddest works, a linguistic survey and defense of the use of "thee" and "thou" entitled *A Battle-Door for Teachers and Professors to Learn Singular and Plural* (London: N.p., 1660), coauthored with John Stubbs and Benjamin Furly.

21. Parker to Margaret Fell, 12 Oct. 1660, Swarthmore MS., I, 172, LSF.

22. *Journal,* 226. There were two sets of executions in October, on the 13th and 19th; see Latham and Matthews, eds., Pepys, *Diary,* 1:265, 269.

23. *Journal,* 229, 224–25.

24. Fox, *Our Covenant with God and with all men in Peace* (London: N.p., 1660), Broadside, no pagination.

25. *Journal,* 225.

26. Fox, Epistle, n.d., Swarthmore MS., VII, 165, LSF. This epistle dealt with the reasons Quakers paid taxes.

27. Hutton, *Restoration,* 147, 149; Thomas Moore, memorandum, 14 Dec. 1660, Swarthmore MS., IV, 196, LSF.

28. Margaret Fell to Fox, 31 July 1660, Portfolio MS., XXIII, 37, LSF.

29. Latham and Matthews, eds., Pepys, *Diary,* 2:18; *Proclamation against all Meetings of Quakers, Anabaptists, etc.* (N.p., [1661]), Broadside.

30. Greaves, *Deliver Us,* 55–56.

31. *Journal,* 229, 231. Apparently the first run of the broadside was confiscated by zealous officials.

32. *A Declaration from the Harmles & Innocent People of God* (N.p., [1661]). A slightly edited version appears in Nickalls, *Journal,* 398–404.

33. *Journal,* 46.

34. Agnes Wilkinson, Epistle, 1653, Swarthmore MS., IV, 228, LSF. This may have been the first clear statement of a firm pacifist testimony from a Quaker. Unfortunately,

almost nothing is known about Wilkinson. Apparently a northerner, probably from Westmorland, she was charged the next year with some kind of lewdness in Yorkshire; see Aldam to Margaret Fell, 30 Oct. 1654, Swarthmore MS., IV, 89, LSF. A later critic pointed out the inconsistency of some Quakers, like Fox, supporting governments' right to raise armies, while others opposed; see Pickworth, *Charge of Error*, 66–67.

35. Fox, "How the Lord," in Cadbury, ed., *Narrative Papers*, 28.

36. *Journal*, 231.

37. Smith, *Descriptive Catalogue*, 2:445. The need for translations was underscored a month later when a report came from the Rhineland that rumors had spread there that Friends had risen against the king; see William Ames to Fox, 14 Feb. 1661, Swarthmore MS., IV, 195, LSF.

38. Frederick B. Tolles and E. Gordon Alderfer, eds., *The Witness of William Penn* (New York: Macmillan, 1957), 100.

39. *Plus Ultra, or the Second Part of the Character of a Quaker* (London: N.p., 1672), 8.

40. Hutton, *Restoration*, 236.

41. Fell, *Collection*, 202.

42. *Journal*, 234.

43. Fox, *Gospel-Liberty and the Royal-Law of Love* (N.p., 1668), 6.

44. On Penington, see Penney, ed., *Journal*, 1:445; Smith, *Descriptive Catalogue*, 2:334–61.

45. More to Conway, 9 Nov. 1675, in Nicholson, ed., *Conway Letters*, 404–6.

46. *The Works of . . . Isaac Penington*, 2 vols., 2d ed. (London: Samuel Clark, 1761), 1:444–45, 449. Penington also included a section on "What the People Called Quakers Desire in Reference to Civil Government" (453–55), but he concentrated on liberty of conscience and plotting and did not mention war.

47. William Mucklow, *Tyranny and Hypocrisy Detected* (London: N.p., 1673), 225.

48. *Journal*, 232.

49. For only one example, see Fox to Edward Brown, 4 April 1661, Swarthmore MS., VII, 168, LSF.

50. On these points, see Horle, *Quakers*, 17–18, 162.

51. For an example, see Fox, *Truths Triumph in the Eternal Power over the Dark Inventions of Fallen Man* (London; N.p., 1661).

52. Fox, Epistle, 1653, Swarthmore MS., VII, 40; *Journal*, 239–40; Penney, ed., *Journal*, 1:373–74.

53. Fox to dear Friends, 28 Jan. 1661, in *Journal*, 232.

54. *Journal*, 238–39.

55. Fox to friends, Dec. 1661, Portfolio MS., XXIV, 46, LSF.

56. *Journal*, 241.

57. Caton to Fox, 25 Jan. 1661, Swarthmore MS., IV, 273, LSF. Caton denied any intention to be rebellious or disobedient, but he did not go.

58. *Journal*, 241–43.

59. William Coddington to John Winthrop, Jr., 29 July 1672, *Collections of the Massachusetts Historical Society*, 4th ser., 10 vols. (Boston: Massachusetts Historical Society, 1865), 7:287–89.

60. Benjamin Furly to Friends, n.d., Cross MS., 22–25, LSF. Furly, a prosperous Englishman at the center of the small Quaker groups in Holland, sided with Perrot for a time but soon realized the insignificance of the hat.

61. Sewell, *History*, 330. Perrot was also one of the few Quakers to sign a petition addressed to Cromwell to remit Nayler's punishment; see Penney, ed., *Extracts*, 21–23.

62. The standard study, Kenneth L. Carroll, *John Perrot, Early Quaker Schismatic*

(London: Friends Historical Society, 1971), miscasts Perrot as "the greatest schismatic in seventeenth century Quakerism" (44) and looks at the conflict through the eyes of one who assumes his subject was in error.

63. Burrough to Dring and Roberts, 21 Jan. 1656, Markey MS., 103–4, LSF.

64. Harwood, *To All People,* 8.

65. Sewell, *History,* 293.

66. On this period, see Carroll, *Perrot,* 14–33. In 1658 Fox publicly expressed approval of his work in Rome; see Fox, *Answer to a Paper,* 17. And the next year he wrote Perrot a letter of sympathy and encouragement; see Cadbury, ed., *Annual Catalogue,* 71 (item 10,34D).

67. Fox to Theory John, n.d., Markey MS., 112–13, LSF. Given Fox's poor spelling, it is impossible to be sure what Perrot in fact called himself. But in ancient Greece a "theor," according to the *Oxford English Dictionary,* referred to an envoy sent on a religious mission by a state; the *OED* lists its first use in English as 1847. Perrot could speak Latin, and may have adopted the Anglicized version of that language's "theorus" to describe himself and his mission. Carroll (*Perrot,* 41) mentions Perrot's habit of signing his letter simply "John" but does not comment on the name Theor John.

68. John Perrot to unknown, n.d., Crosse MS., 47, LSF.

69. Perrot, "I would not that the true Israel," n.d., Swarthmore MS., V, 17, LSF. Perrot's stance did conflict with Paul's recommendation that men should uncover their heads when they were praying or prophesying. For the relevant passage, see 1 Corinthians 11:4–7. But the Quaker practice likewise conflicted with a lite.al reading of this passage, for they never decreed that men who prophesied should uncover, as the apostle recommended.

70. Perrot to Friends of God, n.d., in William Salt, *Some Breathings of the Life, from a Naked Heart* (London: N.p., 1662), 15–17. Furly emphasized the same point; see Furly to Friends, n.d., Crosse MS., 22–25, LSF.

71. Carroll, *Perrot,* 50.

72. Fox, *Spirit of Envy,* 7.

73. Fox, *Works,* 7:189–91. Fox struggled no more successfully with the same contradiction in a muddled 1663 essay; see Fox, *Friends, The matter concerning not putting off the Hat* (N.p., [c. 1663]). Ellis Hookes attached a note endorsing the essay (4).

74. On Pennyman, see Penney, ed., *Journal,* 2:431; Pennyman, *Short Account.* For William Penn's critical but probably basically accurate assessment, see William Penn to Mary Pennyman, 22 Nov. 1673, in Mary M. Dunn and Richard S. Dunn, eds., *The Papers of William Penn,* 5 vols. (Philadelphia: University of Pennsylvania Press, 1981), 1:263–67, esp. 265–66. Pennyman definitely had reservations about remitting taxes for war and clashed with Fox in the early 1660s over this issue; see Pickworth, *Charge of Error,* 225.

75. William Beck and T. Frederick Ball, *The London Friends' Meetings* (London: F. Bowyer Kitto, 1869), 36, 240; G. E. Alymer, *The State's Servants: The Civil Service of the English Republic, 1649–1660* (London: Routledge and Kegan Paul, 1973), 222.

76. Penney, ed., *Short Journal,* 317.

77. Ellwood, *History of Ellwood,* 146.

78. Penneyman, *Short Account,* 10–11; Hookes to Margaret Fell, 25 Nov. 1662, in Penney, ed., *Extracts,* 153–55. Hookes, of course, said he intended to report to Fox. On Latey, see Penney, ed., *Journal,* 2:401. In 1664 this issue was still hanging fire, although now it seemed to center on the best political strategy for lobbying Parliament. Several unnamed and so-called wise men, George Whitehead wrote sarcastically, "who would willingly enough assume to be judges over us," wanted to excise Fox's preamble from a list of sufferings lest it displease Catholics and prevent them from uniting with Quakers

in opposition to a pending bill against sectarians; see Whitehead to Fox, 4 May 1664, Swarthmore MS., IV, 96, LSF.

79. Penneyman, *Short Account*, 10.

80. Cadbury, ed., *Annual Catalogue*, 74 (item 52D). The date of Perrot's arrival is unclear, but he was in London by August 22; see Fox to frends, 22 Aug. 1662, Swarthmore MS., VII, 111.

81. Fox, Stubbs, and Furly, *Battle-Door*.

82. J. H. [John Harwood], "The Life of innocency vindicated," Feb. 1667, BL.

83. George Fox the younger, *The Dread of Gods Power* (London: N.p., [1660]), 1–2.

84. George Fox the younger, untitled poem, in Salt, *Some Breathings*, 19.

85. Except where noted, my account of Perrot's first days in London are from Perrot to Fox, 1664, in Rich, *Hidden Things*, 2–8. Part of this long account is also confirmed by a clearly more contemporary but undated letter; see Perrot to Burrough and Fox, n.d., Crosse MS., 101, LSF.

86. Besse, *Sufferings*, 1:292.

87. Dewsbury to brethren and sisters, 21 Oct. 1661, Portfolio MS., XXXVI, 102, LSF.

88. Perrot to Burrough and Fox, n.d., Crosse MS., 101, LSF.

89. Joseph Nicholson to Margaret Fell, 14 Oct. 1662, Swarthmore MS., IV, 104, LSF. Fox, interestingly, crossed this line out, but whether because he disagreed with it, did not want to believe it, or wanted the phrase omitted when the letter was recopied for distribution is not clear.

90. Perrot to Fox, 1664, in Rich, *Hidden Things*, 8.

91. Isaac Penington, "Some things have been very observable and wonderful unto me concerning John Perrot," n.d., Isabel Harker to A. D., 1 Jan. 1662, Crosse MS., 6, 100, LSF. For Penington's subsequent reflections on his involvement with Perrot, see Penington to Thomas Curtis, 25 Feb. 1678, Penington MS., IV, 144–45, LSF. He thought none would be able to understand his trials in this period.

92. Isaac Penington, *Many deep Considerations* (N.p., [1663]). Needless to say, Fox's supporters were upset at Penington's stance, particularly his prediction that some unspecified "eminent ones" were destined to fall and his view that no certain knowledge of the Lord was sure in any administration. One, Francis Howgill, wrote to ask him to desist his writing because he was raising doubts in some and weakening others; see Howgill to Penington, 20 June 1663, Portfolio MS., III, 83, LSF. For a subsequent explanation of his support of Perrot, see Penington to Thomas Curtis, 25 Feb. 1678, Penington MS., IV, 144–45, LSF.

93. J. L., memorandum, 11 Sept. 1665, Swarthmore MS., VI, 60, LSF. The year of this document is extremely difficult to determine: it could be 1661, or 1665, or possibly 1663; see Carroll, *Perrot*, 64n1, who mistakingly calls it a letter and decides on a 1661 date. In addition, the endorsement on the reverse reads "Account of King sending for John Perrot out of Newgate"; there is no evidence that Perrot was in Newgate in 1661, certainly not prior to September 11, although he was arrested and put there in June 1662; see Sewell, *History*, 398. In any event the memo is post-1661, and the later the date, the farther from the incident described. On the king and Perrot, see Carroll, *Perrot*, 46–47.

94. Perrot to Burrough and Fox, n.d., Crosse MS., 101, LSF.

95. Perrot to All Friends, 8 Nov. 1661, Crosse MS., 98, LSF.

96. Perrot to R. D., 28 Nov. 1661, Crosse MS., 99, LSF.

97. Others included Isabel Harker, Mary Booth, Ann Michael, and Robert Cobbet. Unfortunately, as with others dissidents, little was saved concerning them, so little is known about them.

98. The most recent study is Jeffrey E. Crosby, "'Friends see it not safe to print': the

historical development of censorship among the Quakers in the seventeenth century" (Master's thesis, Brigham Young University, 1983), 38–62.

99. My account of this crucial meeting is taken from Perrot to Fox, 1664, in Rich, *Hidden Things*, 9–11, and Harker to A. D., 1 Jan. 1662, Crosse MS., 100, LSF. Although Perrot did not date the meeting, as did Harker, it is clear from comparing the two that they were referring to the same one.

100. Harker to A. D., 1 Jan. 1662, Crosse MS., 100, LSF.

101. Ibid. In 1660 a German doctor had written to Fox requesting a meeting for his wife; see German doctor to Fox, 1660, Swarthmore MS., III, 125, LSF. For the location of the sites mentioned, see William Crouch, *Memoirs of William Crouch*, in Evans and Evans, ed., *Friends Library*, 11:301.

102. Perrot to Fox, 1664, in Rich, *Hidden Things*, 11.

103. Ibid.; Harker to A. D., 1 Jan. 1662, Crosse MS., 100, LSF.

104. Fox, *Works*, 7:213–15.

105. Perrot to unknown, n.d., Markey MS., 87, LSF.

106. John Perrot, *An Epistle for the most Pure Amity and Unity* (London: N.p., [1662]). For Fox's response, see Fox, *Spirit of Envy*.

107. Rich, *Hidden Things*, 17. Significantly, some of Fox's firmest supporters shared Perrot's imprisonment at Newgate and were won over by him during their stay. Edward Burrough and John Crook signed with Perrot a long counseling letter that indicated their unity; see Burrough, John Crook, and Perrot to dear Friends, n.d., Swarthmore MS., V, 44, LSF. The letter was published for wider circulation; see Burrough, *To all dear Friends and Brethren* (N.p., [1661]).

108. Benjamin Furly, Epistle to Friends, n.d., Crosse MS., 22–25, LSF.

109. Mary Tompkins to Fox, 18 Jan. 1664, Swarthmore MS., IV, 259, LSF.

110. William Mucklow, *The Spirit of the Hat: or, the Government of the Quakers* (London: N.p., 1673); William Penn, *The Spirit of Alexander* and *Judas and the Jews*, in *A Collection of the Works of William Penn*, 2 vols. (London: J. Sowle, 1726), 2:189–227.

111. For Penn's attacks on these labels, see *Judas*, in *Works of Penn*, 2:211. Penn also spoke of "a very great meeting" where the God of Peace humbled both sides in a way that made the Perrotists recant their views "in fear and trembling"; see "Judas," 205. It is not clear when it took place, although one authority implies it was before 1670; see Braithwaite, *Second Period*, 255.

112. Penington, *Deep Considerations*, 3–4.

CHAPTER 14

1. John Stubbs to Margaret Fell, 28 July 1662, in Penney, ed., *Journal*, 2:20–22; *Journal*, 253. Stubbs's letter, the only near-contemporary account of the incident, was written the next day. Two later emendations, in an unknown hand, were added, no doubt to make the letter conform with the subsequent Fox position. Later Stubbs wrote Fell but added little to his earlier account; see Stubbs to Margaret Fell, 2 Aug. 1662, in Cadbury, ed., *Swarthmore Documents in America*, 62–63.

2. The contemporary charges and countercharges concerning this incident are in Rogers, *Christian Quaker*, pt. 5, pp. 55–59; George Whitehead, *The Accuser of our Brethren* (London: N.p., 1681), 157–59, 237–46; Pearson, *Anti-Christian Treachery*, 110–11, 142–50; and Thomas Ellwood, *An Antidote Against the Infection of William Roger's Book* (London: N.p., 1682), 225–28. The only historian to comment, Braithwaite (*Second Period* [219–20]), rejects Rogers's charges; the note in the second edition (*Second Period*, 669) by Henry J. Cadbury, drawing on Russell Mortimer, takes the same point of view,

suggesting that Rogers may have confused the two Sundays that Fox was in Bristol at the end of July 1662. This explanation was ventured, much less charitably, by Whitehead and Pearson. Fox apparently testified in the matter, but his lost affidavit, quoted by Pearson (*Anti-Christian Treachery*, 149), does not raise this point, concentrating on his assertion that he did not leave before the meeting was closed and that he saw or heard no officials. He does not indicate whether he went down the back stairs, merely confusing that issue by asserting that he came down the stairs. Hence it is clear that Fox was conceding a major point of Rogers's and his five deponents' charges, namely, that he had left the meeting by means of the back stairs, ahead of the soldiers and that he told the gathering to "keep in the meeting." On the controversy that provoked these charges, see below.

3. On this point, see also Johnson, "From Seeker to Finder," 313–14.

4. On this theme there is a vast literature, beginning with Ernst Troeltsch, *The Social Teachings of the Christian Churches*, 2 vols. (London: George Allen and Unwin, 1931). As to Quakers, Troeltsch wrote, "[T]he spirit of toleration and 'inwardness' which is produced by opposition to compulsory Christianity is not favourable for the maintenance of an organic body" (2:783).

5. For only one example of this phrase, see Thomas Morford to Margaret Fell, 4 Jan. 1659, Swarthmore MS., IV, 75, LSF.

6. Margaret Fell to Perrot, n.d., Spence MS., III, 30, LSF. They were in London at the same time.

7. See, for example, Henry Fell to T. R., 19 Aug. 1656, Swarthmore MS., I, 42, LSF, in which the author reported that one Quaker was to be "disposed of" as Fell saw fit.

8. Margaret Fell, Jr., to Margaret Fell, 26 July 1659, Spence MS., III, 61, LSF. Fox wisely did not push his views but suggested that Fell do as she was moved.

9. Margaret Fell, Jr., to Margaret Fell, 27 Aug. 1659, Spence MS., III, 2G, LSF.

10. Fox to Roberts, n.d., Swarthmore MS., VII, 141, LSF.

11. Bridgett Fell to Margaret Fell, 22 July 1660, Margaret Fell to children, 25 Sept. and 8 Oct. 1660, Spence MS., III, 69, 73, 75; Salthouse to Margaret Fell, 3 Sept. 1660, Swarthmore MS., III, 166, LSF.

12. On these themes, see Horle, *Quakers*, chap. 2.

13. Ibid., 46–47, 50–51.

14. Ellington, *Christian Information*, 7.

15. Hookes to Margaret Fell, 28 Oct. 1662, in Barclay, ed., *Letters*, 114–17. On this occasion, at least eighty Baptists were also caught in the roundup. Ellwood (*History of Ellwood*, 134–37) adds to Hookes's account.

16. Ellwood, *History of Ellwood*, 156–57, 161–63, 166–67.

17. Braithwaite, *Second Period*, 42.

18. Anonymous to Baxter, 18 Oct. 1670, Baxter Papers, 2:55, DWL.

19. Baxter, *Reliquiae Baxterianae*, 435–37.

20. In his study of Quakers in Essex, for example, Davies ("Quakers in Essex," 33) shows that the largest jump in membership there occurred in the decade of severest persecution.

21. Fox to Roberts, n.d., and Hookes to Fox, n.d. [post-Restoration], Swarthmore MS., IV, 141, 118, LSF.

22. On this point, see Christopher Hill, "Milton, Bunyan and the Literature of Defeat," *Mosaic* 24 (1991): 1–12.

23. Fox, *Works*, 7:201–11.

24. Fox, *Gospel-Liberty*, 9–10, 13, 45, 47–48.

25. Fox, "Concerning the Act," in *Works*, 4:346–65.

26. Ellwood, *History of Ellwood*, 193–95.

27. Docwra, *Apostate-Conscience*, 7.

28. Fox to friends in prison, n.d., Swarthmore MS., V, 107, LSF.

29. Fox, *A Declaration from the People of God, Called Quakers, Against All Seditious Conventicles* (N.p., n.d.), no pagination.

30. Rogers, *Christian Quaker*, pt. 5, p. 57.

31. For this phrase, see *Journal*, 253. Braithwaite (*Second Period*, 220n1) defends Fox's actions at Bristol; he argues that Fox blended courage with prudence.

32. *Journal*, 255–58. Although Fox said he did not know whether the justices saw the letter, his copy was addressed to them. Why Henry Hastings, at this time lord lieutenant of Leicestershire, would support freeing Fox is a fascinating mystery. Hastings was a strong royalist and something of a military genius for the king during the Civil War. See his entry in *DNB*, 9:128–29.

33. Penney, ed., *Short Journal*, 65–66; *Journal*, 259–61.

34. *Journal*, 261–62; Penney, ed., *Short Journals*, 79–80. Fox labeled as a "horrid lie" Rogers's charges that he hid in a ditch to avoid arrest. He conceded that the lane down which the soldiers came had a bank alongside its hedge behind which he watched them pass (Rogers, *Christian Quaker*, pt. 5, pp. 57, 60).

35. *Journal*, 262–63.

36. On these plots, see Greaves, *Deliver Us*, 176–206.

37. Fox to Latey, 1663, in "Abraham Manuscripts," *Journal of the Friends' Historical Society* 11 (1914): 148–49.

38. *Journal*, 262–69; Fell, *Collection*, 6–7; Penney, ed., *Journal*, 2:37.

39. Latham and Matthews, eds., Pepys, *Diary*, 4:200, 205, 206; Penney, ed., *Short Journal*, 68.

40. Fleming to Williams, 14 Nov. 1663, in Penney, ed., *Extracts*, 177.

41. *Journal*, 270; Penney, ed., *Journal*, 2:44, 390; Penney, ed., *Short Journal*, 68.

42. Fox to Latey, 1663, in "Abraham Manuscripts," 148–49; Penney, ed., *Short Journal*, 69; *Journal*, 270–71.

43. Fleming to Williamson, 16 Jan. 1664, in Penney, ed., *Extracts*, 186. According to Ross (*Fell*, 163), the lowest level of government in that part of the county was a family affair.

44. Fox to Latey, 1663, in "Abraham Manuscripts," 148–49; Penney, ed., *Short Journal*, 69; *Journal*, 271–73. For a deposition giving information on some of these sessions, see Penney, ed., *Journal*, 2:43–44.

45. Fiennes, *Illustrated Journeys*, 164–65; Speed, *Counties of Britain*, 109–12.

46. Fleming to Williamson, 16 Jan. 1664, in Penney, ed., *Extracts*, 186. For an example of one of Fell's lobbying efforts, this one after the fact, see Margaret Fell to Richard Kirkby, 20 Jan. 1664, in Penney, ed., *Extracts*, 187–88.

47. Fleming to Williamson, 16 Jan. 1664, in Penney, ed., *Extracts*, 186; *Journal*, 273–74; Penney, ed., *Short Journal*, 71. Fox's recollection inflated the numbers, although he may have included others sentenced later; see Penney, ed., *Journal*, 2:48.

48. For a convenient chronology, see Penney, ed., *Journal*, 2:394.

49. *Journal*, 275–76, 281–82; Penney, ed., *Journal*, 2:393; John Wigan, *Antichrist's strongest Hold overturned* (London: N.p., 1665), 12. Fox termed Wigan a deceiver, as he probably did others; see Fox to John Wigan, n.d., Swarthmore MS., VII, 3, LSF.

50. See, for examples, Fox, *The Examination and Tryall of Margaret Fell and George Fox* (at . . . *Lancaster*) (N.p., 1664); *Works*, 7:244–46; *Journal*, 278–81.

51. Penney, ed., *Short Journal*, xxi. The scrivener was probably Henry Fell.

52. Penney, ed., *Journal*, 2:58; a partial transcript appears on 57–60.

53. *Journal*, 276–78. Fox's reference to the Breda Declaration certainly indicated that

he was thinking along the same lines as the late schemers, although this fact did not of course make him part of the plot.

54. Fox, *Examination and Tryall*, 3–7. On Twisden, see Penney, ed., *Journal*, 2:393.

55. Penney, ed., *Journal*, 2:65–72.

56. Fox, *Examination and Tryall*, 20; Fell, *Collection*, 288; see also *Journal*, 289.

57. Fox, *Examination and Tryall*, 12–24; *Journal*, 288–93.

58. *Journal*, 293, 295, 296. Despite Fox's comment that he answered several books while in Lancaster jail, and the context suggests he meant while he was in the tower (*Journal*, 295), only four letters in 1665 are mentioned in Cadbury, ed., *Annual Catalogue* (86), two epistles (Fox, *Works*, 7:272–73), and one letter in Penney, ed., *Journal*, 2:396; Smith (*Descriptive Catalogue*) lists no books. Fox may have been referring to *A Controversy which hath been betwixt the Quakers Protestants and Papists* (N.p., [1665]).

59. *Journal*, 293–96. The list of the indictment's errors is given in Penney, ed., *Journal*, 2:86–89.

60. *Journal*, 296–98; Penney, ed., *Journal*, 2:94.

61. Penney, ed., *Journal*, 2:94, 399; Finnes, *Journeys*, 101–2. Concerning the day of Fox's removal to Scarborough, see Hookes to Margaret Fell, 22 May 1665, in Barclay, ed., *Letters*, 146–48.

62. *Journal*, 298–304; Penney, ed., *Journal*, 94–101; Fox, *Works*, 7:274. Despite his hardships, Fox may have been better off in his cold, smoky upstairs room—at least he faced less danger from the plague because the fleas that carried it were less active in colder weather. On this point, see the table in Barclay, ed., *Letters*, 155.

63. Hookes to Margaret Fell, 14 Aug. 1666, in Penney, ed., *Journal*, 2:102–3.

64. Penney, ed., *Journal*, 2:104–6, 110.

65. Fleming to Williamson, 15 Sept. 1666, Penney, ed., *Extracts*, 256–57.

66. *Journal*, 307–10.

67. Penney, ed., *Journal*, 2:111, 112–13, 137, 413. He also wrote at least two letters in 1668 dealing with the question of wearing hats when men prayed; see Cadbury, ed., *Annual Catalogue*, 89 (items 23,134E, 23,135E).

68. "Testimony from the Brethren who were met together at London in the 3rd month, 1666," Portfolio MS., XLI, 94, LSF (reprinted in Barclay, ed., *Letters*, 318–24). On the author, see Hookes to Margaret Fell, 14 Aug. 1666, in Penney, ed., *Journal*, 2:102–3. A later critic charged, but offered no evidence, that Fox had a "great hand" in the declaration; see Pickworth, *Charge of Error*, 101.

69. George Bishop, Epistle, 3 Jan. 1667, in Mucklow, *Tyranny and Hypocrisy*, 34–36. It is a commentary on the power of those whom Bishop criticized that his epistle survived only in the pages of a book written by a later harsh critic. See also Oliver, "Quakers and Quietism," 29, and Morgan, "The Quakers and the Establishment," xxii–iii.

70. *Journal*, 310–11; Beck and Ball, *London Meetings*, 227–29.

71. *Querers and Quakers*, 25.

72. See, for examples, Underhill, *Hell broke loose*, 10; Henry Hallywell, *An Account of Familism as it is Revived and Propagated by the Quakers* (London: N.p., 1673).

73. Margaret Fell to [Judge Wyndham], 1653, Spence MS., III, 131, LSF.

74. Fox, *Works*, 7:34. Twenty-two years later, as he endeavored to justify his later, and controversial, stance on marriage, Fox remembered the situation differently; see Fox, *Works*, 8:81. His first statement on procedure, which has not survived, occurred in 1657; see Cadbury, ed., *Annual Catalogue*, 66, (item 115C). He apparently issued one also in 1659, which has also not been found; see Cadbury, ed., *Annual Catalogue*, 72, (item 10,97D). This may have been the one Francis Bugg said was issued on 7 Jan. 1660; see Francis Bugg, *Innocency Vindicated and Envy Rebuked* (N.p., 1684), 2–3.

75. Thomas Robertson to Margaret Fell, 1655, Swarthmore MS., IV, 206, LSF.

76. For one exception, see statement of Friends from Horsham, May 1659, in Barclay, ed., *Letters*, 283.

77. Nickalls, ed., *Journal*, 421–22.

78. Anne Whitehead and Mary Elson, *An Epistle for True Love, Unity and Order in the Church of Christ* (London: N.p., 1680), 9.

79. Hubberthorne and Nayler, *Short Answer*, 8–9.

80. Fox, *Concerning Marriage* (London: N.p., 1661).

81. Fox to Richard Richardson, 16 Oct. 1679, Dix MS., 226, LSF.

82. Beck and Ball, *London Meetings*, 344–50; Fox, *Works*, 7:283–84. Fox took the same position as late as 1673; see *Works*, 8:45–46.

83. Unless otherwise noted my account of Fox's Irish trip comes from *Journal*, 327–32; and Penney, ed., *Journal*, 2:137–51. The latter (2:147) does refer to an apparently existing women's meeting in Dublin. One local, William Edmundson, said later that Fox set up women's meetings, but no other evidence is extant that he did so; see William Edmundson, *A Journal of the Life . . . of . . . William Edmundson* (London: N.p., 1715), 51. Given the controversy about these meetings when Fox dictated his *Journal*, he would have probably mentioned it if he had established any.

84. Isabel Grubb, "The Settlement of Church Discipline among Irish Friends," *Journal of the Friends' Historical Society* 45 (1953): 77.

85. For an overview of Ireland, particularly as it relates to Quakers, see "The Background," in William Penn, *My Irish Journal, 1669–1670*, ed. Isabel Grubb (London: Longmans, Green and Co., 1952), 8–17.

86. On this topic, see, for example, Hill, *God's Englishman*, 108–22.

87. Braithwaite, *Second Period*, 260.

88. Details of the voyage itself and the first two days can be found in Fox to Friends, 11 May 1669, Portfolio MS., XV, 138, LSF. The paucity of placenames in his accounts suggests that Fox was worried about giving away the location of meetings even years later when he dictated his *Journal*.

89. Grubbs, "Settlement of Discipline," 78. Fox's clandestine movements through Ireland do not support Braithwaite's unapt description of it (*Second Period*, 261) as "glad courage."

90. Rous to Margaret Fell, 24 Aug. 1669, Gibson MS., II, 71, LSF.

91. Unless otherwise noted, my account of the marriage is taken from Memorandum, n.d., Portfolio X, 53, LSF; *Journal*, 334; Penney, ed., *Journal*, 2:153–54; Fox, epistle, 2 Oct. 1669, in Cadbury, ed., *Narrative Papers*, 78–88. The rumors were publicized by John Harwood, who mentioned two occasions when he had heard that Fox and Fell spent several hours with each other, walking "unseemly and indiscreetly"; see Harwood, *To All People*, 7. Fox effectively answered these charges in *Spirit of Envy*, 11.

92. Timothy Langley to Thurloe, 19 Sept., 1658, in Birch, ed., *Thurloe Papers*, 7:403.

93. The most recent study of Fell is Knuze, "Family, Social and Religious Life," but it must be used with care. An older, filiopietiestic work is Ross, *Fell*. See also Craig Horle in Greaves and Zaller, eds., *Dictionary of British Radicals*, 1:272–75.

94. *Journal*, 312, vii; Penney, ed., *Journal*, 2:154.

95. The will is reprinted in Ross, *Fell*, 398–400.

96. Penney, ed., *Journal*, 2:154, 416–17.

97. Penn, *Irish Journal*, 19.

98. The certificate, containing their promises, is reprinted in Helen G. Crosfield, *Margaret Fox of Swarthmore Hall* (London: Headley Brothers, [1913]), 254–55.

99. *Journal*, vii, ix.

100. Penney, ed., *Journal,* 2:154. Fox used the term "puritan."

101. Cadbury, ed., *Narrative Papers,* 88.

102. On the conflict in the Fell family, see H. Larry Ingle and Jaan Ingle, "The Excommunication of George Fox, 1678," *Journal of the Friends' Historical Society* 56 (1991): 71–77.

103. Fell, *Collection,* 9. This imprisonment was the only time in her brief memoir that she referred to an incident of ill health.

104. That Margaret Fox believed herself pregnant should resolve speculation (Ross, *Fell,* 218; Knuze, "Fell," 78–79, 81) that the couple's marriage remained unconsummated—unless she likewise imagined that they engaged in sex.

105. For the letter, see Elizabeth Bowman to William Penn, 16 July 1670, Penn Papers, microfilm, in Historical Society of Pennsylvania. The original is in the Public Records Office in London and reprinted in Henry J. Cadbury, ed., "Intercepted Correspondence of William Penn, 1670," *Pennsylvania Magazine of History and Biography* 70 (1946): 352–56, and in Dunn and Dunn, *Papers of Penn,* 1:158–59. The letter's account is a bit ambiguous, but it seems to be referring to Margaret Fox's pregnancy rather than to the pregnancy of her daughter Margaret Rous, who had a son in September. It reports that an unnamed woman "haeth bene here to mete Margret Rous Abought her mouthers Besenes that is in oder to Geat her relese and E. J. and her Mouther ondertanden Margrett Foxes Condeshon and that she being weth child and so nere ass she is her time beinge out All Most thay are very endorstret [interested] to prokure her liberty which I hope thay well done." This letter confirms two quite hostile sources, one written nearly thirty years later, the other slightly later. See Young, *The Foxonian Quakers,* 34–35, who asserts that Margaret, "though past child bearing, was to have an Isaac, the midwife was sent for, but nothing comes, yet this was the marriage that was a type of Christ and the Church." Another writer, indentified as a "North Country gentleman," stated that the story of Margaret Fox's condition was widely known in the north, indeed "afforded the wicked occasion of ridicule and merriment." He reports that the midwife was called—remained a month—the baby clothes were laid out, but, he claims, "nothing came forth, all proved wind"; North Country gentleman to Francis Bugg, 10 Jan. 1707, in Francis Bugg, *The Finishing Stroke* (London: author, 1712), 239–42. Cadbury thinks that the Bowman letter confirms the account in Bugg; he does not refer to Young's account, perhaps because he did not know of it. Kunze, "Fell," 79–80, comes to no conclusion but ventures that Margaret Fox may have suffered a menopausal miscarrriage. A modern authority avers firmly, however, that "pregnancies are rare in women over 50, and extremely rare after the age of 52"; see Jack A. Pritchard, et al., *Williams Obstetrics,* 17th ed. (Norwalk, Conn.: Appleton-Century-Crofts, 1985), 811. Fell, it will be recalled, was fifty-five years old. The age a woman reaches menopause, other authorities report, has not changed in hundreds of years, although it varies slightly in various parts of the world; see Gail Megrow and Robert W. Rebar, "The Menopause," in William Droegemueller and John J. Sciarra, eds., *Gynecology and Obstetrics,* 6 vols., rev. ed. (Philadelphia: J. B. Lippincott, 1990), 1:1. In addition, a late miscarried pregnancy must leave physical evidence, hard to hide in a crowded prison. The editors of the *Penn Papers,* the only other scholars to comment on this matter, think it strange that no other mention of it appeared in Quaker letters; see Dunn and Dunn, eds., *Penn Papers,* 1:159. It must be recalled that almost all the documents were carefully screened by Fox five years later, and it is likely that he destroyed those he did not want to see the light of day; on this topic, see Ingle, "Fox as Historian." Thus it is probable that the main reason the Bowman letter survives is that it was confiscated and became a part of government files.

Although most often occurring in a woman's childbearing years, pseudocyesis has been reported in cases of women in their seventies; nearly 1 percent happen between ages fifty-five and fifty-nine. The best-known historical figure who suffered from this condition was Mary Tudor, queen of England from 1553 to 1558. Women who imagine themselves pregnant report all the symptoms of the actual condition, including supposed movements of the fetus, and often deceive even trained physicians. Occuring only about once in every five thousand obstetrics cases, this fantasy delusion is often a symptom of psychological depression, either because of infertility or loss of some object, real or imaginary, about which the woman cares deeply. For a somewhat similar case, from Germany in 1879, see George D. Bivin and M. Pauline Klinger, *Pseudocyesis* (Bloomington, Ind.: Principia Press, 1937), 47. On the phenomenon of pseudocyesis, see Bivin and Klinger, *Pseudocyesis*; Pritchard, *Obstetrics*, 218; Martin L. Pernoll, et al., eds., *Current Obstetrics and Gynecologic Diagnosis and Treatment 1987* (Norwalk, Conn.: Appleton Lange, 1987), 1041; Jack LaFerla, "Menstrual Disturbance and the Psyche," in Droegemueller and Sciarra, *Gynecology and Obstetrics*, vol. 6, chap. 85.

CHAPTER 15

1. Penney, ed., *Journal*, 1:165–67; Beck and Ball, *London Meetings*, 301.

2. M. Rous to Margaret Fell, 14 Oct. 1670, Swarthmore MS., I, 110, J. Rous to Sarah Fell, 4 Nov. 1670, Abraham MS., 14, LSF.

3. Stubbs to Margaret Fell, 25 Oct. 1670, Abraham MS., 13, LSF.

4. Penney, ed., *Journal*, 2:166–67.

5. Hookes to Margaret Fell, 27 May 1670, Swarthmore MS., IV, 122, LSF; Penney, ed., *Journal*, 2:159–61.

6. Penney, ed., *Journal*, 2:170–72. Five years later, in Worcester jail, he dictated a book containing his only extended biblical exegesis, on Revelation; see Fox, *A Testimony of what we believe of Christ* (N.p., 1677).

7. Penney, ed., *Journal*, 2:175. Ellwood, significantly, omitted mention of the vision from his edition of the *Journal*. That Fox's mind was troubled by thoughts of sex can be seen in a prayer dated in April, in which he petitioned against "all debauchery, vice, whoredoms, fornication, and this raping spirit" in England; see *Journal*, 348.

8. Penney, ed., *Journal*, 1:173–75.

9. Ibid., 175–76.

10. *Journal*, 347. Fox's subsequent recollection of having recommended laying marriages before both men's and women's meetings in 1667 (*Journal*, 315) is simply not supported by more-contemporary documents. A careful reading of this source suggests that, even if he did endorse this procedure, he did so only in London.

11. Fox to Friends in Norwich, 23 June 1671, in Arthur J. Eddington, *The First Fifty Years of Quakerism in Norwich* (London: Friends Historical Society [1932]), 273–74.

12. Fox to Penn, 24 May 1671, Dunn and Dunn, eds., *Penn Papers*, 1:208–09.

13. *Journal*, 316. These schools, two of more than fifteen in operation, were another illustration of a mature Society of Friends concerned less with molding the larger community and more with its own future.

14. For examples, see "American Journey of Fox," 33, 34, 36. Unless otherwise indicated, my account of Fox's journey is from this source, *Journal*, 349–83, and Penney, ed., *Journal*, 2:176–258 (including notes, 425–46).

15. Fox, "For Friends in the Ministry," 1667, Richardson MS. (transcript), 129–31, QC.

16. "Journal of John Burnyeat," in Evans and Evans, eds., *Friends Library*, 10:144, 145–46.

17. Penney, ed., *Journal*, 2:354. John Hull, whose journal of the early part of the trip is reprinted in Penney, 2:176–87, called the ship a "ketch," which would have made it a two-master.

18. Edmundson, *Journal*, 53.

19. J. Eric S. Thompson, ed., *Thomas Gage's Travels in the New World* (Norman: University of Oklahoma Press, 1958), 20–21.

20. Thomas Herbert, *A Relation of Some Yeares Travaile into Afrique, Asia, Indies*, facsimle ed. (New York: Da Capo Press, 1971), 7.

21. Braithwaite, *Second Period*, 618; Jerome S. Handler and Frederick W. Lange, *Plantation Slavery in Barbados: An Archaeological and Historical Investigation* (Cambridge, Mass.: Harvard University Press, 1978), 17, 179; Rufus Jones, *The Quakers in the American Colonies* (London: Macmillan, 1911), 112n; Henry J. Cadbury, *Friendly Heritage: Letters from the Quaker Past* (Norwalk, Conn.: Silvermine Publishers, 1972), 15–16; Edward A. Mance, "George Fox, Quakers, Negroes, and Slavery in Barbados, 1671–1675" (Bachelor's thesis, Yale University, 1945), 3, 44–45. Some Friends were among the island's poor whites; see Hilary McD. Beckles, *White Servitude and Black Slavery in Barbados, 1627–1715* (Knoxville, Tenn.: University of Tennessee Press, 1989), 130.

22. Margaret E. Hirst, *The Quakers in Peace and War* (London: Swarthmore Press, 1923), 310–13.

23. Coddington to Winthrop, 15 July 1674, in *Collections of Massachusetts*, 7:293–96.

24. "What G.ff declared at ye women's meeting at Thomas Rouses," 28 Oct. 1671, Baltimore Women's Half-Yearly Meeting Minutes, 1–11, Friends Historical Library, Swarthmore College (hereafter cited as FHL).

25. Edmundson, *Journal*, 56.

26. On this judge, Ralph Fretwell, see Dunn and Dunn, eds., *Penn Papers*, 2:547.

27. Fox, *To the Ministers, Teachers, and Priests . . . of Barbados* (N.p., 1672), 48–49.

28. Some have doubted Fox's role in writing this letter, which he admitted he "and some other Friends" drew up (*Journal*, [357]). For the clearest statement of these doubts, see Brinton, *Religious Philosophy*, 100. Rufus M. Jones ("George Fox's Letter to the Governor of Barbados," *Friend* 64 [1924], 759–60) rejects Fox's authorship of the first, doctrinal part. That Fox may not have written it seems beside the point: it was not contrary to his purposes and other actions on Barbados or the other places he visited. Jones and Arthur J. Mekeel (*Quakerism and a Creed* [Philadelphia: Friends Book Store, 1936], 18–20) have questioned whether it accurately reflected Quaker doctrine because it was prepared when Fox was not well and was addressed to a conservative audience. Such doubts reflect a desire to recruit Fox posthumously to Mekeel's "real Quaker message."

29. This focus on the theological 60 percent of the letter, carried in all editions of the *Journal*, also distracted scholars, particularly those desirous of emphasizing Fox's orthodoxy, from looking for other creedal statements he wrote. For two examples, see Fox, *Some Principles of the Elect People of God Who in Scorn Are Called Quakers* (London: N.p., 1661) and *Some Principles of the Elect People of God In Scorn Called Quakers* (N.p., 1671), both less orthodox than the more famous letter.

30. In a 1673 letter to Barbadian Quakers, Fox implied that fortnightly meetings for blacks there was an established policy, although later he repeated his advice given at Rous's house that slaves should have two or three hours weekly to wait on the Lord when Friends met. This advice implied separate meetings, where, without white oversight, mischief might occur; see Fox, *Gospel Family-Order, Being a Short Discourse concerning of the Ordering of Families, Both of Whites, Blacks and Indians* (N.p., 1676), 20, 22.

31. Fox, *To the Ministers*, 77.

32. On this shift, see Winthrop Jordan, *White over Black: American Attitudes toward the Negro, 1550–1812* (Baltimore: Penguin Books, 1969), 92–93.

33. Fox, Sermon at Thomas Rous', 21 Oct. 1671, Baltimore Women's Half-Yearly Meeting Minutes, 11–19, FHL. This sermon was virtually reprinted as *Gospel Family-Order.* The conservative implications of these views were especially appealing to Philadelphia's Quaker elite thirty years later, as J. William Frost ("George Fox's Ambiguous Anti-Slavery Legacy," [Paper delivered at the George Fox Conference, Lancaster, England, March 1991]) makes clear. In this instance, to their credit, Quaker historians have a better record than non-Quakers, who have praised Fox for being, as Winthrop Jordan put it, "convinced that the principle of equality must be applied to the poor Negro slaves"; see *White over Black*, 194.

34. Fox, Epistle [1671], 315, MS Q4–5, LSF. In an unpublished epistle at this time, either Fox or his scribe inexplicably marked through a statement grouping whites, blacks, and Indians with Jews, Gentiles, Turks, papists, and Protestants who were dead in Adam; see Fox, Epistle [1671], 314–15, MS Q4–5, LSF.

35. Fox to Friends, 18 Feb. 1674, in *Gospel Family-Order*, 21–22. For the most recent, and best, overview of Fox and slavery, see Frost, "Fox's Legacy."

36. Fox, "For families," n.d., Caton MS., II, 107–8, LSF.

37. Five years later, under pressure from planters, proselytizing of slaves was outlawed; see Handler and Lange, *Plantation Slavery*, 179.

38. On this "Western Design," see Sidney W. Mintz, *Sweetness and Power: The Place of Sugar in Modern History* (New York: Penguin Books, 1985), 37–38.

39. Hirst, *Quakers in Peace*, 307, 314–15.

40. On Maryland, see Wesley F. Craven, *The Southern Colonies in the Seventeenth Century, 1607–1689* (Baton Rouge: Louisiana University Press, 1949), chap. VI, 299–309.

41. Early population figures are murky; these are from thirty years later, but percentages probably hold; see Evarts B. Greene, *American Population Before the Federal Census of 1790* (New York: Columbia University Press, 1932), 128.

42. One researcher ventured that Fox's opposition to slavery could be seen in the will of a Quaker who manumitted his slaves in 1674 after the leader's visit (Kenneth L. Carroll, "Maryland Quakers and Slavery," *Quaker History* 72 [1983]: 27), but no documentary evidence exists for this connection.

43. Burnyeat hoped the West River gathering would bring together Quakers in Maryland; see "Journal of Burnyeat," in Evans and Evans, eds., *Friends Library*, 11:144–45.

44. There is some confusion about exact dates for this meeting. Both Fox and Burnyeat give the date as third month, or May, but assuming the half-yearly meeting convened every six months, and the last meeting was held in October, then April would have been the time for the gathering. Jones (*Quakers in Colonies*, 230) decided on April. There is also some confusion over exactly how long the meeting lasted. I am following the more contemporaneous sources.

45. I have here supplemented the usual sources of this trip from "Journal of Burnyeat," in Evans and Evans, eds., *Friends Library*, 11:145–46.

46. Henry Fell to Margaret Fell, 19 Feb. 1657, Swarthmore MS., I, 68, LSF.

47. In fact, Williams charged that the Quakers were the parents of ranterism. For his views, see Williams, "Fox Digg'd," in *Writings of Williams*, 5:2, 43, *et passim*.

48. For this wedding, see Cadbury, *Friendly Heritage*, 258–59.

49. On Rhode Island Quakers, see Arthur J. Worrall, *Quakers in the Colonial Northeast* (Hanover, N.H.: University Press of New England, 1980), 31–38.

50. Williams, "Fox Digg'd," in *Writings of Williams*, 5:18.

51. For Williams, see Cyclone Covey, *The Gentle Radical: A Biography of Roger Williams* (New York: Macmillan, 1966).

52. Williams claimed in 1676 when he published his side (and the only side to survive) of the to-do that Fox's associates in Newport purposely waited until their leader had gone to present the invitation to the deputy governor; see Williams, "Fox Digg'd," *Writings of Williams*, 5:6–7, 35, 53. Given Fox's disputatious nature, he would no doubt have relished confronting Williams. Fox and Burnyeat published a joint response in 1678: George Fox and John Burnyeat, *A New-England Fire Brand Quenched* (London: N.p., 1678).

53. Williams, "Fox Digg'd" in *Writings of Williams*, prefatory letter.

54. On Dyer, see Williams, *Divine Rebel*, 136–37, 185–87, 200.

55. Coddington to Winthrop, 29 July 1672, *Collections of Massachusetts*, 7:287–89.

56. Edmundson, *Journal*, 64.

57. Jean R. Soderlund, *Quakers and Slavery: A Divided Spirit* (Princeton, N.J.: Princeton University Press, 1985), 73–74.

58. For more on this incident, see Cadbury, *Miracles*, 110–11.

59. On the Ablemarle region, see Craven, *Southern Colonies*, 408–9.

60. Fox to Friends in Virginia, 1673, in *Works*, 8:54–55. On Batts, see *Dictionary of North Carolina Biography*, ed., William S. Powell, 3 vols. (Chapel Hill: University of North Carolina Press, 1979–   ), 1:119.

61. Fox to friends, 7 Jan. 1673, Portfolio MS., XL, 115, LSF.

62. Ibid.

63. Cadbury, ed., *Annual Catalogue*, 115 (item 10,17F), 116 (item 10,41F), 117 (item 10,71F).

64. One is tempted to wonder in Fox's ready depiction of his perils if he did not exaggerate, both to demonstrate what he put himself through and to show that, because he survived, God looked after him. He kept a separate three-page account of his trials, including being imperiled by tigers and lions, which of course did not live in the New World; see Penney, ed., *Journal*, 2:252–55.

65. On these visions, see Frederick W. Tolles, *Quakers and the Atlantic Culture* (New York: Macmillan, 1960), chap. 1.

66. Fox, *Works*, 8:46–47; Tolles, *Quakers and Culture*, 17.

67. *Journal*, 384. On the fair, see Ross, *Fell*, 246n.

68. For Penn's protest, see Penn to Commons of England, March 1673, in Dunn and Dunn, eds., *Penn Papers*, 1:259–61.

69. Russell Mortimer, ed., *Minute Book of the Men's Meeting of the Society of Friends in Bristol, 1667–1686* (Bristol, England: Bristol Record Society, 1971), 54–56.

70. *Journal*, 386–87; Penney, ed., *Journal*, 2:261–63.

71. The principal work to which Fox was probably referring was Mucklow, *Spirit of the Hat*, although other hostile pamphlets appeared. The Quaker dispute with that curious sect the Muggletonians also heated up during this period. Despite the fact that Fox wrote at least one book responding to them (*Something in Answer to Lodowick Muggleton's Book, Which He Calls The Quakers Neck Broken* [London: N.p., 1667]), I have not gone into this dispute, primarily because its bitter vituperation adds little to an understanding of Fox. For the best work on the Muggletonians, see Christopher Hill, Barry Reay, and William Lamont, *The World of the Muggletonians* (London: Temple Smith, 1983).

72. Wildes, *Penn*, 77–78; Anthony Lowther to Penn, 18 Oct. 1675, in Dunn and Dunn, eds., *Penn Papers*, 1:354–55.

73. Penn to father, 23 April and 6 May 1665, in Dunn and Dunn, eds., *Penn Papers*, 1:33–35.

74. For a filiopietistic comparison, see Edwin B. Bronner, "George Fox and William Penn, unlikely yokefellows and friends," *Journal of the Friends' Historical Society* 56 (1991): 78–95.

75. A nearly complete listing of Penn's works in their many editions requires forty-five pages in Smith, *Descriptive Catalogue*, 2:282–326.

76. Parker to Fox, 20 Oct. 1674, in Penney, ed., *Journal*, 2:305–7.

77. On this theme, see Horle, *Quakers*, 176–78.

78. Penn to William Mucklow, 11 Oct. 1672, in Dunn and Dunn, eds., *Penn Papers*, 1:254. See also Melvin B. Endy, Jr., *William Penn and Early Quakerism* (Princeton, N.J.: Princeton University Press, 1973), 334–36.

79. The only biography of Barclay is D. Elton Trueblood, *Robert Barclay* (New York: Harper and Row, 1968).

80. *Journal*, 388; Croese, *History*, book 2, p. 115.

81. Penney, ed., *Journal*, 2:265, 447. The most recent study of this imprisonment and its implications is Craig Horle, "Changing Quaker Attitudes toward Legal Defense: The George Fox Case, 1673–75, and the Establishment of the Meeting for Sufferings," in *Seeking the Light: Essays in Quaker History in Honor of Edwin B. Bronner*, eds., J. William Frost and John W. Moore (Wallingford and Haverford, Pa.: Pendle Hill Publications and Friends Historical Association, 1986), 17–39.

82. Penney, ed., *Journal*, 2:275.

83. Parker's warning is in *Journal*, 388–89.

84. Fox to dear friends, n.d., Portfolio MS., X, 56, LSF.

85. Hookes to Margaret Fell, 9 Jan. 1674, Swarthmore MS., I, 58; Thomas Moore to James Parke, 24 Jan. 1674, Spence MS., III, 169–70, LSF; Speed, *Counties of Britain*, 192. For a Quaker judgment of Parliament's mood, see John Rous to Margaret Fell, 24 Jan. 1674, Spence MS., III, 172, LSF.

86. Hookes to Margaret Fell, 9 Jan. 1674, Swarthmore MS., I, 58, LSF.

87. Fox to Whitehead, Hookes, and Thomas Moore, 17 Jan. 1674, in Penney, ed., *Journal*, 2:268–72. Fox's statement of loyalty is in Penney, 2:272. He apparently wrote it about the end of 1674; see Fox to Penn, 11 Dec. 1674, Penn–Forbes MS., II, 52, Historical Society of Pennsylvania, Philadelphia (hereafter cited as HSP).

88. Horle, "Changing Attitudes," 17–39, expertly charts a way through the legal jungle.

89. *Journal*, 404; Fox and Lower to Penn, 28 Aug. 1674, Penn–Forbes MS., II, 49, HSP.

90. Fox to Margaret Fell, 8 Feb. 1674, Abraham MS., 18, LSF. Fox later scratched through some of his strong words. He also marked out a sentence promising enough "Spanish black cloth" to make his wife a gown.

91. Fox to Margaret Fell, 9 June 1674, Portfolio MS., XXXVI, 35, LSF.

92. Thomas Lower to Mary Lower, 7 Jan. 1674, Abraham MS., 17, LSF. Unfortunately Fox's letter did not survive.

93. Nickalls, ed., *Journal*, 281–83; Rebecca Travers to Margaret Fell, 21 Feb. 1674, Swarthmore MS., I, 388, LSF.

94. Fox to King [1674], in Penney, ed., *Journal*, 2:274; Fox to Margaret Fell, 6 March 1674, in Nickalls, ed., *Journal*, 684; *The Case of the People Called Quakers, Relating to Oathes and Swearing* (N.p., 1673).

95. Margaret Rous to Margaret Fell, 21 March 1674, Spence MS., III, 178–79, LSF.

96. Nickalls, ed., *Journal*, 689–94; Fox to Margaret Fell, 9 June 1674, in Cadbury, ed., *Narrative Papers*, 120.

97. Nickalls, ed., *Journal*, 694–98.

98. *Journal,* 404–5.

99. Margaret Fell to Lord Keeper, 25 Dec. 1674, Spence MS., III, 129, LSF.

100. Fox and Lower to Margaret Fell, 30 Jan. 1675, Spence MS., 167–68, LSF; Penney, ed., *Journal,* 2:285.

101. *Journal,* 406; Lower to Fox and Margaret Fell, 4 March 1675, Spence MS., III, 174, LSF.

102. Epistle, 27 May 1675, in Dunn and Dunn, eds., *Penn Papers,* 1:328–32; Epistle, 4 June 1675, Leek MS., 63–65, LSF.

103. Fox, "My Dear Friends," 25 May 1675, Penington MS., IV, 89–90, LSF.

104. Nickalls, ed., *Journal,* 406.

105. *Journal,* 407.

CHAPTER 16

1. *Journal,* 407. On Fox's historical method, see Ingle, "Fox, Historian."

2. Penney, ed., *Journal,* 2:347–52.

3. For a similar analysis, see James Olney, *Metaphors of Self: The Meaning of Autobiography* (Princeton, N.J.: Princeton University Press, 1972), 175–81.

4. For an account of the history of the *Journal,* see Nickalls, ed., *Journal,* vii–vi. On the various editions of the *Journal,* see Pickvance, *Reader's Companion,* 147–148.

5. Rogers, *Christian Quaker,* part 4, 30.

6. Penney, ed., *Journal,* 2:314–15.

7. *Journal,* 129. See Cadbury, ed., *Narrative Papers,* 209–32.

8. A striking demonstration of this point can be seen in the selection of documents, collected in the mid-nineteenth century by London Yearly Meeting, to illustrate the evolution of the early organization of Quakers. Fox signed not a single one; see *Epistles of the Yearly Meeting,* 1:xxix–lvi. I am using "architect" here in its original sense of chief carpenter rather than one who plans. Concentration on Fox's perceived predominance in the Society of Friends has obscured the contributions of others, less studied. My interpretation differs in emphasis from that of Nicholas Morgan ("Quakers and the Establishment," xxii–iv), who overstates what he labels Fox's "intensely authoritarian attitudes" as the reason for the increased power in the central organizations.

9. Fox to Christopher Taylor, et al., 20 May 1685, *Pennsylvania Magazine of History and Biography* 29 (1905): 105–6.

10. Fox to Barclay, 31 June 1680, in *Reliquiae Barclaianae,* 52–54.

11. It remains unclear why the split received this name. True, two of the principal challengers were John Wilkinson and John Story, "the Two Johns," both Westmorland farmers, and they carried the banner of discontent far and wide. But the controversy originated in Bristol, probably with William Rogers, backed early on by all the men in that meeting. Wilkinson also took a back seat to Story, as was recognized at the time. (As one example, from one of the principal documents on Fox's side, see Pearson, *Anti-Christian Treachery,* 174.) It may well be that the two had their names attached to the challenge because, as rustic provincials, they made easy targets politically. Wilkinson, because of a rather extravagant, even parvenu, style of living, was certainly a better scapegoat than Rogers, a wily, well-established and urbane businessman. There is one tantalizing but incomplete source that dates Wilkinson's disagreements back to 1664; see Daniel Baker to M. F., 17 Feb. 1664, Swarthmore MS., IV, 183, LSF.

12. Caton to Margaret Fell, 26 Jan. 1661, Swarthmore MS., I, 324, LSF.

13. Beck and Ball, *London Meetings,* 344.

14. Fox, Epistle, 5 Oct. 1676, Box Meeting Minutes MS., 33, LSF.

15. *Journal*, 322. He recalled, as he put it, that in 1667 "the Lord had opened to me and let me see" to establish separate meetings for both sexes, but almost all the ones he specified were men's; see *Journal*, 311, 320–21. In his trip to Ireland in 1669, he apparently gave some attention to setting up women's meetings; see Edmundson, *Journal*, 51.

16. Fox, "Concerning writs or summons," 18 Jan. 1670, Kendal Monthly Meeting Minutes, 1670–1726, 37, PRO, Kendal.

17. Fell, *Collection*, 331–50. The effort to prove that Margaret Fell played a major role in planning the establishment of women's meetings, a product of the recent attention to women's history, is weak and almost entirely circumstantial. For the fullest attempt to enlarge her role, see Kunze, "Fell," chap. 4, esp. 196–98. (For lack of adequate research in the sources, I accepted more of Kunze's position than the evidence permits; see H. Larry Ingle, ed., "A Quaker Woman on Women's Roles: Mary Penington to Friends," *Signs* 16 [1991], 587–96, esp 588.) Her account contains a seriously inaccurate implication, namely, that Fox and Fell were at Lancaster prison just before he issued his first epistle exhorting Quakers to form women's meetings and that Fell thus influenced his decision; see "Fell," 197. No evidence exists that Fox saw his future wife from May 1665, when he was moved to Scarborough until sometime in 1667, when she visited him briefly in Cheshire. Fell may have influenced him, but Kunze has not proved such influence. Moreover, Margaret Fell's pamphlet did not discuss the role of women within a church except regarding their right to preach; Fox needed no convincing on that score. By Kunze's reasoning, George might just as well have been responsible for Fell's position.

18. Fox, "To the men and women's meeting," 30 Jan. 1674, Kendal Monthly Meeting Minutes, 1670–1726, 59–64, PRO, Kendal.

19. Fox to Friends in Norwich, 23 June 1671, in Eddington, *Quakerism in Norwich*, 273–74.

20. Mortimer, ed., *Minute Book*, 54–56. The men claimed Fox's letter was directed only to them and that they had intended the women to consider another one of his, one warning against vanity and excess. On Christmas Day, the women submitted a paper on the subject—its contents not recorded—asking permission to have it read at the Tuesday or Saturday meeting. The petition was denied until they "be directed in the wisdom and power of God to publish it." A year earlier the men's meeting had allowed approved marriages to be publicized in the women's meeting, this procedure to continue until they all were again able to occupy their meetinghouse; see Mortimer, ed., *Minute Book*, 34. Approval of marriages had to proceed publishing them; see *Minute Book*, 91.

21. His brothers Francis and George, for example, were traders in Ireland; see Marion Balderston, ed., *James Claypoole's Letterbook: London and Philadelphia, 1681–1684* (San Marino, Calif.: Huntington Library, 1967), 29; Penney, ed., *Short Journal*, 360; Joseph Pike, *Some Account of the Life of Joseph Pike*, ed., John Barclay (London: Darton and Harvey, 1837), 42; and John Raunce to Fox, 30 May 1680, in "A.R. Barclay MSS," *Journal of the Friends' Historical Society* 48 (1958): 218–19.

22. Kendal Monthly Meeting Minutes, 1670–1726, 6 Oct. 1671, 47–49, PRO, Kendal. The first signature on this order of the quarterly meeting, which also required Friends to give an account of whether they paid tithes or not, was John Wilkinson's.

23. Although Rogers did not begin publishing for seven years, he brought out, from 1680 to 1684, eight parts of his *Christian Quaker*; see William Rogers, *Christian-Quaker: The Sixth Part of the Christian-Quaker* (London: N.p., 1681), *The Seventh Part of the Christian-Quaker* (London: N.p., 1682), *The Eighth Part of the Christian-Quaker* (London: N.p., [1684]).

24. Thomas Crisp, *The First Part of Babel's-Builders Unmasking Themselves* (London: Enock Prosser, 1682), 8.

25. Penney, ed., *Journal*, 2:195. Epistle 264, placed by its compliers with those of 1669, does contain this regulation, but the letter is a composite of numerous epistles Fox wrote both then and later, as the editors conceded; see *Works*, 8:331–50, esp. 331, 338.

26. Fox to Margaret Fell, 4 May 1674, in Cadbury, ed., *Narrative Papers*, 117–18.

27. Fox, *Works*, 8:79–83.

28. Epistle, 27 May 1675, in Dunn and Dunn, eds., *Penn Papers*, 1:328–32.

29. Fox, "God's everlasting seed reigns," Richardson MS. (transcript), 455–56, QC.

30. Jean Simcock to M. F., 1672, Swarthmore MS., I, 365, LSF. Unfortunately, little is known for sure about either the issues involved or Simcock. It is likely the proposal concerned use of money by women, a matter of intense controversy. On Simcock, see Penney, ed., *Journal*, 2:407. On Parke, see Braithwaite, *Second Period*, 224, and Dunn and Dunn, eds., *Penn Papers*, 1:557.

31. Since the victors usually control history, information on Story is difficult to come by, but see John Story and John Wilkinson to Margaret Fell, 25 Aug. 1655, Swarthmore MS., I, 36, LSF, and Wilkinson's memoir of his friend in *The Memory of That Servant of God, John Story, Revived* (London: N.p., 1683), 2–8. On the two, see Dunn and Dunn, eds., *Penn Papers*, 1:290.

32. When expedient, Fox could back down on this minor issue; see Fox to Quarterly Meeting in Staffordshire, 11 June 1688, Portfolio MS., XV, 126, LSF.

33. Pearson, *Anti-Christian Treachery*, 29–31; Rogers, *Christian Quaker*, pt. 4, pp. 7–14; Penn to Fox, 4 March 1676, in Dunn and Dunn, eds., *Penn Papers*, 1:359–61. On the ship metaphor, see also Ellwood, *Antidote*, 198. The Pearson paper is lost, as is Fox's. Suffolk Quarterly Meeting followed her lead within months by instructing its subordinate meetings to require couples to appear before the women; see Whitehead, *Accuser of our Brethren*, 94.

34. Beatrice S. Snell, ed., *The Minute Book of the Monthly Meeting of the Society of Friends for the Upperside of Buckinghamshire, 1669–1690* (N.p.: Buckinghamshire Archaeological Society, 1937), 29–30.

35. I am following here the analysis of Horle, *Quakers*, 163.

36. Ann Docwra, *An Apostate-Conscience Exposed* (London: T. Sowle, 1699), 41; More to Conway, 9 Nov. 1675, in Nicholson, ed., *Conway Letters*, 404–6; Pickworth, *Charge*, 101. Whitehead's memoir, *Christian Progress*, ignored the issues within the Society of Friends. For a woefully inadequate biography, see William Beck, *George Whitehead: His Work and Service* (London: Headley Brothers, 1901).

37. On Claypoole, see Balderston, ed., *Claypoole's Letterbook*, 3–24; James Claypoole to Gawen Lawrie, 24 Feb. 1684, Balderston, ed., *Claypoole's Letterbook*, 235–38.

38. Hookes to Friends, 14 May 1675, Leek MS., 59–60, LSF.

39. Fox to Friends, n.d., in "George Fox's Caution Respecting Printing of Books and Papers," *Journal of the Friends' Historical Society* 21 (1924): 12. Although undated, this letter's reference to Robert Dring marks it as early, for he disappeared from the records by 1660.

40. Beck and Ball, *London Meetings*, 339. The first minute preserved from this meeting, that of May 17, 1675, described the procedure, as though it had long been used, for those who wished to testify for God or the ministry: they were to meet with the brethren every Sunday and Monday mornings "when they can" or send a note indicating which meetings they planned to attend; see Minutes, Morning Meeting, transcript, 5, LSF. Beck and Ball suggest that this procedure was the the Society of Friends's way of tacitly approving someone's ministry.

41. Minutes, Morning Meeting, 31 May 1675, transcript, 6, LSF. It was revealing that

Friends supported liberty of conscience in the political realm but sought to suppress heterodoxy in their own religious organization.

42. Minutes, Morning Meeting, 27 Dec. 1675 and 29 Jan. 1677, transcript, 8, 13, LSF.

43. Fox to Rebecca Travers et al., 28 April 1676, Box Meeting MS., 29, LSF. Meeting for Sufferings also reviewed Fox's books; see Minutes, Meeting for Sufferings, 15 March 1689, VI, 262, LSF.

44. "A Memorand: of those generall things discoursed and assented upon by the Late Meeting about Sufferings," 18 Oct. 1675, Leek MS., 76–79, LSF.

45. Minutes, Meeting upon Sufferings, 12 June 1676, Leek MS., 91–94; Minutes, Meeting for Sufferings, 18 Jan. 1677, Book A, 16, LSF. On this point, see the analysis in Oliver, "Quakers and Quietism," 195–96. On the Meeting for Sufferings, see Braithwaite, *Second Period*, 281–86; Lloyd, *Social History*, 11–13; Horle, *Quakers*, 173–77.

46. See, for examples, Minutes, Meeting for Sufferings, Book B, 25, 28 April, 2, and 9 May 1682, LSF.

47. "Articles for the Meet of 12 to proceed by," 20 April 1677, Portfolio MS., XVI, 43, 44, LSF.

48. This is the message of Horle, *Quakers*. In fact, a mere cursory examination of the records of the meeting will show that its principal responsibility for many years remained collecting and publicizing sufferings.

49. "The Dissatisfactions of William Rogers and Others," 1 Feb. 1678, in Dunn and Dunn, eds., *Penn Papers*, 1:525–26.

50. Minutes, Meeting for Sufferings, Book B, 17 and 24 Nov. 1682, LSF.

51. At least individuals were asked occasionally to account for the funds they had; see Minutes, Meeting for Sufferings, Book E, 296, 3 Dec. 1686, LSF.

52. "Testimony from the Brethren," 1666, Portfolio MS., XLI, 94, LSF.

53. Salthouse to Sarah Fell, 30 Sept. [1668?], Swarthmore MS., I, 104, LSF; John Faldo, *A Vindication of Quakerism No Christianity &c* (London: B. Griffin, 1673), 45 [actually 48].

54. For an example that women too considered tattling a feminine activity, see Women Friends in London to Women Friends in the Country, 4 Jan. 1675, in Barclay, ed., *Letters*, 344–45.

55. Reprinted in Beck and Ball, *London Meetings*, 47–52; for a slightly different version, see Arnold Lloyd, *Social History*, Appendix A.

56. Claypoole to Lawrie, 24 Feb. 1684, in Balderston, ed., *Claypoole's Letterbook*, 235–38.

57. Epistle, 26 May 1673, Portfolio MS., XXIII, 134, LSF.

58. General Meeting Epistle, 27 May 1675, William Penn MS., VI, 5, HSP.

59. Jeffery Bullock, *One Blow more against Antichrists Ministers* (London: N.p., 1678), 9, 13. On Bullock, see Smith, *Descriptive Catalogue*, 1:347.

60. On Bugg, see Docwra, *Apostate-Conscience*, 8, 25–26, 46–47. For a listing of Bugg's books, see Smith, *Catalogue*, 1:332–46.

61. Bugg, *Pilgrim's Progress*, 145.

62. Docwra, *Apostate-Conscience*, 6; Bugg, *Pilgrim's Progress*, 146.

63. Bugg, *Innocency Vindicated*, 9–12. This poem, significantly entitled "The Laboring Man's Caveat concerning Women's Meetings," first appeared four years earlier in another anti-Fox pamphlet, Thomas Crisp, *The Fourth Part of Babel's-Builders Unmask't* (N.p., n.d.), 25–27.

64. Penn to William Mucklow, 11 Oct. 1672, in Dunn and Dunn, eds., *Penn Papers*, 1:249–59.

65. Mucklow, *Spirit of the Hat*, 15, 20–21.

66. Penn to Mucklow, 11 Oct. 1672, in Dunn and Dunn, eds., *Penn Papers*, 1:252.

67. Penn, *The Spirit of Alexander the Copper-Smith*, in *Works of Penn*, 2:191–92.

68. Fox to Edward Cooper, 9 June 1678, Portfolio MS., XXXI, 54, LSF.

69. Crisp, *First Part*, 10.

70. Fox, *Several Plain Truths Manifested and Declared from the Spirit of God* (London: Andrew Sowle, 1684), 26.

71. Fox to dear Friends, 12 Jan. 1675, Portfolio MS., X, 19, LSF.

72. Fox, *Several Plain Truths*, 27.

73. Fox, *Works*, 7:332.

74. *Epistles of Yearly Meeting*, 1:48.

75. Fox, *Answer to a Paper*, 3.

76. Fox, Sermon at Thomas Rous', 21 Oct. 1671, Baltimore Women's Half-Yearly Meeting Minutes, 11–19, FHL; Penney, ed., *Journal*, 2:195.

77. Fox, *Friends fellowship must be in the spirit* (N.p., [1669]), 7.

78. Fox to Margaret Fell, 4 May 1674, in Cadbury, ed., *Narrative Papers*, 117–18.

79. For this approach, see Fox to Penn, 28 Aug. 1674, Penn–Forbes MS., II, 49, HSP.

80. Lower to Margaret Fell, 11 Feb. 1675, Spence MS., III, 165, LSF.

81. Penington to Thomas Curtis, n.d., Penington MS., IV, 145–47, LSF.

82. Cadbury, ed., *Annual Catalogue*, 143 (item 139F); Fox to Friends in Reading, 13 Feb. 1678, Portfolio MS., XXIV, 48, LSF.

83. Fox to dear Friends, 12 Jan. 1675, Portfolio MS., X, 19, LSF.

84. Joseph Bowden to Curtis and Arthur Estmead, 20 Nov. 1678, Portfolio MS., XXIII, 156, LSF.

85. Penington to Curtis, 25 Feb. 1678, Penington MS., IV, 144–45, LSF.

86. Fox, *The Saints…their Heavenly and Spiritual Worship, Unity and Communion* (London: John Bringhurst, 1683), 7–8.

87. John Burnyeat to M. F., 6 June 1678, Spence MS., III, 177, LSF. On Bristol, see Thomas Robertson to Fox, 2 Feb. 1686, in "A. R. Barclay MSS," 50 (1963): 168–70.

88. Barclay to Penn, 6 Sept. 1676, in Dunn and Dunn, eds., *Penn Papers*, 1:368–69.

89. Fox, memorandum, 5 Oct. 1680, Barclay MS., 199A, LSF.

90. Henry Stout, et al., to Fox, Oct. 1678, Barclay MS., 202, LSF.

91. Fox to John Story, 10 Dec. 1678, Barclay MS., 214, LSF.

92. Bugg, *Innocency Vindicated*, 15.

93. Whitehead, *Accuser*, 170. For similar incidents, see Pearson, *Anti-Christian Treachery*, 139–41.

94. Crisp, *Fourth Part*, 19.

95. Fox to Strout, 27 Nov. 1678, Barclay MS., 216, LSF. See also Fox to Robert Arch, 20 June 1683, Barclay MS., 198, LSF.

96. Robert Barrow to Penn, n.d., Portfolio MS., XXXI, 116, LSF.

97. Fox to Henry Sidon, 25 May 1677, in Dunn and Dunn, eds., *Penn Papers*, 1:376–77.

98. Ellwood, *Antidote*, 200; Cadbury, ed., *Annual Catalogue*, 134 (items 25,36F, 25,37F).

99. Penney, ed., *Journal*, 2:311.

100. Parker to Fox, 27 Dec. 1675, Gibson MS., II, 10, LSF. Parker told Fox he did not realize the extent of his authority; see Parker to Fox, 5 Oct. 1675, Gibson MS., II, 11, LSF.

101. Penn to Fox, 4 March 1676, in Dunn and Dunn, eds., *Penn Papers*, 1:359–61; Cadbury, ed., *Annual Catalogue*, 143 (items 138F, 139F).

102. Minutes, Morning Meeting, 18 Oct. 1675 and 9 Feb. 1676, LSF; Penn to Fox, 4 March 1676, in Dunn and Dunn, eds., *Penn Papers*, 1:359–61.

103. Penney, ed., *Account Book of Fell*, 259.

104. Fox to Barclay, 29 March 1679, in *Reliquiae Barclaianae*, 47–48.

105. E[dward] B[ourne] to Fox, 17 April 1676, Spence MS., III, 175, LSF.

106. For the text, see "Statement of Two Johns," 7 April 1676, Penn MS., IV, 7, HSP. For an account of Draw-well from the victors' perspective, see Braithwaite, *Second Period*, 305–8.

107. Fox to Story and Wilkinson, 16 Dec. 1676, in Rogers, *Christian Quaker*, pt. 4, pp. 44–61; Fox to Story, 10 Dec. 1678, Barclay MS., 214, LSF.

108. Wilkinson, *Memory of that Servant*, 5.

109. Ibid., 38. See also Crisp, *First Part*, 9. According to Fox at one point, women's meetings were set up to care for the urban poor; see Penney, ed., *Journal*, 2:342.

110. Wilkinson, *Memory of that Servant*, 41.

111. Epistle, 12 June 1677, Portfolio MS., VI, 41; Penney, ed., *Short Journal*, 234. Braithwaite (*Second Period*, 309n2) concedes that the epistle was of questionable legitimacy because it issued from no regular meeting.

112. Fox to Story, 10 Dec. 1678, Barclay MS., 214, LSF.

113. Claypoole to Francis and George Rogers, 3 Dec. 1681, in Balderston, ed., *Claypoole's Letterbook*, 75; Pearson, *Anti-Christian Treachery*, 177.

114. For a listing of Rogers's works, see Smith, *Descriptive Catalogue*, 2:509–11. The best known answer was Pearson's *Anti-Christian Treachery*; see Fox to Barclay, n.d., 29 March and 8 April 1679, *Reliquiae Barclaianae*, 42–44, 47–49.

115. Balderston, ed., *Claypoole's Letterbook*, 143, 146, 210.

116. Smith, "Wilkinson–Story in Bristol," 61.

117. Minutes, Morning Meeting, 14 Aug. 1676 and 11 July 1687 LSF; Jeffrey Bullock, memorandum, 10 Nov. 1686, Portfolio MS., XV, 122, LSF.

118. Unless otherwise noted, my account of this period is taken from *Journal*, 423–32, and Penney, ed., *Short Journal*, 225–36.

119. Margaret Fell to Sarah and Susanna Fell, 31 March 1677, *Journal of the Friends' Historical Society* 2 (1905): 23–25.

CHAPTER 17

1. Docwra, *Apostate Conscience*, 9, 44–47.

2. Penney, ed., *Household Account Book*, 319; Ross, *Fell*, 277.

3. Minutes, Meeting for Sufferings, Book C, 2 Nov. 1683, 60; Book D, 15 May 1685, 44, LSF.

4. On this last period, the best secondary source is Henry J. Cadbury, "George Fox's Later Years," in Nickalls, ed., *Journal*, 713–56.

5. Dunn and Dunn, eds., *Penn Papers*, 2:92.

6. Penney, ed., *Short Journal*, 295.

7. The best picture of the scattering of Fox's goods can be seen from an examination of his testamentary papers in Penney, ed., *Journal*, 2:347–61.

8. Penney, ed., *Journal*, 2:352, 354–55, 489; Hookes to Lower, 16 Dec. 1674, Portfolio MS., II, 76; Hookes to Fox, 17 Oct. 1669, Swarthmore MS., I, 385, LSF; Fox to Margaret Fell, 8 Feb. 1674, in Cadbury, ed., *Narrative Papers*, 112–13.

9. Sarah Meade to Margaret Fell, 15 March 1687, Abraham MS., 170–71, LSF.

10. Rogers, *Christian Quaker*, pt. 5, p. 31; pt. 6, 23.

11. Webb, *Fells*, 366–67; Penney, ed., *Journal*, 2:365–67.

12. Penney, ed., *Journal*, 2:351. When the will became public, his critics, led by wide-awake Francis Bugg, made much of it for what it revealed about Fox's literacy rather than his property; see Bugg, *Last Will and Testament of that Impostor George Fox*, 3d ed. (N.p., 1703), Broadside.

13. Croese, *History*, bk. 2, 179 [209]–213, 234.

14. Barclay to Penn, 6 Sept. 1676, in Dunn and Dunn, eds., *Penn Papers*, 1:368–69; Fox to Friends in Holland, 2 Sept. 1676, in *Works*, 8:128–30.

15. On Keith, see Ethyn W. Kirby, *George Keith: (1638–1716)* (New York: D. Appleton-Century Co., 1942); on Elizabeth Keith, see Penney, ed., *Short Journal*, 362.

16. Penney, ed., *Short Journal*, 305–6.

17. Penney, ed., *Household Account Book*, 413.

18. Penn, "An Account of my Journey into Holland and Germany," in Dunn and Dunn, eds., *Penn Papers*, 1:428–508. Unless otherwise indicated, my account of this journey is taken from Penn's account; *Journal*, 432–54; and Penney, ed., *Short Journal*, 237–55.

19. Penn to Pieter Hendricks, 19 Nov. 1677, in Dunn and Dunn, eds., *Penn Papers*, 1:516–17.

20. Fox to Patrick Livingstone, 5 Aug. 1677, Portfolio MS., IX, 7, LSF; Trueblood, *Barclay*, 75.

21. C. Brinkmann, "Charles II and the Bishop of Münster in the Anglo-Dutch War of 1665–66," *English Historical Review* 21 (1906): 686.

22. Cadbury, *Friendly Heritage*, 259–61.

23. Sewell, *History*, 638–39. On the debate, see also Cadbury, *"Book of Miracles,"* 28.

24. Fox to Barclay, 8 April 1679, in *Reliquiae Barclaianae*, 48–49.

25. Fox to Dear Friends, 23 Oct. 1677, Portfolio MS., IX, 2, LSF.

26. Margaret Fell to Penn, 11 Nov. 1677, Penn–Forbes MS., II, 58, HSP.

27. Penney, ed., *Short Journal*, 256; Fiennes, *Illustrated Journeys*, 131–32.

28. A good sense of Fox's life in this period can be had from Penney, ed., *Short Journal*, 257–60. On the Buckinhamshire duo, see Penn to John Raunce and Charles Harris, 11 Sept. 1676, in Dunn and Dunn, eds., *Penn Papers*, 1:370–73.

29. Penn to Hendricks, 19 Nov. 1677, in Dunn and Dunn, eds., *Penn Papers*, 1:516–17.

30. Minutes, Morning Meeting, [1,] 26, 45, 46, 60, 65, LSF.

31. Fox, "Memorand for the Frds of ye Second Days Meeting," 19 Jan. 1684, Portfolio MS., X, 3, LSF. Fox was referring to Francis Mercurius van Helmont, who allegedly said that "the soul of man is [in] a woman's underpetticoat"; on van Helmont, see Dunn and Dunn, eds., *Penn Papers*, 1:326.

32. See William Rogers, Memorandum, 1 Feb. 1678, Dunn and Dunn, eds., *Penn Papers*, 1:521.

33. Snell, ed., *Minutes*, 83, 145n.

34. *Journal*, 455; Penney, ed., *Short Journal*, 261.

35. Raunce to Fox, 30 May and 9 June 1680, Barclay MS., 135, 136, LSF.

36. Henry and Anne Sweeting, Memorandum, 23 Feb. 1678, Barclay MS., 209, LSF.

37. Dunn and Dunn, eds., *Penn Papers*, 1:520–31.

38. Fox to Barclay, 8 April 1679, in *Reliquiae Barclaianae*, 48–49.

39. Fox to Rogers, n.d., Barclay MS., 222, LSF.

40. Penney, ed., *Short Journal*, 262–64; Fox to Story, 10 Dec. 1678, Barclay MS., 214, LSF.

41. Penney, ed., *Short Journal*, 262–65; Fox to M.F., 3 April 1678, Add. Mss 41063, BL.

42. More to Penn, 22 May 1675, in Dunn and Dunn, eds., *Penn Papers*, 1:304–23; Conway to More, 29 Nov. 1675, in Nicholson, ed., *Conway Letters*, 407–9. On Conway and her circle, see Nicholson, ed., *Conway Letters, passim*, and Hull, *Furly and Quakerism*, 105–23.

43. Fox, "Memorand for the Frds of ye Second Days Meeting," 19 Jan. 1684, Portfolio MS., X, 3, LSF.

44. Nicholson, ed., *Conway Letters*, 322.

45. Penney, ed., *Short Journal*, 267–70.

46. John Gratton to Penn, 19 Dec. 1678, Dunn and Dunn, eds., *Penn Papers*, 1:544–45.

47. Penn, Speech to a Committee of Parliament, 22 March 1678, in Dunn and Dunn, eds., *Penn Papers*, 1:533–34.

48. For perhaps the best example, see Fox, *Gospel-Liberty*.

49. Penney, ed., *Short Journal*, 270; *Yearly Meeting Epistles*, 1:xxiii–xxv.

50. Penney, ed., *Short Journal*, 270; *Journal*, 457–58.

51. Fox to John III, n.d., in *Journal*, 459–63.

52. Minutes, Meeting for Sufferings, Book C, 17 Oct. 1684, 264, LSF.

53. Fox to [Friends], 9 June 1678, in *Journal*, 466–67.

54. Fox to All Friends, 11 July 1678, in *Journal*, 468.

55. Fox to Richard Snead, 7 Jan. 1679, Bristol MS., V, 20–21, microfilm.

56. *Journal*, 467, 468; Fox to Stout, 17 Sept. 1678, Barclay MS., 209, LSF; M. F. to Fox, 18 July 1678, in Webb, *Fells*, 293–94. The Hartford controversy can be followed in letters in Barclay MS., 199A, 200, 202, 205, 208, LSF.

57. For the most up-to-date discussion of this matter, see Ingle and Ingle, "Excommunication of Fox."

58. Fox to Barclay, n.d., 29 March 1679, in *Reliquiae Barclaianae*, 42–44, 47–48.

59. See Smith, *Descriptive Catalogue*, 1:285–86.

60. Fox to Barclay, 8 April 1679, in *Reliquiae Barclaianae*, 48–49.

61. Fox to Lady Conway, 16 Jan. 1680, in Cadbury, ed., *Annual Catalogue*, 160 (item 7,25G); Fox, *Works*, 8:153–55.

62. See examples of his numerous papers on this topic in Cadbury, ed., *Annual Catalogue*, 156–58, 162–65, and compare with Fox, *A Distinction between the New Covenant and the Old* (N.p., [1679]).

63. Fox to Richardson, 16 Oct. 1679, Dix Ms., 226, LSF.

64. Fox, *The True Marriage Declared* (N.p., [1679]), 3, 5.

65. Fox, *An Answer to the Speech or Declaration of the Great Turk, Sultan Mahomet* ([London:] A. Sowle, 1688), 6, 9, 14.

66. Manuscript fragments, n.d., Portfolio MS., XXXVI, 175, LSF.

67. On Marsh Grange, see Ross, *Fell*, 5, 357–58, back endpaper.

68. Cadbury, ed., *Annual Catalogue*, 159 (item 5,139G).

69. Unless otherwise indicated, the final portion of this chapter will be drawn from *Journal*, 478–613, and Penney, ed., *Short Journal*, 75–222.

70. For a summary of the issues, see Isaac Lindley, et al., *Truth Exalted, and the Peaceable Fellowship and Exercise Thereof Vindicated* (N.p., 1685), 1–3. See also Braithwaite, *Second Period*, 475–78.

71. Fox, *Several Plain Truths*, 26–27.

72. Fox to Thomas Robinson, 14 July 1687, Bristol MS., V, 25–26, microfilm.

73. Fox to Barclay, 31 June 1680, in *Reliquiae Barclaianae*, 52–54.

74. Minutes, Morning Meeting , [1:] 45, 46, 55, 60, 65, LSF.

75. Coward, *Stuart Age*, 283, 286.

76. Penn to King, Lords, and Commons [Nov 1680], in Dunn and Dunn, eds., *Penn Papers*, 2:54.

77. On this complicated situation, see Horle, *Quakers*, 87–88, 284.

78. Fox, "Testimony at a Yearly Meeting," May 1681, Richardson MS., 533–48, QC.

79. Claypoole to Penn, 1 April 1683, in Dunn and Dunn, eds., *Penn Papers*, 2:369–72.

80. Sarah Meade to Margaret Fell, 31 May 1684, Spence MS., III, 188, LSF.

81. Dunn and Dunn, eds., *Penn Papers*, 1:500.

82. Fox, *Works*, 2:273.

83. Penn to John Fenwick, 20 Jan. 1675, in Dunn and Dunn, eds., *Penn Papers*, 1:384–85.

84. Fox to Barclay, 18 Jan. 1680, in *Reliquiae Barclaianae*, 50–51.

85. Fox to Margaret Fell, 26 Oct. 1684 [date corrected in Ross, *Fell*, 325n1], in Webb, *Fells*, 348–49; Margaret Fell to unknown, n.d., Spence MS., III, 1, LSF.

86. Ross, *Fell*, 325.

87. Minutes, Meeting for Sufferings, Book C, 26 Dec. 1684, 315, LSF.

88. Fox to Barclay, 19 Dec. 1685, in *Reliquiae Barclaianae*, 58–59.

89. Coward, *Stuart Age*, 294–95.

90. Cadbury, ed., *Annual Catalogue*, 188 (item 4,5H).

91. Penn to James Harrison, 23 Sept. 1686, Dunn and Dunn, *Penn Papers*, 3:122–23.

92. Minutes, Meeting for Sufferings, Book C, 13 June 1684, 189; Book C, 6 Feb. 1685, 348; Book D, 12 June 1685, 63, LSF.

93. On the trial, see Braithwaite, *Second Period*, 69–73.

94. For this dispute, see Ross, *Fell*, 373–76. See also Wildes, *Penn*, 244–45, 356.

95. Penn to M. F., 29 Oct. 1684, in Dunn and Dunn, eds., *Penn Papers*, 2:605–6; Penn to Harrison, 19 May 1685, Dunn and Dunn, eds., *Penn Papers*, 3:55–57. For Penn's assessment of Taylor, see also Penn to unknown, 9 Aug. 1685, Dunn and Dunn, eds., *Penn Papers*, 3:49–50. For a hint that Penn and Whitehead had their troubles, see Henry Gouldney to John Rodes, 25 April 1694, in Mrs. Godfrey L. Lampson, ed., *A Quaker Post-Bag*, (London: Longmans, Green and Co., 1910), 56–58.

96. Cadbury, ed., *Annual Catalogue*, 187 (item 3,72H), 192 (item 6,2H).

97. Fox to Barclay, 19 July 1868, in *Reliquiae Barclaianae*, 59–60.

98. "The Ending of Differences, 1688," *Journal of the Friends' Historical Society* 16 (1909): 16.

99. Minutes, Meeting for Sufferings, 10 June 1687, VI, 71, LSF.

100. Cadbury, ed., *Annual Catalogue*, 185 (item 3,39H), 189 (item 4,41H).

101. Quakers to James II, 19 May 1687; Penn's speech, 24 May 1687, in Dunn and Dunn, eds., *Penn Papers*, 3:154–56.

102. Dunn and Dunn, eds., *Penn Papers*, 153; Cadbury, ed., *Annual Catalogue*, 197 (item 11H).

103. Sarah Meade to Margaret Fell, 6 March 1689, Spence MS., III, 192, LSF.

104. Cadbury, ed., *Annual Catalogue*, 196 (item 9,62H), 198 (items 14,33H, 14,34H).

105. Penney, ed., *Journal*, 2:347–50, 357–65.

106. Fox to Lower, 28 April 1687, Portfolio MS., XXXVI, 1, LSF.

107. Fox to John Norris, 4 March 1689 (Fox may have misdated this letter since the book he reacted to was published in 1690); Cadbury, ed., *Annual Catalogue*, 198 (item 14,35H); John Norris, *Reflections upon the Conduct of Human Life* (London: N.p., 1690), 141, 160–61; Norris to Fox, 15 April 1690, Portfolio MS., IV, 36, LSF. On Norris, see *DNB*, 14:577–78.

108. Minutes, Meeting for Sufferings, 30 Oct. 1689, 7:73, LSF.

109. Cadbury, ed., *Annual Catalogue*, 202 (item 22H).

EPILOGUE

1. Beck and Ball, *London Meetings*, 144–46, 150.

2. See the description of one home in Balderston, ed., *Claypoole's Letterbook*, 7.

3. Penney, ed., *Short Journal*, 213–22.

4. *Journal*, 612–13.

5. Winifred M. White, *Six Weeks Meeting, 1671–1971* (London: Six Weeks Meeting, 1971), 19–20.

6. My account of Fox's death and burial comes from Penn to Margaret Fell, 13 Jan. 1690, Portfolio MS., XVII, 100; Robert Barrow to Henry Coward, et al., 16 Jan. 1690, Thirnbeck MS., 22, LSF; Second Day Morning Meeting, Epistle, in *Journal*, xi–xv; John Ayrey to Friends, 15 Jan. 1691, in Penney, ed., *Journal*, 2:369–71; Gouldney to Rodes, 15 Jan. 1691, in Lampson, ed., *Post-Bag*, 51–52; Beck and Ball, *London Meetings*, 155–57, 330–31.

7. Unfortunately, there is no overall study of the Keithan dispute, but see J. William Frost, "Unlikely Controversialists: Caleb Pusey and George Keith," *Quaker History* 64 (1975), 16–36, and Jon Butler, "Into Pennsylvania's Spiritual Abyss: The Rise and Fall of the Later Keithians, 1693–1703," *Pennsylvania Magazine of History and Biography* 101 (1977): 151–70.

Bibliography

PRIMARY SOURCES

Manuscripts

British Library

George Fox to Margaret Fell, 3 April 1678, Add. MS.
H., J. [Harwood, John]. "The Life of innocency vindicated." 12th month, 1666/67.
Wales, Elkanah. "Memoirs of the Reverend Mr. Elkanah Wales." Add. MS., 4460.
Wales, Elkanah. "Notes of Sermons," Add. MS., 4933 A & B.

Public Records Office, Kendal

Kendal Men's Preparative Meeting Minute Book, 1697–1715.
Kendal Monthly Meeting Minutes, 1670–1726.
Book of Minutes of the General Meeting of Northern Counties, 1658–1700.
Brigflatts Men's Monthly Meeting Minute Book, 1676–1713.
Minute Book of Windermere Women's Preparative Meeting, 1677–c.1724.
Book of Extracts, Kendal.

Public Records Office, Leicester

Bishops Transcripts, Fenny Drayton.

Public Records Office, London

Records of Equity Proceedings of the Chancery Court of the County Palatine of Lancaster.
Records of the Chancery Court of the Palatine County of Lancaster.

Public Records Office, Preston

Marsden Monthly Meeting Minutes, 1676–1746, vols. 1–2.
Lancaster Men's Monthly Meeting Minutes, 1675–1718.
Lancaster Women's Monthly Meeting Minutes, 1676–1740.

Library of Society of Friends, London

A. R. Barclay Manuscripts.
Audland Manuscript.
Lewis Benson papers.
Box Meeting Manuscript, 1671–1753.
W. C. Braithwaite Papers, Kendal Early Record Book.
Bristol MSS., vol. 5 (microfilm).
Catalogue of Books and Papers belonging to Friends at the Chamber in Whitehart Court, Gracechurch Street, London.
A Catalogue of Papers in Manuscript in the Chamber forward up 2 fgs of Stairs at the Meeting house in Gracious Street.
A Catalogue of Printed Books and papers Belonging to Friends in the Back Chamber of Gracious Street Meetinghouse.
William Caton MSS.
Edward Cook MS.
Edmond Crosse MS., 1 vol.
Crossfield MS., 1 vol.
James Dix MS., 1 vol.
Thomas Ellwood MS., 1 vol.
Epistles by George Fox et al., 2 vols.
George Fox Epistles, Manuscript Box Q4/5.
Leek MS., 1 vol.
Letters and Documents of Early Friends, MSS., 5 vols.
Patrick Livingston MS., 1 vol.
London and Middlesex Quarterly Meeting Digest Register.
Markey MS.
Meeting for Sufferings Minutes, Books A–E, vols. 6–7.
Morning Meeting Minutes.
Original Record of Sufferings MS.
John Penington MSS., 4 vols.
Portfolio MSS., 49 vols.
Richard Reynolds MSS., 1 vol.
Spence MSS., 3 vols.
Swarthmore MSS., 8 vols.
John Tapper MS., 1 vol.
Thompson MS., Sufferings, 1 vol.
Thompson MS., Writings, 1 vol.
Thirnbeck MSS., 2 vols.
To All the Women's Meetings in the Resturation.

Dr. Williams's Library, London

Richard Baxter MSS., 6 vols.

Historical Society of Pennsylvania, Philadelphia

Early Quakers—Etting Papers.
Miscellaneous MSS., Etting Papers.
William Penn MSS., vol. 6.
Penn–Forbes Papers, vols. 1–2.

Friends Historical Library, Swarthmore College

Half-Years Women's Meeting in Maryland (microfilm).

Quaker Collection, Haverford College

Little Egg Harbor Monthly Meeting (George Fox's Testimonies).
Richardson MS. (transcript).

Fox's Published Writings

Fox as Sole Author

All Friends everywhere This is the Word of the Lord Unto You All. [London: John Bringhurst, 1683].

All you people that have a tenderness formerly. N.p.: [1660]. [Broadside]

An Answer to a Paper which came from the Papists Lately out of Holland. London: N.p., 1658.

An Answer to Dr. Burgess his Book, entituled A Case concerning of buying Bishop Lands. London: N.p., 1659.

An Answer to several New Laws and Orders Made by the Rulers of Boston in New-England. N.p.: 1678.

An Answer to the Arguments of the Jewes. London: N.p., [1661].

An Answer to the Speech or Declaration of the Great Turk, Sultan Mahomet. [London]: A. Sowle, 1688.

An Answer to Thomas Tillams Book Called, The Seventh-day-Sabbath. London: N.p., 1659.

The Beginning of Tythes in the Law, and Ending of Tythes in the Gospel. N.p.: 1676.

Caesar's Due Rendered unto Him . . . and God & Christs Due. N.p.: 1679.

Cain Against Abel, Representing New-England's Church Hierarchy in Opposition to Her Christian Protestant Dissenters. N.p.: 1675.

A Catechisme for Children. London: N.p., 1657.

The Cause why Adam & Eve Were Driven out of Paradise. London: N.p., 1683.

The Christian Judges, So Called, Their Words Judged. N.p.: 1676.

Christian Liberty Commended, and Persecution Condemned. N.p.: 1675.

Christs light the only Antidote. N.p.: 1662.

Christ's Parable of Dives and Lazarus. N.p.: 1677.

A Clear Discovery . . . with a Warning. N.p.: 1662.

Concerning the Antiquity of the People of God, called Quakers. London: N.p., 1689.

Concerning the Apostate Christian. London: A. Sowle, 1688.

Concerning Christ the Spiritual and Holy Head over his Holy Church. N.p.: 1677.

Concerning Daily Sacrifices and Offerings. N.p., n.d. [Broadside]

Concerning Good-Morrow, and Good-Even; the World's Customs. London: N.p., 1657.

Concerning Marriage. London: N.p., 1661.

Concerning Meeting in Houses, Ships, Streets, Mountains, By-wayes. [London: John Bringhurst, 1683.]

Concerning Persecution in All Ages to this Day. London: John Bringhurst, 1682.

Concerning Revelation, Prophecy, Measure, and Rule, and the Inspiration and Sufficiency of the Spirit. N.p.: 1676.

Concerning Sons and Daughters and Prophetesses speaking and Prophecying. London: M. W., n.d.

Concerning such as have forbidden Preaching or Teaching. London: N.p., [1685]. [Broadside]

Concerning such as shall enter into the Kingdom of God. N.p.: [1684].

Concerning the Antiquity of the People of God, Called Quakers. London: N.p., 1689.

Concerning the Pure and Undefiled Religion. London: John Bringhurst, 1685.

Concerning the Traditions the Jews Taught. [London: A. Sowle, 1688.]

Concerning the True Baptism and the False. N.p.: [1676].

Concerning the Upright and Good Conversation of the Saints. London: John Bringhurst, 1682.

A Controversy which hath been betwixt the Quakers Protestants and Papists. N.p.: [1665].

A Cry for Repentance, unto the Inhabitants of London chieflie. London: N.p., 1656.

A Declaration Against all Professions and Professors. London: N.p., 1655.

A Declaration concerning Fasting and Prayer. London: N.p., 1656.

A Declaration of the Difference of the Ministers of the Word from the Ministers of the World. London: N.p., 1656.

A Declaration of the Ground of Error & Errors, Blasphemy, Blasphemers and Blasphemies. London: N.p., 1657.

A Declaration to the Jews for them to Read Over. London: N.p., 1661.

A Declaration from the People of God, Called Quakers, Against All Seditious Conventicles. N.p., n.d.

A Demonstration to the Christians in Name without the Nature of it. N.p.: 1678.

The Devil Was and Is the Old Informer Against the Righteous. London: John Bringhurst, 1682–1683.

A Distinction between the New Covenant and the Old. N.p.: [1679].

A Distinction between the Phanatick Spirit and the Spirit of God. London: N.p., 1660. [Broadside]

A Distinction between True Liberty and False. N.p.: [1685].

A Distinction betwixt the Two Suppers of Christ. N.p.: 1685.

An Encouragement for all to Trust in the Lord. London: N.p.: 1682.

An Epistle by way of Caution, to Shopkeepers, Merchants, and Factors. N.p.: 1710. [Broadside]

An Epistle Concerning the Government of Christ. London: N.p., 1681.

An Epistle from the People in Scorn Called Quakers. N.p.: 1668.

An Epistle of Love to Friends in the Womens Meeting in London. N.p., n.d.

An Epistle to all Christians to keep to Yea, Yea, and Nay, Nay. London: N.p., 1682.

An Epistle to all my Dear Friends . . . in America. N.p.: [1675].

An Epistle to all People on the Earth. London: N.p., 1657.

An Epistle to all Planters and such who are Transporting Themselves into Foreign Plantations in America. London: N.p., 1682. [Broadside]

An Epistle to all Professors in New-England, Germany, and other parts of the Called Christian World. N.p.: 1673.

An Epistle to be Read in all the Assemblies of the Righteous. N.p.: 1666.

An Epistle to Friends For Them to Read. N.p.: [1679].

An Epistle to the Household of the Seed of Abraham. London: John Bringhurst, 1682.

An Epistle-General to them who are of the Royal Priesthood. London: N.p., 1660.

The Examination and Tryall of Margaret Fell and George Fox (at . . . Lancaster). N.p.: 1664.

The Eternal, Substantial Truths of God's Kingdom. London: N.p., 1661.

An Exhortation to All People. London: John Bringhurst, 1685.

An Exhortation to you who contemne the power of God, and speak evil of it. N.p., n.d. [Broadside]

A Few Queries for Thomas Moor the Elder, Thomas Moor the Younger, John Horn. . . . N.p., n.d.

A Few Words to All such (whether Papists or Protestants) as observe Dayes Contrary to Christ and his Apostles. London: N.p., 1669.

For all the Bishops and Priests in Christendom. N.p.: [1674].

For the Emperour of China, and his Subordinate Kings & Princes. London: N.p.: 1660.

For the holy Women that trust in God and do profess Godliness. N.p.: [1686].

For the Pope, Cardinals and Jesuites, and all the rest of his Family of Papists. London: N.p., 1661.

For your whoredoms in the City of London. N.p.: [1660]. [Broadside]

Friends fellowship must be in the spirit. N.p.: [1668–1669].

Friends, The matter concerning not putting off the Hat. N.p.: [ca. 1663].

A General Epistle To be read in all the Christian Meetings in the World. N.p.: 1662.

A General Epistle to Friends, And all People. London: N.p., 1667.

George Fox's "Book of Miracles." Edited by Henry J. Cadbury. Cambridge: Cambridge University Press, 1948.

George Fox's Journal. Edited by Percy L. Parker. London: Salvation Army Publishing Department, 1905.

The Glorie of the Lord Arising, Shaking terribly the Earth, and Overturning All, Until Righteousness Be set up. London: N.p., 1655.

Gospel Family-Order, Being a Short Discourse concerning of the Ordering of Families, Both of Whites, Blacks and Indians. N.p.: 1676.

Gospel-Liberty and the Royal-Law of Love. N.p.: 1668.

Gospel-Truth Demonstrated. London: T. Sowle, 1706.

The Great Mistery of the Great Whore Unfolded. London: N.p., 1659.

The ground of desperation is out of the light. N.p.: 1655. [Broadside]

The Ground of High Places: and the End of High Places. London: N.p., 1657.

The Heathens Divinity Set upon the Heads of all called Christians. N.p.: 1671.

Here all may see, that Justice and Judgement is to Rule. London: N.p., 1656.

Here Is Declared the manner of the naming of Children in the old time, without a Priest. London: N.p., 1658.

How God's People are not to take the Names of the Heathen Gods in their Mouths. London: N.p., 1687.

Iconoclastes; or A Hammer To break down all invented Images, Image-Makers, and Image-Worshippers. N.p.: 1671.

An Instruction to Judges & Lawyers. London: N.p., [1657].

Inward and Spiritual Warfare, and the False Pretense of it. N.p.: 1690.

A Journal or Historical Account of the Life, Travels, Sufferings, Christian Experiences and Labour of Love in the Work of the Ministry of that Ancient, Eminent and Faithful Servant of Jesus Christ, George Fox. [Edited by Thomas Ellwood.] London: N.p., 1694.

Journal of George Fox. Rev. ed. Edited by John L. Nickalls. Cambridge: Cambridge University Press, 1952.

Journal of George Fox. 2 vols. Edited by Norman Penney. New York: Octagon Books, 1973.

The Judgement, Or, the Spiritual-Man Judging all Things. London: N.p., 1654.

The Lambs Officer Is gone forth with the Lambs Message. London: N.p., 1659.

The Law of God, the Rule for Law-makers. London: N.p., 1658.

The Line of Righteousness and Justice Stretched forth over all Merchants, etc. N.p.: 1674.

Looking-Glas for the Jews. N.p.: 1674.

The Man Christ Jesus the Head of the Church and True Mediator. N.p.: 1678.

A Measuring-Rule concerning Liberty and Persecution. N.p.: [1662].

A Message from the Lord, to the Parliament of England. London: N.p., 1654.

Narrative Papers of George Fox. Edited by Henry J. Cadbury. Richmond, Ind: Friends United Press, 1972.

News coming up out of the North, Sounding towards the South. London: N.p., 1654.

Of Bowings. London: N.p., 1657.

Old Simon the Sorcerer. London: N.p., 1663.

Our Covenant with God and will all men in Peace. London: N.p., 1660. [Broadside]

A Paper Sent Forth into the World, from them that are scornfully called Quakers. London: Giles Calvert, 1654.

A Paper to Friends, and Others, Against the Pomps of the World. London: John Bringhurst, 1682–1683.

The Papists Strength, Principles, and Doctrines. London: N.p., 1658.

The Pearle Found in England. London: N.p., 1658.

The People of God in Scorn Called Quakers Their Love to all Mankind. N.p.: 1676.

Possession above Profession. N.p.: 1675.

A Postscript. N.p.: [ca. 1663].

The Priests and Professors Catechisme. London: N.p., 1657.

The Priests Fruits Made Manifest. London: N.p., 1657.

A Primer for the Schollers and Doctors of Europe. London: N.p., 1659.

Primitive Ordination and Succession of Bishops, Deacons, Pastors and Teachers in the Church of Christ. N.p.: 1675.

The Promise of God Proclaimed. London: N.p., 1660. [Broadside]

Queries for John James. [London: N.p., 1658].

A Reply to the pretended Vindication of the Answer. London: N.p., 1658.

The Royal Law of God Revived. N.p.: 1676.

The Saints (or they that are Born of the Spirit) their Heavenly & Spiritual Worship, Unity & Communion. London: John Bringhurst, 1683.

A Scripture Testimony against Persecution for Religion. N.p., n.d.

A Scripture Testimony to the Saints Practice. N.p., n.d.

The Second Covenant. London: N.p., 1657.

The Serious Peoples Reasoning and Speech with the Worlds Teachers and Professors. London: N.p., 1659.

Several Papers Given Forth. London: N.p., 1660.

Several Papers given forth for the Spreading of Truth, and Detection of Deceit. N.p.: 1671.

Several Plain Truths Manifested and Declared from the Spirit of God. London: Andrew Sowle, 1684.

Several Treatises Worthy of every True Christians Serious Consideration. London: N.p., 1691.

A Short Epistle to Friends to keep in the Power of God. N.p., n.d. [Broadside]

The Short Journal and Itinerary Journals of George Fox. Edited by Norman Penney. Cambridge: Cambridge University Press, 1925.

A Small Treatise Concerning Swearing. N.p.: 1675.

Some Papers Given Forth in English & Latine, to the Magistrates of the Isle of Milita. London: N.p., 1660.

Some Principles of the elect People of God who in Scorn are called Quakers. London: N.p., 1661.

Some Principles of the Elect People In scorn called Quakers. N.p.: 1671.

Some Queries to all the Teachers and Professors. N.p., n.d. [Broadside]

Something by way of Query to the Bishops Courts. N.p.: 1671.

Something in Answer to a Law Lately made at the first Sessions of the General Court held at Boston. N.p.: [1679].

Something in Answer to a Letter (Which I have seen) of John Leverat Governour of Boston. N.p., n.d.

Something in Answer to all such as falsly say, The Quakers Are No Christians. London: Andrew Sowle, 1682.

Something in Answer to Lodowick Muggleton's Book, Which he calls The Quakers Neck Broken. London: N.p., 1667.

Something in Answer to that Book, Called the Church-Faith. London: N.p., 1660.

Something in Answer to the Old Common-Prayer Book. London: N.p., 1660.

The Spirit of Envy, Lying, and Persecution Made Manifest. London: N.p., 1663.

The Spirit of Man, The Candle of the Lord: The Candle of the Wicked Often Put Out. N.p.: 1677.

The Spiritual Man Christ Jesus. N.p.: 1677.

A Spiritual or Heavenly Saluation to all the Tender-Hearted in Christendom. London: N.p., 1690.

The State of the Birth Temporal & Spiritual. London: Andrew Sowle, 1683.

The Summ of such Particulars as Are Charged against George Fox in the Mittimus by which He Stands Committed. N.p.: [1660].

Surely the magistrates of Nottingham are blinde. London: N.p., 1659. [Broadside]

A Testimony concerning Justification. N.p.: 1677.

A Testimony concerning our dear Friend and Brother George Watt. [London: N.p., 1688.]

A Testimony concerning the Blood of the Old-Covenant, and the Blood of the New-Covenant. N.p.: [1678].

A Testimony for all the Masters of Ships and Seamen to Read Over. N.p.: 1677.

A Testimony for God's Truth. [London]: A. Sowle, 1688.

A Testimony of the True Light of the World. London: N.p., 1657.

A Testimony of what we believe of Christ. N.p.: 1677.

That all might see Who They Were That had a Command, and did pay Tythes. London: N.p., 1657.

The Teachers of the World Unvailed. London: N.p., 1656.

These Queries are given forth for any, either Preist or People to Answer. N.p.: [1655].

This for each Parliament-Man. London: N.p., 1656.

This is a Controversy Betwixt the Quakers and the Papists. N.p.: 1664.

This is a Warning to all that Profess Christianity and Others. N.p.: [1679].

This is an Encouragement to all the Womens-Meetings in the World. N.p.: 1676.

This is to all Officers and Souldiers of the Armies in England, Scotland, and Ireland. London: N.p., 1657.

This is for all people who stumble at God's Command. N.p.: 1660.

This is to all the Prisoners and Sufferers. London: J. B., 1684.

To all Freinds and People in the whole of Christendome. London: N.p., n.d.

To all Kings, Princes, Rulers, Governours, Bishops and Clergy that Profess Christianity in Christendom. London: John Bringhurst, 1685.

To All Magistrates and People in Christendom. N.p.: 1676.

To all people in all Christendom. [London: M. W.], n.d.

To All Rulers and Magistrates, To be Tender and Take Heed of Persecuting and Imprisoning, and Spoiling the Goods of God's People. London: John Bringhurst, 1683.

To all that Make Mention of the Name of the Lord. N.p.: n.d. [Broadside]

To all that Professe Christianity. London: N.p., 1661.

To all that would know the Way to the Kingdome. N.p.: [1654].

To all that would know the Way to the Kingdome. London: N.p., 1655.

To all that would Know the Way to the Kingdome. London: N.p., 1660.

To all that would know the Way to the Kingdom. N.p., 1671.

To all that would know the Way to the Kingdom, without Forms, or got above all Forms. N.p.: [1654].

To all the Ignorant people, the word of the Lord. N.p., n.d.

To All the Kings, Princes, and Governours in the whole World. N.p.: 1677.

To all the Nations under the whole Heavens. London: N.p., 1660.

To all the People Who meet in Steeple-Houses in England and elsewhere. London: N.p., 1657.

To all the Professors & Teachers of Christ's Words. London: N.p., 1660.

To all them who are Blinde. N.p., n.d. [Broadside]

To Friends in Barbadoes, Virginia, Maryland, New-England, and elsewhere. N.p.: 1666.

To both Houses of Parliament. London: N.p., 1660. [Broadside]

To the Chief Magistrate, Rulers, Ministers, Justices of the Peace and other Officers. N.p.: [1684]. [Broadside]

To the Councill of Officers of the Armie and the Heads of the Nation. N.p.: [1659].

To the Flock of Christ, Everywhere to be Read in their Assemblies. N.p.: 1681.

To the High and Lofty Ones. N.p.: [1655].

To the Ministers, Teachers, and Priests . . . of Baradoes. N.p.: 1672.

To the Parliament of the Comon-Wealth of England. London: N.p., 1659.

To the People of Uxbridge. London: N.p., [1659]. [Broadside]

To the Pope and all his Magistrates and the Protestants. London: N.p., 1661.

To the Protector and Parliament of England. London: N.p., 1658.

To the Turk, and all that are under his Supream. London: N.p., 1660.

To those That have been formerly in Authority, and Have Broken Covenant with God & Man. London: N.p., n.d.

To you that are crying, What is become of our forefathers. London: N.p., 1657.

A True Account of the Sensible, Thankful and Holy State of God's People. N.p.:1686.

The True Honour Amongst the Jews. London: N.p., 1660.

True Judgement, Or, the Spiritual-Man Judging all Things. London: N.p., 1654.

The True Marriage Declared. N.p.: [1679].

Truths Triumph in the Eternal Power over the Dark Inventions of Fallen Man. London: N.p., 1661.

Trying of Spirits In our Age now as in the Apostles Days. London: N.p., 1683.

Tythes, Offerings, and First Fruits, Commanded by the Law in the Old Testament, Is Not Gospel. London: N.p., 1683.

The Unmasking and Discovering of Anti-Christ. London: N.p., 1653.

The Vials of the Wrath of God. London: N.p., 1655.

A Visitation to the Jews. London: N.p., 1656.

A Voice of the Lord to the Heathen. London: N.p., 1656.

A Warning from the Lord to all such as hang down the head for a Day. London: N.p., 1654.

A Warning from the Lord to the People: and to all His Train of Idolatries. London: N.p., 1656.

A Warning to All in the proud City called London. N.p.: [1655]. [Broadside]

A Warning to all Teachers of Children. London: N.p., 1657.

A Warning to all the Merchants in London. London: N.p., 1658.

A Warning to England, and to all that profess themselves Christians. N.p.: 1674.

A Warning to the Rulers of England. N.p.: 1653.

A Warning to the World. London: N.p., 1655.

A Way to prevent the Indignation and Judgments of God from coming on a Kingdom, Nation, or Family. London: N.p., 1682. [Broadside]

What the Unchangable God is, and how all People may know him. N.p.: [1685].

Why Election and Reprobation is, Clearly Discovered. N.p.: 1679.

The Woman learning in Silence: or, the Mysterie of the Womans Subjection to her Husband. London: N.p., 1656.

A Word of Admonition to such as Wander. London: N.p., 1684.
The Works of George Fox. 8 vols. Philadelphia: Marcus T. C. Gould, 1831.

Fox as Coauthor

et al. *Copies of Some few of the Papers given into the House of Parliament in the time of James Naylers Tryal there.* N.p., n.d.

et al. *A Declaration Against all Popery and Popish points.* N.p.: [1655].

et al. *A Declaration from the Harmles & Innocent People of God Called Quakers.* N.p.: [1661].

et al. *An Epistle to all the Christian Magistrates and Powers in the whole of Christendom.* London: N.p., 1659.

et al. *For the King, and Both Houses of Parliament.* London: N.p., [1661].

et al. *A Letter Relating to Marriages, of Those who are Near of Kin.* N.p.: 1748. [Broadside]

et al. *Several Letters Written to the Saints of the Most High.* London: N.p., 1654.

et al. *Several Papers; Some of them given forth by George Fox.* N.p.: A. P., 1654.

et al. *To you that are called by the name of Baptists.* N.p., n.d.

et al. *A True Declaration of the bloody Proceedings of the Men in Maidstone.* London: N.p., 1655.

and Richard Farnworth and James Nayler. *To you that are called by the name of Baptists.* N.p.: [1654].

and Margaret Fell. *A Paper concerning such as are made Ministers by the will of man.* London: N.p., 1659.

and Ellis Hookes. *The Arraignment of Popery.* London: N.p., 1667.

and Ellis Hookes. *An Epistle From the People in scorn called Quakers to all People Upon the Earth.* N.p.: 1666.

and Richard Hubberthorne. *Truth's Defense Against the Refined Subtilty of the Serpent.* York: N.p., 1653.

and James Nayler. *Severall Papers.* N.p.: A. P., 1653.

and James Nayler. *Some Papers Given forth to the World, to be read.* London: N.p., 1655.

and James Nayler. *A Word from the Lord, unto all the faithlesse Generation of the World.* N.p.: 1654.

and R. R. *To All Magistrates, Teachers, Schoolmasters and People in Christendom.* London: N.p., 1660.

and John Stubs and Benjamin Furly. *A Battle-Door, for Teachers & Professors to Learn Singular & Plural.* London: N.p., 1660.

Published Primary Sources

Edited Texts

Abbott, Wilbur C., ed. *The Writings and Speeches of Oliver Cromwell.* 4 vols. Cambridge, Mass.: Harvard University Press, 1937–1947.

"Abraham Manuscripts," *JFHS* 11 (1914) 145–90.

"The American Journey of George Fox," *JFHS* 9 (1912) 5–52.

Elias Ashmole (1617–1692). 5 vols. Edited by C. H. Josten. Oxford: Clarendon Press, 1966.

Balderston, Marion, ed. *James Claypoole's Letterbook: London and Philadelphia, 1681–1684.* San Marino, Calif.: Huntington Library, 1967.

Barbour, Hugh, and Arthur Roberts, eds. *Early Quaker Writings, 1650–1700.* Grand Rapids, Mich.: Eerdmans Publishing, 1973.

Barclay, John, ed. *Letters, &c., of Early Friends.* London: Harvey and Darton, 1841.

————. *Selections from the Works of Isaac Penington.* London: Darton and Harvey, 1837.

[Barclay, Robert.] *Barclay's Apology in Modern English.* Edited by Dean Freiday. N.P.: 1967.

Beard, Thomas. *The Holy Seed.* 3d ed. Edited by Joseph Porter. London: N.p., 1715.

Beaumont, Agnes. *Narrative of the Persecution of Agnes Beaumont.* Edited by G. B. Harrison. London: Constable and Co., [1929].

Besse, Joseph. *A Collection of the Sufferings of the People Called Quakers.* 2 vols. London: Luke Hinde, 1753.

Birch, Thomas, ed. *Collection of the State Papers of John Thurloe.* 7 vols. London: N.p., 1742.

Book of Common Prayer 1559. Edited by John E. Booty. Charlottesville: University Press of Virginia, 1976.

Bunyan, John. *"The Doctrine of Law and Grace Unfolded" and "I Will Pray with Spirit."* Edited by Richard L. Greaves. Oxford: Clarendon Press, 1976.

————. *The Pilgrim's Progress.* 2d ed. Edited by Roger Sharrock. Oxford: Clarendon Press, 1967.

Burton, Thomas. *Diary of Thomas Burton.* 4 vols. Edited by John T. Rutt. London: Henry Colburn, 1828.

Cadbury, Henry J., ed. *Annual Catalogue of George Fox's Papers.* Philadelphia: Friends Book Store, 1939.

————, ed. "Intercepted Correspondence of William Penn, 1670." *PMHB* 70 (1946): 349–72.

————, ed. *Letters to William Dewsbury and Others.* London: Bannisdale Press, 1948.

————, ed. *Swarthmore Documents in America.* London: Friends Historical Society, 1940.

Calendar of State Papers, Domestic Series, 1649–1660. 13 vols. London: Longman and Co., 1875–86.

Carlyle, Thomas, ed. *Oliver Cromwell's Letters and Speeches.* 4 vols. New York: Charles Scribner's Sons, 1899.

Clarke, George, ed. *John Bellers: His Life, Times and Writings.* London: Routledge and Kegan Paul, [1987].

Epistles from the Yearly Meeting of Friends. 2 vols. London: Edward Marsh, 1858.

Evans, William, and Thomas Evans, eds. *The Friends Library.* 14 vols. Philadelphia: Joseph Rakestraw, 1837.

————. *The Lives of Early Friends: Volume 1.* Farmington Falls, Maine: Friends of Jesus Christ, 1986.

Evelyn, John. *The Diary of John Evelyn.* 2 vols. Edited by William Bray. London: J. M. Dent and Co., n.d.

Fiennes, Celia. *Illustrated Journeys of Celia Fiennes, 1685–c. 1712.* Edited by Christopher Morris. London: MacDonald and Co., 1982.

Foster, C. W., ed. *Lincoln Episcopal Records, 1571–1584.* London: Canterbury and York Society, 1913.

————, ed. *The State of the Church in the Reigns of Elizabeth and James I: Volume 1.* Lincoln, England: Lincoln Record Society, 1926.

Fox, Levi, ed. "Diary of Robert Beake, Mayor of Coventry, 1655–1656." In *Miscellany 1,* ed., Robert Bearman, 114–37. Dugdale Society Publications, Vol. 31. Oxford: Dugdale Society, 1977.

Fuller, Thomas. *History of the Worthies of England.* 3 vols. Edited by P. Austin Nuttall. London: T. Tegg, 1840.

Hacket, [Thomas]. *Memoirs of the Life of Archbishop Williams.* London: Samuel Briscoe, 1715.

Heywood, Oliver. *Autobiography*. Edited by J. Horstall Turner. Brighouse, England: A. B. Baynes, 1882.

Hobbes, Thomas. *Behemoth, or the Long Parliament*. 2d ed. Edited by Ferdinand Tönnies. London: Frank Cass and Co., 1969.

Josselin, Ralph. *Diary of the Rev. Ralph Josselin*. Edited by E. Hockliffe. Camden Society, 3d Series, vol. 15. London: Camden Society, 1908.

Kiffin, William. *Remarkable Passages in the Life of William Kiffin*. Edited by William Orme. London: N.p., 1823.

Letters of Isaac Penington. Philadelphia: Friends' Book Store, n.d.

Letters, Speeches and Declarations of King Charles II. Edited by Authur Bryant. London: Cassell, 1968.

Luke, Samuel. *Journal of Sir Samuel Luke*. 3 vols. Edited by I. G. Philip. Banbury, England: Cherry and Sons, 1947–53.

Lyde, Nehemiah. *A Narrative of the Life of Mr. Richard Lyde of Hereford*. London: N.p., 1654.

Marx, Karl. *Selected Writings*. Edited by David McLellan. Oxford: Oxford University Press, 1977.

Massachusetts Historical Society. *Collections*. 4th series, vol. 7. Boston: Massachusetts Historical Society, 1865.

Milward, James. *Diary of James Milward, Esq*. Edited by Caroline Robbins. Cambridge: Cambridge University Press, 1938.

Mortimer, Russell, ed. *Minute Book of the Men's Meeting of the Society of Friends in Bristol, 1667–1686*. Bristol, England: Bristol Record Society, 1971.

————, ed. *Minute Book of the Men's Meeting of the Society of Friends in Bristol, 1686–1704*. Bristol, England: Bristol Record Society, 1977.

Nayler, James. *A Collection of Sundry Books, Epistles and Papers Written by James Nayler*. Edited by George Whitehead. London: J. Sowle, 1716.

Nicolson, Marjorie H., ed. *Conway Letters: The Correspondence of Anne, Viscountess Conway, Henry More, and their Friends, 1624–1684*. New Haven, Conn.: Yale University Press, 1930.

Norwood, Richard. *Journal of Richard Norwood*. Edited by Wesley F. Craven and Walter B. Hayward. New York: Scholar's Facsimilies and Reprints, 1945.

Owen, Dorothy M., ed. *Records of the Established Church of England, excluding parochial records*. [Cambridge:] British Records Association, 1970.

Penington, Mary. *Experiences in the Life of Mary Penington*. Edited by Normam Penney. London: Headley Brothers, 1911.

Penn, William. *The Papers of William Penn*. 4 vols. Edited by Mary M. Dunn and Richard S. Dunn. Philadelphia: University of Pennsylvania Press, 1981–86.

Penney, Norman, ed. *Extracts from State Papers Relating to Friends, 1654 to 1672*. London: Headley Bros., 1913.

————, ed. *"The First Publishers of Truth."* London: Headley Brothers, 1907.

————, ed. *The Household Account Book of Sarah Fell*. Cambridge: Cambridge University Press, 1920.

[————,] ed. "Meetings in Ely, Cambridge and Huntingdon, 1668." *JFHS* 6 (1909): 12–14.

[————,] ed. "Meetings in Yorkshire, 1668." *JFHS* 2 (1905): 32–36, 73–76, 101–03.

[————,] ed. "Wilkinson-Storyism in Wiltshire c. 1680." *JFHS* 16 (1919): 143–47.

Pennington, D. H., and I. A. Roots, eds. *The Committee at Stafford, 1643-1645: The Order Book of the Staffordshire County Committee*. Manchester, England: Manchester University Press, 1957.

Pepys, Samuel. *Diary of Samuel Pepys.* 11 vols. Edited by Robert Latham and William Matthews. Berkeley and Los Angeles: University of California Press, 1983.

Petrie, Charles, ed. *The Letters, Speeches, and Proclamations of King Charles I.* New York: Funk and Wagnalls, 1968.

Pike, Joseph. *Some Account of The Life of Joseph Pike.* Edited by John Barclay. London: Darnton and Harvey.

A Quaker Post-Bag. Edited by Mrs. Godfrey L. Lampson. London: Longmans, Green and Co., 1910.

"Records of the Jacob-Lathrop-Jessey Church 1616–1641." *Transactions of the Baptist Historical Society* 1 (1910): 203–25.

Reliquiae Barclaianae. N.p.: 1870.

Rowntree, John Stephenson. *John Stephenson Rowntree: His Life and Work.* Edited by Phebe Doncaster. London: Headley Brothers, 1908.

Rowntree, John Wilhelm. *John Wilhelm Rowntree: Essays and Addresses.* Edited by Joshua Rowntree. London: Headley Brothers, 1905.

Sachse, William L., ed. *The Diary of Roger Lowe.* New Haven, Conn: Yale University Press, 1938.

Snell, Beatrice S., ed. *The Minute Book of the Monthly Meeting of the Society of Friends for the Upperside of Buckinghamshire, 1669–1690.* N.p.: Buckinghamshire Archaeological Society, 1937.

Speed, John. *The Counties of Britain: A Tudor Atlas.* Edited by Nicol Nicolson. New York: Thames and Hudson, 1989.

Stocks, Helen, ed. *Records of the Borough of Leicester.* Cambridge: Cambridge University Press, 1923.

Symonds, Richard. *Diary of the Marches of the Royal Army during the Great Civil War.* Edited by Charles E. Long. [London:] Camden Society, 1859.

Thompson, J. Eric S., ed. *Thomas Gage's Travels in the New World.* Norman: University of Oklahoma Press, 1958.

Tolles, Frederick B., and E. Gordon Alderfer, eds. *The Witness of William Penn.* New York: Macmillan Co., 1957.

Tomkins, John, ed. *Piety Promoted, in a Collection of Dying Sayings of Many of the People Called Quakers.* London: William Phillips, 1812.

Tuke, Samuel, ed. *Selections from the Epistles of George Fox.* 2d ed. London: Edward Marsh, 1848.

Underhill, Edward B., ed. *Confessions of Faith . . . of the Baptist Churches of England.* London: Haddon Bros. Co., 1854.

Usher, Ronald G., ed. *The Presbyterian Movement in the Reign of Queen Elizabeth as Illustrated by the Minute Book of the Dedham Classis, 1582–1589.* London: Royal Historical Society, 1905.

Verae fidei gloria est corna vitae. Compiled by Alexander Demaine. London: J. Smith, 1820.

Ward, John. *Diary of the Rev. John Ward, A.M.* Edited by Charles Shevern. London: Henry Colburn, 1839.

West, Jessamyn, ed. *The Quaker Reader.* New York: Viking Press, 1962.

Whiteman, Anne, ed. *The Compton Census of 1676: A Critical Edition.* London: Oxford University Press, 1986.

Williams, Roger. *The Complete Writings of Roger Williams.* 7 vols. Edited by J. Lewis Diman. New York: Russell & Russell, 1963.

Winstanley, Gerrard. *The Works of Gerrard Winstanley.* Edited by George H. Sabine. Ithaca, NY: Cornell University Press, 1941.

————. *Winstanley: The Law of Freedom and Other Essays.* Edited by Christopher Hill Hammondsworth, England: Penguin Books, 1973.

Woodhouse, A. S. P., ed. *Puritanism and Liberty: Being the Army Debates (1647–9).* Chicago: University of Chicago Press, 1974.

Unedited Texts

Adamson, William. *An Answer to a Book, Titled, Quakers Principles Quaking.* London: N.p., 1656.

Aldam, Thomas et al. *False Prophets and false Teachers Described.* N.p.: 1652.

Andrews, T. *A Serious Expostulation With the People call'd Quakers.* London: D. Midwinter, 1708.

Anti-Quakerisme, or, a Character of the Quakers Spirit. N.p.: 1659. [Broadside]

Articles of Christian Religion, Approved and Passed by both Houses of Parliament. London: N.p., 1648.

Atkinson, Elizabeth. *A Brief and plain discovery of the Labourers in mistery, Babilon Generally Called by the name of Quakers.* London: P. L., 1669.

Audland, John. *The Innocent Delievered out of the Snare.* London: N.p., 1655.

Austin, Ra. *The Strong Man Armed not Cast Out, but Removed to a Stronger Hold.* London: Peter Parker, 1676.

B., E. *A Declaration of the present Sufferings of above 140 persons . . . called Quakers.* London: N.p., 1659.

Baiteman, George. *An Answer to (Vindicate the Cause of the Nick-named Quakers of such scandalls and untruths as is falsly cast upon them in a lying Pamphlet, otherwise called) A Discourse concerning the Quakers.* N.p.: 1653.

Barclay, Robert. *An Apology for the True Christian Divinity.* Philadelphia: Friends' Book Store, n.d.

————. *A Treatise on Church Government, formerly called Anarchy of the Ranters.* Philadelphia: Solomon W. Conrad, 1822.

————. *Truth Triumphant.* London: N.p., 1792.

Baxter, Richard. *The Cure of Church Divisions.* London: N.p., 1670.

————. *One Sheet for the Ministry Against the Malignants of all sorts.* London: Robert White, 1657.

————. *Practical Works of Richard Baxter.* 23 vols. London: James Duncan, 1830.

————. *The Quakers Catechism, or the Quakers Questioned.* London: A. M., 1655.

————. *Reliquiae Baxterianae: or, Mr. Richard Baxter's narrative of the most memorable passages of his life and times.* London: N.p., 1696.

————. *A Second Sheet for the Ministry Justifying our Calling.* London: R. White, 1657.

————. *A Winding Sheet for Popery.* London: Robert White, 1657.

Beckman, Edward et al. *A Brief Discovery of Some of the Blasphemous and Seditious Principles of the People, Called Quakers.* London: John Harris, 1699.

Benson, Gervase. *The Cry of the Oppresssd From under the Oppression.* London: N.p., 1656.

Berwick, John. *An Answer to a Quakers Seventeen Heads of Queries.* London: T. R., 1660.

Bishop, George. *Jesus Christ, The same today, as yesterday.* London: N.p., 1655.

Bishop, George, et al. *The Cry of Blood.* London: N.p., 1656.

[Blome, R.] *The Fanatick History: or An Exact Relation and Account of the Old Anabaptists, and the New Quakers.* London: J. Sims, 1660.

[————]. *Gagg for the Quakers.* London: J. C., 1659.

[————]. *Questions Propounded to George Whitehead and George Fox, etc. Who Disputed by Turnes against one Universitie Man in Cambridge.* N.p.: [1659].

Bolton, John. *A Justification of the Righteous Judgement of God on Nathaniel Smith.* N.p.: 1669.

Bolton, John, et al. *A Declaration from the Children of Light.* London: N.p., 1655.

Bossuet, Jacques Benignes. *Quakerism A-la-Mode: Or, a History of Quietism.* London: J. Harris, 1698.

Bourignon, Antonia. *A Warning against the Quakers.* London: N.p., 1708.

Bourne, Immanuel. *A defense of the Scriptures, and the Holy Spirit speaking in them.* London: John Wright, 1656.

Boyce, Thomas. *The Quakers Cruelty, Deceit & Wickedness.* London: N.p., 1675.

Bradshaw, Ellis. *The Quakers Quaking Principles Examined and Refuted.* London: N.p., 1656.

————. *The Quakers Whitest Divell Unvailed.* N.p.: 1654.

Brownsword, William. *The Quaker-Jesuits, or, Popery in Quakerism.* London: J. M., 1660.

Bugg, Francis. *Battering Rams Against New Rome.* London: John Gwillim, 1691.

————. *The Finishing Stroke.* London: Author, 1712.

————. *Innocency Vindicated and Envy Rebuked.* N.p.: 1684.

————. *Jezebel Withstood and her Daughter Anne Docwra Publicly Reprov'd.* N.p.: [1699].

————. *Last Will and Testament of that Impostor George Fox.* 3d ed. N.p.: 1703. [Broadside]

————. *One Blow More at New Rome.* London: N.p., 1691.

————. *The Painted-Harlot Both Stript and Whipt.* London: J. Gain, 1683.

————. *Pilgrim's Progress, from Quakerism to Christianity.* London: N.p., 1698.

————. *The Quakers Set in their true Light.* London: C. Brome, 1696.

————. *Tyranny and Hypocrisy Detected.* London: N.p., 1673.

Bullock, Jeffery. *One Blow more against Antichrists Ministers, the Downfall of whose Ministry hastens.* London: N.p., 1678.

Bunyan, John. *Grace Abounding to the Chief of Sinners.* London: J. F. Dove, 1827.

————. *A Vindication of the Book Called, Some Gospel-Truths Opened.* London: Matthias Cowley, 1657.

Burnet, William. *The Capital Principles of the People Called Quakers.* London: N.p., 1668.

Burrough, Edward. *A Declaration to all the World of our Faith.* London: Thomas Simmons, 1658.

————. *A Description of the State and Condition of all Mankind.* London: N.p., 1657.

————. *Memorable Works of a Son of Thunder and Consolation.* N.p.: 1672.

————. *Stablishing against Quaking.* London: N.p., 1656.

————. *To all dear Friends and Brethren.* N.p.: [1662].

————. *To the Whole English Army.* London: N.p., 1659.

[————]. *The True Christian Religion Againe Discovered.* London: Robert Norton, Jr., 1658.

————. *Truth (the strongest of all) Witnessed forth in the Spirit of Truth, against all Deceit.* London: N.p., 1657.

————. *The Woefull Cry of Unjust Persecutions.* London: N.p., 1657.

Burrough, John, John Crook, and John Perrot. *To all Dear Friends & Brethren.* N.p.: [1662].

C., J. *One Sheet Against the Quakers.* London: Richard Butler, 1677.

————. *Quakerism Subverted.* London: N.p., 1677.

————. *A True Discovery of the Ignorance, Blindness, and Darkness of those who are Called Magistrates about Carlisle.* London: N.p., 1654.

C., R. *Quaeries Propounded to George Fox and His Ministers.* London: N.p., 1669.

Caffyn, Matthew. *The Deceived, and Deceiving Quakers Discovered.* London: R. I., 1656.

[Camm, John, and Francis Howgill?]. *An Answer to a Book which Samuel Eaton Put up to the Parliament.* London: N.p., 1654.

Canons and Institutions Drawn up and Agreed upon the General Assembly or Meeting of the Heads of the Quakers. London: N.p., 1669.

Carpenter, Richard. *The Anabaptist washt and washt and shrunk in the Washing.* London: William Hunt, 1653.

The Case of the People Called Quakers, Relating to Oathes and Swearing. N.p.: 1673.

A Catalogue of the severall Sects and Opinions in England and other Nations. [London]: R. A., 1647.

Caton, William. *Journal of the Life of . . . Will. Caton.* London: N.p., 1689.

Certain Quaeries and Antiquaeries, Concerning the Quakers. London: N.p., 1653.

The Character of a Quaker. London: T. Egglesfield, 1671.

[Cheyney, John]. *Quakerism Proved to be Gross Blasphemy and Antichristian Heresie.* London: N.p., 1677.

Chidley, Katherine. *The Justification of the Independent Churches of Christ.* London: N.p., 1641.

Clap, Roger. *Memoirs of Roger Clap.* Boston: David Clapp, Jr., 1844.

Clapham, Jonathan. *A Full Discovery and Confutation of the wicked and damnable Doctrines of the Quakers.* London: T. R. and E. M., 1656.

Claridge, Richard. *Mercy Covering the Judgement-Seat, and Life and Light Triumphing Over Death and Darkness.* London: T. Sowle, 1700.

Clark, Henry. *A Description of the Prophets, Apostles and Ministers of Christ.* London: N.p., 1655.

———. *Englands Lessons, Set to be learned by her Rulers, Nobles, Judges, Counselors, Scribes, Astrologers, Priests and People of all Sorts. . . .* London: Giles Calvert, 1656.

Claxton, Lawrence. *The Quakers Downfall.* London: N.p., 1659.

Cockson, Edward. *The Quakers Pedigree Trac'd, Or, Some Brief Observations on their Agreement with the Church of Rome.* London: Edw. Ebets, 1703.

Collier, Jeremy. *An Ecclesiastical History of Great Britain.* 9 vols. London: Gilbert and Riverton, 1852.

Collier, Thomas. *A Looking-Glasse for the Quakers.* London: N.p., 1657.

Comber, Thomas. *Christianity No Enthusiasm.* London: T. D., 1678.

Controversy Ended. London: N.p., 1673.

A Copy of a Letter, with its Answer, concerning a contest at Worcester beween a Minister and a Quaker. N.p., n.d.

Cotton, Priscilla and Mary Cole. *To the Priests and People of England.* London: N.p., 1655.

Cox, John. *Articles of Chrsitian Faith Believed and Written by me.* London: N.p., 1686.

Cramp, Harold St. G. *A Yeoman Farmer's Son: A Leicestershire Childhood.* Oxford: Oxford University Press, 1986.

[Crisp, Stephen]. *A Short History of a Long Travel from Babylon, to Bethel.* London: J. Sowle, 1711.

Crisp, Thomas. *The Discovery of the Accursed Thing in the Foxonian Quakers Camp Enlarged.* London: N.p., 1695.

———. *The First Part of Babel's-Builders Unmasking Themselves.* London: Enock Prosser, 1682.

———. *The Fourth Part of Babel's-Builders Unmask't.* N.p., n.d.

———. *Innocency Vindicated.* N.p.: 1684.

———. *Several Testimonies concerning Liberty of Conscience, and Church-Government.* 3d ed. London: N.p., 1782.

————. *The Sixth Part of Babel's-Builders Unmask't*. N.p., n.d.

————. *The Third Part of Babel's-Builders Unmask't*. N.p., n.d.

Croese, Gerard. *The General History of the Quakers*. London: N.p., 1696.

Crouch, William. *Posthuma Christiana*. London: J. Sowle, 1712.

D., E. *Innocents No Saints: or, a, Paire of Spectacles for a Dark-Sighted Quaker*. London: N.p., 1658.

D., W. *The Quakers Converted*. London: J. Robinson, 1690.

[Danson, Thomas]. *The Quakers Proved Deceivers*. London: John Allen, 1660.

————. *The Quakers Wisdom Descended not from Above*. London: J. Allen, 1659.

————. *A Synopsis of Quakerism*. London: N.p., 1668.

Deacon, John. *An Exact History of the life of James Naylor*. London: Edward Thomas, 1657.

————. *The Great Imposter Examined*. London: N.p., 1656.

————. *A Public Discovery of a Secret Deceit*. London: N.p., 1656.

A Declaration of the Maids of the City of London, etc. N.p.: 1659. [Broadside]

[Defoe, Daniel]. *A Tour Thro' the Whole Island of Great Britain*. 3 vols. London: G. Strathan, 1727.

Denne, Henry. *The Quaker No Papist, in Answer to the Quaker Disarm'd*. London: Francis Smith, 1659.

Dent, Arthur. *The Plaine Mans Path-way to Heaven*. London: N.p., 1610.

Dewsbury, William. *The Discovery of the great enmity of the Serpent*. London: N.p., 1655.

————. *The Mighty Day of the Lord, is Coming*. London: N.p., 1656.

Dewsbury, William, et al. *Several Letters Written to the Saints of the Most High*. London: N.p., 1654.

A Discovery of some Fruits of the Profession, Religion, Ministry, Government of this Nation. London: N.p., 1656.

Disney, Gervase. *Some Remarkable Passages in the Holy Life and Death of Gervase Disney*. London: J. D., 1692.

Docwra, Ann. *An Apostate-Conscience Exposed*. London: T. Sowle, 1699.

————. *An Epistle of Love and Good Advice*. London: Andrew Sowle, [1683].

————. *A Looking-Glass for the Recorder and Justices of the Peace*. N.p.: [1682].

————. *The Second Part of an Apostate-Conscience Exposed*. London: T. Sowle, 1700.

[Dugdale, William]. *A Short View of the Late Troubles in England*. Oxford: The Theatre, 1681.

Duke, Francis. *An Answer to some of the Principal Quakers*. London: T. N., 1660.

————. *The Fulness and Freeness of Gods Grace Declared*. London: T. N., 1656.

Eaton, Samuel. *The Quakers Confuted*. London: R. White, 1654.

Edmundson, William. *A Journal of the Life . . . of . . . William Edmundson*. London: N.p., 1715.

Edwards, Thomas. *Gangraena*. London: T. R. and E. M., 1646. (2 parts)

Ellington, Francis. *Christian Information Concerning these Last times*. London: N.p., 1664.

Ellwood, Thomas. *An Antidote Against the Infection of William Roger's Book*. London: N.p., 1682.

————. *A Caution to Constables and Other Inferior Officers, Concerned in the Execution of the Conventicle-Act*. London: William Sheat, 1683.

————. *A Discourse concerning Riots*. London: Thomas Hawkins, 1683.

————. *A Fresh Pursuit*. N.p.: [1674].

————. *The History of Thomas Ellwood: Written by Himself*. London: George Routledge and Sons, 1885.

————. *Rogero Mastix. A Rod for William Rogers*. N.p.: 1685.

————. *A Seasonable Disswasive from Persecution*. London: William Sheat, 1683.

Elys, Edmund. *Edmund Elys His Vindication of Himself.* London: T. Sowle, 1697.

[————]. *One Wonder More.* N.p., n.d.

————. *Reflections upon Some Passages in G. Keith's Narrative.* N.p.: [1696].

————. *Reflections Upon some Passages in George Keith's Third Narrative.* London: T. Sowle, 1698.

————. *Some Reflections Upon Francis Bugg's Book.* N.p.: [1699].

Emmot, G. *A Northern Blast, or the Spiritual Quaker Converted.* London: N.p., 1655.

[Evans, Theophilus]. *History of Modern Enthusiasm, from the Reformation to the Present Time.* 2d ed. London: N.p., 1757.

F., R. *Antichrists Man of War . . . by a Souldier of the Armie of the Lamb.* London: N.p., 1655.

Faldo, John. *XXI Divines . . . Cleared of the Unjust Criminations of Will. Penn.* London: J. D., 1675.

————. *A Vindication of Quakerism No Christianity &c.* London: B. Griffin, 1673.

Farmer, Ra. *The Great Mysteries of Godlinesse and Ungodlinesse.* London: S. G., 1655.

————. *Sathan Inthron'd in his Chair of Pestilence.* London: N.p., 1657.

Farnworth, Richard. *The Antipathy Betwixt Flesh and Spirit.* London: N.p., 1654.

————. *A Discovery of Truth and Falsehood.* London: N.p., 1653.

————. *England's Warning Peece Gone Forth.* London: N.p., 1653.

————. *God's Covenanting with his People.* London: N.p., 1653.

————. *The Holy Scriptures from Scandals are cleared.* London: N.p., 1655.

————. *Light Risen Out of Darkness Now in these latter Days.* London: N.p., 1654.

————. *The Scriptures Vindication Against the Scotish Contradictors.* London: N.p., 1655.

————. *Several Petitions Answered, That were put up by the Priests of Westmoreland.* London: N.p., 1653.

————. *Spirituall Man Judgeth All Things.* London: N.p., 1655.

————. *A true Separation between the Power of the Spirit, and the imitation of Antichrist.* N.p., n.d.

Farnworth, Richard, and James Parnell. *The Immediate Call to the Ministry of the Gospel.* London: N.p., 1654.

Fawne, Luke, et al. *A Second Beacon Fired.* London: N.p., 1654.

Feake, Christopher, et al. *A Faithful Discovery of a treacherous Design.* London: Thomas Brewer, 1655.

Fell, Margaret. *A Brief Collection of Remarkable Passages and Occurrences Relating to . . . Margaret Fell.* London: J. Sowle, 1710.

————. *For Manasseth Ben Israel: The Call of the Jewes out of Babylon.* London: N.p., 1656.

[————]. *A Loving Saluation to the Seed of Abraham among the Jews.* London: N.p., 1657.

A Few Words Concerning the Trial of Spirits. N.p.: [1673?].

[Field, John]. *Some Observations on the Remarks upon the Quakers.* London: T. Sowle, 1700.

Fiennes, Celia. *Through England on a Side Saddle.* London: Field & Tuer, 1888.

Firmin, Giles. *Stablishing against Shaking.* London: J. G., 1656.

Fox, George, the younger. *The Dread of Gods Power.* London: N.p., [1660].

————. *A Noble Salutation and a Faithful Greeting unto thee Charles Stuart.* London: Giles Calvert, 1660.

————. *The Testimony of God.* London: N.p., 1660.

————. *A Visitation of Love unto All People.* London: N.p., 1659.

G., J. *A Just Defense and Vindication of Gospel Ministers and Gospel Ordinances.* London: W. G., 1660.

A Gagge for Lay-Preachers. [London]: N.p., 1652.

Gauden, John. *A Discourse Concerning Publick Oaths.* London: R. Royston, 1662.

Gibson, William. *The Life of God.* N.p.: 1677.

Gilpin, John. *The Quakers Shaken.* London: Simon Waterson, 1653.

Gordon, Robert. *Christianity Vindicated.* London: Robert Boulton, 1671.

Gouge, William. *Of Domesticall Duties.* London: George Miller, 1634.

Grayes, Isaac. *One Outcry More against Tithes.* London: Author, 1657.

Griffith, John. *A Voice from the Word of the Lord to those grand Imposters Called Quakers.* London: N.p., 1654.

Grigg, William. *The Quaker's Jesus.* London: M. Simmons, 1658.

H., H. *The Beast That was, & is not, & yet is, looked upon: or, The Bo-peeping Beast.* London: Daniel White, 1659.

Haggar, Henry. *The Holy Scriptures Cleared It self of Scandals.* London: J. C., 1655.

Hallywell, Henry. *An Account of Familism As it is Revived and Propagated by the Quakers.* London: N.p., 1673.

Hammond, Samuel. *The Quakers House Built upon the Sand.* London: Stephen Bulkley, 1658.

Harris, Francis. *Some Queries Proposed to the Consideration of the Grand Proposers of Queries, the Quakers.* London: N.p., 1655.

Harwood, John. *To All People That profess the Eternal Truth of the Living God.* N.p.: 1663.

———. *A Warning from the Lord to the town of Cambridge.* N.p.: [1655].

Haworth, William. *Animadversions upon a late Quibling Libel from the Hartford Quakers.* N.p.: 1676.

[Hedworth, Henry]. *Controversy Ended.* London: N.p., 1673.

———. *The Spirit of the Quakers Tried.* London: Maurice Atkins, 1672.

[Helmont, Francisco M. van] *A Cabbalistical Dialogue.* London: N.p., 1682.

[———.] *Two Hundered Queries . . . Concerning the Doctrine of the Revolution of Human Souls.* London: N.p., 1684.

Herbert, Thomas. *A Relation of Some Yeares Travaile into Afrique, Asia, Indies.* Facsimile ed. New York: Da Capo Press, 1971.

Higgenson, T. *A Testimony to the true Jesus.* London: [T. Brewster], 1656.

Higginson, Francis. *A Brief Relation of the Irreligion of the Northern Quakers.* London: T. R., 1653.

[Hobbs, Richard]. *The Quakers Looking-Glass.* London: Francis Smith, 1673.

Hobson, Paul. *The Fallacy of Infants Baptisme Discovered.* London: N.p., 1645.

———. *A Garden Enclosed, and Wisdom Justified Only of her Children.* London: James and Joseph Moxon, 1647.

———. *Practical Divinity.* London: N.p., 1646.

———. *A Treatise Containing Three Things.* London: W. Hunt, 1653.

Hobson, Paul, et al. *A Copie of Two Letters.* N.p., n.d. [Broadside]

Hollister, Dennis. *The Skirts of the Whore Discovered.* London: N.p., 1656.

Hookes, Ellis. *The Spirit of the Martyrs Is Risen.* London: N.p., 1661.

Horne, John, and Thomas Moore, Jr. *A Briefe Discovery of the People Called Quakers.* London: J. Brudenell, 1659.

Hosannah to the Son of David: Or a Testimony to the Lord's Christ. London: William Godbid, 1657.

Howard, Luke. *Love and Truth in Plainness Manifested.* London: T. Sowle, 1704.

Howell, James. *Familiar letters; or, Epistolea Ho-Elianae.* 3 vols. London: J. M. Dent, 1903.

Howet, Henoch. *Quaking Principles dashed in pieces by the standing and unshaken Truth.* London: Henry Hills, 1655.

[Howgill, Francis]. *The Inheritance of Jacob Discovered.* London: Giles Calvert, 1656.

———. *One Warning More unto England Before they give up the Ghost, and be Buried in the Pit of Darkness.* London: Thomas Simmons, 1660.

Hubberthorne, Richard. *A Collection of the Several Books and Writings.* London: William Warwick, 1663.

———. *The Common-Wealtsh's Remembrancer.* London: N.p., 1659.

———. *The Good Old Cause Briefly demonstrated.* London: N.p., 1659.

———. *The Real Cause of the Nations Bondage and Slavery, here Demonstrated.* London: N.p., 1659.

Hubberthorne, Richard, and James Nayler. *A Short Answer to a Book called the Fanatick History.* London: N.p., 1660.

The Image of Jealousie Sought Out. London: N.p., 1660.

Ives, Jeremiah. *The Quakers Quaking: or, the Foundation of their Deceit Shaken.* London: J. Cottrel, 1656.

Jackson, Henry. *A Testimony of Truth with an Exhortation of Love.* N.p.: [1662].

[Jackson, John]. *Hosannah to the Son of David.* London: William Godbid, 1657.

[———]. *A Sober Word to a Serious People.* London: J. Cottrel, 1651.

[———]. *Strength in Weakness or the Burning Bush not Consumed.* London: J. Macock, 1655.

[James, R.]. *The Quakers Subterfuge of Evasion Over-Turned.* London: Francis Smith, 1672.

Karp, William. *A Plain Answer to the Eighteen Queries of John Whitehead.* London: N.p., 1654.

Keimer, Samuel. *A Brand pluck'd from the Burning: Exemplify'd in the . . . Case of Samuel Keimer.* London: W. Boreman, 1718.

Keith, George. *The Benefit, Advantage, and Glory of Silent Meetings.* London: N.p., 1670.

———. *A Second Narrative of the Proceedings at Turners-Hall.* London: N.p., 1697.

L., T. *Anti-Quakerisme.* N.p.: 1653.

[Lamboll, William, and John Buy]. *Something in Answer to Thomas Curtis and B.C.'s Reasons why the Meeting House Doors were shut up at Reading.* London: Andrew Sowle, 1686.

———. *A Stop to the False Characterizers Hue-and-Cry.* [London]: Andrew Sowle, 1685.

Lawson, Thomas, and John Slee. *An Untaught Teacher Witnessed Against.* London: N.p., 1655.

[Ledger, Thomas]. *A discourse Concerning the Quakers.* London: N.p., 1653.

[Leslie, Charles]. *Satan Disrob'd from the Disguise of Light: or, the Quakers Last Shift to Cover their Monstrous Heresies.* London: N.p., 1698.

———. *Theological Works of the Reverend Mr. Charles Leslie.* 2 vols. London: W. Bowyer, 1721.

A Letter from Shrewsbury, Setting forth the Design which the Anabaptists and Quakers had to secure the Castle. London: N.p., 1660. [Broadside]

Ley, John. *A Discourse of Disputations.* London: N.p., 1658.

A Light Shining out of Darknes. London: N.p., 1699.

Lindley, Isaac, et al. *Truth Exalted, and the Peaceable Fellowship and Exercise thereof Vindicated.* N.p.: 1685.

A List of some of the Grand Blasphemers and Blasphemies Which was given into the Committee for Religion. London: Robert Ibbitson, 1654.

Lupton, Donald. *The Quaking Montebanck, or the Jesuite turn'd Quaker.* London: E. B., 1655.

M., J. *The Ranters Last Sermon.* London: J. C., 1654.

Mad-Tom. *Twenty Quaking Queries.* London: N.p., 1659.

Magna Britannia et Hibernia. 6 vols. London: Elizabeth Nutt, 1720.

Maning, Edward. *The Mask'd Devil, or Quaker.* London: N.p., 1664.

Mascall, Leonard. *The First Book of Cattell.* London: John Harrison, 1605.

Mather, William. *A Vindication of William Mather and his Wife.* London: B. Aylmer, 1701.

Mayer, John. *The English Catechisme Explained.* London: Miles Flesher, 1635.

The Memory of that Servant of God, John Story, Revived. London: N.P., 1683.

Miller, Joshuah. *Antichrist in Man the Quakers Idol.* London: J. Macock, 1655.

Moore, Thomas, Jr. *An Antidote Against the Spreading Infections of the Spirit of Antichrist.* London: R. Ibbitson, 1655.

———. *A Defence Against the Poyson of Satans Designe, Cast out of his Mouth by James Nayler.* London: Livewel Chapman, 1656.

———. *A Lamentation Over the Dead in Christ.* London: R. I., 1657.

Morris, Samuel. *A Looking-Glasse for the Quakers or Shakers.* London: N.P., 1655.

Mucklowe, William. *Liberty of Conscience Asserted Against Imposition.* London: N.p., 1673/4.

———. *The Spirit of the Hat.* London: N.p., 1673.

[———]. *Tyranny and Hypocrisy Detected.* London: Francis Smith, 1673.

Muggleton, Lodowick. *A Looking-Glass for George Fox.* N.p.: 1756.

———. *The Neck of the Quakers Broken.* Amsterdam: N.p., 1663.

Musgrave, John. *A True and Exact Relation of the Great and Heavy Pressures.* London: N.p., 1650.

Musgrave Muzl'd: or the mouth of Iniquitie stoped. London: John Macock, 1650.

Myers, George. *A Serious Examination of a Pretended Answer to a Paper of Judgement past at Yorke, With a Reply thereto.* N.p.: 1686.

A Narrative of the Holy Life, and Happy Death of . . . John Angier. London: N.p., 1685.

Nayler, James. *An Answer to Twenty Eight Queries.* London: N.p., 1655.

———. *Antichrist in Man, Christs Enemy.* London: N.p., 1656.

———. *The Boaster Bared.* London: N.p., 1655.

———. *Deceit Brought to Daylight: in answer to Thomas Collier.* London: T. L., 1656.

———. *A Discovery of the Beast.* London: N.p., 1655.

———. *A Foole Answered according to his Folly.* London: Giles Calvert, 1655.

———. *Foot yet in the Snare.* London: N.p., 1656.

———. *The Lambs Warre against the Man of Sinne.* London: N.p., 1658.

———. *The Light of Christ, and the Word of Life.* London: N.p., 1656.

———. *The Power and Glory of the Lord Shining Out of the North, or the Day of the Lord Dawning.* London: N.p., 1653.

———. *A Saluation to the Seed of God.* London: N.p., 1655.

———. *A Second Answer to Thomas Moore.* London: N.p., 1655.

———. *Something further in answer to John Jackson's Book.* N.p.: [1655].

[———]. *A True Discoverie of Faith.* London: Giles Calvert, 1655.

———. *What the Possession of the Living Faith is.* London: N.p., 1659.

Norris, John. *Reason and Religion: or, the Ground and Measures of Devotion, Consider'd from the Nature of God, and the Nature of Man.* London: N.p., 1689.

———. *Reflections Upon the Conduct of Human Life.* London: N.p., 1690.

———. *Two Treatises Concerning the Divine Light.* London: N.p., 1692.

Norton, John. *The Heart of New England Rent at the Blasphemies of the Present Generation.* London: J. H., 1660.

Ogilby, John. *Britannia, or an Illustration of the Kingdom of England.* London: J. Ogilby, 1675.

Overton, Constant, et al. *The Priests Wickednesse and Cruelty, Laid Open.* London: N.p., 1655.

Pagitt, Ephraim. *Heresiography.* 5th ed. London: N.p., 1654.

A Parallel Between the Faith and Doctrine of the Present Quakers, and that of the Chief Hereticks of the Church. London: John Nut, 1700.

Parker, A. *A Discovery of Satans Wiles and his Subtile Devices.* London: Thomas Simmons, 1657.

Parnell, James. *Christ Exalted in His Throne, and the Scripture owned in its place.* N.p.: [1655].

———. *The Fruits of a Fast.* London: N.p., 1655.

———. *Goliahs Head Cut off with his own Sword.* London: N.p., 1655.

———. *A Shield of the Truth, or the Truth of God cleared from Scandals and Reproaches.* London: N.p., 1655.

———. *A Trial of Faith.* London: N.p., 1654.

———. *The Trumpet of the Lord Blown.* London: N.p., 1655.

Parresiastes, Philophus. *Enthusiasmus Triumphatus, or, a Discourse of the Nature, Causes, Kindes, and Cures of Enthusiasme.* London: J. Fletcher, 1656.

Paye, Edward. *Antichrist in Spirit unmasked.* London: N.p., 1692.

Payne, John. *A Discovery of the Priests.* London: Jo. Streater, 1655.

Pearson, Anthony. *The Great Case of Tithes Truly Stated, Clearly Open'd, and fully Resolved.* London: N.p., 1732.

———. *To the Parliament of the Common-wealth of England.* N.p.: [1653].

Pearson, John, et al. *Antichristian Treachery Discovered, and the Way Block'd up.* N.p.: [1686].

Pendarues, John. *Arrows Against Babylon.* London: J. C., 1656.

Penington, Isaac. *Many deep Considerations.* N.p., n.d.

———. *A Voyce out of the Thick Darknesse.* London: N.p., 1650.

———. *The Works of the Long-Mournful and Sorely-Distressed Isaac Penington.* 2 vols. 2d ed. London: Samuel Clark, 1761.

Penington, John. *John Penington's Complaint Against William Rogers.* London: N.p., 1681.

Penington, Mary. *Some Account of Circumstances in the Life of Mary Penington.* London: Harvey and Darton, 1821.

Penn, William. *A Collection of the Works of William Penn.* 2 vols. London: J. Sowle, 1726.

———. *Judas and the Jews Combined against Christ and his Followers.* N.p.: 1673.

Pennyman, John. *Abstracts of Some Letters Written by Mr. Robert Rich.* London: N.p., 1680.

———. *The Ark is begun to be opened.* London: N.p., 1671.

———. *A Short Account of the Life of Mr. John Pennyman.* London: N.p., 1696.

———. *This is for the People Called Quakers.* London: N.p., 1675.

Perrot, John. *An Epistle for the most Pure Amity and Unity.* London: N.p., [1662].

[———]. *John, To all Gods Imprisoned People.* London: N.p., 1660.

———. *The Vision of John Perrot, Wherein is Contained the Future State of Europe.* London: N.p., 1682.

A Phanatique League and Covenant, Solemnly enter'd into by the Assertors of the Good Old Cause. N.p.: 1659. [Broadside]

Pickworth, Henry. *A Charge of Error.* London: N.p., 1715.

Plant, Thomas. *A Contest for Christianity or a Faithful Relation of two late Meetings Between the Baptists and the Quakers.* London: N.p., 1674.

A Pleasant Discourse of a Young Gentle-woman to her Husband, the Quaker. N.p., n.d.

Plus Ultra or the Second Part of the Character of a Quaker. London: N.p., 1672.

Pomroy, John, et al. *A Faithful Discovery of a treacherous Design.* London: H. Hills, 1653.

Poor Robin. 1677, or, a Yea-and-Nay Almanack. Westminister: George Larkin, 1677.

A Proclamation Prohibiting the Disturbing of Ministers and other Christians in their Assemblies and Meetings. White-hall: N.p.: 1654. [Broadside]

Prynne, William. *A New Discovery of Some Roman Emissaries, Quakers.* London: N.p., 1656.

———. *Quakers Unmasked.* 2d ed. London: Edward Thomas, 1655.

[Purnel, Robert, et al.]. *The Church of Christ in Bristol*. London: Thomas Brewer, 1657.

The Quaker Disarmed, or a True Relation of a Late Publick Dispute Held at Cambridge. London: Daniel White, 1659.

The Quakers Appeal Answer'd. London: Peter Parker, 1674.

Quakers are Inchanters and Dangerous Seducers. London: T. M., 1655.

The Quakers Art of Courtship. London: N.p., 1689.

The Quakers Dream, or, the Devil's Pilgrimage in England. London: N.p., 1655.

The Quakers Fiery Beacon: Or, the Shaking-Ranters Ghost. London: N.p., 1657.

The Quakers Quaking: or, the most just and deserved punishment inflicted on the Person of James Nayler. London: N.p., 1657.

The Quakers terrible Vision; or, the Devil's Progress to the City of London. London: N.p., 1655.

The Quakers wanton Wife. [London]: J. Deacon, n.d.

The Quakers Wedding, October 24, 1671. London: N.p., 1671. [Broadside]

The Querers and Quakers Cause at the Second Hearing. London: I. G., 1653.

A Relation of a Quaker, That to the shame of his Profession, Attempted to Bugger a Mare Near Colchester. N.p., n.d. [Broadside]

Remarks upon the Quakers: Wherein the Plain-Dealers Are Plainly Dwelt with. London: Walter Kettilby, 1700.

A Reply to Part of a Book signed William Lambol, John By. N.p.: 1686.

Rich, Robert. *Hidden Things Brought to Light on the Discord of the Grand Quakers among Themselves*. N.p.: 1678.

———. *Mr. Robert Rich: His Second Letters from Barbadoes*. London: N.p., 1669.

Rich, Robert, et al. *Copies of Some few of the Papers given into the House of Parliament in the time of James Naylers tryal there*. N.p.: [1657].

Richardson, Richard. *A Few Ingredients Against the Venom in William Roger's Book*. London: N.p., 1681.

Roberts, Gerrald, et al. *A Declaration from the People Called Quakers*. London: N.p., 1660.

Rogers, John. *Some Account of the Life and Opinion of a Fifth-Monarchy-Man*. London: Longman, Green, Reader and Dyer, 1867.

Rogers, William. *The Christian-Quaker*. London: N.p., 1680.

———. *The Sixth Part of the Christian-Quaker*. London: N.p., 1681.

———. *The Seventh Part of the Christian-Quaker*. London: N.p., 1682.

———. *The Eighth Part of the Christian-Quaker*. London: N.p., [1684].

Rosewell, Thomas. *An Answer unto Thirty Quaeries*. London: N.p., 1656.

Ross, Alexander. *A View of all Religions of the World*. 2d ed. London: John Seywell, 1655.

[Russel, William]. *Quakerism is Paganism*. London: N.p., 1674.

Rych, Robert. *The Letter Sent by Robert Rych to William Bayly and Mary Fisher*. London: Richard Lowndes, 1669.

S., T. *A Review of that which Richarch Hubberthorn Did affirme to the King*. London: J. C., 1661.

The Sad Effects of Cruelty Detected. N.p.: 1675.

Salt, William. *The Light, the Way, that Children Ought to be Trained up in*. London: N.p., 1660.

———. *Some Breathings of the Life, from a Naked Heart*. London: N.p., 1662.

Salthouse, Thomas. *The Hidden Things of Esau brought to Light*. London: N.p., 1657.

[Simpson], William. *A Declaration unto All, both Priests and People*. London: N.p., 1655.

Scandrett, Stephen. *An Antidote against Quakerisme*. London: Thomas P. Parkhurst, 1671.

Second Days Morning Meeting. *An Epistle by Way of Testimony . . . Concerning the Decease of our Faithful Brother George Fox*. London: N.p., 1690. [Broadside]

A Serious Expostulation with E. B. an Eminent Quaker. N.p.: [J. C., 1673].

Shawe, John. *Memoirs of the Life of Master John Shawe.* Hull: J. Ferraby, 1824.

Sherlock, R. *The Quakers Wilde Questions Objected Against the Ministers of the Gospel.* London: E. Coates, 1654.

Shirreff, Alexander. *Quakerism Canvassed.* N.p.: 1675.

A Short Answer to a book set forth by seven Priests . . . with a Word to the Reader. London: N.P., 1654.

A Short Relation of some part of the Sad Sufferings and Cruel Havock and Spoil. N.p.: 1670.

1678. A Yea and Nay Almanack For the people call'd by the men of the World Quakers. London: N.p., 1678.

1679. A Yea and Nay Almanack For the people call'd by the men of the World Quakers. London: Margaret White, 1679.

1680. A Yea and Nay Almanack For the people call'd by the men of the World Quakers. London: Anne Godbid and John Playford, 1680.

Smith, Humphrey. *Something further laid open of the cruel Persecution of the People called Quakers.* London: N.p., 1656.

Smith, Nathaniel. *Quakers Spiritual Court Proclaim'd.* London: N.p., [1668].

Smith, Richard. *The Light Unchangeable.* London: N.p., 1677.

[Smith, Thomas]. *A Review of that which Richard Hubberthorn Did affirme to the King.* London: J. C., 1661.

Smith, William. *Balm from Gilead.* N.p.: 1675.

Snead, Richard, et al. *An Exalted Diotrephes Reprehended.* London: N.p., 1681.

Some Few of the Quakers Many Horrid Blasphemies, Heresies, and their Bloody Treasonable Principles, Destructive to Government. London: Richard Janeway, 1699.

Some Papers Given forth to the World, to be read. London: N.p., 1655.

Something in Answer to a Book called Fiat Lux. London: N.p., 1667.

Something in Answer to a Petition to Oliver Cromwell, From the Subscribers in Cumberland. London: N.p., 1654.

Stephens, Nathaniel. *A Plain and Easie Calculation of the Name, Mark, and Number of the Name of the Beast.* London: Ja. Cottrel, 1656.

―――. *Vindiciae Fundamenti: Or a threefold defense of the Doctrine of Original Sin.* London: T. R. and E. M., 1658.

Stoddard, Amor, et al. *Something Written in Answer to a Lying, Scandalous Book.* N.p.: [1655].

[Stubbs, John, and William Caton]. *A True Declaration of the Bloody Proceedings of the Men of Maidstone in the County of Kent.* London: N.p., 1655.

Stubbs, Thomas. *A Call into the Way to the Kingdome.* London: N.p., 1655.

Swinton, John. *Some Late Epistles to the Body.* N.p.: 1663.

―――. *A Testimony for the Lord.* N.p., n.d.

Taverner, [Phillip]. *The Quakers Round.* London: G. Dawson, 1658.

Taylor, C. *An Epistle of Caution to Friends.* London: N.p., 1681.

Taylor, Christopher. *A Warning from the Lord to this Nation.* N.p.: [1655].

―――. *The Whirl-wind of the Lord gone forth.* London: N.p., 1655.

Taylor, John. *The Carriers Cosmographie.* London: A. G., 1637.

Taylor, Thomas. *Truth's Innocency and Simplicity Shinning.* London: T. Sowle, 1697.

These several Papers was sent to Parliament. London: N.p., 1659.

Thomas, Ra. *Sathan Inthron'd in his Chair of Pestilence.* London: S. G., 1655.

Thomas, William. *Rayling Rebuked: or, a Defence of the Ministers of this Nation.* London: T. M., 1656.

Toldervy, John. *The Foot Out of the Snare.* London: J. C., 1656.

——. *The Naked Truth Laid Open, Against What is Amiss.* London: N.p., 1656.

——. *The Persecution of the People They Call Quakers in Lancashire.* N.p.: [1656].

——. *The Snare Broken: or Light discovering Darknesse.* London: N.p., 1656.

Townsend, Sampson. *The Scriptures Proved to be the Word of God.* London: S. G., 1654.

Townsend, Theophilia. *An Epistle of tender Love to all Friends.* London: N.p., 1690. [Broadside]

[Trotter, Thomas]. *The Quaker Turn'd Jew.* London: W. L., 1675.

A True and Impartial Narrative of the Eminent Hand of God that Befell a Quaker and his Family. London: Francis Smith, 1672.

A True and Lamentable Relation of the Most desperate death of James Parnel, Quaker. London: T. C., 1656. [Handwritten copy, LSF]

A true Copie of a Paper . . . from a People who . . . have been hitherto kept from the Great Apostacie. London: N.p., 1659.

A true Copie of a Paper delivered to Lt. Gen. Fleetwood to be Communicated to the General Council of Officers. London: N.p., 1659.

A True Relation of the Dispute Between Francis Fullwood . . . and one Thomas Salthouse. London: A.M., 1656.

A True Relation of the Transaction of the Commands of both Houses of Parliament in the Execution of the Militia in the County of Leicester. London: N.p., 1642.

A True Testimony of What was done concerning the Servants of the Lord . . . at Northampton. London: N.p., 1655.

Truth Cleared from Reproaches and Scandals. London: N.p., 1654.

The Truth Exalted in the Writings of . . . John Burnyeat. London: N.p., 1691.

Turner, Jane. *Choice Experiences of the Kind Dealings of God.* London: H. Hils, 1653.

Underhill, Thomas. *Hell broke loose: or an History of the Quakers, Both Old and New.* London: Simon Miller, 1660.

Vincent, Thomas. *The Foundation of God standeth sure.* London: N.p., 1668.

The Voyce of the Light Unto the People Called Quakers, in relation to Tythes. London: James Collins, 1678.

Wade, Christopher. *Quakery Slain irrecoverably.* London: N.p., 1657.

——. *To all those called Quakers, Even in the whole World.* London: N.p., 1659.

Walton, Izaak. *The Complete Angler.* 2 vols. Boston: Little, Brown, and Co., 1889.

——. *The Lives of Dr. John Donne, Sir Henry Wotton, Mr. Richard Hooker, Mr. George Herbert, and Dr. Robert Sanderson.* New York: Protestant Episcopal Press, 1832.

A Warning from the Lord to the Teachers & People of Plimouth. London: N.p., 1656.

Weare, George, et al. *The Doctrines and Principles of the Priests of Scotland.* London: N.p., 1659.

Weld, Thomas, et al. *A Further Discovery of that Generation of Men called Quakers.* Gateside: S. B., 1654.

——. *The Perfect Pharise, under Monkish Holines.* London: N.p., 1654.

The West Answering to the North in the Fierce and Cruell Persecutions of the manifestation of the Son of God. London: N.p., 1657.

Whitehead, Anne, and Mary Elson. *An Epistle for True Love, Unity and Order in the Church of Christ.* London: N.p., 1680.

Whitehead, George. *The Accuser of our Brethren Cast Down in Righteous Judgment.* London: N.p., 1681.

——. *A Christian Epistle to Friends in General.* [London:] Andrew Sowle, 1687.

——. *The Christian Progress.* London: J. Sowle, 1725.

——. *The Quakers Plainness Detecting Fallacy.* N.p.: 1674.

——. *The Path of the Just Cleared.* London: N.p., 1655.

―――. *Truth and Innocency Vindicated: And the People Called Quakers Defended.* London: T. Sowle, 1699.

Whitehead, George, et al. *The Grounds and Causes of our Sufferings Related in Short.* London: N.p., 1656.

Whitehead, John. *The Enmitie Between the Two Seeds.* London: N.p., 1655.

[Whiting, John]. *An Exalted Diotrephes Reprehended.* London: N.p., 1681.

―――. *Persecution Exposed in some Memoirs Relating to the Sufferings of John Whiting.* London: J. Sowle, 1715.

Wickham Wakened, or, The Quakers Madrigall in Rime Dogrell. N.p.: 1672.

Wigan, John. *Antichrist's strongest Hold overturned.* London: N.p., 1665.

Willington, George. *The Gadding Tribe Reproved by the Light of the Scriptures.* London: W. Hunt, 1655.

Winder, Henry. *The Spirit of Quakerism, and the Dangers of their Divine Revelations Laid Open.* London: N.p., 1696.

Winterton, Thomas. *The Quaking Prophets Two wayes proved False Prophets.* London: Robert Wood, 1655.

Women Friends, Yearly Meeting at York. *A Testimony for the Lord and his Truth.* N.p.: [1688].

Work for a Cooper. London: J. C., 1679.

[Young, Samuel]. *The Foxonian Quakers, Dunces, Lyars and Slanderers, Proved out of George Fox's Journal.* London: N.p., 1697.

SECONDARY SOURCES

Guides

Benson, Lewis. "Notes on George Fox." Pendle Hill Library.

Catalogue of the Pamphlets, Books, Newspapers, and Manuscripts Relating to the Civil War, the Commonwealth, and Restoration, Collected by George Thomason, 1640–1661. 2 vols. London: British Museum, 1908.

George Fox Epistles: An Analytical Phrase Index. Compiled by Arthur Windsor. Gloucester, England: George Fox Fund, 1992.

Horle, Craig, comp. A List of the Original Records of Sufferings. 3 vols. 1976. LSF.

―――, comp. "Spence MSS., Volume 3: Listing and Index." 1975. LSF.

―――, comp. "William Caton MSS., Volume 3: Listing and Index." 1975. LSF.

Nuttall, Geoffrey F. "Early Quaker Letters from the Swarthmore MSS to 1660." LSF.

Pickvance, Joseph. *A Reader's Companion to George Fox's Journal.* London: Quaker Home Service, 1989.

Smith, Joseph. *Bibliotheca Anti-Quakeriana; or, A Catalogue of Books Adverse to the Society of Friends.* London: Joseph Smith, 1873.

―――. *A Descriptive Catalogue of Friends' Books.* 2 vols. New York: Kraus Reprint Co., 1970.

―――. *Supplement to a Descriptive Catalogue of Friends' Books.* New York: Kraus Reprint Co., 1970.

Wing, Donald. *Short Title Catalogue.* 3 vols. New York: Columbia University Press, 1951.

Unpublished Material (not cited in notes)

Bailey, Richard G. "The Making and Unmaking of a God: New Light on George Fox and Early Quakerism." Paper delivered at Lancaster Conference, Lancaster, England, March 1991.

Barbour, Hugh S. "The Early Quaker Outlook Upon 'the World' and Society, 1647–1662." Ph.D. diss., Yale University, 1952.

Benefiel, Margaret J. "The Early Quaker Suspicion of Theology in Light of the Work of Bernard Lonergan and J. B. Libanio," Ph.D. diss., Catholic University of America, 1989.

Benson, Lewis. "A descriptive and partial outline of the projected book now in preparation; George Fox: Prophet of the Spiritual Reformation by Lewis Benson," LSF.

Cole, W. A. "The Quakers and Politics, 1652–1660." Ph.D. diss., Cambridge University, 1955.

Creasy, Maurice A. "Early Quaker Christology, with special reference to the Teaching and Significance of Isaac Penington, 1616–1679." Ph.D. diss., University of Leeds, 1956.

"Dictionary of Quaker Biography." Typescript. LSF and Quaker Collection, Haverford College.

Elser, Eugene C. "Charismatic Communication: A Critical Analysis of the Rhetorical Behaviors of George Fox, Founder of the Society of Friends." Ph.D. diss., Ohio State University, 1972.

Graves, Michael P. "The Rhetoric of the Inward Light: An Examination of Extant Sermons." Ph.D. diss., University of Southern California, 1972.

Guelzo, Allen C. "'Repent Thou Beast': Puritans, Quakers, and Controversy in the Interregnum." Master's thesis, University of Pennsylvania, 1979.

Gwyn, Douglas P. "The Apocalyptic Word of God: The Life and Message of George Fox (1624–1691)." Ph.D. diss., Drew University, 1982.

Hurst, Philip. "Family Continuity in the Parliamentary Representation of the North-West Counties in the Seventeenth Century." M. Litt. thesis, Lancaster University, 1980.

Hurwick, Judith J. "Nonconformists in Warwickshire, 1660–1720." Ph.D. diss., Princeton University, 1970.

Horle, Craig W. "Partridges upon the Mountains: The Quakers and the English Legal System, 1660–1688." Ph.D. diss., University of Maryland, 1985.

Howell, Cicely A. H. "The Economic and Social Condition of the Peasantry in South East Leicestershire A.D. 1300–1700." Ph.D. diss., Oxford University, 1974.

Ingle, H. Larry. "Unraveling George Fox: The Real Person." Paper read at the George Fox Commemorative Conference, Lancaster University, 26 March 1991, Lancaster, England.

Johnson, W. G. "Post Restoration Nonconformity and Plotting, 1660–1675." Master's thesis, Manchester University, 1967.

Jones, T. Canby. "George Fox's Teaching on Redemption and Salvation." Ph.D. diss., Yale University, 1956.

Laydon, John P. "The Kingdom of Christ and the Powers of the Earth: The Political Uses of Apocalyptic and Millenarian Ideas in England 1648–53." Ph.D. diss., Cambridge University, 1976.

Ludlow, Dorothy P., "'Arise and Be doing': English 'Preaching' Women, 1640." Ph.D. diss., Indiana University, 1978.

McCollum, Adele B. "Gerrard Winstanley and the Diggers: A Study of Psyche and Myth in 17th Century Sectarianism." Ph.D. diss., Syracuse University, 1972.

McGregor, J. F. "Fox and the Ranters." Paper read at George Fox Commemorative Conference, Lancaster University, Lancaster, England, 25 March 1991.

Martin, Joseph W. "The English Revoluton and the Rise of Quakerism (1650–1660)." Ph.D. diss., Columbia University, 1965.

Mason, Gilliam. "Quaker Women and Education, 1642–1840." Master's thesis, Lancaster University, 1987.

Meinke, Robert J. "The Sociology of Inner-Worldly Mysticism: Freedom, Power and Authority in the Society of Friends." Ph.D. diss., New School for Social Research, 1983.

Moore, Rosemary. "Decision-Making and Defining the Faith among Quakers, 1652–165?" Unpublished paper, 1991.

"Morning Meeting Minutes, 1673–92." Typescript. LSF.

Morrill, John. "Charles I, Tyranny, and the English Civil War." Paper delivered at the Tudor-Stuart Seminar, University of London, March 1988.

Mortimer, R. S. "Quakerism in Seventeenth Century Bristol," Master's thesis, University of Bristol, 1946.

Nuttall, Geoffrey F. "Record and Testimony: Quaker Persecution Literature, 1650–1700." LSF.

Oliver, Pamela M. C. "Quaker Testimony and the Lamb's War." Ph.D. diss., University of Melbourne, 1977.

Poe, Harry L. "Evangelistic Fervency among the Puritans in Stuart England, 1603–1688." Ph.D. diss., Southern Baptist Theological Seminary, 1982.

Sheeran, Michael J. "Friendly Persuasion: Voteless Decisions in the Religious Society of Friends," Ph.D. diss., Princeton University, 1977.

Smith, Hilda L. "Feminism in Seventeenth-Century England." Ph.D. diss., University of Chicago, 1975.

Smith, Roberta. "Female 'Intransigence' in the Early Quaker Movement from the 1650s to about 1700, with Particular Reference to the North West of England." Master's thesis, Lancaster University, 1990.

Spurrier, William W. "The Persecution of the Quakers in England: 1650–1714." Ph.D. diss., University of North Carolina, 1976.

Trevett, Christine. "Fox and the fate of the female prophet: some questions." Paper read at the Fox Commemorative Conference, Lancaster University, Lancaster, England, 27 March 1991.

Articles (*not cited in notes*)

Abbreviations

CH Church History
JEH Journal of Ecclesiastical History
JFHS Journal of the Friends Historical Society
JR Journal of Religion
LAHS Leicestershire Archaeological and Historial Society
PP Past & Present
PMHB Pennyslvania Magazine of History and Biography
QH Quaker History
SCH Studies in Church History
TLAS Transactions of the Leicestershire Archaeological Society
VHC Victorian History of the Counties of England

Alsop, J. D. "Gerrard Winstanley: Religion and Respectability." *Historical Journal* 28 (1985): 705–09.

Anderson, Alan B. "A Study in the Sociology of Religious Persecution: The First Quakers." *Journal of Religious History* 9 (1977): 247–62.

Aston, Margaret. "Lollardy and the Reformation: Survival or Revival?" *History* 49 (1964): 149–70.

Aston, M. E. "Lollardy and Sedition, 1381–1432." PP, no. 17 (1960): 1–44.

Aylmer, G. E. "Did the Ranters Exist?" *PP*, no. 117 (1987): 208–19.

Baker, J. N. L., "England in the Seventeenth Century." In *An Historical Geography of England Before A.D. 1800*, ed. H. C. Darby, 387–443. Cambridge: Cambridge University Press, 1936.

Bass, Jeff D., "'Levellers': The Economic Reduction of Political Equality in the Putney Debates, 1647." *Quarterly Journal of Speech* 77 (1991): 427–45.

Bauman, Richard. "Observations on the Place of Festival in the Worldview of the Seventeenth-Century Quakers." *Western Folklore* 43 (1984): 133–38.

Baxter, Nicola. "Gerrard Winstanley's Experimental Knowledge of God (The Perception of the Spirit and the Acting of Reason)." *JEH* 39 (1988): 184–201.

Bell, Maureen. "Mary Westwood: Quaker Publisher." *Publishing History* 23 (1988): 5–66.

Berg, J. van den. "Quaker and Chiliast: the 'contrary thoughts' of William Ames and Petrus Serrarius." In *Reformation, Conformity and Dissent: Essays in honor of Geoffrey Nuttall*, ed. R. Buick Knox, 180–98. London: Epworth Press, 1977.

Bitterman, M. G. F. "The Early Quaker Literature of Defense." *CH* 42 (1973): 203–28.

Braithwaite, Alfred W. "The Mystery of Swarthmoor Hall." *JFHS* 51 (1965): 22–29.

Brauer, Jerald C. "Puritan Mysticism and the Development of Liberalism." *CH* 19 (1950): 151–70.

Brink, Andrew. "The Question of Isaac Penington: A Study based on his Pamphlets of 1648–1650." *JFHS* 51 (1965): 30–53.

Burtt, Ruth G., "The Quaker Marriage Declaration," *JFHS* 46 (1954): 53-59.

Cadbury, Henry J. "The *Editio Princeps* of Fox's Journal." *JFHS* 53 (1974): 197–218.

———. "George Fox's Library Again." *JFHS* 30 (1933): 9–19.

———. "George Fox's Library: Further Identifications." *JFHS* 29 (1932): 63–71.

———. "An Obscure Chapter of Quaker History." *JR* 24 (1944): 201–13.

Carroll, Kenneth L. "Maryland Quakers in the Seventeenth Century." *Maryland Historical Magazine* 47 (1952): 297–313.

Christianson, Paul. "The Causes of the English Revolution: A Reappraisal." *Journal of British Studies* 15 (1976): 40–75.

———. "The Peers, the People, and Parliamentary Management in the First Six Months of the Long Parliament." *Journal of Modern History* 49 (1977): 575–99.

———. "Reformers and the Church of England under Elizabeth I and the Early Stuarts." *JEH* 31 (1980): 463–80.

Clark, Richard, "'The Gangreen of Quakerism': An Anti-Quaker Anglican Offensive in England during the Glorious Revolution." *Journal of Religious History* 11 (1981): 404–29.

Cogley, Richard W. "Seventeenth-Century English Millenarianism." *Religion* 17 (1987): 379–96.

Cohen, Alfred. "Prophecy and Madness: Women Visionaries during the Puritan Revolution." *Journal of Psychohistory* 11 (1984): 411–30.

Cole, Alan. "The Quakers and the English Revolution." *PP*, no. 10 (1956): 39–54.

Coleman, D. C., "Labour in the English Economy of the Seventeenth Century." *Economic History Review* 8 (1956): 280–95.

Collinson, Patrick. "A comment: Concerning the Name Puritan." *JEH* 31 (1980): 483–88.

Cooper, Wilmer, ed. "Lewis Benson Issue." *Quaker Religious Thought* 22 (1987): 1–60.

Cope, Jackson I. "Seventeenth-Century Quaker Style." *Proceedings of the Modern Language Association* 71 (1956): 725–54.

Crompton, James. "John Wyclif: A Study in Mythology." *LAHS Transactions* 42 (1966–1967): 6–34.

———. "Leicestershire Lollards." *LAHS Transactions* 44 (1968–1969): 11–44.

Dailey, Barbara R. "The Husbands of Margaret Fell: An Essay on Religious Metaphor and Social Change." *Seventeenth Century* 2 (1987): 55–71.

Davis, J. C. "Fear, Myth and Furore: Reappraising the 'Ranters.'" *PP*, no. 129 (1990): 79–103.

———. "Radicalism in a Traditional Society." *History of Political Thought* 3 (1982): 193–213.

Davis, J. F. "Lollard Survival and the Textile Industry in the South-east of England." *SCH* 3 (1966): 191–201.

De Welles, Theodore. "Sex and Sexual Attitudes in Seventeenth-Century England: The Evidence from Puritan Diaries." *Renaissance and Reformation* 12 (1988): 45–64.

Disbrey, Claire. "George Fox and Some Theories of Innovation in Religion." *Religious Studies* 25 (1989): 61–74.

Ditchfield, G. M. "Parliament, the Quakers and the Tithe Question, 1750–1835." *Parliamentary History* 4 (1985): 87–114.

Durnbaugh, Donald F. "Baptists and Quakers—Left Wing Puritans?" *QH* 62 (1973): 67–82.

Edwards, Irene L. "The Women Friends of London: The Two-Weeks and Box Meetings." *JFHS* 47 (1955): 3–21.

Ellis, Gertrude. "George Fox and Leicestershire." *TLAS* 13 (1923–1924): 83–89.

Evans, R. H., "Nonconformists in Leicestershire in 1669." *TLAS* 25 (1949), 98-143.

———. "The Quakers of Leicestershire, 1660-1714," *TLAS* 28 (1952): 63–83.

Farnell, James E. "The Social and Intellectual Basis of London's Role in the English Civil War." *Journal of Modern History* 49 (1977): 641–60.

Gentles, Ian. "London Levellers in the English Revolution: the Chidleys and their Circle." *JEH* 29 (1978): 281–309.

George, C. H. "Gerrard Winstanley: A Critical Retrospect." In *The Dissenting Tradition*, ed. C. Robert Cole and Michael E. Moody, 191–225. Athens: Ohio University Press, 1975.

———. "Puritanism as History and Historiography." *PP*, no. 41 (1968): 77–104.

Gerry, Thomas. "The Religious Beliefs of David Willson and the Children of Peace." *York Pioneer* 80 (1985): 32–44.

Greaves, Richard L. "John Bunyan and the Fifth Monarchists." *Albion* 13 (1981): 83–95.

———. "The Ordination Controversy and the Spirit of Reform in Puritan England." *JEH* 21 (1970): 225–41.

———. "The Puritan–Nonconformist Tradition in England, 1560–1700: Historiographical Reflections." *Albion* 17 (1985): 449–86.

Greene, Douglas G. "Muggletonians and Quakers: A Study in the Interaction of Seventeenth-Century Dissent." *Albion* 15 (1983): 102–22.

Grubb, Edward. "The Evangelical Movement and Its Impact on the Society of Friends." *Friends' Quarterly Examiner* 58 (1924): 1–34.

Hall, Basil. "Puritanism: The Problem of Definition." *SCH* 2 (1965): 283–96.

Harvey, T. Edmund. "The Young George Fox and Nathaniel Stephens." *Friends Quarterly Examiner* 80 (1946): 69–78.

Heal, Felicity. "The Family of Love and the Diocese of Ely." *SCH* 9 (1972): 213–22.

Henretta, James A. "Families and Farms: *Mentalité* in Pre-Industrial America." *William and Mary Quarterly* 35 (1978): 3–32.

Heriot, Duncan B. "Anabaptism in England during the 17th Century." *Transactions of the Congregational Historical Society* 13 (1937–1939): 22–40.

Hexter, J. H. "Power Struggle, Parliament, and Liberty in Early Stuart England." *Journal of Modern History* 50 (1978): 1–50.

Hill, Christopher. "John Bunyan and the English Revolution." *Marxist Perspectives* 7 (1979): 8–26.

———. "The Radical Critics of Oxford and Cambridge in the 1650s." In *Universities in Politics: Case Studies from the Late Middle Ages and Early Modern Period,* ed. John W. Baldwin and Richard A. Goldthwaite, 107–32. Baltimore: Johns Hopkins University Press, 1972.

Hirst, Derek. "The Failure of Godly Rule in the English Republic." *PP,* no. 132 (1991): 33–66.

Holdsworth, Christopher J. "Mystics and Heretics in the Middle Ages: Rufus Jones Reconsidered." *JFHS* 53 (1972): 9–30.

Huber, Elaine C. "'A Woman Must Speak': Quaker Women in the English Left Wing." In *Woman of Spirit: Female Leadership in the Jewish and Christian Tradition,* ed. Rosemary Ruether and Eleanor McLaughlin, 153–81. New York: Simon and Schuster, 1979.

Hudson, Winthrop S. "Mystical Religion in the English Commonwealth." *JR* 28 (1948): 51–56.

———. "The Weber Thesis Reexamined." *CH* 57 (1988): 56–67.

Hull, William I. "Egbert van Heemskerk's 'Quaker Meeting.'" *Bulletin of the Friends Historical Association* 27 (1938): 17–33.

Ingle, H. Larry. "From Mysticism to Radicalism: Recent Historiography of Quaker Beginnings." *QH* 76 (1987): 79–94.

Isichei, Elizabeth. "From Sect to Denomination among English Quakers." In *Patterns of Sectarianism: Organisation and Ideology in Social and Religious Movements,* ed. Bryan R. Wilson, 161–81. London: Heinemann, 1967.

Johnson, George A. "From Seeker to Finder: A Study in Seventeenth-Century English Spiritualism before the Quakers." *CH* 17 (1948): 299–315.

Jones, Rufus M. "The Psychology of George Fox." *Holborn Review* 64 (1924): 320–33.

Kaufman, Peter I. "Social History, Psychohistory, and the Prehistory of Swiss Anabaptism." *JR* 68 (1988): 527–44.

Kendall, Joan. "The Development of a Distinctive Form of Quaker Dress." *Costume,* no. 19 (1985): 58–74.

Kennedy, Thomas C. "History and Quaker Renaissance: The Vision of John Wilhelm Rountree." *JFHS* 55 (1983–1984): 35–56.

Kent, Stephen A. "Mysticism, Quakerism, and Relative Deprivation: A Sociological Reply." *Religion* 19 (1989): 157–78.

———. "Psychology and Quaker Mysticism: The Legacy of William James and Rufus Jones." *QH* 76 (1987): 1–17.

———. "The Quaker Ethic and the Fixed Price Policy: Max Weber and Beyond." *Sociological Inquiry* 53 (1983): 16–32.

———. "Relative deprivation and resource mobilization: a study of early Quakerism." *British Journal of Sociology* 33 (1982): 29–44.

———. "Weber, Goethe, and the Nietzschean Allusion: Capturing the Source of the 'Iron Cage' Metaphor." *Sociological Analysis* 44 (1983): 297–320.

Kohut, Thomas A. "Psychohistory as History." *Amerian Historical Review* 91 (1986): 226–54.

Kunze, Bonnelyn Y. "'Poore and in Necessity': Margaret Fell and Quaker Female Philanthropy in Northwest England in the Late Seventeenth Century." *Albion* 21 (1989): 559–80.

———. "Religious Authority and Social Status in Seventeen-Century England: The Friendship of Margaret Fell, George Fox, and William Penn." *CH* 57 (1988): 170–86.

———, ed. "An Unpublished Work by Margaret Fell." *Proceedings of the American Philsophical Society* 130 (1986): 424–52.

Lippard, Paula V. "The Rhetoric of Silence: The Society of Friends' Unprogrammed Meeting for Worship." *Communication Quarterly* 36 (1988): 145–56.

Liu, Tai. "The Calling of the Barebones Parliament Reconsidered." *JEH* 22 (1971): 223–36.

Ludlow, Dorothy P. "Shaking Patriarchy's Foundations: Sectarian Women in England, 1641–1700." In *Triumph over Silence: Women in Protestant History,* ed. Richard L. Greaves, 93–123. Westport, Conn.: Greenwood Press, 1985.

McAdams, Dan P., and Richard L. Ochberg, eds. "Psychobiography and Life Narratives." *Journal of Personality* 56 (1988): 1–326.

Macaulay, Thomas B. "George Fox." In *Critical, Historical, and Miscellaneous Essays and Poems,* 3 vols. ed. Thomas B. McCaulay, 3: 517–21. Boston: Estes and Lauriat, n.d.

McGregor, J. F. "Ranterism and the Development of Early Quakerism." *Journal of Religious History* 9 (1976–1977): 349–63.

MacIntyre, Alasdair. "The Logical Status of Religious Belief." In *Metaphysical Beliefs,* 158–201. New York: Schocken Books, 1970.

Mack, Phyllis. "Women as Prophets during the English Civil War." *Feminist Studies* 8 (1982): 19–45.

Maclear, James F. "'The Heart of New England Rent': The Mystical Element in Early Puritan History." *Mississippi Valley Historical Review* 42 (1956): 621–52.

———. "The Making of the Lay Tradition." *JR* 33 (1953): 113–36.

———. "Quakerism and the End of the Interregnum: A Chapter in the Domestication of Radical Puritanism." *CH* 19 (1950): 240–70.

Matar, N. J. "Milton and the Idea of the Restoration of the Jews." *Studies in English Literature 1500–1900* 27 (1987): 109–24.

Middleton, Warren C. "The Denunciations of George Fox Viewed Psychologically." *JR* 11 (1931): 589–609.

Moore, Barrington, Jr. "Austerity and Unintended Riches." *Comparative Studies in Society and History* 29 (1987): 787–810.

Moss, Jean D. "The Family of Love and English Critics." *Sixteenth Century Journal* 6 (1975): 35–52.

Mulligan, Lotte, and Judith Richards. "A 'Radical' Problem: The Poor and the English Reformers in the Mid-Seventeenth Century." *Journal of British Studies* 29 (1990): 118–46.

Murray, John J. "The Cultural Impact of the Flemish Low Countries on Sixteenth- and Seventeenth-Century England." *American Historical Review* 62 (1957): 837–54.

Muscamp, Robert. "Historical Notes on the Society of Friends or Quakers in Manchester in the Seventeenth Century." *Transactions of the Lancashire and Cheshire Antiquarian Society* 31 (1914): 45–62.

———. "The Society of Friends in the Seventeenth Century, with a few Later Notes." *Transactions of the Lancashire and Cheshire Antiquarian Society* 44 (1929): 78–92.

Naulty, R. G. "Stephen A. Kent and the Mysticism of the Early Quakers." *Religion* 19 (1989): 151–56.

Nickalls, John L. "George Fox: Manchester or Mancetter?" *JFHS* 31 (1934): 43.

Norlind, Emilia F. "Quakerism and Democracy: Some Points Concerning Revelation and Organisation." *JFHS* 42 (1950): 17–40.

"Notes and Queries" *PMHB* 29 (1905): 105–7.

Nuttall, Geoffrey F. "The Last of James Nayler: Robert Rich and the Church of the First-Born." *Friends Quarterly* 23 (July 1985): 527-34.

———. "A Letter by James Nayler Appropriated to George Fox." *JFHS* 55 (1988): 178–79.

———. "Millenarianism in the English Commonwealth." *Dutch Review of Church History* 67 (1987): 71–79.

———. "Overcoming the World: The Early Quaker Programme." In *Sanctity and Secularity: The Church and the World*, ed. Derek Baker, 145–64. Oxford: Oxford University Press, 1973.

———. "Puritan and Quaker Mysticism." *Theology* 78 (1975): 518–31.

O'Mallery, Thomas. "'Defying the Powers and Tempering the Spirit': A Review of Quaker Control over their Publications." *JEH* 33 (1982): 72–88.

Palmer, William G. "The Burden of Proof: J. H. Hexter and Christopher Hill." *Journal of British Studies* 19 (1979): 122–29.

Pearlstein, Richard M. "Of Fear, Uncertainty, and Boldness: The Life and Thought of Thomas Hobbes." *Journal of Psychohistory* 13 (1986): 309–24.

Penney, Norman. "George Fox's Writings and the Morning Meeting," Friends Quarterly Examiner 36 (1902): 63-72.

Perry, R. "The Gloucestershire Woolen Industry, 1100–1690." *Transactions of the Bristol and Gloucestershire Archaeology Society* 66 (1945): 49–137.

Pickvance, T. Joseph. "George Fox's Hills of Vision." *Friends Quarterly* 6 (1952): 152–60.

Popkin, Richard H. "The Religious Background of Seventeenth-Century Philosophy." *Journal of the History of Philosophy* 25 (1987): 35–50.

———. "Spinoza, the Quakers, and the Millenarians, 1656–1658." *Manuscripts* 6 (1982): 113–33.

Reay, Barry. "The Authorities and Early Restoration Quakerism." *JEH* 34 (1983): 69–84.

"Robert Barclay on the Internal History and Development of the Society of Friends." *Friend* 17 (1877): 123–25.

"Robert Barclay on the Mysticism of the Early Friends." *Friend* 17 (1877): 188–89.

Rogers, R. Michael. "Quakerism and the Law in Revolutionary England." *Canadian Journal of History* 22 (1987): 149–74.

Ross, Isabel. "Early Quakerism in Northern England." *Friends Quarterly* 6 (1952): 134–43.

Rowntree, Arthur. "Quakerism on Moor and Wold." *JFHS* 29 (1932): 1–28.

Royce, Josiah. "George Fox as a Mystic." *Harvard Theological Review* 6 (1913): 31–59.

Rutter, Elizabeth B. "A Glimpse of Ancient Friends in Dorset." *JFHS* 5 (1908): 35–40, 87–92, 151–57.

Schwarz, Marc L. "Some Thoughts on the Development of a Lay Religious Consciousness in Pre-Civil-War England." *SCH* 8 (1972): 171–78.

Scott, Jonathan. "Radicalism and Restoration." *Historical Journal* 31 (1981): 453–67.

Sharpless, Isaac. "The Handwriting of George Fox." *JFHS* 1 (1903–1904): 6–10.

Sippell, Theodor. "The Testimony of Joshua Sprigge." *JFHS* 38 (1946): 24–28.

Soderlund, Jean R. "Women's Authority in Pennsylvania and New Jersey Quaker Meetings, 1680–1760." *William and Mary Quarterly* 44 (1987): 722–49.

Solt, Leo F. "Anti-Intellectualism in the Puritan Revolution." *CH* 24 (1956): 306–16.

————. "John Saltmarsh: New Model Army Chaplain." *JEH* 2 (1951): 69–80.

Sommerville, C. John. "Anglican, Puritan, and Sectarian in Empirical Perspective." *Social Science History* 13 (1989): 109–35.

Speizman, Milton D., and Jane C. Kronick, eds. "A Seventeenth-Century Quaker Women's Declaration." *Signs* 1 (1975): 231–45.

Stayer, James M., Werner O. Pachull, and Klau Deppermann. "From Monogenesis to Polygenesis: The Historical Discussion of Anabaptist Origins." *Mennonite Quarterly Review* 49 (1975): 83–121.

Stone, Lawrence. "The English Revolution." In *Preconditions of Revolution in Early Modern Europe*, ed. Robert Forster and Jack P. Greene, 55–108. Baltimore: Johns Hopkins University Press, 1970.

————. "Social Mobility in England, 1500–1700." *PP*, no. 33 (1966): 16–55.

Thirsk, Joan. "Younger Sons in the Seventeenth Century." *History* 54 (1969): 358–77.

Thomas, Keith. "Women and the Civil War Sects." *PP*, no. 13 (1958): 42–62.

Tolles, Frederick B. "1652 in History: Changing Perspectives on the Founding of Quakerism." In *Then and Now: Quaker Essays, Historical and Contemporary*, ed. Anna Brinton, 73–94. Philadelphia: University of Pennsylvania Press, 1960.

Tual, Jacques. "Sexual equality and conjugal harmony: The way to celestial bliss. A View of early Quaker matrimony." *JFHS* 55 (1988): 161–74.

Underwood, T. L. "'It pleased me much to contend': John Bunyan as Controversalist." *CH* 57 (1988): 456–69.

————. "Quakers and the Royal Society of London in the Seventeenth Century." *Notes and Records of the Royal Society of London* 31 (1976): 133–50.

Vann, Richard T. "Diggers and Quakers—A Further Note." *JFHS* 50 (1962): 65–68.

Whitney, Janet Payne. "The Apprenticeship of George Fox." *JFHS* 51 (1965): 3–20.

Wilkes, John W. "The Transformation of Dissent: a Review of the Changes from the Seventeenth to Eighteenth Centuries." In *The Dissenting Tradition*, ed. C. Robert Cole and Michael E. Moody, 108–20. Athens: Ohio University Press, 1957.

Williams, J. B. "George Fox and Walker the Ironmonger." *Friends Quarterly Examiner* 44 (1910): 518–26.

Woolwych, Austin. "The Cromwellian Protectorate: A Military Dictatorship?" *History* 75 (1990): 207–31.

Worden, Blair. "Providence and Politics in Cromwellian England." *PP*, no. 109 (1985): 55–99.

Zaller, Robert. "What Does the English Revolution Mean? Recent Historiographical Interpretations of Mid-Seventeenth Century England." *Albion* 18 (1986): 617–35.

Books (*not cited in notes*)

Acworth, Richard. *The Philosophy of John Norris of Bemerton 1657–1712*. New York: Georg Olms Verlag Hildesheim, 1979.

Ashley, Maurice. *England in the Seventeenth Century*. 3rd ed. Harmondsworth, England: Penguin Books, 1970.

Ashton, Robert. *The English Civil War: Conservatism and Revolution, 1603–1649*. New York: W. W. Norton and Co., 1978.

Aylmer, G. E. *Rebellion or Revolution? England 1640–1660*. Oxford: Oxford University Press, 1986.

Baker, W. King. *George and Margaret Fox*. London: George Routledge and Sons, n.d.

Berens, Lewis H. *The Digger Movement in the Days of the Commonwealth*. London: Simpkin, Marshall, Hamilton, Kent, and Co., 1906.

Bernstein, Eduard. *Cromwell and Communism: Socialism and Democracy in the Great English Revolution.* Translated by H. J. Stenning. New York: A. M. Kelley, 1966.

Boisen, Anton T. *The Exploration of the Inner World: A Study of Mental Disorder and Religious Experience.* New York: Harper and Bros., 1936.

———. *Religion in Crisis and Custom: A Sociological and Psychological Study.* New York: Harper and Brothers, 1955.

Brailsford, Mabel R. *A Quaker from Cromwell's Army: James Nayler.* London: Swarthmore Press, 1927.

———. *Quaker Women, 1650–1690.* London: Duckworth and Co., 1915.

Brayshaw, A. Neave. *The Quakers: Their Story and Message.* London: Friends Home Service, 1969.

Brinton, Crane. *The Anatomy of Revolution.* Rev. ed. New York: Vintage Books, 1960.

Brinton, Howard, ed. *Byways in Quaker History.* Wallingford, Pa.: Pendle Hill, 1944.

———, ed. *Children of Light: Essays in Honor of Rufus M. Jones.* New York: Macmillan Co., 1938.

Brockbank, Elisabeth. *Richard Hubberthorne of Yealand: Yeoman-Soldier-Quaker, 1628–1662.* London: Friends' Book Centre, 1929.

Brown, Elisabeth P., and Susan M. Stuard, eds. *Witnesses for Change: Quaker Women over Three Centuries.* New Brunswick, N.J.: Rutgers University Press, 1989.

Brunskill, R. W. *Traditional Buildings of Britain.* London: Victor Gollancz, 1985.

Butler, D. *George Fox in Scotland.* Edinburgh, Scotland: Oliphant, Anderson and Ferrier, 1913.

Carlton, Charles. *Charles I: The Personal Monarch.* London: Routledge and Kegan Paul, 1983.

Carroll, Kenneth L. *Quakerism on the Eastern Shore.* N.p.: Maryland Historical Society, 1970.

Casson, Edmund. *George Fox: A Poem in Twelve Books.* Kendal, England: Titus Wilson and Son, 1947.

Clarkson, Thomas. *A Portraiture of the Christian Profession and Practice of the Society of Friends.* Glasgow, Scotland: Robert Smeal, 1869.

Cliff, J. F. *Puritans in Conflict: The Puritan Gentry during and after the Civil War.* London: Routledge, 1988.

Cohn, Norman. *The Pursuit of the Millennium.* Fairlawn, N.J.: Essential Books, 1957.

Craven, Maxwell. *Derby: An Illustrated History.* Derby, England: Breedon Books, 1988.

Cross, F. L., ed. *The Oxford Dictionary of the Christian Church.* London: Oxford University Press, 1957.

Davis, J. C. *Fear, Myth and History: The Ranters and the Historians.* Cambridge: Cambridge University Press, 1986.

Deacon, Henry. *George Fox and the Quaker Testimony: A Lecture.* London: Elliot Stock, 1896.

Debus, Allen G. *The English Paraclesians.* London: Oldbourne, 1965.

Denbigh, Kathleen. *A Hundred British Spas: A Pictorial History.* London: Spa Publications, 1981.

Douglas, Eileen. *George Fox: The Red Hot Quaker.* 2d ed. London: Salvation Army, n.d.

Dunn, Mary M. *William Penn: Politics and Conscience.* Princeton, N.J.: Princeton University Press, 1967.

Dunn, Richard S., and Mary Maples Dunn, eds. *The World of William Penn.* Philadelphia: University of Pennsylvania Press, 1986.

Durnbaugh, Donald F. *The Believers' Church: The History and Character of Radical Protestantism.* New York: Macmillan Co., 1968.

Finlayson, Michael G. *Historians, Puritanism, and the English Revolution: the Religious Factor in English Politics before and after the Interregnum.* Toronto: University of Toronto Press, 1983.

Firth, C. H. *Cromwell's Army.* 3d ed. London: Methuen and Co., n.d.

Fox. Charles. *George Fox No Precursor of the Salvation Army.* Edinburgh, Scotland: Robert M. Cameron, 1881.

Fussell, G. E., and K. R. Fussell. *The English Countryman: His Life and Work.* London: Andrew Melrose, 1955.

Gager, John G. *Kingdom and Community: The Social World of Early Christianity.* Englewood Cliffs, N.J.: Prentice-Hall, 1975.

George, Charles H., and Katherine George. *The Protestant Mind of the English Reformation, 1570–1640.* Princeton, N.J.: Princeton University Press, 1961.

Gillett, Edward. *East Yorkshire and North Lincolnshire, 1660–1668.* Hull, England: Department of Adult Education, 1981.

Gooch, G. P. *English Democratic Ideas in the Seventeenth Century.* 2d ed. New York: Harper and Brothers, 1959.

Greer, Mrs. J. R. *The Society of Friends: A Domestic Narrative Illustrating the Peculiar Doctrines Held by the Disciples of George Fox.* 2 vols. London: Saunders and Otley, 1853.

Gregg, Pauline. *Free-born John: A Biography of John Lilburne.* London: George G. Harrap and Co., 1961.

Gura, Philip F. *A Glimpse of Sion's Glory: Puritan Radicalism in New England, 1620–1660.* Middletown, Conn.: Wesylan University Press, 1984.

Hacket, [Thomas]. *Memoirs of the Life of Archbishop Williams.* London: Samule Briscoe, 1715.

Haller, William. *The Rise of Puritanism.* New York: Harper Torchbooks, 1957.

Hexter, J. H. *On Historians: Reappraisals of Some of the Makers of Modern History.* Cambridge, Mass.: Harvard University Press, 1979.

Hill, Christopher. *The Experience of Defeat: Milton and Some Contemporaries.* New York: Penguin Books, 1985.

———. *Intellectual Origins of the English Revolution.* Oxford: Oxford University Press, 1965.

———. *Milton and the English Revolution.* New York: Penguin Books, 1979.

———. *A Nation of Change and Novelty: Radical Politics, Religion and Literature in Seventeenth-Century England.* London: Routledge, 1990.

———. *Oliver Cromwell, 1658–1958.* N.p.: Routledge and Kegan Paul, 1958.

———. *Reformation to Industrial Revolution.* Harmondsworth, England: Penguin Books, 1972.

Hine, Reginald L. *A Mirror for the Society of Friends.* London: George Allen and Unwin, 1930.

Holder, Charles F. *The Quakers in Great Britain and America.* New York: Neuner Company, 1913.

Holdsworth, L. V. *Gulielma: Wife of William Penn.* London: Longmans, Green and Co., 1947.

Hollings, J. F. *The History of Leicestershire during the Great Civil War.* Leicester, England: Combe and Crossley, 1840.

Hoskins, W. G. *Essays in Leicestershire History.* Liverpool, England: Liverpool University Press, 1950.

———. *The Heritage of Leicestershire.* Leicester, England: Edgar Backus, 1946.

———. *Midland England.* London: B. T. Batsford, 1949.

Huehns, Gertrude. *Antinomianism in English History, With special reference to the period 1640–1660.* London: Cresset Press, 1951.

Hutton, William L. *The English Church, from the Accession of Charles I to the Death of Anne.* London: Macmillan, 1934.

Jones, Colin, Malyn Newitt, and Stephen Roberts, eds. *Politics and People in Revolutionary England.* Oxford: Basil Blackwell, 1986.

Jones, Rufus M. *The Flowering of Mysticism: The Friends of God in the Fourteenth Century.* New York: Macmillan Co., 1939.

———. *The Life and Message of George Fox, 1624–1924.* New York: Macmillan Co., 1924.

———. *Mysticism and Democracy in the English Commonwealth.* Cambridge, Mass.: Harvard University Press, 1932.

———. *Spiritual Reformers in the Sixteenth and Seventeenth Centuries.* Gloucester, Mass.: Peter Smith, 1971.

———. *Studies in Mystical Religion.* London: Macmillan Co., 1923.

Jordan, W. K. *The Development of Religious Toleration in England.* 4 vols. Gloucester, Mass.: Peter Smith, 1965.

———. *The Social Institutions of Lancashire: A Study of the Changing Patterns of Aspirations in Lancashire, 1480–1660.* Manchester, England: Cheltham Society, 1962.

King, Rachel H. *George Fox and the Light Within, 1650–1660.* Philadelphia: Friends Books Store, 1940.

Kishlansky, Mark A. *The Rise of the New Model Army.* Cambridge: Cambridge University Press, 1979.

Kramer, Stella. *The English Craft Guilds: Studies in Their Progress and Decline.* New York: Columbia University Press, 1927.

Lamont, William M. *Godly Rule: Politics and Religion, 1603–60.* London: Macmillan and Co., 1969.

———. *Richard Baxter and the Millennium.* Totowa, N.J.: Rowman and Littlefield, 1979.

Laurence, Anne, W. R. Owens, and Stuart Sim, eds. *John Bunyan and his England, 1828–88.* London: Hambledon Press, 1990.

Levy, Barry. *Quakers and the American Family.* New York: Oxford University Press, 1988.

Lewis, Georgina K. *George Fox.* London: Friends' Book Centre, 1939.

Loewenberg, Peter. *Decoding the Past: The Psychohistory Approach.* New York: Alfred A. Knopf, 1983.

Lomas, James. *A History of Quakers in Nottingham, 1648–1948.* [Nottingham, England]: Friends Meeting, [1948].

Lynch, Louis. *The Barbados Book.* New York: Coward, McCann and Geoghegan, 1973.

Macfarlane, Alan. *The Culture of Capitalism.* Oxford: Basil Blackwell, 1987.

———. *The Family Life of Ralph Josselin: A Seventeenth Century Clergyman.* New York: W. W. Norton and Co., 1977.

———. *The Origins of English Individualism.* Oxford: Basil Blackwell, 1978.

McCusker, John J. *How Much Is That in Real Money: A Historical Price Index for Use as a Deflator of Money Values in the Economy of the United States.* Worchester, Mass.: American Antiquarian Society, 1992.

Millward, Roy. *A History of Leicestershire and Rutland.* Chicester, Sussex, England: Phillimore and Co., 1985.

Moore, John M., ed. *Friends in the Delaware Valley.* Haverford, Pa.: Friends Historical Association, 1981.

Morrill, John, ed. *Reactions to the English Civil War, 1642–1649.* New York: St. Martin's Press, 1983.

Mortimer, Russell. *Early Bristol Quakerism: The Society of Friends in the City, 1654–1700.* Bristol, England: Bristol Branch, Historical Association, 1967.

Mullett, Michael, ed. *Early Lancaster Friends.* Lancaster, England: Centre for Northwest Regional Studies, 1978.

————. *Radical Religious Movements in Early Modern Europe.* London: George Allen and Unwin, 1980.

Murray, Ruth S. *Valiant for the Truth; or, Some Memorials of George Fox and the Early Friends.* New York: Burr Printing House, 1883.

Nightingale, B. *Early Stages of the Quaker Movement in Lancashire.* London: Congregation Union, [1921].

————. *Lancashire Nonconformity: The Churches of Preston, North Lancashire, and Westmorland.* Manchester, England: John Heywood, [1890].

Noble, Vernon. *The Man in Leather Breeches: The Life and Times of George Fox.* London: Elek, 1953.

Notestein, Wallace. *The English People on the Eve of Colonization, 1603–1630.* New York: Harper and Row, 1954.

Nuttall, Geoffrey F. *The Puritan Spirit: Essays and Addresses.* London: Epworth Press, 1967.

————. *Studies in Christian Enthusiasm: Illustrated from Early Quakerism.* Wallingford, Pa.: Pendle Hill, 1948.

————. *The Welsh Saints, 1640–1660: Walter Cradock, Vavasor Powell, Morgan Llwyd.* Cardiff: University of Wales Press, 1967.

Nuttall, Geoffrey F., Roger Thomas, R. D. Whitehorn, and H. L. Short. *The Beginnings of Nonconformity.* London: James Clark and Co., 1964.

Ollard, S. L., et al., eds. *A Dictionary of English Church History.* London: A. R. Mowbray and Co., 1948.

Paget, Guy, and Lionel Irvine. *Leicestershire.* London: Robert Hale, 1950.

Parry, R. H., ed. *The English Civil War and after, 1642–1658.* Berkeley and Los Angeles: University of California Press, 1970.

Peare, Catherine O. *William Penn: A Biography.* Ann Arbor, Mich.: Ann Arbor Paperbacks, 1966.

Pennington, Donald, and Keith Thomas, eds. *Puritans and Revolutionaries: Essays in Seventeenth Century History Presented to Christopher Hill.* Oxford: Oxford University Press, 1978.

Pestana, Carla G. *Quakers and Baptists in Colonial Massachusetts.* Cambridge: Cambridge University Press, 1991.

Petegorsky, David W. *Left-Wing Democracy in the English Civil War: A Study of the Social Philosophy of Gerrard Winstanley.* New York: Haskell House Publishers, 1972.

Phillips, John. *The Reformation of Images: Destruction of Art in England, 1535–1660.* Berkeley and Los Angeles: University of California Press, 1973.

Pickvance, T. Joseph. *George Fox on the Light of Christ Within.* Gloucester, England: George Fox Fund, 1978.

Pingriff, G. N. *Cambridge County Geographies: Leicestershire.* Cambridge: Cambridge University Press, 1920.

Pinto, Vivian de Sola. *Peter Sterry: Platonist and Puritan, 1613–1672.* New York: Greenwood Press, 1968.

Popkin, Richard H., and Michael A. Signer, eds. *Spinoza's Earliest Publication?* Wolfeboro, N.H.: Van Gorcum, 1987.

Pugh, Ralph B. *Imprisonment in Medieval England.* Cambridge: Cambridge University Press, 1968.

R[ailton], George. *George Fox: His Life, Travels, Sufferings, and Death.* London: Salvation Army, 1881.

Redwood, John. *Reason, Ridicule and Religion: The Age of Enlightment in England, 1660–1750.* London: Thames and Hudson, 1976.

Reviving the English Revolution: Reflections and Elaborations on the Work of Christopher Hill. Edited by Geoff Eley and William Hunt. London: Verso, 1988.

Roberts, Arthur O. *Through a Flaming Sword: A Spiritual Biography of George Fox.* Portland, Oreg.: Barclay Press, 1959.

Rogow, Arnold A. *Thomas Hobbes: Radical in the Service of Reaction.* New York: W. W. Northon and Co., 1986.

Roots, Ivan. *The Great Rebellion, 1642–1660.* London: B. T. Batsford, 1968.

Rosen, George. *Madness in Society: Chapters in the Historical Sociology of Mental Illness.* Chicago: University of Chicago Press, 1968.

Salter, J. L., ed. *Atherstone: An Outline History of a North Warwickshire Market Town.* N.p.: 1985.

Selleck, George A. *Quakers in Boston, 1656–1964.* Cambridge, Mass.: Friends Meeting at Cambridge: 1976.

Sharp, Buchanan. *In Contempt of All Authority: Rural Artisans and Riot in the West of England, 1586–1660.* Berkeley and Los Angeles: University of California Press. 1980.

Sharrock, Roger. *John Bunyan.* London: Macmillan, 1968.

Simmons, Jack. *Leicester; Past and Present.* Vol. 1, *Ancient Borough to 1860.* London: Eyre Melhuen, 1974.

Skillington, S. H. *A History of Leicester.* Leicester, England: Edgar Backus, 1923.

Spurgeon, C. H. *George Fox: A Lecture Delivered to the Society of Friends.* London: Passmore and Alabaster, [1866].

Summers, W. H. *Our Lollard Ancestors.* London: Thomas Law, 1906.

Tallack, William. *George Fox, The Friends, and the Early Baptists.* London: S. W. Partridge, 1868.

Tawney, R. H. *Religion and the Rise of Capitalism.* New York: New American Library, 1947.

Thirsk, Joan. *The Rural Economy of England: Collected Essays.* London: Humbledon Press, 1984.

Thistlewaite, W. Pearson. *Yorkshire Quarterly Meeting, 1665–1966.* Harrogate, England: Author, 1979.

Thomas, Keith. *Religion and the Decline of Magic.* New York: Charles Scribner's Sons, 1971.

Thompson, E. P. *The Making of the English Working Class.* New York: Vintage Books, 1963.

Toon, Peter, ed. *Puritans, the Millennium and the Future of Israel: Puritan Eschatology 1600 to 1660.* London: James Clarke and Co.,1970.

Trevett, Christine. *Women and Quakerism in the 17th Century.* York, England: Sessions, 1991.

Trollope, Andrew. *An Inventory of the Church Plate of Leicestershire.* Leicester, England: Clark and Hodgson, 1890.

Tuke, Henry. *Biographical Notices of Members of the Society of Friends,* vol. 2. York, England: W. Alexander, 1815.

Underdown, David. *Pride's Purge: Politics in the Puritan Revolution.* Oxford, England: Clarendon Press, 1971.

———. *Revel, Riot, and Rebellion: Popular Politics and Culture in England, 1603–1660.* Oxford, England: Clarendon Press, 1985.

———. *Royalist Conspiracy in England, 1649–1660.* New Haven, Conn.: Yale University Press, 1960.

VHC: Lancashire. Edited by William Page. London: Dawsons of Pall Mall, 1966. (Vols. 2, 8.)

VHC: Leicester. Edited by William Page. London: Archibald Constable and Co., 1907. (Vol. 1.)

VHC: Leicester. Edited by W. G. Hoskins. London: Oxford University Press, 1954. (Vol. 2.)

VHC: Northampton. Edited by William Page. London: St. Catherine Press, 1930. (Vol. 3.)

VHC: Stafford. Edited by William Page. London: Archibald Constable and Co., 1908. (vol. 1.)

Watkins, Owen C. *The Puritan Experience.* London: Routledge and Kegan Paul, 1972.

Watts, Brenda, and Eleanor Winyard. *The History of Atherstone.* London: HMSO, 1988.

Weeks, Stephen B. *Southern Quakers and Slavery: A Study in Institutional History.* New York: Bergman Publishers, 1968.

White, A. P. *The Story of Northampton.* West Ardsley, Yorkshire, England: S. R. Publishers, 1970.

Wilbur, Earl M. *A History of Unitarianism: Socinianism and Its Antecedents.* Cambridge, Mass.: Harvard University Press, 1947.

Wildes, Harry E. *Voice of the Lord: A Biography of George Fox.* Philadelphia: University of Pennsylvania Press, 1965.

Woolrych, Austin. *Commonwealth to Protectorate.* Oxford, England: Clarendon Press, 1982.

Wragge, J. Philip. *George Fox.* London: Friends Home Service Committee, 1950.

Wright, Luella M. *The Literary Life of the Early Friends, 1650–1725.* New York: AMS Press, 1966.

Young, Peter. *Civil War England.* London: Longman, 1981.

Index